INDUSTRIAL/ORGANIZATIONAL PSYCHOLOGY

Understanding the Workplace

SECOND EDITION

PAUL E. LEVY
University of Akron

HOUGHTON MIFFLIN COMPANY
Boston New York

Publisher: Charles Hartford
Sponsoring Editor: Jane Potter
Development Editor: Rebecca Berardy
Senior Project Editor: Jane Lee
Editorial Assistant: Kristen Truncellito
Senior Art and Design Coordinator: Jill Haber
Senior Photo Editor: Jennifer Meyer Dare
Senior Composition Buyer: Sarah Ambrose
Senior Manufacturing Coordinator: Marie Barnes
Marketing Manager: Laura McGinn
Marketing Assistant: Erin Lane

Credits are found following the references at the end of the book.

Custom Publishing Editor: Dee Renfrow
Custom Publishing Production Manager: Tina Kozik
Project Coordinator: Jonathan Sellers

Cover Designer: Emily Quillen

Printed in the United States of America.

ISBN 13: 978-0-618-73374-3
ISBN 10: 0-618-73374-4
N-06023

5 6 7 8 9 – CCI – 09 08

New Ways to Know

222 Berkeley Street • Boston, MA 02116

Address all correspondence and order information to the above address.

BRIEF CONTENTS

CONTENTS

PREFACE

Everything I Need to Know I Learned Between the First and Second Editions. . . .

In the first edition, I began the Preface with a discussion of why I took three years out of my life to write the text. Since my motivation for writing the first edition remains an important driving force, I'd like to explain my purpose for originally writing the book as well as the changes I've made to the second edition as a result of what I've learned throughout the process.

I've been teaching Introduction to Industrial and Organizational (I/O) Psychology at The University of Akron since 1996 and also taught it for a few years in the late 1980s at Virginia Tech. I've always loved teaching it but was never quite happy with the available textbooks. My students have always had concerns about the textbooks as well, so I wondered if I might be able to make a meaningful contribution to the I/O texts available. I have always found most I/O texts to be quite dry, and a dry textbook for a technical field is not the best pairing. Therefore, my first goal in writing the first edition was to write a textbook that was more interesting, more accessible to students, and a consistently "better read." I worked very hard at producing a book that would engage students, excite them, and, of course, teach them a great deal of what I/O psychology is all about. The potential to write a book that would draw students into the story of I/O psychology was what attracted me to this task from the very beginning, and it has been my guiding principle throughout my work on both the first and second editions.

Focusing on writing a student-friendly text alone would have been difficult enough. However, my second goal was to write a student-friendly book that was also of the highest quality in terms of its research orientation. I have been fortunate enough to be a member of one of the finest I/O programs in the country for 16 years, and thus, high-quality I/O research is important to me and to my colleagues. So the real task for me was to maintain the rigorous research focus that is critical to understanding I/O psychology, but to do it in a way that students would find interesting and stimulating. This book was written to serve as the main text in an Introduction to I/O class, which is usually taught at a sophomore or junior level, but I know quite a few colleagues who have used the first edition in basic or introductory graduate level courses. It is very comprehensive in its coverage of the domain of I/O psychology. It is also more current than most of the other I/O books on the market. Because I teach graduate courses in Industrial Psychology, Organizational Psychology, and Research Methods—arguably the three major content domains of I/O Psychology—I have to stay current on the research in all three areas. I made especially strong efforts to do so while writing the second edition and am very pleased with the final product. While being readable, it is also sophisticated and truly a book for the 21st century.

I stuck to the same overriding principles in the design and writing of the second edition—to develop an interesting, reader-friendly, current, research-based coverage of industrial/organizational psychology. In particular, I revised each chapter based on comments that were provided informally by colleagues who used the first edition and formal reviews submitted by a diverse cross section of I/O psychology instructors from community colleges, four-year schools, and universities with graduate programs in I/O psychology. I attempted to tighten up the writing a bit, expand on the real-world examples, and broaden the coverage to other areas that have emerged more recently on the I/O scene.

What Is Included in the Book and How Is the Book Organized?

I've kept the chapter structure from the first edition because it seemed to work for the reviewers and the instructors who used the book. I've divided the book into three sections. The first section focuses on the history of I/O psychology (Chapter 1) as well as the basics of the research process (Chapter 2), including measurement, methods, and stats. Chapter 1 differs in its treatment of I/O history from most other I/O books because it not only includes a history of the development of the field, but also presents very important information about how I/O psychologists are trained. This gives students a flavor of not only how the field develops, but also how I/O psychologists develop. Dr. Jim Austin, who specializes in the history of I/O psychology, was gracious enough to develop a historical time line that is a great complement to the text of Chapter 1. Chapter 2 is the longest chapter in the book and certainly more detailed about the research process than the analogous chapter in other I/O texts. I did this on purpose because I think that without enough of a foundation to appreciate what a correlation is, what extraneous variables are, why they are a problem, and so on, students get lost later on in the course.

The second section of the text is built around what we have traditionally called industrial psychology. A few things that I've done differently here are worthy of note. First, I emphasize the importance of the job analysis (Chapter 3) throughout this entire section. Second, I include a full-sized chapter on criterion measurement (Chapter 4), which most I/O texts either roll into the performance appraisal or selection chapters. Many of the reviewers really seemed to appreciate having this chapter and liked the structure of the chapter a great deal. This chapter provides the foundation for the rest of the second section and even many elements of the third section of the book. Third, I provide a framework for the second section in Chapter 3 that shows how everything begins with the job analysis, and how each succeeding chapter in this section of the book builds on and adds to it. Fourth, while I cover rating formats, along with errors and biases, in the performance appraisal chapter (Chapter 5), there is more emphasis on the social-contextual approach to performance appraisal and a particular focus on current research in this area. Fifth, I've broken selection into two chapters: the first is a traditional chapter covering the major predictors used in selection (Chapter 6); the second focuses on how predictors are used in selection, which is a topic that I don't think I/O books cover very well. Chapter 7 also has a lengthy section on legal issues in selection, which is an interesting area for students and an important one for the field. Reviewers seemed to particularly like this chapter, noting that I was able to take difficult material and make it accessible, and that this chapter hits just the right note for the students. Finally, in the last chapter of this section of the text (Chapter 8), I present a traditional look at training with an emphasis on 21st-century themes, including sexual harassment and diversity training.

The third section of the text provides an overview of organizational psychology. I've tried to make the motivation chapter (Chapter 9) a little more applied than what I've seen in most I/O texts, which tend to present just a list of motivational theories. Chapter 10 on job attitudes begins with some basic social psychological attitudes work by Fishbein and his colleagues. Their work is then applied throughout the chapter to the relationships between predictors, like job satisfaction and organizational commitment, and organizational outcome variables such as turnover and absence. In the stress chapter (Chapter 11), I spend a good deal of time on work-family issues, which are such an important element of work in the 21st century. Violence in the workplace has also become a much-talked-about and examined phenomenon in recent years, and I discuss it within the context of the 21st-century workplace. Groups and work teams are the focus of Chapter 12 in which I again start with basic social psychological work and show how it has been applied to issues at work such as self-managing work teams. Leadership is presented in Chapter 13 where theories are categorized as either traditional or contemporary. I also discuss at some length 21st-century issues revolving around gender and leadership as well as culture and leadership. The final chapter (Chapter 14) talks about organizational theory and applies these theories, as well as others from earlier chapters, to a discussion on how organizations change and develop. There is an emphasis in the latter half of this chapter on why organizations need to adapt in order to survive. This discussion is also linked to some recent writings by highly respected organizational gurus who talk about how organizations need to change for survival in the 21st century. Cutting-edge topics such as knowledge management and continuous learning are discussed here as well, and this chapter was very well received by both instructors and reviewers when it appeared in the first edition.

New to the Second Edition

Although the second edition was intended to be a light revision, I ended up revising the book considerably more than I had intended. The first edition was well received by most of the instructors who used the text, and I was also fortunate to receive a good deal of informal feedback from them and a great deal of very useful feedback from the reviewers. This feedback, along with the dynamic nature of the field and several ideas I had already begun to consider soon after I completed the first edition, resulted in the blueprint for the second edition. In addition to updating each practitioner forum, updating the references throughout the text, restructuring sections and chapters to better communicate the material, and tightening up the writing, the following chapter-by-chapter changes were made:

CHAPTER 1

- Extended the timeline to 2004.
- Updated the demographics with most recent SIOP data.
- Used the forthcoming book on the history of I/O Psychology extensively in the revision process (Ed., Laura Koppes).

CHAPTER 2

- Tightened up the writing around technical issues like reliability and research design.
- Added discussion on inter-rater reliability.

CHAPTER 3

- Expanded the information on O*Net and hybrid approaches to job analysis.
- Made extensive use of a few new and respected resources on job analysis.
- Emphasized that the choice of the job analysis technique should be based largely on the purpose for the job analysis.
- Revised the graphical representation of wage equity to better explain the concept.
- Updated the data on working women's wages.

CHAPTER 4

- Further discriminated between objective and subjective criteria.
- Included a discussion of counterproductive behaviors.
- Included most recent conceptualizations of OCBs.

CHAPTER 5

- Made use of the most recent conceptual and review papers in the revision process.
- Expanded the section on appraisal formats especially with respect to forced distribution (ranking) and companies' experiences with them.
- Added 22 new references.

CHAPTER 6

- Updated both the history and current status of testing in the United States.
- Provided a graphical example and discussion of how specific tests tap particular KSAs that are linked directly to the job specifications from the job analysis.
- Expanded the discussion of personality tests for selection and covered legal issues and faking in more detail.
- Updated estimates of validity coefficients of various selection tests based on recent research.
- Added 16 new references.

CHAPTER 7

- Updated and expanded the section on recruitment and included recent work on Internet recruiting.
- Updated and expanded the legal section to include the latest affirmative action information (e.g. the recent Supreme Court rulings in the University of Michigan cases), national origin discrimination, and age discrimination.
- Added 24 new references.

CHAPTER 8

- Completely reorganized the chapter to better present the material.
- Heavily updated or provided brand new content in the following sections:
  - Learning Context
  - Instructional Design
  - Active Learning
  - Individual Difference in Trainees
  - Employee Development-Based Approaches
  - Characteristics of Trainers
  - Transfer of Training
  - Self-Directed Training Techniques
  - Technology-Based Approaches
- Updated the statistics on training in organizations.
- Expanded the discussion of how selection and training fit together.
- Added 24 new references.

CHAPTER 9

- Added a section on Cognitive Evaluation Theory.
- Expanded the section on Organizational Justice.
- Expanded the coverage of Social Cognitive Theories.
- Added 11 new references.

CHAPTER 10

- Added a section on Perceived Organizational Support (POS).
- Expanded the section on Emotions at Work.

- Expanded the section on individual differences and job satisfaction.
- Expanded job satisfaction-performance section based on recent research.
- Added a bit more discussion on the relationship between job satisfaction and organizational commitment.
- Added 28 new references.

CHAPTER 11

- Reorganized the chapter around recent work in this area.
- Updated work-life statistics, job-loss statistics, and women in the workforce statistics.
- Enhanced the discussion on work-family issues by:
  - Distinguishing between WF conflict and WF enrichment
  - Distinguishing between the family roles of working men and working women
  - Expanding the discussion on WF supports
- Expanded the discussion of workplace violence.
- Added 24 new references.

CHAPTER 12

- Reduced the coverage of traditional social-psychological work on groups and added a good deal more on I/O work on groups and teams.
- Supplemented the discussion on group process with more information on Gersick's Punctuated Equilibrium model.
- Expanded on the pros and cons of brainstorming.
- Expanded the discussion of group composition and group performance.
- Added 14 new references.

CHAPTER 13

- Updated trait theories, behavioral, and contingency theories with very recent research.
- Updated the women in leadership statistics.
- Expanded the gender and leadership section with recent research on the potential of a feminine leadership advantage.
- Expanded the culture and leadership section with recent research from the GLOBE project.
- Added 22 new references.

CHAPTER 14

- Included more coverage of other OD techniques like Outdoor Experiential Training (OET).
- Presented recent data on TQM effects.
- Expanded the discussion of gainsharing.

- Expanded the discussion of knowledge management by including some applied examples.
- Added 13 new references.

Special Features to Benefit the Students

A series of features has been included to help make the book more accessible to students and to help teach the material in an effective and interesting way. Each of these features was revised for the second edition. First, each chapter includes a marginal glossary that is designed to help students highlight and understand the important terms *as they read* through the book rather than having to go to the end of the chapter to see the key terms and formal definitions. A complete glossary for the entire book is also presented at the end of the text. Second, each chapter includes a set of learning objectives and review questions. The learning objectives should help students to see what the goals of the chapter are upfront—that is, they highlight what I want students to understand after having worked through the chapter. The review questions are designed to help students study and to encourage them to think about the material at a deeper level rather than just memorize key points. Some of these questions are designed to be *thought* questions as opposed to *factual* questions.

Third, perhaps the most innovative feature that I've included in this text is what I've called the "Practitioner Forum," in which an I/O psychologist practitioner provides a bit of his or her insight and experience in an area relevant to that particular chapter. I've included a Practitioner Forum for 11 of the 14 chapters, and each one is written by a practitioner who has wonderful experiences and information to share. We've tried to keep this feature short and concise, and the practitioners have done a terrific job tying their experiences and the situation they describe back to the content of the chapter. We think students will find this feature very interesting. I've also provided a short list of valuable readings at the end of each chapter, along with a very brief summary of each. These readings vary from technical journal articles to very general overviews of the different topics covered in the book. I updated these for the second edition where I felt new, important works had been recently published. Complete citations are included to help make it easier for students to pursue additional depth or understanding of I/O information. Finally, I've also incorporated many Internet citations and websites, which furnish yet another novel way to approach learning. These citations provide a wealth of information that would be difficult to access via print media. Each of these sites is an active link as of this writing. Websites like that of the Equal Employment Opportunity Commission (EEOC), for instance, are great resources for students and can provide a rich source of cutting-edge information.

What Supplements Are Available to Enhance the Teaching and Learning Processes?

The *Instructors Manual with Test Bank* (Norris-Watts, Levy, and Cober) contains suggestions for classroom activities and discussions, and multiple-choice and short-answer test items. Three types of objective questions are provided: factual, conceptual, and applied, and all answers are keyed to learning objectives, text pages, and question type, for easier test creation. The test questions are also available electronically as a *Computerized Test Bank* in an easy-to-use menu-driven format that allows for customization to each instructor's needs.

Instructor and Student Websites were created specifically for this text and contain PowerPoint slides and the Instructor's Resource manual for professors, to help facilitate classroom lectures, as well as Weblinks, which provide an array of helpful websites where both students and professors can go to find related information. These sites may be accessed by going to *http:psychology.college.hmco.com.*

Who Are the People Without Whom I Couldn't Have Written This Book?

This book is clearly my view of I/O psychology and no one else's. Upon finding out that my book was going to be a sole-authored text, many people asked me how I could possibly write this book by myself. Well, I couldn't have, and fortunately I didn't really have to write the first edition or the second edition by myself. While it was in many ways a labor of love for me, it would have been also completely impossible without the help and support of so many friends, family, and colleagues. I'll start first with my current and former graduate students who have always provided me with the crystal-clear reason for why I am a psychology professor. They have been instrumental in helping to shape my thoughts and ideas over the years, and a few have helped with some of the specific tasks associated with the second edition. I thank them all, but especially thank those who have had their hands in this text in various ways: Samantha Chau, Rich Cober, Christina Norris-Watts, and Brian Whitaker.

Next, I must thank all of the undergraduates in my Introduction to Industrial/Organizational Psychology class over the years who have experienced this book, in the sense that they lived through the rough draft as I lectured and talked about these topics over the course of each semester. Without their encouragement and favorable response to the class I would have never considered writing this text.

Third, my I/O colleagues at The University of Akron, with whom I have been so fortunate to have worked over the last 16 years, have contributed in so many ways—from helpful expertise on certain sections, to ideas about how to present information, to those key cites from their areas of expertise that often just helped bring sections to life, to just plain-old social support. I'd like to thank: Dennis Doverspike, Joelle Elicker, Rosalie Hall, Bob Lord, Aaron Schmidt, Andee Snell, and Harvey Sterns. All of my non-I/O colleagues in the Department of Psychology at Akron have been instrumental in this process as well by helping me think through ideas, providing resources, and encouraging my efforts. In particular, I'd like to formally thank Sue Hardin, Linda Subich, Charlie Waehler, and Dave Baker. Other colleagues and friends have also been instrumental in the development of this book such as Stan Silverman, Jim Austin, and Meaghan Alegi.

The authors of the Practitioner Forums were terrific contributors to the book through their expertise and insight, which is reflected not only in their written contributions, but also in their willingness to pitch in and to do so on our sometimes-tight schedule including their revisions for the second edition. I appreciate the efforts of: Allan Church, Shelly Funderburg, Scott Goodman, Rhonda Gutenberg, Jeff Hill, David Hyatt, Elizabeth Kolmstetter, Joe Lualhati, Tom Ruddy, Pat Shannon, and Steve Walker.

The following individuals served as reviewers at various stages of this project—I was amazed at the level of detail and care that these individuals put into this project. Without their ideas, suggestions, and criticisms, the finished product would be considerably "less finished." And I would be remiss if I did not again thank the reviewers whose invaluable input shaped the first edition as well as those who helped mold the second edition. I can't thank these individuals enough!

Kimberly Cummings, University of Tampa
Kelly Bouas Henry, Missouri Western State College
Alice Stuhlmacher, DePaul University
John J. Donovan, Virginia Polytechnic and State Institute
Donald Truxillo, Portland State University
Howard M. Weiss, Purdue University
Sharon E. Lovell, James Madison University
Teresa M. Heckert, Truman State University
Kraig L. Schell, Angelo State University
Michael Beitler, University of North Carolina, Greensboro
Corey E. Miller, Wright State University
Martin Wikoff, University of Wisconsin—Greenbay; St. Norbert College
Michael McCall, Ithaca College
Joe S. Bean, Shorter College
Bruce H. Johnson, Gustavus Adolphus College
Robert Keefer, Mount Saint Mary's College
Gilad Chen, Georgia Tech
Reeshad S. Dalal, Purdue University
James M. Diefendorff, Louisiana State University
Michael S. Goodstone, Farmingdale State University of NY
Leslie Hammer, Portland State University
Michael Horvath, Clemson University
Scott B. Shadrick, Western Kentucky University
Comila Shahani-Denning, Hofstra University
David Campbell, Humboldt State University
James K. Esser, Lamar University

As with the first edition, I relied on the folks at Houghton Mifflin a great deal and was never led astray in the preparation of the second edition. All of my questions were answered; all of my fears removed; and most of my stress reduced! They were all terrific to work with, and I'd like to thank: Kerry Baruth, Rebecca Berardy, Laura Hildebrand, and Jane Lee for their outstanding work in helping me bring this second edition to fruition. Yes, I'm the sole author, but no, I didn't do it alone.

Finally, I'd like to thank my extended family, whose faith in me in everything I've ever done has never wavered—that means more to me than they realize. My wife, Sylvia, has continued to put up with me through this long process, as I sometimes juggle more things than seems reasonable—she has done so with the dignity, class, love, and respect that she has spoiled me with since we first met 20 years ago. I could not have done this without her and would not have even tried. Our three boys, Christopher, Sean, and Jared, have provided the unmeasurable joy in our lives that we've needed to get through this project and every other project that we tackle. "Dad, can you play ball with us?" continues to be music to my ears after long days of reading, writing, and editing.

Dedication

To Helen and Jerry Levy: My parents never let on that being a parent was the hardest job in the world; they made it look easy, and I thank God for being their son.

P. E. L.

ABOUT THE AUTHOR

Paul E. Levy was born and raised in Baltimore, Maryland, as the last of his family's five children. He received his B.A. in psychology and economics from Washington & Lee University, and his M.A. and Ph.D. in industrial/organizational psychology from Virginia Tech. He has been a faculty member at The University of Akron since 1989 where he has served as Chair of the I/O Psychology program since 1995 and Associate Chair of the Department of Psychology since 2000. He has been very involved in the development and training of hundreds of graduate students during his time at Akron, while also providing many undergraduates with their first exposure to the field of I/O psychology through his Introduction to Industrial/Organizational Psychology course. Dr. Levy's consulting and research interests include performance appraisal, feedback, recruitment, organizational justice, and organizational surveys/attitudes. Dr. Levy has published his scholarly work in many psychology and management journals such as the *Journal of Applied Psychology, Journal of Personality and Social Psychology, Personnel Psychology, Organizational Behavior and Human Decision Processes*, and the *Journal of Management*. Dr. Levy is married to Sylvia Chinn-Levy and has three young boys (Christopher, Sean, and Jared) who are, amazingly, more interested in basketball, baseball, music, and reading than they are in psychology. Dr. Levy is an avid baseball and basketball fan, youth sports coach, basketball player, and a lifelong fan of the Baltimore Orioles.

The History of I/O Psychology

1

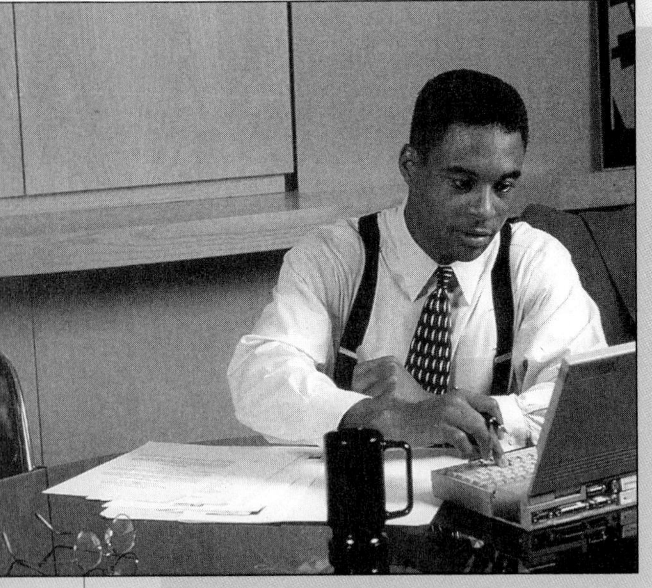

CHAPTER OUTLINE

For most of us, who we are is in large part defined by what we do. If you were to ask me to describe myself in a few sentences, I would say something like the following:

> My name is Paul Levy. I have been fortunate enough to be married to Sylvia Chinn-Levy for 16 years and have three terrific young boys named Christopher, Sean, and Jared. I am a psychology professor at The University of Akron, where I specialize in industrial/organizational psychology. I teach both undergraduate and graduate students and do research in the area of performance appraisal and feedback. I'm a big sports fan, a youth sports coach, I play basketball, and am a fanatic about the Baltimore Orioles.

You can see from this simple example how prominent my job is in my self-description. I think of myself as a husband, father, and psychology professor (in that order!). Most of us spend over one-third of our day at work, traveling to and from work, or preparing to go to work. Many individuals bring work home with them or are called into work at night, on weekends, or even in the early morning hours. We have cell phones and pagers so that our co-workers can reach us when they need to, even if we are at the ball game or a wedding or having a picnic with our families. Although most of us would concur that family is the most important element in our lives, work is probably second. In this book, I present the world of work from the perspective of I/O psychology and attempt to provide you with a better understanding of the complexities that are inherent in the interactions between employees and organizations. Chapter 1 of the book introduces I/O psychology by focusing on its definition, its approach to training, and its history.

LEARNING OBJECTIVES

This chapter should help you understand:

- how I/O psychologists are trained.
- the work of I/O psychologists and how it benefits organizations and employees alike.
- the diverse historical trends associated with the development and growth of I/O psychology.
- the very important role currently being played by I/O psychology in the changing workplace, as well as the field's great potential to contribute to organizational functioning in the 21st century.

WHAT IS I/O PSYCHOLOGY?

industrial/organizational (I/O) psychology
The application of psychological principles and theories to the workplace.

Industrial/organizational (I/O) psychology is the application of psychological principles and theories to the workplace. I/O psychologists study, among other things, the attitudes and behaviors of employees and employers; interpersonal relationships at work; the structure of organizations and organizational policies; the complex processes of motivation and leadership; both individual and organizational performance; the context, culture, and climate of organizations; and the match between people and jobs. Traditionally, industrial psychology and organizational psychology have been distinguished from each other based on their respective content areas. *Industrial psychology* (sometimes called *personnel psychology*) has long been associated with job analysis, training, selection, and performance measurement/appraisal, whereas *organizational psychology* deals with motivation, work attitudes, and leadership, as well as organizational development, structure, and culture. In a sense, however, the dichotomy is a false one given the great overlap among the issues involved in each area. In addition, most I/O psychologists are trained as exactly that—I/O psychologists—not as industrial psychologists only or as organizational psychologists only. Finally, there is no broad line that divides workplace problems into organizational or industrial ones. For instance, a performance problem that might traditionally be defined within the industrial domain (the term *performance* has always been more closely aligned with industrial psychology) is likely to be caused by attitudinal or motivational factors that are traditionally associated with organizational psychology. Nevertheless, I use the distinction here to be consistent with other treatments of the topic and, even more important, to provide a framework for the discussion. I want to reiterate that *I* and *O* are put together into *I/O* for good reason: They are interdependent, related areas that form one applied subspecialty of psychology.

Before tracing the history of I/O psychology, we must consider at length how I/O psychologists are trained and what it is that I/O psychologists do.

HOW ARE I/O PSYCHOLOGISTS TRAINED?

The *Society for Industrial and Organizational Psychology (SIOP)*, Division 14 of the American Psychological Association (APA), is the professional association with which most I/O psychologists affiliate. Most I/O psychologists have obtained a Ph.D. (or a Psy.D, which is a similar degree with less research emphasis) from one of the 65 or so I/O psychology programs currently available in the United States and Canada, but there are other programs elsewhere in the world as well. For a detailed look at these numerous programs, see *Graduate Training Programs in Industrial-Organizational Psychology and Related Fields* (Society for Industrial and Organizational Psychology, 2000). The work of I/O psychology can also be done by people without Ph.D.s in I/O (e.g., there are many I/O psychologists with master's degrees), as well as by people without specific training in I/O. Many of those without training in I/O receive their instruction in a graduate program housed in a business school.

SIOP publishes guidelines for doctoral training in I/O psychology, called *Guidelines for Education and Training at the Doctoral Level in Industrial-Organizational Psychology* (Society for Industrial and Organizational Psychology, 1999). These guidelines clearly stipulate that the underlying approach to training I/O psychologists is the **scientist/practitioner model,** which maintains that I/O psychologists are often both the generators of knowledge (scientists) and the consumers of such knowledge (practitioners). Accordingly, doctoral education in I/O psychology must focus on both the theory and applications associated with the various content areas; the dual emphasis on theory and practice is needed regardless of one's career path. Indeed, to be a strong researcher, one needs to understand both the theory involved in the research and how to apply the knowledge that could potentially come from that research. To effectively teach future I/O psychologists, one must be able to share insights at both a theoretical and an applied level. Similarly, to apply the knowledge in an organization, one must have a theoretical understanding of I/O issues and practices in order to make them work and to enable other employees to understand the potential benefits of the procedures or interventions being implemented.

scientist/practitioner model
An approach used to train I/O psychologists that maintains that because I/O psychologists are both generators and consumers of knowledge, training must be focused on both theory and application.

Earlier, I made the point that few are trained as industrial psychologists only or as organizational psychologists only; rather, most are trained as both. Along the same lines, the ideal background for I/O psychologists is to be trained as scientist/practitioners who are skilled in both theory and application—and thus can become both generators and consumers of knowledge. Returning to the beginning of the chapter, we see that even the definition of I/O psychology—*the application of psychological principles and theories to the workplace*—emphasizes both theory and application; hence SIOP's emphasis on the scientist/practitioner model of training in its guidelines.

These guidelines also maintain that the goal of graduate training in I/O psychology is to develop **competencies,** which are the skills, behaviors, knowledge, abilities, and capabilities that allow employees to effectively perform specific functions—or, in this case, to be effective members of the I/O psychology profession. Table 1.1 summarizes the competencies that have been identified as important for I/O psychologists. This comprehensive list is, in reality, only a guide to be used by graduate programs in the training of I/O psychologists. It is safe to say that no I/O psychologist graduates from school having attained complete competence in every one of these areas, but certainly most graduates have attained some degree of competence in most.

competencies
The skills, behaviors, and capabilities that allow employees to perform specific functions.

Another issue addressed by SIOP's guidelines is the importance of *diversity* in the training of I/O psychologists. The guidelines point out that, just as science and practice are inherent in each competency, an appreciation of diversity can be applied to each as well. Diversity in this sense refers to an awareness and understanding not only of ethnic, racial, and cultural differences among employees but also of age and gender differences.

TABLE 1.1 Areas of Competence to Be Developed in Doctoral Level I/O Psychology Programs

Consulting and Business Skills	
Ethical, Legal, and Professional Contexts of I/O Psychology	Individual Differences
Fields of Psychology	Job Evaluation and Compensation
History and Systems of Psychology	Job/Task Analysis and Classification
Research Methods	Judgment and Decision Making
Statistical Methods/Data Analysis	Leadership and Management
Attitude Theory, Measurement, and Change	Organizational Development
Career Development	Organizational Theory
Consumer Behavior	Performance Appraisal and Feedback
Criterion Theory and Development	Personnel Recruitment, Selection, and Placement
Health Stress in Organizations	Small Group Theory and Team Processes
Human Performance/Human Factors	Training: Theory, Program Design, and Evaluation
Individual Assessment	Work Motivation

Source: Society for Industrial and Organizational Psychology, Inc. (1998).

Developing competency in the areas outlined by SIOP and graduating with a Ph.D. in I/O psychology usually require at least four to five years of graduate school (following completion of an undergraduate degree). The last portion of this time is spent on a dissertation. Because it's my experience that many undergraduates are not familiar with what a dissertation entails, I will give you just a brief look. A **dissertation** is a unique piece of scholarly research; in I/O psychology, it is usually an empirical piece of research. The doctoral student finds a topic of interest and exhaustively reviews the current literature in that area. The student then decides what needs to be done in that area and designs a study to answer a series of research questions, working closely with a faculty member who has some degree of expertise in the area. This process, from the initial search for an idea to the actual completion of the study (the completion is marked by a formal defense of the written paper in front of the student's advisory committee) can range in time from one year to many, many years. Now that you have an idea of what I/O psychology is and how I/O psychologists are trained, we will consider what I/O psychologists actually do after completing their training.

dissertation
A unique piece of scholarly research that is usually the last hurdle before obtaining a Ph.D.

WHAT DO I/O PSYCHOLOGISTS DO?

Although I/O psychologists are trained according to the scientist/practitioner model, most choose a career that, in a relative sense, emphasizes either science

FIGURE 1.1 Primary Employment of SIOP Members

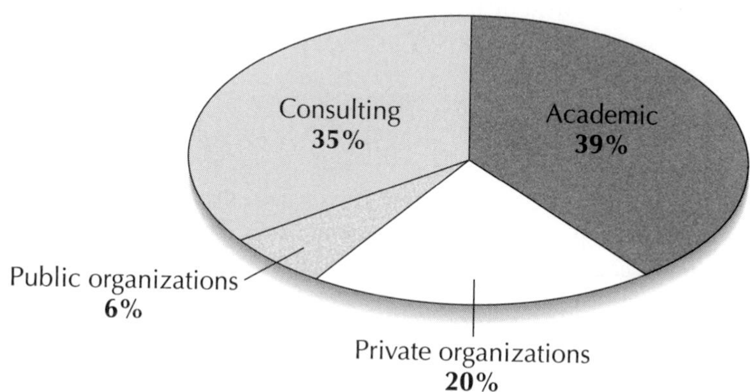

Source: Society for Industrial and Organizational Psychology (2004).

and research *or* practice. The point here is not that academics don't ever deal with the application of research and theory to the real world, because most do on a regular basis; rather, it's that their emphasis is still on the research. Similarly, there are practitioners who are also involved in research and establish excellent research reputations by publishing their applied work in scholarly journals, as well as in more practice-oriented journals, but who maintain a focus on the application of I/O to their organizations. Figure 1.1 categorizes I/O psychologists by the various employment settings in which they work. As you can see, a large percentage of I/O psychologists—39.1%—are employed as professors by universities. These individuals typically teach in psychology or business departments, in addition to doing empirical and theoretical research. Other research-oriented I/O psychologists are employed by research consortia or institutes or by public or private organizations.

Those I/O psychologists who do not work in academic settings devote the majority of their time to applying psychology to the workplace, doing so in consulting firms (35%), private organizations (20%), and public organizations (6%). Many of these practitioners work in the human resource departments of companies in the manufacturing industry, financial services industry, telecommunications industry, and consumer products industry, among others. Among those in the public sector, many work in federal, state, and local government, as well as in the military. Job titles for I/O practitioners include, but are not limited to, the following: Director of Personnel, Vice President of Personnel, Manager of Human Resources, Organizational Development Specialist, Personnel Psychologist, Senior Consultant, Compensation Analyst, Project Manager, Senior Scientist, Management Consultant, Research Scientist, and Behavioral Scientist. Many I/O psychologists have typically been employed by large Fortune 500 and multinational companies such as British Petroleum, United Airlines, Frito-Lay, IBM, Xerox,

AT&T, Johnson & Johnson, Goodyear Tire and Rubber, Ford Motor Company, Dow Chemical, S. C. Johnson Wax, The Gap, and Manpower International. This is just a sampling. The field of I/O has grown dramatically since the 1970s, and more and more companies are employing I/O psychologists. But what exactly are these I/O psychologists doing?

You got a sense of what I/O psychologists do from the competencies presented in Table 1.1. From this table, it is clear that I/O psychologists have very broad training, but let's get a little more specific and discuss the major areas in which they work. In the ensuing chapters, these areas will be examined in greater detail.

SIOP publishes a pamphlet called *Building Better Organizations* (Society for Industrial and Organizational Psychology, 2003) in which major areas are listed, and I will highlight the most significant. First, the area in which more I/O psychologists work than any other is *selection.* Here, experts work on the development and administration of tests used for employee selection and placement. An important element in this process is the validation of selection instruments to ensure that they adequately predict job performance. Many I/O psychologists spend a great deal of time administering tests to applicants and current employees and then relating those test scores to performance on the job as a way of seeing if the test is a good one. We will examine issues of selection in Chapters 6 and 7. A second area in which many I/O psychologists work is *training and development.* Companies spend a great deal of time and money on training programs that teach new employees how to do their jobs and more established employees how to do new jobs with new equipment. I/O psychologists develop these training programs. First they carefully analyze the organization and the job; then they conduct the training program with the company's employees to improve performance on the job; and, eventually, they evaluate the effectiveness of the program. Training will be the focus of Chapter 8.

Organizational development (OD) is a third area of importance to many I/O psychologists. Experts in this area analyze organizational structures, cultures, and climate and develop interventions appropriate for a particular organization that might make the organization run more effectively. Organizational change is a large part of OD and one that companies are very interested in, given the many changes that are taking place in organizations of the 21st century. We will discuss organizational development in Chapter 14. A fourth area of emphasis for I/O psychologists is *performance appraisal* (sometimes also referred to as *performance management*). The emphasis here is on developing both individual and organizational measures of performance and using these measures to improve performance. An I/O psychologist might be responsible for developing an appraisal measure, deciding how to implement it, and overseeing its actual conduct. Performance appraisal will be discussed in Chapters 4 and 5.

The last area I'll mention is what I call *quality of worklife.* The chief concerns for people who work in this area are the measurement and improvement of job-related attitudes, such as job satisfaction and organizational commitment. An I/O psychologist might develop and administer an attitude survey to employees in an attempt to understand what employees like and don't like about their jobs. These

Many people do some of their work at home or, as we see here, while commuting to work on the train or subway.

data from surveys of this kind are often linked to performance, and then a plan is devised to improve attitudes by enhancing not only the work climate but also organizational efficiency. Chapter 10 provides a detailed analysis of quality of work-life in the context of job attitudes.

Certainly there are other areas that I/O psychologists work in, such as *consumer psychology* and *engineering or human factors psychology,* but the five areas discussed above account for the largest portion of work conducted by I/O psychologists. In the remainder of this text we will take a much more detailed look at what I/O psychologists do; but first we should examine at some length the history of I/O psychology, for nothing is as relevant to the future as its past.

100 YEARS OF HISTORY

Although the field of I/O psychology is relatively young compared with other areas within psychology, its history is a rich and interesting one. For those interested in a more detailed history of the field, I refer you to a fine resource by Laura Koppes (in press) on the first 100 years of I/O psychology. I will use an organizational structure, which breaks down the last 100 years into six periods, that was suggested by R. A. Katzell and J. T. Austin (1992). Table 1.2 presents a timeline of important historical events in the field of I/O psychology.

TABLE 1.2 Timeline for I/O Psychology in the United States

Year	Event
1892	American Psychological Association founded (Hugo Munsterberg a founding member)
1903	*The Theory of Advertising* published by Walter Dill Scott
1913	*Psychology and Industrial Efficiency* published by Hugo Munsterberg
1915	Walter VanDyke Bingham starts Division of Applied Psychology at Carnegie Institute of Technology (closes in 1924) Lillian Gilbreth earns Ph.D. in Psychology at Brown
1917	One group of psychologists, under Robert Yerkes, develops the Alpha and Beta tests; a second, the Committee on Classification of Personnel under Scott, works on a complete personnel system for the Army *Journal of Applied Psychology* publishes first issue
1919	The Scott Corporation founded as first consulting organization (closes in 1922)
1920	International Association of Applied Psychology created (www.ucm.es/info/Psyap/iaap)
1921	Bruce V. Moore earns Ph.D. in applied psychology at Carnegie Tech Graphic Rating Scale method published by Max Freyd
1924	Hawthorne Studies begin as investigations into lighting and productivity
1927	Equal interval scale proposed by Louis L. Thurstone
1931	Minnesota Employment Stabilization Research Institute created to study unemployment
1932	*Industrial Psychology,* the first comprehensive textbook in this field, published by Morris Viteles
1935	Robert Hoppock publishes research on job satisfaction
1938	Comparison of democratic and authoritarian leadership published by Kurt Lewin and Ronald Lippitt
1939	*Dictionary of Occupational Titles* first published by Department of Labor *Management and the Worker* published by Fritz Roethlisberger and William Dickman
1940	Walter V. Bingham and Robert Yerkes assist in preparing for world war, again
1941	John Flanagan creates Aviation Psychology Unit of Army Air Forces (summaries of the work are published as a 20-volume set following the war)
1945	Research Center on Group Dynamics founded by Kurt Lewin at MIT (became part of Institute of Social Research, under Rensis Likert, at University of Michigan) Ohio State Leadership studies initiated by Carroll L. Shartle
1946	Division 14 founded as part of reorganization of American Psychological Association, and Bruce V. Moore elected as first president
1947	General Aptitude Test Battery released by Department of Labor's Employment Service
1948	*Assessment of Men* describes selection of agents for Office of Strategic Services *Personnel Psychology* begins publication
1950	*Handbook of Applied Psychology* edited by Douglas Fryer and Edwin Henry
1954	Technical Recommendations for Psychological Tests and Diagnostic Techniques developed by APA Critical Incident Technique developed during World War II, published by John Flanagan
1956	AT&T Management Progress Study begins under the direction of Douglas Bray, with a 30-year follow-up published by Ann Howard and Bray in 1988
1958	*Organizations* published by James March and Herbert Simon
1959	Evolution toward scientific focus in management education initiated by publication of two reports sponsored by Ford Foundation (Gordon and Howell) and Carnegie Foundation (Pierson)
1963	Behavioral Expectation Scale method developed by Patricia Smith and Lorne Kendall
1964	Civil Rights Act enacted by Congress (Employment Title VII, revised in 1991)

TABLE 1.2 Timeline for I/O Psychology in the United States *(cont.)*

Year	Event
	Work and Motivation, presenting expectancy-value theory, published by Victor Vroom
1969	Job Descriptive Index measure of job satisfaction published by Patricia Smith, Lorne Kendall, and Charles Hulin
	"Signs, samples, and behavior" published by Paul Wernimont and John Campbell
	Position Analysis Questionnaire job analysis instrument published by Ernest McCormick
1973	Division 14 of APA changes name to Division of Industrial-Organizational Psychology
1975	First edition of *Principles for the Validation and Use of Personnel Selection Procedures* published by SIOP
1976	*Handbook of Industrial and Organizational Psychology* edited by Marvin Dunnette
1976	Job Diagnostic Survey instrument for assessment in job design published by Richard Hackman and Greg Oldham
1977	Technique for meta-analysis of test validity presented by Frank Schmidt and John Hunter
1980	Situational Interview technique published by Gary Latham, Lise Saari, Elliot Pursell, and James Campion
1982	Division 14 sponsors series of books on innovations in methodology; incorporates as Society for Industrial and Organizational Psychology, or SIOP (www.siop.org)
1986	First volume in SIOP Frontiers series, *Careers in Organizations,* edited by Douglas T. Hall
	First midyear I/O conference for SIOP members
1987	*Workforce 2000* projections published by Hudson Institute
	Attraction-Selection-Attrition (A-S-A) framework proposed by Benjamin Schneider
1988	American Psychological Society founded in response to perceived APA inadequacies
1990	*Handbook of Industrial-Organizational Psychology* (2nd ed.) published (Vol. 1 of 4)
	American Psychologist special issue edited by Lynn Offerman and Marilyn Gowing
	Summary of goal-setting theory published by Edwin Locke and Gary Latham
	Americans with Disabilities Act establishes individuals with declared physical/mental disabilities as a protected group and mandates reasonable accommodations
1991	First volume in SIOP Practice series, *Working with Organizations and Their People,* edited by Douglas Bray
1995	Occupational Information Network "content model" created by Department of Labor as basis of computerized replacement for the *Dictionary of Occupational Titles*
1997	*Workforce 2020* projections published by Hudson Institute (updated by Johnston and Packer)
1998	O*Net Ver 1.0 software and database released (1,100 occupations)
1999	*Standards for Educational and Psychological Testing* revised
2001	Anderson, Ones, Senagil, & Viswesvaran publish second edition of *Handbook of Industrial, Work, and Organizational Psychology*. Contributions reflect field's cross-cultural diversity.
2002	O*NET Ver 4.0 software and database released; associated no-cost assessments of work interests, work values, and job-relevant abilities available for a "whole person" approach.
2003	*Handbook of Psychology* published with a volume dedicated to I/O (Vol. 12, Borman, Ilgen, & Klimoski) that aims to update the 1990–1994 second edition of Dunnette's handbook. Society for Industrial and Organizational Psychology releases fourth edition of *Principles for Validation and Use of Personnel Selection Procedures.*
2004	Increasing emphasis on computer- and Internet-based recruiting, assessment, and testing.

Pre–World War I

The initial phase of this history started around the turn of the century and ended with World War I. In 1901, Walter Dill Scott, a professor at Northwestern University and former student of Wilhelm Wundt, was invited by the Western advertising manager of a chain of magazines to give a talk at the Agate Club in Chicago on the psychological aspects of advertising. Many refer to the date of this talk—December 20, 1901—as the beginning of business and industrial psychology, or what we now call industrial/organizational psychology. Scott published *The Theory of Advertising* in 1903. Twelve years later, in 1915, the Division of Applied Psychology was established at Carnegie Tech (now Carnegie Mellon University), with Walter VanDyke Bingham as its head, and in 1916 Scott became its first professor of applied psychology. At about the same time, Hugo Munsterberg (another Wundt student) moved to the United States, continued doing the applied work he had begun in Germany, and published his textbook *Psychology and Industrial Efficiency* (Munsterberg, 1913). It's interesting to note that, as virtually all psychologists at this time were trained as experimental psychologists, Scott, Munsterberg, Bingham, and others with applied interests had to fit these interests in amidst their full-time jobs in experimental psychology (Katzell & Austin, 1992).

World War I Through the 1920s

The second historical phase ranges from the World War I years through the 1920s. This is the period when I/O psychology really came of age and moved out from the hallowed halls of academia into the applied world. During this time, Scott and Bingham established a psychological program under the Army's personnel officer. Their staff was responsible for such things as the development of personnel files for military personnel and the creation of performance rating forms. Another group of psychologists led by Robert Yerkes (at that time the president of the American Psychological Association) worked for the government doing selection and placement of military personnel, using their newly developed tools—the **Army Apha and Army Beta** mental ability tests. These tests, which were developed as multiple choice–based intelligence tests that could be administered in groups, differed from the more typical individually administered intelligence tests that existed at this time. It became very clear during this period that those who studied and practiced I/O psychology had a great deal to offer the military—including the use of these and other tests for the screening and classification of many people.

Army Alpha and Army Beta
Mental ability tests developed by I/O psychologists during World War I that were used to select and classify army personnel.

It was also at this time that I/O psychology began to expand beyond the academic and military realms into government and private industry. I/O psychologists started consulting firms such as The Scott Company (founded by Walter Dill Scott), which worked in the areas of mental ability testing, personnel planning, training, and personnel administration. The Psychological Corporation was founded in 1921 and still exists today, specializing in test development.

Testing for selection and classification was an important part of what psychologists did for the military during World War I and World War II.

In the same year, Bruce V. Moore received from Carnegie Tech what is believed to have been the first Ph.D. in industrial psychology. His is an interesting story, as he rose from assistant professor to become department chair at Pennsylvania State University (the psychology building at Penn State is named after him) and eventually, in 1945, the first president of Division 14 of the APA. While at Carnegie Tech, he was approached by the Westinghouse Electric and Manufacturing Company with a problem: The company could not distinguish very well between new employees who should be directed toward careers in sales engineering and those who were better suited to design engineering (Gilmer, 1981). Moore and others worked on this problem, discovering that these different employees were best differentiated on the basis of items that reflected their interests. This early work by Moore was expanded on in later years by Edward Strong in what became the *Strong Vocational Interest Blank for Men* (Strong, 1927). In high school, I took a version of this inventory that told me my interests matched up with the interests of those who like to work with people and that teaching might be a good profession for me! And I'm sure that many of you may have taken what is now called the *Strong Interest Inventory* (Hansen & Campbell, 1985), which is commonly administered to high school and college students by guidance departments in an attempt to help students identify what careers they might find stimulating.

Interestingly, historians estimate that prior to 1917 there were fewer than 10 I/O psychologists in existence and that by 1929 there were about 50—a very large increase in just over 10 years (Katzell & Austin, 1992). In addition to the program at Carnegie Tech, I/O programs at Ohio State University, the University of

Minnesota, and Pennsylvania State University were launched during this time (Lowman, Kantor, & Perloff, in press).

The 1930s to Pre–World War II

The defining event of the next phase was a series of experiments collectively referred to as the Hawthorne Studies (see Table 1.3). This period in our history, of course, was marked by the Great Depression, during which unemployment rose to all-time highs and growth in the economy was nonexistent. As a result of these historical trends, our culture became focused less on employee testing and training and more on the human condition (Austin & Davies, 2000). The Hawthorne Studies were a series of experiments, some of which examined the impact of illumination on productivity, that were conducted at the Western Electric Plant in Hawthorne, Illinois. These experiments, among other things, highlighted the importance of social relations and employee attitudes. The interesting part of the story is that after observing employees' behaviors, researchers realized that the social and psychological conditions of work were often more important than the physical conditions (Roethlisberger & Dickson, 1939). We need to keep in mind that, to this point, the history of I/O had read more like the history of "I" alone! In other words, it wasn't until the Hawthorne Studies that team development, supervision, group process, worker morale, and other organizational phenomena played much of a role in the I/O field. As Haller Gilmer (1981), one of the early I/O psychologists, noted in his later years, "thinking about industrial-psychology problems changed. Simple answers to simple problems were not enough. Questions about motivation, leadership, supervision, and human relations began to emerge" (p. 13). Many view this time period, and the Hawthorne Studies in particular, as the birth of organizational psychology.

World War II to the Mid-1960s

Like the previous war, World War II was an important and dynamic time for the development of I/O psychology. Bingham, Scott, and Yerkes were brought back to the military to help match recruits to jobs. Selection, placement, evaluation, and appraisal were all largely begun during the World War I years, whereas World War II saw a great refinement in terms of their knowledge base and how best to apply them to specific situations. Organizational psychology took on the role of a more equal partner with industrial psychology and began to emphasize such areas as organizational dynamics, work groups, and employee morale. Whereas much of the military work initiated during World War I was shut down after that war, World War II work continued as the armed services created centers of research such as the Army Research Institute (ARI) and the Air Force Human Resources Laboratory (AFHRL), where studies are conducted to this day. During the 1950s many companies, including AT&T, General Electric, Metropolitan Life, and Stan-

TABLE 1.3 Hawthorne Illumination Study

Description	Manipulation	Expectation	Results
Experiment 1			
Test group would work under different light intensities, whereas Control group would work under constant light.	Test group experienced three different intensities (24, 46, and 70 foot candles), whereas Control group experienced no change in light intensity.	Test group would show increased productivity, whereas Control group's productivity would remain unchanged.	Test group's productivity increased, but Control group's productivity increased by about as much.
Experiment 2			
Test group would work under less intense light, whereas Control group would work under same light intensity.	Test group's lighting was decreased from 10 to 3 foot candles, whereas Control group's lighting did not change at all in intensity.	Test group would show a decrease in productivity, whereas Control group's productivity would remain unchanged.	Test group's productivity still increased, as did Control group's productivity.
Experiment 3			
Workers' lighting expectations were the focus of this study.	Workers were led to believe that the lighting was being increased, but in fact it was still the same intensity.	Original expectation was that there would be no effect; but if expectations were really important, then they might affect productivity or other variables.	Productivity remained the same, but workers reported favorable reactions to the increase in lighting. (Lighting, of course, did not increase.)
Experiment 4			
Workers' lighting expectations were the focus of this study.	Workers were led to believe that the lighting was being decreased, but in fact it was still the same intensity.	Original expectation was that there would be no effect; but if expectations were really important, then they might affect productivity or other variables.	Productivity remained the same, but workers reported unfavorable reactions to the decrease in lighting. (Lighting, of course, did not decrease.)

dard Oil of New Jersey, also established large research groups to do I/O work (Dunnette, 1962).

The number and diversity of universities training students in I/O psychology increased during the same period. New programs were developed at the University of Maryland, Michigan State University, and George Washington University. In addition, several university-based programs were developed that emphasized organizational issues (as opposed to industrial ones), such as the Research Center for Group Dynamics established by Kurt Lewin at the Massachusetts Institute of Technology (Katzell & Austin, 1992). Lewin, chiefly considered a social psychologist, was instrumental in developing theory and methodology in the area of work groups and leadership. His early work still influences modern I/O psychology through its impact on more recent motivational theories such as goal setting and expectancy theory (we'll consider these in Chapter 9). Finally, personnel counseling developed during this time as an outgrowth of the Hawthorne Studies. The focus here was on helping employees deal with personal problems that had the potential to affect their work performance (Highhouse, 1999).

The Mid-1960s to the Mid-1980s

One strong indication of the increasing role of organizational psychology was the fact that, in 1970, Division 14 of the APA changed its name from "the Division of Business and Industrial Psychology" to "the Division of Industrial and Organizational Psychology." Organizational psychology had truly arrived.

On the industrial side, this period marked a great deal of work on selection and performance appraisal. These continue to be two of the largest and most researched topic areas in I/O psychology. One major theme at the time was a concern with ethnic and racial differences on selection tests and the fairness of those tests. This interest emerged as a result of the social, political, and legal climate of the 1960s. As you know, this period was defined by the civil rights movement; it was a time of great racial tension. Issues of discrimination and fairness permeated society and the workplace. I/O psychology began addressing these issues as well. In Chapters 6 and 7, we will discuss Title VII of the Civil Rights Act of 1964, which was the legal framework for much of this work.

Organizational topics of interest during this period included work motivation, job attitudes, and job characteristics. As we will note in Chapter 9, on motivation, more than a few of the most popular theories of motivation—including goal setting and expectancy theory—came of age during this period. Indeed, Richard Hackman and Greg Oldham's work on the motivating potential of jobs as a result of their characteristics is among the most cited work in the history of I/O psychology (Sackett, 1994). Similarly, much of the work on job attitudes, such as job satisfaction and organizational commitment (see Chapter 10), was conducted during this time.

These two decades were a time of tremendous growth in I/O psychology. New doctoral training programs emerged at such places as Bowling Green State University (1966), North Carolina State University (1966), and The University of Akron (1968). In 1960, there were about 756 members of Division 14; by 1980 they totaled 2,005 (Katzell & Austin, 1992).

The Mid-1980s to the Present

During the last 15 to 20 years, the field of I/O psychology has grown very rapidly, with more work in traditional areas such as selection, performance appraisal, motivation, and leadership, as well as in new domains. For instance, the fairness of employment tests—and the legal climate involved in personnel or labor law—has become an even greater focus among I/O psychologists. Cognitive processes, too, are now the focus of much research in the I/O area as this cognitive framework has emerged within all aspects of psychology. Historians estimate that in 1939 there were fewer than 100 I/O psychologists in the world (Katzell & Austin, 1992). That estimate grew to 760 by 1960. In 1992, there were about 2,500 members of SIOP and probably a few hundred more I/O psychologists who weren't members, totaling around 3,000 I/O psychologists. The most recent SIOP data indicate about 3,500 professional members and 2,500 student members (Society for Industrial and Organizational Psychology, 2003). In earlier sections, I highlighted the development of some of the early I/O programs, beginning with Carnegie Tech. The latest SIOP data reveal more than 65 doctoral programs in I/O psychology and many others that offer master's degrees. Whereas Walter Dill Scott was the first professor of applied psychology, there are more than 1,000 such professors in psychology departments and business schools around the globe today. And whereas Bruce V. Moore received the first Ph.D. in I/O from Carnegie Tech in 1921, 1,311 members of SIOP received their doctoral degrees between 1995 and 2003 (Esther Benitez, personal communication, March 15, 2004). In addition to being one of the fastest-growing areas within psychology, I/O holds the potential for making a great impact on 21st-century society.

THE IMPORTANCE OF I/O PSYCHOLOGY IN THE 21ST CENTURY

Although the history of I/O psychology presented here seems to reflect a great deal of change over the past 100 years, it is fair to say that this change is just the tip of the iceberg. The 21st century promises to be fast, frenzied, competitive, and turbulent. Dramatic changes are taking place in the world of work. Wayne Cascio (1995), former president of SIOP, has given an excellent account of those changes and what the I/O field needs to do to keep up with them while continuing to make contributions to human welfare.

First, whereas war defined the geopolitical scene of the 20th century, economics will be the crowning issue of the 21st century. We hear the term *global competition* thrown about a great deal, and for good reason. Our workers and firms in the United States can no longer expect to freely and easily make a profit. Global competition will continue to require that we have a skilled, well-trained, and competent workforce to compare favorably with the many, many countries that are now our competitors. Second, new technology has decreased the number of traditional jobs for workers and organizations. At the same time, *downsizing* has occurred at an alarming rate; between 1987 and 1992 alone, more than 6 million employees were laid off (Baumohl, 1993). A glimpse at the local newspaper makes it very clear that this trend is continuing into the 21st century. We have empathy, and rightfully so, for those who are laid off due to organizational cutbacks; but the rest of the story is that when these individuals are fortunate enough to be reemployed, they are reemployed at a lower wage rate (Cascio, 1995). In addition, we need to remember that those cutbacks leave other workers behind to complete the job, sometimes requiring them to do more for less. Companies are always looking to be more competitive, more efficient, and leaner, but the result is that fewer employees are left to do the work that needs to be done. I/O psychology is thus important for (1) helping laid-off workers to become competitive for other jobs and (2) helping those left behind to handle more diverse jobs and sometimes a heavier workload.

The global marketplace has changed the nature of work in the 21st century.

Third, one of the latest trends in organizations is "flatter" organizational structures, which means that middle-level management is often cut out of the organization entirely. In order for companies to run with this sleeker structure, they often emphasize the empowerment of workers. No longer is it typical for organizations to have a manager for every 10 employees; now an upper-level manager may supervise 50 employees in teams of 10. Employees—team members—are given greater responsibility for their performance, as well as for objective setting and decision-making. Employees and teams manage themselves! This is not to say that management and leadership are no longer relevant to organizations and, thus, should no longer be a focus of what we, as I/O psychologists, do. On the contrary, it makes what we do more integral to the functioning of organizations: No longer can we focus just on the management and leadership training for traditional "managers," but we must also develop programs for employees to guarantee that they can function in these new leaderless groups. In short, industrial/organizational psychologists need to prepare current and future employees for this very different approach to organizational functioning.

Finally, the workplace is becoming more diverse in terms of race, gender, age, ethnicity, and culture. This diversity requires much more coordination and sensitivity to "differences" on the part of management and employees. Education and training regarding diversity among workers has become a very important area for I/O psychologists and will continue to grow in importance in the 21st century.

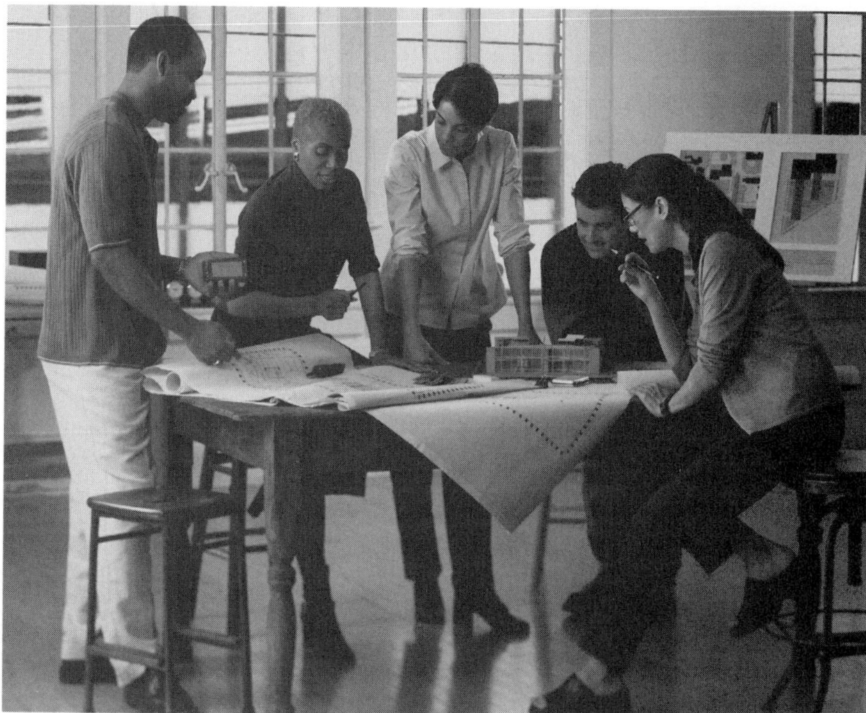

Many companies have diverse work groups like this one.

As American society and the American workplace continue to change, the field of I/O psychology will have potentially more to offer. Earlier, we traced the history and development of the field, noting various areas in which I/O psychologists work. These areas—including training, evaluation, appraisal, leadership, and motivation—have been important to the world of work for many years, but now with the 21st century having begun and the workplace so thoroughly transformed, I/O psychology is poised to make a real difference.

SUMMARY

I/O psychology, the application of psychology to the workplace, encompasses such diverse areas as performance appraisal, employment testing, organizational development, and motivation. I/O psychologists receive extensive training in a wide range of areas, but their central approach is based on the scientist/practitioner model, which emphasizes both theory and practice. Most obtain an advanced degree such as a Ph.D. The training is quite intensive and includes a great deal of course work, practical experience, and research experience. The culmination of the training is usually the completion of a dissertation.

Almost 40% of I/O psychologists work in academic settings such as psychology departments and business schools, where they teach graduate and undergraduate students and conduct research for the purposes of creating and applying knowledge. The majority of I/O psychologists, however, work outside of academia in the public or private sector, applying what they've learned in graduate school to their particular organization. Many of these I/O psychologists also work for consulting firms that provide services to organizations on a project-by-project basis.

I/O psychology has a rich, albeit relatively short, history. Although its beginnings date to around the turn of the 20th century, its growth as a field emerged with World War I, when I/O psychologists were employed by the government to do training, testing, and performance measurement. Other historical hallmarks include World War II, the civil rights movement of the 1960s, and the emergence of the global economy in the past 15 years. I/O psychology is positioned to play an ever-increasing role in the constantly changing world of work in the 21st century. In the remainder of this book we will discuss the various topics and areas in which I/O psychology has, and will continue to have, an impact.

REVIEW QUESTIONS

1. What is the distinction between industrial psychology and organizational psychology?
2. What is the scientist/practitioner model, and how is it used in the training of I/O psychologists?

3. Discuss what I/O psychologists do in organizations, consulting firms, and academia.

4. Briefly describe the contributions of the following to the development of I/O psychology: (a) Walter Dill Scott, (b) Walter VanDyke Bingham, (c) Kurt Lewin, (d) World War I, (e) the civil rights movement, (f) the changing world of work.

5. Why is I/O psychology likely to have a great impact in the 21st century?

SUGGESTED READINGS

Arthur, W., Jr., & Benjamin, L. T., Jr. (1999). Psychology applied to business. In D. A. Bernstein (Ed.), *Psychology: Fields of application* (pp. 98–115). Boston: Houghton Mifflin. A nicely written review of I/O psychology in an interesting book about psychology and its diverse subfields.

Katzell, R. A., & Austin, J. T. (1992). From then to now: The development of industrial-organizational psychology in the United States. *Journal of Applied Psychology, 77*(6), 803–835. A thorough history of the I/O field with an emphasis on the role of the people involved in each time period.

Koppes, L. L. (Ed.). (in press). *The science and practice of industrial and organizational psychology: Historical aspects of the first 100 years.* Mahwah, NJ: Erlbaum. The most comprehensive and up-to-date text ever written on the history of I/O psychology—this is a must-read for history buffs who are interested in I/O psychology.

Research Methods in I/O Psychology

2

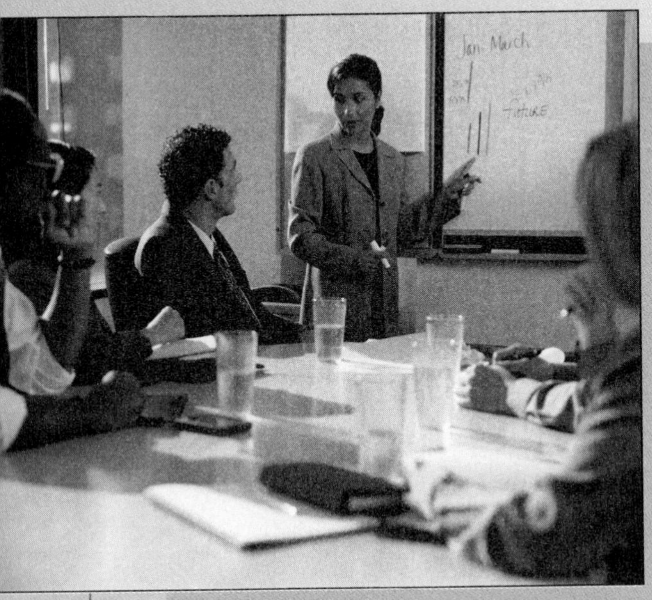

CHAPTER OUTLINE

Chapter 1 introduced you to I/O psychology, provided you with some history about I/O psychology, and discussed some of the topics that I/O psychologists explore. This chapter presents the scientific method as the framework used by I/O psychologists in doing their work.

Suppose that an organization is having a problem with absenteeism such that, on average, its employees are missing about 15 days of work per year. Absenteeism is a very expensive problem for organizations because it slows down production and costs additional dollars to replace employees who are missing. Suppose further that this company has hired you as an I/O psychologist to help it diagnose the problem, provide a potential solution, and implement and evaluate that solution. First, then, you have to figure out what the problem is. You may do this by interviewing current plant employees, by talking to managers, and by administering surveys. In addition, you may need to look at the organization's absence data and do some statistical analysis to uncover how frequent the absences are, when they tend to occur (e.g., Mondays and Fridays versus days in the middle of the week), and whether they are occurring in certain departments more than in others. Second, you may need to collect some historical data about the company and its absence policy (usually a written policy in the employee handbook) because this may help you to understand the problem better. Third, you might use this information and your expertise in I/O psychology to develop and implement an approach to the problem. Further, you will need to look at the absence data again a few months after the new approach is under way to see whether absence has decreased. In addition, you may want to survey and interview employees to see if they have noticed any differences since (and as a result of) the new approach. At each of these steps in the process, you will need to gather data in order to understand the problem and to evaluate the solution. In this chapter, I will talk about how I/O psychologists gather data and use it to improve their understanding of organizational functioning.

LEARNING OBJECTIVES

This chapter should help you understand:

- the scientific method and its goals and assumptions.
- the importance of theory to science and psychology.
- internal and external validity.
- the complex interplay among experimental variables.
- how research is conducted with an emphasis on induction and deduction, and involving a five-step process.
- a variety of measurement issues such as reliability and validity.
- basic-level statistics ranging from descriptive statistics to correlation and regression.

CHAPTER TWO

WHAT IS SCIENCE?

science
A process or method for generating a body of knowledge.

Science is a process or method for generating a body of knowledge. It's important to note that this term refers not to a body of knowledge but, rather, to the process or method used in producing that body of knowledge. Science represents a *logic of inquiry*—a way of going about doing things to increase our understanding of concepts, processes, and relationships. What makes psychology scientific is that we rely on formal, systematic observation to help us find answers to questions about behavior. Science is not about people in white coats in a laboratory, or brilliant teachers in the thought-provoking world of academia, or mind-boggling technological advances; science is about understanding the world in which we live. But scientists are not satisfied with a superficial understanding; they strive for a complete understanding. For instance, the nonscientist may note that employees seem to be more productive when they are allowed to participate in important organizational decisions. The scientist, on the other hand, works at understanding why this is the case, what kind of participation is most important for employees, when participation might not benefit the organization, why it is that participation seems important for some employees but not for others, and so on. In the next section, we will examine the four major goals of science.

GOALS OF SCIENCE

There are many different lists of the goals or objectives of science, but I will use the list described by Larry Christensen (1994) because it is most consistent with my thinking on the subject. First, there is *description,* the accurate portrayal or depiction of the phenomenon of interest. In our example, this is the focus of the nonscientist's approach to understanding, in that he simply noted and described the phenomenon whereby employees are more productive when given some voice by the organization. But the scientist goes further than this—which brings us to the second goal. In an attempt to better understand the phenomenon, the scientist focuses on an *explanation*—that is, on gathering knowledge about why the phenomenon exists or what causes it. This usually requires an identification of one or more antecedents, which are conditions that come prior to the phenomenon. Again, in our example, it may be that giving employees the opportunity to participate in decisions makes the employees feel needed and important, which leads to or causes increased effort. Of course, as scientists we realize that almost all behaviors are complex and that there tend to be many causes or antecedents for any given behavior.

The third goal of science is *prediction,* which refers to the ability to anticipate an event prior to its actual occurrence. Accurate prediction requires that we have some understanding of the explanation of the phenomenon so that we can anticipate when the phenomenon will occur. In our example, we may be able to predict an increase in effort on the part of the employees if we know that the company just recently sent out a survey asking for their input on important decisions about medical benefits. Without the ability to predict, we have a gap in our knowledge and are left with very little helpful information that we can provide to the company. In other words, if we have described and explained the phenomenon but cannot help the company predict this behavior in the future, our usefulness is somewhat limited.

The last goal of science is *control* of the phenomenon—specifically, the manipulation of antecedent conditions to affect behavior. Ideally, we'd like to have a sufficiently complete understanding of the phenomenon so that we can manipulate or control variables to increase or decrease the occurrences of the phenomenon. In other words, we'd like to be able to help the company provide the appropriate antecedents so that employees will work harder and perform better. Indeed, by providing employees with opportunities for participation throughout the year, the company should be able to maintain high levels of effort and performance.

In sum, we have attained some degree of scientific understanding only when a phenomenon is accurately described, explained, predicted, and can be controlled.

Assumptions of Science

In order for scientists to do their work and to make sense of the world, they must have some basic assumptions about the world. First, scientists must believe in *empiricism,* which is the notion that the best way to understand behavior is to generate predictions based on theory, to gather data, and to use the data to test these predictions. Psychologists who do not accept the principle of empiricism would find science a fruitless venture. Second, scientists must believe in *determinism,* which suggests that behavior is orderly and systematic and doesn't just happen by chance. Imagine what psychology would be like if its basic assumption was that behavior was a chance occurrence. It would counter what all psychologists believe, because it would suggest that we can neither explain nor predict behavior. In effect, if we didn't believe that behavior is orderly, psychology would have nothing to offer society.

The third basic assumption of scientists is *discoverability,* which suggests not only that behavior is orderly but also that this orderliness can be discovered. I'm not suggesting that behavior is so orderly that a psychologist can easily predict what an individual will do at any given moment; if it was that easy, think about how it would change the way you interact with others. For instance, if you knew exactly how your girlfriend or boyfriend would react to a marriage proposal, you would feel much less stress and be certain that you would never hear the answer "no" (since, in that event, you wouldn't ask the question!). Psychologists do not suggest that behavior is that orderly, only that there is some order to it; so the last major assumption here is that we can experience, examine, and discover—to some extent—that orderliness.

Theories

theory
A set of interrelated constructs (concepts), definitions, and propositions that present a systematic view of a phenomenon by specifying relations among variables, with the purpose of explaining and predicting the phenomenon.

A **theory** is a set of interrelated constructs (concepts), definitions, and propositions that present a systematic view of phenomena by specifying relations among variables, with the purpose of explaining and predicting the phenomena (Kerlinger, 1986). Fred Kerlinger goes as far as to suggest that the four goals of science discussed earlier are subsumed under the one major objective of science, which he says is theory development. He argues that without an emphasis on theory, science would become nothing more than a simple search for answers, lacking any framework or carefully executed process. It is theory and its accompanying propositions, according to Kerlinger, that allow us to describe, explain, predict, and control the phenomenon under investigation. Even though, as I/O practitioners, our focus may be on conducting research that will help us to solve an applied problem, that research should be based on a theory, or its results should be used to help develop new theories and alter existing theories. It's important to realize that theories are as important to applied disciplines like I/O psychology as they are to basic-level scientific disciplines, like microbiology.

What Makes a Good Theory? As with everything else in science, there are good theories and there are bad theories. Bad theories can be responsible for a lot of wasted effort as we try to understand a particular phenomenon. Sometimes our theories are not very helpful, and for a variety of reasons—not the least of which is that they may be wrong. Scientists generally agree that a good theory should meet certain criteria or standards. First, a theory is of little use if it is not *parsimonious.* In other words, the theory should be able to explain a lot in as simple a way as possible. The fewer statements in a theory, the better. If a theory has to have a proposition or statement for every phenomenon that it tries to explain, it will become so big as to be unmanageable. Generally, if two theories make the same predictions, the more parsimonious one is the better theory. After all, if people can't understand the theory or use it in their research, the theory will not help advance science by improving their understanding.

The second criterion for a good theory is *precision.* A theory should be specific and accurate in its wording and conceptual statements so that everyone knows what its propositions and predictions are. You might notice a tradeoff here between parsimony and precision, but, in fact, theorists try to develop theories that are both simple and precise: Too much of either is a potential weakness of the theory. If the theory is not very precise and instead is wordy and unclear, scientists will not know how to use the theory or be able to make predictions based on the theory. They would be left in the position of having to try to interpret the theory based on what *they think* it tries to say. *Testability* is the third criterion for a theory, because if it can't be tested, it can't be useful. Testability means that the propositions presented in the theory must be verifiable by some sort of experimentation. If you have developed a theory that predicts rainfall in inches as a function of the number of Martians that land on the earth per day, you have developed a theory that is untestable (unless you know something I don't know!)

and that, therefore, is not a good theory. Notice that I have not said that the theory must be capable of being proven. The reason is that theories are not proven but, rather, are either supported or not supported by the data. We can never prove a theory; we can only gather information that serves to make us more confident that the theory is accurate or that it is misspecified.

It is very possible to have a theory that stands the test of time for many years and then is refuted by additional data collection and theoretical work. From about the 2nd century A.D. to the 15th century A.D., Ptolemy's theory of the solar system (a geocentric system), with the Earth as the immovable center of the universe, was uniformly accepted across the world (Britannica Online, 1998b). However, in the 15th century, Copernicus demonstrated that there was more support for his heliocentric system, with the Sun as the center of the universe and the Earth revolving around it. This "Copernican Revolution" caused shock among many who had steadfastly believed that the Earth was the center of the universe (Britannica Online, 1998a). With more and more observations and mathematical formulae supporting it, Copernicus's view of the universe eventually supplanted Ptolemy's.

One of the great scientific philosophers, Karl Popper, argued that science is really about ruling out alternative explanations, leaving just one explanation or theory that seems to fit the data (Popper, 1959). He further said that the ultimate goal for a scientific theory is to be "not yet disconfirmed." In making this statement, Popper seemed to realize that most theories are likely to be disconfirmed at some point, but that it is in the disconfirmation that science advances.

A slightly different list of the stages involved in the research process.

Of course, a theory must also be *useful,* such that it is practical and helps in describing, explaining, and predicting an *important* phenomenon. You may be able to generate a theory about how often and when your psychology instructor is likely to walk across the room while lecturing; but I would wonder, even if your theory describes, explains, and predicts this phenomenon pretty well, whether anyone really cares. The behavior itself is not important enough to make the theory useful; so no matter how well it predicts, by this criterion of usefulness it would be a bad theory. The theory may also be testable, but the phenomenon it predicts is not important enough for the theory to be useful.

Finally, a theory should possess the quality of *generativity;* it should stimulate research that attempts to support or refute its propositions. We may develop a theory that seems to meet all of the other criteria, but if no one ever tests the theory or uses it in any way, then the theory itself would be of little value.

In sum, science is logic of inquiry, and the primary objective of science is theory building. As a set of propositions about relationships among variables, a theory is developed to describe, explain, predict, and control important phenomena. Theories can be evaluated as to their parsimony, precision, testability, usefulness, and generativity. But how do we put all of this together and start to conduct research? That will be the focus of the rest of the chapter. First, however, we need to clarify the relationship between theories and data.

Which Comes First—Data or Theory? Theory and data are of the utmost importance to science and can't be overemphasized. Science uses both theory and data, but individual scientists have disagreed about which should come first and which is more important. Sir Francis Bacon, in the 1600s, was one of the early scientists who believed in the importance of empirical observation—that is, for Bacon, data was key. This approach to science is still popular today. Referred to as **induction,** it involves working from data to theory. Basically, the argument here is that we must collect data, data, and more data until we have enough data to develop a theory. Others, however, take the opposite approach, known as **deduction,** which involves starting with a theory and propositions and then collecting data to test those propositions. In this case, reasoning proceeds from a general theory to data that test particular elements of that theory—working from theory to data.

induction
An approach to science that consists of working from data to theory.

deduction
An approach to science in which we start with theory and propositions and then collect data to test those propositions—working from theory to data.

In their purest forms, there are problems with both the inductive and deductive approaches to research. Collecting data and then generating theories (i.e., induction) is useless unless those theories are tested and modified as a result of additional data. But generating a theory and collecting data to test its propositions (i.e., deduction) is only a partial process, too, unless those data are used to alter or refute those propositions. The approach taken by most distinguished scientists is one that combines inductive processes with deductive processes.

Both approaches are depicted in Figure 2.1, which illustrates the *cyclical inductive-deductive model of research.* Note that although it doesn't really matter whether one starts with data (induction) or with a theory (deduction), neither is

FIGURE 2.1 The Cyclical Inductive-Deductive Model of Research

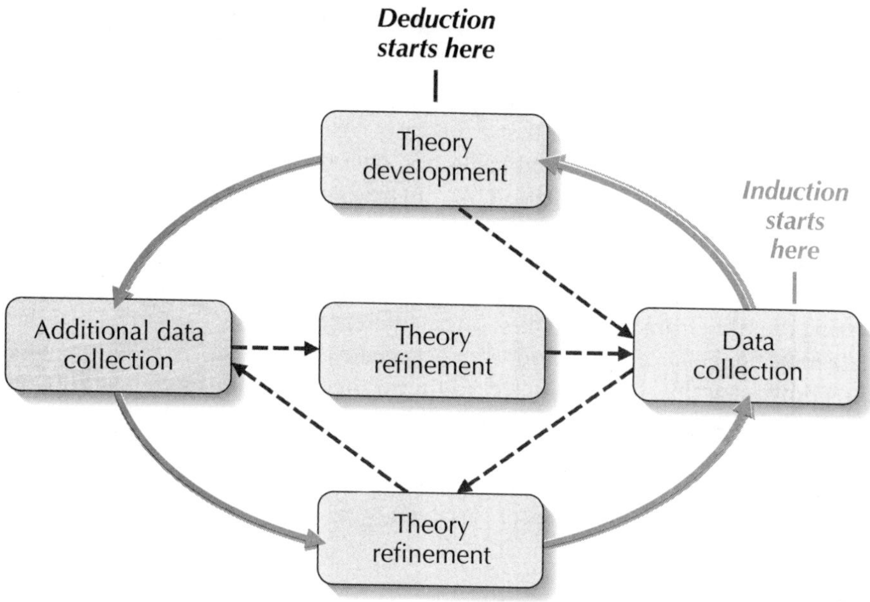

used exclusively at the expense of the other. If one starts with a general theory (inside path of the figure), data are collected to test the theory; the data are used to make changes to the theory if necessary; more data are collected; the theory is amended again; and the process continues. If one begins with data collection (outside path of the figure), the data are used to develop a theory; additional data are collected to test this theory; the theory is amended if necessary; even more data are collected; and the process continues.

At least initially, most research tends to be driven by inductive processes. Think about it. Even in research using the deductive approach—theory to data—the original development of the theory was probably based on some data. Hence induction is an initial part of the process, with an ensuing emphasis on deductive methods. So here, too, we see the cyclical model in action.

By now it should be obvious that there is no perfect way to "do science." However, being aware of the goals of science, the assumptions of scientists, the criteria for good theories, and how induction and deduction feed into each other should help you to understand the ways in which the scientific process is best applied. The specific types of research designs and data collection techniques will be discussed soon, but first you need to be familiarized with some important terminology.

RESEARCH TERMINOLOGY AND BASIC CONCEPTS

causal inference
A conclusion, drawn from research data, about the likelihood of a causal relationship between two variables.

To begin to understand what is involved in conducting experiments, you have to know what is meant by drawing a **causal inference** because this is what we typically want to be able to do at the completion of our experiment. Recall my earlier point that we can never prove that a theory is right or wrong but can only gain confidence in the theory through collecting data that support the theory. With causality, we have a similar situation. We can never prove a causal relationship between two variables because there may be some other variable, of which we aren't even aware, that's causing the relationship. Thus our greatest hope is that we have conducted our experiment carefully enough so that we feel confident about inferring causality from it. We make a causal inference when we determine that our data indicate that a causal relationship between two variables is *likely*. Again, we can't prove causality, but we can feel confident that there is a causal relationship. This inability to prove causality explains why psychologists spend a great deal of time working to design their experiments very carefully. Being able to confidently draw a causal inference depends on careful experimental design, which, in turn, begins with the two major types of variables.

INDEPENDENT AND DEPENDENT VARIABLES

independent variable
A variable that is systematically manipulated by the experimenter or, at the least, measured by the experimenter as a precursor to other variables.

An **independent variable** is anything that is systematically manipulated by the experimenter or, at the least, measured by the experimenter as an antecedent to other variables. The intention is to determine whether the independent variable causes changes in whatever behavior we are interested in. For example, we might vary the amount of participation that we give employees in deciding how to do their work: One group might be given no input and simply told how to do its work, a second group might be given some input into deciding how to accomplish the tasks, and a third group might be given complete control over how to do the job. In this experiment, our independent variable would be the degree of participation granted to employees.

dependent variable
The variable of interest, or what we design our experiments to assess.

The **dependent variable** is the variable of interest—what we design our experiment to assess. In short, we are usually interested in the effect of the independent variable on the dependent variable. For example, we might predict that participation (the independent variable) will influence employees' job satisfaction (the dependent variable). In other words, the more opportunities employees are given to decide how to do their own work, the more satisfied they will be with their jobs. If we were to find these results, we would conclude that participation causes job satisfaction. Keep in mind, however, that when I say *causes* I mean that we are making a causal inference, because we can't be certain that participation causes satisfaction. This shortcut in terminology is typically used by psychologists: We talk about causation when we really mean causal inference. In I/O psychology, common dependent variables include performance, profits, costs, job attitudes, salary, promotion, attendance behaviors, and motivation. Usually, we manipulate the independent variable and measure its effect on the dependent variable.

Another type of variable is called an **extraneous variable.** An extraneous variable—also known as a confounding variable—is anything other than the independent variable that can contaminate the results or be thought of as an alternative to our causal explanation. Extraneous variables get in the way and prevent us from being confident that our independent variable is affecting our dependent variable. In our participation–job satisfaction experiment, for example, performance might be an extraneous variable if better performers were given more opportunity for participation. In this case they may be more satisfied not because of their participation but, rather, because they are getting more organizational rewards as a result of being better performers.

extraneous variable
Anything other than the independent variable that can contaminate our results or be thought of as an alternative to our causal explanation.

In I/O psychology, we often refer to independent and dependent variables by other, more specific names. Independent variables are frequently called *predictors, precursors,* or *antecedents,* and dependent variables are often called *criteria, outcomes,* or *consequences.* In the selection context (which we will discuss in Chapters 6 and 7, we often talk of predictors and criteria. We use a predictor variable to forecast an individual's score on a criterion variable. For instance, we might say that intelligence is an important predictor of successful job performance. *Predictors* and *criteria* are discussed in much more detail later in the book, but for now it's important that you realize that these terms are often used interchangeably with *independent variable* and *dependent variable,* respectively.

Internal and External Validity

With respect to research, it's important that we distinguish the two types of validity associated with research studies from the validity of a test, which is explained later in the chapter. With any experiment, the first thing we are interested in is whether our results have **internal validity,** which is the extent to which we can draw causal inferences about our variables. In other words, can we be confident that the result of our experiment is due to the independent variable that we manipulated and not due to some confounding or extraneous variable? Returning to our participation–job satisfaction study, we would have high internal validity if we were confident that participation was the variable that was affecting employees' satisfaction levels. If, however, it was actually the rewards associated with better performance that led to high satisfaction (as I suggested, these rewards might be an extraneous variable), then we couldn't rule out rewards as an alternative explanation for differences in satisfaction, and we would thus have internal-validity problems.

internal validity
The extent to which we can draw causal inferences about our variables.

The other major type of validity that is important when designing experiments is **external validity,** the extent to which the results obtained in our experiment generalize to other people, settings, and times. Suppose we conduct a study in which we find that those employees who are given specific, difficult goals to

external validity
The extent to which the results obtained in an experiment generalize to other people, settings, and times.

work toward perform better than those who are simply told to do their best. We want to be able to say that this effect will generalize to other employees in other companies at other times. Obviously, external validity is extremely important to the development of science; to the extent that we devise studies that are low in external validity, we are not moving science forward. For instance, some criticize I/O research done with student participants as not being generalizable to "real-world" employees. If the work that is done with students does not generalize to employees, it is not very useful for increasing our understanding of the phenomenon under study. (For a different view, see Dobbins, Lane, & Steiner, 1988.) However, external validity is always an empirical question. We can't simply conduct a study and argue that it is or is not externally valid. Rather, the external validity of this one study is demonstrated by replicating it with different participants, in different settings, at different times. We can also try to use representative samples of the population to which we want to generalize and argue that our results probably generalize to others. However, to be sure, we have to collect additional data.

There is an important tradeoff between internal and external validity that often demands the researcher's attention (Cook & Campbell, 1979). As we rule out various alternative explanations by controlling more and more elements of the study to successfully increase our internal validity, what happens to the generalizability of our results? It may decline because, now, a one-of-a-kind situation has been created that is *so artificial* it is not likely to be externally valid. Put more simply, the findings may not generalize to other situations because no other situation is likely to be very similar to the one we've created. So, as we gain control for internal validity purposes, we may lose the potential for external validity. Of course, if we don't control and rule out alternative explanations, we will not be confident in our causal explanation (internal validity), even if the results have the potential to generalize to other settings and participants. And in any case, if we aren't sure what the results mean, what good is external validity? My point here is that we have to start with internal validity because, without it, our research really can't make much of a contribution to the knowledge in the field. But we also need to balance the two types of validity, as too much control can reduce the extent to which the results are likely to generalize. Now, let's talk about how we use control in our research.

Control

Control is a very important element of experimental design. To ensure that we can make a causal inference about the effect of our independent variable on our dependent variable—a matter of internal validity—we need to be able to exercise control over the experiment. Indeed, John Stuart Mill, a great philosopher of science, argued that in order to be able to confidently draw a causal inference, we must eliminate other potential explanations of the effect (Cook & Campbell, 1979). And one major way of doing this is to control extraneous variables.

Let's say we're interested in the effect of leadership style on employee performance. To examine this relationship, we could use a survey of employees to measure their leaders' style and then match that up with the performance of individuals who work for each leader. We could then look to see if a particular leadership style results in better employee performance. However, there are many potential extraneous variables in this situation, such as employees' ability or experience. It may be that all of the employees who work for the leader with the most favorable style also happen to be the employees with the most ability. Therefore, although it looks as though leader style leads to a particular level of performance, certain leaders' employees may actually be performing well because of their own ability rather than because of the leader's style. Consider the case of a really bad baseball player who gets traded all the time but always lands on good teams. If these teams go on to win the World Series, do we say that they won because of this bad player? Certainly not; they won the World Series because most of their other players were very good. The extraneous variable here is the overall quality of these teams: good pitching, hitting, and defense. The relationship isn't between the bad player's ability and the performance of the teams he plays on, but between the quality of the players on the team that he joins and team performance.

There are various ways in which we can attempt to control for extraneous variables. First, the potentially extraneous variable can be *held constant* in our experiment. For instance, if we think that employees' experience might be an extraneous variable in our leadership–job performance study, we could control for this by using as participants only those employees who have the same amount of job experience—exactly 10 years. In other words, rather than allowing experience to confound our results, we hold it constant. Then, if we find that leadership style and employee performance are related, although we cannot say for sure that style causes performance, we *can* be certain that employee experience is not an alternative explanation. Because all of the participants in our study have the same amount of experience, any differences on performance must be due to something else.

A second way in which we try to control for extraneous variables is by systematically *manipulating different levels of the variable.* For example, if we think that gender might be a confounding variable in our leadership–job performance study, we might treat gender as an independent variable and use a more complicated experimental design in which we look at the relationship between leadership style and job performance among female leaders versus male leaders. This would be the opposite of holding the variable constant; here, we make the variable *part of the experimental design* and examine whether it plays a role in affecting the dependent variable. For instance, if we find the same relationship between leadership style and job performance among male leaders as we find among female leaders, then we have successfully ruled out gender as an alternative explanation of our effect.

A third way, though it's too complicated for our present purposes, is to use *statistical control.* For instance, with statistical techniques such as the analysis of covariance, we can remove or control the variability in our dependent variable that is due to the extraneous variable.

A Model of the Research Process

There are various ways to go about conducting a research project, but in this section we will discuss a general approach that should act as a guide for you in developing and conducting your own research. It should also help you to understand how research in psychology progresses through various stages. The model is presented in Figure 2.2.

hypothesis
A tentative statement about the relationship between two or more variables.

Usually, the first step in any research project is to formulate testable hypotheses. A **hypothesis** is a tentative statement about the relationship between two or more variables. Hypotheses are most often generated as a result of a thorough review of the literature. Sometimes, however, they arise from the experimenter's own experiences or from a question that has not yet been answered in the published literature. Regardless of how one gets there, hypothesis generation is the first formal step in this process.

The second step involves the actual designing of the study, which we've talked about previously with respect to control, internal validity, and external validity. The two basic choices that need to be made at this stage are who the participants in your study are going to be and what is going to be measured. Although research participants in general can include children, older adults, animals, and people suf-

FIGURE 2.2 Stage Model of the Research Process

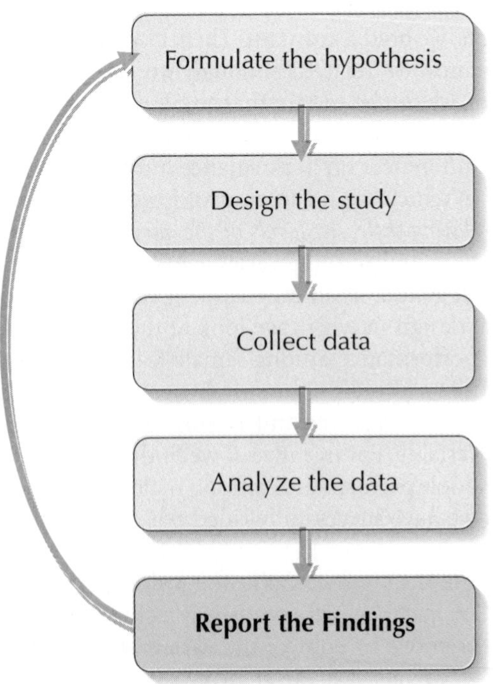

fering from various disorders, participants in most I/O psychology experiments are either college undergraduates or organizational employees. As for measures, we typically have one or more independent variables and dependent variables.

After the study is designed, it's time to actually go about collecting the data. This can be done in many different ways. Some studies require data collection over more than one time period, whereas others may require the use of more than one group of participants. Some data are collected through face-to-face interactions, other data are collected by mail, and still other data are collected via e-mail or the Internet. We'll talk briefly about some of the more common approaches to data collection in the following sections.

Once the data are collected, the researcher needs to make sense out of them. This is usually done through some sort of statistical analysis, an area in which I/O psychologists are well schooled because the field of I/O is one of the more quantitative fields within psychology. I/O psychologists make great use of the various analytic methods that are available. At this stage of the process, the researcher goes back to the original hypotheses and research questions and uses statistical techniques to test those hypotheses and answer those research questions.

The last step in the research process is writing up the results. This is the point at which the I/O researcher goes back to the original ideas that were used to generate the hypotheses and describes those ideas and the research on which they were based. She will then present the hypotheses and describe in detail the procedures that were used to carry out the research. The last two sections of the write-up will include a presentation of the results and a discussion of what they mean, how they fit into the existing literature, how they help to solve a problem, and what implications they have for organizational functioning. Ideally, this paper can be published in a journal that is an outlet for research of this type and that allows researchers to communicate their findings to other scholars and practitioners. Sometimes these research reports are presented at national conferences (e.g., the annual meetings of SIOP, the Academy of Management, or the American Psychological Association), serve as work toward a student's master's or doctoral degree, or meet the requirements of a psychology course or an honors curriculum. Whether one is writing up the results of an honors project, a small study that was done for an experimental psychology class, or a paper to be published in one of the top I/O journals such as the *Journal of Applied Psychology, Personnel Psychology, Organizational Behavior and Human Decision Processes,* the *Academy of Management Journal,* or the *Academy of Management Review,* the process is the same in terms of the steps involved in the research, as well as in the actual written presentation of the research project. (For guidelines, see American Psychological Association, 2001.)

It is through the dissemination of information in this form that any scientific field grows and develops. Of course, throughout the rest of the book we will be discussing a great deal of this published research, which will help you to understand the complexities of I/O psychology and the world of work. First, however, we still need to consider how research is conducted in I/O psychology.

TYPES OF RESEARCH DESIGNS

There are various ways in which studies are designed to answer a particular research question. In this section we will consider the most frequently employed methods and look at some examples to further your understanding.

Experimental Methods

We have already examined the inductive-deductive cycle of research, as well as the five major steps in the research process. (A mnemonic that might help you remember these steps, as summarized in Figure 2.2, is ***How Dilbert Conducts All Research.***) Now, however, we turn to the experimental methods that the researcher can employ in order to answer her particular research questions. **Experimental methods** are characterized by two factors: random assignment and manipulation.

experimental methods
Research procedures that are distinguished by random assignment of participants to conditions and the manipulation of independent variables.

Random assignment refers to the procedure by which research participants, once selected, are assigned to conditions such that each one has an equally likely chance of being assigned to each condition. For instance, if we were interested in measuring the effect of training on job performance, we would want to randomly assign participants to training and no-training conditions so as to provide a fair test of our hypothesis. If we assigned all of the good performers to the training condition and found that their performance was better than that of the no-training group, the reason could be that the training group was composed of better performers than the no-training group even before training. In other words, pretraining performance could be an extraneous variable. To control for this and other potential extraneous variables, we use random assignment to conditions.

random assignment
The procedure by which research participants, once selected, are assigned to conditions such that each one has an equally likely chance of being assigned to each condition.

The second necessary factor associated with experimental methods is the **manipulation** of one or more independent variables. With experimental designs, we don't just measure our independent variables; we systematically control, vary, or apply them to different groups of participants. In our training–job performance example, we systematically provide training to one group of participants and no training to another. Random assignment and manipulation of independent variables are the keys to controlling extraneous variables, ruling out alternative explanations, and being able to draw causal inferences. In other words, these two techniques increase the internal validity of our experiment. They are the reason that experimental designs almost always have higher internal validity than observational designs.

manipulation
The systematic control, variation, or application of independent variables to different groups of participants.

Laboratory Experiments. One type of experimental methodology is the laboratory experiment. Random assignment and manipulation of independent variables are used in a laboratory experiment to increase control, rule out alternative explanations, and increase internal validity. Most laboratory experiments take place in a somewhat contrived setting rather than a real-world work setting. For instance, a colleague and I conducted a study in which undergraduates were presented with some performance information about a fictitious employee and then were asked to provide an annual performance review (Makiney & Levy, 1998). We then manipulated additional information by telling one group of participants that peers rated each employee better than the participants had rated each employee and a second group of participants that the employees rated themselves better than the participants had rated them. We were interested in the extent to which participants would use this additional information in making a final performance judgment. The findings revealed that participants paid more attention to the additional peer information than to the additional self-rating information. Because of our random assignment of participants to experimental conditions and our careful manipulation of the additional information, we were able to rule out other plausible alternatives and argue that the difference in final judgments was due to different degrees of trust in the sources of the additional information.

Recall the internal validity–external validity tradeoff that we discussed earlier. Laboratory experiments give rise to that very problem. Although they are typically very high in internal validity because of the extent to which researchers have control of the laboratory context, they are often questioned in terms of external validity, or generalizability, because of the contrived nature of the laboratory setting. In an attempt to counter this criticism in the study described above, my colleague and I invited as participants only those students who were also employed at least part time. In addition, the majority of our participants had real-life experience conducting performance appraisals. This factor improved the external validity of our study because our participants were very much like the population to whom we wanted to generalize. That they had actual real-world performance appraisal experience made the task we asked them to do (i.e., make performance judgments) more reasonable, thus increasing external validity. Inducing enough control to maintain high levels of *internal validity,* having realistic scenarios, and using participants who are representative of the working world for *external validity* are important issues in experimental designs.

Field Experiments and Quasi-Experiments. To overcome the problems associated with the artificiality of laboratory settings, I/O researchers sometimes take advantage of the realism of field settings and do field experiments. Here, we still use random assignment and manipulations of independent variables to control for extraneous variables, but we do so within a naturally occurring real-world setting. Admittedly, these experiments are not used a great deal in I/O research because it is difficult to find real-world settings in which random assignment and manipulations are reasonable. Organizations are typically not willing to allow a researcher to come in and randomly assign employees to a training or no-training group, because such arrangements could disrupt productivity and organizational efficiency.

quasi-experiment
A research design that resembles an experimental design but does not include random assignment.

A more viable alternative is a **quasi-experiment,** which resembles a field experiment but does not include random assignment (Cook & Campbell, 1979). Quasi-experiments usually involve some manipulation of an independent variable, but instead of random assignment of participants to conditions, they often use *intact* groups. In our training–job performance study, for example, it would be difficult to gain access to an organization that would allow random assignment of individuals to conditions, but it might be more manageable to assign departments, work groups, or plants to conditions. In this case, perhaps four work groups could be assigned to the training condition and four others to the no-training condition. And to control for potential extraneous variables, we could measure and control for any preexisting differences between the two experimental conditions in terms of experience, gender, performance, attitudes, and so on. Quasi-experiments are very common in I/O psychology because they are more feasible to conduct than field experiments but still allow for reasonable levels of internal validity.

Observational Methods

Studies that employ observational methods are sometimes called *correlational designs* because their results are usually analyzed by correlational approaches, which we will talk about a bit later in this chapter. This kind of research is also referred to as *descriptive,* because we focus exclusively on the relationships among variables and thus can only describe the situation. Descriptive studies are not true experiments because they don't involve random assignment or the manipulation of independent variables. In these designs, we make use of what is available to us, and we are very limited in drawing causal inferences. All we can conclude from such studies is that our results either do or do not indicate a relationship between the variables of interest. We can use this approach in either the laboratory or the field. It is much more common in the field, however, because it is here that we are usually limited in terms of what we can control.

Let's say that we're interested in the relationship between job satisfaction and performance. To examine this issue, we could administer a job satisfaction survey to 200 employees at a company and then measure their performance using their supervisor's rating. Through statistical analysis, we could conclude that job satisfaction is related to performance, but we could not conclude that satisfaction causes performance because we have not manipulated satisfaction nor have we randomly assigned employees to satisfaction conditions. Indeed, it might be that performance causes job satisfaction, as the better performers are rewarded for their performance and, therefore, are more satisfied (Lawler & Porter, 1967). The only way we could actually examine causality in this situation would be to manipulate job satisfaction—an option that seems both nonsensical and potentially unethical. Can you think of a company that would allow you to come in and make some employees satisfied with their jobs and others dissatisfied so that you could examine the effects of these conditions on performance? Probably not. In such situations, we typically use observational methods and draw conclusions about relationships rather than about causality.

Descriptive research can be very important in a couple of ways. First, although we can't infer causality from such research, we can often gather data that describes

One way in which supervisors evaluate employees is through observation and discussion.

a relationship or pattern of relationships. These data can then be used to generate more causal hypotheses, which in turn can be examined with experimental designs. Second, in some cases, there is a great deal to be gained by description alone. Recall that description is one of the basic goals of science. Indeed, some important scientific findings are entirely descriptive, such as the Periodic Table of Elements in chemistry. Descriptive research in I/O psychology can be very important as well, such as when we use surveys to measure the work-related attitudes of organizational employees. This information is certainly useful for employers who may be trying to decide if it is worth it to implement a new reward program for their employees. In addition, it can be integral to us as researchers who are trying to enhance our understanding of work processes.

Prediction, you may remember, is another goal of science—and such studies can be very useful in predicting behavior in certain situations. So, although observational research is not as strong as experimental research with respect to inferring causality, it is important for other reasons.

DATA COLLECTION TECHNIQUES

There are a variety of ways in which data can be collected for a research study. In this section we will focus on some methods of data collection in I/O psychology, proceeding from the least to the most common approaches.

Naturalistic Observation

Perhaps the most obvious way to gather data to answer a research question about a behavior is to watch individuals exhibiting that behavior. We use observation in both laboratory and field settings in which we are interested in some behavior that can be observed, counted, or measured. *Naturalistic observation* refers to the observation of someone or something in its natural environment. One type of naturalistic observation that is commonly used in sociology and anthropology, though not so much in I/O psychology, is called *participant observation;* here, the observer tries to "blend in" with those who are to be observed. The observational technique more often used by I/O psychologists is called **unobtrusive naturalistic observation,** in which the researcher tries not to draw attention to himself or herself and objectively observes individuals. For example, to collect performance data on faculty teaching, a researcher might visit an instructor's class, sit in the back, and, without asking any questions, simply observe the interactions between the instructor and the students. Similarly, a consultant interested in the effect of leadership style on the functioning of staff meetings might measure leadership style through a questionnaire and then observe the behaviors and interactions that take place during a series of staff meetings conducted by various leaders. Note that, although unobtrusive naturalistic observation can be a very fruitful approach for gathering data, the researcher needs to be aware of the possibility that she is affecting behaviors and interactions through her observation. No matter how unobtrusive she tries to be, some people may react differently when an observer is present.

unobtrusive naturalistic observation
An observational technique whereby the researcher unobtrusively and objectively observes individuals but does not try to blend in with them.

Case Studies

case studies
Examinations of a single individual, group, company, or society.

Somewhat similar to naturalistic observation, **case studies** are best defined as examinations of a single individual, group, company, or society (Babbie, 1998). A case study might involve interviews, historical analysis, or research into the writings or policies of an individual or organization. The main purpose of case studies is description (as with other observational methods), although explanation is a reasonable goal of case studies, too. Sigmund Freud is well known for his use of case studies in the evaluation of his clients, but an I/O psychologist might use a case study to analyze the organizational structure of a modern company or to describe the professional life of a Fortune 500 CEO. Case studies are not typically used to test hypotheses, but they can be very beneficial in terms of describing and providing details about a typical or exceptional firm or individual. Of course, a major concern with this approach is that the description is based on a single individual or organization, thus limiting the external validity of the description.

Archival Research

Sometimes social scientists can answer important research questions through the use of existing or "secondary" data sets. **Archival research** relies on such data sets, which have been collected for either general or specific purposes identified by an individual or organization (Zaitzow & Fields, 1996). One implication is immediately clear: The quality of research using an archival data set is strongly affected by the quality of that original study. In other words, garbage in–garbage out. Researchers cannot use a weak data set for their study and expect to fix the problems inherent in it. Indeed, lack of control over the quality of the data is the chief concern with archival research.

archival research
Research relying on secondary data sets that were collected either for general or specific purposes identified by an individual or organization.

This issue aside, archival data sets can be very helpful and, in fact, are used a great deal by I/O psychologists. Available to them are data sets that have been collected by market researchers, news organizations, behavioral scientists, and government researchers. One of the largest and most extensively used in the employment area is the data set containing scores on the General Aptitude Test Battery (GATB), which was developed by the U.S. Employment Service in 1947. It includes information on personal characteristics, ability, occupation, and work performance for over 36,000 individuals and has been used in a quite a few publications in the I/O area (e.g., Avolio, Waldman, & McDaniel, 1990; McDaniel, Schmidt, & Hunter, 1988).

Certainly, the use of secondary data sets can be very beneficial to the researcher in that she does not have to spend huge amounts of time developing measures and collecting data. Going back to Figure 2.2, we find that steps 2 and 3 are already completed for the researcher who embarks upon an archival study. In addition, many of the archival data sets available for use were collected by organizations with a great deal more resources than any one researcher would tend to have. Such data are not only based on large samples, which improve the quality of the research, but may also be richer in that many more variables may be involved than a single researcher would be able to include. A final strength of archival data sets is that they often include both *cross-sectional data*—collected at one point in time from a single group of respondents—and *longitudinal data*—collected over multiple time periods so that changes in attitudes and behaviors can be examined. Again, given the limited resources of most researchers, these types of data would typically be difficult to obtain.

SURVEYS

surveys
A data collection technique that involves the selection of a sample of respondents and the administration of some type of questionnaire.

Well, it sure seems obvious that if you want information from people, one way to gather it is to ask them. This is the very basis of survey methodology. **Surveys** involve the selection of a sample of respondents (or participants) and the administration of some type of questionnaire. They are terrific tools for gathering data on employees' attitudes and beliefs about their organizations, their supervisors, their co-workers, and many other aspects of the world of work. It follows that surveys are probably the most frequently used method of data collection in I/O psychology. I'm certain that you have had at least some experience with surveys. You might have filled one out at a restaurant to rate the quality of the food or service, completed one on the warranty card that came with your new stereo, or answered questions on the telephone about what you watch on TV or what candidate you are likely to vote for and why. Surveys are, quite frankly, everywhere. Have you ever been stopped at the mall to answer questions about your buying preferences? Or asked about your religious preferences and practices? Chances are that if you have conducted any experimental research at all (such as an undergraduate research project, an honors project, or an experiment for another psychology class), you used a survey to some extent in this research. Let's look at the two survey approaches that are most frequently used by I/O psychologists.

Self-Administered Questionnaires. *Self-administered questionnaires* are surveys that are completed by respondents in the absence of an investigator. The primary example is the mail survey, which is mailed (or perhaps e-mailed) to respondents, who complete it and return it to the experimenter. Sometimes, however, we use the term *self-administered questionnaire* to refer to situations in which the respondent fills out the survey in the presence of the researcher (as in research you may have participated in for extra credit toward your Introduction to Psychology grade). In these situations, the respondent is provided with a written survey that asks a series of questions requiring responses along some scale of agreement or frequency. This is a very common approach to collecting survey data.

Self-administered questionnaires are also common in field settings, in which employees are often asked about their attitudes and beliefs about their jobs and organizations. For instance, job satisfaction is typically measured with a self-administered survey. Aside from the research goals linked to surveys, organizations routinely provide surveys to their employees to gather useful information for future organizational planning and decision making, as well as for the purpose of giving employees a voice in company policies. Self-administered surveys are particularly useful for three reasons. First, they are relatively easy to administer (although developing them carefully can be quite time-consuming; see Hinkin, 1998). Second, they can be administered to large groups of people at the

Surveys are often used by restaurants to gather information about performance.

same time. Finally, they can provide respondents with anonymity, which makes them feel more comfortable and increases the likelihood that their responses will be honest. On the negative side, with mail surveys in particular, the researcher is dependent on the respondents returning the surveys. These response rates can be quite low. When only a small percentage of the sample complete and return the survey, conclusions drawn from the data may be very inaccurate. Also, unless the researcher is available during the administration of the survey, respondents cannot easily get clarification of questionnaire items that they do not understand. Despite these limitations, however, self-administered surveys are both popular and useful within the field of I/O psychology.

Interviews. An alternative to the self-administered questionnaire is the investigator-administered survey or *interview* in which the investigator asks a series of questions verbally rather than in written form. Interviews are usually conducted

Interviews can be an effective way to collect data such as customer satisfaction feedback.

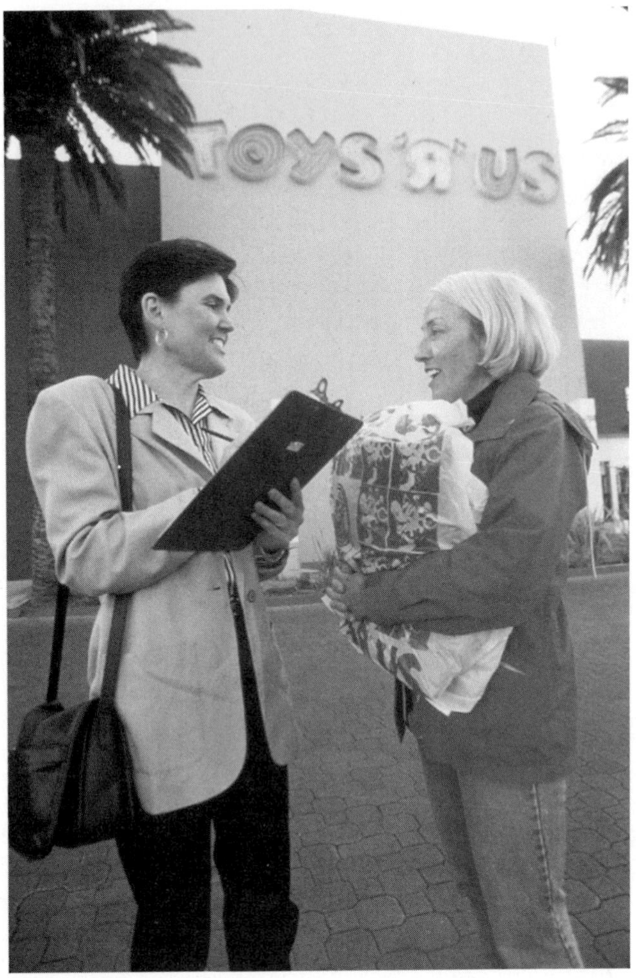

face-to-face but sometimes are conducted over the telephone. But either way, the process is much the same. Interviews tend to be more time-consuming than self-administered questionnaires because they are usually done one-on-one. Still, there are some clear benefits to this approach. First, response rates tend to be higher, as people are less likely to turn down a face-to-face interview than to throw away a mail survey (Babbie, 1998). Second, ambiguities about what a question means that may arise with mail surveys can easily be resolved in interviews because the interviewer is available to provide answers. In the I/O domain, interviews are commonly used to gather data about employees' attitudes, concerns over the need for more management attention, applicants' skills and abilities, whether or not applicants fit a particular job very well, and employees' promotability.

MEASUREMENT

We have talked about science, theories, and research design in this chapter, but although these are all very important to the research enterprise, they are worthless without careful measurement. **Measurement** is defined as the assignment of numbers to objects or events using rules in such a way as to represent specified attributes of the objects (Stevens, 1968). For I/O psychology, this often means that we are quantifying individuals along some attribute. An **attribute** is a dimension along which individuals can be measured and along which individuals vary. Thus, for instance, we could devise a test of cognitive ability in which job applicants respond to a series of questions or problems, allowing us to *measure* their intelligence; or, we could have undergraduate participants complete a survey of their satisfaction with school, allowing us to *measure* their school-related attitudes. In either case, we are attempting to assign numbers to individuals that indicate how much or how little of an attribute these individuals possess. Ultimately, our goal is to use these measurements or data in our statistical analyses to answer our research questions.

measurement
The assignment of numbers to objects or events using rules in such a way as to represent specified attributes of the objects.

attribute
A dimension along which individuals can be measured and along which individuals vary.

One very important point here is that psychology is very different from other areas such as the physical sciences. For instance, few measurement problems are likely to occur in the measurement of the weight of an object, provided that one has an accurate scale (an inaccurate scale would be a huge problem). However, when we are measuring an employee's attitude about her supervisor, there are many things that can make that measurement inaccurate—many sources of *measurement error.* By this I mean that if the employee had a particularly bad interaction with the supervisor that day, or wasn't feeling well, or was worried about a sick child, the measurement of her attitude might not be accurate or may differ from the measurement of her attitude next week when a whole host of new variables are involved. Measurement in the behavioral sciences is especially difficult because there isn't a scale, gauge, thermometer, ruler, or calculator that can be used to measure attitudes, beliefs, desires, and behaviors. Thus, when we measure a person's creativity, commitment to the organization, job satisfaction, or motivation, there is greater potential for measurement error than when we measure a person's weight or height. For this reason, we need to be particularly careful in developing our measures.

We have already seen the importance of prediction in science. Prediction takes on added importance in I/O psychology because much of what we try to do is to predict who will be successful in certain kinds of jobs and organizations and with certain kinds of supervisors and co-workers. Prediction is often the major practical goal for I/O psychologists. For instance, if I owned a fleet of buses or cabs, I would probably give potential applicants for mechanic positions a mechanical comprehension test before making hiring decisions about those applicants. My thinking would be that the scores on the mechanical test could be used to predict success on the job. We will discuss selection at length in later chapters, but for now note that this example is a very common one. The process of measuring a quality or construct and using it to predict job performance is indeed common in the field; it is also one in which the accuracy of measurement is very important.

Reliability

reliability
The consistency or stability of a measure.

The consistency or stability of a measure is its **reliability.** Three points are relevant in this context. First, keep in mind that if we are going to use a score on a test as a predictor of on-the-job performance (much like SAT scores are used as predictors of success in college), it is imperative that the predictor be measured reliably. Second, recall that I mentioned measurement error as getting in the way of accurate measurement. Now you should be able to see that measurement error is what renders measurement inaccurate or unreliable. An individual's score on the mechanical comprehension test I just described will not be a perfect representation of the individual's mechanical comprehension; perhaps she missed some questions because she didn't read those questions correctly, or mistakenly filled in the wrong ovals, or, for that matter, got some questions correct simply by guessing. In other words, there is always some measurement error that causes the person's score to be a less-than-perfect indicator of her mechanical comprehension. The further that score gets from her actual level of mechanical comprehension, the more inaccurate or unreliable the test is. Third, reliability is extremely important because we cannot accurately predict attitudes, performance, or behavior with a variable that is not measured very well. In other words, reliability provides a ceiling on our prediction accuracy—what we will call *validity* in subsequent sections. First, however, there are a few types of reliability to briefly discuss.

test-retest reliability
The stability of a test over time; often referred to as a *coefficient of stability.*

Test-retest reliability reflects the stability of a test over time and is therefore often referred to as a *coefficient of stability.* To demonstrate test-retest reliability, we might give our mechanical comprehension test to a group of participants and then administer the same test to the same group 6 weeks later. Assuming that the participants did not somehow improve their mechanical comprehension in the interim (e.g., by taking a training course or gaining additional job experience), their scores at the first test administration should be about the same as their scores at the second administration. Scores that varied, however, would reflect measurement error, indicating that our measure was not perfectly reliable. Virtually no measure we would use in I/O psychology is perfectly reliable. We can only hope to minimize the error as much as possible so that most of the high scorers at the first administration are also the high scorers at the second administration and the low scorers at the first administration continue to be the low scorers at the second administration. This outcome would demonstrate acceptable levels of test-retest reliability.

Figure 2.3 shows what 7 individuals' pairs of scores on mechanical comprehension might look like when the measure has high reliability versus low reliability. Each line represents one person, and the dots on either end represent that person's score at two different time periods. Notice that when the test has high re-

FIGURE 2.3 Test-Retest Reliability

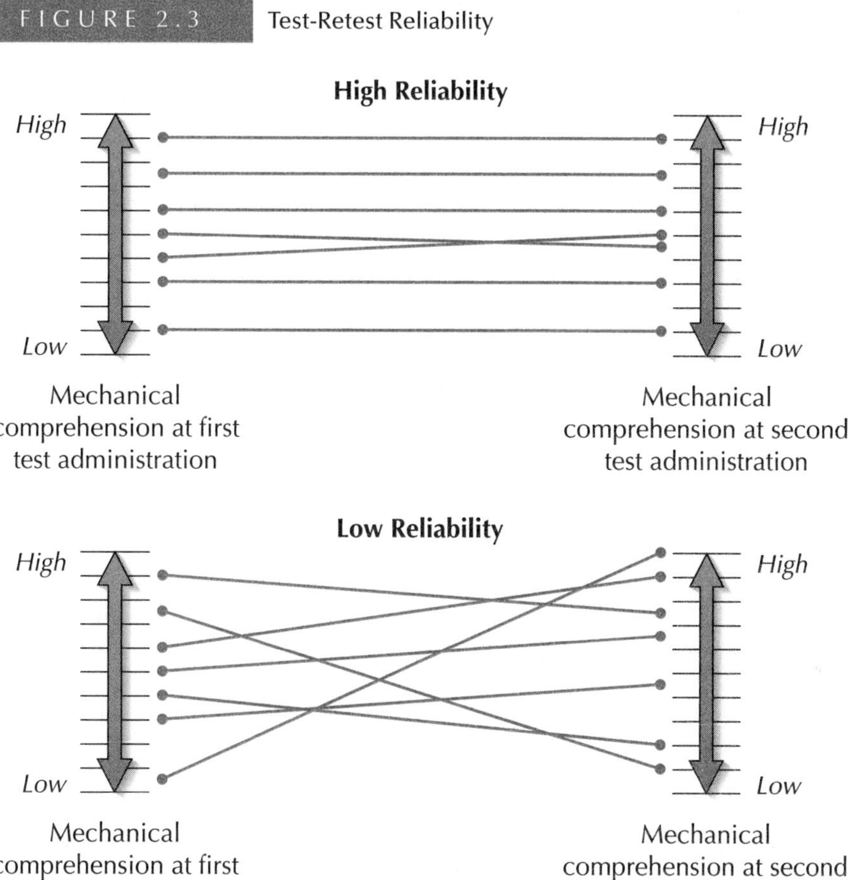

liability, the high scorers are the same people across both test administrations, but that this is not the case when the test has low reliability.

Parallel forms reliability (sometimes called equivalent forms reliability) is often referred to as a *coefficient of equivalence* because it reflects the extent to which two independent forms of a test are equivalent measures of the same construct. In other words, we might want to have two versions of the same test—an approach often used in large, multiple sections of a course to prevent cheating. The important thing is to ensure that the two tests are measuring the same thing. The issue of parallel tests has become very significant in recent years given the increasing concern for fairness in treatment of the disabled. We will consider this issue in the context of selection in Chapters 6 and 7, but for now note that there are situations in which different tests ought to be developed for applicants

parallel forms reliability
The extent to which two independent forms of a test are equivalent measures of the same construct.

or employees who are disabled. Again, we would want to be able to demonstrate that the test for disabled persons is equivalent to the test for nondisabled persons. Similarly, the use of computerized testing has become a hot topic (Bloom, 1998). It is important to be able to demonstrate that when measuring cognitive ability, say, a computerized test is equivalent to the more traditional paper-and-pencil test.

interrater reliability The extent to which multiple raters or judges agree on ratings made about a particular person, thing, or behavior.

An approach to estimating reliability that is similar conceptually to test-retest is what is commonly called **interrater reliability,** which is the consistency with which multiple raters view and thus rate the same behavior or person. This is often relevant in the performance appraisal arena, in which we might be interested in considering how two or three judges might rate someone's performance so that we aren't relying on just one judge who may have his or her own biases—we'll consider this kind of situation in more detail in Chapter 5. Interrater reliability is measured in various ways, but many approaches involve examining the correlation between the ratings of two different judges rating the same person. One way to think about this is to conceive of the judges as multiple tests, which makes this kind of reliability somewhat similar to parallel forms.

internal consistency An indication of the extent to which individual test items seem to be measuring the same thing.

The final form of reliability that we'll discuss is **internal consistency,** which gives an indication of the interrelatedness of the test items. We wouldn't want an item on an IQ test that doesn't seem to fit with the rest of the items, because that would suggest that the item is not measuring the same thing as the other items. Internal consistency tells us how well our test items are hanging together. We can estimate internal consistency in two different ways. First, we can split the test in half by odd or even question numbers and see if the even half of the test is equivalent to the odd half—a measure of *split-half reliability.* Second, we can determine whether there is consistency among the items by looking at the correlations among all of the items—a measure of *inter-item reliability* and referred to as *Cronbach's coefficient alpha* in some situations and *Kuder-Richardson 20* in other situations.

As I've suggested, reliability is very important, and one of our goals should always be to have high reliability. A rule of thumb used by many is that our measures should have reliability levels of at least .70. But because measurement consistency, though important, is not usually our ultimate goal in I/O psychology, we need to spend some time talking about validity—the extent to which our test measures what we believe it measures and how well it predicts other things. Just as a reminder, you can think of this as a two-step process. First, you have to develop a sound, reliable measure. Second, because you will probably want to use that measure to predict attitudes, performance, or behavior, your focus will turn to validity. This is our next topic for discussion.

construct validity The extent to which a test measures the underlying construct that it was intended to measure.

Validity of Tests, Measures, and Scales

The validity of a measure is most precisely considered in terms of **construct validity,** which is the extent to which a test measures the underlying construct that it was intended to measure. A **construct** is an abstract quality, such as intelligence or motivation, that is not observable and is difficult to measure. In a general sense, our test of mechanical comprehension is valid if it really measures mechanical comprehension. There are two types of evidence that we use to demonstrate construct validity. First, **content validity** is the degree to which a test or predictor covers a representative sample of the quality being assessed. In other words, if you were being tested on Chapters 1, 2, and 3 of this book, a content valid test would be one that covers the entire domain of material presented in those three chapters. Have you ever taken a test that seemed to cover the minor stuff and didn't ask anything about large sections of chapters? You were probably upset about that test and, although you didn't know it at the time, you were upset because the test was *not* content valid—it didn't fairly and accurately reflect the domain of material in such a way as to be representative of that domain. In an employment setting, performance appraisal measures should be content valid such that an employee's performance appraisal reflects all of the important elements of his job not just one or two. For instance, to evaluate faculty members based solely on research would be to ignore that part of the performance domain which reflects teaching, resulting in an invalid measure of performance.

construct
An abstract quality, such as intelligence or motivation, that is not observable and is difficult to measure.

content validity
The degree to which a test or predictor covers a representative sample of the quality being assessed.

The second type of evidence that we use to demonstrate construct validity is called *criterion-related validity.* The focus here is on whether the test is a good predictor of attitudes, behavior, or performance. We will discuss this type of validity at greater length in Chapter 7, which is concerned with applicant selection in which the prediction of job performance is the overarching goal. For now, however, let us simply define the two approaches to criterion-related validity. First, **predictive validity** refers to the extent to which test scores obtained at one point in time predict criteria obtained at some later time. For instance, does our test of mechanical comprehension, when given to applicants, successfully predict their on-the-job behavior once they are hired? In traditional selection situations of this kind, I/O psychologists attempt to develop tests or predictors that companies can use to make employment decisions. The same approach is used for admitting students into college and graduate school: SAT scores and GREs have been shown to be predictive of success in college and graduate school, respectively—as have GPAs in both cases (Briel, O'Neill, & Scheuneman, 1993; Kuncel, Campbell, & Ones, 1998). However, for a different view, one that questions how valid these test scores are for prediction, you should see an interesting paper by R. J. Sternberg and W. M. Williams (1997).

predictive validity
The extent to which test scores obtained at one point in time predict criteria obtained in the future.

Second, **concurrent validity** refers to how well a test predicts a criterion that is measured at the same time that the test is administered. We still want to make the argument that our test predicts a future criterion, but sometimes predictive validity studies are extremely time-consuming and difficult (if not impossible) to conduct, leaving concurrent validity studies as the more viable option. We will discuss the differences between these two approaches in Chapter 7, but I want to emphasize here that both approaches are used to demonstrate that a test is related to a criterion such as job performance. Figure 2.4 depicts a situation in which one cognitive ability test predicts job performance well (high validity) and another

concurrent validity
The extent to which a test predicts a criterion that is measured at the same time that the test is conducted.

FIGURE 2.4 Criterion-Related Validity

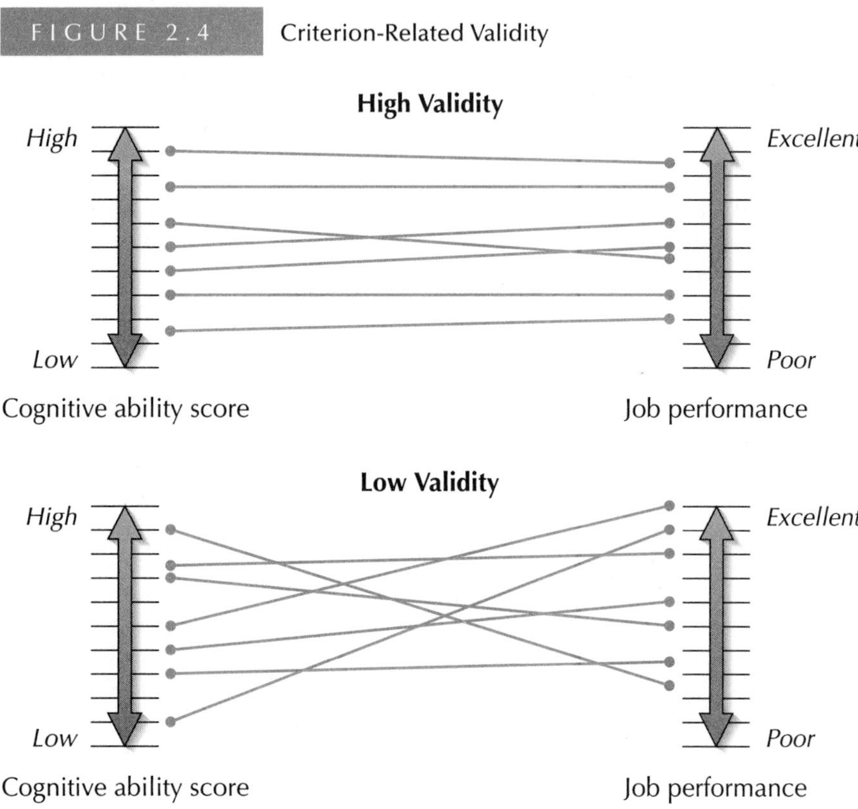

does not (low validity). In the case of the high-validity test, those who score well also perform well on the job, and those who don't score well also don't perform well on the job. In the case of the low-validity test, however, one's score does not seem all that related to one's job performance.

convergent validity
The degree to which a measure of the construct in which we are interested is related to measures of other, similar constructs.

divergent validity
The degree to which a measure of the construct in which we are interested is *not* related to measures of other, dissimilar constructs.

In the preceding paragraphs, we discussed how criterion-related validity (both predictive and concurrent) is used to demonstrate the construct validity of a measure by showing that it is related to or predicts measures of other, similar constructs. This situation describes **convergent validity.** However, in order to demonstrate that a particular measure is construct valid, we must also demonstrate that the measure is not related to measures of dissimilar constructs—a matter of **divergent validity.** For instance, if we were developing a new measure of job satisfaction, we would need to demonstrate convergent validity by showing that our new measure is strongly related to other, existing measures of job satisfaction and divergent validity by showing that our new measure is not strongly related to measures of organizational commitment, job involvement, and satisfaction with the public school system. The point here is that we can be confident that our new measure is measuring the construct that we intended (i.e., job satisfaction) only if it relates to measures of other constructs in the way that it should, based on the definitions of these constructs.

Convergent and divergent validity can be demonstrated through both predictive and concurrent validation designs, which are discussed in more detail in Chapter 7. In the meantime, Figure 2.5 provides a helpful summary of the major types of reliability and the approaches used to demonstrate construct validity that we've discussed.

FIGURE 2.5 Summary of Reliability Types and Approaches to Construct Validity

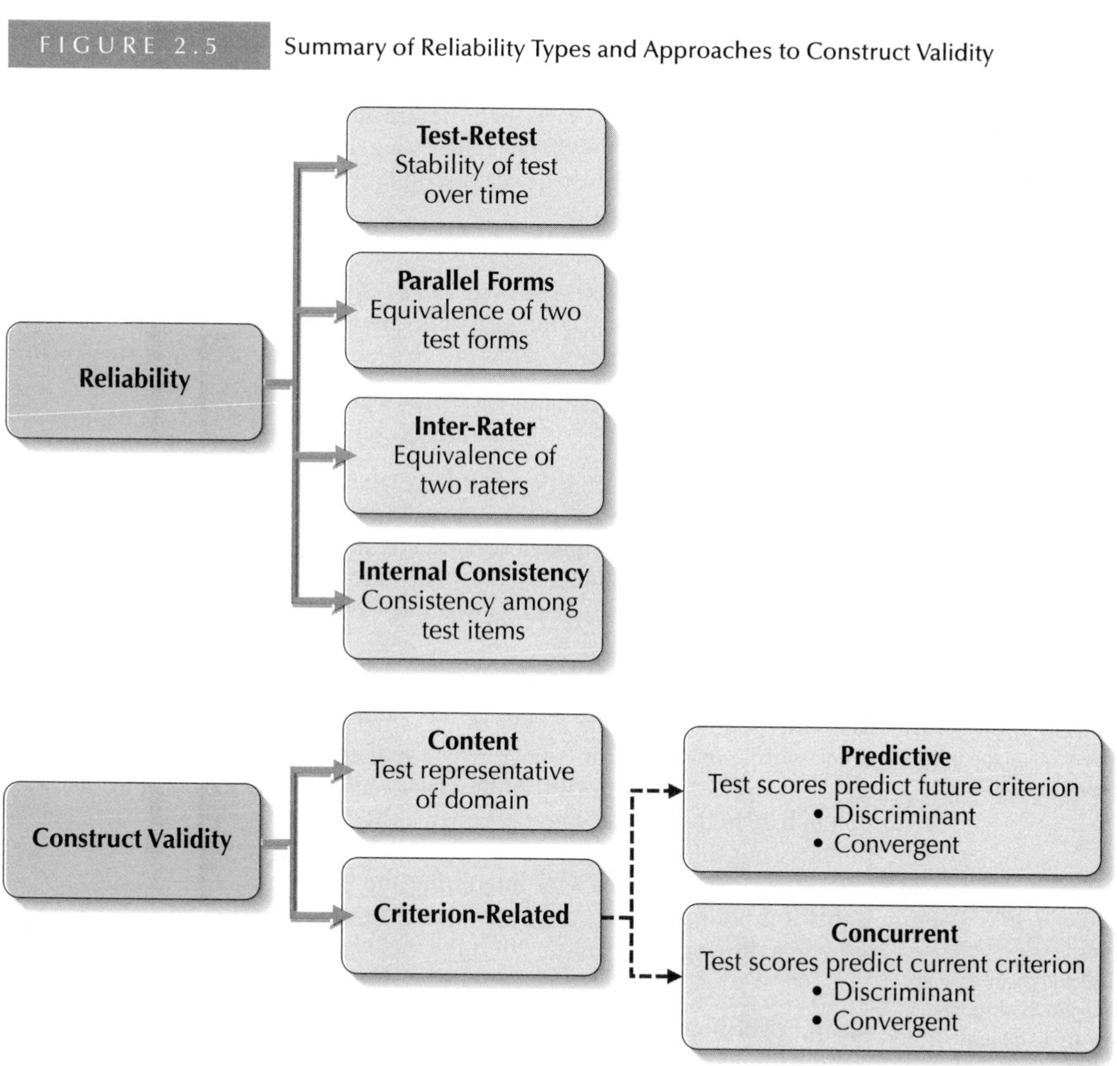

STATISTICS

After we collect our data, we need to present them in a way that allows us to draw conclusions about what our data mean with respect to our hypothesis and the research literature. This usually involves a summary of the data, often referred to as *descriptive statistics.* A **statistic** is an efficient device for summarizing in a single number the values, characteristics, or scores describing a series of cases. The first group of statistics we'll discuss are measures of central tendency.

statistic
An efficient device for summarizing in a single number the values, characteristics, or scores describing a series of cases.

MEASURES OF CENTRAL TENDENCY

Measures of central tendency characterize a *typical* member of the group in that they represent the "best guess" as to the nature of any case chosen at random from the group. They present a way of characterizing the group with just a few relevant numbers. These measures can be very useful in comparing the various conditions or groups in one's study.

mode
The most frequent single score in a distribution.

Mode. The most frequent single score in a distribution is called the **mode.** The following data set reflects the job satisfaction levels of 9 employees on a job satisfaction survey that ranges from a low of 1 to a high of 50. What is the mode in this data set?

1 1 1 10 12 26 33 45 50

Clearly, the mode is 1, as it is the most frequent score in the data set. But this example demonstrates why the mode is not usually the best measure of central tendency for describing psychological data: 1 is not the single number we would choose to describe the data set overall. (The mode tends to be useful only in situations involving categorical data, as when we say that the modal religion among Americans is Protestantism.)

median
The score in the middle of the distribution.

Median. The score in the middle of the distribution is termed the **median.** In other words, it is the score above which half the distribution falls and below which the other half of the distribution falls—it's the score that cuts the distribution in half. In the data set above, the median is 12. In this example, the median is probably not the best measure of central tendency either, though it seems more descriptive than the mode. One interesting and important feature of the median is that it is not particularly sensitive to extreme scores, meaning that an extreme score in a distribution does not affect the median much, if at all.

mean
The arithmetic average of a group of scores, typically the most useful measure of central tendency.

Mean. The most useful measure of central tendency is usually the **mean,** which is the arithmetic average of a group of scores. Almost all inferential statistics that we use are based on it. In our example above, the mean is 19.89—and you can see that this value gives a more accurate picture of the data set than does the mode or median. If you were to pick a single value to describe the data in this simple example, 19.89 would be the best one to choose, as it is more representative than either 1 or 12. One problem with means, however, is that they are sensitive to extreme scores; a single extreme score can have a drastic effect on them. Let's consider another data set. Rather than job satisfaction, let's say that it now reflects the number of days absent in a 3-year period among the same 9 employees:

1 1 1 10 12 26 33 45 400

Note that only one number has been changed—50 has become 400—but that value is by far the most extreme one, such that the mean is now 58.8 rather than 19.89. Clearly, this one value has a huge effect on the mean. What is the median in our new data set? The median doesn't change; it's still 12 because medians are not sensitive to extreme scores. This suggests that in situations involving extreme scores, a median has some advantages over the mean.

Measures of Dispersion

Measures of dispersion inform us about how closely scores are grouped around the measure of central tendency, usually the mean. These are sometimes referred to as measures of variability because they provide information about how much the scores vary from each other. In a sense, we can say that measures of dispersion give us an idea of the "spread-outedness" of the data.

The simplest measure of dispersion is called the **range,** which is the spread of scores from the lowest to the highest. In our original data set, the range is 49, which is the difference between the largest observed score (50) and the smallest observed score (1). This measure appears in published reports of research, but it is not reported as often as the **variance,** which is recognized as the most useful measure of dispersion. To calculate the variance, the researcher subtracts each score from the mean, resulting in differences that are then squared. The next step is to add these squared differences and divide the sum by the total number of scores, which is usually denoted as *N*. In our first data set, the variance is 372.11. The third measure of dispersion is called the **standard deviation,** which is the square root of the variance. Returning again to the first data set, we find that its standard deviation is 19.29. We often use this measure because it retains the original metric of the scores. In other words, 19.29 reflects the spread-outedness of the employees' job satisfaction levels on a satisfaction scale that ranges from 1 unit of job satisfaction to 50 units of job satisfaction. The variance, on the other hand (372.11), is much more difficult to conceptualize because it is in squared units.

range
The simplest measure of dispersion, reflecting the spread of scores from the lowest to the highest.

variance
A useful measure of dispersion reflecting the sum of the squared differences between each score and the mean of the group divided by the number of total scores.

standard deviation
A measure of dispersion that is calculated as the square root of the variance.

normal distribution
A mathematically based distribution depicted as a bell-shaped curve, in which most of the observations cluster around the mean and there are few extreme observations.

Shapes of Distributions

The **normal distribution** is a theoretical mathematical model based on a population of measures that is infinite in size. This distribution is depicted by what appears to be a *bell-shaped curve,* in which most of the observations are clustered around the mean with increasingly fewer observations as we move out along the continuum in either direction. The normal distribution is important in psychology because many psychological variables are distributed in this way. For instance, intelligence, motivation, performance, personal characteristics, and job attitudes are all believed to be normally distributed in the population. Therefore, the properties of the normal distribution take on added significance.

This bell-shaped curve is presented in Figure 2.6, which indicates standard deviation units along the bottom and the percentage of observations that fall within those standard deviation units at the top. In other words, in a normal distribution, 68% (i.e., 34% + 34%) of the observations in our data fall within 1 standard deviation below the mean and 1 standard deviation above the mean, and about 99% of the observations fall within 3 standard deviations of the mean in either direction. The mean and median have the same value in the normal distribution, indicating that half of the observations fall above the mean and half fall below the mean.

Figure 2.7 shows two normal curves with different standard deviations. Note that the taller curve has a smaller standard deviation than the shorter curve, but that both are normal distributions and the same properties of the normal distribution hold for both.

From the properties of the normal curve and an individual's score, we can determine the individual's *percentile* score relative to the rest of the population. You have all taken some type of achievement test for which a percentile score is given, indicating the percentage of other students in the population who did not score

FIGURE 2.6 The Normal Distribution

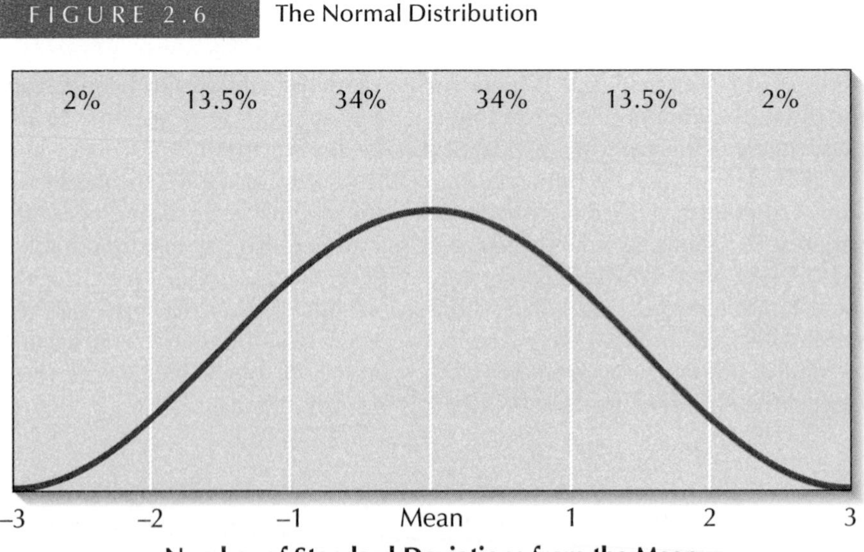

FIGURE 2.7 Normal Distributions with Different Standard Deviations

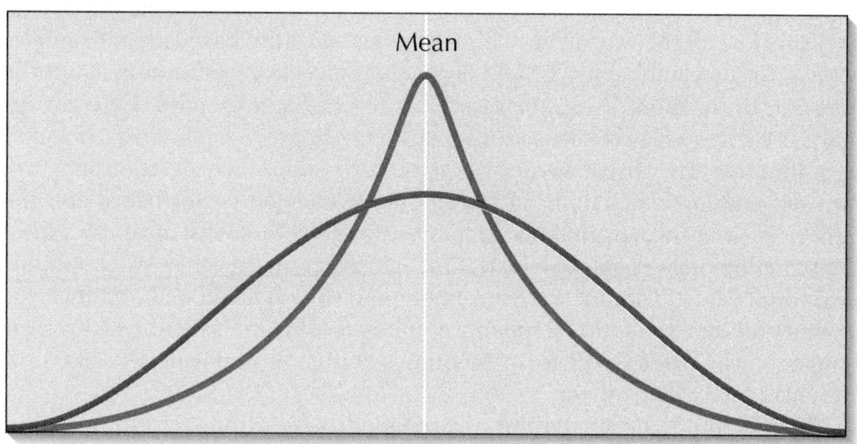

as well as you did. This percentile score is based on the mean, the standard deviation, and the normal distribution. We could apply the same process to the performance of employees at a Fortune 500 company to determine how well, in relation to all employees, a particular employee is performing.

Correlation and Regression

As you undoubtedly are aware by now, I/O psychologists are often interested in the relationship between two (or more) variables. To examine this relationship, we typically use the **correlation coefficient (*r*)**, which measures the strength of the relationship between two variables. A correlation provides information about the *direction* of the relationship, or its sign, and the *magnitude* of the relationship, or its strength. A correlation can indicate a positive or negative relationship between two variables. A positive relationship is indicated when high scores on one variable reflect high scores on the other variable and low scores on one variable reflect low scores on the other variable. For a real-world example of a positive correlation, think of two people on an elevator: As one goes up or down, so does the other. This is a perfect positive correlation. In most of the examples that we've talked about in this chapter, we have hypothesized a positive correlation, as in the relationships between participation and job satisfaction, leadership style and job performance, mechanical comprehension and job performance, SAT scores and school performance, and cognitive ability and job performance. In every case, we predicted that high scores on one variable would be related to high scores on the other variable.

correlation coefficient
A statistic that measures the strength and direction of the relationship between two variables.

A negative relationship is indicated when high scores on one variable are reflected in low scores on the other variable, and vice versa. Think of two children on a teeter-totter. As one goes up, the other goes down. If one is all the way up, the other must be all the way down. This is a perfect negative correlation. Examples of negative correlations may be a little more difficult to generate at first, but the more you think about them, the easier it is to call them to mind. Here, for instance, are a few negative correlations that we might predict: job satisfaction and the amount of time absent from work, supervisor-subordinate relationships and turnover, employee sanctions and promotions, and job performance and the number of grievances against the employee. In all of these instances, we expect high scores on one variable to be related to low scores on the other. We expect satisfied employees to seldom be absent, employees who get along well with their supervisors to stay with the company, employees who are sanctioned by their company to be passed over for promotions, and good performers to have few grievances filed against them.

The magnitude or strength of a correlation ranges from zero to one, with larger numbers indicating a stronger relationship. It's important to realize that although a correlation can range from –1.0 to +1.0, correlations of –.50 and +.50 have the same magnitude—the only difference being the sign. A scatterplot in which all of the data points fall along a straight 45-degree line represents a perfect 1.0 correlation, which is so rare as to be nonexistent in psychology. In the behavioral sciences, correlations among variables are almost never larger than .70. Consider the three scatterplots shown in Figure 2.8. The first, in the shape of a circle, reflects a correlation of 0. This indicates that a high score on the mechanical comprehension test is just as likely to lead to low performance as to lead to adequate performance as to lead to superior performance; in short, there is no relationship between the two variables. The other two scatterplots indicate rather strong relationships—one in the positive direction and the other in the negative direction.

Correlations are relevant for much of I/O psychology because they are intimately involved in prediction, an important goal in I/O psychology. One step beyond computing a correlation among variables is the statistical procedure called *regression,* which allows us to predict one variable from another. Here we calculate how much variance in our criterion variable is accounted for by our predictor variable—a calculation that is based on the correlation between these variables. The percentage of variance accounted for is called the **coefficient of determination,** and it can be computed from the regression as well as from the correlation. In fact, this percentage is actually the correlation squared, commonly expressed as r^2. Returning one last time to our example involving mechanical comprehension as a predictor for job performance, let's measure our employees using a mechanical comprehension test and also measure their on-the-job performance using their supervisors' ratings of their performance. Now imagine that we find a .60 correlation between these two variables, indicating that mechanical comprehension accounts for about 36% (i.e., $.60^2$) of the variance in job performance.

coefficient of determination
The percentage of variance in a criterion that is accounted for by a predictor.

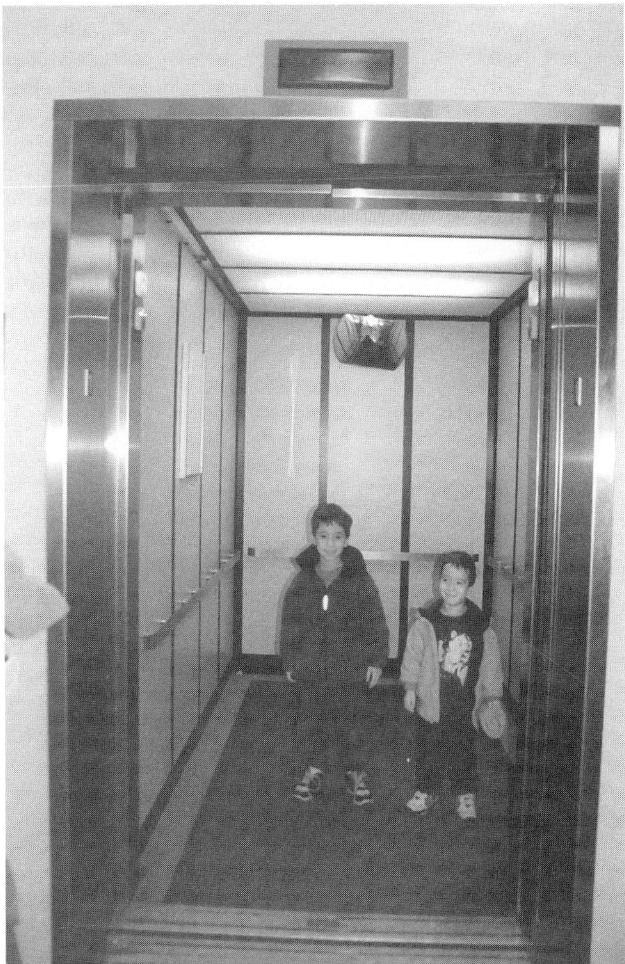

The movement of an elevator represents a positive correlation; teeter-totter activity represents a negative correlation.

Correlation Examples

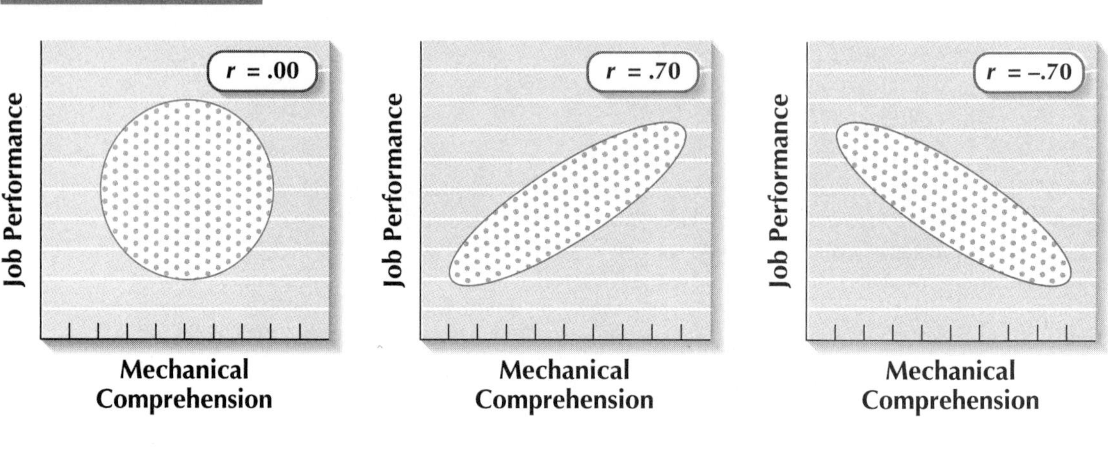

This statistic sounds confusing, and we will spend a little more time on it in Chapter 6; but basically it means that some (i.e., 36%) of the differences among employees on the performance variable (not everyone is going to perform at the same level) could be predicted by the mechanical comprehension test. In other words, knowing an individual's score on the mechanical comprehension test is helpful in predicting that individual's level of job performance. Figure 2.9 describes the relationship between these two variables, using a Venn diagram for each. As you can see, there is some overlap between mechanical comprehension and job performance. This overlap represents the coefficient of determination. I/O psychology uses correlations and regressions extensively, and we will revisit these throughout the rest of the book.

FIGURE 2.9 Coefficient of Determination

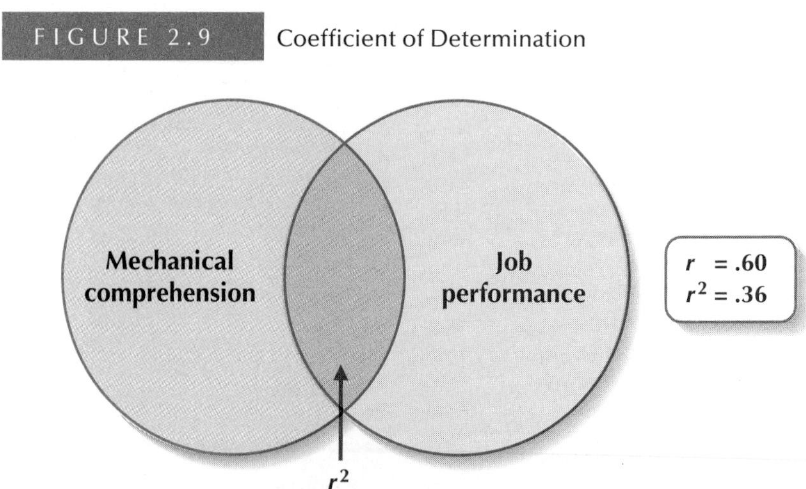

Meta-Analysis

A recently developed statistical and methodological technique that is widely used in the social sciences has also gained a very strong following in the I/O area. I'm referring here to **meta-analysis,** a methodology that is used to conduct quantitative literature reviews (Hunter & Schmidt, 1990; Rosenthal, 1991). Prior to the development of this approach in the late 1970s, a researcher conducting a literature review on the relationship between, say, job satisfaction and job performance would conduct a *narrative review* consisting of summaries of all the different findings in the literature; however, there was no mechanism for combining these different findings and providing a best estimate of the true relationship between job satisfaction and job performance. With the development of meta-analysis came a way to combine these many findings and thereby *quantify* the relationship between the two variables.

meta-analysis
A methodology that is used to conduct quantitative literature reviews.

Researchers can use meta-analysis to combine the results from 25, 100, even 1,000 or more studies to arrive at the best estimate of the true relationship. The point here is that statistically combining findings from previous studies is a more accurate way to estimate the true relationship than is focusing on one or two studies that measure this relationship. In the remainder of the book, I present many meta-analytic results as a way of summarizing various findings in the field of industrial/organizational psychology.

SUMMARY

Research methods are important to I/O psychology—and all scientific endeavors, for that matter—because research conducted without care is unreliable and worthless. But when we are careful to base our theories on data and to use these data to test and revise the theories, the science of I/O psychology can make a prominent contribution to the world of work. Science is more than just a matter of commonsense predictions and beliefs. Among its goals are to describe, explain, predict, and control human behavior at work. It is also important to realize that theories are the domain not just of basic science but also of applied scientific disciplines such as I/O. In fact, it is only through careful theoretical development, testing, and revision that we can use our knowledge to describe, explain, predict, and control organizational behaviors and environments.

A major goal of most research in I/O psychology is to be able to draw causal inferences about the relationship between two or more variables. Thus we design our studies with an emphasis on internal validity, attempting to control for extraneous variables that could provide alternative explanations for our results. In addition to internal validity, we concern ourselves with external validity, or the generalizability of our findings.

There are many ways in which I/O psychologists go about collecting data, but the survey is perhaps the one most frequently used. Surveys are very useful in gathering information about attitudes and beliefs. We may also use observational approaches to measure and record frequency or incidents of particular behaviors or interactions. Archival research is a popular approach as well, given our access to the numerous large-scale data sets that have been collected by the government and private organizations. I/O psychologists often combine these and other data collection techniques in any given study to better examine their research questions.

Without reliable and valid measurement, the research conducted by I/O psychologists would have very little to offer. Researchers must work very hard to eliminate sources of measurement error and to ensure that their measures are tapping the constructs that they were intended to tap. There are a few different approaches to estimating reliability, and each is important for demonstrating the soundness of any particular measure. Validity is important as well, but to talk of validity in general is not very helpful, as the term can mean several different things. In I/O, when we speak of the validity of a test or predictor, we are usually referring to the extent to which the test predicts job performance or some other criterion.

After we have collected our data, the next step is to describe and summarize those data using descriptive statistics such as measures of central tendency and dispersion. Because I/O psychologists are usually interested in the relationships among variables and the prediction of one set of variables from another set, correlation and regression are statistical techniques that are very useful to us. Ultimately, we complete our five-step research process with a written report that summarizes the research project.

In the remainder of this text we will discuss various content areas of I/O psychology and the research that is conducted in those areas, along with their implications for organizational functioning.

REVIEW QUESTIONS

1. What is science, and why is it important? What are its goals and assumptions?
2. Does theory matter in applied disciplines such as I/O? If so, why?
3. What makes a good theory?
4. What major types of experimental validity are important for research?
5. How are data collected in I/O psychology, and what are the benefits of each approach?
6. What are the various types of reliability and validity associated with measures, tests, and predictors?
7. Identify the measures of central tendency and dispersion.
8. Why is the normal distribution important? Describe its major characteristics.

9. What roles do correlation and regression play in I/O psychology?
10. How does I/O research enhance our understanding of work-related processes?

SUGGESTED READINGS

Babbie, E. (2003). ***The practice of social research (10th ed.).*** **Belmont, CA: Wadsworth Publishing Company.** An excellent presentation of research methods that is helpful for both undergraduates and graduate students.

Hinkin, T. R. (1998). A brief tutorial on the development of measures for use in survey questionnaires. ***Organizational Research Methods, 1*****(1), 104–121.** A clear "how-to" paper for those interested in developing survey measures.

Leong, F. T. L., & Austin, J. T. (Eds.). (1996). ***The psychology research handbook: A guide for graduate students and research assistants.*** **Thousand Oaks, CA: Sage.** A complete treatment of the research process targeted at new psychology researchers. The best book of its kind, it was written to be useful for both advanced undergraduate and graduate students; a new edition of this book should be published very soon.

Job Analysis

3

CHAPTER OUTLINE

The second section of this book centers on *industrial psychology,* or what has been traditionally called *personnel psychology.* Before discussing the major applications of industrial psychology, such as criterion measurement, performance appraisal, selection, and training, you must first have an understanding of the foundation for virtually all of this work—job analysis. This is the focus of the current chapter. Think about your own experiences with appraising others' performance. Imagine trying to evaluate their performance without knowing what their job is or what the outcomes of their work were intended to be. Now picture someone appraising your own performance without knowing the details of the job for which you were hired or the complexities involved in operating the machines or making the important decisions that are associated with your job. Unfortunately, job analysis is often taken for granted by I/O researchers and practitioners, but in this chapter I argue that it is the most important building block for industrial psychology.

Doing performance appraisals without such knowledge would be like preparing a dish without knowing what the food was, what the recipe was, or how it was supposed to taste. The job analysis provides information about the ingredients, about the way to combine them, and about the finished product—information that is integral to everything else that follows in industrial psychology. See Figure 3.1 for a picture of how job analysis relates to the major *human resource (HR)* functions that will be covered in this section of the text. The three major outcomes of job analysis—job evaluation, job description, and job specifications—will be discussed in this chapter, along with their respective links to each of the HR functions. Subsequent chapters will focus on the HR functions in much more detail.

LEARNING OBJECTIVES

This chapter should help you understand:

- how important job analysis is to HR functioning.
- the common terminology used in the area of job analysis.
- how to differentiate between job-oriented and worker-oriented job analysis techniques.
- how to conduct a job analysis using the Task Inventory Approach, Functional Job Analysis, Job Element Method, Position Analysis Questionnaire, and Common-Metric Questionnaire.
- what's included in the *Dictionary of Occupational Titles* and how it has been improved through the development of the Occupational Information Network (O*NET).
- what a job description is and how it is used in human resource practices.
- what job specifications are and how they are used in human resource practices.
- the variety of human resource functions for which job analysis is of great importance.
- the role of job evaluation in setting compensation levels.
- the doctrine of comparable worth and the wage gap.

CHAPTER THREE

FIGURE 3.1 Framework for Industrial Psychology

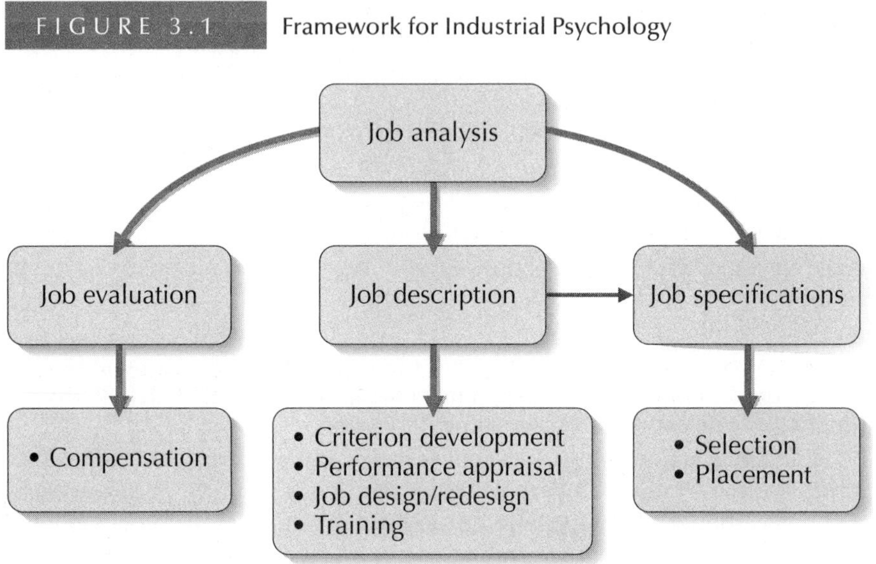

SOME TERMINOLOGY

Before discussing approaches to job analysis, we must familiarize ourselves with some terms that have very specific meanings within the domain of job analysis. First in the list are elements. An **element** is the smallest unit of work activity, such as pressing the button to start the machine or turning the key to start the engine. Multiple elements join together to form a **task,** commonly defined as the activity of work that is performed to achieve a specific objective. For instance, among the necessary elements involved in a cab driver taking his passenger to her destination are turning the key, pressing the accelerator, and shifting the transmission into "drive." Collectively, these elements form a task that is the operation of the vehicle. The tasks performed by an individual in an organization define that person's **position.** A **job** is a collection of positions similar enough to one another to share a common job title. At the risk of making this more confusing, let's try a recap here: The most basic level of work activity are the elements of work, which combine to form tasks, which in turn constitute one's position in the organization; similarly defined positions are what we term a job. Of course, it is the job (and sometimes the position) that is the focus of job analysis. R. J. Harvey (1991) notes that we should be careful to avoid confusing the job and the position with the individuals who occupy them. In other words, job analysis should be focused not on the person who holds the job or occupies the position but, rather, on the job or position itself.

element
In job analysis, the smallest unit of work activity.

task
A work activity that is performed to achieve a specific objective.

position
An individual's place in the organization defined by the tasks performed.

job
A collection of positions similar enough to one another to share a common job title.

Sackett and Laczo (2003) define job analysis as "a broad term commonly used to describe a wide variety of systematic procedures for examining, documenting,

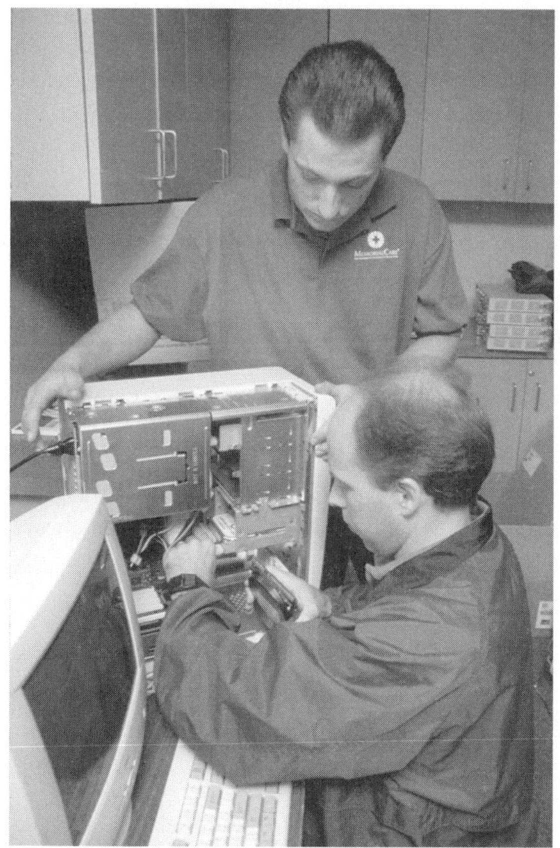

Computer technician jobs score relatively high on *data* and *things*, but not so high on *people*, whereas. . . . (see next photo)

Sales jobs score relatively high on *data* and *people*, but not so high on *things*.

and drawing inferences about work activities, worker attributes, and work context" (p. 21). In other words, **job analysis** is the process of defining a job in terms of its component tasks or duties and the knowledge or skills required to perform them. Brannick and Levine (2002) argue that job analysis is the basis for the solution to any human resource problem.

job analysis
The process of defining a job in terms of its component tasks or duties and the knowledge or skills required to perform them.

APPROACHES TO JOB ANALYSIS

Most procedures in I/O psychology can be conducted in various ways. Job analysis is no exception. Whatever the approach, however, the job analyst needs to consider the purpose of the job analysis when deciding on a strategy. One approach may be more beneficial for a given purpose than a different approach. As Sackett and Laczo (2003) state: "One size does not fit all!" In this section and the one to follow, we will examine a couple of general perspectives taken in the area of job analysis, as well as some specific ways in which job analysis data can be collected.

The traditional taxonomy espoused by most job analysis experts over the years categorizes job analysis methods as either job-oriented or worker-oriented (McCormick, 1976). **Job-oriented** techniques focus on describing the various tasks that are performed on the job. These techniques tend to be job specific because they are based on the particular tasks performed during a particular job. **Worker-oriented** techniques examine broad human behaviors involved in work activities (Gatewood & Feild, 2001). Unlike job-oriented approaches, which focus at the very specific level of tasks, worker-oriented job analyses focus broadly on general aspects of the job, such as the physical, interpersonal, and mental factors necessary for completion of the job and the related worker attributes. In fact, a recent review and analysis in this area also suggests a third category—hybrid methods. These approaches attempt to gather information about the work and the worker at the same time (Brannick & Levine, 2002). Gatewood and Feild (2001) also note that the distinction between the two traditional categories is not always clear and that some job analytic techniques cross over into the other category. Further, one approach is not necessarily better than the other.

job-oriented
Referring to approaches to job analysis that focus on describing the various tasks that are performed on the job.

worker-oriented
Referring to approaches to job analysis that examine broad human behaviors involved in work activities.

JOB ANALYTIC METHODS

For simplicity's sake, this chapter largely employs the traditional job-oriented and worker-oriented distinction, but it also presents the important results of a hybrid approach employed in the development of the Occupational Information Network (O*NET).

JOB-ORIENTED TECHNIQUES

Job-oriented techniques for conducting job analyses tend to be focused on tasks. (Recall our previous definition of a task as the activity of work that is performed to achieve a specific objective.) One job-oriented approach is called the **Task Inventory Approach,** in which task statements are generated by experts who are familiar with the jobs—**subject matter experts (SMEs).** These experts may be **incumbents**—that is, people who are currently occupying the job of interest. Or they may be individuals who have expertise or knowledge about the job for some other reason, such as being a supervisor of individuals in that job or an I/O psychologist who has gathered expertise through her work. Once a list of task statements has been generated, this list, which can include hundreds of task statements, is usually administered to incumbents who put a check next to those statements

Task Inventory Approach
A job-oriented approach to job analysis in which task statements are generated by experts who are familiar with the job in question.

subject matter experts
Individuals who participate in job analyses as a result of their job-related expertise.

incumbents
In job analysis, employees who are currently occupying the job of interest.

FIGURE 3.2 Task Inventory for College Professor

Task Statements	Is task done on this job?	Importance of task to job					Relative to other tasks performed on the job, how much time is spent on each of the following tasks?				
		1	2	3	4	5	1	2	3	4	5
	Yes or No	Not important at all		Somewhat important		Extremely important	Much less time	Somewhat less time	About the same amount of time	Somewhat more time	Much more time
1. Develops written assignments											
2. Grades exams											
3. Meets with students individually to help them understand things											
4. Lectures to groups of students											
5. Designs research studies											
6. Collects data											
7. Mentors and advises students regarding career issues											

that describe a task that they do on their job. A sample task inventory for the job of college professor is provided in Figure 3.2. The task statements that are checked as being done on the job are also often rated as to the importance or criticality of the task to the job and the relative time spent on the job doing each task. This process effectively summarizes the tasks that are completed on the job, the time that is spent on each task, and the incumbents' view of the importance of each task. Together, these pieces of information can provide a thorough analysis or *picture* of the job.

In **Functional Job Analysis (FJA),** a highly structured job-oriented approach developed by Sidney Fine many years ago, data are obtained about *what* tasks a worker does and *how* those tasks are performed. (For a summary of this technique, see Fine, 1988.) Specifically, a series of task statements are developed that are believed to be relevant for the job in question. Incumbents or SMEs rate each of these statements (which are similar to those shown in Figure 3.2) on a series of

Functional Job Analysis
A highly structured job-oriented approach developed by Sidney Fine in which data are obtained about *what* tasks a worker does and *how* those tasks are performed.

dimensions. These dimensions are what set this approach apart from the standard Task Inventory Approach.

A picture of the job is generated when these task statements have been rated with regard to *data, people,* and *things*—three factors with which employees in all jobs are assumed to interact. One way to understand a job is to know the extent to which these interactions take place and the complexity of those interactions. This is the focus of FJA. A task focusing largely on *data* requires the employee to use cognitive resources in handling information, ideas, and facts. Tasks that are coded along this dimension range from simple comparisons to more complex synthesizing. The *people* dimension refers to the extent to which the job requires employees to use interpersonal resources such as understanding, courtesy, and mentoring. Tasks coded along this dimension range from simply taking instructions to more sophisticated behaviors such as mentoring. Finally, a task that is linked to the *things* scale requires the use of physical resources and includes the use of strength, speed, and coordination. Tasks coded along this dimension range from the simple handling of things to more intricate precise operations.

Dictionary of Occupational Titles (DOT) A tool developed by the Department of Labor in the 1930s that has been used to classify occupations and jobs, consisting of narrative descriptions of tasks, duties, and working conditions of about 12,000 jobs.

In the 1930s the Department of Labor used FJA to develop the ***Dictionary of Occupational Titles*** **(DOT),** a tool that matches people with jobs. Consisting of narrative descriptions of tasks, duties, and working conditions of about 12,000 jobs, the DOT codes each of these jobs according to the data, people, and things dimensions developed by Fine. The information presented in the DOT is based on years and years of data collected through job analyses. The DOT presents a hierarchical organization of jobs, with nine major occupational clusters at the uppermost level of the hierarchy (American Institutes for Research, 1996). Figure 3.3 shows the DOT entry for a faculty member, including labels for the particular parts of the entry. The nine-digit *occupational code* is important in that it uniquely identifies this particular job. The first three digits classify the job with respect to its occupational category. The next three digits identify where the job is classified with respect to data, people, and things; in this example the digits 227 indicate that the job is high on both data *(analyze)* and people *(instruct)* but low on things *(handle).* This probably fits your preconceived notion of what faculty members do, which is to spend a great deal of time working with data and people but less time manipulating tools, equipment, and so on. The *industry designation* in this case is "education." The *lead statement* is always the first sentence of the description itself, followed by a colon. This statement provides the best simple description of the job. The *task element statements,* which come next, describe with more precision what is done on the job to meet the objectives presented in the lead statement. In other words, college professors teach subjects, prepare lectures, stimulate class discussion, and so on, in order to conduct college courses. Finally, the *"May" items* indicate activities that may be done in some organizations by individuals who occupy this job but are not routinely part of this job in most organizations.

The Department of Labor is currently undertaking a new initiative to replace the DOT, which it views as incompatible with the current workplace. This new initiative, known as the Occupational Information Network (O*NET), aspires to identify and describe the key components of modern occupations (Occupational Information Network, 1998). In contrast to the DOT, the O*NET is not based on

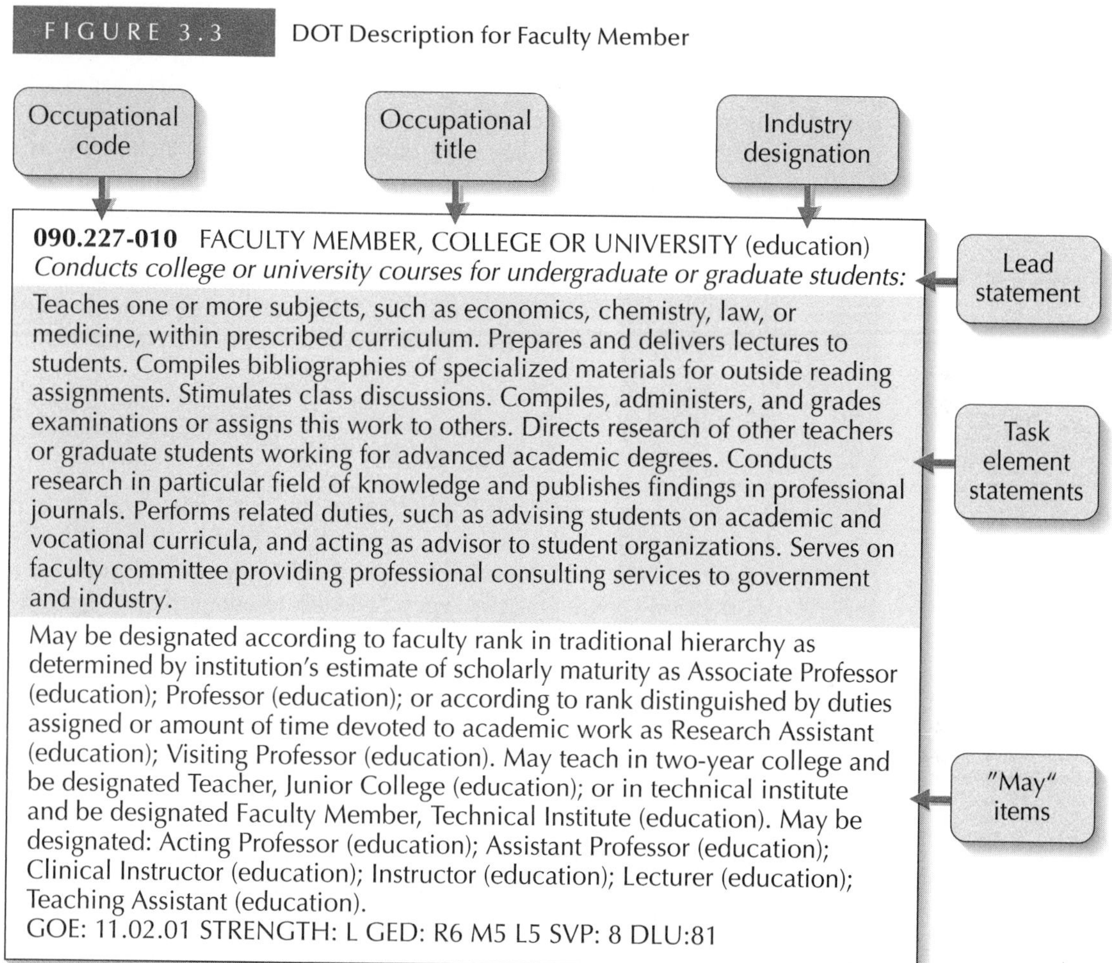

090.227-010 FACULTY MEMBER, COLLEGE OR UNIVERSITY (education)
Conducts college or university courses for undergraduate or graduate students:
Teaches one or more subjects, such as economics, chemistry, law, or medicine, within prescribed curriculum. Prepares and delivers lectures to students. Compiles bibliographies of specialized materials for outside reading assignments. Stimulates class discussions. Compiles, administers, and grades examinations or assigns this work to others. Directs research of other teachers or graduate students working for advanced academic degrees. Conducts research in particular field of knowledge and publishes findings in professional journals. Performs related duties, such as advising students on academic and vocational curricula, and acting as advisor to student organizations. Serves on faculty committee providing professional consulting services to government and industry.
May be designated according to faculty rank in traditional hierarchy as determined by institution's estimate of scholarly maturity as Associate Professor (education); Professor (education); or according to rank distinguished by duties assigned or amount of time devoted to academic work as Research Assistant (education); Visiting Professor (education). May teach in two-year college and be designated Teacher, Junior College (education); or in technical institute and be designated Faculty Member, Technical Institute (education). May be designated: Acting Professor (education); Assistant Professor (education); Clinical Instructor (education); Instructor (education); Lecturer (education); Teaching Assistant (education).
GOE: 11.02.01 STRENGTH: L GED: R6 M5 L5 SVP: 8 DLU:81

FIGURE 3.3 DOT Description for Faculty Member

FJA; rather, it is based on data gathered in a variety of ways, including an initial review of existing literature in the domains of human performance and occupational analysis. Thus it is categorized as a hybrid approach by Brannick and Levine (2002), because it focuses simultaneously on both the work and the worker. This database is now available online, making it much more accessible than the older DOT (O*NET Online, 2000). In addition to having data on thousands of jobs, it will allow individuals to search for occupations through key words relating to skill requirements, and it will be connected to *America's Job Bank* and *school-to-work* initiatives that use schools to train students to be better prepared for the workplace and to successfully find employment. Indeed, O*NET has widespread implications for the world of work and the practice of I/O psychology. Research on the O*NET is just now emerging, such as a recent study by Jeanneret and Strong (2003) that reported that the O*NET General Work Activities were related to particular employee knowledge, skills, and abilities that were required for effective work performance.

In his thorough review of job analytic techniques and research, Harvey (1991) criticizes job-oriented approaches to job analysis as being potentially too narrowly focused on the tasks for a particular job. It follows, he argues, that by focusing microscopically on the tasks of a particular job, we rule out the possibility of making a real comparison across jobs, because no job is likely to emerge as similar at such a fine-grained level. In other words, we may miss similarities in jobs because of the high level of technological and behavioral specificity of the tasks and thereby fail to detect more abstract similarities across jobs. Worker-oriented approaches to job analysis address this very problem.

Worker-Oriented Techniques

These job-analytic techniques focus less on the specific tasks done on a job and more on the human characteristics that contribute to successful job performance (Sackett & Laczo, 2003). E. J. McCormick and his colleagues (1972) provided a very clear distinction between the two types: "The job-oriented concept typically would be reflected by the use of specific task statements. . . . In turn, the worker-oriented concept typically would be reflected by the use of descriptions of reasonably definitive human behaviors of many kinds" (p. 348). Worker-oriented methods of job analysis are more effective than task-focused job-oriented methods if the analyst is interested in comparing across jobs, because jobs can then be compared with respect to their reliance on the various talents and abilities of the incumbents.

Job Element Method (JEM)
A worker-oriented approach to job analysis that was designed to identify the characteristics of superior workers in a particular job.

The **Job Element Method (JEM)** was designed to identify the characteristics of superior workers in a particular job (Primoff & Eyde, 1988). Note that in this context, the word *element* refers to general work behaviors, not to the smallest unit of work activity as defined earlier. More specifically, job elements in the JEM refer to the knowledge, skills, abilities, and other characteristics (KSAOs) that are required for successful job performance (Primoff & Eyde, 1988). KSAOs are very important in I/O psychology because they are the basis for much of the work done in employee selection (see Chapters 6 and 7). In short, organizations prefer to hire those employees who possess KSAOs that are likely to make them successful performers. Indeed, this is largely what selection and placement in organizations are all about. The JEM's aim is to directly connect job analysis to the selection context by identifying the KSAOs that are necessary for successful job performance. The procedure is rather simple. First, SMEs are asked to develop a comprehensive list of job elements, as well as subelements or employee characteristics that are more specific than the job elements. For instance, one element for a college professor might be "ability to communicate clearly," and subelements within this element might include "can express ideas in an interesting manner to large groups of people" and "able to explain complex issues to students in a one-on-one environment." Once the final list of elements and subelements has been generated, the SMEs are instructed to provide work examples of each. Together, the elements, subelements, and work examples provide a complete picture of the job.

A common criticism of this approach is that the JEM ignores the specific job tasks that make it difficult to demonstrate that a particular element is related to the job (Gatewood & Feild, 2001)—a point that will become clear when we discuss the issues involved in test validation in Chapter 7. This criticism is consistent with Harvey's (1991) concern that job analysis needs to remain focused on observables instead of inferring hypothetical worker traits or abilities. However, much of what we do in psychology involves inferences of some sort, so excluding them seems unreasonable. We can resolve this paradox by realizing that an important focus of job analysis is to ensure that when inferences are drawn, they are based on observable work-related data. The job analyst can choose to focus only on work activities or only on worker attributes or can employ both, which is consistent with the hybrid approach discussed earlier.

Perhaps the best-known job analysis method is the **Position Analysis Questionnaire (PAQ),** a standardized instrument that focuses on general work behaviors (McCormick et al., 1972). Because of this focus it is useful in describing many types of jobs. The PAQ consists of 195 items or elements, 187 of which describe general work behaviors, work conditions, and job characteristics. The incumbent employee or SME decides whether each item pertains to the job in question, and those that do are evaluated in terms of various dimensions, such as the extent to which it is used on the job, its importance to the job, and the amount of time on the job that is spent on this behavior. These 187 job elements are organized along six dimensions: information input, mental processes, work output, relationships with other persons, job context, and other job characteristics. Table 3.1 lists these six dimensions, along with two examples of each. A profile of the job emerges as a result of this rather large data collection effort.

Position Analysis Questionnaire (PAQ)
A widely used job analysis instrument that focuses on general work behaviors.

Despite its historically widespread use, the PAQ has been the target of at least three major criticisms. First, some data indicate that the reading level of the PAQ is at least college level, if not graduate level (Ash & Edgell, 1975). This is a problem because it limits who can competently do the job analysis and rules out the less educated incumbents in many jobs. Second, the PAQ does not seem well suited for managerial jobs; and, third, the items themselves are too abstract (Harvey, 1998). These criticisms have led other job analysis researchers and practitioners to develop alternative worker-oriented instruments.

The Common-Metric Questionnaire (CMQ), developed by Harvey (1998), is one such instrument. Two basic beliefs about worker-oriented approaches to job analysis are reflected in the CMQ: (1) The instrument must comprehensively describe work activities using a common set of items written at a more behaviorally abstract level than the typical task statements, and (2) the rating scale must have the same meaning across all jobs. The focus here is on describing jobs at a level that allows the descriptions to be compared across jobs, as opposed to describing them so abstractly that differences across jobs are lost. Think back to such job-oriented approaches as the Task Inventory Approach and Functional Job Analysis. In these cases, the focus is on extremely specific tasks conducted on the job, making it very

Common-Metric-Questionnaire
A newly developed worker-oriented job-analysis instrument that attempts to improve the generalizability of worker-oriented approaches through the use of items focused on slightly less general work behaviors.

TABLE 3.1 PAQ Dimensions and Elements

Information input	(Where and how does the worker get the information he uses in performing his job?)
Examples:	Use of written materials Near-visual differentiation
Mental processes	(What reasoning, decision-making, planning, and information-processing activities are involved in performing the job?)
Examples:	Level of reasoning in problem solving Coding/decoding
Work output	(What physical activities does the worker perform, and what tools does she use?)
Examples:	Use of keyboard devices Assembling/disassembling
Relationships with other persons	(What relationships with other people are required in performing the job?)
Examples:	Instructing Contacts with public, customers
Job context	(In what physical or social contexts is the work performed?)
Examples:	High temperature Interpersonal conflict situations
Other job characteristics	(What activities, conditions, or characteristics other than those described above are relevant to the job?)
Examples:	Specified work pace Amount of job structure

Source: McCormick (1979).

difficult to uncover any similarities across jobs. But the worker-oriented approaches, best exemplified by the PAQ, may be so abstract as to result in the emergence of dissimilar jobs with very similar profiles. For instance, what jobs do you think might emerge with a profile similar to that of police officer? You probably listed things like firefighter, prison guard, and private detective. However, research indicates that one answer is the job of *homemaker* (Arvey & Begalla, 1975). This is probably not one of the jobs that you had on your list, but the profiles tend to be similar because both police officers and homemakers are often involved in handling emergencies and troubleshooting. However, I would argue that if the PAQ elements were a little less abstract, these jobs would not emerge as similar.

The CMQ is computer-based, consisting of 2,077 items that are organized along 80 dimensions. Obviously, one issue with respect to this instrument is its length, but the author reports that over 90% of those who have used it completed it in under 3 hours (Harvey, 1998). Two screens of the program are presented in Figure 3.4. The first one features a question about whether a particular job requires skill in instruction at a college or university, along with the response scale

FIGURE 3.4 Common-Metric Questionnaire Job Analysis

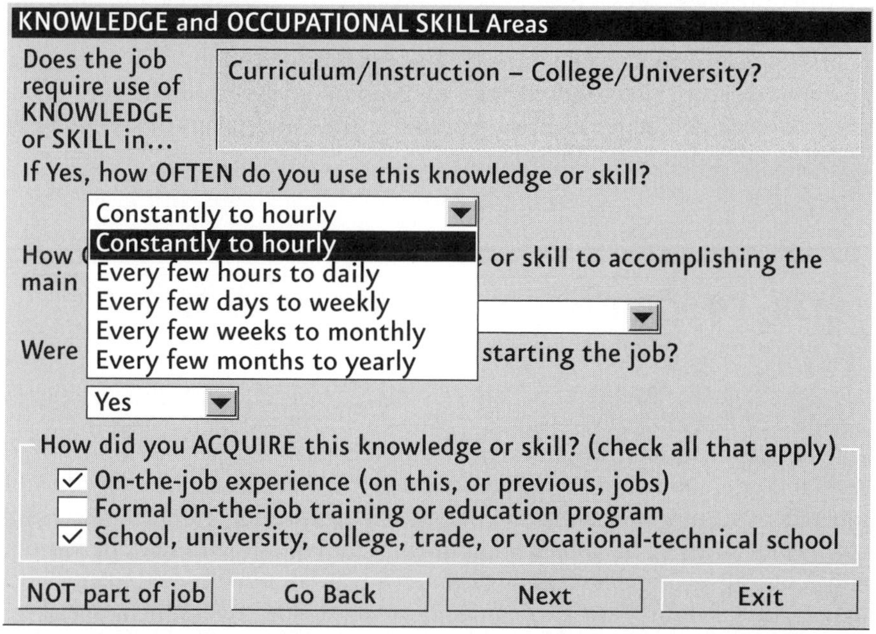

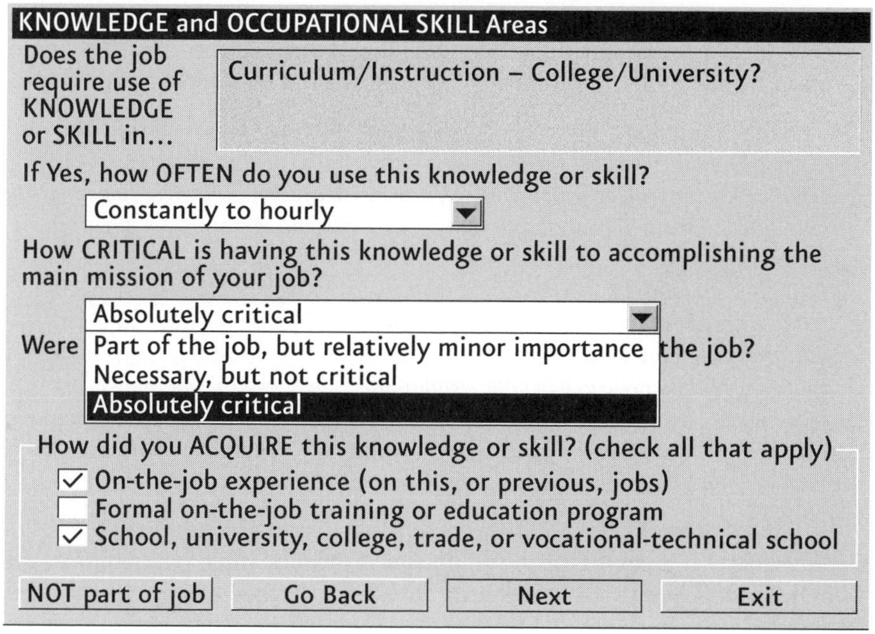

KNOWLEDGE and OCCUPATIONAL SKILL Areas

Does the job require use of KNOWLEDGE or SKILL in...

Curriculum/Instruction – College/University?

If Yes, how OFTEN do you use this knowledge or skill?

Constantly to hourly

Constantly to hourly
Every few hours to daily
Every few days to weekly
Every few weeks to monthly
Every few months to yearly

How (… or skill to accomplishing the main

Were … starting the job?

Yes

How did you ACQUIRE this knowledge or skill? (check all that apply)

- [x] On-the-job experience (on this, or previous, jobs)
- [ ] Formal on-the-job training or education program
- [x] School, university, college, trade, or vocational-technical school

NOT part of job | Go Back | Next | Exit

KNOWLEDGE and OCCUPATIONAL SKILL Areas

Does the job require use of KNOWLEDGE or SKILL in...

Curriculum/Instruction – College/University?

If Yes, how OFTEN do you use this knowledge or skill?

Constantly to hourly

How CRITICAL is having this knowledge or skill to accomplishing the main mission of your job?

Absolutely critical

Part of the job, but relatively minor importance
Necessary, but not critical
Absolutely critical

Were … the job?

How did you ACQUIRE this knowledge or skill? (check all that apply)

- [x] On-the-job experience (on this, or previous, jobs)
- [ ] Formal on-the-job training or education program
- [x] School, university, college, trade, or vocational-technical school

NOT part of job | Go Back | Next | Exit

for that item. The second screen shows the response scale for the criticality of this particular skill. The items for all 80 dimensions are set up in a similar way. Although rather new, the CMQ has been piloted on over 900 occupations involving over 6,700 positions. Its items are more behaviorally specific than those included on the PAQ, its reading level is much lower, and it is relevant for both managerial and nonmanagerial jobs. Indeed, the CMQ appears to have potential for providing a worker-oriented job analysis instrument that avoids many of the problems plaguing those that have come before it.

DEFINING THE JOB: DESCRIPTIONS AND SPECIFICATIONS

job description
As an outcome of job analysis, a written statement of what jobholders actually do, how they do it, and why they do it.

The basic goal of job analysis is to define the job in terms of its component parts. As noted earlier, job analysis yields three major outcomes: job evaluation, job description, and job specifications. The first of these will be discussed in a separate section. The second outcome, **job description,** is a written statement of what the jobholders do, how they do it, and why they do it (Cascio, 1998). It presents the *task requirements* of the job. The job description typically includes the job title and descriptions of the tasks and machinery involved, and it sometimes includes information about the working conditions and physical environment, social environment, and conditions of employment. Think about the job of college professor and ask yourself what college professors do, how they do it, and why they do it. Upon answering those questions, you might arrive at the following job description, which looks very similar to the DOT entry for faculty member presented earlier.

> *College Professor: Teaches college or university courses within a particular curriculum (e.g., psychology, mathematics, history) to classes of undergraduate and graduate students. Prepares and delivers lectures that conform to a predetermined course outline. Stimulates class discussions in smaller informal groups. Evaluates students' knowledge and achievement through reading, writing, and other assignments as well as through examinations that are graded so as to provide feedback. Conducts research in his or her area of expertise and disseminates the findings of that research in appropriate outlets (e.g., scientific journals, books) to further the knowledge in the field. Provides mentoring and advising to students who are seeking academic degrees. Serves on university committees that serve the interests of students, the university, the government, and the community.*

job specifications
An outcome of job analysis delineating the KSAOs deemed necessary to perform a job.

The third outcome derived from the job analysis is a description of the *people requirements* that are reflected in the **job specifications** (often referred to as "job specs"). The job specifications delineate the KSAOs deemed necessary to perform the job. Let's return to our college professor example. We've generated a job description, but what would comprise the job specifications or KSAOs necessary to be a successful college professor? Here is one such list:

- reading and writing at the postcollege level
- advanced knowledge verified by an advanced degree (master's or doctorate)
- willingness or desire to work with others
- ability to communicate clearly
- ability to communicate in an interesting manner
- methodological and statistical skills
- mentoring and advising skills
- a deep knowledge/understanding of one's own discipline

One way to view the relationships among job analysis, job description, and job specifications is to view the job description as stemming directly from the job analysis and the job specifications as being inferred indirectly from the job analysis through the job description and stemming directly from the job analysis. Look back at Figure 3.1 for this organizational scheme. For instance, we might use the JEM to develop a picture of the job and to write a job description (like the preceding one) that includes mentoring and advising students who are seeking academic degrees. From the job analysis and this job description, we might infer that successful college professors must have mentoring and advising skills. In short, the job analysis, job description, and job specifications are necessarily intertwined. As you may recall, Harvey (1991) argued that job analysis should be focused only on observables and warned against making inferences about KSAOs from the job analysis. Of course, one of the major purposes of job analysis is to identify KSAOs that can be used in the selection of employees. This process is covered in Chapter 6, but it's worth noting here that even if one limits job analysis to observables that result in a job description, the job analysis and job description must be used to infer job specifications that are of paramount importance for selection and placement. The bottom line is that as I/O psychologists we are not simply focused on describing the job; indeed, our longer-term goal is the use of this job analysis information for selection, placement, performance appraisal, and other HR functions. Let's turn to a brief discussion of the purposes of job analysis.

THE MANY PURPOSES OF JOB ANALYSIS

As I suggested earlier, job analysis is the foundation for much of industrial psychology. There are two reasons for this. First, a job analysis is necessary to the success of human resource functions. In other words, without a job analysis, many of the HR functions in organizations would be carried out ineffectively. Second, an increased emphasis on laws associated with the workplace has made it more desirable for companies to use job analyses as their first line of defense when accused of an unfair practice. Table 3.2 presents a few cases in which the existence and quality of a job analysis played a major role in the court's decision. We will discuss legal issues in more depth in the next few chapters; for now, let's consider job classification, an important purpose served by job analysis.

TABLE 3.2 Legal Importance of Job Analysis to Organizations

Case Description:	Legal Ruling
Kirkland v. New York Dept. of Correctional Service (1974): Test used for promotion resulted in many fewer minority promotions than Caucasian promotions. Defendant argued that the test was job-related because it tapped important skills necessary to do the job.	Court ruled that the company had not performed an adequate job analysis demonstrating that the test items were linked to job performance and that the test was, therefore, not valid to be used for promotion.
Harless v. Duck (1977): A physical test (push-ups, sit-ups, broad jump, and obstacle course) was used in hiring patrol officers, but it resulted in many fewer women hires than men hires. Defendant argued that the test was job-related.	Court ruled that the job analysis was adequate for demonstrating that the skills and abilities measured by the physical test were necessary for successful job performance. Thus the test was deemed reasonable and valid for the hiring of patrol officers.
Adams v. City of Chicago (1996): Sergeant Promotional Test resulted in far fewer minorities promoted than Caucasians, but the City argued that the test was job-related.	Court ruled that the job analysis identified important and relevant skills and abilities that were adequately measured by the Sergeant Promotional Test. Thus the test was found to be valid for making promotion decisions to the rank of Sergeant.

Job Classification

Jobs are often categorized in terms of job families, each of which can then be used as a level of analysis for various personnel decisions. For instance, Word Processing Specialist I, Word Processing Specialist II, and Data Technician I may all be declared parts of a job family called "computer support staff." Note, however, that they would be classified as parts of this job family only if the job analyses conducted on each job demonstrated enough overlap to warrant such a designation. If they did, all jobs within this job family would operate under the same benefits package, including number of allowable sick days, number of vacation days, and amount of health benefits. In addition, if a company's 2,000 jobs can be grouped into 100 job families, many of the company's personnel practices would be simplified.

Criterion Development and Performance Appraisal

Performance appraisal is certainly one of the most frequent uses of job analysis data. As we will discuss in Chapters 4 and 5, performance appraisal is one of the most important functions performed by human resource departments. Of course,

PRACTITIONER FORUM

SHELLY FUNDERBURG
Ph.D., 1995, I/O Psychology, University of Akron
Director of Hiring Solutions
Manpower

Manpower is a global provider of staffing and workforce management solutions with over 3,700 offices in 59 countries. We placed more than 2.7 million employees at customer sites in 2003. I oversee the development, validation, and implementation of hiring systems used by Manpower and our customers' employees. Given our focus on helping companies find the right employees for their needs, job analysis is a major foundation for our work at Manpower. With respect to job analysis, we have three main objectives: (1) to analyze jobs and develop selection and appraisal systems for national and global projects, (2) to use job analytic information to train our field staff on making appropriate staffing decisions, and (3) to continue monitoring and updating our human resource systems to reflect current job skills and relevant work changes.

Our first objective, analyzing jobs and developing human resource systems that work well together, is the most arduous and time-consuming one. At Manpower, we blend the job and work-oriented approaches to ensure not only that we understand the tasks necessary for the job but also that we have a good comprehension of the underlying skills and abilities that contribute to successful performance of those tasks. To do this, we conduct site visits, develop and administer surveys, and conduct focus groups.

After we use job analysis to define the basic elements of each job, our second objective is to train our field staff to match the elements of the job with each customer's staffing needs. When a customer requests help in staffing a particular job, our field specialists must quickly and easily determine which selection and training process is appropriate for the requested position. We use job analysis to develop checklists that assist these field specialists in comparing each new request with the analyzed jobs.

Third, it is important to ensure that our job analysis research reflects the dynamic workplace of the future. As new staffing requests are placed and additional jobs are researched, we look for changes in the daily work of our employees. As you can imagine, any change in the job itself, or what is done on that job, significantly impacts the skills and abilities required to perform the job and, therefore, changes the selection process.

Job analysis is the first and most important step in developing any of Manpower's human resource (HR) processes and is one reason that our HR processes work so well.

APPLYING YOUR KNOWLEDGE

1. What other job analysis methods might prove helpful to Manpower?
2. How can this approach to job analysis be tied to compensation systems?
3. Given the changing nature of work, why is job analysis especially important? How is Manpower demonstrating this fact?

to conduct a useful and fair performance appraisal, organizations must have clearly stipulated goals, objectives, and criteria on which employees can be evaluated. These criteria should come directly from the job analysis. For instance, if college professors are going to be evaluated annually with respect to their success in teaching, the college must be able to demonstrate that teaching is an important part of the professors' job. (This should be an easy thing to do, but it still needs to be verified by the job analysis.) Suppose that I was evaluated based on the reactions of my students to my classes (and in fact, I am evaluated in this way every semester), but the job analysis done by my school does not demonstrate that teaching is an integral part of my job. This would suggest that I was being evaluated according to criteria that were not a substantial part of the job—an outcome that would be neither fair nor appropriate. Here, of course, I would argue that the problem was not with the criteria but with the job analysis, which did not identify an important element of the job. This example, too, demonstrates the importance of doing a thorough and accurate job analysis because the job analysis is used in important ways.

Selection and Placement

There is perhaps no area of industrial psychology for which job analysis is more important than selection and placement (see Chapters 6 and 7). Indeed, a major purpose of job analysis is to help industrial psychologists identify the KSAOs that are necessary for successful performance on the job. As I mentioned earlier, this involves drawing inferences from observables, thus allowing industrial psychologists to identify the skills that employees need to have in order to be successful on the job.

In Chapter 1, I defined *competencies* as the skills, behaviors, and capabilities that allow employees to perform specific functions. Obviously, this definition is very similar to the one I have specified for KSAOs in this chapter. In fact, many experts consider competencies and KSAOs to be the same thing (e.g., Schippmann et al., 2000). Another way to think about this relationship, though, is to view competencies as sets or groupings of specific KSAOs that allow employees to perform specific organizational functions (Reilly & McGourty, 1998). For example, interpersonal communication may be considered a competency. That competency, in turn, may consist of several KSAOs such as (1) the knowledge of different communication styles, (2) the skill to communicate positive and negative feedback to individuals, and (3) the ability to understand what individuals need to hear from their supervisor to increase their motivation.

Competency modeling is parallel to job analysis in that both involve describing jobs in a careful and methodical way so that HR practices can be based on this information (Schippmann et al., 2000). Differences have been observed as well. For example, competency modeling is believed to be more worker-oriented and job analysis more job-oriented (Schippmann et al., 2000). Competency modeling may be a bit broader in focus because it tries to build a full framework for HR functioning by defining the responsibilities, skills, knowledge, abilities, personal attributes, and business challenges that are relevant for a particular organization. Although some distinctions have been drawn between using job analysis to identify KSAOs and competency modeling to build competencies, the two terms are similar enough that I will use them interchangeably throughout the text.

Let's turn to the world of construction for an example. In doing a job analysis for the job of an architect, we conclude that spatial skills and a knowledge of some basic engineering principles are required. Therefore, when screening applicants we look for individuals who seem to be knowledgeable and skilled in these areas and hire them. This scenario makes sense, but it may also be too simplistic. For instance, we might ignore the part of our job analysis indicating that architects also need to have some drafting (or drawing) skills, because they need to be able to develop plans for new buildings. Given this flaw in our process, we may hire knowledgeable and spatially skilled individuals who do not have the drafting skills to put their ideas on paper. In short, because we weren't careful in conducting and interpreting our job analysis, we may have made costly personnel decisions, leaving our organization without a capable employee in a very important position in the organization. Does this cost our company money? It sure does, and it also may cost individuals their jobs. Using job analysis data to identify KSAOs for the selection and placement of personnel is indeed one of the most important functions of human resource departments.

Job Design and Redesign

Job analysis may sometimes uncover problems with a particular job that the organization may want to address. For instance, interviews with incumbents may reveal that some of the current equipment used on the job needs to be updated because it no longer works at a pace that is fast enough to keep up with other equipment during the production process. A company may use this information to purchase newer equipment or to redesign the job so that the current equipment will work more efficiently within the process. Alternatively, PAQ or CMS data may indicate that employees spend far too much time on a particular facet of the job, information that the company may use to initiate a job redesign intervention to make the work process more efficient. We can see that in this area of I/O psychology, job analyses are often used to make alterations in the work process with the intent of making the company run more efficiently.

Training

In many instances, employees are hired into an organization without all of the KSAOs necessary to do every facet of their jobs. Sometimes, even highly skilled new employees require training to learn the procedures used in a particular organization (see Chapter 8). Job analysis can be used to identify areas in which training programs need to be developed. Ideally, the job analysis should identify what work behaviors occur on the job so that the human resource department of the organization can develop training programs around these general and specific work behaviors. In addition, given that jobs are *dynamic* in that they change considerably with changes in technology, in the workforce, and in economic demands, job analysis can be used to identify the extent to which job behaviors have changed to match the times. This information can then be used to develop and target training programs for existing employees.

JOB EVALUATION

Although we like to think that our job is as important to our particular organization as anyone else's, the reality is that some jobs are more important than others. **Job evaluation** is a technique based on job analysis that attempts to determine the value or worth of particular jobs to organizations so that salaries can be set accordingly. Most of us would agree that the clerk who works in the hospital restaurant makes a less important contribution to the organization than the chief surgeon. Job evaluation is about trying to quantify differences of this sort so that salaries can be set in a fair manner based on the value or contribution of jobs. Because compensation is often the largest budget item in many companies, it has an important effect on profits and, therefore, attracts a good deal of attention from organizational administrators and HR practitioners.

job evaluation
As an outcome of job analysis, a technique that attempts to determine the value or worth of particular jobs to organizations so that salaries can be set accordingly.

Point System

There are various approaches to job evaluation, but I will focus on the one most frequently used: the **point system.** This approach involves estimating the value of jobs based on points assigned to various predetermined dimensions (Milkovich & Newman, 1984). Among the most common of these dimensions—referred to as **compensable factors** to indicate that employees are compensated based on them—are effort, skill, responsibility, and working conditions. The idea here is that jobs requiring more effort and skill, involving more responsibility, and taking place in less desirable working conditions (e.g., outdoors in subzero temperatures versus climate-controlled office buildings) should be more highly compensated than jobs that don't have these characteristics.

point system
The most common approach to job evaluation, which involves estimating the value of jobs based on points assigned to various predetermined dimensions.

compensable factors
Dimensions or factors that are used to rate jobs, indicating that employees are compensated based on these factors. Examples include effort, skill, responsibility, and working conditions.

The steps involved in conducting a point-system job evaluation are rather simple. First, managers or some other group of SMEs use a job analysis to identify the compensable factors. Second, each job is assigned points by a compensation committee with respect to the degree that each has these compensable factors. Third, the points assigned to each job are summed across the factors to arrive at a total score. Fourth, these points are then used to assign wages, with the goal being to maintain equity so that jobs of greater value are better compensated than those of lesser value. Finally, the scores can be plotted against the current wage for existing jobs, providing a clear picture of whether a job is currently undercompensated, overcompensated, or adequately compensated.

Figure 3.5 shows an example of this kind of plot to determine how jobs within the organization stack up to each other in terms of the factors and compensation. The line marked "perfect wage equity" represents the ideal situation whereby the number of job evaluation points is exactly proportional to the level of compensation, such that the highest rated jobs are also the highest paid jobs. The line marked "imperfect wage equity," on the other hand, is more realistic but much less desirable. As you can see, jobs evaluated at 125 points are overcompensated at

Construction worker and nurse (see next page) are two gender-typed jobs. This sometimes affects the compensation and expectations for these jobs.

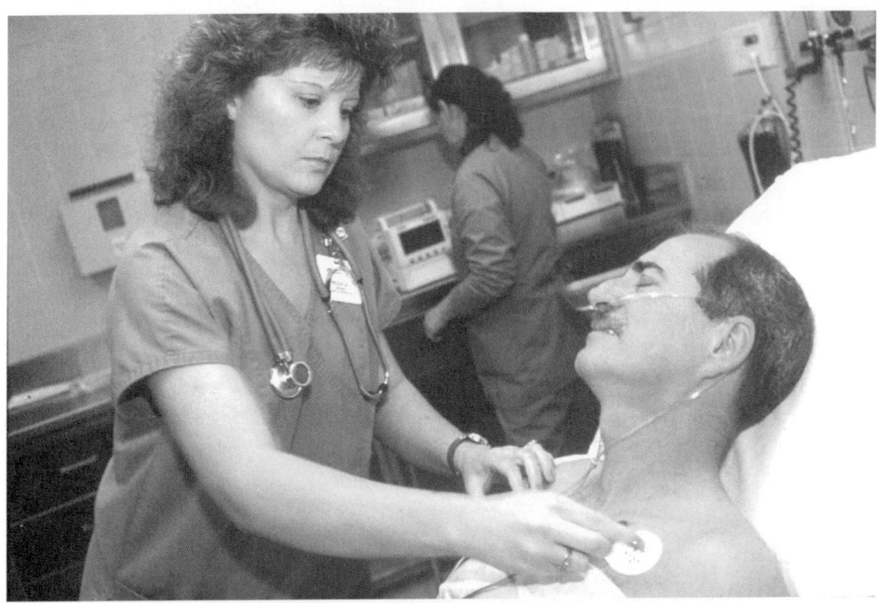

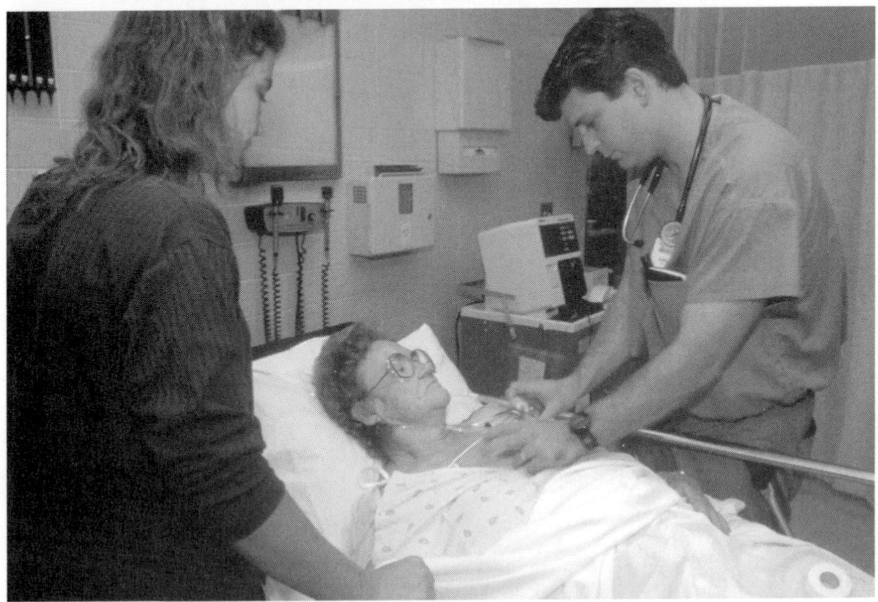

$8.75 per hour rather than the expected $6.25 per hour, and jobs evaluated at 350 points are undercompensated at $13.75 per hour rather than the expected $17.50 per hour. Clearly, there are compensation issues to be resolved in this particular organization: Some positions are compensated at a rate that is higher than the job evaluation indicates they should be, and others are compensated at a rate that is

FIGURE 3.5 Wage Equity and Job Evaluation

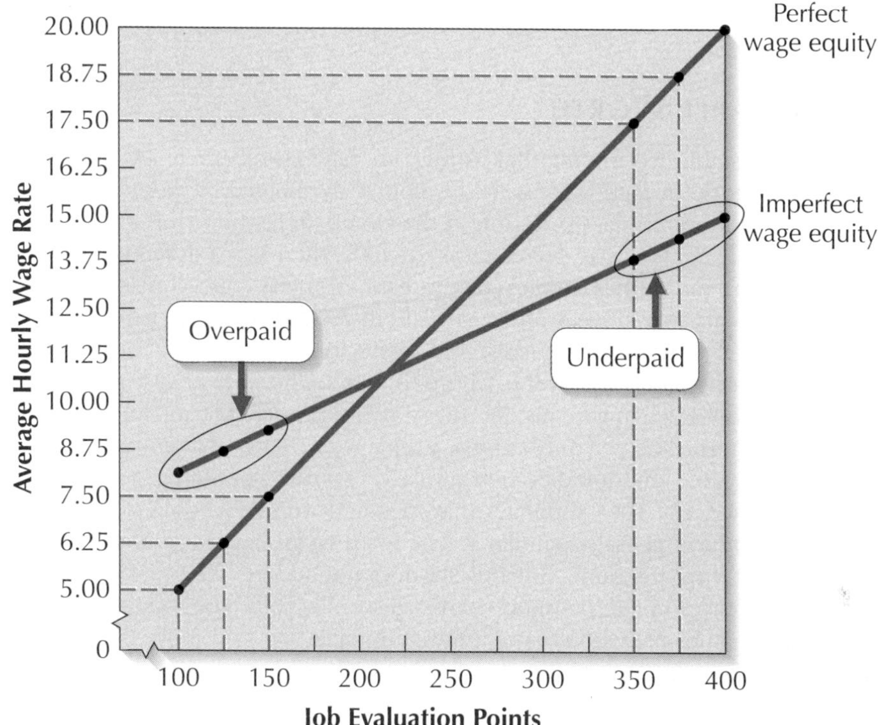

lower than the job evaluation indicates they should be. You can imagine the reactions of employees when they become aware of this situation. Yet once organizations have accumulated and examined such data, they can begin to develop ways to bring wages back in line. For instance, jobs that are undercompensated can be targeted for wage increases, whereas those that are overcompensated can be targeted for wage freezes. Those jobs that seem to be compensated at the appropriate levels would not be targeted for any particular compensation adjustments.

So far, this sounds very scientific, and in some ways it is. But as is often the case with I/O psychology, when we move into the applied arena things are not quite so simple. In the actual labor market, for instance, individuals in jobs with job evaluation scores between 100 and 200 points sometimes have to be "overpaid"; in other words, there are so few people who will take these lower-level jobs that, to be competitive with other companies, we have to pay these jobs more than our job evaluation tells us they are worth. At the same time, there may be so many managers interested in upper-level jobs that we can save money by "underpaying" them. Retention of good workers is yet another important issue: We will probably pay what we think is necessary to keep them on the job. In a practical sense, then, companies are likely to use not only job analysis and job evaluation information but also labor market information when setting compensation levels for jobs.

Comparable Worth

It is a long-established finding that women are paid considerably less than men for similar work. In fact, when a field becomes dominated by women, as happened with the secretarial profession in the twentieth century (for a review, see Lowe, 1987), the rate of pay decreases. As of 2002, there was a difference of 23% between men's and women's wages (Institute for Women's Policy Research, 2003). This means that, on average, women earn about 77% of what men earn, and this figure has been pretty stable since the mid-1990s, raising concerns about whether women's compensation will ever catch up to men's. The wage gap is smaller, but still sizable (16%), when we consider only starting salaries (Marini & Fan, 1997). This issue is a troublesome one, as most people would agree that employees who are doing the same job should be paid similarly regardless of their gender. In fact, the Equal Pay Act of 1963 stipulates that men and women who do work that is *equal* must be compensated similarly. The word *equal* has been interpreted to mean jobs that are the same. But this act does not address the broader issue of gender differences in compensation across dissimilar jobs. For instance, should computer technicians (who are predominantly male) be paid more than executive secretaries (who are predominantly female)? Granted, these jobs aren't the same—but are they equal in terms of their value to the organization? And if they are equal in this sense, shouldn't they be compensated similarly?

A recent study (Ostroff & Atwater, 2003) demonstrated that compensation is also affected by the gender composition of one's co-workers. In particular, managers (regardless of gender) who work largely with women are paid considerably less than are managers who work largely with men. Apparently, gender issues in compensation extend beyond just the gender of the employees to the gender composition of the work group, as well.

comparable worth
A doctrine maintaining that jobs of equal (or comparable) worth to the organization should be compensated equally.

These kinds of questions have given rise to the doctrine of **comparable worth,** which maintains that jobs of equal (or comparable) worth to the organization should be compensated equally. This issue has been linked quite closely to gender differences in compensation. Proponents of comparable worth insist that job evaluation should play a larger role, and the market a smaller role, in setting compensation. They argue that the market is biased, and that it artificially sets the compensation for female-dominated jobs lower than for male-dominated jobs. They argue that by focusing on job behaviors rather than on job performers, job evaluation decreases the likelihood of gender bias in compensation (Cascio, 1998). Interest in comparable worth has been growing over the past 20 years. One paper, for instance, reviewed the experiences of 8 states that have implemented comparable worth legislation and noted that 45 states have been involved in some pay equity activities (Gardner & Daniel, 1998). Opponents of comparable worth argue that there is no bias against female-typed jobs and that women can choose whatever jobs they prefer. They encourage women to choose not to work in lower-compensated jobs. But the issue of comparable worth is unlikely to be solved quickly or easily, complicated as it is by market factors and historical trends, potential biases in job evaluation, and both real and imagined gender differences.

SUMMARY

Although job analysis tends to receive little empirical attention, it is among the most important areas of I/O psychology, providing the foundation on which all other HR processes are built. This chapter was largely structured around Figure 3.1, which shows the interrelationships among job analysis, job descriptions, job specifications, job evaluation, and the HR functions that are built on these. It should be clear by now that without a carefully designed and executed job analysis, HR practitioners and I/O psychologists would have very little to go on in making HR decisions.

Both job-oriented and worker-oriented approaches to job analysis were presented in this chapter, along with a discussion of different methods within each category. Also discussed were the advantages and disadvantages of each approach, the choice of which should depend upon the job analyst's purpose. Some recent developments in the area of job analysis were considered as well. First, although the DOT has been of great importance to the I/O field for many years, the Department of Labor's current undertaking, the O*NET, should provide more updated, useful, and accessible data on occupations and jobs. Second, the CMQ was presented as one of the newer job analysis instruments with great potential to serve the purposes of worker-oriented job analysis methods while avoiding criticisms regarding reading level and work behaviors that are too general.

Job descriptions and job specifications are derived either directly or indirectly from the job analysis and are directly or indirectly connected to a myriad of HR functions. This chapter provided a brief discussion of the links between job analysis and these HR functions; the remainder of the second section will cover these HR functions at length. Finally, we considered the role of job analysis in job evaluation. The Equal Pay Act of 1963 mandates that individuals who do equal work should receive equal pay, but it does not speak to wage gaps between "male-typed" and "female-typed" jobs. The emergence of the doctrine of comparable worth in recent years suggests that organizations and society need to do a better job in setting compensation for jobs while taking gender-based job classes into account.

The stage is now set for examining the many important and interesting HR functions within organizations. Along the way we will discuss how to develop criteria to use for performance evaluations, how to assess job applicants and make selection decisions, and how to determine the training needs of an organization and the employees within it. Now that we know how to determine what the ingredients are, the way to combine them, and what the finished product should look like, we are ready to get on with the business of industrial psychology, which is the focus of the rest of the second section.

REVIEW QUESTIONS

1. Discuss how job analysis provides the building blocks for most of the work done by industrial psychologists and HR practitioners.
2. How do job-oriented and worker-oriented job analysis approaches differ? What is a hybrid approach to job analysis? What are the advantages and disadvantages associated with each?
3. How would one use the Task Inventory Approach, Functional Job Analysis, the Job Element Method, the Position Analysis Questionnaire, and the Common-Metric Questionnaire to conduct a job analysis? Discuss the differences among these approaches.
4. What is a subject matter expert (SME)?
5. What are the major DOT entries? How does the O*NET project expand and improve on the DOT as a classification of occupations?
6. What is a job description? Where does it come from? What is it used for?
7. What are job specifications? Where do they come from? What are they used for?
8. What role does job evaluation play in setting compensation levels? Discuss the difficulties involved in using job evaluation for this purpose.
9. What is the doctrine of comparable worth, and how does it relate to the wage gap between male and female workers?
10. What are the political implications of comparable worth?

SUGGESTED READINGS

Brannick, M. T., & Levine, E. L. (2002). ***Job analysis: Methods, research, and applications for human resource management in the new millennium.*** **Thousand Oaks, CA: Sage.** An outstanding treatment of job analysis that is useful for both researchers and practitioners.

Gatewood, R. D., & Feild, H. S. (2001). ***Human resource selection*** **(2nd ed.). Fort Worth, TX: Harcourt College.** An excellent reference for everything that constitutes industrial psychology, though it is perhaps strongest in its coverage of job analysis and other technical areas.

Sackett, P. R., & Laczo, R. M. (2003). Job and work analysis. In W. C. Borman, D. R. Ilgen, & R. J. Klimoski (Eds.), *Handbook of psychology: Industrial and organizational psychology* (Vol. 12, pp. 21–37). New York: Wiley. A thoughtful up-to-date review that does more than just provide the technical issues. It synthesizes our knowledge and makes important recommendations.

Criterion Measurement

4

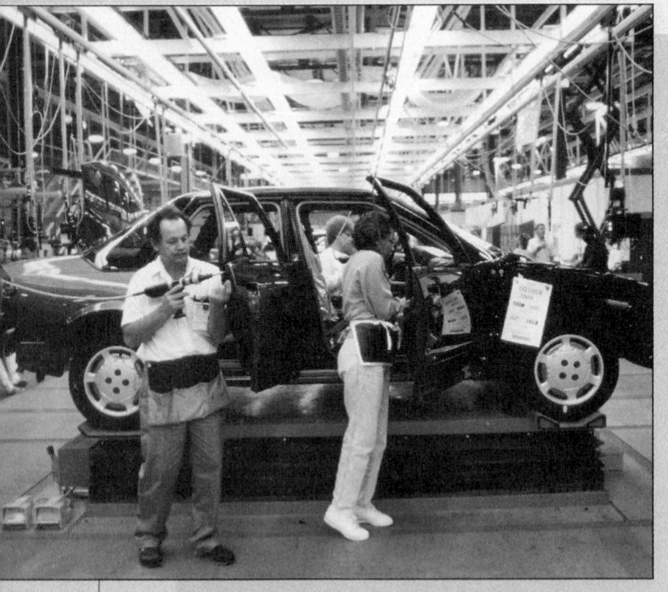

CHAPTER OUTLINE

As noted in the last chapter, job analysis provides the foundation upon which everything in the field of industrial psychology is built. In this chapter, I will talk about the first aspect of this "everything": criteria. Criteria are quite important to industrial psychology because they reflect organizational or individual performance—and, in a competitive market, companies are driven by performance and profits. Thus I/O psychologists are often hired to help organizations develop criteria, as well as to implement HR processes that are directly linked to those criteria. Criteria are typically dependent variables that provide an indication of success or performance. This chapter will present the nuts and bolts of criteria—what they are, how they are developed, how they are evaluated, and what they are used for—along with a discussion of the different types.

LEARNING OBJECTIVES

This chapter should help you understand:

- what the criterion problem is.
- how criteria are defined in I/O psychology.
- what the criteria for the criteria are.
- the difference between the ultimate criterion and the actual criterion.
- how to differentiate between criterion contamination and criterion deficiency.
- the important issues that revolve around multiple criteria.
- different ways to weight criteria to arrive at a composite criterion.
- what dynamic criteria are and how they can affect HR functioning.
- the differences between objective and subjective criteria.
- the potential role of contextual performance (including counterproductive behavior) in criterion development.

CHAPTER FOUR

THE CRITERION PROBLEM

It may seem an odd strategy to begin such an important chapter by talking about "*the* criterion problem," but in this instance I'll take the chance, because understanding the criterion problem is really where you have to start in order to comprehend the role of criteria in industrial/organizational psychology. The notion that there is a basic problem associated with criteria is a long-standing one (e.g., Flanagan, 1956). The problem is that there are great difficulties involved in the process of defining and measuring performance criteria in that they tend to be both multidimensional and differentially appropriate for various purposes (Austin & Villanova, 1992). In other words, performance (the criterion in which organizations, employees, managers, and I/O psychologists are most often interested) usually comprises more than one dimension, and some performance criteria are suitable for one type of organizational decision, while other criteria are suitable for a different type of organizational decision, such that no one performance criterion fits the bill for all organizational purposes. Given these difficulties, the measurement of performance criteria can be quite complicated.

You might remember from your Introduction to Psychology class that human behavior is determined by multiple causes, such that it is impossible to point to a particular behavior and demonstrate beyond a shadow of a doubt that the behavior was determined by any one particular cause. Similarly, it is impossible to point to any one performance criterion and argue that it is the perfect measure of performance; performance is simply more complicated than that. So, because of this criterion problem, I/O psychologists have had to work creatively and diligently to gather enough information over the past 70 years to form a tentative school of thought regarding performance criteria. We do not have performance criteria entirely figured out any more than we have human behavior entirely figured out; but just as we can often predict, understand, and explain human behavior, we can develop, use, and understand criteria in the world of work. We still have a ways to go, but we've also traveled quite a distance. Let's now turn to an examination of how far we've come.

DEFINING CRITERIA AND THEIR PROPERTIES

Every time you evaluate something or someone, you are using criteria—though you're probably not aware of doing so. When, for the first time, you walked into your dorm room as a freshmen or your office cubicle as a new employee, you very likely wondered whether you and the students in that dorm room or the coworkers in the nearby cubicle would get along. In other words, you wondered whether you would like those people. When you did finally decide that Bob was a pretty cool roommate, you may have made that decision based on his personality (funny, serious, kind, trustworthy), intelligence (smart about academic things, smart about everyday things), hobbies (enjoys sports, music, movies), hang-ups (dislikes people who are stuck on themselves and people who don't clean up after themselves), and so on. You made your decision based on all of these criteria. Consciously or unconsciously, you defined various criteria that led you to the overall evaluation that Bob was a cool roommate.

Of course, we don't always agree on the decisions we make. For instance, you may have another roommate, Tim, who doesn't think Bob is cool at all. Often, when we disagree in this way, it is because we have different criteria. Different judgments may be involved in determining whether Tim thinks someone is cool versus whether you think someone is cool. For example, Tim may think it's important to be a jock, which Bob isn't. In other words, you and Tim come to different conclusions about Bob because you are using different criteria. At other times, however, we disagree about things not because our criteria differ but because we evaluate people and things differently on the basis of those criteria. Certainly we see this during elections when the "spin doctors" from the two campaigns come to drastically different conclusions despite using the same information and the same criteria. And when Ebert and Roeper disagree on their movie reviews, the disagreement is often based not on different criteria but on how the same criteria are evaluated. For instance, one may think the movie is good because the characters are believable, and the other may think the movie is bad because the characters aren't at all believable. Character believability is an important criterion for both reviewers, but their perceptions about the extent to which the movie scores high on this criterion differ, resulting in different evaluations of the film.

In industrial/organizational psychology, **criteria** are defined as evaluative standards that can be used as yardsticks for measuring employees' success or failure. We rely on them not only for appraising employees' performance but also for evaluating our training program, validating our selection battery, and making layoff and promotion decisions. Therefore, if we have faulty criteria these other HR functions would be flawed as well because they depend directly on the adequacy of the criteria. For instance, it seems reasonable to fire an employee because she is not performing at an acceptable level on the performance criterion. However, if that performance criterion is not a good measure of job performance, there is the potential for making a huge mistake in firing someone who may actually be a good worker. This highlights the importance of criteria: Because important organizational decisions will be made directly on the basis of criteria, organizations need to be sure that these yardsticks are measuring the right thing and measuring it well. With poor criteria come erroneous and costly organizational decisions such as hiring, firing, promoting, and giving raises to the wrong people.

criteria
Evaluative standards that can be used as yardsticks for measuring an employee's success or failure.

In general, the criterion in which I/O psychologists are most interested is **performance,** which can be defined as actual on-the-job behaviors that are relevant to the organization's goals. Performance is the reason that organizations are interested in hiring competent employees. Throughout this chapter, I will use the terms *criterion, performance,* and *performance criterion* interchangeably.

performance
Actual on-the-job behaviors that are relevant to the organization's goals.

Performance is multidimensional, and even these employees can be evaluated along different dimensions of performance.

THE FAR SIDE® By GARY LARSON

"You know, Russell, you're a great torturer. I mean, you can make a man scream for mercy in nothing flat ... but boy, you sure can't make a good cup of coffee."

Ultimate Criterion

ultimate criterion
A theoretical construct encompassing all performance aspects that define success on the job.

The **ultimate criterion** encompasses all aspects of performance that define success on the job. R. L. Thorndike (1949) discussed this very notion in his classic text *Personnel Selection,* arguing that the ultimate criterion is very complex and not even accessible to us. What he meant is that the ultimate criterion is something we can shoot for, but in actuality we can never completely define and measure every aspect of performance. Doing so would require detail and time that simply are not available. As an example, let's say we're interested in defining the ultimate criterion for an administrative assistant's job. Toward that end, we might generate the following list:

- Typing speed
- Typing quality
- Filing efficiency
- Interactions with clients
- Interactions with co-workers
- Creativity

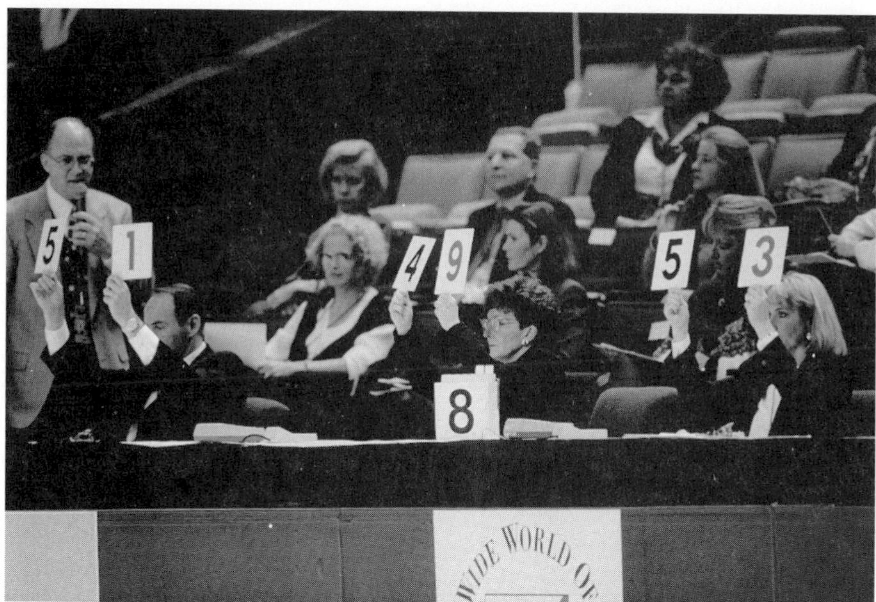

Criteria are used to evaluate many things, and we don't always agree on our ratings.

- Written communication skills
- Oral communication skills
- Knowledge of procedures
- Organizational skills
- Interactions with supervisors
- Punctuality
- Initiative

This appears to be a pretty complete list, but when I asked two administrative assistants in our Psychology Department office if they had any to add, they came up with quite a few more that I hadn't thought of, including experience with spreadsheet computer programs, experience with database computer programs, and knowledge about the operation of office equipment. My guess is that if I gave this list to additional people, they would come up with still other dimensions or subcriteria; perhaps you have thought of a few as well. The point here is that merely listing all the criteria that define success on the job is difficult enough; *measuring* all of them would be virtually impossible. Thus the ultimate criterion is a theoretical construct that we develop as a guide or a goal to shoot for in measuring job success.

Actual Criterion

The **actual criterion** is our best real-world representative of the ultimate criterion, and we develop it to reflect or overlap with the ultimate criterion as much as possible. Figure 4.1 illustrates this concept with respect to the administrative assistant job that we discussed earlier. Because we cannot possibly measure every

actual criterion
Our best real-world representative of the ultimate criterion, which we develop to reflect or overlap with the ultimate criterion as much as possible.

FIGURE 4.1 Criterion Properties

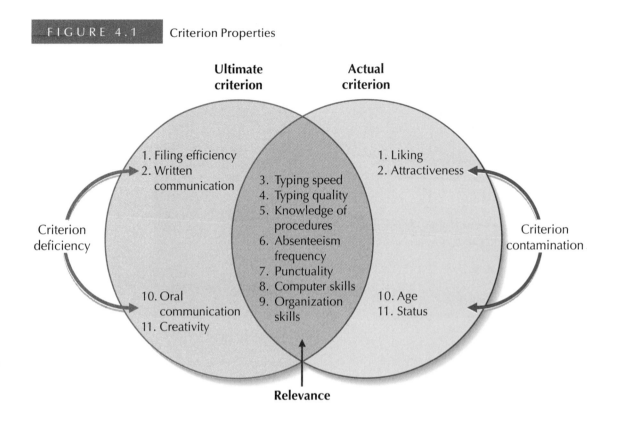

skill that we think is involved in the administrative assistant job and probably could not even list every skill that would indicate one's success on the job, we consider only those elements that seem most important and that are most easily measured. Again, as applied psychologists we need to keep practical issues in mind, and we do this by thinking about the time, effort, and cost associated with measuring the different elements of the criteria involved. Time, effort, and cost are of great importance to the company with which we are working, so they need to be important concerns of ours, as well. In a perfect world, everything that is listed as being a part of the ultimate criterion would be included in the actual criterion, but typically this isn't possible. Thus our actual criterion includes only those elements of the ultimate criterion that we intend to measure. Again, the actual criterion is the best available representation of the ultimate criterion.

Criteria for the Criteria

In this section we focus on what makes a good criterion. There are many lists of dimensions along which criteria can be evaluated. One of the earliest of these lists features 15 dimensions (Blum & Naylor, 1968). In a later work, John Bernardin and Dick Beatty (1984) delineate more than 25 characteristics that have been examined as yardsticks for measuring the effectiveness of criteria. For our purposes here, I will highlight what I think are the five most fundamental of these criteria for the criteria (see Table 4.1 for a summary).

Relevance. The crucial requirement for any criterion is *relevance,* or the degree to which the actual criterion is related to the ultimate criterion. Relevance reflects the degree of correlation or overlap between the actual and ultimate criteria. In a more technical, statistical sense, relevance is the percentage of variance in the ultimate criterion that can be accounted for by the actual criterion (see our discussion of the *coefficient of determination* in Chapter 2). Ideally, we would like to see complete overlap such that all of the variance in the ultimate criterion is accounted for or tapped by the actual criterion; but as this is only a goal we can shoot for, we have to be content with having as much overlap as is practical to achieve. Look back at Figure 4.1 and note the six dimensions—typing speed, typing quality, knowledge of procedures, punctuality, computer skills, and organizational skills—in the intersection of the ultimate criterion and the actual criterion. These constitute relevance. The overlap itself thus represents the portion of the ultimate criterion that is tapped by our actual criterion. We want this portion of the Venn diagram to be as large as possible, indicating that our actual criterion

TABLE 4.1 Criteria for the Criteria

Dimension	Definition	Example/Explanation
Relevance	The extent to which the actual criterion measure is related to the ultimate criterion	A measure that seems to capture the major elements of the ultimate criterion; that is, it represents job performance very well
Reliability	The extent to which the actual criterion measure is stable or consistent	A measure that does not give drastically different results when used for the same employees at close time intervals
Sensitivity	The extent to which the actual criterion measure can discriminate among effective and ineffective employees	A measure that consistently identifies performance differences among employees; that is, everyone is not rated the same
Practicality	The degree to which the actual criterion can and will be used by those whose job it is to use it for making important decisions	A measure that can be completed in a reasonable amount of time by a supervisor and does not require excess paperwork
Fairness	The extent to which the actual criterion measure is perceived by employees to be just and reasonable	A measure that does not result in men always being rated higher than women, and vice versa

mirrors the ultimate criterion pretty well. Relevance in this sense is analogous to validity.

criterion deficiency
A condition in which dimensions in the ultimate measure are not part of or are not captured by the actual measure.

Two conditions can limit the relevance of a criterion. The first is **criterion deficiency,** which refers to dimensions in the ultimate measure that are not part of the actual measure. A criterion is deficient if a major source of variance in the ultimate criterion is not included in the actual criterion. We want this part of the Venn diagram to be very small. Figure 4.1 shows the criterion deficiency as a list of dimensions that are in the ultimate criterion but are not part of our actual measure—namely, filing efficiency, written communication, oral communication, and creativity. Our criterion is deficient to the extent that these dimensions are not tapped by our criterion measure and are important to the criterion construct. If these particular dimensions are not terribly important to the criterion construct, then our criterion is not very deficient; but if they are important, then we may have a problem with criterion deficiency.

criterion contamination
A condition in which things measured by the actual criterion are not part of the ultimate criterion.

The second condition that can limit the relevance of a criterion is **criterion contamination,** which refers to those things measured by the actual criterion that are not part of the ultimate criterion. This is the part of the actual criterion variance that is not part of the ultimate criterion variance. Criterion contamination occurs in two ways. First, it can be caused simply by random measurement *error:* No matter how carefully we develop precise and accurate measurement, there is always some error in that measurement—what we called *unreliability* in Chapter 2. This measurement error is random in the sense that it tends to even itself out over time, but any single performance measurement may not reflect true performance. For instance, we might measure performance every 6 months for 2 years and find that there are some differences in our four performance measurements, even though true performance (i.e., the ultimate criterion) may not have changed.

The second cause of criterion contamination, *bias,* is more troubling given its systematic rather than random nature. Bias is most prevalent when the criteria of interest are judgments made by individuals. It is not unusual for raters to allow their biases to color their performance ratings. For instance, bias would result in criterion contamination if an evaluator, when rating administrative assistants on the dimension of organizational skills, gave a higher rating to those she liked or to those who were more attractive, regardless of actual performance levels. (Two additional examples, age and status, are listed in Figure 4.1.) Sometimes this is done on purpose, while at other times it is unconscious; we will discuss both instances of bias in more detail in the next chapter.

Criterion contamination occurs when the measure of the actual criterion reflects things other than what it should measure according to the ultimate criterion. Recall that in Chapter 2 *construct validity* was defined as the extent to which a test measures the underlying construct that it is intended to measure. In a parallel sense, when we are talking about criteria, a criterion is contaminated if it measures something other than what it is intended to measure, such as liking or attractiveness. Contamination is often a problem in the context of performance ratings, which we will discuss at length in the next chapter. (For recent reviews of performance ratings, see Motowidlo, 2003; Scullen, Mount, & Goff, 2000; Viswesvaran, 2002.)

Sometimes employees are rated differently based on non–performance-related dimensions such as age, race, and attractiveness.

Reliability. Although unreliability was mentioned as a potential cause of criterion contamination, its opposite—reliability—is important enough to be listed as a criterion itself. As discussed in Chapter 2, reliability refers to the stability or consistency of a measure. Indeed, an unreliable criterion is not very useful. For instance, suppose that we measured an administrative assistant's typing speed on six successive occasions and found that he typed at 50, 110, 40, 100, 60, and 45 words per minute. Such variability in the criterion measure would lead me to conclude that this particular measure is unreliable. When a measure is unreliable, we can't confidently use it in important decisions. Another way to conceptualize the situation is to ask if this administrative assistant is a fast typist, as the 110 and 100 words per minute might indicate, or a below-average typist, as the 40 and 45 words per minute might indicate. Because the criterion is unreliable, we simply don't know—and the criterion is thus not useful.

Sensitivity. A criterion must be *sensitive* enough to discriminate among effective and ineffective employees. If everyone is evaluated similarly according to the criterion, then it is not very useful. Suppose Goodyear wants to make a series of promotion decisions based on a performance criterion consisting of the number of tire valves produced by each employee in an 8-hour shift. At first glance, this seems a reasonable criterion; but upon closer examination, we find that all 100 employees produce between 22 and 24 tire valves per 8-hour shift. In short, there doesn't appear to be much variability in the performance of these 100 employees on this criterion. The criterion isn't sensitive enough to discriminate between effective and ineffective performers, so Goodyear could not reasonably make promotion decisions based on this criterion. (After all, would it make sense to promote those employees who produce 24 tire valves over those who produce 23?) Yet there are probably other criteria in this situation that *could* distinguish among the employees. Can you think of any? The first one that comes to my mind is quality. Although all 100 employees produce about the same number of tire valves, there may be some serious differences in the quality of these valves. A second criterion, and one that may be even more sensitive, is the amount of waste each employee leaves behind after producing tire valves. Quite a few other alternative measures would work as well. Every situation is different, of course—but the bottom line is that I/O psychologists work hard to develop sensitive criteria so that confidence can be placed in the criteria upon which decisions are based.

Practicality. I have alluded to the importance of practical issues throughout the book thus far, but here the concept is tied more directly to organizational functioning. *Practicality* refers to the extent to which a criterion can and will be used by individuals making important decisions. Consider the following example. Let's say I spend an extraordinary amount of time conducting a thorough job analysis using the Common-Metric Questionnaire; then I develop a set of relevant and reliable criteria that have hardly any criterion deficiency or contamination. But there is one problem: The organization's employees choose not to use the criteria on the grounds that they are too difficult to measure and too abstract to be useful. My error here was that I neglected to consider the usefulness or practicality of the measures and failed to work with the organization's management and other employees in the development process. Indeed, criteria must always be relatively available, easy to obtain, and acceptable to those who want to use them for personnel decisions.

Fairness. The last element in my list of criteria for the criteria is *fairness*—in other words, the extent to which the employees perceive the criteria to be just and reasonable. Whereas relevance (along with the interplay of deficiency and contamination), reliability, and sensitivity are rather technical concepts, fairness and practicality have more to do with the human element involved in the use of criteria. Here, the issue is whether the employees who are being evaluated along certain criterion dimensions think that they are getting a fair shake. Fairness, or justice, has received a great deal of attention in the I/O literature of the past 20 years (Cropanzano, 2001), and the importance of this concept seems quite relevant for evaluating criteria, as well. A criterion that is viewed by the employees as unfair, inappropriate, unreasonable, or unjust will not be well received by these employees. This point, of course, has widespread implications for organizational functioning and interpersonal dynamics. For instance, Simons and Roberson (2003) found that employees' perceptions of justice were linked to important organizational criteria such as turnover intentions and customer satisfaction ratings.

TWO MAJOR COMPONENTS OF THE CRITERION PROBLEM

In the preceding sections I discussed the criterion problem and alluded to the difficulty in measuring performance criteria. In this section I will highlight two of the most important elements of the criterion problem.

Multiple Versus Composite Criteria

The idea of developing a unidimensional actual criterion to match as closely as possible the unidimensional ultimate criterion is the traditional view of criteria, or what John Campbell (1990) calls the "Classic I/O View." He criticizes this view (see also Campbell, McCloy, Oppler, & Sager, 1993) for suggesting that there is one general criterion factor that will account for all of the performance variance. Further, he suggests that this traditional view has led many I/O practitioners and scientists alike to refer to job performance as if it were a single tangible thing (which it is not), resulting in the misperception that any intervention that might be used to target changes in specific aspects of performance can change that one general thing called performance. Campbell makes some interesting points in his considerable writings on performance (see also Campbell et al., 1996), many of which are too technical for our purposes here. However, let's look in more depth at one issue that he and others have focused on—the dimensionality of performance.

Most I/O psychologists believe that performance is multifaceted—in other words, that it is made up of more than one dimension. Look back at the list of criteria I presented for the job of administrative assistant, and it should be clear that there are many related, as well as potentially unrelated, dimensions of performance for this job. Belief in a multiple-factor model (Campbell et al., 1996)—the view that job performance is composed of multiple criteria—has been common among I/O psychologists for years. However, many experts in the area have noted that studies of criteria-related issues and, especially, examinations of multiple-factor models have been minimal at best (Austin & Villanova, 1992; Campbell, 1990; Campbell et al., 1993).

Campbell, one of the leaders in this area, has developed an eight-factor model that he suggests should account for performance variance in every job listed in the *Dictionary of Occupational Titles* (DOT; Campbell, 1990). He asserts that although not every dimension will be relevant for every job, every job can be described adequately in terms of a subset of these eight dimensions. (These are listed in Table 4.2, along with definitions and examples.) In addition, he maintains that three of these dimensions—job-specific task proficiency, demonstrating effort, and maintaining personal discipline—are necessary components of every job. It is beyond the scope of this book to discuss Campbell's job performance taxonomy at length, but it is important to note that he developed one! Although we might quibble about the existence or labeling of various dimensions, the fact remains that Campbell has helped I/O psychologists begin to conceptualize the true meaning of performance. His model is built on some of his early research with the U.S. Army, and there appears to be some empirical support for the dimensions he suggests (Campbell, McHenry, & Wise, 1990). Of course, more research is needed in this area and is currently being conducted.

The fact that performance is multidimensional complicates the practicalities of HR decisions. Returning to our administrative assistant example, let's assume that the job has five criteria that are reflective of performance and that each is important and relatively unrelated to each other. Now, when it comes time to hire, promote, fire, lay off, or increase salaries, which criteria will be used to make these decisions? You see, things would be much easier if performance was one-dimensional, because then we could make all of these decisions based on the one criterion without any confusion. However, because performance is multidimensional, we have to make some tough decisions about which criteria to use or how to combine them for the purposes of HR decisions. This is a part of the criterion problem: Performance is best represented by multiple criteria, but organizations need to make decisions based on one score, number, or combination of these multiple criteria.

composite criterion A weighted combination of multiple criteria that results in a single index of performance.

There are at least two alternatives for dealing with this criterion issue. Both focus on creating a **composite criterion,** which is a weighted combination of the multiple criteria, resulting in one index of performance. First, if the five criteria are scored on the same scale, they can be combined using equal weighting. Here, they are simply added up to compute one number that represents the performance of each individual. But on what grounds do we base this decision? Does it seem appropriate to take these five dimensions, which are largely unrelated, and just add them up and call it performance? Doing so would seem to take us back to Campbell's concern that we often mistakenly assume that performance is a single construct (Campbell et al., 1993) when, in fact, it is not.

A second alternative composite criterion can also be created through unequal weighting, whereby some procedure is employed to weight the criteria differentially. For instance, it might make sense to employ only those criterion dimensions that seem especially relevant for the particular HR decision that needs to be made and to weight them according to their importance so that the overall weights sum to one. Note that the way in which the information is weighted is a value judgment made by the organization and that this decision should be based on the organization's goals and on research conducted by the organization (Campbell et al., 1990). Further, the weighting scheme may vary across HR decisions, such that different weights may be employed for making a promotion decision than for making a termination decision about employees. An example is provided in Table 4.3, which demonstrates how different dimensions might be used depending on

TABLE 4.2 Campbell's Taxonomy of Performance

Performance Factor	Definition	Example
Job-Specific Task Proficiency	Degree to which individual can perform core tasks central to a particular job	An Administrative Assistant who does word processing
Non-Job-Specific Task Proficiency	Degree to which individual can perform tasks that are not specific to a particular job	A Plumber who handles phone inquiries and sets up appointments to provide estimates for work
Written and Oral Communication Tasks	Proficiency with which one can write and speak	A Military Officer who gives a formal talk to recruits
Demonstrating Effort	Consistency and persistence in an individual's work effort	A College Professor who goes into the office to continue working on her book even though the university is closed due to a winter storm
Maintaining Personal Discipline	Avoidance of negative behaviors such as alcohol abuse, substance abuse, and rule infractions	An off-duty Nurse who avoids excessive alcohol in the event that he is needed in an emergency
Facilitating Peer and Team Performance	Helping and supporting peers with job problems	A Journalist who helps a co-worker with his story to meet the co-worker's deadline
Supervision	All the behaviors that go along with managing or supervising other employees	A Retail Store Manager who models appropriate behavior, provides fair and timely feedback, and is available to handle the questions of his or her subordinates
Management/Administration	All the behaviors associated with management that are independent of supervision	A Plant Manager who gets additional resources, sets department goals and objectives, and controls expenditures

Source: Campbell (1990).

the HR decision in question. In this example, the decision to terminate a particular employee would be based largely on such dimensions as punctuality and performance quality, somewhat on computer skills and organizational skills, and not at all on interpersonal skills and leadership behaviors. On the other hand, leadership behaviors and interpersonal skills would be much more important for deciding to promote this person into a supervisory position, whereas punctuality would be much less important.

Still, unequal weighting does not remove the concern that we have now created an index that is somewhat illogical. Let's say that we combine one's score on organizational skills with one's score on productivity. What is this index? What should we call it? What is the construct that it really measures? Finally, haven't we

TABLE 4.3 Combining Criterion Dimensions for the Job of Administrative Assistant

Criterion Weights for Promotion to Supervisor	Criterion Dimension	Criterion Weights for Termination Decision
.00	Punctuality	.30
.20	Performance Quality	.40
.20	Interpersonal Skills	.00
.30	Leadership Behaviors	.00
.15	Computer Skills	.20
.15	Organizational Skills	.10

lost the very thing that we wanted to capture with our measures, the multidimensionality of performance? You can see that combining multiple criterion dimensions is a tricky business.

Given these complexities and concerns, you might think it best to keep the criteria separate; but of course this causes problems for making HR decisions, as you'd need to make that one hire/don't hire, retain/fire, promote/don't promote decision based on some number or score. A classic article by F. L. Schmidt and L. B. Kaplan (1971) suggests that the issue becomes one of *purpose*. These authors argue that if psychological understanding is the primary goal, then multiple criteria should be examined in light of predictor variables without combining them into a composite. On the other hand, if the primary goal is decision making with an economic focus, the I/O psychologist should combine the criteria into one measure and use that as an index of economic success. However, the authors also point out that most applied psychologists are interested in both psychological understanding and economic decision making and, therefore, should use their weighted composite to make hire/don't hire decisions while at the same time using the multiple dimensions to examine how they relate to various predictors, enhancing the psychological understanding of the performance process. Schmidt and Kaplan conclude by saying that this approach, in which we combine multiple criteria into a composite for decision-making purposes but take advantage of the wealth of knowledge available in our multiple criteria, is consistent with the approach of I/O psychologists who embody the ideal of the scientist-practitioner—an ideal whereby both psychological understanding and applied decision making are important.

Dynamic Criteria

dynamic criteria
Measures reflecting performance levels that change over time.

The issue of **dynamic criteria** has been the focus of much debate in I/O psychology for the past 15 years, but the notion that performance levels change over time was introduced many years ago (for reviews, see Austin & Villanova, 1992; Steele-

Johnson, Osburn, & Pieper, 2000). This notion may seem unimportant, but let's consider a situation in which an employee performs well for the first 9 months on the job but by the end of 18 months is performing at unacceptable levels. The problem becomes clearer if we consider a selection context in which measures are developed to predict an individual's performance on the job. The measure—say, a measure of intelligence—might predict performance early on in the employee's career (in fact, we believe that it will, which is why we hired the employee based on an intelligence test to begin with), but not over the long haul. In other words, the validity with which our measure predicts job performance deteriorates over time. This, of course, is a big problem for those trying to staff an organization with people who are most likely to be successful on the job. We will address the selection process in greater detail in Chapters 6 and 7, but for now just note that the concept of dynamic criteria raises some important issues.

Some I/O psychologists have argued that criteria are not really dynamic at all (Barrett, Caldwell, & Alexander, 1985), but this argument has largely been refuted by more recent empirical work (Deadrick, Bennett, & Russell, 1997; Deadrick & Madigan, 1990; Hoffman, Jacobs, & Baratta, 1993) demonstrating that the relative performance of individuals changes over time. In short, the best worker for the first 6 months on the job is sometimes not among the best workers for the next 6 months on the job. Perhaps the most interesting of these studies is the one that examined the batting averages of major-league hitters and the earned-run averages of major-league pitchers (Hoffman, Jacobs, & Gerras, 1992). This study found that both hitters and pitchers changed their relative performance levels over time. But even more telling was the fact that some players consistently improved over time, others consistently declined over time, and still others whose performance changed seemed to do so in less systematic ways. In the world of baseball, this finding would seem to complicate the general manager's choices when it comes time to sign those incredibly expensive free agents, as performance doesn't appear to be very stable. The studies cited above certainly suggest that part of "the criterion problem" is reflected in performance changes over time. Predicting performance, which is integral to what I/O psychologists do, is all the more difficult when the performance criterion changes. Keep this point in mind when we discuss the various predictors used in the selection of employees in Chapter 6.

DISTINCTIONS AMONG PERFORMANCE CRITERIA

Among the many different criteria relevant for various jobs are two traditional types of criteria, which I discuss next. After that, I discuss a third criterion type that has only recently captured the attention of I/O psychologists and organizations—namely, contextual performance.

Objective Criteria

objective criteria
Performance measures that are based on counting rather than on subjective judgments or evaluations.

Objective criteria are taken from organizational records; often based on counting, they are not supposed to involve any subjective judgments or evaluations. They have traditionally been viewed as the "cleanest" criterion measures because they tend not to necessitate making a judgment call about another employee's performance. Objective criteria are also sometimes referred to as *hard* or *nonjudgmental* criteria, reflecting the belief that they are somehow more solid and believable than other types. Table 4.4 presents some examples of often-used objective criteria.

Some types of objective criteria are relevant for many different jobs. (These will be discussed in more detail in Chapter 11 when we examine common outcomes of job-related attitudes.) For instance, *absenteeism rate* is often deemed an important criterion by organizations; it refers simply to the total number of times (or number of days) an employee is absent over a predetermined time period. Related criteria include *turnover rates* and *lateness rates,* which are also used by organizations to evaluate employees and organizational efficiency. Turnover is of particular interest here: Although it generally costs organizations a great deal of money, it can be beneficial to the extent that it involves the replacement of low performers with potentially better performers. Probably the most typical objective criterion is *productivity,* which is usually measured in terms of the number of acceptable products produced in a given time period. This criterion is commonly used by manufacturing plants and assembly lines, where individuals or groups of employees can be evaluated according to how many cars are produced, how many

TABLE 4.4 Examples of Objective Criteria and Measurement

Criteria	Measurement Examples
Absence	number of days absent per year; number of incidents of absence per year
Lateness	number of minutes late per month; number of incidents of lateness per month
Turnover	percentage of employees who leave the organization over a 12-month period
Accidents	number of accidents per year; number of workers' compensation claims per year
Grievances	number of grievances filed per year; number of grievances lost per year
Productivity	number of products produced per day; sales volume in dollars per month
Counterproductive Behaviors	dollars lost in theft per year; number of unlikely events (e.g., arson) per year without a reasonable explanation

pipes are made, how many computers are assembled, how many bookshelves are completed, and so on.

Nonmanagerial jobs lend themselves to objective criteria, but managerial and other higher-level jobs do not. One reason is that most managerial jobs are not based solely on a 40-hour work week during which the manager punches a time clock; another is that these jobs are not directly linked to a particular item that was produced. Nor are objective criteria appropriate for evaluating college professors, physicians, real estate agents, attorneys, and restaurant managers—with perhaps two exceptions: grievances and counterproductive behavior. The number of *grievances* is a measure of the number of times others have filed complaints about a particular manager; these complaints are usually handled within the organization's grievance process, but they can also be resolved in the court system. *Counterproductive behavior* is a term that refers to actions, such as theft and sabotage, that reflect the intent to harm the organization in some way.

You may have noted that when I defined objective criteria I said that these criteria are "not supposed" to require any judgment by others. Indeed, we describe these criteria as objective, and for the most part they are; but they're not completely objective. For instance, a manager can record an employee's absence as being excused, he can record it as being unexcused, or he can fail to record it at all. Other measures of productivity require judgment, as when someone has to determine which of the 87 computers assembled by a particular work team meet the quality criteria of being functional—perhaps the 87 is reduced to 75, but this reduction involved some judgment.

On average, objective criteria tend to involve less judgment than subjective criteria (which we will turn to next). But we need to realize that subjectivity can come into play in virtually all measures of performance. Further, objective criteria can be limited by unexpected factors or situational constraints. For instance, a production employee may not produce at her usual level because her machine has been malfunctioning frequently, thus slowing down her production. The objective criterion would not likely take this into account, but a supervisor could consider it in rating the employee's performance. Performance ratings are typically considered subjective measures of performance, but the subjectivity in this instance is probably a good thing.

Subjective Criteria

Subjective criteria refer to performance measures that are based on the judgments or evaluations of others rather than on counting. Most published studies on criteria use subjective criteria, also referred to as *judgmental* or *soft* criteria. Because subjective criteria are predominantly used in performance appraisals, which we cover in detail in the next chapter, they are only introduced here. Typical subjective criteria include ratings or rankings of employees by other employees such as supervisors, co-workers, and subordinates. Of course, these kinds of measures are much more likely to be affected by the biases, attitudes, and beliefs

subjective criteria
Performance measures that are based on the judgments or evaluations of others rather than on objective measures such as counting.

of the raters than are the more objective criteria. On the other hand, they can be an excellent alternative to objective criteria for jobs in which objective criteria don't exist or are insufficient (as in evaluations of managers). As you will see in the next chapter, we tend to rely largely on subjective criteria, although we may work very hard to make them as objective as possible.

Contextual Performance

I noted earlier in the chapter that the field of I/O psychology has spent more time and effort on predictors than on criteria. However, it appears that criteria are beginning to earn their due. As discussed earlier, Campbell's work on the modeling of performance (Campbell et al., 1990; Campbell et al., 1993) is an indication of this and, hence, a step in the right direction. Another indication is the recent work in the area of contextual performance that has attempted to expand the criterion domain to include more than just those traditional objective and subjective criteria.

task performance
The work-related activities performed by employees that contribute to the technical core of the organization.

contextual performance
Activities performed by employees that help to maintain the broader organizational, social, and psychological environment in which the technical core operates.

counterproductive behaviors
A group of behaviors that detract from the goals of the organization.

Task performance encompasses the work-related activities performed by employees that contribute to the technical core of the organization (Borman & Motowidlo, 1997), while **contextual performance** encompasses the activities performed by employees that help to maintain the broader organizational, social, and psychological environment in which the technical core operates (Motowidlo, Borman, & Schmit, 1997). Slightly different renditions of the concept known as contextual performance are *organizational citizenship behaviors (OCBs)* and *prosocial organizational behaviors (POBs*; Borman & Motowidlo, 1997). Up to this point, we've focused largely on task performance. An administrative assistant is rated high on task performance if he types quickly and answers phones efficiently, but he is rated high on contextual performance (OCBs or POBs) if he demonstrates enthusiasm, helps his co-worker with a problem that she may be having, and works hard to support his organization. Perhaps we can view the basic distinction as one between what is required in the way of on-the-job behaviors (task performance) and other behaviors that are specifically of value to one's workplace and co-workers (contextual performance). I think of contextual behaviors as reflective of employees who go that extra yard rather than putting forth only what is required or expected of them. However, some **counterproductive behaviors** (see Sackett & DeVore, 2002, for a review) are considered to fall within contextual performance and include those behaviors that somehow harm or detract from the organization, such as creating a negative environment in the workplace and making others look bad to their supervisors.

There are many different categorical schemes for the dimensions of contextual performance. One such scheme, presented by W. C. Borman and S. J. Motowidlo (1997), divides these multiple dimensions into five categories. The first pertains to individuals who work with extra enthusiasm and effort to get their jobs done; the second, to those who volunteer to do things that aren't formally part of their jobs, sometimes taking on extra responsibility in the process; the third, to those who help others with their jobs (reflecting what some researchers call sportsmanship or organizational courtesy); the fourth, to those who meet deadlines and comply with all the organization's rules and regulations (reflecting civic virtue or conscientiousness); and the fifth, to those who support or defend the organization for which they work (as when they stay with the organization through hard times or "sell" the organization to others).

Borman and Motowidlo (1997) have done extensive work on contextual performance, differentiating it from task performance and arguing for its inclusion in the domain of performance criteria. They suggest three major distinctions between task performance and contextual performance. First, task activities vary a great deal across jobs (think of the job descriptions for a plumber and for a musician), but contextual behaviors tend to be similar across jobs (a plumber can help a colleague just as much as a musician can). Second, compared with contextual activities, task activities are more likely to be formally instituted by the organization as items on a job description or performance appraisal form. Third, they have different antecedents. One recent study, for example, demonstrated that cognitive ability was more strongly related to sales performance (task activities) than to OCBs such as volunteerism and, similarly, that a personality measure of conscientiousness was more strongly related to OCBs than to sales performance (Hattrup, O'Connell, & Wingate, 1998).

Borman and Motowidlo (1997) specifically argue for the inclusion of contextual performance as part of the criterion space, suggesting that these criterion elements can be differentiated from task performance. They also make the point that, given changes in the workplace such as global competition and an increased

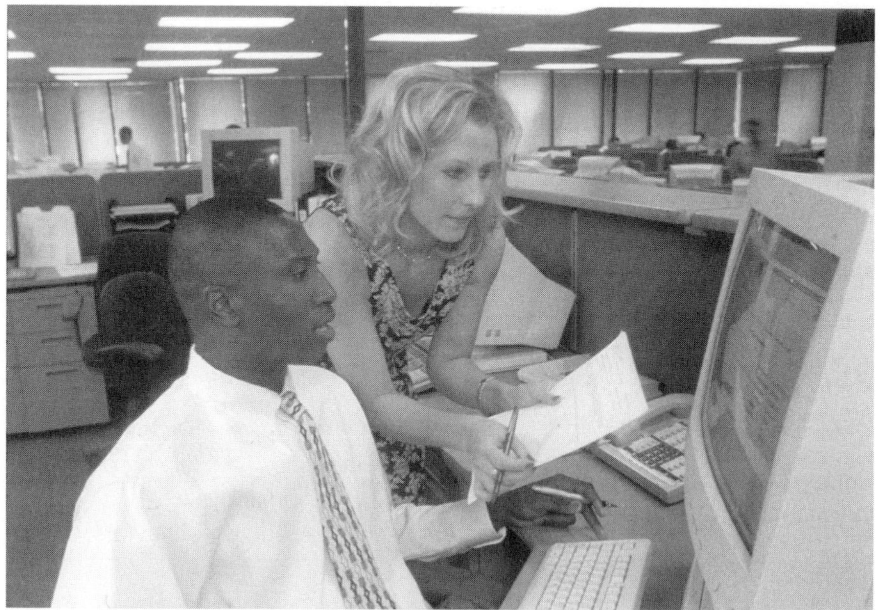

Some co-workers show altruism, courtesy, or sportsmanship by helping others with their work.

emphasis on teams, contextual performance will eventually increase in importance and have a large role to play in determining organizational effectiveness. A recent framework proposes that OCBs result in favorable relationships among co-workers, which serve as "social capital," and that this capital then affects the organization's performance and effectiveness (Bolino, Turnley, & Bloodgood, 2002). You may recall from the historical review of I/O psychology in Chapter 1 that industrial psychology was developed within a measurement framework, resulting in a rather narrow conceptualization of performance as productivity—a measurable outcome. Many now argue, however, that an expansion of the criterion space is more consistent with organizations of the current age (e.g., Tepper, Lockhart, & Hoobler, 2001). This more expansive view of performance criteria is illustrated in Figure 4.2.

In expanding the criterion to include contextual performance, we should examine how various predictors are related to the various criterion dimensions. Because Borman and his colleagues take a selection perspective, they emphasize the last point above—that task and contextual performance have different antecedents (Motowidlo et al., 1997). In fact, their performance model includes two different performance dimensions—task performance and contextual performance—along with two categories of determinants or predictors of these two performance dimensions—cognitive ability variables and personality variables. They report some empirical support for their notion that personality variables are better predictors of contextual performance and that cognitive ability variables are better predictors of task performance (Motowidlo et al., 1997). In-

FIGURE 4.2 Expansion of the Criterion Domain

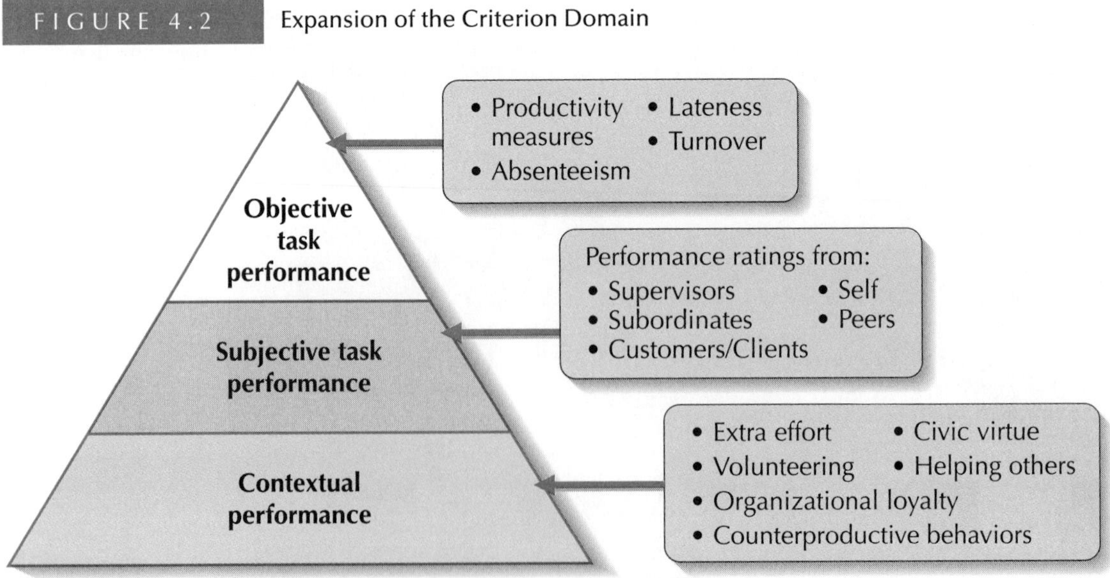

deed, without looking at *both* dimensions of performance, we would likely have a serious criterion deficiency problem and fail to understand how various predictors map onto the different criteria. In identifying the antecedents and consequences of OCBs, a recent review outlines an interesting future research agenda (Podsakoff, MacKenzie, Paine, & Bachrach, 2000).

SUMMARY

Traditionally, I/O psychologists have emphasized predictors at the expense of criteria. But this is less the case now that more and more scientists and practitioners have recognized the great importance of developing valid criteria and understanding their role in organizations. Consistent with this observation is the fact that all of the HR functions to be discussed in the remainder of this section depend completely on adequate criteria.

In this chapter, the criterion problem was discussed at length and identified as a potential stumbling block to advancing research in this area. The measurement of performance criteria is as complex as it is important, which is why the criterion problem is so pervasive. Nevertheless, we are making progress, as the chapter has demonstrated, in the process of presenting generally accepted definitions of criteria, examples of criteria, and evaluative standards for criteria, such as relevance, reliability, sensitivity, practicality, and fairness. The ultimate criterion and the actual criterion were defined and discussed, and the traditional view of criteria was explained in detail; also discussed were more recent concerns about the impression that this view can give about the nature of criteria. An actual criterion that does not cover a representative sample of the ultimate criterion was described as deficient, and one that measures things other than what is in the ultimate criterion was described as contaminated.

In discussing the criterion problem, I highlighted two major issues that contribute to that problem. First, I considered the debate regarding multiple criteria versus a composite criterion and suggested that even though, from an applied perspective, a decision needs to be made that has to be based on some score or number, the variety of information that comes from using multiple criteria must not be ignored. Performance is surely multidimensional, and multiple criteria are needed to measure it well. Campbell's work in the area of performance modeling and approaches to criteria was highlighted as providing a model for how we need to proceed in this arena (Campbell, 1990; Campbell et al., 1993). Second, I presented the common belief that criteria are dynamic in that they change over time. This belief is reflected in the relative changes that an individual's performance undergoes; issues of measurement and prediction were also considered in this context.

Finally, I examined the differences between objective and subjective criteria while considering various examples of each (e.g., measures of productivity, absenteeism, and lateness), as well as supervisor ratings of employees' performance. (The latter are discussed in the next chapter.) In addition, I presented a newer component of performance criteria called contextual performance. Recent research in this area suggests that contextual performance is more closely related to personality variables, while task performance is more closely related to cognitive variables.

REVIEW QUESTIONS

1. What are criteria? How do we use them in our everyday lives? How are they used in I/O psychology?
2. What is meant by "the criterion problem," and why is it such a problem?
3. What is being done by organizations to deal with "the criterion problem"?
4. Explain the distinction between the ultimate criterion and the actual criterion.
5. Identify the five major "criteria for the criteria." What can be done to ensure that these evaluative standards are met?
6. How is criterion contamination different from criterion deficiency, and how can we avoid these two major problems?
7. What are the issues involved in choosing to use multiple criteria as opposed to choosing to combine multiple criteria into a composite?
8. Are criteria dynamic? If so, what impact do they have on I/O psychology at both the theoretical and applied levels?
9. Explain the distinction between objective and subjective criteria.
10. How can organizations expand the criterion domain, and why should they?

SUGGESTED READINGS

Austin, J. T., & Villanova, P. D. (1992). The criterion problem: 1917–1992. *Journal of Applied Psychology, 77,* 836–874. This is the most thorough published review on the historical use of criteria in organizations. The article contains a great deal of valuable information, but it isn't an easy read.

Campbell, J. P. (1990). Modeling the performance prediction problem in industrial and organizational psychology. In M. D. Dunnette & L. M. Hough (Eds.), *Handbook of industrial and organizational psychology* (2nd ed., Vol. 1, pp. 687–732). Palo Alto, CA: Consulting Psychologists Press. This presentation of Campbell's work on modeling performance provides a good overview of his theoretical ideas, along with some empirical findings.

Motowidlo, S. J., Borman, W. C., & Schmit, M. J. (1997). A theory of individual differences in task and contextual performance. *Human Performance, 10,* 71–83. A nice overview of contextual performance with some interesting data. Borman and Motowidlo have written extensively in the area, and this is a representative piece of their work.

Rotundo, M., & Sackett, P. R. (2002). The relative importance of task, citizenship, and counterproductive performance to global ratings of job performance: A policy-capturing approach. *Journal of Applied Psychology, 87*(1), 66–80. A well-done empirical piece that shows how these various performance measures can be combined to make overall ratings for personnel decisions.

Performance Appraisal

5

CHAPTER OUTLINE

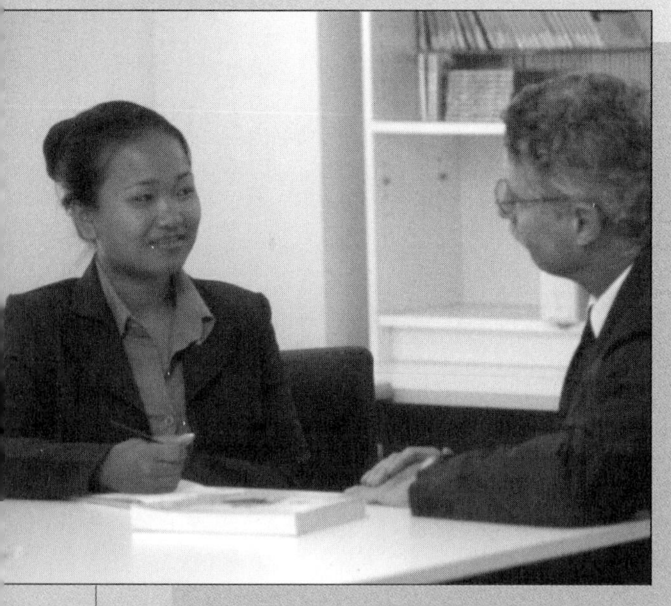

In the previous chapter we talked about criteria and identified the properties of good criteria (i.e., criteria for the criteria). In addition, we noted that the most important criterion for organizations is *performance* and that performance criteria are used extensively to evaluate employees. The process of evaluating employees' performance—performance appraisal—is the focus of this chapter. Having our performance appraised is something we've all experienced at one time or another. Of course, we may not have fond memories of our fathers telling us that we didn't weed the vegetable garden well enough, or of our high school shop teacher pointing out that our birdhouse had no place for the birds, or of our Psychology 100 professor telling us that our test scores so far give us only a C in the course. The types of performance appraisal just described are all examples of negative appraisals. But sometimes we did a nice job mowing the lawn, acting in a play, and writing a term paper—instances in which we probably received positive appraisals.

There are many domains in which we are held accountable for our performance, but in this chapter we will talk specifically about the role of performance appraisal in organizational life—in which it plays a very important role indeed. In this domain, **performance appraisal** is defined as the systematic review and evaluation of job performance, as well as the provision of performance feedback. However, as I think you'll soon see, performance appraisal is a lot more interesting than that definition makes it sound.

performance appraisal
The systematic review and evaluation of employees' job performance, as well as the provision of feedback to the employees.

LEARNING OBJECTIVES

This chapter should help you understand:

- the purposes of performance appraisal.
- the various formats used in the evaluation of performance.
- the effect of rating errors on the appraisal process.
- how the broader context in which performance appraisal takes place has various and diverse implications for performance appraisal and organizational functioning.
- the important role played by legal issues in the performance appraisal process.

CHAPTER FIVE

USES OF PERFORMANCE APPRAISAL

Performance appraisal is one of the most important processes conducted within organizations. It has many purposes, of which the three most significant are discussed here. First, performance appraisals are used to make important *personnel decisions* such as who gets promoted, fired, demoted, or laid off; who gets a large raise, a small raise, or no raise at all; who gets reassigned to an exciting new department and who stays behind to continue the "same old" work; who gets the opportunity for training on the new equipment and who continues running the old, soon-to-be-outdated equipment. In efficient organizations these decisions are not made haphazardly; they are made on the basis of performance appraisal data.

Second, performance appraisals are used for *developmental purposes.* Employees are provided with information about their performance strengths and weaknesses so that they can be proud of what they are doing well and can focus their efforts on the areas that need some work. On the whole, organizations benefit when employees perform better, and performance appraisal data are used to help employees become better performers. In addition, organizations are interested in seeing their employees advance within the company to other important jobs—an outcome that performance appraisal can facilitate. For example, an employee may be told that she needs to improve her interpersonal skills so that she will be eligible when the next promotion becomes available.

A third purpose of performance appraisal is what I'll call *documentation* of organizational decisions—a purpose that has recently evolved out of personnel decisions and the growing area of personnel law. Now that companies are very aware of the possibility of being sued over personnel business decisions, managers are increasingly using performance appraisals to document employees' performance patterns over time. In cases in which poor performers are fired for inadequate performance, the organization—if it has kept careful track—can fall back on a detailed account of the employees' inferior performance, making it difficult for them to claim that they were fired without just cause. (We will discuss legal issues in performance appraisal later in this chapter.)

On the other hand, performance appraisals that are not carefully developed and implemented can have negative repercussions for both the organization and its employees. For instance, a poorly conceived appraisal system could get the wrong person promoted, transferred, or fired. It could cause feelings of inequity on the part of good employees who erroneously receive smaller raises than bad employees. It could lead to legal suits in which the company has a very weak defense for why a particular individual was not promoted. Also, it could result in disgruntled employees who decrease their effort, ignore the feedback, or look for other jobs. Even customers are poorly served when an ineffective appraisal system causes employees to operate at less than their peak level of efficiency. Indeed, an ineffective performance appraisal system has widespread implications for

Performance can be measured and evaluated in many different ways.

everyone involved with the organization, which is why performance appraisal has received so much research attention (for reviews, see Levy & Williams, 2004; Murphy & Cleveland, 1995).

THE ROLE OF I/O PSYCHOLOGY IN PERFORMANCE APPRAISAL

I/O psychologists play a significant role in the area of performance appraisal. They are often hired to help develop and implement performance appraisal systems. I/O psychologists have measurement expertise, as well as a background in both human resources and organizational psychology—areas of knowledge that are integral to successful performance appraisals. Many companies have I/O psychologists in their HR departments who are responsible for what is known as **performance management,** a system of individual performance improvement. This system typically includes (1) objective goal setting, (2) continuous coaching and feedback, (3) performance appraisal, and (4) developmental planning. The key points here are twofold: These four components are linked to the company's goals and objectives, and the system is implemented on a continuous cycle rather than just once per year.

performance management
A system of individual performance improvement that typically includes (1) objective goal setting, (2) continuous coaching and feedback, (3) performance appraisal, and (4) development planning.

Researchers who specialize in performance appraisal pursue research questions like the following: (1) What is the best format or rating scale for performance appraisals? (2) To what extent do rater errors and biases affect the appraisal process? (3) How should raters be trained so that they can avoid these errors and biases? (4) What major contextual variables affect the appraisal process? (5) How important is the organizational context or culture in the appraisal process? In addition to addressing such questions, I/O psychology, as an empirically based applied discipline, attempts to use basic psychological principles to help organizations develop and implement motivating, fair, accurate, and user-friendly appraisal systems.

A CONTEXTUAL APPROACH

In the remainder of this chapter, performance appraisal is treated as a social-psychological process (Murphy & Cleveland, 1995). This approach views performance appraisal as a communication process that takes place within a **context.** The idea here is that performance appraisal is not a stand-alone process that can be examined in isolation but, rather, a complex process that takes place in a very rich and sophisticated social climate. Therefore, to better understand performance appraisal, researchers and practitioners alike must recognize and examine this important context.

context
The social-psychological climate in which performance appraisal takes place.

For many years, practitioners and researchers believed that rating-scale formats were integral to the success of performance appraisal systems and that *accuracy* should be the chief goal of any performance appraisal system. Because of these two common beliefs, much of the early research in this area focused on the context of performance appraisal as it related to rating formats and rater errors. We have learned a great deal from this research, and, indeed, formats and errors will be covered in the next two sections, respectively. Nevertheless, we now realize that there is much more to the process of performance appraisal than just rating formats and rater errors. Hence the remaining sections of this chapter will focus on contemporary issues that better emphasize the social-psychological processes and the social context described earlier (see Levy & Williams, 2004; Murphy & Cleveland, 1995).

Rating Formats

When it comes time for an evaluator to appraise someone's performance, he or she typically uses some type of rating form. There are quite a few options here; in this section we will discuss the ones most frequently employed.

Graphic Rating Scales. Graphic rating scales are among the oldest format used in the evaluation of performance. These scales consist of a number of traits or behaviors (e.g., dependability), and the rater is asked to judge how much of each particular trait the ratee possesses or where on this dimension the ratee falls with respect to organizational expectations. The early versions of these scales included tick marks all along the base of the scale. The performance rating score was the measurement in inches or centimeters (i.e., the number of ticks) from the left edge of the scale to the respondent's check on the scale (Farr & Levy, in press). Today, graphic rating scales usually include numerical/verbal anchors at various points along the scale, such as "1/below expectations," "4/meets expectations," and "7/exceeds expectations," and the score is whatever number is circled. Graphic rating scales are commonly used in organizations due, in part, to their simplicity in use and development. Figure 5.1 provides an example of a graphic rating scale—in this case, one that appraises the extent to which employees are "following procedures."

FIGURE 5.1 Graphic Rating Scale for "Following Procedures"

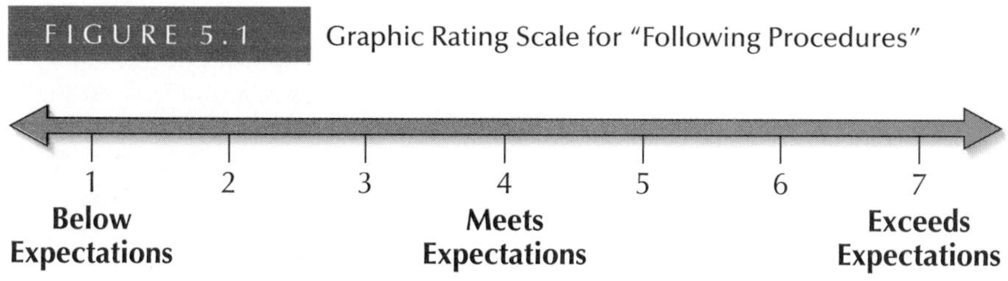

Behaviorally Anchored Rating Scales. Behaviorally anchored rating scales, or BARS (Smith & Kendall, 1963), are similar to graphic rating scales except that they provide actual behavioral descriptions as anchors along the scale. An example of a 9-point BARS for a nuclear power plant operator's tendency to "follow procedures" is shown in Figure 5.2.

BARS are perhaps best known for the painstaking process involved in their development (see Smith & Kendall, 1963). I will summarize this process as taking place in five steps (Bernardin & Beatty, 1984). First, a group of participants—such as employees, supervisors, or subject matter experts (SMEs)—identifies and carefully defines several dimensions as important for the job ("follows procedures," "works in a timely manner," etc.). Second, another group of participants generates a series of behavioral examples of job performance (similar to the items in Figure 5.2) for each dimension. These behavioral examples are called **critical incidents.** Participants are encouraged to write critical incidents at high-, medium-, and low-effectiveness levels for each dimension. In Figure 5.2, for example, "Never deviates from the procedures outlined for a particular task and takes the time to do things according to the employee manual" represents high effectiveness, whereas "Takes

critical incidents
Examples of job performance used in behaviorally anchored rating scales or job-analytic approaches.

FIGURE 5.2 Behaviorally Anchored Rating Scale for "Following Procedures"

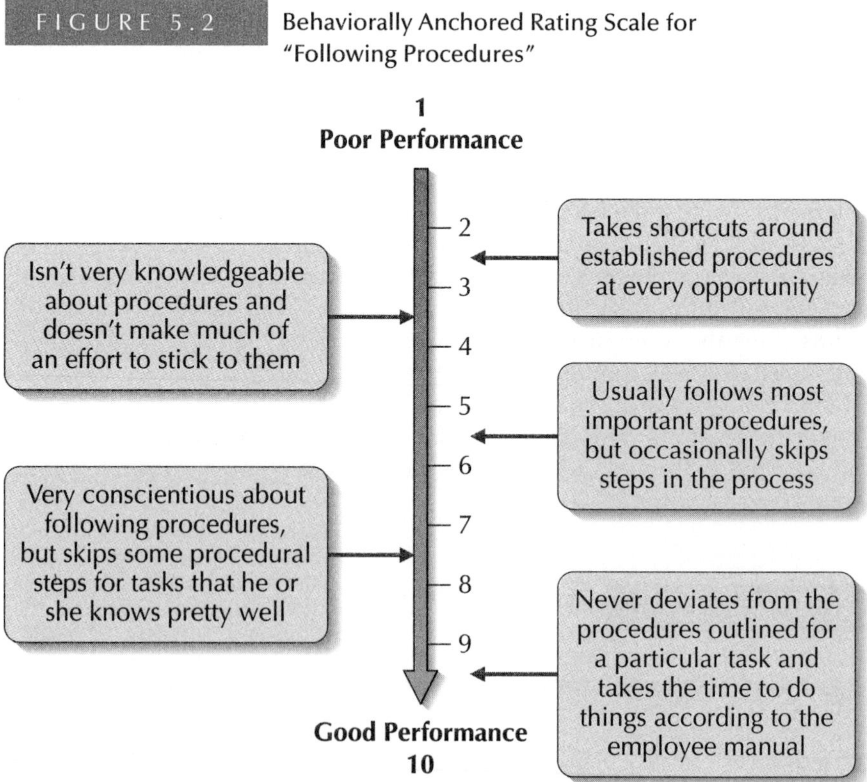
1
Poor Performance
2
3
4
5
6
7
8
9
Good Performance
10
Takes shortcuts around established procedures at every opportunity
Isn't very knowledgeable about procedures and doesn't make much of an effort to stick to them
Usually follows most important procedures, but occasionally skips steps in the process
Very conscientious about following procedures, but skips some procedural steps for tasks that he or she knows pretty well
Never deviates from the procedures outlined for a particular task and takes the time to do things according to the employee manual

shortcuts around established procedures at every opportunity" represents low effectiveness. Third, yet another group of participants is asked to sort these critical incidents into the appropriate dimensions. During this *retranslation* stage, the goal is to make sure that the examples generated for each dimension are unambiguously associated with that dimension. Usually a criterion, such as 80%, is used to weed out items that are not clearly related to a particular dimension: If fewer than 80% of the participants place the critical incident in the correct dimension, the item is dropped. A fourth group of participants then rates each remaining behavioral example on its effectiveness for the associated dimension. This rating is usually done on a 5- or 7-point scale. Any item with a large standard deviation is eliminated because a large standard deviation indicates that some respondents think the item represents effective performance, whereas others think it represents ineffective performance—obviously, a problematic situation. Fifth, items that specifically represent performance levels on each dimension are chosen from the acceptable pool of items, and BARS are developed and administered.

This very deliberate and thorough development process is both the biggest strength and the biggest weakness of BARS. Usually such a detailed process involving at least four different groups of participants results in a useful and relevant scale. However, the costs in both time and money are too high for many organizations, so they often employ a simple graphic scale instead.

Checklists. Checklists are another popular format for performance appraisals. Here, raters are asked to read a large number of behavioral statements and to check off each behavior that the employee exhibits. One example from this category is the *weighted checklist,* which includes a series of items that have previously been weighted as to importance or effectiveness; specifically, some items are indicative of desirable behavior, whereas others are indicative of undesirable behavior. Figure 5.3 presents an example of a weighted checklist for the evaluation of a bookstore manager.

In a real-life situation, the scale shown in Figure 5.3 would be modified in two ways. First, the items would be scrambled so as not to be in numerical order; and, second, the scale score column would not be part of the form. To administer this type of scale, raters would simply check the items that apply; in our current example, the sum of items checked would be the bookstore manager's performance appraisal score. Note that as more and more of the negative items are checked, the employee's summed rating gets lower and lower.

Forced-choice checklists are also used by organizations, though not as frequently as weighted checklists. Here, raters are asked to choose two items from a group of four that best describe the target employee. All four appear on the surface to be favorable, but the items have been developed and validated such that only *two* are actually good discriminators between effective and ineffective performers. The purpose of this approach is to reduce purposeful bias or distortion on the part of raters. In other words, because all the items appear favorable and the raters don't know which two are truly indicative of good performance, they

FIGURE 5.3 A Weighted Checklist

Bookstore Manager		
Check Box (if applicable)	**Behavioral Descriptor**	**Scale Score**
☐	Maintains full inventory of heavy demand items	+8.5
☐	Employees create a positive atmosphere for customers	+6.7
☐	Is accessible to customers	+4.4
☐	Is in the store at least 40 hours per week	+1.5
☐	Doesn't consistently anticipate likely problems	–1.2
☐	Pays little attention to labor dollars/sales dollars ratio	–2.4
☐	Rarely attends to customers' needs	–4.6
☐	Isn't able to make changes necessary to show a profit	–6.7
	TOTAL SCORE:	

cannot intentionally give someone high or low ratings. One drawback to this approach is that some raters don't like it because they feel as though they've lost control over the rating process. How would you feel if you had to choose two statements that describe your poorly performing subordinate, but all four statements seem positive? A recent appraisal format has been developed that appears to reduce the bias sometimes associated with other approaches, but without the negative reactions on the part of the raters. Borman and his colleagues have developed the Computerized Adaptive Rating Scale (CARS), which, although in its infancy, seems to be more psychometrically sound than other approaches and provides more discriminability (Borman, et al., 2001; Schneider, Goff, Anderson, & Borman, 2003).

Employee Comparison Procedures. The final category of rating formats, *employee comparison procedures,* involves evaluation of ratees with respect to how they measure up to or compare with other employees. One example of this type of format is *rank-ordering,* whereby several employees are ranked from best to worst. Rank-ordering can be particularly useful for making promotion decisions and discriminating the very best employee from the rest. A second example, *paired comparisons,* involves comparison of each employee with every other employee. If a manager has only 3 employees to evaluate, this isn't too difficult a task. (Think about doing this for each of your instructors this semester—comparing each to every one of the others.) However, as the number of ratees increases, so does the complexity of the task. The formula $N(N-1)/2$ can be used to calculate the total number of comparisons. For example, whereas 3 employees entails 3 comparisons, 10 employees entails 45! Although this method is one way to arrive at a "clear winner" among employees, it obviously becomes very cumbersome as the number of employees grows.

A third example is called *forced distribution*. Here, raters are instructed to "force" a designated proportion of ratees into each of five to seven categories. A similar procedure is grading on the normal curve, whereby teachers assign grades based on meeting the normal curve percentages (i.e., 68% of the grades assigned are Cs, 13.5% are Bs, 13.5% are Ds, 2.5% are As, and 2.5% are Fs). Sometimes organizations require supervisors to use the same sort of procedure, resulting in the categorization of one-third of the subordinates as average, one-third as below average, and one-third as above average (see the *Time* article by Greenwald, 2001). This is often done because performance ratings are tied to raises and, with a limited raise pool, the company wants to make sure that not too many employees are rated as eligible for a raise and to potentially remove inferior employees from the organization. To appreciate how employees might feel about this approach, think about how you would feel if your psychology instructor told you that you were to be graded on a "normal curve." In other words, if you averaged a 95 in the course but 3% of your classmates averaged 96 or better, you would *not* receive an A in the course because only 3% can get As. Needless to say, forced distribution is not a popular approach among ratees, whether students or employees; but it is currently being used by as many as 20% of Fortune 500 companies, such as General Electric, 3M, Texas Instruments, and Hewlett Packard (Meisler, 2003). However, some very public lawsuits over the use of these systems have created a controversy regarding the extent to which underrepresented groups tend to be disproportionately ranked in the low category. Companies such as Ford and Goodyear (both the targets of legal proceedings) have discontinued their use. You can continue to follow these issues in the popular press (see Bates, 2003).

An Evaluation of the Various Alternative Methods. Since the 1950s, perhaps no area within performance appraisal has received more research attention than rating type or format. Because no single format appears to be clearly superior to the others (Landy & Farr, 1980; Murphy & Cleveland, 1995), I will make no attempt to argue for one. Instead, I provide in Table 5.1 a summary of the advantages and disadvantages of the four major types discussed here. You can use this to decide for yourself which format you would use to evaluate your employees; in some cases, your choice would depend on the situation. Note, however, that companies most often use a graphic rating scale with various behavioral anchors—basically a hybrid combination of a graphic rating scale and a BARS.

Rating Errors

Evaluating another individual's performance accurately and fairly is not an easy thing to do; moreover, errors often result from this process. An understanding of these errors is important to appreciating the complexities of performance appraisal.

Cognitive Processes. In a typical company situation, once or twice per year supervisors have to recall specific performance incidents relating to each employee; somehow integrate those performance incidents into a comprehensible whole; arrive at an overall evaluation; and, finally, endorse a number or category that represents the employee's performance over that period. Further, this has to be done for each of 6 to 12 different employees, and perhaps more! With the trend toward "flatter" organizations (see Chapters 1 and 14), the number of subordinates for each supervisor is increasing steadily, making the task that much more difficult.

Although more complex *cognitive processing* models of performance appraisal have been developed (see DeNisi, Cafferty, & Meglino, 1984; Landy & Farr, 1980), all such models are consistent with the scheme depicted in Figure 5.4. Note that this figure includes two examples of potential error or bias that may come into

TABLE 5.1 Summary of Appraisal Formats

	Advantages	Disadvantages
Graphic Rating Scales	1. Easy to develop 2. Easy to use	1. Lack of precision in dimensions 2. Lack of precision in anchors
BARS	1. Precise and well-defined scales—good for coaching 2. Well received by raters and ratees	1. Time and money intensive 2. No evidence that BARS are more accurate than other formats
Checklists	1. Easy to develop 2. Easy to use	1. Rater errors such as halo, leniency, and severity are quite frequent
Employee Comparison Methods	1. Precise rankings are possible 2. Useful for making administrative rewards on a limited basis	1. Time intensive 2. Not well received by raters (Paired Comparison) or ratees (Forced Distribution)

play at each of the steps shown (see the left and right columns). In the 1980s this model was at the core of a great deal of research stemming from Frank Landy and Jim Farr's (1980) call for more cognitive process-oriented research. The first step in this model is the *observation* of employees' behaviors. In many situations, this is done well; the rater may observe a large portion of the ratee's behavior, as when a grocery store manager observes his subordinates' performance every day. In other situations, however, raters are unable to observe ratees' performance directly. For instance, professors are often evaluated by their department heads, even though the department heads have little opportunity to view the professors engaging in job-related tasks like teaching.

Second, the observed behavior must be *encoded.* This means that the behavior must be cognitively packaged in such a way that the rater is able to store it. Note that if an observed behavior is encoded incorrectly (e.g., an adequate behavior is somehow encoded as inadequate), the appraisal rating will be affected at a later time.

Third, after encoding, the behavior must be *stored* in long-term memory. Because it is unreasonable to expect that anyone could perfectly store all of the relevant performance incidents, some important incidents may not get stored at all.

Fourth, when the appraisal review is being conducted, the stored information must be *retrieved* from memory. In many situations, the rater cannot retrieve

FIGURE 5.4 Cognitive Processing Model of Performance Appraisal

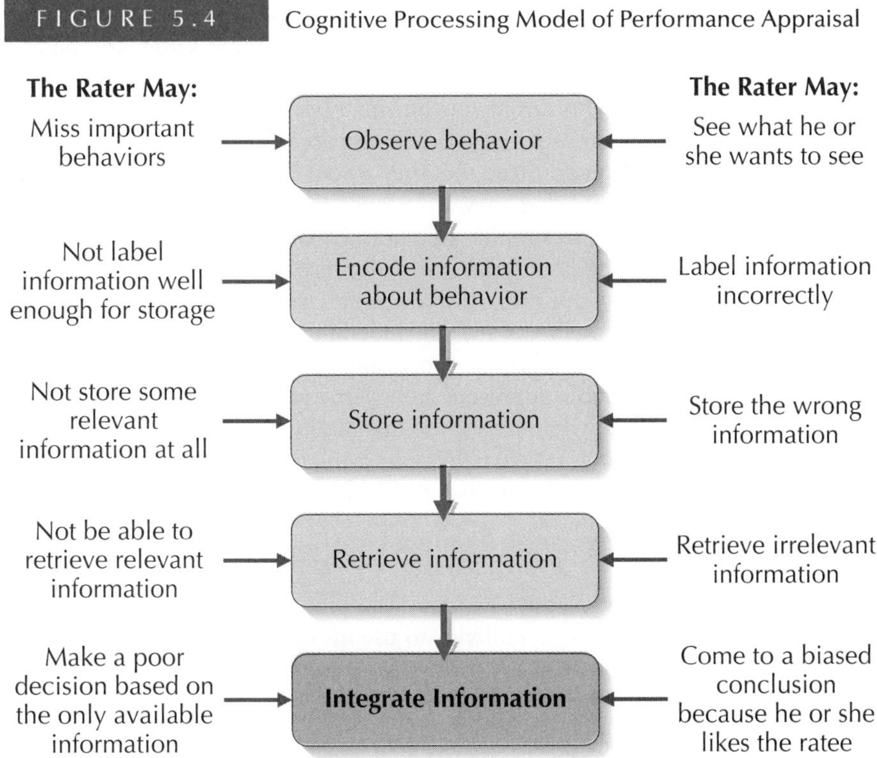
The Rater May:
Miss important behaviors
Not label information well enough for storage
Not store some relevant information at all
Not be able to retrieve relevant information
Make a poor decision based on the only available information
Observe behavior
Encode information about behavior
Store information
Retrieve information
Integrate Information
The Rater May:
See what he or she wants to see
Label information incorrectly
Store the wrong information
Retrieve irrelevant information
Come to a biased conclusion because he or she likes the ratee

some of the important information, leading to an appraisal rating that is based on an inadequate sample of behavior. Also, since performance reviews are difficult and time-consuming, it's not unusual for raters to retrieve irrelevant information and to use it as the basis for the performance rating. Think about doing a review of your subordinate's administrative assistant—someone with whom you have very little interaction. In doing this review, you would certainly get input from your subordinate; but later, when doing the final evaluation, you might recall a memo from your subordinate that explained an expensive mix-up in his office in terms of scheduling conflicts. You may consider this when doing the administrative assistant's evaluation (after all, it makes sense that he would be in charge of scheduling), even though you don't know whether this mix-up was his fault. For that matter, he may have been the one who caught the problem and saved the company money. If you stored irrelevant information, you may unwittingly use it later in making a performance judgment.

Finally, the rater has to *integrate* all of this information and come to a final rating. If the rater has done a good job of observing, encoding, storing, and retrieving relevant performance information, the integration step should be relatively easy. However, sometimes raters let attitudes and feelings cloud their judgments. If your boyfriend, girlfriend, spouse, or even a close acquaintance worked under your direct supervision, would you be able to be objective in arriving at a performance judgment that would be used in a promotion decision? You'd like to think that you could, but many of us probably can't. This is one reason that many companies frown upon hiring both members of a married couple. Other companies, if they do hire the couple, will not allow them to work in the same plant; still others will draw the line just short of having one member of the couple supervise the other. In one case that I know of, the U.S. Military accepted a married couple into the army as captains and guaranteed that they would be in the same geographical region, but also guaranteed that they would not be assigned to the same base. Many organizations prefer to simplify things and avoid these potential problems altogether, thus preventing potential biases and acts of favoritism.

An extensive review of appraisal-process research conducted in the 1980s (Ilgen, Barnes-Farrell, & McKellin, 1993) concluded that this research has helped us to understand fundamental cognitive processing as applied to performance appraisal. For instance, we now appreciate how demanding the task of appraisal is and recognize more about what makes it so demanding. Meanwhile, I/O psychologists have been developing ways to help raters avoid the cognitive errors involved in performance appraisal. Let's consider some of the most common of these errors (Hoyt, 2000).

halo
The rating error that results from either (1) a rater's tendency to use his or her global evaluation of a ratee in making dimension-specific ratings for that ratee or (2) a rater's unwillingness to discriminate between independent dimensions of a ratee's performance.

Halo. One error that has received a great deal of attention is called **halo.** Halo results from either (1) a rater's tendency to use his or her global evaluation of a ratee in making dimension-specific ratings for that ratee or (2) a rater's unwillingness to discriminate between independent dimensions of a ratee's performance (Saal, Downey, & Lahey, 1980). Halo effects can be positive or negative in nature. Here's a personal example of positive halo that students usually find helpful. I had a tendency to do well in school, and when I was in fifth grade I was Sister Agnelia's prized pupil. Because I was such a good student in English and math, Sister Agnelia thought I could do no wrong—she let halo get in the way of her evaluation of me on other dimensions such as spelling and handwriting, in which I was not particularly strong. Some of my classmates were unhappy that I received better grades than they did even though my handwriting was no better than theirs. You can see how halo can lead to chaos in the fifth grade; but, more important, you can imagine how it can lead to inaccurate appraisals in the workplace, as well as to hard feelings on the part of employees who feel mistreated either because they are not benefiting from the positive halo surrounding other co-workers or because they have been subjected to a negative halo whereby a supervisor has allowed a negative impression to color judgments on other specific dimensions.

The early research in this area assumed that all halo was error. However, some people are competent across *all* dimensions—leadership, communication skills, motivating employees, completing paperwork, and so on. Traditionally, I/O psychologists noted high correlations across ratings on these dimensions and concluded that there was a great deal of halo error. However, from a hiring standpoint (see Chapters 6 and 7), organizations tend to target those applicants whom they believe will be "good at everything"—those are the people they want. And, indeed, there are employees in all organizations who do seem to be good performers on all performance dimensions. (Consider Tom Hanks, who as an actor can do it all well—from intense, serious drama to light comedy.) The point here is that some halo results from accurate intercorrelations among performance dimensions (see Goffin, Jelley, & Wagner, 2003; Murphy & Jako, 1989; Murphy & Reynolds, 1988), or what we call **true halo.** Thus we no longer view all halo as error.

true halo
Halo that results from accurate intercorrelations among performance dimensions rather than from rating error.

Rating errors such as leniency, central tendency, and severity (discussed below) are categorized as **distributional errors** because they result from a mismatch between actual rating distributions and expected rating distributions. In other words, the grouping of ratings is much farther toward one end of the distribution or much closer to the middle than what we assume the true distribution to be. Remember our discussion of the normal distribution in Chapter 2, where I pointed out that many qualities are distributed in this bell-shaped distribution, such as intelligence, height, weight, political attitudes, and so on. Performance is another quality that we expect to be distributed in this way: Most employees are adequate performers, and few are extremely good or extremely bad.

distributional errors
Rating errors, such as severity, central tendency, and leniency, that result from a mismatch between actual rating distributions and expected rating distributions.

Leniency. Raters commit the error of **leniency** when (1) the mean of their ratings across ratees is higher than the mean of all ratees across all raters or (2) the mean of their ratings is higher than the midpoint of the scale. In other words, if your boss rates her employees higher than all the other bosses rate their employees, or if she gives ratings with a mean of 4 on a 5-point scale, she would be described as a lenient rater. Raters may be lenient because they like their employees or want to be liked. They may think that giving everyone favorable ratings will keep "peace" in the workplace or that doing so will make them "look good" as supervisors who have high-performing subordinates. In fact, Neil Hauenstein

leniency
The rating error that results when (1) the mean of one's ratings across ratees is higher than the mean of all ratees across all raters or (2) the mean of one's ratings is higher than the midpoint of the scale.

(1992) found that there are at least two explanations for leniency: (1) *intentional* distortion of ratings as a result of the rater's motivation and (2) *information-processing* distortion as a result of unintentional encoding or memory biases. In a recent applied study, Chambers and Schmitt (2002) reported that students rated professors more leniently when they perceived themselves to be receiving higher grades than they've received in other classes for which they've expended the same amount of effort.

As with halo, we need to be careful in assuming that distributional errors are really errors. Indeed, it is possible, perhaps likely, that some supervisors really do have better employees or work groups than others, resulting in more favorable ratings that are "accurate" rather than "lenient." For example, the airline chosen as the best in the nation with respect to service should show higher performance ratings for its service employees than other airlines. So what may appear to be the result of leniency among the evaluators of this airline is in fact the result of accurate evaluation. Research also suggests that personality can have an impact on one's tendency to be lenient. Specifically, individuals categorized as "agreeable" have been shown to be more lenient than those categorized as "conscientious" (Bernardin, Cooke, & Villanova, 2000).

central tendency
The tendency to use only the midpoint of the scale in rating one's employees.

Central Tendency. Raters who use only the midpoint of the scale in rating their employees commit what is called the error of **central tendency.** An example is the professor who gives almost everyone a C for the course. In some cases the raters are lazy and find it easier to give everyone an average rating than to spend the extra time necessary to review employees' performance so as to differentiate between good and poor workers. In other cases the raters don't know how well each of their subordinates has performed (perhaps because they are new to the work group or just don't see their employees' on-the-job behavior very often) and take the easy way out by opting for average ratings for everyone. Consider a bank manager who has very little opportunity to observe her subordinates—loan officers—as they interact with their customers. She may tend to rate these officers in the middle of the scale on "customer skills," thus committing a central tendency error. Some recent research suggests that central tendency error is sometimes a result of the rating scale itself and that simpler semantic differential scales (e.g., EFFECTIVE EMPLOYEE . . . INEFFECTIVE EMPLOYEE) result in a considerable amount of this bias (Yu, Albaum, & Swenson, 2003).

Of course, a given work group or department may largely be populated by average employees. In fact, the normal distribution suggests that most employees really are average, so it is reasonable to have a large percentage of employees rated as such. At times, then, central tendency is a rating error; but at other times it reflects the actual distribution of performance, which is largely centered around "average."

severity
The tendency to use only the low end of the scale or to give consistently lower ratings to one's employees than other raters do.

Severity. Less frequent than leniency and central tendency is the rating error of **severity,** which is committed by raters who tend to use only the low end of the scale or to give consistently lower ratings to their employees than other raters do. Some supervisors intentionally give low ratings to employees because they believe that doing so motivates them (you will see when we get to Chapter 9, on motivation, that this strategy is not likely to work), or keeps them from getting too cocky, or provides a baseline from which new employees can improve. For some, severity represents an attempt to maintain the impression of being tough and in charge—but what tends to happen is that such raters lose, rather than gain, the respect of their subordinates.

Some work groups include a larger number of low performers than other work groups, so low ratings from the supervisor of such work groups may be accurate rather than "severe." Thus, although we don't see these terms in the literature, we could speak of true leniency, true central tendency, and true severity in much the same way as we speak of true halo. For any given situation, in fact, it is difficult to determine whether the ratings are affected by rating errors or are an accurate reflection of performance.

The chief problem stemming from distributional errors is that the ratings do not adequately *discriminate* between effective and ineffective performers. In such cases, the majority of ratees are lumped together in the bottom, middle, or top of the distribution. This general problem is often referred to as *range restriction* because only a small part of the scale range is used in the ratings. The difficulty for the organization is that it intends to use performance rating information for personnel decisions such as promotions, raises, transfers, layoffs and other terminations, but if all of the employees are rated similarly (whether as a result of central tendency, leniency, or severity), the ratings do not help in making these personnel decisions. For instance, if everyone is rated in the middle of the scale, who gets promoted? If everyone is rated very favorably, who gets the big raise? If everyone is rated as ineffective, who gets fired?

Employee morale is also affected by nondiscriminating ratings, in that employees who believe they are good employees will feel slighted because their reviews are no better than those of employees whom they view as much less effective. Think about those forced ranking systems we talked about earlier: How would you feel if you were at the very top of that middle category and got a B but then realized that people at the very bottom of that huge category (e.g., 70% of the total workforce) also received a B and the same pay raise? Or think about this: Have you ever been passed over for a promotion, only to discover that the person who was promoted, though less deserving than you, was rated similarly to you? You likely experienced feelings of *injustice,* which may have affected not only your subsequent on-the-job performance but also your attitude. These additional implications of nondiscriminating ratings will be discussed in more detail in Chapters 10 and 11.

Other Errors. Many other rating errors are discussed in the literature, but I will touch on just three more. One is *recency error,* whereby raters heavily weight their most recent interactions with or observations of the ratees. A supervisor who, in rating his subordinate, largely ignores 9 months of superior performance and bases his evaluation of this subordinate on only the past 3 months of less-than-adequate performance could be described as making a recency error. This is similar to the somewhat misguided belief in organizations that all that matters is the question "What have you done for me lately?"

Another error of note, called *first impression error,* is the opposite of leniency error. Here, raters pay an inordinate amount of attention to their initial experiences with the ratee. A construction foreman may think back to that first day when the new electrician helped out on the site at a crucial time and use this as the basis for his evaluation of the electrician while largely ignoring some major performance problems over the past few months. First impressions tend to be heavily weighted in our everyday lives, as when we form friendships with people with whom we just seem to "hit it off" from the very beginning; they are also used, sometimes ineffectively, in performance appraisal.

Finally, there is the *similar-to-me* error, which occurs when raters tend to give more favorable ratings to ratees who are very much like themselves. This shouldn't come as a surprise to you. Think about the people with whom you hang out. Typically, there is a great deal of similarity between yourself and your friends. You might have a similar background, a similar taste in clothes and music, similar hobbies, and so on. We know from social psychology that people tend to be interested in making friends with and being around people who are much like themselves: "Birds of a feather flock together" (Aronson, Wilson, & Akers, 1997). A similar effect occurs in performance appraisal situations, resulting in more favorable ratings of employees similar to the rater than of those dissimilar.

Rater Training

We have just discussed some of the common errors that raters make in evaluating the performance of others. An important question asked by I/O researchers and practitioners alike is whether rater training can reduce such errors and improve the rating process (Hauenstein, 1998; Schleicher, Day, Mayes, & Riggio, 2002). There are two main types of rater training in the performance appraisal area. One, known as **Rater Error Training (RET),** was originally developed to reduce the incidence of rater errors (Spool, 1978). The focus was on describing errors like halo to raters and showing them how to avoid making such errors. The assumption was that by reducing the errors, RET could increase accuracy.

Rater Error Training (RET)
A type of training originally developed to reduce rater errors by focusing on describing errors like halo to raters and showing them how to avoid making such errors.

As suggested early on in the development of this approach, however, RET can reduce errors, but accuracy is not necessarily improved (Bernardin & Pence, 1980). In fact, studies have shown that accuracy sometimes *decreases* as a function of reducing error (e.g., Bernardin & Pence, 1980). How can this be? Well, recall what I said about halo, for instance: Halo can be a rating error, or it can be *true halo.* Think also about the good performers at your job. Are these people good at only one thing, or do they tend to be effective across a bunch of job dimensions? Usually there is some relationship across such dimensions. Certainly, we wouldn't expect correlations as high as .70, but we would expect some relationship such that the good fast-food employee can produce 24 hamburgers quickly and with high quality and that the good UPS driver can deliver all her packages efficiently, quickly, and to the correct households. When raters are instructed not to allow for halo, they are in effect being taught that there is no relationship among performance dimensions and that their ratings across dimensions should not be correlated. But in many cases there is true halo, and the ratings *should* be correlated. Thus rater training may have reduced the correlation across dimensions that we used to assume was error, resulting in artificially uncorrelated ratings that are now inaccurate.

A second type of rater training, called **Frame of Reference (FOR) Training,** was designed by John Bernardin and his colleagues to enhance raters' observational and categorizational skills (Bernardin & Beatty, 1984; Bernardin & Buckley, 1981). Bernardin's belief was that to improve accuracy of performance ratings, raters have to be provided with a frame of reference for defining performance levels that is consistent across raters and consistent with how the organization defines the various levels of performance. In other words, for our fast-food employee on the dimension of cleanliness, all raters must know that, on a 5-point scale, a 5 would be indicated by the following behaviors:

Frame of Reference (FOR) Training
A type of training designed to enhance raters' observational and categorizational skills so that all raters share a common frame of reference and improve rater accuracy.

> Table top is wiped down in between runs of burgers. Ketchup and mustard guns are always placed back into their cylinders and never left sitting on the table. Buns are kept wrapped in plastic in between runs of burgers. Floor around production area is swept at least once per hour and mopped once in the morning and afternoon. All items in the walk-in refrigerators are placed on the appropriate shelves and the walk-ins are organized, swept, and mopped periodically.

FOR training attempts to make that description part of all raters' performance schema for the level of "5/exceptional" performance. The hope is that by etching this performance exemplar in the raters' minds, the training will render each rater better able to use it consistently when observing, encoding, storing, retrieving, and integrating behaviors in arriving at a final rating. The goal is to "calibrate" raters so that a score of 5 from one rater means the same as a score of 5 from any other rater. Popular procedures for FOR training have since been developed (Pulakos, 1984, 1986). In these, raters are provided with descriptions of the dimensions and rating scales while also having them read aloud by the trainer. The trainer then describes ratee behaviors that are representative of different performance levels on each scale. Raters are typically shown a series of videotaped practice vignettes in which individuals are performing job tasks. Raters evaluate the stimulus persons on the scales; then the trainer discusses the raters' ratings and provides feedback about what ratings should have been made for each stimulus person. A detailed discussion ensues about the reasons for the various ratings.

Rater training is becoming more common in organizations such as the Tennessee Valley Authority, JP Morgan Chase, Lucent Technologies, and AT&T. It has also been applied to public safety jobs in both the United States and Canada. For instance, Neil Hauenstein and Roseanne Foti have worked with police departments in which they had incumbents generate target effectiveness ratings for a list of performance statements, resulting in performance standards that were then used for the FOR training program (Hauenstein & Foti, 1989). Similarly, Lorne Sulsky and Dave Day (1994) developed FOR training programs for officers in the Canadian Forces Military Police Assessment Centre. Specifically, they showed police officers videotapes of soldiers and provided the officers with the "correct" FOR for evaluating their performance. This program was well received by the police force and used in subsequent performance evaluations.

Research has consistently shown that FOR training improves appraisal accuracy (Athey & McIntyre, 1987; Sulsky & Day, 1994). A couple of recent studies have suggested that combining FOR training with *behavioral observation training (BOT)*, which focuses on teaching raters how to watch for certain behaviors and avoid behavioral observation errors, may improve the recognition or recall of performance behaviors (Noonan & Sulsky, 2001; Roch & O'Sullivan, 2003). One current concern, however, is that very little field data is available on the FOR technique. Except for the studies mentioned in the previous paragraph, the research showing that FOR training improves accuracy has been conducted with students in laboratory settings (see Hauenstein, 1998). The next step is to find a way to bring FOR training research into more organizational settings, but doing so requires some modification to the rather expensive and time-consuming process. Stay tuned as current research tries to accomplish just that.

Contemporary Performance Appraisal Research

Format and error research of the 1980s has taught us a great deal about the processes and errors involved in arriving at a performance judgment. However, numerous questions remain; these stem from the social context of the appraisal process (Ilgen et al., 1993) and are now the focus of appraisal researchers' work.

The Importance of the Social-Psychological Context. Many experts have suggested a more direct research focus on the context in which the appraisal takes place, arguing that this context colors the entire appraisal process (Folger, Konovsky, & Cropanzano, 1992; Ilgen et al., 1993; Judge & Ferris, 1993; Levy & Steelman, 1997; Murphy & Cleveland, 1995). The context in which performance appraisal takes place includes not only the social and legal climates in which the organization exists but also the climates and cultures within the organization itself (Murphy & Cleveland, 1995).

These context-related topics include an examination of (1) the use of employees' reactions to the appraisal rather than *accuracy* as a criterion to evaluate performance appraisal systems, (2) how the relationship between the supervisor and subordinate affects performance appraisal, (3) the role of organizational politics in the appraisal process, (4) the importance of trust in the appraisal process,

(5) the use of multiple feedback sources rather than just the supervisor's feedback in the appraisal process, and (6) the value of providing employees with knowledge about the appraisal system and the opportunity to participate in the appraisal process. This list represents just a small sampling of the context issues at the core of current performance appraisal research (see Levy & Williams, 2004, for a complete and current review). With our movement away from an emphasis on formats and errors, we are beginning to increase our understanding of the process itself and to apply that understanding to the use of appraisals in organizations. The next few sections will consider some of this new context-based research.

Reaction Criteria. Traditionally, performance appraisals were evaluated with respect to how "accurate" they were, in the sense of being free from errors. But as you now know, there are problems with accuracy and error measures. As early as 1984, John Bernardin and Dick Beatty suggested that future appraisal research should begin to move beyond psychometric criteria due to the measurement problems inherent in that approach and instead focus on what they termed *qualitative criteria* (Bernardin & Beatty, 1984) and what others have called *reaction criteria* (Cawley, Keeping, & Levy, 1998). Both phrases refer to the role played by raters' and ratees' reactions in the appraisal process (Hedge & Teachout, 2000; Keeping & Levy, 2000).

One research focus of late is the potential importance of raters' and ratees' favorable responses to the appraisal system or process (e.g., Findley, Giles, & Mossholder, 2000). In fact, until recently, the relative lack of research attention directed toward reaction criteria instead of psychometric and accuracy criteria led Kevin Murphy and Jan Cleveland (1995, p. 310) to refer to reaction criteria as one class of "neglected criteria" that might be critical in evaluating the success of an appraisal system. It seems reasonable to expect that subordinates' reactions to appraisal systems would have just as much impact on the success and effectiveness of an appraisal system as the more technical aspects of the system. However, Bernardin and Beatty (1984) have suggested that reactions are usually better indicators of the overall viability of an appraisal system than narrower psychometric indices such as leniency or halo. After all, one may develop the most technically sophisticated appraisal system, but if that system is not accepted and supported by employees, its effectiveness will ultimately be limited (Cardy & Dobbins, 1994; Carroll & Schneier, 1982; Cawley et al., 1998; Murphy & Cleveland, 1995). Indeed, due to the changing nature of performance appraisals and organizations, worker attitudes toward performance appraisal may play an increasingly important role in appraisal processes as the procedures and systems continue to develop (Hedge & Borman, 1995).

Despite the relative neglect of reaction criteria, several studies have attempted to investigate various appraisal characteristics that elicit or at least contribute to positive employee reactions. For instance, Greg Dobbins, Bob Cardy, and Stephanie Platz-Vieno (1990) demonstrated that for a sample of bank tellers,

The performance appraisal process can be strongly affected by the supervisor-subordinate or leader-member relationship.

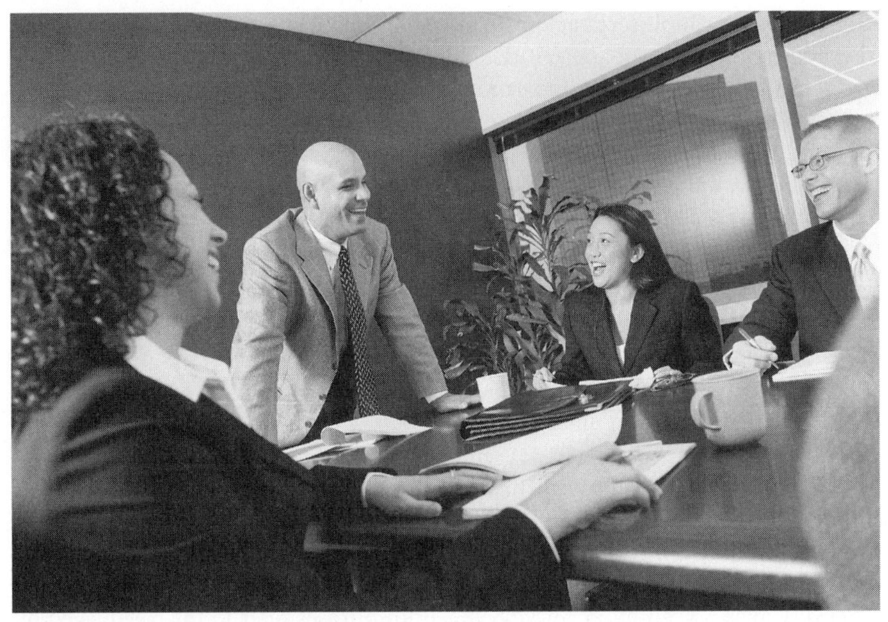

appraisal satisfaction was affected by both appraisal characteristics (e.g., frequency of appraisals) and organizational variables (e.g., employees' understanding of their jobs). Further, bank tellers who reported a positive relationship with their supervisors and a low amount of ambiguity about their roles in the organization were more satisfied with the appraisal system. A recent study demonstrated that subordinates reported less anger and higher perceptions of justice when supervisors provided justification for their ratings (Tata, 2002). Further, Brown and Benson (2003) also found that performance appraisals viewed as unfair by subordinates tended to be related to emotional exhaustion. This research approach has great implications for appraisal in organizations because it suggests that there are things that organizations and supervisors can do to increase the likelihood that employees will respond favorably to the performance appraisal process—namely, provide frequent performance feedback and relevant job-related information to employees.

The Supervisor-Subordinate Relationship. The relationship between supervisors and subordinates has been discussed in terms of *leader-member exchange (LMX) theory,* which emphasizes the idea that supervisors have different types of relationships with different subordinates (Engle & Lord, 1997; see also Chapter 13). Performance appraisal research has virtually ignored the role of leader-member exchange in subordinate reactions toward the appraisal process (Wexley & Klimoski, 1984), but LMX is important in this connection. For instance, a study found that telephone employees who experienced a high level of LMX with their supervisors were rated high in terms of performance regardless of objective performance indicators, whereas those who experienced a low level of LMX received performance ratings that matched their objective level of performance (Duarte, Goodson, & Klich, 1993). In short, the relationship that an employee has with his or her supervisor plays a role in the performance appraisal process. A recent study demonstrated that the frequency of communication between a subordinate and supervisor interacts with LMX to affect performance ratings. A positive LMX relationship led to favorable ratings when there was also frequent communication, but ratings were less favorable even with a positive LMX when there was little communication (Kacmar, Witt, Zivnuska, & Gully, 2003). This is an excellent example of the connection between the context in which the appraisal takes place and the outcome of the appraisal process. The implication in this case is that understanding the appraisal process within a work group requires an understanding of the relationships among those involved, because these relationships affect the appraisal process.

Organizational Politics. Organizational politics—"deliberate attempts by individuals to enhance or protect their self-interests when conflicting courses of action are possible"—help delineate the context in which performance appraisal takes place (Longenecker, Sims, & Gioia, 1987, p. 184). Because organizations are political entities, politics plays a role in all important organizational decisions and processes, including performance appraisal (Longenecker, Sims, & Gioia, 1987). It's important to note that both supervisors and subordinates are affected by the politics of performance appraisal. In particular, Clint Longenecker and his colleagues (1987) have demonstrated through interviews that executives intentionally manipulate appraisals for political reasons (e.g., to send a message to subordinates or to make their own department look good). Research has also indicated that subordinates use *impression management* strategies in an effort to bring about favorable appraisals; in other words, they control their behavior to make a good impression on their superiors (see Eder & Fedor, 1990; Villanova & Bernardin, 1989; Wayne & Kacmar, 1991; Wayne & Liden, 1995). Finally, a recent study of more than 800 employees demonstrated that among those who perceived a high level of organizational politics in their company, the ones who were also high on conscientiousness performed better than did those who were not high on conscientiousness (Hochwarter, Witt, & Kacmar, 2000). It appears that the high-conscientiousness employees were able to overcome the politics and perform well. Thus, to gain a better understanding of the appraisal process in an organization, and to affect that process, one needs to have information about the politics of the organization and the work group.

Trust. *Trust* in the appraisal process is the extent to which raters believe that fair and accurate appraisals have been or will be made in their organization (Bernardin, Orban, & Carlyle, 1981). Alternatively, if a rater feels that other raters in the organization are inflating their ratings, that rater may do the same. Bernardin and his colleagues developed a scale called *Trust in the Appraisal Process Survey,* or TAPS, to measure raters' perceptions of the rating behavior of the other raters in their department (Bernardin, 1978; Bernardin et al., 1981). They found that raters who scored low on the TAPS were more lenient raters than those who scored high. This finding indicates the importance of trust on appraisal ratings. Trust also seems to be related to employees' acceptance of the appraisal system (Murphy & Cleveland, 1995). In addition, performance appraisal systems that are well received by employees appear to affect employees' trust of top management, suggesting that the performance management system may be an effective tool for enhancing organizational trust (Mayer & Davis, 1999).

In another line of work related to trust issues, researchers have looked at how comfortable raters are with the performance appraisal process (Villanova, Bernardin, Dahmus, & Sims, 1993). In particular, Peter Villanova and his colleagues have shown that scores on a scale they call the *Performance Appraisal Discomfort Scale (PADS)* are related to leniency in such a way that those raters who express great discomfort in evaluating others and providing them with feedback also tend to be among the most lenient raters. In other words, not all raters are equally comfortable "doing" performance appraisals, and the extent to which raters experience discomfort in this setting is likely to affect the quality of the ratings and other elements of the appraisal process (e.g., interpersonal interactions).

360-degree feedback
A method of performance appraisal in which multiple raters at various levels of the organization evaluate a target employee and the employee is provided with feedback from these multiple sources.

Multiple Source Feedback. One of the "hottest" areas in performance appraisal is multiple source feedback, or what is sometimes called **360-degree feedback** (Fletcher & Baldry, 1999). This method involves the use of multiple raters at various levels of the organization who evaluate and provide feedback to a target employee. As presented in Figure 5.5, these multiple sources typically include subordinates, peers, supervisors, clients or customers, and even self-raters.

These systems are becoming of great importance to the modern organization in terms of performance assessment and management (Church & Bracken, 1997; Ghorpade, 2000). Many companies—such as Home Depot, Procter & Gamble, Johnson & Johnson, BP Amoco, Motorola, AT&T, DuPont, Honeywell, Intel, General Electric, and Boeing, among others—are using these systems for a variety of purposes, including developmental feedback to employees, performance appraisal, leadership and management development, and "succession planning" (i.e., figuring out likely promotions and lateral moves within the company). The use of multiple sources of feedback is consistent with such notions as participation and empowerment, which became popular in organizations of the late 20th century (see Chapter 1). In fact, Herb Meyer, one of the best-known performance appraisal researchers in the last 50 years, published an article in 1991 in which he argued convincingly that the traditional "top-down" performance appraisal system is inconsistent with the more humanistic and participative organizations of the late 20th century (and, presumably, the early 21st as well). It no longer seems reasonable for the supervisor to call all of the shots these days, now that employ-

FIGURE 5.5 360-Degree Feedback

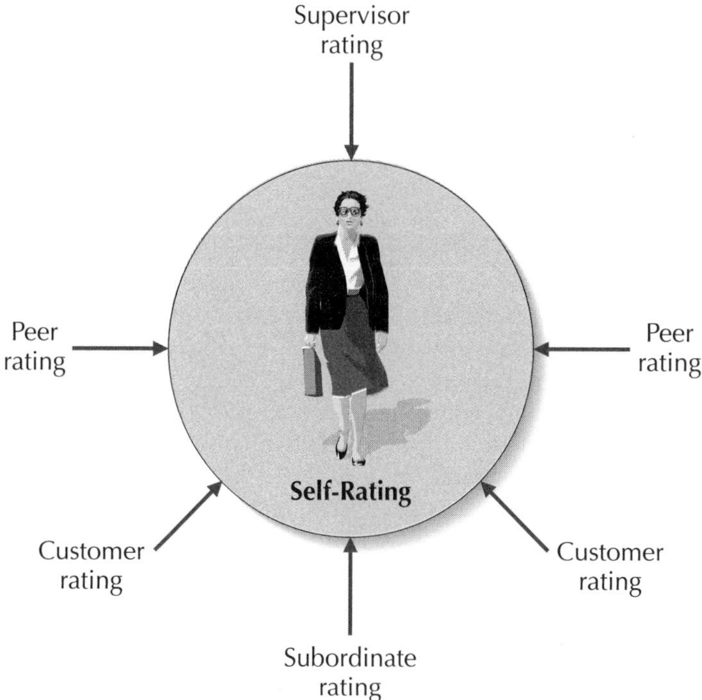

ees expect to participate more and to have their viewpoints heard. Indeed, 360-degree feedback is consistent with both greater employee expectations and the more sophisticated organizations of the 21st century.

Three basic assumptions are held by advocates of 360-degree feedback systems. First, when multiple raters are used, the participants are happier because they are involved in the process—and this calls to mind the importance of participation alluded to earlier. Second, and perhaps more important, when multiple raters from different levels of the organization rate the same target employee, the idiosyncrasies (and biases) of any single rater are overcome. For instance, if my supervisor doesn't like me and rates me severely for that reason, additional ratings from other individuals that aren't severe should overcome my supervisor's rating and highlight the possibility that there may be a problem with that rating. Third, multiple raters bring with them multiple perspectives on the target employee, allowing for a broader and more accurate "view" of performance. For instance, who is best able to evaluate my teaching performance? Certainly not my department chair, who *never* sees me in the classroom. Rather, the best judges are my students (some would call them "customers"; see Schneider, Hanges, Goldstein, & Braverman, 1994)—which is why many universities require student

upward appraisal ratings
Ratings provided by individuals whose status, in an organizational-hierarchy sense, is below that of the ratees.

ratings of teaching performance in all classes. These are sometimes called **upward appraisal ratings,** because they refer to ratings provided by individuals whose status is, in an organizational-hierarchy sense, below that of the ratees (Atwater, Daldman, Atwater, & Cartier, 2000).

Research attention to 360-degree feedback began to accelerate with two special journal issues devoted entirely to this technique in the mid-1990s: *Human Resource Management,* Vol. 32 (1993) and *Group and Organization Management,* Vol. 22 (1997). Although 360-degree feedback has been used in organizations for a few decades, research efforts to understand it have only recently begun to catch up with practitioner usage. For instance, one study demonstrated that lack of agreement among raters regarding a particular ratee is sometimes not error but a result of the role played by the raters themselves (Salam, Cox, & Sims Jr., 1997). Another study showed that contextual factors such as supervisory style and feedback environment were more important than personality variables in terms of their effect on 360-degree attitudes (Funderburg & Levy, 1997). A survey of employees found that upward appraisals produced more favorable outcomes and fewer negative ones than peer appraisals (Bettenhausen & Fedor, 1997). To this point, the majority of empirical work on 360-degree feedback has focused on measurement properties of the ratings such as the extent of agreement among rating sources (Levy & Williams, 2004). However, Angelo DeNisi and Avi Kluger (2000) have taken an approach consistent with the theme of this chapter, focusing on the social context of appraisal, and have provided a list of recommendations to follow for implementing 360-degree feedback. This list includes (1) being honest about how the ratings will be used, (2) helping employees interpret and deal with the ratings, and (3) avoiding the presentation of too much information.

Each year it seems that more and more companies are incorporating 360-degree feedback into their performance management systems. Let's look at a couple of current examples: JP Morgan Chase and Goodyear.

JP Morgan Chase has developed a 360-degree feedback process that is used to provide information to individuals on a number of management and leadership dimensions. The brief questionnaire includes ratings and written comments on several dimensions (including technical skills, client skills, responsiveness, management, decision making, and so on) and additional ratings on 12 to 25 leadership behaviors, depending on one's level in the organization. Feedback is used for two purposes: performance appraisal and employee development. First, using the company's intranet, individual employees nominate raters (themselves, up to 3 managers, up to 10 peers, and up to 10 direct reports or subordinates). Second, managers review and edit the ratee's list of potential raters to establish a quality check on who rates each individual. Third, raters complete the 360-degree questionnaires—again, using the intranet. All results are analyzed by a third-party consultant (JP Morgan Chase hires an outside firm to do this, keeping the process more objective), and feedback reports are sent to managers and employees simultaneously. These are discussed during the final performance appraisal interview. This is a typical approach to 360-degree feedback, used by thousands of companies nationwide.

PRACTITIONER FORUM

ALLAN H. CHURCH

Ph.D., 1994, Organizational Psychology, Columbia University
Vice President, Organization and Management Development at PepsiCo, Inc; prior to this, an external Organization Development Consultant

For several years our management consulting group was involved in a major leadership assessment and development process for a global pharmaceuticals organization. Fierce competition in the pharmaceuticals industry had caused this organization to reevaluate its competitive standing relative to other drug companies in the marketplace. In an effort to establish its momentum, the organization initiated an organizational change effort that included the introduction of a new performance management and development system. As part of this process, we helped develop a core set of leadership and management behaviors that were tied to the four core strategic objectives of the organization.

These behaviors were then used to assess and develop the company's entire management and executive population over a multiyear period. They became the underlying basis for both (1) the formal performance appraisal system, which was used for personnel decision making such as promotions, terminations, and new assignments, and (2) a developmental 360-degree feedback system, which was used to help improve leader and manager skills. Our organization was primarily involved in the developmental feedback portion of the process. As part of the assessment, data were collected from each executive, as well as from his or her subordinates, peers, and supervisor. Score averages were then delivered by I/O psychologists and counselors to each executive in a personal and individualized coaching setting. The role of the psychologist/coach was to help executives to accept their positive and negative ratings and to make specific targeted plans for their improvement. This is one of the key differences between training in I/O psychology and training in other, related disciplines such as business. Specifically, I/O psychologists are interested in the social-psychological and interpersonal relationship aspects of leadership and management.

After several years of work, the development assessment program and the appraisal system became fully institutionalized into this organization's system. Although by assessment standards the organization change effort has been very successful, only time will tell whether the organization's culture and performance in the marketplace will shift as well. This will be the true indicator of success.

APPLYING YOUR KNOWLEDGE

1. Given the increase in global competition, what important role can performance management play in companies that want to be successful?
2. What does the approach taken here suggest about the relationship between performance appraisal and coaching/development?
3. In what ways are I/O psychologists trained to do coaching/development?

Goodyear employs a 360-degree feedback system that consists of four main tools: (1) a 360-Degree Development Questionnaire, which is administered to multiple rating sources and measures 13 skill dimensions, such as leadership and business acumen; (2) a 360-Degree Feedback Report, which provides the results of the ratings from the various sources, as well as some summary information about ratees' strengths and weaknesses; (3) a Development Workbook, which helps employees work with and understand the Feedback Report; and (4) a Development

TABLE 5.2 How to Conduct a Performance Appraisal Interview

Prior to the Interview	During the Interview
1. Supervisor should give employee adequate notice about meeting date. 2. Employee should do a self-appraisal. 3. Supervisor should receive copy of self-appraisal. 4. Supervisor should review documentation of performance.	1. Supervisor should explain the purpose of interview. 2. Employee should summarize accomplishments and needs with respect to major responsibilities. 3. Supervisor should do same summary as above, but from his or her viewpoint. 4. Supervisor and employee should discuss whether developmental need exists with respect to each major responsibility. 5. Supervisor and employee should diagnose the causes of any discrepancy or

Guide, which provides suggested readings and activities to improve skills in the targeted areas (see "Practitioner Forum").

What does the future hold for 360-degree feedback? The frequency with which it's used in organizations suggests that it will continue to play an important role. Recent research endeavors suggest that the following important issues will continue to attract attention: construct validity of ratings (Atkins & Wood, 2002; Scullen, Mount, & Judge, 2003), determinants of multisource ratings such as rating purpose (Greguras, Robie, Schleicher, & Goff, 2003), as well as liking and personality (Bates, 2002; Warr & Hoare, 2002), and the effect of multisource ratings on employee attitudes and development (Bailey & Fletcher, 2002; Maurer, Barbeite, & Mitchell, 2002). As I said earlier, the research is finally catching up with the practice of 360-degree feedback.

Participation. One contextual process variable that has received a great deal of attention in the performance appraisal literature is employee participation (e.g., Dipboye & dePontbriand, 1981; Giles & Mossholder, 1990; Korsgaard & Roberson, 1995). Overall, this research suggests an association between allowing employees to participate in the appraisal process and positive employee reactions toward the appraisal system (Cawley et al., 1998). Specifically, as demonstrated by a recent meta-analysis (remember from Chapter 2 that a meta-analysis is a quantitative review of research findings), there is a strong positive relationship between participation and a host of performance appraisal reactions including (1) satisfaction with the appraisal system and session, (2) motivation to improve as a result

	After the Interview
"gap" between objectives and actual performance. 6. Supervisor and employee should develop action plans to enhance performance on each major responsibility. 7. Supervisor and employee summarize performance on each major responsibility and review agreed-upon action plans. 8. Supervisor should compliment employee on accomplishments. 9. Supervisor should set time and date for future meetings to discuss responsibilities and performance.	1. Supervisor and employee should independently review major responsibilities and objectives. 2. Supervisor and employee should schedule additional meetings to set objectives for the next review period. 3. Supervisor and employee should agree on the organizational link between achieving objectives and receiving organizational rewards (compensation, promotions, etc.). 4. Communication channels between supervisor and employee should remain open throughout the review period.

of the appraisal, (3) fairness of the appraisal, and (4) usefulness of the appraisal (Cawley et al., 1998). In short, when employees are allowed to participate in the appraisal process—by completing a self-assessment or expressing their ideas during the appraisal session or interview—they react more positively to the appraisal than when they are not given the opportunity to participate. Here, too, the important implication is that organizations and supervisors have interventions available to them that can improve the quality of the appraisal process—in this case, by giving employees a voice in the process.

Table 5.2 presents the steps to be followed during a performance appraisal interview. Compiled from various sources (primarily Silverman, 1991), these steps make it very clear that the performance appraisal interview should be a participative process that includes substantial input from the employee. This observation is consistent with findings regarding the importance of participation in the performance appraisal process (Cawley et al., 1998), as well as with the recent change in management style and structure from autocratic to humanistic that has become pervasive in organizations (Meyer, 1991).

Knowledge of the Appraisal System. In 1992, Jane Williams and I introduced a construct called *Perceived System Knowledge (PSK)*. The implication of this construct is that employees' understanding of the performance appraisal system is an important contextual variable in the appraisal process. In particular, we have demonstrated that when employees perceive that they understand the appraisal system and its objectives, their own ratings of their performance tend to agree with their supervisors' ratings of their performance. In other words, the leniency commonly found in self-ratings (indeed, it's typical for individuals to rate themselves more favorably than their supervisors do) is significantly reduced when employees understand the appraisal system. In the years since this first study was conducted, my colleagues and I have further demonstrated that managers report higher levels of PSK than do nonmanagers (Williams & Levy, 1995), that PSK is positively related to job attitudes (Levy & Williams, 1998), and that PSK is positively related to appraisal reactions (Levy & Steelman, 1994). This construct is related to the notion of participation and is thus consistent with the move away from the traditional "supervisor calls the shots" approach to performance appraisal. The idea here is that when employees are provided with information about the system, they not only understand the appraisal system better but also feel as though they are an integral part of that system: It becomes *their* appraisal system, not just something handed down to them without explanation by management.

Just as early work in performance appraisal helped researchers and practitioners to better understand the cognitive complexities of the rating process, current research in this area is focused on expanding our knowledge regarding contextual variables and their significant role in the appraisal process—a focus that will continue in the future.

Legal Issues in Performance Appraisal

It is illegal in the United States to discriminate in performance appraisals on the basis of non-performance-related factors such as age, gender, race, ethnicity, religion, and disability. In short, no employee can be promoted, demoted, fired, transferred, or laid off on the basis of any of these factors.

In their article on legal requirements and technical guidelines related to performance appraisal, Jim Austin, Pete Villanova, and Hugh Hindman (1995) make the following recommendations for performance appraisal. First (as I have suggested many times throughout this text), start with a job analysis. Austin and his colleagues especially recommend developing criteria from a documented job analysis. Second, communicate performance standards to employees in writing. Third, instead of relying on just an overall rating of performance, recognize that

Reductions in force or layoffs are a serious business, and humor as a part of this process is not likely to work very well.

there are separate dimensions of performance that should be evaluated on an individual basis. Fourth, use both objective criteria and subjective judgments where possible and ensure that the subjective judgments evaluate job-related behaviors rather than global personality traits. Fifth, give employees access to an appeal mechanism. Sixth, use multiple raters rather than one rater with absolute authority. Seventh, document everything pertinent to personnel decisions. This recommendation can't be emphasized enough, as one never knows who is likely to bring suit and on what basis. The courts have been clear in such cases: If there is no documentation to support the personnel decision in question, the defendant (i.e., the organization that is being sued for discrimination) is likely to lose the case. Finally, where possible, train the raters—and if training is not possible, provide them with written instructions for conducting the performance appraisal.

In an extensive review of court decisions between 1980 and 1995, Jon Werner and Mark Bolino (1997) uncovered more than 300 Court of Appeals decisions related to performance appraisal. Of these, 109 were related to age discrimination, 102 to race discrimination, and 50 to sex discrimination. Werner and Bolino attempted to determine what factors were most closely associated with judgments made for or against the plaintiffs (i.e., the employees bringing suit against the company). What they concluded was that, in general, the practical recommendations provided in the literature (e.g., Austin et al., 1995; Barrett & Kernan, 1988; Malos, 1998) seemed consistent with the ways in which the courts make these judgments. For instance, judgment was more likely to be made for the defendant when (1) a job analysis was used, (2) written instructions regarding the appraisal process were provided, (3) employees were provided with an opportunity to review their appraisals, (4) multiple raters agreed on performance ratings, and (5) rater training was used. In addition, these researchers found that rating format (e.g., BARS versus graphic rating scales) didn't seem to matter, as this topic never came up in the judges' written decisions. On the other hand, the court's view of the fairness of the appraisal process was extremely important.

These findings regarding the importance of fairness in court judgments are consistent with the work of Rob Folger, Mary Konovsky, and Russell Cropanzano (1992), who have presented a framework that emphasizes the social context of performance appraisal discussed earlier (e.g., Murphy & Cleveland, 1995), but with a particular emphasis on justice. In particular, they argue that because performance appraisal was developed within the tradition of industrial psychology, in which testing and measurement have always been the focus, performance appraisals have previously been viewed as tests with an emphasis on rating accuracy, rating formats, and rating errors. Folger and his colleagues refer to this as the *test metaphor* view of performance appraisal. What they recommend, however, is the *due process metaphor* view of performance appraisal, in which the emphasis is on (1) adequate notice, (2) a fair hearing, and (3) judgments based on evidence. Each of these three components of due process—a familiar term in the legal arena—is built around perceptions of justice. In short, courts value the presence of justice in appraisal systems—an observation that supports continued research on contextual variables of this type.

SUMMARY

Performance appraisals are used to make personnel decisions, to provide employees with important job-related feedback, and to document employee performance as a way of protecting the organization from potential legal suits. Industrial/organizational psychologists often play an active and important role in the performance management systems of organizations.

Performance appraisals are available in many formats, including graphic rating scales, BARS, checklists, and employee comparison procedures. Each format has advantages and disadvantages (see Table 5.1); none has clearly been identified as the single best approach. The process of appraising an individual's performance is very complex and can result in rating errors such as halo, leniency, central tendency, and severity. Two types of rater training, Rater Error Training (RET) and Frame of Reference (FOR) Training, have been established as potentially useful in reducing these errors and/or improving accuracy.

Contemporary performance appraisal research continues to focus on the social-psychological context in which the appraisal takes place. This research indicates that ratee and rater reactions toward the appraisal process are important in measuring the success of an appraisal system. Also relevant to the appraisal process are the relationship between the supervisor and subordinate, the political climate within the organization, and the degree of trust among raters.

Participation is another integral element in the appraisal process. One interesting development in this area is the 360-degree feedback system, in which employees receive performance feedback from peers, subordinates, supervisors, and clients/customers. Self-ratings are commonly included in this system, especially when the only other participant is the supervisor. Although 360-degree feedback is relatively new, early research results indicate not only that many employees like it but also that it has a great deal of potential for improving the feedback process in general.

Adherence to legal guidelines is also critical to the performance appraisal process. Recent work has identified fairness as important not only to ratees but also to the courts, which appear to weight it quite heavily in making judgments for or against plaintiffs.

As we have seen, performance appraisal has widespread implications for organizations because appraisal information is used for such important personnel decisions as promotions, demotions, layoffs, dismissals, and raises. Obviously, invalid performance appraisal information is likely to result in poor organizational decisions. Our understanding of the appraisal process is thus enhanced by our appreciation of the context in which it takes place.

REVIEW QUESTIONS

1. What are the major purposes of performance appraisal?
2. How would you distinguish among graphic rating scales, BARS, and checklists?
3. In what ways do employee comparison procedures differ from other rating formats?
4. Why is performance appraisal so cognitively complex?
5. What are distributional errors? Describe the various types.
6. Describe the two major types of rater training, and discuss their differences.
7. Why are *reaction criteria* important in the study of performance appraisal?
8. List and describe three contextual variables that can play a role in performance appraisal.
9. What is 360-degree feedback, and why are so many companies implementing this approach to performance appraisal?
10. Describe some of the guidelines you would follow to ensure that the appraisal system you developed for your company would meet legal scrutiny.

SUGGESTED READINGS

Farr, J. L., & Levy, P. E. (in press). Performance appraisal. In L. L. Koppes (Ed.), *The science and practice of industrial-organizational psychology: The first hundred years.* Mahwah, NJ: Erlbaum. A review of the historical development of performance appraisal methods and approaches since the beginning of the 20th century.

Hedge, J. W., & Borman, W. C. (1995). Changing conceptions and practices in performance appraisal. In A. Howard (Ed.), *The changing nature of work,* pp. 451–481. San Francisco: Jossey-Bass. The authors of this student-friendly chapter discuss changes in the workplace and their implications for I/O psychology. They also suggest ways to keep up with these changes.

Levy, P. E. & Williams, J. R. (2004). The social context of performance appraisal. *Journal of Management (Annual Review Issue, 2004), 30(6)* 881–905. A comprehensive review of the performance appraisal research since 1995 with particular emphasis on the social context of performance appraisal.

Malos, S. B. (1998). Current legal issues in performance appraisal. In J. W. Smither (Ed.), *Performance appraisal: State of the art in practice,* pp. 49–94. San Francisco: Jossey-Bass. This readable and current review of the legal issues involved in performance appraisal is a great place to start for students interested in personnel law.

Predictors

6

CHAPTER OUTLINE

Up to this point we have talked about the importance of job analysis in setting the stage for all else that follows. In addition, we have spent a great deal of time talking about criteria and their many uses in I/O psychology. Performance appraisal was the first of those major uses; the validation of our selection processes, which will be the focus of this chapter and the next one, is the second. Certainly, criteria are central to organizations and I/O psychology, but in a selection context we typically don't have access to criteria and instead must use predictors as proxies or substitutes for criteria.

Think about a large law firm that is in the market to hire a new associate right out of law school. Ideally, the firm would like to have some criterion data on the potential applicants before making a decision about which one to hire. However, criterion data (e.g., number of lawsuits won, number of cases argued in district court, billable hours logged per month, etc.) aren't available on the applicants because they haven't been employed as lawyers yet. You can see the "catch-22" in which the firm is entangled: It wants to hire the right person, the one who will do the best job; but without bringing the applicant on board and seeing how he or she will do, the firm has no criterion data with which to make a decision. This is where *predictors* come into the picture. Predictors are used in place of criteria; in fact, they are used to forecast criteria. In this situation the law firm might rely on such predictors as performance in law school, performance in mock trials, letters of recommendation from law professors, and tests of cognitive ability. Selection is all about prediction, or forecasting. Available data are used to predict who is likely to be successful on the job so that the individual in question can be hired.

As I mentioned in Chapter 4, I/O psychologists have focused more attention and resources on predictors than on criteria. I also discussed how this has slowed the development of the field, given that a thorough understanding of performance criteria is necessary to understand organizational functioning. However, predictors are also of great importance, because we place so much trust in their ability to model criteria. Just as faulty criteria can result in bad organizational decisions such as firing or promoting the wrong employee, faulty predictors can result in hiring the wrong person or not hiring the right person. Of course, we don't know that we've hired the wrong person until we've collected some criterion data. Sound complicated? Well, it is, but it's also fascinating and integral to the success of industry and our society. Let's begin our discussion of employee selection by focusing first on the world of predictors.

LEARNING OBJECTIVES

This chapter should help you understand:

- the definition of a test and how to find existing tests used for personnel selection.
- the differences between various types of tests, such as speed versus power tests, individual versus group tests, and paper-and-pencil versus performance tests.
- the importance of validity coefficients to employee selection.
- definitions, estimates of validity, and examples of the following types of predictors: cognitive ability (both general and specific) tests, psychomotor tests, personality tests, integrity tests, work samples, assessment centers, biographical information, and interviews.

CLASSIFICATION OF TESTS

test
A systematic procedure for observing behavior and describing it with the aid of numerical scales or fixed categories.

A **test** is a systematic procedure for observing behavior and describing it with the aid of numerical scales or fixed categories (Cronbach, 1990). A test is systematic in that it is administered in the same way across groups of people, following some sort of script or listing of procedures. In the broad area of employee selection, tests are used as predictors to forecast performance on the job or some other work-related criterion. Thus I will use the terms *predictor* and *test* interchangeably in our discussion. This discussion should be of interest to all readers, even those of you who aren't budding I/O psychologists, because at some

FIGURE 6.1 Linking job analysis to specific measures of KSAOs

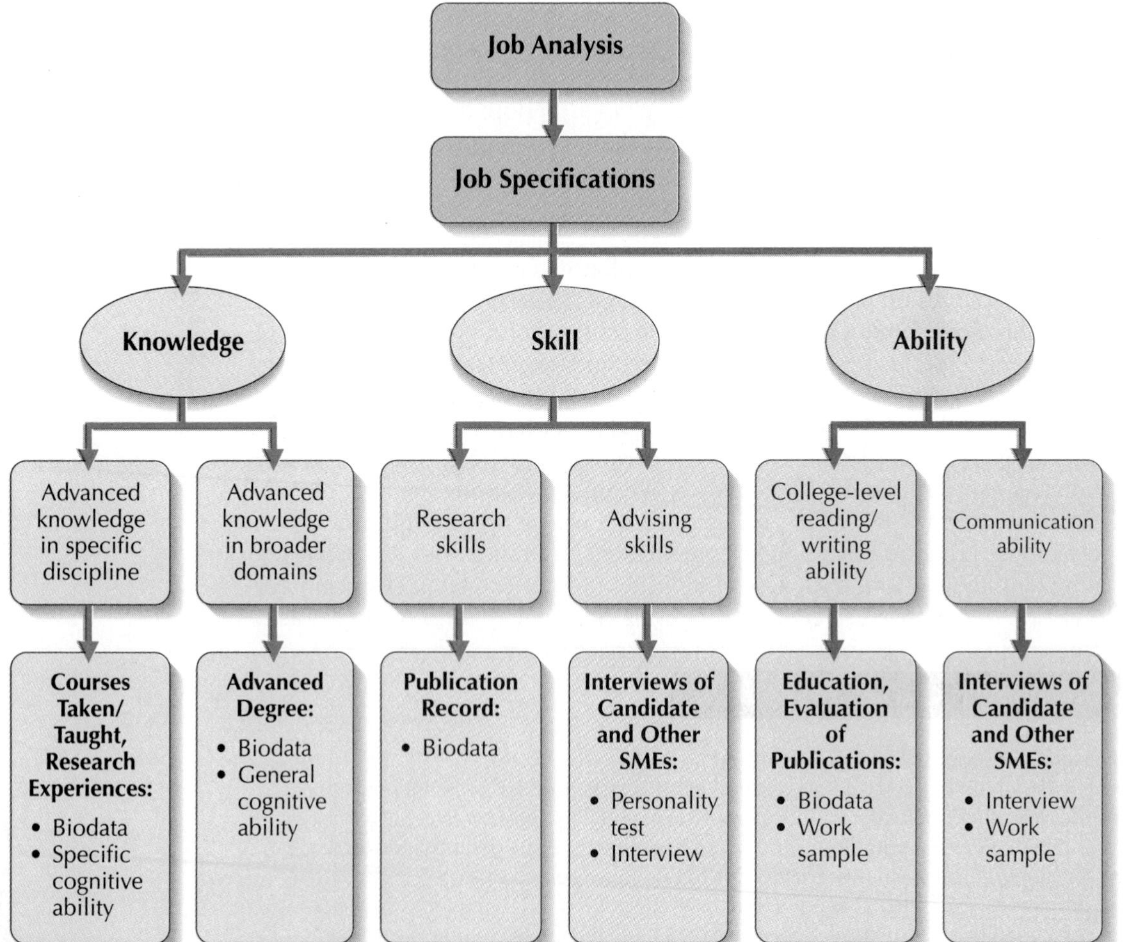

point you will need to apply (or already have applied) for a job, a scholarship, or admission to a school. In all of these situations, you probably provided the prospective employer, organization, or school with predictor information. Have you ever filled out an application blank for a summer job or taken a test that measured your ability or personality? Chances are that these predictors were used to forecast your potential criterion performance. Testing has become very popular in recent years. In fact, 1.4 million students in the class of 2003 took the SAT in that year, and 1.2 took the ACT (College Board, 2003; Cox, Matthews, & Associates, 2003). The use of tests for employee selection seems to be increasing as well. In Great Britain, almost 90% of employers surveyed used some sort of employee test for selection purposes ("Selection Test Increase," 2003). In the United States, it's estimated that companies spend 1.2 billion dollars per year on drug testing alone (Penttila, 2000) and that 80% of large companies use drug testing (Ehrenreich, 2001). Finally, personality tests are being used with great frequency, as over 2,500 tests are part of the $400 million-a-year personality-assessment industry ("Selection Tests Increase," 2003).

To select or develop predictors, we start—once again—with a *job analysis.* We use the job analysis not only to define the job but also to identify relevant criteria that are important for job success. This information, in turn, helps us to locate, develop, create, or modify predictors that we hope are valid indicators of the criteria. Sometimes we might develop our own tests to tap the KSAOs (knowledge, skills, abilities, or other characteristics) in which we are interested, whereas at other times we might find an established test and modify it or use it in its entirety to tap a particular KSAO. Figure 6.1 shows a graphical representation of how specific tests may be chosen to measure particular KSAOs that are linked directly to the job specifications stemming from the job analysis. The boxes in this figure give examples of specific data that could be used to quantify the KSAOs identified from the job analysis. In addition, an example or two of the type of predictors that might be useful for each of these specific KSAOs are provided. There are some established sources available in which thousands of existing tests are described. Perhaps the best example of these sources is the *Mental Measurements Yearbook* (Mitchell, 1998), which has been published annually for over 50 years and provides evaluations of tests in a variety of areas. These evaluations include the psychometric properties, cost, and administration time of the tests, as well as information on how to obtain them.

Tests fall into different categories based on their various dimensions. Several of these categories are described in the following sections.

Speed Versus Power Tests

A **speed test** is a test composed of easy items with a short time limit in which individuals are told to do as many as they can in a given time period. One example would be a typing test for a word-processing job. Applicants are instructed to type as much of a writing sample as they can in five minutes, and they are scored

speed test
A test containing relatively easy items in which individuals are told to complete as many as they can in a given time period.

on the basis of how much they finished and the number of errors they made. A **power test,** by contrast, has no fixed time limits and tends to be more difficult. Test takers are expected to be able to complete all the items on a power test, but not on a speed test. Most college exams are power tests; although the items are somewhat difficult, students are given what is believed to be enough time to complete them all. In our typing example, however, test takers are not expected to have time to type the entire written sample in the five minutes allotted.

power test
A test with no fixed time limits and relatively difficult items.

Individual Versus Group Tests

Individual tests are administered to one person at a time and, thus, are very costly in terms of time and money. Though often used for upper-level managerial positions, these tests tend to be avoided at lower levels because of the costs involved. Intelligence tests such as those developed by Wechsler (WAIS-III and WISC-III) are good examples of individually administered tests in which an examiner assesses one individual at a time. (For more information on these tests, see Kaufman, 1994; Kaufman & Lichtenberger, 1999.) Individual tests may take as much as two or three hours to complete and often have to be administered and scored by someone trained specifically on the test in question. More frequently used in organizations are **group tests,** on which many applicants can be tested at one time. These tests are more conducive to employee selection and thus more cost effective—especially in situations in which a company may have 50 or more applicants who need to be assessed for a few job openings.

individual tests
Tests that are administered to one person at a time.

group tests
Tests on which many applicants can be tested at one time.

Paper-and-Pencil Versus Performance Tests

Paper-and-pencil tests are the ones we've all most commonly experienced. In such tests, we respond to questions in a test booklet or by marking computer sheets to be scanned. These questions can take several different forms, including essay, multiple choice, true-false, and short answer. Most cognitive ability tests are of this type. Both the ACT and the SAT are paper-and-pencil tests; so are most of your course examinations. **Performance tests,** on the other hand, require the manipulation of an object or a piece of equipment. These include tests of manual dexterity or psychomotor skills, which we will talk about later in this chapter. Most of us would insist that our surgeons have a certain degree of manual dexterity with the instruments necessary for their surgical specialty. This skill could not be evaluated with a paper-and-pencil test but, instead, would require some sort of performance test. (Does the children's game *Operation* ring a bell?) Similarly, manufacturing jobs and trades such as plumbing and electrical work often require manipulation of objects or pieces of equipment.

paper-and-pencil tests
Frequently used tests in which individuals respond to questions in a test booklet or mark answers on computer sheets to be scanned.

performance tests
Tests that require the manipulation of an object or a piece of equipment.

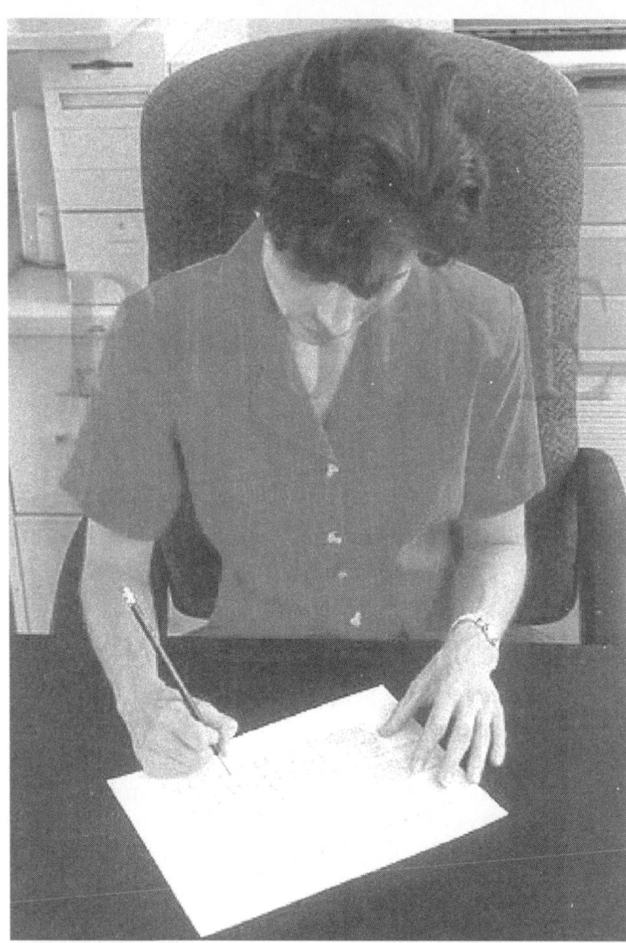

Paper-and-pencil tests and performance tests are often used to assess job applicants' skills and abilities.

TYPES OF PREDICTORS

Many kinds of tests are used for selection purposes, and we will discuss several of these in the following sections; but first let's revisit a couple of concepts. Recall our lengthy discussion of reliability and validity in Chapter 2 and our application of these concepts to *criteria* in Chapter 4. Indeed, reliability and validity are just as important for the predictors that we will discuss here. An unreliable predictor will not be successful in predicting job performance. Imagine a situation in which you are trying to select automobile mechanics by giving them printouts from a diagnostic machine and asking them to use this information to diagnose the car's problem. This makes sense: Diagnostic skills are important (i.e., they are KSAOs) for mechanics and thus ought to be used to predict on-the-job performance. However, suppose that we don't realize that the diagnostic machine is not working properly in about half of the trials. An applicant may appear to make the wrong diagnosis about half the time, thus scoring low on this predictor. In other words, her misdiagnoses may be a result of the diagnostic machine's errors rather than her own errors. In this situation, our predictor score would be unreliable (due to a measurement problem caused by the faulty diagnostic machine) and thus not very useful for predicting performance.

When we talk about the validity of a predictor we are usually thinking in terms of *criterion-related validity,* which was discussed in Chapter 2. Keep in mind that the sole purpose of predictors in I/O psychology is to predict some performance criterion. And because we don't have access to performance criteria prior to hiring employees, we use predictors as proxies for the criteria—and it is here that criterion-related validity takes on great importance. If a predictor is not related to a criterion, then the predictor serves little purpose. To avoid this problem, I/O psychologists spend a great deal of effort finding, developing, and validating predictors. In this way, organizations can be confident that selecting applicants based on predictor scores will result in the selection of those with the greatest potential to be successful on-the-job performers.

validity coefficient
A correlation that serves as an index of the relationship between a predictor and a criterion, used by selection researchers and practitioners as evidence that a particular test is a valid predictor of a performance criterion.

Recall from Chapter 2 that the *correlation* between two variables provides an index of the relationship between those two variables. This correlation is important to selection because it can be used for prediction, which is often the major goal of any selection or testing initiative. In fact, in the context of selection, it has a special name—**validity coefficient (*r*).** As an index of the relationship between a predictor and a criterion, it is used by selection researchers and practitioners as evidence that a particular test is a good predictor of job performance. In Chapter 2 we also discussed the *coefficient of determination,* which is the square of the correlation coefficient (r^2). The coefficient of determination can be thought of as the percentage of variance in the criterion variable that is accounted for by the predictor variable. It reflects how well one variable predicts the other. For example, we could use a measure of general cognitive ability to predict job performance, calculate the validity coefficient, and square that coefficient to estimate the amount of variance in a group of applicants' criterion scores that can be accounted for by this group's cognitive ability scores. In other words, we could determine how well measures of general cognitive ability predict individuals' performance on the job, as summarized by the validity coefficient. Let's take a closer look at predictors in the context of cognitive ability.

Cognitive Ability

Tests of *cognitive ability* are among the most frequently used predictors in selection contexts (e.g., employee selection, college admissions) because of the common belief that mental functioning or intelligence is important for most jobs, as well as for success in school. There are two classes of cognitive ability tests, or what are sometimes called intelligence tests. The first are general cognitive ability tests and the second are specific cognitive ability tests.

General Cognitive Ability Tests. If you think back to the history of I/O psychology (see Chapter 1), you'll recall that measures of cognitive ability are linked with two of the most important early periods in the history of I/O psychology—World War I and World War II. Early applied psychologists such as Walter Dill Scott and Robert Yerkes worked for the government as specialists in the selection and placement of military personnel, using newly developed tests of general cognitive ability—*Army Alpha* and *Army Beta* tests. Measures of general cognitive ability have continued to gain favor in the world of employee selection (Borman, Hanson, & Hedge, 1997); among these, the *Wonderlic Personnel Test* (Wonderlic, 1984) has been one of the most frequently used for many years. Figure 6.2 presents a few examples of items similar to those found on the Wonderlic test (as well as other tests of general cognitive ability). A debate over the importance of general cognitive ability in employee selection contexts continues to rage (Goldstein, Zedeck, & Goldstein, 2002; Murphy, 2002).

There's a fair amount of evidence suggesting that general cognitive ability accounts for a large proportion of variance in criterion performance (Ree, Earles, & Teachout, 1994; Salgado & Anderson, 2003). For instance, a meta-analysis of various studies in this area indicates that the validity coefficient for measures of general cognitive ability is .53 (Hunter & Hunter, 1984). This means that over 25% of the performance variance of people (i.e., the differences in performance across people) is accounted for or can be predicted by measures of general cognitive ability. Clearly, general cognitive ability is a valuable predictor of performance, which is why so many of us have taken some type of test measuring general intelligence for school or work. Notice, however, that if 25% of the criterion variance is accounted for by this measure, 75% is left unaccounted for. Is it reasonable to ask if we can do better? This question has been discussed for years, and researchers are continually working to determine what other predictors might help

FIGURE 6.2 Items Similar to Those Found on the Wonderlic Personnel Test

1. Focused is the opposite of:

a. *scattered* b. concerned c. helpful d. gracious

2. Automobile is to road as boat is to:

a. air b. tracks *c. water* d. gasoline

3. Which of the following months has 31 days?

a. September b. April c. June *d. December*

4. Which number completes the series: 2, 4, 8, 4, 8, 16, 8,

a. 16 b. 12 c. 8 d. 20

5. If Bill runs 3 miles in 30 minutes how many miles will he run in 1 1/2 hours?

a. 12 b. 6 *c. 9* d. 8

**This figure regarding the Test of Mechanical Concepts has been reproduced with the permission of NCS Pearson, Inc.*

account for a greater percentage of the criterion variance, or what is called *incremental validity* (Borman & Motowidlo, 1997; Cortina, Goldstein, Payne, Davison, & Gilliland, 2000; Mount, Witt, & Barrick, 2000; Schmidt & Hunter, 1998).

mechanical ability
A specific cognitive ability involving a focus on mechanical relations, recognition of tools used for various purposes, and sometimes actual mechanical skills.

Specific Cognitive Ability Tests. Whereas general cognitive ability tests attempt to predict the likelihood that an individual will perform well in a particular job by measuring the individual's *general* capacity to learn, tests of specific cognitive abilities attempt to predict the likelihood that an individual will do well in a particular job given his or her *specific* abilities. For instance, tests of **mechanical ability** tap comprehension of mechanical relations, recognition of tools used for various purposes, and sometimes actual mechanical skills. The Bennett Mechanical Comprehension Test (The Psychological Corporation, 1980) is probably the best known of this type. Sample items from the SRA Test of Mechanical Concepts, another popular test, are presented in Figure 6.3. (SRA stands for "Science Research Associates.") A test of mechanical ability would be relevant for such jobs as machine operator, factory worker, and engineer, in which mechanical principles are important. Glance back at the framework of industrial psychology presented in Figure 3.1, and you'll see that two of the three major outcomes of job analysis—job description and job specifications—should tell us whether or not

FIGURE 6.3 Sample Items from the SRA Test of Mechanical Concepts

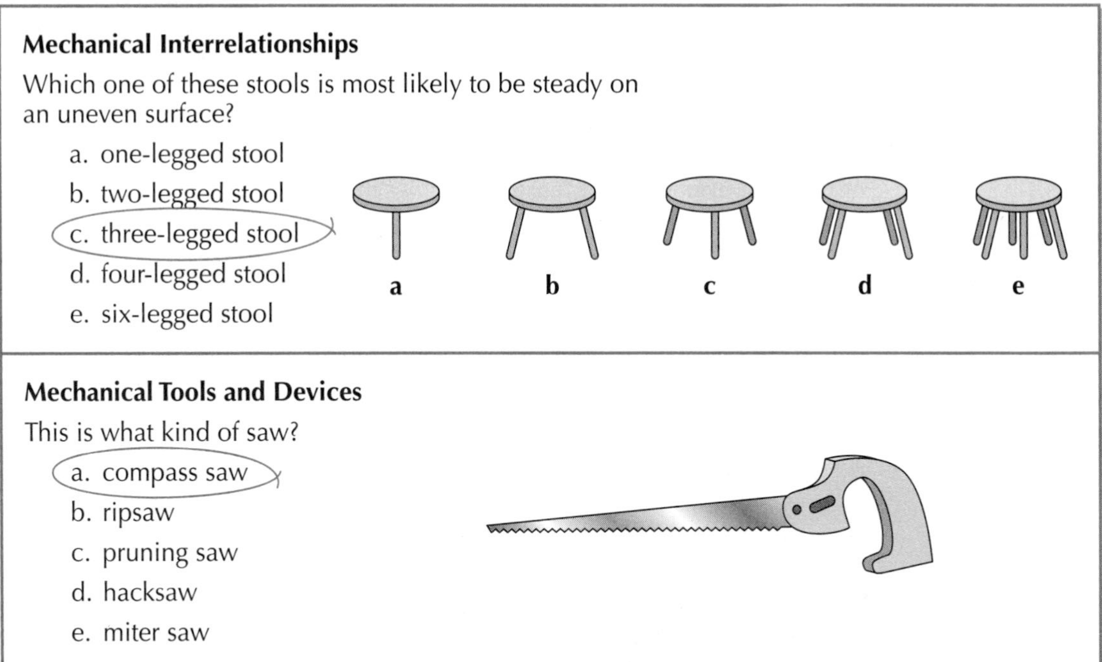

mechanical ability is important for the particular job of interest. Indeed, if we are doing our job analysis properly, we should conclude that mechanical ability is important in selecting machine operators but not relevant for hiring college faculty members.

Mechanical Interrelationships
Which one of these stools is most likely to be steady on an uneven surface?
a. one-legged stool
b. two-legged stool
c. three-legged stool
d. four-legged stool
e. six-legged stool
a
b
c
d
e
Mechanical Tools and Devices
This is what kind of saw?
a. compass saw
b. ripsaw
c. pruning saw
d. hacksaw
e. miter saw

Closely related to mechanical ability is **spatial ability,** a second specific cognitive ability that plays an important role in many jobs. Measures of spatial ability often deal with geometric relations, such as visualizing objects and rotating them spatially to form a particular pattern. Jobs for which these types of tests might be relevant include mechanic and architect. A third specific cognitive ability, **clerical ability,** is relevant for numerous important positions such as secretary, administrative assistant, bookkeeper, and clerk. Most measures of clerical ability focus on both perceptual speed and accuracy in processing verbal and numerical data (Gatewood & Feild, 2001). The most frequently used test is probably the Minnesota Clerical Test, which was developed in 1933 (The Psychological Corporation, 1979). This test comprises 200 items, each of which consists of a pair of numbers or names; the respondent is asked to place a check next to the pairs that are identical. Items similar to those found on the Minnesota Clerical Test are presented in Figure 6.4. An individual's score is the number right minus the number wrong. This is a speed test in which respondents are not expected to get through

spatial ability
A specific cognitive ability involving a focus on geometric relations such as visualizing objects and rotating them spatially to form a particular pattern.

clerical ability
A specific cognitive ability relevant for jobs such as secretary, administrative assistant, and bookkeeper involving a focus on both perceptual speed and accuracy in processing verbal and numerical data.

the entire list of pairs in the time allotted. Performance on the names subtest has been shown to be related to speed of reading and spelling, whereas scores on the numbers subtest are related to arithmetic skills and computations (Gatewood & Feild, 2001). Thus, if you are trying to fill positions in which ability to read, spell, and do simple arithmetic are important for the job, a measure of clerical ability such as the Minnesota Clerical Test might be a reasonable predictor to use.

The validity of measures of specific cognitive abilities tends to hover around .40 to .50 (for a review of the relevant research, see Gatewood & Feild, 2001). One of the most extensive and thorough studies in the selection area in the past 20 years, the Project A study, was conducted in the military and involved over 4,000 army enlisted personnel (McHenry, Hough, Toquam, Hanson, & Ashworth, 1990). Here, the validity coefficients for general cognitive ability and spatial ability predicting core job performance were .63 and .56, respectively. It is clear that both general and specific cognitive abilities are important predictors of job performance across a wide variety of jobs. However, the same large military study also revealed that these two cognitive predictors did not predict a different criterion, incumbents' personal discipline, very well. As I emphasized in the last chapter, the match between the predictor and the criterion is important. No abilities or skills are predictive of all aspects of performance—I/O psychologists have to rely on the job analysis to identify the important KSAOs for predicting particular

FIGURE 6.4 Items Similar to Those Found on the Minnesota Clerical Test

INSTRUCTIONS: Please place an "X" on the line between each pair of items that are exactly the same. Do as many as you can in the allotted time.

Comparison of Names

Bekky Huber	________	Becky Huber
Verna MacDonald	________	Verna McDonald
Frank Giorno	________	Frank Giorno
Bel Air, Maryland	________	Belair, Maryland
Sylvia Chinn	________	Sylvia Chin

Comparison of Numbers

13574	________	13574
245693	________	245663
5193754	________	5193457
4396207	________	4396207
8730916375	________	8739016375

on-the-job behaviors. A test of spatial ability would not be predictive of my success as a teacher (and it's a good thing or I'd still be looking for work!) but would likely be very helpful in hiring engineers, architects, or cartographers.

Psychomotor Tests

Jobs such as packer, machine operator, computer assembler, and electrician require great hand, arm, and finger dexterity. Other positions, such as air traffic controller, nuclear plant operator, and fighter pilot, require excellent sensory abilities such as superior vision and hearing. Measures of sensory abilities known as **psychomotor tests** are often used in the selection of applicants for such positions. Psychomotor tests evaluate both the speed and the accuracy of motor and other sensory coordination. One of the best-known tests of psychomotor ability is the Purdue Pegboard (Mathiowetz, Rogers, Dowe-Keval, Donahoe, & Rennels, 1986), which measures an individual's ability to make controlled movements with the hands, arms, and fingertips. Test takers are placed in front of a pegboard on a table and asked to manipulate pegs, washers, and collars in and around the pegboard. Traditional vision and hearing tests are also used for selection in jobs where a certain proficiency of these senses is required. (There is a logical reason for why you don't see many baseball players wearing eyeglasses: The ability to hit a baseball requires many skills, but chief among them is excellent vision. Ted Williams, a Red Sox Hall of Famer and one of the game's greatest hitters, is often said to have had vision so acute that he could pick up the spin of the pitch a fraction of a second earlier than anyone else, resulting in more time to adjust his swing accordingly.) The Project A study mentioned previously (McHenry et al., 1990) reported a validity of .53 for a psychomotor test battery predicting core job performance across nine jobs. In addition, John Hunter and Ronda Hunter (1984) reported validities of psychomotor tests averaging about .40 across several jobs—a figure that varied according to the type of job. Combining these data, we find that psychomotor tests predict between 16% and 28% of the variance in job performance. Keep in mind that these percentages are not precise, given the diversity of the psychomotor measures, performance criteria, and jobs investigated.

psychomotor tests
Tests that measure both the speed and the accuracy of motor and other sensory coordination.

Because a psychomotor test used for the wrong job would likely result in a validity of zero, a careful job analysis is recommended here, also. For example, the Purdue Pegboard would not likely predict the success of a waitress or a telephone operator. But when used for appropriate jobs, it can be a very useful tool.

Personality Tests

Compared to many of the other predictors discussed in this chapter, **personality tests** have received a great deal of recent attention from the research community (Hurtz & Donovan, 2000; Mount et al., 2000). Even as early as the 1930s and 1940s personality tests were being used in an attempt to identify individuals who were likely to become known as assertive union members, "thugs," or "agitators"

personality tests
Tests in which numbers are systematically assigned to individuals' characteristics.

(Zickar, 2001). The word *personality* refers to an individual's traits—or predispositions to behave in a particular way across situations—and personality measurement involves procedures that systematically assign numbers to such characteristics (Hogan, Hogan, & Roberts, 1996). The most typical measures are self-report questionnaires such as the NEO Personality Inventory (for a recent review, see Piedmont, 1998), the Hogan Personality Inventory (Hogan & Hogan, 1995), and the Sixteen Personality Factory Questionnaire (Cattell, Eber, & Tatsuoka, 1970; for a review, see Schuerger, 1995). Other measures, such as the MMPI (Minnesota Multiphasic Personality Inventory), have been used in employee selection even though there has been criticism of the use of measures for employee selection that were normed on a clinical sample and developed for clinical purposes. This interesting issue has been considered by the courts in *Soroka v. Dayton Hudson* (1989), in which using the MMPI for selection was ruled a violation of privacy because of the questions about religion and sexual behaviors.

Although there are many different personality measures, personality researchers tend to agree that many of them measure five broad dimensions that make up the "Big Five" model: Openness to Experience, Conscientiousness, Extraversion, Agreeableness, and Neuroticism. (A helpful mnemonic is to note that the first letters of each dimension spell O-C-E-A-N.) Of all the personality classification schemes, this is the one used most often by practitioners and researchers alike.

Many personality researchers argue that on rational grounds it makes sense to use personality to predict performance because job analysis interviews of incumbents usually generate statements like "being a team player," "being responsive to client's needs," and "taking initiative" as reflective of excellent job performance and, indeed, of personality itself (Hogan et al., 1996). In addition, a great deal of empirical research suggests that personality measures are valid predictors of job performance (e.g., Barrick & Mount, 1991; Hough, 1998). Although it is generally difficult to estimate the size of the validity coefficient between personality and on-the-job performance, especially because so many personality dimensions have been examined in this light, one meta-analysis indexed the relationship between personality and managerial performance as .24 (Tett, Jackson, & Rothstein, 1991). Furthermore, Conscientiousness (being dependable and hard working) and Extraversion (being sociable and active) have been reported to be the best predictors of performance (Barrick & Mount, 1991). Accordingly, these two dimensions have received the most research attention.

It seems clear that personality predicts performance on the job to some degree, but some personality researchers argue that estimates such as the .24 noted above are *under*estimates given that, in most studies, specific personality dimensions are not linked to specific criteria. In particular, Leaetta Hough (1998) argues that the "Five Factor" model comprises dimensions that are "too fat," adding that prediction will be improved to the extent that specific personality dimensions are used to predict targeted performance criteria such as effort and leadership, personal discipline, and counterproductive behavior. The Project A data seem to support Hough's arguments: General cognitive ability, spatial ability, and psychomotor ability predicted core job performance, given *rs* = .63, .56, and .53, respectively, but did not predict personal discipline (the extent to which the individual follows Army regulations and demonstrates responsibility) or effort/leadership (perseverance in adverse situations and leadership toward peers) very well, given coefficients ranging from .12 to .31. On the other hand, personality dimensions such as achievement orientation and dependability predicted both personal discipline and effort/leadership better (*rs* = .33 and .32, respectively) than any of the cognitive and psychomotor tests (McHenry et al., 1990). Again, I strongly emphasize that no predictor works for all criteria and that job analysis has to allow for the appropriate match between predictor constructs such as personality dimensions and criterion constructs such as a particular element of task or contextual performance (Borman et al., 1997).

One potential problem with noncognitive selection tests such as those used to measure personality is that they are prone to being *faked.* That is, individuals can potentially guess the responses that are likely to result in high scores. For instance, most applicants would know how to answer the following question in such a way as to "look good" to the organization: "I often think of ways in which I can outsmart my supervisor—strongly agree or strongly disagree?" According to recent work in this area, faking requires two things: (1) the ability to fake and (2) the motivation to fake (Snell, Sydell, & Lueke, 1999). Yet research has also shown that some individuals, even when told to fake-good on a measure (i.e., to respond in a way that will make them look as good as possible), either can't or won't. It appears, then, that dispositional variables, as well as experience and test characteristics, affect one's ability to fake. Indeed, Andee Snell and her colleagues (1999) argue that the motivation to fake is influenced by demographic characteristics (e.g., age and gender), individual differences (e.g., integrity and manipulativeness), and perceptual variables (e.g., perceptions of others' behavior and perceptions of organizational justice). A recent study (Mueller-Hanson, Heggestad, & Thornton, 2003) demonstrated differences between predictor scores on a personality test for a control group and a group that was given a motivation to fake (i.e., they were told that their opportunity to participate in more research and win some money was tied directly to how well they scored on the test). Overall, those in the faking condition scored higher than those in the control condition on the personality test. Based on predictor scores, more of the faking participants would have been selected for employment, but they scored worse on the criterion measure than did those from the control (or honest) group who were selected. There is still much debate in the literature about the effect of faking on the validity coefficients of noncognitive tests (Rees & Metcalfe, 2003), but most experts agree that faking occurs frequently and has problematic potential. This is one of the hottest issues in the testing area; research over the next few years should prove both interesting in itself and beneficial to employee selection.

integrity tests
Tests used in an attempt to predict whether an employee will engage in counterproductive or dishonest work-related behaviors like cheating, stealing, or sabotage.

Integrity Tests

Among the newest tests used in employee selection are **integrity tests** (also called *honesty tests*), which attempt to predict whether an employee will engage in counterproductive or dishonest work-related behaviors such as cheating, stealing, or sabotage. Since 1988, when the passage of the Employee Polygraph Protection Act prohibited the use of polygraphs for most private-sector jobs, integrity testing has taken on a much more important role in selection (Cascio, 1998). There are two types of integrity tests. One type is the *overt integrity test,* which attempts to measure both attitudes toward theft and self-reports or admissions of actual theft behaviors. Overt integrity tests might ask respondents to report how often they have stolen from previous employers, whether they believe that lying is okay if one doesn't get caught, and the extent to which they perceive theft to be easy. The second type of integrity test is the *personality-type integrity test,* which measures personality characteristics believed to predict counterproductive behaviors (e.g., risk taking, emotional instability, dishonesty, and irresponsibility). The purpose of these tests is more hidden from respondents than that of overt tests. Interestingly, a recent investigation found that test takers perceived overt integrity tests to have greater face validity (i.e., they appear more believable and useful) and predictive validity than personality-type integrity tests (Whitney, Diaz, Mineghino, & Powers, 1999).

Researchers have found clear empirical support for the use of integrity tests. For instance, when Judy Collins and Frank Schmidt (1993) administered a personality-based integrity test to more than 300 prisoners who were convicted of white-collar crime (stealing, bribery, extortion, etc.) and to more than 300 white-collar workers in positions of authority in the working world, they found that these groups scored very differently on the integrity test. The authors conceptualized the differences as being reflective of "social conscientiousness"—or a lack of it—such that the prisoners exhibited greater tendencies toward irresponsibility and disregard for rules and social norms than did the working managers. The most extensive review of integrity tests to date is a meta-analysis that reported validity coefficients of .47 and .34 for integrity tests that predict counterproductive behavior and job performance, respectively (Ones, Viswesvaran, & Schmidt, 1993). Moreover, as Paul Spector and James Wanek (1996) noted in a more recent review, the finding that integrity testing appears to be valid for predicting both counterproductive behavior and traditional task performance suggests a very important role for this type of predictor. There is still much we don't know about integrity testing, but with the accumulation of data over the past 20 years, it's become clear that integrity tests have much to offer organizations that are concerned about the role played by potential employees whose tendencies may include theft and other counterproductive behaviors. Note that the previous discussion of faking on personality tests is relevant here as well, inasmuch as some integrity tests appear to be fakable (Alliger & Dwight, 2000).

Work Samples

Thus far we have talked about identifying various types of measures that are intended to predict a performance criterion. Notice, however, that none of these predictor measures look much like the criterion measures. In other words, although a cognitive ability test, a vision test, and a personality test may be useful predictors for the position of police officer, none of these tests actually measure on-the-job behaviors; rather, they are used as proxies or replacements for criteria because we don't have access to criteria at this stage in the selection process. With **work sample tests,** we take a very different approach: Instead of measuring constructs that we hope will predict our performance criterion, we try to duplicate the performance criterion measures and use them as predictors. Work samples are thus miniature replicas of the job. To develop them, we create smaller standardized tests that measure the actual job performance criteria identified by the job analysis. As an example, recall that you had to physically get behind the wheel of a car and drive it around before you could get your license. The Motor Vehicle Administration test you took was your work sample—and what better way could there be to determine whether people are deserving of the privilege of a driver's license than actually evaluating them driving? This is the rationale for the use of work sample tests.

work sample tests
Tests that attempt to duplicate performance criteria measures and use them as predictors, thus forming miniature replicas of the job.

Let's turn to the world of work. In addition to using measures of personality, general cognitive ability, and specific clerical ability, we may find it useful to develop a work sample test for hiring administrative assistants. In fact, this type of test is typically included in a selection battery for the administrative assistant position. A work sample of typing is one of the best ways to determine whether someone can type accurately and quickly. Similarly, we could present applicants with descriptions of a thorny issue that they might run into while working with, say, the spreadsheet software used on the job. This would provide an opportunity for us to see how individual applicants are likely to handle on-the-job crises.

In most academic departments, potential new faculty members are required to present to faculty and students a research study that they have conducted. This approach serves two purposes. First, it provides an opportunity for the department to evaluate the applicant's research after hearing him or her present it for an hour or so. Second, it provides a work sample in the sense that the applicant, if hired, will have to stand up before a group of students and lecture/teach about topics that are in his or her area of expertise. This small sample of behavior is our first clue as to how effective the applicant might be as a teacher in the department.

You can see how useful work samples can be in selecting individuals for various jobs. In fact, when work samples are carefully developed, they can demonstrate validities as high as the .50s. In the exhaustive meta-analysis conducted by Hunter and Hunter (1984), for example, work sample tests were identified as the most valid tests for the prediction of promotion criteria, with an overall validity coefficient of .54. This means that an individual's performance on a work sample test is a very strong indicator of whether or not this person is likely to be promoted within the company. Another meta-analysis reported a validity coefficient of .38 across a series of performance criteria (Schmitt, Gooding, Noe, & Kirsch, 1984). The results of these reviews make it clear that work sample tests are among the most valid predictors of criterion performance.

A specific type of work sample test has regained the attention of I/O psychologists in recent years—namely, *situational judgment tests.* These include

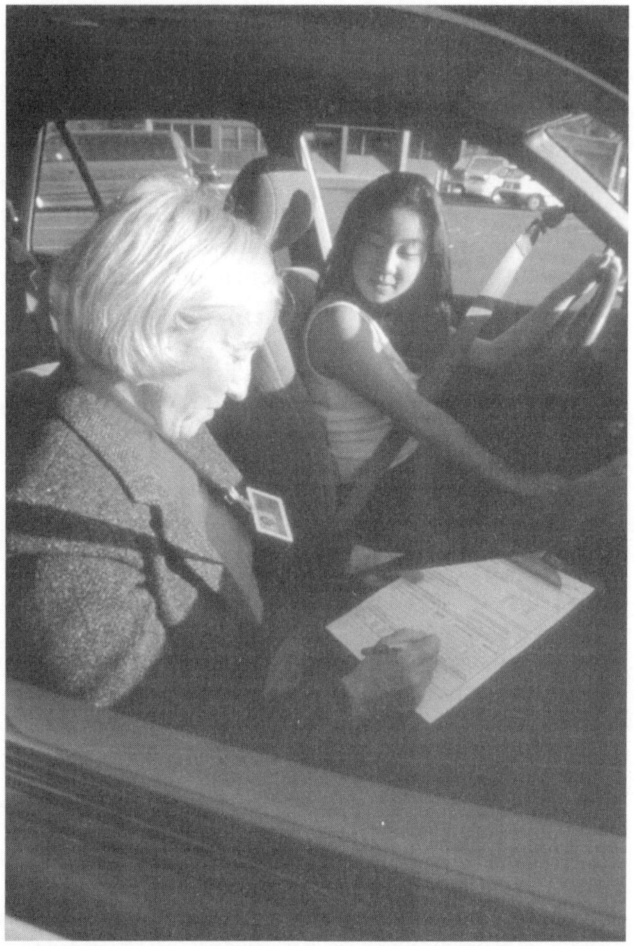

The driving test given prior to obtaining a driver's license is an example of a work sample test.

paper-and-pencil tests that measure applicants' judgment in work settings (McDaniel, Morgeson, Finnegan, Campion, & Braverman, 2001). For instance, applicants might be asked how they would handle a situation in which an employee seemed unable to understand how to solve a particular problem, and they would have to choose from the following response options: (1) Continue explaining the problem to the employee, (2) ask someone else to get involved and explain the problem to the employee, (3) discipline the employee for his or her deficiency, or (4) place the employee in a remedial training program. Typically, one of these response options would be scored as the correct answer based on subject matter expert (SME) judgments regarding the best response. Situational judgment tests have been used since the 1920s, but a renewed interest in them appears to have emerged in the past 10 to 15 years. For instance, Chan and Schmitt (2002) used 160 employees to demonstrate that scores on a situational judgment test predicted both task performance and contextual performance. Further, situational judgment tests demonstrated incremental validity over measures of personality, job experience, and cognitive ability. A recent meta-analysis that uncovered over 60 studies examined the validity of situational judgment tests and found it to be about .34 for the prediction of job performance. Further, as would be expected given the importance of job analysis, situational judgment tests that were developed on the basis of a job analysis were more valid ($r = .38$) than those that were not ($r = .29$; McDaniel et al., 2001).

Assessment Centers

The term **assessment center (AC)** refers to an approach or method in which multiple raters (called *assessors*) evaluate applicants or incumbents (called *assessees*) on a standardized set of predictors (called *exercises*). Assessment centers differ in many ways, but a typical one might have the following characteristics. Twelve to fifteen assessees are involved in the center at any given time. The assessment is done by a team of four to six assessors who do not know the assessees and are likely to be two levels above the assessees in the organizational hierarchy. Almost without exception, multiple methods of assessment are used, such as a measure of general cognitive ability, an interview, and various work sample-type exercises. The overall assessment usually lasts two to three days. The assessors receive at least a half-day of training and often stay a half-day after the assessment is complete to finalize scores and write up reports. Many large companies employ assessment centers (Arthur, Woehr, & Maldegen, 2000; Woehr & Arthur, 2003), often using their own sites, such as an HR building or a world headquarters that includes a series of rooms designed for this purpose.

assessment center (AC) An approach or method in which multiple raters (*assessors*) evaluate applicants or incumbents (*assessees*) on a standardized set of predictors (*exercises*).

As with much of the testing movement in I/O psychology, assessment centers were developed within the military. They were first created in Germany in the 1930s and later refined during World War II by the British and U.S. military departments (Gatewood & Feild, 2001). The coming of age of assessment centers is primarily associated with Doug Bray, who conducted a Management Progress Study of AT&T in 1956. (For a review of this work, see Bray, Campbell, & Grant, 1974.) This study focused on the career development of young employees as they moved up through the ranks of the company. Data were collected on these young men from 1956 through 1965, and more than 300 of them who were tested in the early years of the assessment center remained with the company through 1965. This is the most extensive study of managerial development ever conducted; it created a rich data set that still provides a wealth of information about the relationships between employees' scores on the various exercises and their career progression. The results of Bray's study are very impressive: Of the 72 men who were not promoted by the year 1965, the assessors had correctly identified 68 (i.e., 94%) as unlikely to be promoted based on their assessment center performance.

Surveys indicate that 50% or more of major companies employ assessment centers (Fletcher & Anderson, 1998; see also "Practitioner Forum"). The United

Assessment centers involve the observation of job candidates or incumbents interacting and exhibiting job-related behaviors.

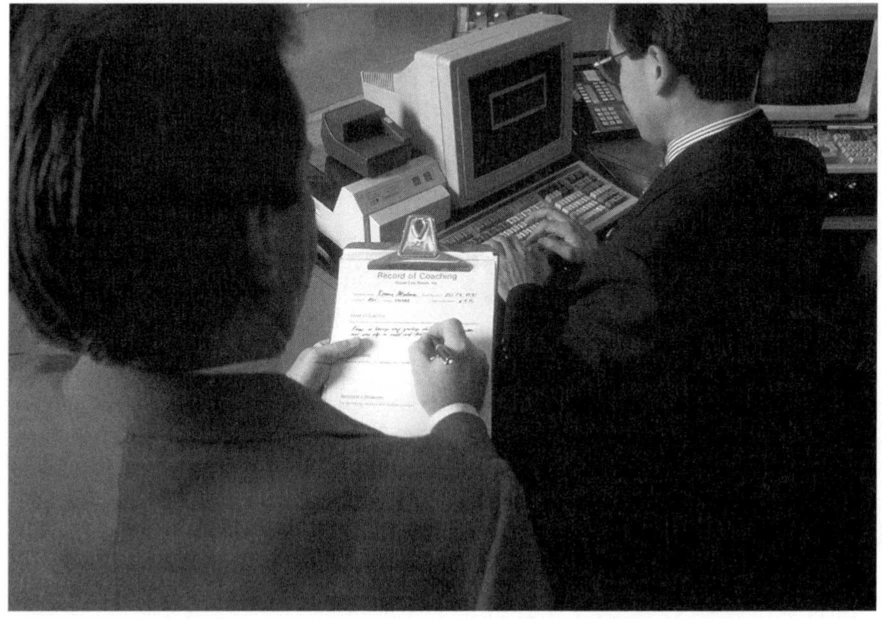

Nations uses them to select managers for their worldwide operations (Jackson & Schuler, 2000). They are also implemented throughout Europe. In the United Kingdom, for instance, a major bank uses them to identify management potential and development needs among upper-level clerical staff. In this bank, each assessment lasts one day and includes group discussion exercises, in-baskets (see below), interviews, and paper-and-pencil tests. Seven dimensions are used for the assessment (such as reasoning ability, innovativeness, decision making, and so on). Another example of the use of assessment centers is the rather extensive work being done by Novotel, a worldwide hotel chain. Novotel's "School of Life" program utilizes assessment centers to identify how managers deal with a variety of situations—a method that provides very useful information not only to Novotel executives but also to the managers themselves (Littlefield, 1995). This program has been employed at hotels in the United Kingdom, the United States, and Canada.

In addition to their widespread use in the private sector, assessment centers have been extensively employed by metropolitan fire and police departments—specifically for the selection, as well as the promotion, of firefighters and police officers into high-ranking positions such as fire chief, deputy chief, and so on. A survey of the fire departments of 75 of the largest cities in the United States and Canada revealed that almost half use assessment centers in making promotion decisions (Yeager, 1986).

As we have seen, assessment centers attempt to predict performance criteria by focusing on multiple exercises that simulate activities and situations found on the job. Obviously, an assessment center is only as effective as the exercises that make it up are valid. In general, considerable evidence suggests that well-established centers are valid predictors for many different performance criteria. The most cited review of assessment center validity reports a validity coefficient of .37 for overall assessment center validity (Gaugler, Rosenthal, Thornton, & Bentson, 1987). A more recent review found a similar overall relationship and also demonstrated that combining multiple assessment center dimensions into a composite resulted in a validity coefficient of .45 (Arthur, Day, McNelly, & Edens, 2003). It's clear that assessment centers are good tools for predicting an individual's performance on the job and exceptional tools for predicting an individual's likelihood of successfully moving up the organizational hierarchy. Of course, they can also be very expensive in terms of both the time and money involved in assessing employees in a fair and valid way.

Let's now take a closer look at two of the most often used assessment center exercises: the in-basket and the leaderless group discussion.

In-Basket. An **in-basket** is an individual exercise in which an assessee is presented with a scenario such as being newly hired to replace a manager who has had to leave the company abruptly due to a serious illness. The assessee is also provided with information such as an organizational chart and a description of the company mission, along with the kinds of things that would typically appear in a manager's in-basket, such as memos, letters, requests for information, files on grievances, and employee applications. At that point, the assessee is asked to take the one or two hours that are available to him or her prior to hopping on a flight to New York for a board of directors' meeting to review all of the in-basket materials and to respond accordingly with memos, letters, decisions, delegations, interview scheduling, and so on. When the time is up, the assessee is asked to describe (using a checklist or a narrative) all of his or her actions and to present a rationale for each.

> **in-basket**
> An individual exercise in which an assessee is asked to act as if he or she is a manager in a particular company with certain issues or ideas that need to be considered and responded to.

The idea here, of course, is to place the assessee in a set of circumstances similar to those he or she would experience as a manager and to evaluate how well he or she responds. Some refer to in-baskets as simulations or even work samples, because they mimic actual on-the-job settings. Figure 6.5 presents the background information and instructions presented to participants for an in-basket task that I have used for research purposes. Notice that the instructions have the clear purpose of asking the assessee to take actions and make decisions about how to proceed. This is typical of in-basket exercises.

> **leaderless group discussion (LGD)**
> A group exercise designed to tap managerial attributes that requires the interaction of a small group of individuals.

Leaderless Group Discussion. Whereas an in-basket is an individual exercise, a **leaderless group discussion (LGD)** is a group exercise designed to tap managerial attributes that requires the interaction of a small number of individuals

FIGURE 6.5 An In-Basket Test: The Bradford Consolidated Fund

While working on this exercise, you are to be Pat Chandler, who has just assumed the duties of General Manager for the Bradford Consolidated Fund (BCF) in Bradford, New Jersey. The BCF is a nonprofit organization devoted to charitable enterprises. The Fund is now in the middle of the 1999 annual fund-raising drive. You were recently hired to replace George McKinley, the former General Manager, who was in an automobile accident and had to resign from his position with the BCF.

Today is Sunday, March 16, 1999, the first opportunity you have had to come to Bradford. Your administrative assistant, Hazel Stein, has left you a memo along with a number of items on your desk for you to look at and work on during the afternoon. Ms. Stein has also left you a list of members of the staff connected with the 1999 fund-raising drive. You will find this on your desk along with some stationery, pencils, paper clips, etc. for your use.

The Current Situation: Your task on this Sunday afternoon is to go through the items, taking appropriate actions as necessary. Keep in mind that you may not finish everything in front of you in the allotted time and it is up to you to decide the order in which to work on the items. You are now actually on the job. Everything you decide to do must be in writing and also recorded on the *Reasons for Actions* form enclosed. Use the stationery provided for memos, letters, lists, etc. Outline plans or set agendas for meetings you may want to call. Sign papers, if necessary. Wherever possible, clip letters, memos, or notes to the items that they concern.

Behave as though you are actually on the job. Remember, it is Sunday afternoon, March 16, 1999, and you have 30 minutes in the office to get as much work done as you can.

(Gatewood & Feild, 2001). Typically, a group of five or six assessees is seated at a conference table, surrounded by assessors at the perimeter of the room who observe the interactions. The group is then presented with an issue to resolve. Sometimes each assessee is given a particular role to play, such as the director of one of the departments involved in the issue; at other times roles are not assigned. But in all cases, no one is assigned the role of leader (hence the term *leaderless*). After the

PRACTITIONER FORUM

STEVEN E. WALKER

Ph.D., 1989, I/O Psychology, Virginia Tech
Vice President, JP Morgan Chase
Leadership and Organization Development

The Credit and Rate Markets division of JP Morgan Chase is a $7 billion organization in which individuals originate, structure, sell, and trade products such as commodities, loans, bonds, and currencies—usually to institutional investors. Originators, salespersons, and traders take calculated risks to make large sums of money for the firm and, for doing so, are paid handsomely. Accordingly, these are critical jobs, and we invest a great deal of time in selecting and training such individuals prior to their placements.

As I/O psychologists we have knowledge of selection practices and validities, and this knowledge has led us to using assessment centers (ACs) as our selection tool. When we hire junior traders, salespersons, research analysts, and originators into credit and rate markets, we put all of our candidates who pass an initial screen through a one-day assessment center. The center consists of two structured interviews and three exercises: a leaderless group discussion, a sales role-play, and a simulated trading game. Candidates are "tested" in groups ranging from 10 to 16, and for every two candidates there is one trained assessor. Assessors are senior-level salespersons or traders, approximately three levels above the incoming candidates, who receive training about how to conduct ACs.

The key to the success of our assessment centers is that the exercises are mini-replicas of the job, or what are sometimes called "work samples." For instance, the trading game is viewed by the assessors as a great way of measuring trading aptitude, and candidates easily see how what they do in this game is very similar to what they would do on the job. Our exercises also serve as a realistic job preview for our candidates and are perceived as very fair.

When ACs are well done, they are very good predictors of performance. We take a lot of time (and staff!) to make sure our centers run as smoothly as possible. Clearly, one pitfall can be the training of assessors. If, for example, assessors vary in terms of believing that some KSAOs are more critical than others for making hiring decisions, they would disagree on their hiring decisions, resulting in conflict. The goal of the AC is to do everything (administer exercises, train assessors, etc.) with consistency so that only candidate performance can vary. When this goal is achieved, we make excellent hiring decisions, and the AC becomes an integral part of our success.

APPLYING YOUR KNOWLEDGE

1. In what ways are training and measurement important to the success of ACs?
2. Why are work samples like those used in JP Morgan Chase's AC effective predictors?
3. How are competencies used in ACs?

group has been provided with background information about the issue in question and given a fixed amount of time to resolve it, the assessors simply sit and observe the interactions; they do not participate at all. The assessees are typically rated on such dimensions as aggressiveness, persuasiveness, interpersonal skills, communication skills, flexible thinking, and listening skills. Scores on these dimensions are used to predict performance-related criteria.

Biographical Information

biographical information
In the context of selection, any information that is descriptive of an individual's personal history.

The major premise behind the use of **biographical information** for selection is that past behavior is the best predictor of future behavior. Biographical information can be thought of as any information that is descriptive of an individual's personal history. The idea is that if I want to predict how you will respond in a certain situation, one of the best ways for me to do so is to find out how you have responded in similar situations in the past. Those who work with biographical information often go one step further in considering *any* information indicative of a person's history as potentially useful—even information about hobbies or other activities that are not directly related to the job (Mael, 1991). In the selection context, biographical information is typically collected in one of two ways: through an application blank or a BioData questionnaire.

Application Blank. Without a doubt, the application blank is one of the most frequently and widely used selection devices. Whether you are applying for a restaurant job or a faculty position or an executive position at a Fortune 500 company, the chances are good that you will be asked to fill out some sort of application blank (although applications for professional positions may differ from those for nonprofessional positions). Typically this form will request historical (as well as current) information such as your educational background, work experience, experience relevant to the job in question, and the names and addresses of previous employers. Most of us have filled out such forms at one time or another. Unfortunately, many companies spend little time developing their application blanks. Some even hand out generic ones, which are available at office supply stores; but keep in mind that if these are being used for selection purposes, all the same ethical and legal rules apply. The presence of generic application blanks suggests that the information the company is asking for has not been developed from a job analysis. But as we now know, a job analysis is critical. If educational background and work experience are going to be defended as valid predictors of future on-the-job performance, these items have to be backed up by a job analysis. As you can imagine, many companies get themselves into legal skirmishes by using "off the shelf" application blanks rather than developing their own or at least validating the "off the shelf" predictors.

BioData
Personal history information obtained through a biographical information blank (BIB) that asks respondents about their attitudes, hobbies, experiences, and so on.

BioData. Although it may be appropriate to think of application blank information as biographical data, the term **BioData** is usually reserved for the personal history information that is obtained through biographical information blanks (BIBs). BIBs are different from application blanks in that (1) they usually have a multiple-choice, yes-no, or Likert-scale format (the last contains answers ranging from "strongly agree" to "strongly disagree"); (2) they ask questions in much broader areas, such as health, hobbies, family history, interests, and social experience; and (3) they contain many more questions (up to about 150) than do application blanks (10–15). Table 6.1 presents some BioData items for the job of customer service representative. This position involves a person who responds to service complaints or requests from customers over the phone. In the left column of the table are seven predictor dimensions; in the right column are BioData items related to each of those dimensions. In a real-life situation, of course, both the predictor dimensions and criterion dimensions would be developed on the basis of a job analysis. The premise here is that past behavior is a good predictor of future behavior. Thus, for instance, someone with a history of exhibiting patience

TABLE 6.1 BioData Items for the Position of Customer Service Representative

Dimension	Items
Helping Others	How often have you helped someone you didn't know by carrying something for them (e.g., boxes, luggage, groceries)? How often have you stopped to give aid or called someone to assist a stranded motorist?
Negotiation Skills	When you feel strongly about something, how easily can you persuade others to see your point of view? As a child, when your parents/guardians originally refused to let you do something, how easily could you convince them to change their minds?
Interpersonal Intelligence	In the past, how easily have you been able to judge the moods of your friends, co-workers, or family members? In the past, when meeting people for the first time, to what extent were you aware of the kind of impression you made?
Patience	When you have been in a frustrating interpersonal situation, how often have you been able to be patient with the person or persons causing the frustration? When asked for travel directions by a stranger, how likely are you to voluntarily repeat them if you suspect the person is confused?
Empathy	To what extent would your friends describe you as sympathetic? In the past, how easily have you been able to reach out to or express compassion for someone who was upset? In the past, when you've seen a friend or family member upset, to what extent have you actually "felt their pain"?
Extraversion	When socializing with a group of people, how often do you feel the group is relying on you to keep the conversation flowing? In the past, how comfortable have you felt in social situations?
Oral Communication	While in school, if given a choice, how often would you choose to do an oral presentation rather than a written report? In the past, to what extent have you been comfortable in sharing job-related information by having discussions in person?

in socially frustrating situations is likely to respond patiently to customers who are yelling about the lack of quality service they've received from the company. Similarly, someone with a history of helping strangers is not only more likely to be satisfied with a customer service job but also more likely to perform well than someone who has never considered it important or rewarding to help others. In short, BioData items should predict on-the-job performance.

For BioData the validity evidence is quite consistent: It predicts performance quite well (Allworth & Hesketh, 2000). A review of performance predictors for salespeople reported that BioData was the strongest predictor ($r = .52$) of managerial ratings of sales performance (Vinchur, Schippmann, Switzer, & Roth, 1998). And in more extensive reviews, Hunter and Hunter (1984) reported a .37 validity coefficient across a series of criteria, whereas Neal Schmitt and his colleagues (1984) reported a .32 validity coefficient for predicting performance ratings. A great resource for further information is the *BioData Handbook,* one chapter of which provides a summary of meta-analytic reviews of BioData (Stokes & Cooper, 1994). This chapter makes it clear that BioData consistently demonstrate validities between .20 and .46—these tend to be highest for criteria like supervisory ratings of performance and measures of productivity.

INTERVIEWS

interviews
A procedure designed to predict future performance based on an applicant's oral responses to a series of oral questions.

As you may have guessed, **interviews** are among the most popular selection devices and are typically used across all job levels. I was a high school student when I experienced my first job interview at a fast-food restaurant, and every job I've had since then (e.g., camp coordinator, construction apprentice, college teaching assistant, faculty member) was preceded by an interview. I'm sure that most of you have had interviews of some sort, too—either for a job or for school or for some club or organization for which selection decisions need to be made. It's been estimated that over 80% of U.S. organizations use some type of interview process; some estimates range as high as 99% (for a review, see McDaniel, Whetzel, Schmidt, & Maurer, 1994). An interview can be defined as a procedure designed to predict future performance based on an applicant's oral responses to a series of oral questions. The rationale is that the person conducting the interview can gather information through such questions that will allow the organization to make accurate predictions of successful job performance.

Two types of interviews merit special attention. First is the *structured interview,* which consists of a series of standardized job analysis–based questions that are asked of all job candidates. For instance, when interviewing someone for the job of camp counselor, an interviewer might use questions like "What is it about working with adolescents that attracts you?" "What kinds of nature experiences have you had that prepare you for this particular job?" and "Which of your strengths match well with the social and physical requirements of this job?" Each candidate would be asked these questions in the same order, the responses would be noted by the interviewer, and the candidates would receive a score on the interview based on these responses. It is this score that would be used in the selection process. The key to a structured interview is that everyone is asked the same set of questions. This technique not only increases the reliability of the interview process but also allows for a fair comparison among the applicants.

The more traditional *unstructured interview* is constructed haphazardly, with no consistency of questioning across applicants. One candidate may be asked what his particular strengths are and why he is interested in the job, while a second candidate may be asked what her particular weaknesses are and whether she's had any experiences that are especially relevant for the job. The unstructured interview process sometimes results in the organization comparing apples and oranges. For this reason, it is generally considered a less useful technique than the structured interview approach.

According to the many reviews of job interview validity conducted between 1960 and 1990, interviews of both types have rather low validity. One well-cited study reported a validity coefficient of only .14 for interviews in predicting supervisor ratings of performance (Hunter & Hunter, 1984). Nevertheless, organizations continued to use interviews in selection. Among the many possible explanations for this persistence, the most convincing is that the interview is more than a selection device. Indeed, it is a communication process in which the organization gains useful information about the applicant and the applicant gathers useful information about the organization (Cascio, 1998). The interview format may even provide the applicant with a **realistic job preview (RJP),** which is simply an accurate glimpse of what the job would actually be like. In this way the applicant can begin to get a feel for the organization's climate, the attitudes among employees, and the interpersonal relationships between subordinates and supervisors. In short, even if the interview lacks predictive validity with respect to job performance, it is potentially useful for both the organization and the applicant.

realistic job preview (RJP)
During an employment interview, the presentation of an accurate glimpse of what the job would be like.

Since 1990, more sophisticated meta-analytic techniques have been developed (Ganzach, Kluger, & Klayman, 2000), and recent reviews using these techniques have reported better validity for the employment interview. One meta-analysis found that interviews overall were predictive of job performance ($r = .37$) and, as expected, that structured interviews were more predictive ($r = .44$) than unstructured interviews ($r = .33$; McDaniel et al., 1994). Another study demonstrated that structured interviews predict performance over and above general cognitive ability and conscientiousness, thus indicating the incremental validity of the interview (Cortina et al., 2000). These results suggest that interviews can be very useful in employee selection contexts and that practitioners should attempt to use structured rather than unstructured interviews when possible because they are better predictors of job performance criteria. Of course, some of the biases discussed in the context of performance appraisal (Chapter 5)—including halo error, contrast effects, and similarity effects—may come into play during interviews as well. For instance, a recent study demonstrated that interview ratings

This couple should have hired a consulting firm to administer personality tests to or conduct an employment interview with their babysitter applicants—this is clearly a selection decision gone bad!

"Now let me get this straight. ... We hired you to babysit the kids, and instead you cooked and ate them *both*?"

are affected by nonverbal factors such as physical attractiveness (Burnett & Motowidlo, 1998). However, despite the subjective nature of interview ratings, they tend to be good predictors of on-the-job performance.

One additional point should be made before we leave this topic: Although the employment interview can include many different questions, there are important legal issues involved in deciding what questions shouldn't be asked. Table 6.2 contains a list of legally suspect questions that could be challenged in courts and used by plaintiffs to allege discrimination, and in the next chapter we will discuss various employment laws that define what organizations can and cannot ask of applicants.

Table 6.3 presents validity coefficients for all of the predictors that I have reviewed in this chapter. Notice that general cognitive ability appears to be the best

TABLE 6.2 Interview Questions That Shouldn't Be Asked

Legally Suspect Questions	Explanation and Alternatives*
How old are you? When were you born?	The Age Discrimination in Employment Act (ADEA) does not specifically prohibit an employer from asking an applicant's age or date of birth. However, because such inquiries may deter older workers from applying for employment or may otherwise indicate possible intent to discriminate based on age, requests for age information will be closely scrutinized by the Equal Employment Opportunity Commission (EEOC).
Have you ever been arrested?	Being arrested does not imply guilt of any crime; could ask if the applicant has been convicted of a felony within the past 5 years.
Do you plan on having children? Are you pregnant?	An employer cannot refuse to hire a woman because of her pregnancy-related condition as long as she is able to perform the major functions of her job. An employer cannot refuse to hire her because of its prejudices against pregnant workers or the prejudices of co-workers, clients, or customers.
Are you a U.S. citizen?	This may lead to discrimination based on national origin. Employer is allowed to ask if applicant is eligible to work in the United States either as a U.S. citizen or under a government immigration qualification.
Do you have a disability?	Employers may not ask job applicants about the existence, nature, or severity of a disability. Applicants may be asked about their ability to perform specific job functions. A job offer may be conditioned on the results of a medical examination, *but only* if the examination is required for all entering employees in similar jobs. Medical examinations of employees must be job related and consistent with the employer's business needs.
Do you have children? What daycare arrangements will be made if you are hired for this job?	It is unlawful to inquire if an applicant has children (an issue that is certainly not job related). Employer may ask if candidate has any commitments or responsibilities that might result in considerable absenteeism, but this should be asked of all candidates regardless of gender.
Are you actively involved in the National Association for the Advancement of Colored People (NAACP)?	Requesting preemployment information that discloses or tends to disclose an applicant's race suggests that race will be unlawfully used as a basis for hiring. Solicitation of such preemployment information is presumed to be used as a basis for making selection decisions. Therefore, if members of minority groups are not hired, the request for such preemployment information would likely constitute evidence of discrimination.

TABLE 6.2 Interview Questions That Shouldn't Be Asked *(cont.)*

Legally Suspect Questions	Explanation and Alternatives*
Have you ever been treated by a psychologist or psychiatrist?	All of these questions are probably illegal under the Americans with Disabilities Act (ADA). It is illegal to ask any preemployment questions about illness.
Have you ever been hospitalized? If so, for what?	
Please list any conditions or diseases for which you have been treated in the past three years.	
How many days were you absent from work due to illness in the past year?	
Are you taking any prescribed drugs?	

**Some of this information was adapted from the Equal Employment Opportunity Commission (EEOC) website (*http:www.eeoc.gov/*).*

predictor of job performance, followed closely by psychomotor ability, assessment centers, and BioData. Of course, even these consistent predictors seldom account for more than 25% of the variance in a criterion. In one study, for example, Frank Schmidt and John Hunter (1998) examined the extent to which adding predictors to general cognitive ability would help in predicting job performance. What they found was that work sample tests, integrity tests, personality tests, and structured interviews demonstrated incremental validity by accounting for an additional 14% or more of the variance in job performance and that the best two-predictor combination was general cognitive ability and integrity tests (multiple $R = .65$), which together accounted for about 42% of the variance in job performance. The lesson here is that companies should be careful and diligent in choosing what predictors to use in their selection batteries, realizing that using multiple predictors is likely to account for more variance in the criterion and that some predictors tend to be more useful than others.

TABLE 6.3 Estimates of Validity Coefficients for Common Predictors

Predictor	Validity Coefficient Estimate	Source of Estimate	Description
General Cognitive Ability	.53	Hunter & Hunter, 1984	Meta-analysis
	.25	Schmitt et al., 1984	Meta-analysis
Specific Cognitive Ability	.40–.50	Gatewood & Feild, 2001	Narrative Review
	.27	Schmitt et al., 1984	Meta-analysis
Psychomotor Ability	.40	Hunter & Hunter, 1984	Meta-analysis
	.53	McHenry et al., 1990	Project A data
Personality Tests	.24	Tett et al., 1991	Meta-analysis
	.25–.37	McHenry et al., 1990	Project A data
Conscientiousness	.23	Barrick & Mount, 1991	Meta-analysis
Integrity Tests	.34–.47	Ones et al., 1993	Meta-analysis
Work Samples	.32–.38	Schmitt et al., 1984	Meta-analysis
	.44	Hunter & Hunter, 1984	Meta-analysis
Assessment Centers	.37	Gaugler et al., 1987	Meta-analysis
	.38-.45	Arthur et al., 2003	Meta-analysis
BioData	.52	Vinchur et al., 1998	Meta-analysis (Sales)
	.37	Hunter & Hunter, 1984	Meta-analysis
	.20–.46	Stokes & Cooper, 1994	Narrative Review
Interviews	.37	McDaniel et al., 1994	Meta-analysis
Structured	.44	McDaniel et al., 1994	Meta-analysis
Unstructured	.33	McDaniel et al., 1994	Meta-analysis

SUMMARY

In this chapter, tests were classified in terms of form as well as the predictor type they represent. The most frequently used selection instruments—cognitive ability tests, psychomotor tests, personality tests, integrity tests, work sample tests, assessment centers, biographical information, and interviews—were discussed in the context of their role in employee selection. The validity coefficients of these selection instruments are listed (in Table 6.3) in the order in which they were presented in the chapter. Note that the variability of these coefficients may be due to the diversity of the studies included in the meta-analyses (e.g., Hunter & Hunter, 1984, versus Schmitt et al., 1984) as well as to differences among the predictors and criteria.

We can draw a few general conclusions. First, it is clear that ability measures (e.g., general cognitive, specific cognitive, and psychomotor) are among the most valid predictors of performance criteria in an employment setting. Second, the validity coefficients for personality tests are not as high as those for most of the other predictors included in our review. Third, nontraditional predictors, such as integrity tests, BioData, work samples, and assessment centers, are consistently valid predictors of on-the-job performance. In Chapter 7 we will discuss the actual selection process, focusing also on the legalities involved in how organizations use these predictors to hire employees.

REVIEW QUESTIONS

1. Along what dimensions can tests be classified?
2. How valid is general cognitive ability for the prediction of job performance?
3. How does general cognitive ability differ from specific cognitive ability?
4. How valid are psychomotor tests for predicting job performance?
5. What evidence is there that personality tests are good predictors of job performance?
6. What are the differences between overt integrity tests and personality-type integrity tests?
7. What are work sample tests, and how are they used for selection? Are they valid for selection?
8. Describe in-basket and leaderless group exercises, and discuss their usefulness to selection.
9. In what ways can biographical information be collected from applicants?
10. Describe the major types of interviews. Do their validities differ?

SUGGESTED READINGS

Cascio, W. F. (1998). *Applied psychology in human resource management* (5th ed.). Upper Saddle River, NJ: Prentice-Hall. Now in its 5th edition, this is still the most thorough human resource management (HRM) textbook available—and the one I pull off my shelf most frequently.

Gatewood, R. D., & Feild, H. S. (2001). *Human resource selection* (5th ed.). Fort Worth, TX: Harcourt College. Another solid HRM text. Somewhat more focused than Cascio's, its emphasis is on job analysis and employee selection.

Guion, R. M. (1998). *Assessment, measurement, and prediction for personnel decisions.* Mahwah, NJ: Erlbaum. This book, written by one of the most distinguished industrial psychologists ever, focuses largely on criterion measurement and selection, providing a very thorough treatment of the issues involved.

Thomas, J. C. (2004). *The comprehensive handbook of psychological assessment: Vol. 4. Industrial/organizational assessment.* New York: Wiley. This is part of a four-volume set that wonderfully reviews psychological assessment with sophistication and simplicity. The I/O volume is a great reference, providing a source of tests and data on the most often used tests for assessment at work.

Selection Decisions and Personnel Law

7

CHAPTER OUTLINE

In the last few chapters we have discussed in detail the importance of predictors and criteria in I/O psychology. At this point, you should realize that I/O psychologists are very concerned with selecting employees who have a strong likelihood of being successful on the job. Recall that Chapter 6 presented a detailed discussion of the common predictors, or tests, that are used in employee selection (see Table 6.3 for a list of those predictors and their validity estimates). In this chapter we will discuss how an organization might go about using those predictors to select employees.

Let's return briefly to our example from the last chapter involving the hiring of a new associate by a large law firm. Because the applicants are directly out of law school, there are no criterion data available; thus the law firm has to rely on predictors. Of course, this is the typical situation in which organizations and I/O psychologists are placed. If criterion data *were* available, we wouldn't need predictors, and selection would be both easier and less expensive: We would simply hire the lawyer who was performing best on the job. However, we need to use other information to predict performance on the job. Based on what we discussed in the last chapter, you might suggest that we use predictors like performance in law school, a legal in-basket, performance in mock trials, and tests of cognitive ability as predictors. The focus of this chapter is how we go about using these predictors to make hiring decisions. But how do we know that our predictors are valid ones, and what legal issues come into play in this context of employee selection? For answers to these questions, we need to put the predictors and the criteria together in ways that enable us to do accurate and legal employee selection. The health, success, and long-term viability of organizations depend on how well employee selection is conducted.

LEARNING OBJECTIVES

This chapter should help you understand:

- the steps involved in validating a selection battery.
- some of the best recruitment strategies used by organizations to recruit individuals to apply for jobs.
- the differences between predictive validation and concurrent validation and the steps involved in each.
- the importance of cross-validation.
- what validity generalization is and how important it has become to I/O psychology.
- the three main approaches to selection (multiple cutoff, multiple hurdle, and multiple regression) and the differences among them.
- the importance of the utility concept for I/O selection.
- the factors that affect the utility of a selection battery (namely, validity, base rate, selection ratio, and cost).
- important related concepts such as employment at-will, adverse impact, and affirmative action.
- what has been rendered illegal by certain U.S. employment laws.
- the different forms of sexual harassment.
- how the courts seem to be interpreting reasonable accommodation, essential functions of the job, and undue hardship under the Americans with Disabilities Act.

A BRIEF REVIEW

We will talk about selection decisions in this chapter, but first I want to clarify that much of what is discussed here can also be applied to other personnel decisions, such as promotion decisions and decisions about whom to lay off when reductions in force become a reality. For instance, we may give employees a promotion test to use in determining whom to promote into a management job. The same procedures that apply to validating a selection test can be applied to the validation of a promotion test. Accordingly, in this chapter I present a general process that can be used to make personnel decisions, and I use the selection decision as an example because it is very important to organizations and because research and litigation have focused on this type of personnel decision in particular.

Let's say that we all work for a consulting firm called "PE Levy and Associates," which has been hired by CS&J Products, a large manufacturing company, to devise, implement, and evaluate a selection battery that is to be used for the selection of *middle-level managers.* A **selection battery** is a set of predictors, or tests, that are used to make employee hiring decisions. In Chapter 6, we discussed the various types of predictors one by one, but note that in actuality it is rare for any of these predictors to be used alone. It is much more likely that organizations will employ a set of predictors or battery of tests as a way of predicting criterion performance. Of course, by this time, you know what the first step is. It's the job analysis—the foundation for everything we do in industrial psychology. Thus we would choose a job-oriented, worker-oriented, or hybrid job analytic technique as discussed in Chapter 3. From the job analysis we would generate a *job description* and *job specifications,* and from these we would develop performance criteria. We would also be sure to consider the "criteria for the criteria" in developing our measures (see Chapter 3).

selection battery
A set of predictors, or tests, that are used to make employee hiring decisions.

Using the job analysis—chiefly, the job specifications information—we would develop predictors or select predictors from those that already exist. We would need to decide what type of predictors to use, choosing among work samples, assessment centers, BIBs, ability tests, interviews, and so on. In this case, because the job is a managerial one, we should seriously consider the use of work samples and assessment centers, as these seem particularly relevant for the job in question. Also, we would opt for multiple tests, as multiple tests would likely increase the proportion of criterion variance that we could account for.

Figure 7.1 demonstrates why a selection battery yields better prediction than a single test. Remember that a correlation (r) is used as an index of the relationship between a predictor and a criterion, whereas the coefficient of determination or the squared correlation (r^2) provides information about how much variance in the criterion is accounted for by the predictor. In the figure, the squared correlations between each predictor and the performance criterion vary from .10 to .36. Together they account for about 55% of the variance in criterion performance (r^2). The validity coefficient for the battery of predictors is about .74 (i.e., the square root of .55). When the predictors are combined in this way, the validity coefficient is a multiple R—the correlation between the combination of all the predictors and the criterion. It's clear, based on the validity coefficient (multiple $R = .74$) and the amount of variance accounted for ($r^2 = .55$), that using a test battery results in better prediction than using any single test in isolation. Notice also that there is some overlap among the predictors, which means that they are slightly correlated. This explains why, if we add up the individual r^2s, we would get .71 rather than .55. The difference between these two numbers reflects the overlap in the predictors. For instance, part of the variance that is accounted for by the work sample test is also accounted for by the assessment center (this is the area of overlap in the figure). Ideally, we want as little correlation among the predictors as possible so that we aren't predicting the same piece of the pie with more than one predictor. In this example, the assessment center is somewhat redundant with the other two predictors. It adds to the prediction, but it makes a smaller unique contribution when you consider the overlap it has with both the work sample and the interview. If costs were an issue and CS&J Products wanted to use only one predictor, which would you suggest, based on validity alone? As the figure makes clear, using the work sample would result in accounting for more variance in the criterion than any other single predictor. If costs were not an issue, the three predictors as a package seem to do the best job.

FIGURE 7.1 Selection Battery Example

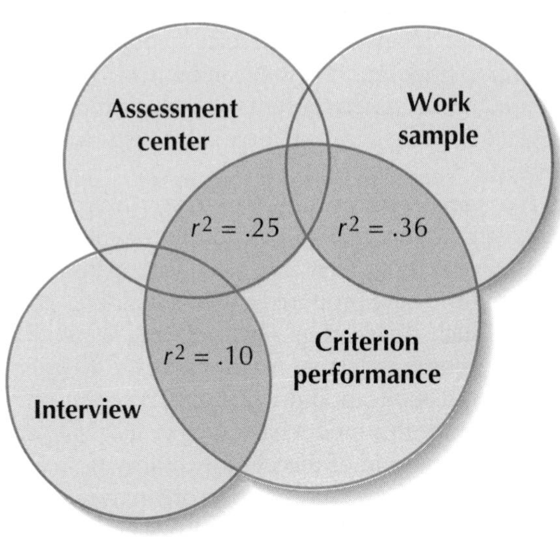

RECRUITMENT

recruitment
The process of encouraging potentially qualified applicants to seek employment with a particular company.

Before we can select employees for CS&J, we must get the applicants interested enough in the jobs to apply. **Recruitment,** the process of encouraging potentially qualified applicants to seek employment with a particular company, has traditionally been an often ignored element of I/O psychology—but one with widespread implications. Obviously, the quality or efficiency of a selection system is limited by the quality of the applicants. We could have a large enough budget to be able to make job offers to five lawyers just coming out of law school, but if the applicant pool is weak and the new lawyers are not qualified, selection doesn't really matter very much. The best selection system in the world is useless if we can't recruit good applicants in the first place.

There are many ways to entice individuals to apply for jobs. Traditionally, jobs have been advertised through college placement offices, newspaper advertisements, employee referrals, and job fairs (Breaugh, Greising, Taggart, & Chen, 2003). Recent work in the recruiting area has begun to enhance our understanding of this process a great deal. For instance, Cable and Turban (2003) have shown that recruits use the organization's reputation as an indicator of what they expect their job to be like, and this reputation also affects recruits' expectations about the pride they will experience working for a particular company (see also Collins & Stevens, 2002). Highhouse and his colleagues (Highhouse, Hoffman, Greve, & Collins, 2002) have demonstrated that organizational values, as shared with potential applicants via a recruitment brochure or newspaper article, affected recruits' attraction to the organization. They (Lievens & Highhouse, 2003) have also shown that individuals aren't attracted to organizations just because of the job attributes (compensation, work environment, etc.) but that they also consider strongly their subjective evaluation of the organization (is it an innovative, cool, prestigious place to work?). In fact, these subjective evaluations appear to be even more important.

The Internet has added a new dimension to recruiting in that it reaches an incredibly large audience—one that knows no geographical boundaries (Cober, Brown, Blumental, Doverspike, & Levy, 2000). Cober and his colleagues have been very active in this arena and have proposed a model that suggests applicant attraction as a function of such variables as aesthetics and useability of the organization's employment website, affective reactions to the website, perceptions of organizational image, and applicant individual differences (Cober, Brown, Keeping, & Levy, 2004). Pieces of this model have been tested, and some of the results suggest that, as predicted, content of the website information, aesthetic quality of the website, and useability of the website all affect organizational attraction (Cober, Brown, Levy, Cober, & Keeping, 2003; Williamson, Lepak, & King, 2003). Although we know more about Internet recruiting than we did only a few years ago, there is still a great deal more to learn. This area promises to attract research attention, as indicated by two special issues of recent journals devoted wholly to the role of technology in staffing (see Stanton & Coovert, 2004; Viswesvaran, 2003).

Job fairs are one of many ways through which organizations can recruit new employees.

Informal communication also results in many contacts and, hence, potential job applicants. Often, employees of the company will pass along job information to friends and colleagues, who in turn will spread it to other friends and colleagues, greatly increasing the potential applicant pool. This process can be helpful, given that employees tend to be somewhat discriminating about whom they encourage to apply. I myself certainly would not encourage a colleague at another university to apply for our open faculty position if I didn't think she was a hard worker or believe that she would be successful in my particular department. In this way, informal contacts can help in the screening process. Of course, for legal reasons, companies do not want to rely only on informal contacts that could be interpreted as resulting in discrimination (if the organization is largely made up of white males, employees' friends and acquaintances are likely to be white males as well); thus more formal channels are typically used, too. In fact, the more channels that are used to advertise a position, the less likely it is that illegal discrimination will occur, given that increased numbers of culturally and racially diverse people will be aware that the position has become available. We will spend a great deal of time on legal issues later in this chapter. For a thorough review of the recruitment literature and a framework for future research, the reader is referred to Rynes and Cable (2003). For the sake of our purposes here, let's go back to our consulting project and assume that through varied and appropriate recruitment techniques, CS&J has identified several applicants for its managerial position.

THE SELECTION DECISION

CS&J wants us to use a selection battery to decide whom to hire and whom not to hire. Indeed, this is the focus of the remainder of the chapter. Because the work of PE Levy & Associates is based on strong scientific practice and is driven by a strong sense of ethics, prior to recommending any particular selection battery, we would set out to demonstrate its validity. There are two general approaches to demonstrating the validity of a selection battery: the conduct of a *validation study* and *validity generalization.* Let's consider each in turn.

THE PROCESS OF TEST VALIDATION

I have already introduced the concepts of validity coefficient, predictors, and criteria. These will become the focus of this section. We use a validation study to determine the extent to which a predictor or battery of predictors is related to the criterion of interest, such as on-the-job performance. In other words, it is from a validation study that the validity coefficients we've been talking about are derived. In addition, recall the notion of *criterion-related validity,* which concerns the extent to which a test is a good predictor of some criterion such as performance (see Chapter 2). There are two approaches to demonstrating criterion-related validity, but both approaches start with the same "up-front" work—and for our consulting gig, we've already done that work. In other words, we've started with a job analysis, which allows us to develop or select both predictors and criteria. The process of validation is how we examine the links between these two sets of variables.

Predictive Validation. As defined in Chapter 2, *predictive validity* refers to the extent to which test scores obtained at one point in time predict criteria obtained at some future point in time. In our current example, if we were to pursue criterion-related validity through a predictive validation design, we would be asking if scores on the work sample, assessment center, and interview predict performance at CS&J Products.

To demonstrate predictive validity, we would follow these steps:

1. *Gather predictor data on all of the applicants.* In our example, this would mean running each applicant through a work sample test, an assessment center, and an interview. Each applicant would be scored on these tests, and a composite score would be arrived at by adding the scores or performing some other computation.
2. *Hire some of the applicants to fill the open positions.* Note, however, that these applicants would be hired on the basis of predictors that are *not* part of our newly developed selection battery. Often this step is implemented by hiring individuals according to the company's current selection system, which is

probably quite different from the one we are proposing. By following this rather unorthodox strategy, we are more likely to get individuals hired into CS&J who range from low to high on our new predictors. This outcome is very important for the validation process because if we were to only hire high scorers on the new predictors, we would not be able to determine whether low scorers were unsuccessful on the job, because no low scorers would be in our sample.

3. *After several months, gather performance data that can serve as the criteria for our validation study.* Remember that these criteria are developed from the job analysis and that they are intended to differentiate successful from unsuccessful performers.
4. *Compute a validity coefficient between the predictor score and the criterion score that indicates the strength of the relationship between our predictor and our criterion.* We can compute a validity coefficient for the battery as a whole or for each predictor separately. Likewise, we can compute validity coefficients for each particular performance criterion or for our composite criterion.

Predictive validity studies investigate how effective our predictors are at forecasting the on-the-job performance of applicants. Predictors are measured prior to hiring, and criteria are measured after a few months on the job.

Concurrent Validation. As defined in Chapter 2, *concurrent validity* refers to how well a test predicts a criterion that is measured at the same time as the test. We still want to draw the same conclusions and use our tests to predict which applicants are likely to be successful job performers. But sometimes predictive validity studies are difficult (if not impossible) to conduct, making concurrent validity studies the more viable option. Predictive validity studies are difficult to conduct because they require selecting employees based on predictors other than those we are intending to validate—and doing so requires two sets of predictor measures. Obviously, this can be expensive in terms of both the dollars involved in the development and administration of the tests and the time spent by applicants and test administrators.

To establish criterion-related validity through a concurrent validation study, we would undergo the following steps:

1. *Data on both predictors and criteria are collected from incumbent employees at the same time.* In our current example, this would mean that incumbents would be run through the work sample test, the assessment center, and the interview, and their performance on these predictors would be scored. In addition, performance data would be collected. For instance, we might gather performance appraisal data already in the incumbents' files or ask supervisors and peers to provide performance ratings of these incumbents.
2. *A validity coefficient is computed between the predictor score and the criterion score*—again, indicating the strength of the relationship between our predictor and our criterion. We can compute a validity coefficient for the battery as

TABLE 7.1 Validation Designs

Element	Concurrent Design	Predictive Design
Participants	Incumbents	Applicants
Predictor Measurement	Time 1	Time 1
Criterion Measurement	Time 1	Time 2
Selection Decision	Made prior to Time 1 and was based on other predictors	To be made between Time 1 and Time 2 and to be based on other predictors
Validity Coefficient	Correlation between predictor and criterion	Correlation between predictor and criterion

a whole or for each predictor separately. Likewise, we can compute validity coefficients for each particular performance criterion or for our composite criterion.

Table 7.1 presents an overview of each validation strategy. Concurrent validation differs from predictive validation in two major ways: In situations involving concurrent validation, (1) incumbents, rather than applicants, are used as participants, and (2) predictors and criteria are measured at the same time. Although empirical research has not demonstrated many differences between concurrent and predictive validation efforts (Schmitt, Gooding, Noe, & Kirsch, 1984), some I/O psychologists are concerned about the use of concurrent validation because, in their view, incumbents and applicants differ in important ways such as amount of job experience and potential motivation (Cascio, 1998).

validity shrinkage
A statistical phenomenon reflecting the likelihood that a given selection battery will demonstrate lower validity when employed with a different sample.

Cross-Validation. In cases in which predictive or concurrent strategies are used to validate a selection battery, it is a statistical truth that the validity of that selection battery will always be the highest for the sample upon which it was validated. In other words, a given selection battery will likely demonstrate lower validity when employed with a different sample—a phenomenon known as **validity shrinkage.** Although the statistical explanation for this phenomenon is beyond the scope of the book, we can consider the general factors involved in our particular situation. Let's say we find that our selection battery has a validity coefficient (in this case, a multiple R) of .74, as depicted in Figure 7.1. If we use this selection battery with another sample of applicants at the same company, the validity coefficient is likely to be smaller. The key question for the generalizability of our results is "How much smaller?" To cross-validate the selection battery *empirically,* we would apply the same predictors and criteria to a different sample at CS&J to see how close the validity coefficient is to the original. Specifically, we would generate a regression equation using the original predictor and criterion data. We would then plug the predictor scores from the new individuals in the cross-validation sample into this original regression equation to obtain a *predicted criterion score.* Correlating this predicted criterion score with the actual criterion score provides the validity coefficient for the new sample, which can be compared with the validity coefficient of the original sample. Of course, we are hoping for only a small amount of validity shrinkage. If the validity doesn't shrink very much, we can feel comfortable that the selection battery is still valid and ready for use by CS&J to select employees.

To cross-validate the selection battery *statistically,* we would correct or adjust the original validity coefficient for measurement error. But the approach we choose, whether empirical or statistical, is less important than our commitment to estimating the cross-validated coefficient. The best estimate of the validity of a particular selection battery is the cross-validated coefficient; yet, because it takes a little extra time and effort, this step is frequently skipped in validation projects.

Validity Generalization

Obviously, it takes a great deal of effort, time, and money to demonstrate criterion-related validity using concurrent or predictive approaches. An alternative to this approach that has been gaining in popularity over the past 20 years is called **validity generalization (VG).** One long-standing belief in the selection area was that test validities varied across situations. If this were the case, the selection battery that PE Levy & Associates developed for CS&J would not likely be valid for another company. Indeed, the work sample we developed would work only for this particular company and this particular situation. The belief that test validities are limited to particular situations is termed **situational specificity.** John Hunter and Frank Schmidt (1990) took issue with this belief, however, developing methods to examine whether validities are truly situationally specific. Their VG technique was both statistically and conceptually tied to the technique of meta-analysis, which they developed in conjunction with this work. In fact, their ideas about meta-analysis began as issues related to VG. Basically, they argued that by using meta-analytic techniques to weigh and combine validity coefficients across situations, we can examine whether validities are situationally specific or generalizable across situations. Their conclusion—and there is a great deal of research to support it—is that validities do tend to generalize across situations (reviewed in Schmidt et al., 1993).

validity generalization
A statistical approach used to demonstrate that test validities do not vary across situations.

situational specificity
The belief that test validities are specific to particular situations.

The evidence that validities can generalize across situations is convincing, but things are never quite that simple. For a thorough review and critical analysis of VG, see Landy's (2003) edited book, which includes chapters by various experts who share their thoughts and data on this topic. I will mention just a few of the relevant issues here. First, many criticisms and concerns have been raised against the statistical methodology used in VG (Cascio, 1998). Second, VG is still limited to jobs that are similar to those on which the test was originally validated. For instance, to say that the validity of an in-basket test generalizes is not to say that because it is valid for managerial selection it is also valid for the selection of custodians and ministers. Sometimes, those who espouse the value of validity generalization make possible the misperception that a particular test is equally valid across all jobs. For instance, in *Van Aken v. Young* (1982), an expert witness for the plaintiff testified that there was a high correlation between cognitive ability (i.e., intelligence) and the ability to be a good lemon picker. The court found this testimony to lack credibility and disregarded it. The conclusion is obvious: No test or measure of any construct, regardless of the measure's soundness, is a good predictor for every job (see also *EEOC v. Atlas Paper Box,* 1989). Third, the legal community is often involved in disputes as to whether a particular selection test is legal—an issue we will consider shortly. For now, though, note that although the courts have traditionally required a validation study to show that a selection battery was valid, in recent years they have viewed VG more favorably, given the caveat that a complete and thorough job analysis is necessary. This job analysis must demonstrate that the job on which the tests were validated is the same as the job for which those tests are being used for selection. In our current example, the implication is that if someone else has validated an in-basket for managerial selection, PE Levy & Associates needs to be able to show that the CS&J managerial jobs for which we want to use this in-basket are very, very similar to the managerial jobs on which the in-basket was originally validated.

Validation of selection batteries is extremely important not only to effective organizational performance but also, as we will soon see, to the legal arena that polices our work. There are three main approaches to validation: predictive validation studies, concurrent validation studies, and validity generalization. Each has its strengths and weaknesses, so one's choice should be determined on a case-by-case basis.

Practical Approaches to Selection

Now that we've demonstrated the validity of our selection battery (including cross-validation), we can provide this information to CS&J Products, ensuring its executives that our selection battery predicts job performance quite well. CS&J, being a profit-driven company, is interested in achieving two main goals. First, it wants us to provide the names of people who are likely to be successful performers. This is, after all, why it hired us. Second, it wants us to demonstrate that our selection battery is cost effective. We will consider both of these goals in the next few pages, starting with two major approaches to employee selection: multiple cutoffs and multiple regression.

multiple cutoff approach
A noncompensatory model of employee selection in which "passing scores," or cutoffs, are set on each predictor.

Multiple Cutoffs. The **multiple cutoff approach** is a noncompensatory method of employee selection in which "passing scores," or cutoffs, are set on each predictor. It is considered noncompensatory because applicants, to be eligible for selection, must score higher than these cutoffs on each predictor. In other words, they have to pass each test, and scoring well on one test does not "make up" or

TABLE 7.2 Multiple Cutoff Approach: Cardiac Surgeon

Applicant	Medical Knowledge Test	Medical School GPA	Interview Score	Psychomotor Test	Total Score
Dr. Pratt	10	8	6	8	32
Dr. Carter	10	10	10	**5**	35
Dr. Quinn	9	8	8	7	32
Dr. Welby	9	8	7	10	34
Dr. Seuss	**6**	10	10	10	36
Predictor Cutoff:	9	7	6	7	

**All test scores are on a 1–10 scale, with higher numbers indicating better performance.*

compensate for scoring low on another test. Back to our example: In order to be rated as acceptable for the middle-level-manager job at CS&J, applicants would have to exceed some minimal level of performance on the work sample test, the assessment center, *and* the interview. If an applicant excels on the work sample and assessment center but bombs on the interview, he won't be hired—regardless of the importance of the KSAOs (knowledge, skills, abilities, and other characteristics) that the interview was designed to tap.

Perhaps the strengths of a multiple cutoff approach are best seen when we consider certain types of jobs. For instance, to select cardiac surgeons, we might use a measure of medical knowledge, grades in medical school, an interview, and a psychomotor test involving fine-grained hand work such as cutting and sewing. I won't speak for you, but a multiple cutoff is the way I want my surgeon selected: An incredibly smart and verbally skilled surgeon who shakes uncontrollably with a scalpel in her hand is of no use to me! It is of paramount importance that candidates pass all of the cutoffs for the position of cardiac surgeon. Table 7.2 presents the names of five applicants for this position, along with their predictor scores. Look this over and decide whom you would select. Let's say we had two open positions in the cardiac surgery department. If we simply added up the applicants' scores and selected the two highest scorers as our surgeons, we would pick Dr. Seuss and Dr. Carter. However, both of them failed to reach a critical cutoff score—Dr. Seuss on medical knowledge and Dr. Carter on the psychomotor test. Although they have the highest total scores, they seem weak in very important areas, and with a noncompensatory model these weaknesses would prevent them from being selected. In this situation I would prefer Drs. Welby, Pratt, and Quinn because they met every criterion cutoff. As I suggested earlier, I don't want a surgeon working on my heart who, though very bright, has poor motor ability and weak cutting skills (like Dr. Carter). How about you? Would you hire the two "top" candidates, or would you invoke a multiple cutoff strategy?

TABLE 7.3 Multiple Hurdle Approach: Production Line Supervisor

Applicant	Cognitive Ability Test *Cutoff = 110*	Personality Test *Cutoff = 55*	Work Sample *Cutoff = 80*	Interview *Cutoff = 18*
Ripken	120	61	88	23
Banks	118	59	76	
Jeter	107			
Tejada	108			
Yount	106			
Belanger	104			
Aparacio	121	40		

Least Expensive → Most Expensive

multiple hurdle approach A rendition of the multiple cutoff approach in which the predictors are administered in a predetermined order and applicants are measured on the next predictor only if they scored above the cutoff on the previous predictor.

One special rendition of the multiple cutoff approach to selection is the **multiple hurdle approach.** As before, passing scores are set on each predictor, and superb performance on one predictor cannot compensate for below-cutoff performance on another predictor. With the multiple hurdle approach, however, predictors are administered in a predetermined order and applicants are measured on a subsequent predictor only if they scored above the cutoff on the previous predictor.

Table 7.3 presents scores for seven applicants on four predictors, as well as the cutoff scores for each predictor. Suppose that we have been hired by CS&J to help it select production line supervisors, and we've identified the relevant predictors as being a cognitive ability test, a personality test, a work sample test, and an interview. The predictors are arranged from least to most expensive because this is typically the way multiple hurdle strategies are conducted. The cognitive ability test can be purchased from a test publisher and administered to applicants in a group, so it is inexpensive in terms of both time and money. But the interview questions probably need to be developed "in-house" rather than bought "off the shelf," and they are typically done one-on-one—so they may require a great deal of time both to develop and to conduct. Applicants proceed to the next predictor only if they successfully jump the previous hurdle (i.e., by scoring above the cutoff on the previous predictor). As you can see in Table 7.3, only Ripken, Banks, and Aparacio pass the cognitive ability test. Thus they go on to the next hurdle. But here only Ripken and Banks pass the personality test. They both go on to the work sample test, on which only Ripken survives to the next hurdle. Ripken also passes the interview and would thus be hired. (One thing is for sure: You won't have an absence problem if you hire Ripken! Absence will be discussed in Chapter 11.) Because of the way multiple hurdles are designed, they tend to save both money and time. See "Practitioner Forum" for an important example of this approach to selection.

PRACTITIONER FORUM

ELIZABETH KOLMSTETTER

Ph.D., 1991, I/O Psychology, Virginia Tech
Deputy Assistant Administrator, Workforce Performance and Training, Transportation Security Administration, Dept. of Homeland Security

In the aftermath of 9/11, Congress passed legislation mandating a new federal agency, the Transportation Security Administration (TSA), to hire and train a federal workforce of more than 50,000 airport security screeners at more than 429 airports nationwide in less than a year. The TSA implemented high standards during all aspects of creating this new workforce, including the recruiting, selection, training, and certification process. A fair, valid, and defensible selection system was the cornerstone of the success of the workforce federalization. Every screener hired went through the same hiring and training process, regardless of airport size or location, from Nantucket, Massachusetts, to Los Angeles, California.

The assessment process was developed and validated following the principles discussed in this chapter regarding a multiple hurdle approach to selection, but here are some of the specifics. Keep in mind that the applicant proceeds to the next hurdle only if he or she passes the previous hurdle.

1. Application (on-line or via telephone)
2. Three-and-a-half-hour multiple-choice test: (a) Aviation Security Screener Employment Test (ASSET; personality-based), (b) Screener English Test (SET), and (c) Screener Object Recognition Test (SORT; x-ray image test)
3. Structured Interview (in-person)
4. Physical Abilities Test (i.e., baggage lift, baggage search)
5. Medical Evaluation (including tests for drugs, vision, hearing, color vision, orthopedic, cardiovascular, etc.)
6. Background Investigation (i.e., credit and criminal checks)
7. 45-Hour Basic Screener Training (including classroom training with labs; including job knowledge test, x-ray image detection test)
8. 60-Hour On-The-Job Training and Initial Certification (including formal practical skills evaluation, x-ray image detection mastery test)
9. Annual Re-certification (job knowledge test, x-ray image detection proficiency test, practical skills demonstration)

Obviously, TSA screeners are chosen carefully, and the multiple hurdle approach is cost effective because the most expensive testing and screening procedures are conducted late in the process after most of the candidates have been screened out. In its first year, TSA processed more than 1.7 million applications, tested more than 340,000 applicants, and hired approximately 50,000 screeners. By implementing a job-related selection process, the TSA ensured that less than 2% of the screeners hired failed the training.

The TSA has been very thorough in the development and validation of this complex selection system, but carrying out this process is done with even greater caution. Test security (Who has access to the tests?), training of test administrators and applicant assessors (How can we ensure that everyone does this the same way?), and quality of test scoring (How can we be certain that there are no errors in how individuals' tests are scored?) are all issues that involve the expenditure of considerable time by the I/O psychologists and other TSA employees and contractors. Although it takes an incredible amount of work, national security is "high stakes" employment and a priority for this country. The TSA screener selection program is a very successful program that selects qualified screeners while serving society's needs.

APPLYING YOUR KNOWLEDGE

1. What are the benefits of the multiple hurdle approach to selection?
2. What other issues are important in the implementation of selection systems?
3. Why should organizations integrate their selection and training programs?

Multiple Regression. We briefly discussed regression analysis in Chapter 2, but we need to spend more time on it here because it is an important technique for determining how we use predictor information to make selection decisions. Recall that the validity coefficient is an index of the strength of the relationship between a predictor and a criterion. For our present purposes, however, we are interested in more than just this relationship, because the focus of selection is on prediction. Accordingly, we use **multiple regression,** which is a statistical technique that allows us to estimate how well a series of predictors forecasts a performance criterion. This process can get rather complicated, but I will try to present the basics using the middle-level-manager selection scenario that we've been working with.

multiple regression
A statistical technique that, when used in the selection context, allows us to estimate how well a series of predictors forecasts a performance criterion.

First, we use our validation data (let's assume a predictive validity design) to generate a regression equation. We do this by regressing the criterion performance of those applicants who were selected on their predictor scores (work sample, assessment center, and interview). The general form of a multiple regression equation is

$$Y = b_0 + b_1X_1 + b_2X_2 + b_3X_3$$

where each X is the individual's score on a specific predictor, each b is the weight for that particular score, Y is the criterion, and b_0 is the intercept (i.e., the point at which the regression line crosses the Y axis). Computing the regression equation with our validation data yields the following result:

$$Y_{predicted} = 1.043 + 1.548 \text{ (work sample score)} + .752 \text{ (assessment center score)} + .320 \text{ (interview score)}$$

This equation indicates the best prediction scheme, based on our validation data, for forecasting any individual's criterion performance. In other words, we use the predictor and criterion data from our validation study to determine the best weights for each predictor in arriving at a predicted criterion score.

Second, we apply that prediction scheme (i.e., the regression equation) to our applicant data to arrive at selection decisions. An example is presented in Table 7.4, which shows the predictor scores for four new applicants, along with their predicted criterion scores derived from the regression equation. These applicants were not part of the validation sample; rather, we are now using the results of the validation to select from our new applicant pool. Specifically, the predicted criterion scores are derived by plugging each individual's predictor score into the regression equation (as presented in the bottom portion of the table). The table clearly shows that Tomlin is predicted to be the best performer.

The final step is to rank-order all of the applicants according to predicted criterion scores and then to select from the top until all of the open positions are filled. It's important to note that the regression equation creates the best combination of the tests for maximizing the prediction of the criterion. Based on these data, if CS&J had two open positions, we would make offers to Tomlin and Stokes because, based on our validation study, these two applicants are predicted to be the best performers on the job.

There are a few loose ends here. First, the executives at CS&J may have a very good idea of what is acceptable performance for their company. Thus they may

TABLE 7.4 Multiple Regression Approach

Applicant	Work Sample	Assessment Center	Interview Criterion	Predicted
Stokes	3	5	7	11.69
Dulany	4	2	6	10.66
Tomlin	5	5	8	15.10
Blake	2	3	5	8.00

Stokes: $Y_{predicted} = 1.043 + 1.548\,(3) + .752\,(5) + .320\,(7) = 11.69$
Dulany: $Y_{predicted} = 1.043 + 1.548\,(4) + .752\,(2) + .320\,(6) = 10.66$
Tomlin: $Y_{predicted} = 1.043 + 1.548\,(5) + .752\,(5) + .320\,(8) = 15.10$
Blake: $Y_{predicted} = 1.043 + 1.548\,(2) + .752\,(3) + .320\,(5) = 8.00$

want to set a cutoff score on the predicted criterion. For instance, based on their standards of what is acceptable employee performance, they may decide that the predicted criterion cutoff is 11.00, which means that no matter how many position openings are available, they will not hire anyone whose predicted criterion score is under 11.00. In terms of our example in Table 7.4 and based on this cutoff, only Tomlin and Stokes would be considered "qualified" to be hired into CS&J Products. Second, it is possible that the executives at CS&J or PE Levy & Associates feel that it is best to set minimum cutoffs on each predictor. This would involve an approach that combines the multiple cutoff technique with the multiple regression technique. For instance, we might set a cutoff of 4.00 on the work sample test. When using the multiple regression, we could still rank-order applicants based on their predicted criterion scores, but prior to selection we would check to make sure that the applicants who fall below 4.00 on the work sample test are withdrawn from the applicant pool regardless of their predicted criterion score. In this case, Stokes and Blake would be removed from the qualified applicant pool. Think back to our cardiac surgeon example. Given the importance of psychomotor skills and medical knowledge, the use of cutoffs on these predictors, as well as a multiple regression approach, would be a very reasonable strategy for the selection of surgeons. (Prior to using the regression equation for selection, of course, we would cross-validate it either statistically or empirically.)

Usefulness of Selection Processes

At this point, we can tell the executives at CS&J that we have developed, validated, and cross-validated a selection battery that will result in successful employee selection. We can present to them a few different ways to use the predictor data in making these employment decisions, such as the multiple cutoff approach, the multiple hurdle approach, the multiple regression approach, or some combination of these. Certainly, they will be pleased with what we have to offer. However,

FIGURE 7.2 Decision Accuracy

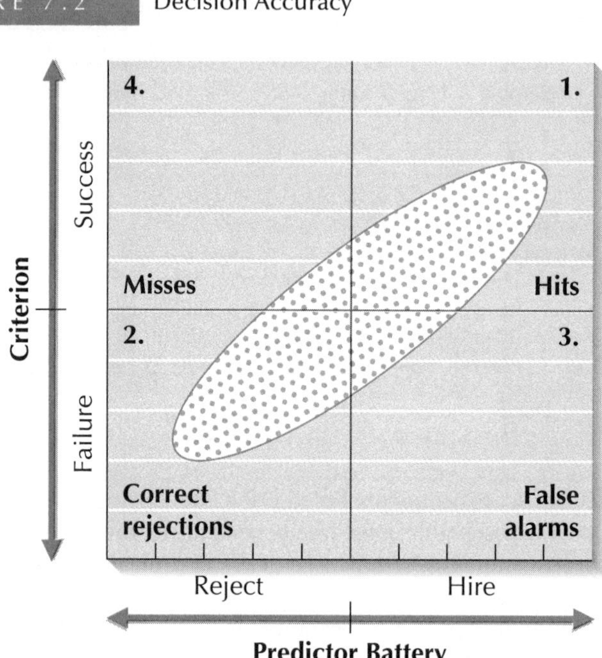

they will probably have one remaining question for us to answer: Is it worth it? The executives at CS&J aren't satisfied with knowing that we have developed a valid selection system for them; they also want to know how much better it is than their current system and how expensive (in time and dollars) it is to switch to and use this new system. These questions all deal with the **utility** of the selection battery—that is, with how useful and cost efficient it is. We will now spend some time discussing the various elements of the selection process that allow us to answer these questions for the organization.

utility
The degree to which a selection battery is useful and cost efficient.

Decision Accuracy. The first element we need to focus on is the accuracy of the selection decision—or, more specifically, the gain in accuracy that is provided by our new selection battery. After all, the whole purpose of our involvement in this project is to improve the quality of the current CS&J workforce by making better employee selection decisions.

Figure 7.2 depicts all possible theoretical outcomes of our selection situation, as represented by quadrants 1 through 4. In other words, every selection decision can be characterized by whether the person is hired or rejected and whether the person is successful or unsuccessful on the job. (Of course, we won't know about job performance until after the person has been on the job for a while.)

The first two quadrants refer to the accurate selection decisions. Quadrant 1, labeled *hits* (sometimes called "true positives"), represents the number of applicants hired on the basis of our selection system who went on to be successful performers. Quadrant 2, labeled *correct rejections* (sometimes called "true negatives"), represents the number of applicants who were not hired and would have been unsuccessful on the job. (Although this number cannot be accessed from our applicant sample because these individuals are never hired, we are able to gather information about such individuals from the validation sample.) The last two quadrants refer to the inaccurate selection decisions. Quadrant 3, labeled *false alarms* (sometimes called "false positives"), represents the applicants who were hired but proved to be ineffective performers. And Quadrant 4, labeled *misses* (sometimes called "false negatives"), represents the applicants we didn't hire but should have hired, as they would have been successful performers. (These individuals, too, can be examined only within the validation sample.)

Companies are often interested in knowing the outcome of the hiring decisions only—that is, whether the hired applicants succeed or fail. This information is provided by the following formula for *decision accuracy for hires,* which reflects the percentage of hiring decisions that are correct:

$$\text{Quadrant 1} / (\text{Quadrant 1} + \text{Quadrant 3})$$

Certainly, for jobs such as cardiac surgeon, airline pilot, air traffic controller, and nuclear power plant operator, this would be the most relevant measure of decision accuracy. Indeed, I would be willing to reject 10 airline pilots who may have proved to be successful (Quadrant 4), but I would *not* be willing to hire even 1 or 2 who prove to be unsuccessful (Quadrant 3). In other words, in the realm of public safety occupations, misses are preferable to false alarms! Therefore, it seems reasonable to focus only on Quadrants 1 and 3—hits and false alarms—as a measure of accuracy.

In other occupations, however, the number of rejected applicants who would have been successful (Quadrant 4) might constitute important information. For instance, my colleagues and I spend a great deal of time reviewing admissions into our doctoral program in I/O psychology. We are certainly concerned about admitting students who prove to be unsuccessful and do not finish the program (Quadrant 3), but we are also concerned about *not* admitting candidates who go elsewhere and do very well, indicating that they may have been very successful in our own program (Quadrant 4). The operationalization for *overall decision accuracy* looks like this:

$$(\text{Quadrant 1} + \text{Quadrant 2}) / (\text{Quadrant 1} + \text{Quadrant 2} + \text{Quadrant 3} + \text{Quadrant 4})$$

Regardless of how we define decision accuracy, however, the goal of the selection battery is to maximize the number of hits and correct rejections and to minimize the number of misses and false alarms. All else being equal, the utility of the selection battery is demonstrated by the extent to which it does both.

Validity. Maximizing hits and correct rejections while minimizing misses and false alarms will occur to the extent that the selection battery is valid. Thus the first factor that affects the utility of the selection battery is its validity. Figure 7.2 depicts the outcomes of a selection battery with a validity coefficient of about .7. (Compare this figure with the middle panel of Figure 2.8). Given this degree of validity, the small number of false alarms and misses is not surprising; the selection battery depicted here certainly maximizes the hits and correct rejections. By contrast, Figure 7.3 depicts the outcomes of a selection battery with zero validity, as represented by a circle. (Compare this figure with the left panel of Figure 2.8.) What makes the lack of validity obvious is the same number of hits, correct rejections, misses, and false alarms. In this case, individuals who score high on the battery of predictors are just as likely to be unsuccessful on the job as they are to be successful, and those who score low on the battery of predictors are just as likely to be successful on the job as they are to be unsuccessful. Thus making a selection decision with a battery that demonstrates zero validity is akin to random hiring and clearly provides no utility to the company.

base rate
The percentage of current employees who are successful on the job.

Base Rate. The **base rate** reflects the percentage of current employees who are successful on the job. In part, this percentage reflects the quality of the previous

FIGURE 7.3 The Case of No Validity

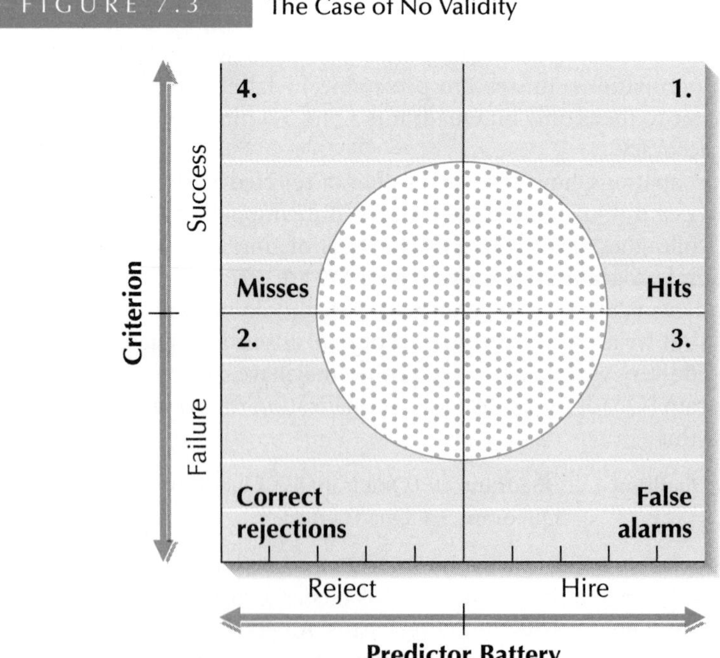

selection battery (and, perhaps, is affected by other HR processes such as performance management and training) and provides a baseline against which the new selection battery can be compared. Of course, the organization needs to set a cutoff on the criterion so that the base rate can be calculated. In most colleges, for instance, a 2.0 GPA is thought of as the criterion cutoff, and the percentage of current students who meet that cutoff is considered the base rate. Suppose that 30% of the current employees at CS&J perform at a level that CS&J has decided is acceptable. The baseline would thus be 30%, and a new selection battery that resulted in an increase in this base rate would be an improvement over the old selection battery. Of course, if CS&J had a base rate of 90%, it is unlikely that we could develop a selection battery to improve on the current one, and the utility of our newly developed selection battery would be low.

Selection Ratio. The **selection ratio** is defined as the number of job openings divided by the number of applicants. If CS&J has 20 open positions and 20 applicants, the selection ratio would be 1.00, suggesting that the cost and effort involved in developing and implementing a selection battery is unnecessary because the company would have to hire all available applicants in order to fully staff its organization. On the other hand, if CS&J has 5 open positions and 20 applicants, the selection ratio would be 25% (5/20)—a situation in which the selection battery could prove useful, especially if tough hiring decisions have to be made. Typically, the smaller the selection ratio, the greater the potential utility of the selection battery. This observation is further evidence of the importance of recruitment for increasing the number of applicants and thus providing organizations with more options. For instance, each year my colleagues and I typically receive about 100 applications for admission into our I/O doctoral program, and we average about 8 open slots. This selection ratio of 8% (8/100) suggests that we have the potential to make better decisions by investing time and money into a complex selection battery than by choosing applicants solely on the basis of their undergraduate GPA or some other easily obtainable predictor.

selection ration
The number of job openings divided by the number of applicants.

Cost. The cost associated with the development and implementation of a selection battery certainly factors into its utility. Even assuming that our selection battery is valid and improves the workforce dramatically, would CS&J be interested in it if the costs are so high as to be greater than the increased revenue from the hiring of better employees? Let us not forget that most organizations are driven, at least in part, by the "bottom line." The money spent by a company on a new selection battery would probably be compared against the additional revenues that are indirectly a function of the new system. In a dollars-and-cents world, this is really the ultimate comparison in terms of utility for CS&J and thousands of other companies like it. Of course, cost is important in another way, too. Many organizations are willing to spend thousands and thousands of dollars on a selection battery because, in the long run, it will save them money. Organizations such as the military and the upper reaches of the federal government, where a great deal of money is invested in the training and development of new employees, are especially willing to invest in selection. Because it costs millions of dollars to train an astronaut, the "false-alarm rate" is very significant. (If you saw the movie *Apollo 13,* you might recall the sophisticated flight simulators and other equipment and programs that were employed in training the astronauts.) Think of it this way: For every new recruit who is selected to be an astronaut, millions of dollars are invested; thus a great deal of money would be wasted in the training of someone who fails. This is the reason NASA prefers to invest considerable money "up front" in the selection system, to ensure that the people chosen are trainable and that the training investment will not be wasted. We'll talk more about training in the next chapter.

Putting It All Together. Now that we have discussed all of the information that comes into play when evaluating the utility of a selection battery, we can look at how this information is combined to estimate this utility. Wayne Cascio (1998) details and summarizes several approaches to this task, but for simplicity's sake we will focus on just one.

With a valid selection battery and knowledge of the organization's base rate and selection ratio, it is possible to estimate the improvement that is likely to follow from the implementation of our newly developed selection battery. Keep in mind that we can only estimate this improvement and that we are still making many assumptions about the performance of the newly hired individuals based on their potential. These high-scoring applicants may not perform well on the job for a whole host of reasons, some of which they have no control over; and in any case, not all of the people who graduate first in their class become the best employees. For now, however, we will have faith that our assumptions and calculations are correct.

Tables have been developed that allow us to estimate the improvement in the workforce that will result from the new selection battery. One version of these is known as the *Taylor-Russell Tables* (Taylor & Russell, 1939). Table 7.5 presents a portion of these tables corresponding to base rates of 30% and 70% for various levels of validity and various selection ratios. Suppose that the base rate at CS&J Products is .30 (i.e., 30% of the current employees are performing at, or better than, a level the company views as adequate), the validity coefficient for our new selection battery is .60, and the selection ratio is .40 (i.e., we have 40 openings and 100 applicants). The tables indicate that the predictive efficiency of our new selection battery is .52, which means that with the new selection battery 52% of the workforce is likely to be successful. Comparing this figure to the current base rate (30%), we see a 22% improvement in the percentage of successful employees. By contrast, a base rate of .70, a validity coefficient for our new selection battery of .20, and a selection ratio of .30 would yield a predictive efficiency of .78. Comparing this to the current base rate (.70), we see only an 8% improvement in the percentage of successful employees.

TABLE 7.5 A Portion of the Taylor-Russell Tables

Base Rate	Validity Coefficient	Selection Ratio										
		.05	*.10*	*.20*	*.30*	*.40*	*.50*	*.60*	*.70*	*.80*	*.90*	*.95*
30%	.00	.30	.30	.30	.30	.30	.30	.30	.30	.30	.30	.30
	.10	.38	.36	.35	.34	.33	.33	.32	.32	.31	.31	.30
	.20	.46	.43	.40	.38	.37	.36	.34	.33	.32	.31	.31
	.30	.54	.50	.46	.43	.40	.38	.37	.35	.33	.32	.31
	.40	.63	.58	.51	.47	.44	.41	.39	.37	.34	.32	.31
	.50	.72	.65	.58	.52	.48	.44	.41	.38	.35	.33	.31
	.60	.81	.74	.64	.58	**.52**	.47	.43	.40	.36	.33	.31
	.70	.89	.62	.72	.63	.57	.51	.46	.41	.37	.33	.32
	.80	.96	.90	.80	.70	.62	.54	.48	.42	.37	.33	.32
	.90	1.00	.98	.90	.79	.68	.58	.49	.43	.37	.33	.32
70%	.00	.70	.70	.70	.70	.70	.70	.70	.70	.70	.70	.70
	.10	.77	.76	.75	.74	.73	.73	.72	.72	.71	.71	.70
	.20	.83	.81	.79	***.78***	.77	.76	.75	.74	.73	.71	.71
	.30	.88	.86	.84	.82	.80	.78	.77	.75	.74	.72	.71
	.40	.93	.91	.88	.85	.83	.81	.79	.77	.75	.73	.72
	.50	.96	.94	.91	.89	.87	.84	.82	.80	.77	.74	.72
	.60	.98	.97	.95	.92	.90	.87	.85	.82	.79	.75	.73
	.70	1.00	.99	.97	.96	.93	.91	.88	.84	.80	.76	.73
	.80	1.00	1.00	.99	.98	.97	.94	.91	.87	.82	.77	.73
	.90	1.00	1.00	1.00	1.00	.99	.98	.95	.91	.85	.78	.74

Source: H. C. Taylor & J. T. Russell (1939).

In both of these situations, as a last step, the organization would consider the costs involved in the development and implementation of our new system and ask whether the expenditure is more than offset by the 22% or 8% improvement. Again, we should note that in most organizations, financial expenditures and revenues play a large part in human resource decisions and programs. In addition, even a 5% improvement for a job like a cardiac surgeon would be well worth a hospital's expenditure because it has such a positive effect on the organization (e.g., improved reputation and fewer malpractice suits), as well as on society at large (e.g., more lives saved). More complex approaches to utility involve estimates of the dollar value of different performance levels, but these are very difficult to calculate. (For a discussion of such approaches and a more sophisticated review and critical analysis, see Boudreau & Ramstad, 2003; Roth, Bobkio, and Mabon, 2002.)

In our discussion so far, you have come to understand not only the various predictors in selection but also various techniques used to make selection decisions and ways of evaluating the effectiveness of these techniques. You should thus have a fairly clear idea about how you could use predictor information to arrive

I/O psychologists have to learn to deal with the financial realities of the corporate sector.

"Mr. Herman, you made me laugh and you made me cry, but you didn't make me money."

at a selection decision and how cost effective this process might be. But the final component in the selection process—legal issues—is equally important. I present these issues specifically within the context of selection because it is here that they have become most relevant; but please note that legal issues apply to *all* personnel decisions, such as performance appraisal ratings used for promotion, layoffs, firings, salary increments, and training (which we will discuss in the next chapter).

LEGAL ISSUES IN INDUSTRIAL PSYCHOLOGY

It's hard to believe, but prior to the early 1960s discrimination in the hiring of employees was *not* illegal in the United States. For instance, it was accepted practice for companies to have "white jobs" for which African-Americans were not even considered. As a reaction to this history of discrimination, the Civil Rights Act of 1964 was designed to provide equality of opportunity and treatment to all people regardless of "race, color, religion, sex, or national origin." Title VII of this act, which deals specifically with employment, led to creation of the Equal Employment Opportunity Commission (EEOC). The EEOC began operating on July 2, 1965 (EEOC, 1998), and in 1978 it published the "Uniform Guidelines on Employee Selection Procedures" (hereafter referred to as the Guidelines), which have been adopted as the legal guidelines for employee selection. In 1987, the Society for Industrial and Organizational Psychology (SIOP) published its *Principles for the Validation and Use of Personnel Selection Procedures* (revised in 2003) to serve as a technical guide for those who work in the field of employee selection, with the caveat that the principles were not intended to be written as law. These two documents have emerged as a "how to" guide for personnel decisions. Both are used extensively by professionals in the field and referred to in court decisions. Much of the content discussed in the remainder of this chapter is based on these documents.

Employment At-Will

According to the common law doctrine of **employment at-will,** employers and employees have the right to initiate and terminate the employment relationship at any time, for any reason or for no reason at all. This approach to employment began in England and was incorporated into the United States during colonial times (Dunford & Devine, 1998). However, the interpretation of this idea has changed such that companies are sued each year by employees who claim "wrongful discharge" by their employers. Therefore, many organizations play it safe and no longer rely on employment at-will. Instead they maintain "just cause" discharge policies, which present to the employees acceptable reasons for discharge (Dunford & Devine, 1998). Although employment at-will is still the default employment condition, there are exceptions, such as the existence or implication of an employment contract that prevents either employer or employee from ending the employment relationship prematurely. The most extensive limitation to employment at-will is federal legislation that renders illegal any employment decisions, such as firings and layoffs, that are based on certain conditions, such as race and gender. We will discuss these federal laws shortly, but first a few other major concepts need to be introduced.

employment at-will
A common law doctrine stating that employers and employees have the right to initiate and terminate the employment relationship at any time, for any reason or for no reason at all.

Adverse Impact

To appreciate the intricacies of employment law as it applies to I/O psychology, you need to understand **adverse impact.** This concept, defined in the Guidelines as the "80% rule of thumb," is the common operationalization of discrimination according to the courts. A selection procedure is said to exhibit adverse impact (i.e., to discriminate) against a group if the selection rate for that group is less than 80% of the selection rate for the group with the highest selection rate. Usually, but not always, it is a minority group that has been hired at a rate lower than

adverse impact
The most accepted operationalization of discrimination, defined in the Guidelines as the "80% rule of thumb." A selection battery exhibits adverse impact (i.e., discriminates) against a group if the selection rate for that group is less than 80% of the selection rate for the group with the highest selection rate.

TABLE 7.6 The Absence and Presence of Adverse Impact

Case	Majority Selection Rate	Minority Selection Rate	80% Rule Cutoff	Legal Status
#1	60 out of 100 Caucasians hired (60%)	50 out of 100 African-Americans hired (50%)	80% of 60% = 48%	(50% > 48%), thus no adverse impact
#2	40 out of 50 men hired (80%)	20 out of 80 women hired (25%)	80% of 80% = 64%	(25% < 64%), thus adverse impact

that for Caucasians. For instance, if we hired 60 out of 100 Caucasian applicants (a selection rate of 60%), we would avoid adverse impact if we also hired at least 48 out of 100 African-American applicants (i.e., 80% of the 60% rate for Caucasians, or 48%).

Table 7.6 illustrates two such cases—one in which adverse impact is absent and the other in which it is present. Notice that the actual minority cutoff is determined by multiplying the majority rate by 80%. If the minority rate is less than this cutoff, there is adverse impact; if it is at least equal to this cutoff, there is no adverse impact. Although adverse impact is important, its presence alone does not indicate illegal discrimination. To understand this better, let's take a general look at how a discrimination case might proceed.

First, the plaintiff (i.e., the employee who feels discriminated against) must demonstrate a *prima facie* case. In other words, the plaintiff must show that "on the face of it" the numbers indicate adverse impact. For instance, a Hispanic plaintiff might argue that her not having been hired by a particular company is indicative of a pattern exhibited by this company—a pattern that shows adverse impact against minorities, including Hispanics. The plaintiff would demonstrate this pattern by providing the company's own data showing that the 80% rule has been violated and that minorities are being hired at a rate less than 80% of the rate for the majority group.

Second, the defendant (i.e., the company) may argue against these statistics by showing that the plaintiff is looking at only some of the data, interpreting the data incorrectly, or considering the wrong data. In this case, however, let's say that the company does not dispute the data but instead admits that adverse impact exists. At this point, the company has a few options to combat the charge of illegal discrimination.

The traditional approach is to demonstrate that, despite the presence of adverse impact, the selection battery is *job related* for all minority groups, as well as for the majority group. The job relevance of the selection battery is usually established through a validation study, by which the case is made that predictors are tapping the KSAOs that have been shown to be important for success on this job.

This is one reason why validation studies are so important. If the company can show that the selection battery is valid such that, regardless of ethnicity, race, and gender, those employees who score high on the selection battery are successful on the job and those who score low on the selection battery are unsuccessful on the job, the courts are likely to recognize this case as an example of adverse impact that is *not* illegal. Recent rulings and legislation has made it clear that the defendant must show that each test that was part of the selection battery was job related—it's not enough to show that the bottom line result was to hire an appropriate percentage of minorities from the pool deemed acceptable (Posthuma, 2002).

Another approach the company can take to rebut the claim of illegal discrimination is to argue that employees of a particular race, ethnicity, or gender are a *business necessity* and that the business cannot adequately be conducted without them. This argument sometimes amounts to showing that a particular race or gender is a *bona fide occupational qualification (BFOQ).* But it is interpreted very narrowly by the courts. Imagine the difficulty of convincing a judge that in order to operate your business you need to hire only females. In fact, this very issue was addressed in an interesting case known as *Diaz v. Pan Am* (1971). Diaz was a man who wanted to be a flight attendant; but because of Pan Am's policy, which favored women to the exclusion of men, he was not selected. The expert witness who testified on behalf of Pan Am argued that providing intangibles such as passenger comfort and psychological well-being were critical to the job and that only people with feminine traits could provide them successfully. In its defense, Pan Am even cited satisfaction data indicating that most customers preferred women flight attendants. In short, Pan Am claimed that gender was a BFOQ and that it was acceptable to hire only women for this job. Think about your most recent flight, and you can probably figure out how this case was decided! The court ruled that the primary function of an airline is to transport passengers safely, and, thus, maintaining safety was the chief job of a flight attendant. A pleasant environment is tangential to this primary function; therefore, gender could not be a BFOQ. It further noted that customer preference has no weight in determining a BFOQ. Can men do the job adequately? Of course they can, so intentionally not hiring them is illegal.

Affirmative Action

Before examining some of the major employment laws, we need to consider a far-reaching concept that is very important in this area: **affirmative action (AA).** It is employed by many organizations to increase the number of minorities or protected class members (i.e., African-Americans, Asian-Americans, Hispanic-Americans, Native Americans, and women) in targeted jobs. Affirmative action is not a quota system, although the popular press tends to characterize it that way. This is not to say that quotas never emerge from or develop in parallel to affirmative action programs. But the important point here is that such programs aim

affirmative action
A practice employed in many organizations to increase the number of minorities or protected class members in targeted jobs.

Diaz v. Pan Am made it easier for males to be hired as flight attendants.

to address the discrimination that has existed in many companies and industries throughout history.

Affirmative action programs vary from relatively uncontroversial (as when a company networks with minorities to increase their awareness of job opportunities) to very controversial (as when minorities are hired preferentially). When implemented appropriately, such programs do not result in the hiring of *unqualified* minorities; they may, however, result in the hiring of minority applicants whose qualifications are equal to those of majority applicants. Affirmative action programs have been popular for many years, as evidenced by the inclusion of the following phrase at the bottom of many job advertisements on TV, in the print media, and elsewhere: "This organization is an EEO/AA employer, and qualified minority candidates are encouraged to apply." (EEO/AA stands for Equal Employment Opportunity/Affirmative Action.)

Much has been written in recent years, both in the popular press and the academic literature, about affirmative action. For instance, some recent studies have examined stigmatization of AA, finding that individuals who benefit from AA are sometimes viewed as incompetent (Evans, 2003) and that individuals view AA as having greater potential benefits to individuals when a justification based on organizational fairness is provided than when it is not (Aberson, 2003). Perceptions of justice also played a role in a study examining the attitudes of black applicants to AA. Black applicants reported as *less fair* an AA plan operationalized as showing preference for a black candidate whose qualifications were the same as those of a white candidate than they did similar plans that emphasized special recruit-

Many organizations publicly emphasize that equal employment opportunity is an important principle underlying how they do business.

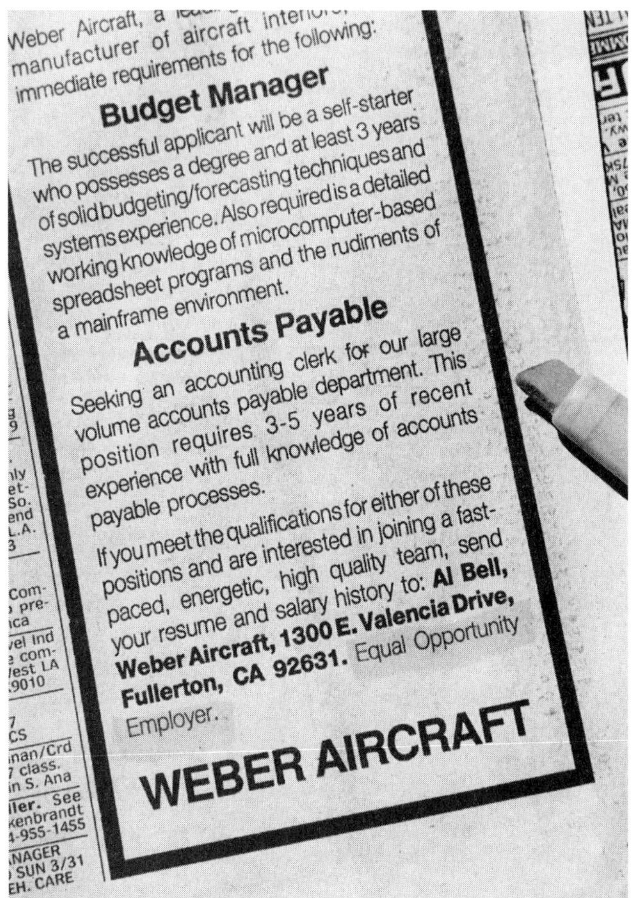

ment of black candidates or that fostered equity between black and white applicants (Slaughter, Sinar, &Bachiochi, 2002).

Two recent court cases have the potential to play a central role in how AA plans are viewed and implemented by organizations. However, both of these cases are about college admissions decisions, and thus it is still unclear to what extent these rulings will affect traditional organizational AA plans (for an early clue as to how these might generalize to organizational selection systems, see *Petit v. Chicago,* 2003). The University of Michigan was sued by two Caucasian males who argued that they were denied admission to the College of Literature, Science, and the Arts because even though they were both qualified, preference was shown to candidates who were classified as "underrepresented minorities" (*Gratz v. Bollinger,* 2003). The Supreme Court ruled for the plaintiffs, citing an admission policy that automatically distributed 20 points (1/5 of the points needed to guarantee admission) to every underrepresented minority as too global in form. Ignoring individual

TABLE 7.7 Major U.S. Employment Legislation

Legislation	Year	Description
Equal Pay Act	1963	Prohibits discrimination in pay and benefits on the basis of sex for jobs in the same establishment that require equal skill, effort, and responsibility and that are performed under similar working conditions.
Civil Rights Act (Title VII)	1964	Makes it unlawful for an employer with 15 or more employees to discriminate against individuals with respect to hiring, compensation, terms, conditions, and privileges of employment on the basis of race, color, religion, national origin, or sex.
Executive Order 11246	1965	Prohibits job discrimination by employers holding federal contracts or subcontracts on the basis of race, color, sex, national origin, or religion and requires affirmative action to ensure equality of opportunity in all aspects of employment.
Age Discrimination in Employment Act	1967	Makes it unlawful for an employer with 20 or more employees to discriminate against individuals who are 40 years or older with respect to hiring, compensation, terms, conditions, and privileges of employment on the basis of age.
Americans with Disabilities Act	1990	Makes it unlawful for an employer with 15 or more employees to discriminate against qualified individuals with disabilities with respect to hiring, compensation, terms, conditions, and privileges of employment.
Civil Rights Act	1991	Amends the 1964 act and the ADA to allow compensatory and punitive damages, but places caps on the amounts that can be awarded. Also provides for jury trials in suits brought under these laws.
Family and Medical Leave Act	1993	Allows eligible employees to take job-protected, unpaid leave for up to a total of 12 weeks in any 12 months because of (1) the birth of a child and the need to care for a newborn, (2) the placement of a child with the employee for adoption, (3) the need to care for a family member with a serious health condition, or (4) the employee's own serious health condition.

differences and qualifications among these minority applicants seemed to go against the purpose inherent in diversity initiatives, which is considering all that individuals bring to the situation and choosing those that are likely to diversify the educational environment.

The University of Michigan Law School was sued by a Caucasian female who argued that she was denied admission due to racial preferences as well (*Grutter v.*

Bollinger, 2003). The Supreme Court saw this case very differently and ruled for the university. First, they noted that diversity is a compelling interest for the law school. In other words, the court said that diversity in graduate education, such as law school, can provide educational benefits to the entire student body and is important. They did not make the same statement regarding the undergraduate admission process (see *Gratz v. Bollinger*). Second, the court noted that the law school system, which considered race as a "plus" in the admission process (and did not allocate a fixed number of points based on one's race) and which considered various elements of diversity on an individualized basis, does not make race the defining feature of its decision. These two decisions are very recent and will, according to Justice Antonin Scalia, generate lawsuits for years to come. We don't know what the outcome of this split decision will be, but the next 5 to 10 years of decisions should prove to be very interesting as our society continues to struggle with these issues. A terrific summary of these cases can be found in Gutman (2003).

Table 7.7 presents a list of the major U.S. employment legislation prohibiting job discrimination. These are described in the following sections, along with legal cases where appropriate.

Equal Pay Act

As we discussed in the section on comparable worth in Chapter 3, the Equal Pay Act (1963) makes it illegal to provide unequal pay and benefits to men and women who are holding jobs that are equal. The disputes that arise regarding this law usually involve the definition of *equal work*. In defining this phrase in terms of skill, effort, responsibility, and working conditions, the Equal Pay Act prevents companies from paying men more than women (or women more than men) unless the companies can show that the work is not equal. Further, what is and is not equal is decided on a case-by-case basis. For instance, the court ruled in *Brennan v. Prince William Hospital Corp.* (1974) that male hospital orderlies who were assigned the extra duty of turning patients over in bed did not merit additional pay relative to female nurse aides who were not assigned this extra duty. Indeed, the courts have made it clear over the years that there must be sizable and reasonable differences in the work to support different pay for men and women; slight differences such as that described above in *Brennan* have not been viewed by the courts as sufficient to merit unequal pay rates (Gutman, 2000).

Civil Rights Act

Title VII of the Civil Rights Act of 1964 further limited discrimination in the United States. From its inception on July 2, 1965, the EEOC has been charged with enforcing the principal federal statutes prohibiting discrimination, and this 1964 act is the most far-reaching one. The Civil Rights Act of 1991, which modified the 1964 act, deals with issues of monetary damages and jury trials, in addition to clarifying each party's obligation in adverse-impact cases. Unless noted, when I refer to the Civil Rights Act (CRA), I am referring to both laws. In general, the CRA prohibits employment discrimination based on race, color, religion, sex, or national origin, thereby mandating that it is illegal to make employment decisions based on these factors because such decisions would result in discrimination and "unequal opportunity" rather than the equal opportunity that is at the basis of the employment laws.

One of the most important cases in this area is *Griggs v. Duke Power* (1971), in which the court ruled that even when a company argues convincingly that it had no intention to discriminate, if adverse impact exists it is incumbent on the company to demonstrate that the selection battery was job related. Cases of this kind are sometimes called **disparate impact cases,** because they involve a minority group discriminated against or unfairly affected by employment procedures that appear to be unintentional; in other words, there is adverse impact regardless of intent. In **disparate treatment cases,** by contrast, the discrimination is intentional and a result of differential treatment (as in *Diaz v. Pan Am,* 1971). Most cases in personnel law are of the disparate impact variety, in which discrimination emerges as a byproduct of employment procedures.

disparate impact cases
Cases involving a minority group discriminated against or unfairly affected by employment procedures that appear to be unintentional.

disparate treatment cases
Cases involving discrimination that results from intentional differential treatment or behavior.

In *Griggs v. Duke Power,* the plaintiff, Mr. Griggs, was an African-American male who had not been hired as a laborer and presented data documenting adverse impact against African-Americans. The defendant, Duke Power, responded by saying that the adverse impact was unintentional, but it lost the case largely because it could not demonstrate the job relatedness of its selection battery, as a validation study was never done. Think about this case for a minute, because it is very, very important. What the court was saying, and this still applies today, is that it is illegal to hire only Caucasians, even when they score better on the selection battery, *if the selection battery has not been demonstrated to predict job performance.* Another conclusion from this decision is that even professionally developed tests can be illegal if the company cannot show that the KSAOs measured by those tests are job related.

In addition to prohibiting discrimination in employment decisions based on race (an issue that certainly receives the most attention in the courts and the popular press), the CRA prohibits discrimination based on *national origin,* such that no one can be denied equal employment opportunity because of ancestry, culture, birthplace, or linguistic characteristics common to a specific ethnic group (EEOC, 2004b). For instance, a company cannot refuse to hire someone because she has an accent unless the company can show that the accent impairs job performance. Over the past 8 years there has been an increase of about 20% in National Origin discrimination cases, but the EEOC attributes most of that increase to a post–9/11 backlash against Muslims and people of Middle Eastern descent (Employment Practices Solutions, 2002). The EEOC has developed a new website for both employers and employees who have questions about the law regarding National Origin discrimination, as well as a new compliance manual (EEOC Updates, 2002). Employment decisions based on *religion* are illegal as well. Further, companies can be required to make reasonable accommodations for individuals' religious practices (EEOC, 2004d). For instance, they may have to provide flexibility in schedules for Jewish employees whose religious practices prevent them from working on the Sabbath, if this can be done without undue hardship to the employer. Protection is also provided to *pregnant women* under the CRA, which stipulates that discrimination on the basis of pregnancy, childbirth, or related medical conditions constitutes unlawful sex discrimination. The bottom line is that pregnant women cannot be treated differently from other applicants or employees with similar abilities (EEOC, 2004c).

Also prohibited by the CRA is **sexual harassment,** which includes such behaviors as unwelcome sexual advances, requests for sexual favors, and other conduct of a sexual nature, submission to or rejection of which affects one's job or creates an offensive work environment (EEOC, 2004e). There are two forms of sexual harassment. The first is *quid pro quo harassment,* which refers to situations in which advancement or continuation in a company is contingent on sexual favors. (*Quid pro quo* means "this for that.") This is the blatant kind of sexual harassment that we tend to hear about most often. (You may recall hearing about Hollywood actresses who were given the unmistakable impression that their chances of getting a particular role would be greater if they slept with the director.)

sexual harassment
Behaviors such as unwelcome sexual advances, requests for sexual favors, and other conduct of a sexual nature, submission to or rejection of which affects one's job or creates an offensive work environment.

The second form is *hostile work environment harassment,* defined by the courts in *Meritor Savings Bank v. Vinson* (1986) as verbal or physical behavior that creates an intimidating, hostile, or offensive work environment or an environment that interferes with one's job performance. Ms. Vinson was abused verbally and sexually by her boss at Meritor Savings Bank, and the court ruled in favor of Vinson, arguing that this behavior was both abusive and "unwelcome." Thus hostile work environment was established as a type of sexual harassment (Cascio, 1998). Do you recall reading about Clarence Thomas's Supreme Court confirmation hearing in 1991? It was during this hearing that Anita Hill, a lawyer employed at the EEOC, where Thomas was her supervisor, raised issues about his sex-related talk, which she alleged created a hostile work environment. Though not a legal proceeding as such, this was certainly the most famous "case" focusing attention on the issue of sexual harassment. Of course, Justice Thomas was confirmed by the Senate after a rather long and difficult hearing and still serves on the Supreme Court of the United States.

Executive Order 11246

Executive Order 11246, enacted in 1965, prohibits job discrimination by employers holding federal contracts or subcontracts on the basis of race, color, sex, national origin, or religion. This piece of legislation is very similar to the CRA but is relevant for federal agencies and those organizations that do work for federal agencies. For instance, universities fall within this legislation.

Age Discrimination in Employment Act

Individuals who are 40 years of age or over are protected from discrimination by the Age Discrimination in Employment Act (ADEA), signed into law by President Lyndon Johnson on December 15, 1967. According to the ADEA, it is unlawful to discriminate against a person because of his or her age with respect to any employment-related decision (EEOC, 2004a). In addition, it is illegal to indicate any age preferences or limitations in job ads or notices. Exceptions are possible only when the company can demonstrate that age is a BFOQ necessary to the conduct of its business. In fact, BFOQs are more accepted by the courts with respect to age than to sex. *EEOC v. U. of Texas Health Science Center at San Antonio* (1983) is one example of a case in which the court allowed age as a BFOQ exception—specifically, by upholding a maximum age of 45 for campus police officers. In its ruling, the court noted that because the job was dangerous and required individuals to be on the beat alone, an age limit of 45 was a reasonable and safe requirement. Another example is the Age 60 Rule, which states that no commercial airline may employ a pilot or copilot who is 60 years old or older. Similarly, individuals cannot be initially hired as air traffic controllers if they are over 30 years old, and individuals can remain in the position only until they turn 56 years old (Sterns, Doverspike, & Lax, in press).

Cleverly v. Western Electric (1979) is a good example of a typical ADEA case. Cleverly, an engineer was fired 6 months before his pension benefits were to become fully vested—despite many years of distinguished service. In any ADEA case, plaintiffs must demonstrate that they (1) are members of the protected class (i.e., 40 or over), (2) were doing satisfactory work, (3) were discharged despite

In most jobs, individuals cannot be forced to retire at a certain age.

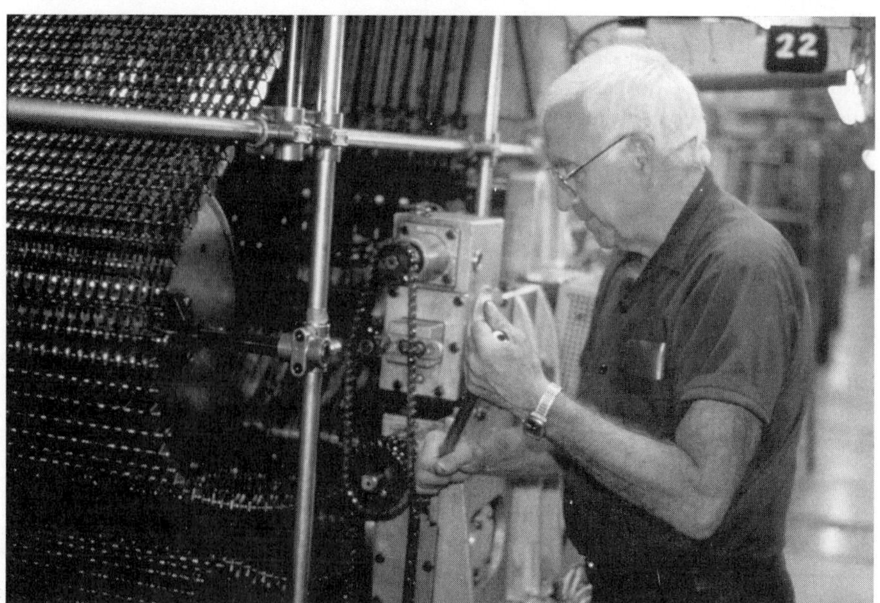

satisfactory work, and (4) were replaced by younger persons (Cascio, 1998). Cleverly was able to meet each of these requirements and was awarded back pay. Western Electric had even made direct statements to him noting that he was being let go to make way for young engineers!

Americans with Disabilities Act

Title I of the Americans with Disabilities Act (ADA), which was signed into law by President George Herbert Walker Bush in 1990 (and took effect on July 26, 1992), prohibits discrimination against qualified individuals with disabilities in employment decisions. To clarify the role played by the ADA in organizations, I will start by defining a few terms. First, according to the EEOC (1997), a person with a *disability* is someone who (1) has a physical or mental impairment that substantially limits one or more major life activities, such as seeing, hearing, speaking, working, learning, and walking; (2) has a record of such an impairment; or (3) is regarded as having such an impairment. Thus, for example, a person with a disability may be blind, have limited use of his or her legs, have a heart condition, have impaired hearing, or have short-term memory problems as a result of a stroke or other illness. As this list makes clear, many illnesses and ailments qualify as disabilities under the law. However, the law applies not to all disabled employees but only to those who are otherwise qualified for the job in question. By *qualified,* the EEOC means that the person can perform the essential functions of the job—if necessary, with the aid of reasonable accommodations.

Essential functions are tasks that are significant and meaningful aspects of the job. In short, then, it is illegal to deny someone a job because he can't perform tasks that are only tangential to the job. For example, in a company in which heavy lifting is seldom necessary but occasionally useful, the company should be able to make other arrangements when heavy lifting is called for. In those instances, someone with a bad back could still do the essential functions of the job, whereas someone else could do the lifting.

essential functions
Tasks that are significant and meaningful aspects of the job.

Reasonable accommodations are changes or exceptions made by the employer that would allow the qualified disabled individual to successfully do the job. They include redesigning existing facilities so that they are readily usable by individuals with disabilities (e.g., installing an elevator in a building that does not currently have one), restructuring jobs and schedules to allow disabled persons to perform their jobs, and acquiring equipment devices, training materials, and qualified readers/interpreters to aid disabled persons. An example in this last category would be voice-activated computer software that allows individuals who have lost the use of their hands to write documents to computer disks without having to type them.

reasonable accommodations
Changes or exceptions made by an employer that allow qualified disabled individuals to successfully do a job.

Employers are required to make reasonable accommodations, but only if such accommodations do not impose undue hardship on themselves. This brings us to our final definition: **undue hardship,** an accommodation that would result in significant difficulty or expense given the employer's size and financial resources.

undue hardship
An accommodation for the disabled that would result in significant difficulty or expense given the employer's size and financial resources.

Because of the ADA, disabled workers who are qualified for a particular job can not be rejected for that job because of their disability.

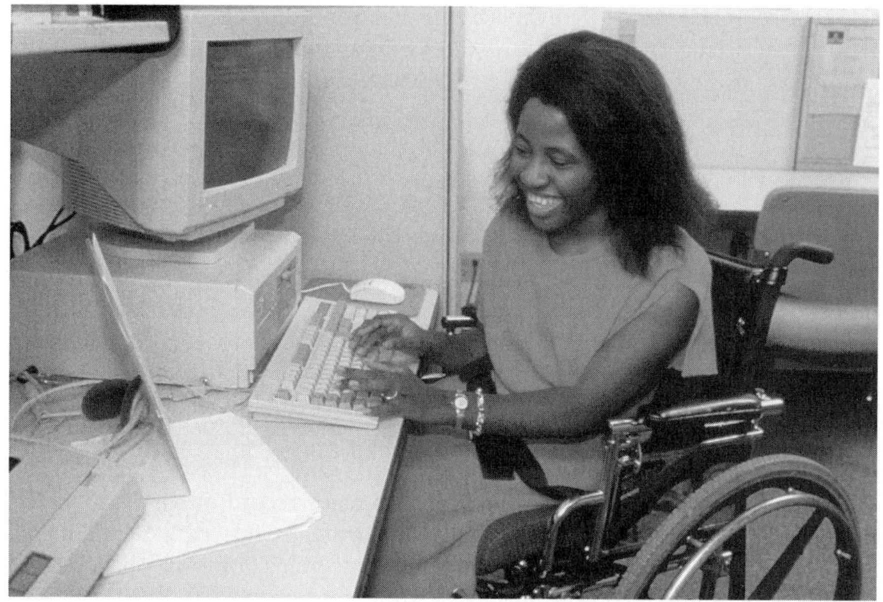

Because the ADA is a relatively new law, it is still unclear how the courts will define essential functions, although they will probably rely, in part, on job analyses and job descriptions. More at issue is what the courts will consider reasonable accommodation. This will likely be interpreted on a case-by-case basis. For instance, in *Ethridge v. State of Alabama* (1994), the court ruled that Ethridge, a police applicant, could not perform the essential functions of the job due to his limited use of one hand and that no reasonable accommodation existed. The essential function cited by the court was shooting in a two-handed position. In a more recent case, *Sutton v. United Air Lines* (1999), Sutton was not hired by United Air Lines because her uncorrected vision was worse than the 20/100 organizational requirement. Sutton claimed that this was a violation of the ADA. However, the Supreme Court ruled that because her vision was correctable with glasses or contact lenses, her vision impairment was not a disability that limited her in any major life activity. Her claim was thus rejected. Some argue that the ADA needs to be amended because many impairments don't meet the narrow definition of a disability (Lee, 2003). Further, some recent research suggests that U.S. citizens' views of what constitutes a disability do not match those covered by the ADA (Popovich, Scherbaum, Scherbaum, & Polinko, 2003).

Probably the most famous ADA case to date is *Martin v. PGA Tour, Inc.* (1998). Casey Martin was a disabled professional golfer whose right leg was so disabled that when he walked he was placed at significant risk of fracturing his leg. Yet he could do everything else required by the game of golf. Martin sued the PGA after it refused his request that a reasonable accommodation be made on his behalf to allow him to use a golf cart on the PGA tour. The PGA asserted that walking is a substantive rule of its competition and that waiving this rule fundamentally alters the competition and gives Martin a competitive advantage. The judge ruled that allowing Martin to use a cart, given his personal circumstances, would *not* fundamentally alter the PGA competition. He further argued that it was a "gross distortion of reality" to think that providing Martin with a cart would give him a competitive advantage, given not only his disability and the pain he experiences simply being on his feet but also the stress that is associated with the very real risk of serious injury. Thus the judge concluded that the requested accommodation of a cart is eminently reasonable in light of Martin's disability. The PGA's recent appeal of this decision (*PGA Tour, Inc. v. Martin,* 2000) was rejected by the Supreme Court, which ruled that allowing Martin to use a cart would not fundamentally alter the nature of the game, given that Martin's disability results in far greater fatigue than the other golfers experience by walking the course.

Family and Medical Leave Act

The first piece of legislation signed by President Bill Clinton was the Family and Medical Leave Act (FMLA) in August of 1993, which allowed eligible employees to take job-protected, unpaid leave for up to 12 weeks owing to family-related issues such as the birth of a child, the serious health condition of a family member, or one's own serious health condition. *Serious health condition* is defined as an illness, injury, impairment, or physical or mental condition that involves in-patient care or continuous treatment by a healthcare provider (Franklin & Gringer, 1999). In general, the employee has the right to return to the same position or an equivalent position with equivalent pay and benefits at the conclusion of the leave. The purpose of the FMLA is to provide employees with the opportunity to balance their work and family life and to promote the security and economic stability of the family (Department of Labor, 2000). California has recently become the first state to pass a paid family and medical leave statute that requires employers to provide 6 weeks of paid family leave to every eligible employee for each 12-month period. This balance between work and family life will be considered in more detail in Chapter 11, on stress and worker well-being.

As we have seen, legal issues are tightly linked with employment decisions, especially employee selection. In general, employment laws attempt to ensure *equal employment opportunity* to all individuals. According to the EEOC (1998), it is illegal to discriminate in any aspect of employment such as, but not limited to, the following:

- hiring and firing
- compensation, assignment, or classification of employees
- transfer, promotion, layoff, or recall
- job advertisements
- recruitment
- testing

- use of company facilities
- training and apprenticeship programs
- fringe benefits
- pay, retirement plans, and disability leave

This is an exciting area that continues to grow and develop. Table 7.7 lists most of the major pieces of employment legislation in existence as of this writing. Because a few of these laws are relatively new, and because legal work is so driven by court decisions and case interpretations, I suggest that you consult the websites cited throughout the references in this chapter for the most recent information on industrial psychology and the law, especially with respect to current court cases.

SUMMARY

Whereas Chapter 6 discussed the many types of predictors used in employee selection, this chapter has presented information about how to use those predictors in making selection decisions. Predictive validation, concurrent validation, and validity generalization were examined in light of how important they are for employee selection. Recruitment was also discussed as an important precursor to employee selection.

Various approaches to the selection process were discussed, including the multiple cutoff, multiple hurdle, and multiple regression techniques. This part of the discussion provided both a "how to" guide and an overview of the differences among these approaches. A lengthy discussion of utility followed; here we noted that if a selection battery is not viewed as useful for an organization, the organization is unlikely to be interested in it. We also looked at two ways in which decision accuracy can be operationalized: decision accuracy for hires and overall decision accuracy. Validity, base rate, selection ratio, and cost were identified as important factors affecting the utility of a new selection battery.

The last half of the chapter was spent on legal issues in industrial psychology. The emphasis was on selection, as it is in this area that legal issues tend to emerge most often. First, we discussed the history of the EEOC. Next, we examined employment at-will, adverse impact, and affirmative action, as these are among the most important concepts one must understand in order to appreciate the context and procedures involved in personnel law. Finally, we considered the major employment laws currently in place (see Table 7.7). Distinctions were drawn between disparate treatment and disparate impact, between *quid pro quo* harassment and hostile work environment harassment, between BFOQ defenses and job-relatedness defenses, and between reasonable accommodation and undue hardship.

REVIEW QUESTIONS

1. What are the steps involved in conducting a predictive validation study and a concurrent validation study? Discuss the differences between these two approaches.
2. Define validity generalization and situational specificity.
3. How do multiple cutoff approaches to selection differ from multiple regression approaches to selection? Where do multiple hurdles fit in?
4. What is utility, and why are organizations interested in this concept?
5. How can decision accuracy be operationalized in selection contexts?
6. What is employment at-will, and what are the exceptions to this rule?
7. Explain adverse impact and the 80% rule.
8. What is affirmative action? Is it the same as a quota system?
9. What are the major employment laws, and what do they prohibit?
10. Review the two types of sexual harassment discussed in this chapter.

SUGGESTED READINGS

EEOC. (2004, May). *U.S. Equal Employment Opportunity Commission: An overview.* EEOC. Available online at http:www.eeoc.gov/overview.html [2004, January 6]. The EEOC website is a valuable source of information relevant to I/O psychology and personnel law, including a history and overview of the EEOC itself.

Robinson, R. H., Franklin, G. M., & Wayland, R. (2002). *The regulatory environment of human resource management.* Orlando, FL: Harcourt College. This text presents a nice framework for understanding and interpreting personnel law. A technical presentation is made more user-friendly by many useful examples.

Schmidt, F. L., & Hunter, J. E. (1998). The validity and utility of selection methods in personnel psychology: Practical and theoretical implications of 85 years of research findings. *Psychological Bulletin, 124*(2), 262–274. This thorough review of selection research was conducted by two well-known and respected experts in the area. It covers reviews from the past 85 years and provides estimates of the validity of 19 selection tests and test combinations.

Training and Development

8

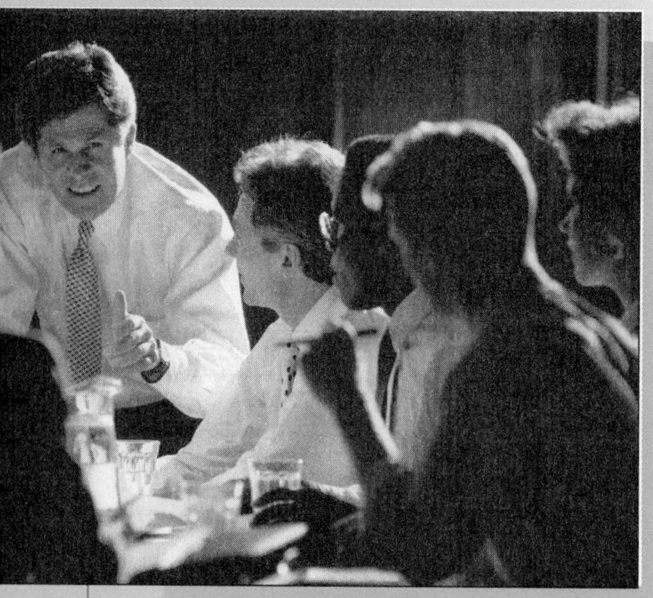

CHAPTER OUTLINE

My purpose in this section on industrial psychology has been to discuss the major human resource (HR) functions in organizations—that is, what HR professionals do at their jobs. We have also examined job analysis in detail, as it is the foundation on which industrial psychology is built. The job analysis (Chapter 3) leads to job descriptions and job specifications, which are used to develop predictors (Chapter 6) and criteria (Chapter 4); to implement performance appraisal systems (Chapter 5), selection systems (Chapter 7), and compensation systems (Chapter 3); and to design, implement, and evaluate training programs (Chapter 8).

The final chapter of this section discusses the extremely important role of training and development in organizations. Surveys consistently report that over 90% of Fortune 500 companies have some type of formal training program. According to the American Society for Training and Development, the typical firm spent about $2.1 million on training in 1998, and the industry, in general, spent about $5.5 billion. The average expenditures by firms considered on the leading edge of training in 1997 approached $2,000 per employee; in 1998, they spent about $4.7 million on training (Bassi & Van Buren, 1998). At a very basic level, we can think of training as being any kind of teaching that is related to one's job—it's about employee development. In previous chapters, we have seen how organizational efficiency is affected by the selection, appraisal, and compensation of employees. This chapter demonstrates how organizational efficiency is also affected by training of employees. Training is pervasive across organizations, and you have probably been trained at some time in your working life. Was the training helpful? Did you need the training that was provided to you? Was the trainer talented and skilled in providing the training material? Did you learn better, more efficient work strategies from the training? Did the training carry over to your work on the job? Was the training program evaluated in any way, and did you have input into the evaluation of that program? Were you a better employee as a result of the training? Was the organization more efficient as a result of the training? The answers to such questions are very important to the development of both employees and organizations.

LEARNING OBJECTIVES

This chapter should help you understand:

- how important training is to both organizations and employees.
- how to diagnose an organization's training needs through the use of organizational, task, person, and demographic analyses.
- the basic principles of learning that affect training success, such as meaningfulness, practice, overlearning, and feedback.
- what makes an organization's learning context conducive for successful training.
- each of the various training techniques, as well as their strengths and weaknesses.
- what are the key elements of transfer of training.
- the increasing importance and prevalence of both sexual harassment training and diversity training.
- the traditional criteria used in training evaluation, along with a newer perspective on these criteria.
- how to design a training evaluation study in a number of different ways.

You might be wondering why training is needed at all if you are careful about your selection system. In other words, if you select high performers, you ought to be able to save a great deal of money on training—because these employees already have the KSAOs (i.e., Knowledge, Skills, Abilities, and Other characteristics) necessary to do the job. If you take this approach, I would argue that your logic appears to be sound except for a few key issues. First, a well-developed, valid selection system is not usually enough to guarantee a skilled workforce that is ready to perform effectively the first day on the job. In other words, although a company may hire people who appear to be the most skilled and able of its applicants, they may still need job- or organization-specific training to be able to effectively do the job. For instance, IBM may hire the best and brightest graduates of computer programming departments worldwide, but if those new hires don't know the IBM paperwork system or the IBM computer networking system or aren't familiar with the culture, norms, and procedures that are part of the IBM way of doing business, they will not be effective performers until they are trained in these areas. Every company has its own way of doing things, and it is through training that those with the necessary KSAOs are taught the necessary procedures and processes.

A second reason that training is so important to organizations, even those with effective valid selection systems, is that experienced employees must sometimes be *retrained* because of changes in the job or organization. This issue will continue to grow in importance as the technological explosion in the workplace changes the nature of many jobs (Kanter, 1999; Pfeffer, 1998), making it necessary for employees to keep up with these technological changes. As a major example of this phenomenon, consider the proliferation of computers and word processors in offices. Secretaries who were trained on typewriters need to be retrained on personal computers and word-processing software in order to do the same job today that they were hired to do 20 years ago.

Third, training is important for the continued development of employees. Experts believe that training programs can lead to increased organizational commitment and job satisfaction, resulting in increased productivity, decreased absenteeism, and less turnover (Jackson & Schuler, 2000). In other words, training and development efforts result in better employees and a more productive workforce.

Although many definitions of *training* are available in the literature, the following is one that I believe is particularly good: **Training** comprises the *formal procedures* that a company utilizes to facilitate *learning* so that the resultant *behavior* contributes to the attainment of the company's *goals and objectives* (McGehee & Thayer, 1961). I've added italics to highlight the fact that when we talk about training in this chapter and elsewhere in the book, we are talking about a formal process that is focused on teaching employees so that their learning can be reflected in behaviors that help the organization achieve its goals. It's important to recognize that training is not something that companies should take lightly; on the contrary, training programs should be carefully linked to the company's goals and objectives.

training
The formal procedures that a company utilizes to facilitate learning so that the resultant behavior contributes to the attainment of the company's goals and objectives.

Effective training is a good deal more complicated and more important than Dilbert seems to realize.

Organizations must do a fair amount of analysis and background work to gather the information necessary to develop training programs. Implementation of the training program is also important, given that there are many different ways to "do training" and that some fit better with certain organizations or goals. For instance, Moreland and Myaskovsky (2000) have presented different techniques that may be useful for training work groups or teams. Moreover, the evaluation of training programs is just as crucial as the evaluation of selection systems or performance appraisal systems. Because of the expense involved, companies certainly want to know if the training program is having the desired effect—and this is where program evaluation comes in (which we will discuss later in the chapter).

ASSESSING TRAINING NEEDS

Before even beginning to develop a training program, organizations must identify what, if any, training needs exist. Organizations differ greatly in terms of what kinds of training needs they have (Brown, 2002). For instance, some organizations may need training at the management level, while others may have training needs at the nonmanagement level. Some organizations may need rater training (which we talked about in Chapter 5), while others may need performance training and still others may need sexual harassment training. In this section we will consider how organizations identify their training needs through four types of needs analyses. (For a thorough treatment of needs analysis, see Goldstein & Ford, 2002.)

ORGANIZATIONAL ANALYSIS

Where is training needed in the organization? The answer to this question is provided by an organizational analysis, which is conducted to determine the organization's short- and long-term goals and then to compare those goals to the organization's accomplishments. In this way, the organization can identify areas in which goals aren't being reached, as these areas are likely to be targets for training.

I myself have done some training work with a manufacturing company. In this case, the organizational analysis indicated that the organization had not been able to achieve one of its important goals, which was to generate a "team-oriented" relationship among managers and subordinates. The organization believed that a stronger working relationship among supervisors and subordinates would improve productivity. It saw this as a clear need and targeted improvement in that area by developing and implementing a training program designed to improve communication among employees, thus creating a shared sense of the organization's purpose and mission. Organization analysis should also consider the culture of the organization. Is it an organizational culture that sees training and development as important? If not, this suggests some potential obstacles to training that will need to be overcome and necessitates careful thought about how best to proceed. The "Practitioner Forum" presents a nice example of the reasons an organization's goals and objectives are integral to a successful training program.

Task Analysis

What duties, tasks, behaviors, and actions need to be improved? At this level, the analysis is much like the job analysis that we have discussed thus far. The organization or consultant examines the task requirements that are necessary for the successful conduct of each job, specifying exactly what it is that the new employees are going to do on their jobs. By identifying these tasks, the organization can distinguish between those the new employees are able to do immediately upon beginning employment and those for which they will require some training. Recall that in Chapter 3 we talked about different types of job analysis. The type most often used for a training needs analysis is a task-oriented job analysis in which subject matter experts (SMEs) such as incumbents or others who are familiar with the job respond to a series of items in a checklist format. The responses are collected into a summary that serves as the outcome or result of the task analysis—a summary that specifically describes the tasks that are completed on the job. For instance, a task analysis might indicate that sales clerks at a department store need to be able to operate a cash register and control the store's inventory. In this case, a training program could be developed to teach new clerks about cash registers and inventory management. Alternatively, your local telephone company may notice that customers frequently complain that mild wind storms are knocking down their telephone lines and disconnecting their service. After drawing a comparison between the task analysis and the manner in which telephone line workers were attaching the lines to the house, the company is able to conclude that the line workers did not know how to effectively do this task. Indeed, this is a clear instance in which retraining would be very beneficial.

It's important at this point to note that we talked extensively about job analysis as the foundation for selection. We used job analysis to identify KSAOs that are necessary to be an effective employee. In a related vein, we use task analysis here to identify the KSAOs that need to be further developed or refined to allow the employee to do his or her job. Quite often employees have what it takes to do the

PRACTITIONER FORUM

DAVID HYATT

Ph.D., 1990, I/O Psychology, Bowling Green State University
Vice President and Partner with DeCotiisErhard, Inc.

At DeCotiisErhard (DE) we work with some of the largest and most successful restaurant companies in the country. As such, we have learned that one of the few critical keys to success in this industry (and probably most industries) is to have fully staffed locations with fully trained people. We all know the importance of the staffing component of what we I/O psychologists do, but as I/O psychologists we sometimes forget the importance of training. However, if you think back to the last time you were dealing with someone in a customer service position who clearly did not know what he or she was doing, you will understand the importance of proper training. But training also has a very large impact on your experience as an employee. Think about it: How does it feel to be held accountable for something you were not trained to do? How likely are you to want to repeat that experience or feel that way regularly? In short, nobody likes to feel clueless on the job, and people who are not trained properly generally leave the organization for other work environments if they have options. Because we feel that training is so important, at DeCotiisErhard we spend a great deal of time training our customers how to: use our products; train their people to live their vision; and create great customer and employee experiences.

One interesting way in which training has developed in recent years is through corporate universities, which have been around for years (GE launched one in 1955) and can be structured in many ways—from a brick and mortar building to a "virtual" university on the Internet. Although their structures can be quite different, they all share a similar mission: to provide a cohesive resource for training in the organization that supports the organization's business objectives. Seems like a no-brainer: Shouldn't all training programs be supportive of the company's business objectives and be cohesive? They *should*, but frequently they aren't.

Most of the questions raised in this chapter on training are similar to those we felt were relevant for designing a corporate university for one of our customers (e.g., Who does the training? What are the organizational needs? How do we ensure effective transfer of training? What types of media will be used?). Two issues that we addressed as we were designing the university were on-site versus off-site training methods and how to design the training to maximize its transfer.

One decision that affected the scope of the university was that it was never going to have a central location where training could be conducted. This decision was made for a number of reasons, one of which was that it was countercultural. Specifically, this company's culture resisted creating a large, centralized training bureaucracy, necessitating a different path. Given that we were dealing with a large international company with over 1,000 locations, we created a university with 1,000 locations for on-site training. That decision led to another issue: If we wanted to maintain standards and make sure everyone received a consistent message, how would we get teachers or trainers to these people? Our answer was pretty simple: Instead of sending teachers to them, create a university that is self-paced and self-taught with a mentoring system so that trainees always had someone they could talk to about the course.

Finally, to maximize transfer, each course offered a series of exercises that required the learner to practice skills on site. For example, in a course on leading a meeting, the learners studied the components of a meeting, the basic processes of communication, and so on, and were then required to practice by leading a meeting. Learners were also critiqued by the workplace mentor and asked to provide self-assessments. In this way, they had the opportunity to apply the material to the workplace and to receive feedback on their performance. In addition, because the exercises could be performed on more than a one-time basis, learners could improve their skills each time they practiced.

In our applied work with large multinational organizations, and as this chapter suggests, we have found that the key to success for any training initiative, whether large or small, is first to focus on the outcomes, such as organizational needs, and then to make sure the curriculum supports the business objectives.

APPLYING YOUR KNOWLEDGE

1. Discuss how an organization's objectives can be linked with a training program.
2. In what ways can a "corporate university" improve its organizational efficiency?
3. What principles of learning seem especially relevant for this training intervention?

job but need a bit more focused training to really do it well. This is a clear example of how selection and training fit together. One way to think about the relationship between selection and training is to view selection as dealing in the raw materials (i.e., the KSAOs that employees bring to the organization) and training as developing or producing the finished product (i.e., the KSAOs that are developed through training and applied to one's job).

Person Analysis

Who needs the training? A person analysis gets quite specific, focusing on those employees who actually need training. Toward this end, it examines how well all employees are carrying out their job responsibilities and duties. For an example, let's return to our telephone company scenario. The line workers are the employees who have been identified as needing some training, and, in particular, they need training on attaching telephone wires to houses so that they aren't easily dislodged. Now, however, we must also ask: Which of the line workers are most in need of this training? If the telephone company has 2,500 line workers but only 500 of them seem unable to grasp this skill, it makes sense to target our training to those 500 employees who appear to need it. So the person analysis goes this one extra step, specifying the employees in whom training dollars should be invested.

Often, performance appraisal data (see Chapter 5) are used to identify good candidates for training. Such data might identify, for example, those department store sales clerks who are consistently rated as ineffective in inventory management and are thus in need of training in this area or those line workers whose territories have the most complaints about dislodged wires. In addition to traditional performance appraisal ratings, some organizations allow employees to nominate themselves for training in specific areas in which they feel they could be further developed as employees. Finally, sometimes organizations will give a test to diagnose employees' strengths and weaknesses using these data, rather than existing performance appraisal data, to indicate who is in need of additional training and development opportunities.

Demographic Analysis

Traditionally, training needs assessment has entailed analyses at the organization, task, and person levels. More recent research, however, has suggested that needs analysis should also take into account the demographic makeup of the organization (Latham, 1988). Basically, this involves determining the specific training needs of various demographic groups such as those protected by civil rights legislation. For instance, since the Age Discrimination in Employment Act (ADEA) has made it illegal to discriminate in the selection of employees based on age, many companies that hire older employees recognize that these individuals may need training that is not necessary for younger employees. One example is technological training. Many older employees may need such training simply as a result of having grown up during an era in which technology was less advanced, whereas younger employees have probably picked up these skills throughout their lives. It's reasonable to assume, for instance, that some older new employees on the sales force in a department store may need to be trained somewhat on the computer skills used to support the main functions of the sales job.

Another example is training for employees with disabilities. As we discussed in Chapter 7, organizations are legally required to make reasonable accommodations for disabled employees. One such accommodation may be provision of training that helps these employees do their jobs. Another is the redesign of existing training programs to accommodate disabled employees. For instance, a visual-based management skills training program may have to be altered in such a way that blind employees can participate in and benefit from the training program. Training practitioners must also avoid discriminating against employees on the basis of gender, race, physical abilities, age, ethnicity, and religion—in keeping with the laws, policies, and mission of equal employment opportunity.

LEARNING CONTEXT

Before we discuss the various training methods available, we need to discuss the learning context, because it is so important to the success of any training program. In short, the context, which includes principles of instructional design, basic principles of learning, and characteristics of the trainee and trainer, largely determines the success of a training intervention.

Instructional Design

Instructional design refers to all activities that are developed and coordinated to support the trainees' learning processes (Goldstein & Ford, 2002). The first important element of the instructional design is determining what is to be learned. Learning can take a variety of forms, but generally it can be categorized as either cognitive, psychomotor, or social. Although Gagne, Briggs, and Wager (1992) present a more sophisticated scheme, they also present a series of design features or learning conditions (e.g., providing feedback, informing trainee of goal) that can be mapped to the various categories of learning. This kind of approach allows an organization to use existing knowledge to build an effective context or environment for the specific learning targeted by the organization.

Instructional design
A set of events that facilitate training through their impact on trainees.

Principles of Learning

Learning
The relatively permanent change in behavior that occurs as a result of experience or practice.

Learning is defined as a relatively permanent change in behavior that occurs as a result of experience or practice (Wexley & Latham, 2002). Therefore, to understand training, which is all about learning, we need to spend some time getting a clearer understanding of what principles enhance the learning process. In academic circles, the research on learning has been chiefly conducted by cognitive, experimental, and social psychologists. As I/O psychologists, however, we try to apply learning principles to the design and implementation of training programs because we recognize that trainees must learn the subject matter if the programs are to be successful.

In the following sections we will focus on some of the more general principles that are important to effective organizational training.

Active Learning. Learning theory has always argued that learning is facilitated if the learner is active during the learning period. This, of course, is why professors always encourage students to take notes or outline reading assignments, talk to others about the material, and write and rewrite key concepts rather than just reading the material over and over again. The suggestions from learning theory about active learning apply very easily to training in organizations as well. One can read about how to conduct a PA interview or be provided a list of the specifications for the development of a particular product, but a better way to learn these things is to actually practice doing them, actively working with the to-be-learned material.

Size of the Unit to be Learned. The question here is whether training should be structured in such a way as to present the whole task or only part of the task in a given training session (Goldstein & Ford, 2002)—a distinction sometimes referred to as *whole versus part learning.* According to learning theorists, it is more effective to practice or be trained on the whole task at one time if the task is highly organized, coherent, and interdependent, whereas for a complex task that is easily divided into independent components, a more effective strategy is to be trained on each component separately, moving on to the next component after mastering the previous one.

For instance, let's say that I have just hired a 55-year-old man as my new secretary, that he graduated from secretarial school almost 30 years ago before personal computers had really caught on, and that he has been out of the workforce for nearly 20 years. Obviously, I need to provide this person with some training on word processing and other computer procedures that I use in my office. Here, it would probably be more efficient to teach bits and pieces of the word-processing software than to try and teach the whole program all at once. (In fact, when I myself upgrade to a new version of my word-processing software, I learn it in a piecemeal sort of way—as it would be overwhelming to try and learn all of the changes at once.) On the other hand, let's suppose that I have hired a new truck driver to deliver my product to the retail establishments that sell it. Assume also that this driver has no experience driving an 18-wheel tractor-trailer, which is the vehicle I want her to use for my deliveries. Does it make sense to train her first on how to use the tractor-trailer's clutch, and then on how to use its accelerator, and then on how to use its side-view mirrors? No, because the overall operation of this vehicle requires that the clutch, accelerator, and side-view mirrors be used in concert. Learning them separately would clearly be ineffective. You can see, then, that the way in which material to be learned is structured can play an important role in the success of a training program.

A related structural question is whether the practice of the task should take place all at once or be spread out over time. **Distributed practice** refers to training that is divided into segments, usually with rest periods in between, whereas **massed practice** refers to training that takes place at one time, without breaks. Research indicates that, overall, distributed practice is better for learning skills and for long-term retention of those skills. However, for practical reasons, many organizations don't make the time for distributed practice and instead cram in as much as possible during one 8-hour session (Wexley & Latham, 1991)—an approach that often results in poorly trained employees. According to a recent meta-analysis of 63 studies, distributed practice is especially effective on tasks that are low in complexity, such as psychomotor tasks (Donovan & Radosevich, 1999).

distributed practice
Training in which the practice is divided into segments, usually with rest periods in between.

massed practice
Training in which all the practice takes place at the same time, without breaks.

Meaningfulness of Material. It makes sense that trainees will be more likely to learn new material if they find it meaningful. Accordingly, organizations should incorporate a few elements into their training programs to make the material more meaningful and relevant for the trainee (Wexley & Latham, 1991). First, the trainer should present an overview of the material. An overview allows the trainees to better understand the objectives of the training program, as well as its procedures. Second, the material should be presented in a way that is easily understandable for the trainees. This involves using terms, examples, and concepts that the trainees will be able to understand and to which they can relate. One obvious application here is the use of job-relevant examples in the training, such as patient-care issues when training nurses and student-related issues when training schoolteachers. Third, sequencing of the material is important. Trainers should present the material in a logical order. For example, in training air conditioner–repair technicians to replace an air conditioner coil, it makes sense to demonstrate, first, how to disassemble the unit; next, how to take out the old coil; then, how to install the new coil; and, finally, how to reassemble the unit. Any other order of steps would not be logical and could result in less understanding on the part of the trainee.

Practice and Overlearning. You've heard it said that "practice makes perfect." Although true perfection is rarely achieved, this phrase does suggest that practice is important in almost any learning situation. How one practices—that is, the quality of the practice—also affects what one learns. This last point is an important one to make in a training context, as employees who either don't practice or practice in an inappropriate way do not learn very well. We all fall prey to some bad habits in our home lives as well as our work lives. Often those bad habits develop from a lack of practice of good habits or from practice in which we repeat a pattern of wrong behaviors. Bad habits—such as when children don't wash their hands after using the bathroom; drivers don't use their turn signals; secretaries don't save their working documents every few minutes on the computer; and UPS drivers lift heavy boxes using just their backs and not their legs—can easily develop from faulty practice. Trainers must be aware of the practice sessions of trainees and make sure that they are practicing appropriately, because although practice doesn't really make perfect, "perfect practice" is a near guarantee of quality performance.

overlearning
The process of giving trainees continued practice even after they have appeared to master the behavior, resulting in high levels of learning.

Overlearning is the process of giving trainees continued practice even after they have appeared to master the behavior, resulting in high levels of learning. You may think this is a waste of time, but, in fact, practicing something so much as to overlearn it increases the likelihood that one will be able to exhibit the behavior quickly, easily, and consistently when called upon to do so. Think back to the subject of bad habits. If I stop practicing the use of my turn signal when I drive, eventually I won't be using it at all. However, if I have overlearned this behavior to the point where it becomes second nature to me and I don't even have to think about it, I'm likely to use that turn signal forever. The same principle holds true in the workplace. If a secretary using a word processor is trained to save his document after every page typed, actually doing so during the training sessions themselves, he is likely to continue this practice because the behavior has been overlearned. Now let's consider a situation that is truly a matter of life and death. ER physicians must be trained in such a way that they overlearn certain behaviors because, given the stress and severity of the situations they find themselves in, these behaviors have to be second nature. If a member of my family is rushed to the ER because he can't breathe or his heart isn't pumping, I don't want the ER physician having to think through the steps involved in intubating or defibrillating him—I want these behaviors to be so overlearned that they happen automatically.

Feedback. You know how important feedback is to you in your daily life. Relationships tend to end (quickly or, worse, very slowly) when partners do not provide each other with feedback about what they like and don't like. Students tend to get annoyed when faculty do not provide timely feedback on their exam performance. In training situations, too, it is imperative that participants be given timely and useful feedback about how they are performing. Feedback, also called knowledge-of-results (KOR), serves three purposes in a training context: (1) It provides information that allows trainees to make whatever adjustments may be necessary in their behaviors during training; (2) it makes the learning process more interesting for the trainees and increases their motivation to learn; and (3) it leads to goal setting for improving performance (Wexley & Latham, 1991). Also worth knowing are three important principles regarding how feedback is best delivered to individuals: (1) Feedback works best when it is given immediately following the individual's behavior; (2) immediate and frequent feedback tends to result in the best performance; and (3) both positive and negative feedback have value when delivered in a sensitive, yet clear manner. (For an excellent and classic overview of the feedback process, see Ilgen, Fisher, & Taylor, 1979.)

Individual Differences in Trainees

Although the structural elements of the learning context are important, as discussed in the instructional design section, characteristics of the learner are also important. There are two major characteristics of the learner that deserve some discussion. First, learning isn't likely to happen if the learner isn't prepared to learn—what is sometimes called trainee **readiness.** We've all known individuals at school or at work who weren't capable of being taught something because they didn't have the necessary knowledge, ability, or experiences to allow them to learn.

readiness
Possessing the background characteristics and necessary level of interest that makes learning possible.

Second, the motivation to learn is important as well. We will talk at length about motivation in Chapter 9, but for now it's important to understand that if employees are not motivated to be trained, the training is almost certain to fail. I could design the slickest multimedia training program ever, making use of nice color videos and computer technology—but if you hate your job and aren't motivated to do any better than you're currently doing, you won't work hard during training, and it isn't likely to have much impact on you. Providing useful, immediate feedback to trainees is one strategy a trainer can use to increase motivation. A second strategy is to demonstrate how the training will pay off for the trainee. This answers the "what's in it for me" question, which is a very reasonable one for the employee to ask. If the trainer can show that, by working hard in training, employees will be able to work more easily, or perform better, or enjoy their jobs more, motivation is likely to follow.

Some recent work has begun to focus on these individual differences in trainees. For instance, some training work has taken a different perspective by encouraging trainees to make errors during training. The rationale is that more exploration (trial and error) may help trainees learn at a deeper level and gain a better understanding of the task at hand. Gully, Payne, Koles, and Whiteman (2002) found that so-called error training was very effective for trainees who were high in cognitive ability and openness (the Big Five construct). Those individuals who were high on conscientiousness, however, demonstrated reduced self-efficacy as a result of error training. For these very conscientious individuals, making errors was just more than they could take!

Herold and his colleagues (Herold, Davis, Fedor, & Parsons, 2002) have focused on the role of individual differences (e.g., Big Five factors) in training success and found that those high on emotional stability and openness acquired skills in training at a faster rate. They concluded from these and other results that individual differences are useful for predicting training success and that early training success has differential effects on later success depending on the various levels of these individual differences.

Characteristics of the Trainer

We've seen how the structural properties of the training context, the principles of learning, and individual differences among trainees affect the training process. In some ways, the last piece of the puzzle is a consideration of trainer characteristics. Certainly it is reasonable to expect that differences among trainers are likely to influence the effectiveness of a training intervention. First, Wexley and Latham (2002) suggest that effective trainers establish specific objectives and take care to communicate them clearly to the trainees. Second, trainers should have a solid understanding of how people learn (including the principles of learning discussed earlier) and what role their own approaches or styles can play. Third, communication skills are extremely important. As you might imagine, trainees' attitudes, motivation, and behaviors are likely to be adversely affected by a trainer who communicates in a rigid, closed, negative, and condescending way. Fourth, trainers must realize that different trainees may require a different style or different treatment from the trainer. Although other issues may be important as well, this list provides a good overview of the kinds of trainer characteristics that are likely to be important to training effectiveness.

Transfer of Training

Transfer of training
The extent to which the material, skills, or procedures learned in training are taken back to the job and used by the employee in some regular fashion.

Transfer of training, is the extent to which the material, skills, or procedures learned in training are taken back to the job and used by the employee in some regular fashion. From the organization's perspective, this principle is integral to the success of the training program. If the trainees do very well in training and appear to learn all the intended material, but never use what they've learned on the job to improve their efficiency and the effectiveness of the organization, what good was the training? This is the reason that training experts and organizations alike are always concerned about transfer of training. *Positive transfer* is the organization's goal—the hope is that what is learned in the training program will improve performance back on the job. Sometimes, however, performance declines as a result of training. This outcome is called *negative transfer.*

Irv Goldstein and Kevin Ford's classic text on training (2002) provides a summary of the literature in this area, as well as some guidelines on how to increase the likelihood of positive transfer. First, trainers should maximize the similarity between the training situation and the job situation. In other words, the training environment should resemble the on-the-job environment as much as possible, an idea that is often called *identical elements theory*. A major cause of negative transfer in many training situations is disparity between these two environments. As an example, let's say we're training employees how to assemble automobile wheels, and we provide all of the materials they need at their work stations, along with an unlimited amount of time to complete the task. However, when these employees who have succeeded in the training program get back to their jobs, they find that the materials are not always at their work stations, and, owing to the assembly-line nature of the workplace, they don't have an unlimited amount of time. When the employees try to use the same procedures they learned in training (where they had a lot of time) to the work situation (where time is limited), their performance declines because there isn't enough time to actually use the procedures they learned in training. This is negative transfer. A recent study demonstrated that transfer was enhanced when the trainee's actual work situation matched what he or she desired in an ideal work situation (Awoniyi, Griego, & Morgan, 2002). Although not completely parallel to identical elements theory, it is certainly related in the sense that the way the relevant situations match up seems important.

Second, trainers should provide employees with an adequate amount of active practice, which is essential to positive transfer. This is especially true for new employees learning new tasks. In such situations, practice to the point of overlearning is a good strategy to enhance transfer because it helps the new employees do these new tasks correctly despite the additional stress associated with novel situations of this kind. Third, trainers should provide different contexts in which employees can practice the desired behaviors. Practice in different contexts with different stimuli (e.g., wheels of different sizes and parts) increases the likelihood that what is learned in training will generalize to a variety of contexts back on the job. Fourth, the trainers, trainees, and manager should work together throughout this entire process. Fifth, expectations for the trainers, trainees, and manager should be made clear up front. And, finally, trainers need to provide on-the-job maintenance programs that are focused on helping employees to continue their learned behaviors.

Baldwin and Ford's (1988) classic paper on transfer of training proposed a model of the transfer process that emphasized, among other things we've just discussed, the importance of social support. Clarke (2002) found that social service employees reported a lack of transfer from their training experiences due to heavy workloads, excessive time pressures, lack of reinforcement, and a lack of feedback. Clearly, these findings suggest that the supportiveness of the work context is important in affecting transfer of training.

TRAINING DELIVERY

No book could do justice to all of the training techniques that are available to HR practitioners, and we certainly can't cover them all in this one chapter. However, I will talk about a representative sample of the various training techniques organized by type of approach. First, I will present a few of the more traditional approaches. Second, technology-based approaches that have become quite popular in the last couple of decades will be presented. Finally, I will conclude with some coverage of techniques that are used specifically to develop employees in various ways, including leadership skills.

For training to be successful, it is important that the training context match the actual job context.

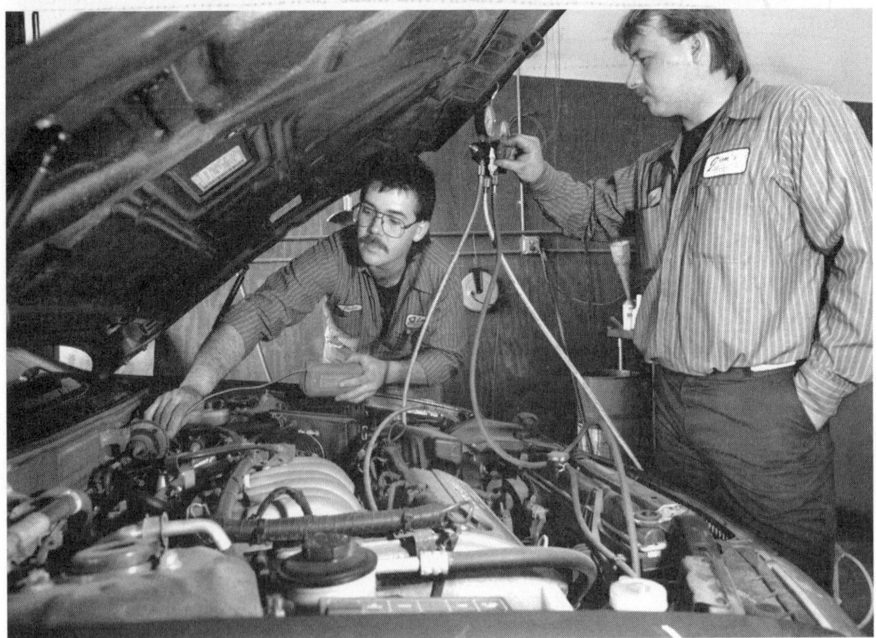

TRADITIONAL APPROACHES

Lecturing. One of the most established and oldest training methods is the use of simple lecturing to teach trainees important work-related information. This approach is very economical because many employees can be trained at one time. However, a fixed time-limit lecture delivered to a moderately sized group of trainees is not likely to include such important learning principles as active practice, overlearning, and feedback. The effectiveness of this technique varies greatly, depending on the training objectives. Specifically, whereas the lecture approach seems useful for teaching trainees facts or helping them to acquire knowledge, it may not be very effective for developing problem-solving or interpersonal skills. In their meta-analysis of training effects, Arthur, Bennett, Edens, and Bell (2003) point out that even though the lecture method has a bit of a negative reputation based on perceptions that it is a boring technique, their data strongly support its effectiveness across many different skills.

On-the-Job Training. On-the-job training (OJT) is, and has been for years, the most widely used training technique in organizations. Almost all employees are exposed to some form of it. How many times has your boss introduced you to new employees and asked you to spend the week working with them and showing them the ropes? The assumption underlying OJT is that the new employee can learn the job by watching an experienced employee doing the job, by talking with that employee about important elements of the job while the employee performs those job elements, and by working with the actual machines, materials, or raw products that are the focus of the job. With this kind of training, too, success is largely dependent on the skills and motivation of the trainer. Reliance on the trainer can be a weakness of OJT unless the trainer is both skilled at training and motivated. Some companies do OJT without much thought or preparation—and in such cases it often fails. In fact, some companies use OJT in place of carefully planned training programs. When new employees report to work, incumbents who happen to be working that shift are asked to work with them—a prime example of poorly designed OJT. By contrast, companies that choose employees to serve as trainers based on their potential to be good teachers, that train the trainers in the proper methods of instruction, that provide incentives for their work as trainers, and that match up trainers with trainees based on their potential to work well together are more apt to have successful training programs (Wexley & Latham, 2002).

Self-Directed Techniques. Self-instructional materials such as programmed texts have been produced for training purposes since the 1950s (Goldstein & Ford, 2002). These techniques allow trainees to work at their own pace and to emphasize identified weaknesses. *Programmed instruction (PI)* of this variety presents information to the learner while using learning principles to reward and motivate. The first step in programmed instruction is to present material broken down into small elements. Second, these elements are arranged in a logical sequence from simple to complex. Third, following completion of each element, a short test is administered to see if the learners have mastered the material at some criterion level. Finally, the learners are given immediate feedback (KOR). If they answer questions incorrectly, they are given additional information to think about and then asked to revisit those questions until a performance criterion is met. If they answer questions correctly, they are asked to skip this additional information and to move on to the next stage of the PI.

Programmed instruction is clearly based on many of the learning principles reviewed earlier in the chapter, such as KOR, distributed practice, and reinforcement. One obvious advantage of this approach is that trainees can work at their own pace: Those who are quite skilled don't have to waste time waiting for everyone else to catch up, whereas those who are not as skilled can take as much time as they need. Overall, research indicates that PI techniques result in shorter training times than other techniques, but PI training groups often do not show a superiority in learning or retention as compared with trainees in control training groups (Goldstein & Ford, 2002). Bell and Kozlowski (2002) suggest that the lack of superiority of this approach is due to the fact that the learner control that is inherent in self-directed training programs is counterproductive. This control often results in less time spent on task and the use of poor learning strategies. They conducted a study that demonstrated that providing self-directed trainees with adaptive guidance or simply information that helps them make more effective learning decisions (guides them toward what to practice, suggests how best to use attentional resources, etc.) during the training process results in higher levels of knowledge and performance and better transfer. This is certainly an area in which we can expect to see more research to further enhance self-directed methods.

Computer-assisted instruction (CAI) stems largely from the PI approach just discussed, but with one difference: Trainees interact with a computer. The computer is the medium through which information is presented to them and by which their performance is monitored. The computer provides information and then asks questions to determine what the trainees have learned and not learned. Given the computer's storage and memory capacity, both information and questions can be presented on the basis of the trainees' responses to previous questions. Thus fast learners can move through the training program quickly, and slower learners can move at a more deliberate rate with additional practice and tests as needed. You may have experienced programs of this type yourself, especially in the form of computerized *tutorials* designed to be used with certain software packages. In these tutorials, the computer "walks" the learner through examples and asks the learner to perform certain tasks; if these are done incorrectly, the computer then provides feedback and additional practice. Although this individualized approach to training has great potential, careful evaluations of it are lacking (Goldstein & Ford, 2002); clearly this technique needs to be a major focus of training research in the new millennium, and the work of Bell and Kozlowski (2002) on adaptive guidance holds great promise here.

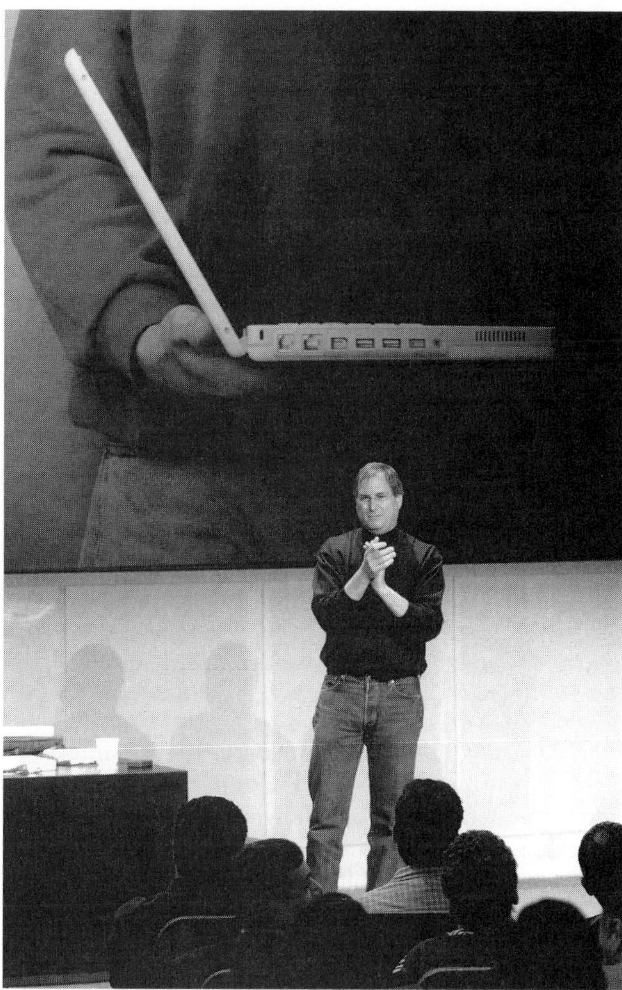

High-tech presentations, such as this one being delivered by Steve Jobs of Apple, are quite common in today's technological age.

Work Simulators. Did you see the movie *Apollo 13?* If so, you might recall that one of the most important factors in the safe return of the astronauts to Earth was the flight simulator, which was used by one of the astronauts who did not make the trip to the moon. Astronaut Ken Mattingly, played by Gary Sinise, worked tirelessly in the simulator to help devise a plan that the astronauts could follow within the limits and constraints experienced by the astronauts in space in order to achieve a successful return. A simulator is designed to be as realistic as possible so that when trainees are using it, they are able to easily transfer the skills they gain to the real-life situation. For many jobs, it would be too dangerous, costly, and inefficient to train individuals on the actual equipment to be used in the real-life situation (Wexley & Latham, 2002). Training astronauts is one obvious example; it simply isn't possible to send individuals into space to learn how to be

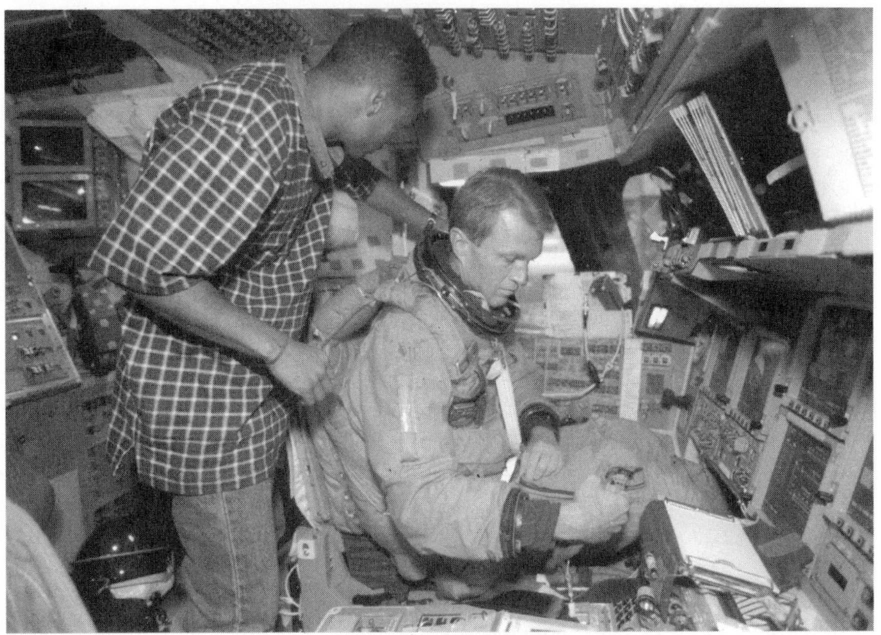

Simulators are used frequently in the training of astronauts.

astronauts. In short, they need to learn off site with carefully developed simulators. Simulators have also played an instrumental part in the training of airline pilots and military fliers, providing repeated practice and individualized feedback without any actual safety hazards. Of course, the simulated hazards are made to seem as real as possible. In fact, two important determinants of the effectiveness of simulators is their **physical fidelity,** the extent to which the operation of the equipment mimics that in the real world, and their **psychological fidelity,** the extent to which the behavioral processes necessary for success on the job are also necessary for success on the training simulation. Table 8.1 presents a description of a flight simulator that demonstrates how realistic these simulators can be when they possess both physical and psychological fidelity. Simulators have been designed to train individuals on procedures, motor skills, conceptual tasks, identification of hazards, and the coordination of team efforts. Despite their costs, they are beneficial to the organization and often contribute to society's greater good, as well.

physical fidelity
The extent to which the operation of equipment in training mimics that in the real world.

psychological fidelity
The extent to which the essential behavioral processes needed to be successful on the job are also necessary for success on the training simulation.

Technology-Based Approaches

We have reviewed traditional approaches to training—those that some might call the "tried and true" training techniques. In this section I present three contemporary approaches that are becoming the "hot" approaches to training for the 21st century. Each of these employs technology to enhance training delivery.

TABLE 8.1 Terror at Zero Feet: A Crew's Simulated Brush with Disaster

In this accident, one can hear rain pelting the windshield. And there is thunder. "We would never take off in conditions like this," Carter said.

But true to the real event, Hill took the plane's controls while Carter spooled up the engines. They began racing down the runway.

"Eighty knots," Carter said. About 92 mph.

As the plane passed 127 knots—the speed that pilots call V1, essentially the point of no return—the air speed indicator abruptly stopped moving.

"Wind shear!" shouted Carter as he slammed the throttles into the full "firewall" position—as much power as he could muster.

"Keep it on the runway," he told Hill, who eased the nose wheel back down onto the runway to gain as much speed as possible on the ground—a maneuver that amounts to "banking energy" for the ordeal ahead. Even with the increased ground speed, the air speed dropped 20 knots—about 23 mph.

As did the real aircraft in the real incident, the simulator began climbing steeply as it neared the end of the runway, pushing everyone back in his seat. Then came the bad news.

"Decreasing air speed," Carter said.

"Sinking," he said: "200 feet . . . 160 feet . . . 140 feet . . . 80 feet."

"Bring your stick higher," he said. Hill, already fighting his control yoke as if it were a bull in a rodeo, pulled the nose higher into the air as the engines roared.

With that, pandemonium broke out in the cockpit. Lights began flashing and the control yoke began vibrating loudly like a giant rattlesnake—the "stick shaker" that warns of a stall.

An artificial voice boomed out in a deliberate but loud monotone, "Don't sink! Don't sink! Don't sink!" It was the ground proximity warning having its say.

As all appeared lost, the plane began emerging from the shear.

"Air speed recovery," said someone out of the din.

A later reading of the simulator tapes showed that the plane dropped within 20 feet of the ground before it recovered and took off.

A lot of people died on the real plane, in the days before pilots were trained to survive wind shear. This was just a simulator. But the cold sweat, fast heartbeat and weak knees were not simulated.

Source: D. Phillips (1991). The Washington Post.

Audiovisual Techniques. One of the fastest-growing areas in training is the use of audiovisual or multimedia presentations as the basis for training programs. In the past, these techniques have involved films, slides, and videotapes. But as we enter the new millennium, video disc presentations, CD presentations, and computer presentations using PowerPoint and other sophisticated software are coming to the fore. Many large consulting firms that specialize in training, such as Development Dimensions International (DDI), have invested extensively in elaborate multimedia training programs. Though not as fancy, videotapes are still quite popular; in fact, they are often used in organizations for behavioral modeling. Audiovisual techniques are believed to be at least as effective as, and often more effective than, traditional live lectures. The flexibility they allow—in terms of reshowing segments, pausing at various segments, repeating earlier segments, and stopping the presentation prior to showing the correct approach—make them particularly appealing. In fact, some training procedures, such as those involved in a medical operation, would be impossible during a live lecture but quite feasible using audiovisual means (Wexley & Latham, 2002). Not surprisingly, trainees often report greater interest in and satisfaction with training that is conducted through multimedia presentations than with training of the live-lecture variety. Even in universities across the country, there is a strong push to transform live-lecture courses into courses that are more multimedia based. This push is fueled by the belief that students are more interested in and pay more attention to the multimedia courses.

distance learning (DL) The delivery of material to all participants at the same time even though participants are separated by geographical distance.

Distance Learning. In addition to video, audio, and computer technologies to train their workforces, many organizations are making use of the Internet for **distance learning,** which is the delivery of educational or training materials, usually through electronic means, to people at different locations at the same time. Burgess and Russell (2003) summarize the many benefits of DL programs as articulated by various organizations. These include: (1) the most efficient use of high-quality instructors and instruction; (2) learners taking more responsibility for personal success; and (3) very clear cost savings. As an example of cost savings, the US Army National Guard reported a cost savings of $1.6 million after implementation of a DL program, with most of the savings being linked to a reduction in travel costs. BellSouth reports a potential savings of $7 million per year related to the training of 50 new employees per year who experience a substantial DL training component (Sutton, 2004).

Web-Based Learning. Training delivered via the World Wide Web has become quite popular. Using an Internet browser, employees at remote sites can sort through, read, and work with information made available by the company. A few benefits of Web-based training are worthy of mention. First, it's easy to update and change information because it's stored in one location and transmitted across company intranets or the Internet. Second, the training can be done at work or at another location that's convenient for the trainee (even at home!). Third, the training can be set up so that trainees can share information with each other via discussion groups, chat rooms, or bulletin boards.

Unfortunately, very little empirical research has been conducted on the success of Web-based training, but some research suggests that it is slightly more effective than traditional classroom-based training (Welsh, Wanberg, Brown, & Simmering, 2003). A great deal of research seems necessary so that organizations have the information they need to allow for reasoned decisions and choices about the potential for Web-based delivery of training. There is some evidence that trainees react favorably to Web-based instruction, but research is lacking here as well (Goldstein & Ford, 2002).

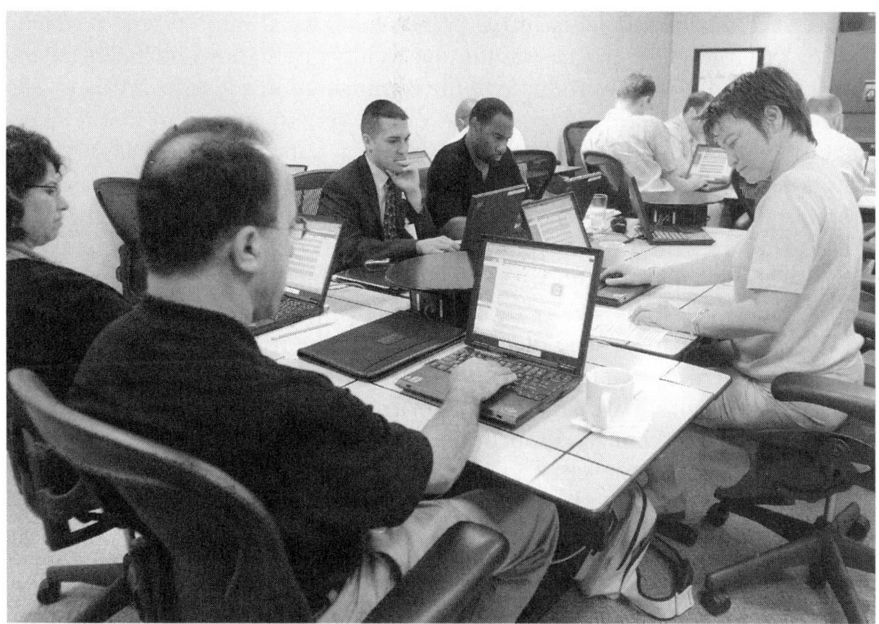

Many employees can experience training while working from their offices or computer labs due to the advances in Web-based training techniques.

Looking to the future, it seems clear that technology-based training is fast becoming the most preferred choice for training delivery across large, and to a lesser extent, smaller corporations. In particular, the growth of DL and Web-based training is staggering and will soon dominate training delivery across the United States and other technology-focused countries.

Employee Development-Based Approaches

The techniques we've discussed thus far are general methods that can be used in a variety of jobs. In this section, however, we will consider some techniques that are specifically associated with employee development and leadership skills training. This type of training, in its many forms, has become a huge factor in HR.

Orientation Training and New Employee Socialization. Though not always treated as a formal training technique, the socialization of new employees is usually the first element of training that new employees experience. **Organizational socialization** is the process by which an individual acquires the attitudes, behavior, and knowledge needed to participate as an organizational member (Goldstein & Ford, 2002). This is done both formally and informally. Formally, it may include new employee orientation meetings conducted by the HR staff in concert with line managers, social receptions for new employees, policy workshops, and

organizational socialization
The process by which an individual acquires the attitudes, behavior, and knowledge needed to participate as an organizational member.

tours of the organizational facilities. (When I was hired into my first academic job, my first formal experience was the new faculty orientation and lunch, during which new faculty were introduced to the administration and to each other.) The socialization process for new employees can be very important in that it determines their first impression of the organization, supervisors, and co-workers. This is also the time when new employees learn the formal and informal rules, procedures, and expectations of the organization or work group. A recent study of new-employee training found that employees who experienced an orientation program that focused on the history, values, principles, and structure of the organization were indeed more aware of the goals, values, history, and people of the organization than those who did not experience the training (Klein & Weaver, 2000). They were also more committed to the organization. In a review of the socialization literature, T. N. Bauer, E. W. Morrison, and R. R. Callister (1998) argue that as uncertainty, change, competition, and global expansion increase for both organizations and employees—a trend among 21st-century organizations—the need to understand how to effectively manage the socialization process of new employees becomes more critical.

Coaching. Like organizational socialization, many classic treatments of organizational training do not consider coaching as a training technique. I'm discussing it in this chapter because its focus is on helping employees to get better at their jobs, which is, in large part, what training is all about. When I talk to I/O practitioners about the issues that are really big in their organizations—the hot topics—I invariably find that coaching is one of the first things they mention. **Coaching** is the process by which supervisors provide subordinates with advice and information about current performance and discuss ideas and goals for improving that performance (Whetten & Cameron, 2002). In short, it is a training and motivational technique used to improve performance. According to Wexley and Latham (2002), coaching serves the following functions:

coaching
The process by which supervisors provide subordinates with advice and information about current performance and discuss ideas and goals for improving that performance.

- It lets subordinates know how well others think they are doing their jobs.
- It encourages subordinates and supervisors to work together in developing a plan for performance improvement.
- It improves communication and collaboration between supervisors and subordinates.
- It establishes a framework for developing both short- and long-term career goals.

Many organizations invest considerable resources in teaching their managers how to conduct effective and useful coaching sessions. In other words, whereas coaching serves a training function for nonmanagerial employees in organizations and is of the on-site variety, managers themselves are trained to do effective coaching. As noted earlier, managerial training is discussed at length in a separate section; but it is logical to talk about training good coaches here as well. One way to approach this topic is to consider Stan Silverman's (1991) Appraising and Developing Performance Training (ADEPT), a comprehensive training program that supports performance appraisal. ADEPT is a video-based, 2-day program that uses various training techniques such as behavior modeling, group discussion, practice, feedback, lectures, role playing, and individual exercises. It consists of eight modules designed to carry out the various steps of a performance management cycle. One step of this cycle is coaching. In the ADEPT module that focuses on this topic, a trainer teaches trainees how to identify performance problems, how to diagnose their causes, and, ultimately, how to solve them. Two videos demonstrate both effective and ineffective ways of taking these three steps. Finally, a series of role plays are employed so that trainees can practice these important coaching behaviors. As a training device, coaching is successful only when the coaches themselves are well trained.

Some recent work by Manny London and his colleagues has begun to clarify the coaching process. London and Smither (2002) suggest that the feedback orientation of the employee, such as the extent to which he or she welcomes guidance and coaching, interacts with the feedback culture of the organization (see Steelman, Levy, & Snell, 2004) to determine the effectiveness of coaching. At least one empirical study (with executives) has shown that coaching has an effect on managerial behaviors such as goals set, amount of feedback shared with subordinates, and extent to which managers ask others for input and ideas. All of these, of course, are important managerial behaviors (Smither, London, Flautt, Vargas, Kucine, 2003). Managers in this study who were coached were rated more favorably by subordinates than were those who did not experience any coaching.

Behavior Modeling. Because interpersonal skills and working with others are such important competencies for managers, they are of great interest to organizations. Behavioral modeling is one technique that seems well suited for improving them. It is based on Albert Bandura's (1986) work on social imitation or social learning theory. You might recall from your introductory psychology class or social psychology class that Bandura did the Bobo doll study in which kids watched adults act aggressively against a blow-up doll and later, when given the opportunity, acted aggressively against the doll themselves. The theory's main argument is that most of social behavior is learned through observation.

This theory has been successfully applied to training for the past 20 years. An especially good example of the use of behavior modeling in organizational training is provided by Gary Latham and Lise Saari (1979), who developed nine training modules to train managers to interact effectively with their subordinates. The modules focused on such things as socializing a new employee, motivating a poor employee, overcoming resistance to change, and dealing with a problem employee. The trainees met for 2 hours for each of 9 weeks. The training format included (1) an introduction to the topic; (2) a film that demonstrated a manager modeling effective behaviors, which were highlighted in earlier and later films as well; (3) a group discussion of the effectiveness of the model; (4) practice in role playing the desired behaviors in front of other trainees and the trainer; and (5) feedback from the training class regarding the effectiveness of each trainee's role play. Latham and Saari assigned half the supervisors to the training condition and half to a control condition that did not involve the behavior modeling training. (The latter group did eventually receive the training, but not until this segment of the study was completed.) The training resulted in positive trainee reactions, better scores than the control group on a learning test given a few months after the training, and better on-the-job performance than the control group when measured one year later. Clearly, the behavior modeling had a significant impact on the employees who experienced this training.

Business Simulations. This technique is somewhat similar to a case study approach used in business education. Managers are given a brief introduction that includes some background about a fictitious company, the situation, organizational problems, and the organizational goals. The managers are presented with this contrived organizational situation and placed within that situation. They are asked to make managerial decisions, and these decisions subsequently affect the situation and context. These simulations or management games are usually set up to be competitive in the sense that managers are organized into teams and the teams develop their own ideas, procedures, and solutions. As decisions are made on a round-by-round basis, they are presented to the trainers, who provide feedback and make alterations to the environment on the basis of those decisions. The next round is begun with new and additional decisions to be made by the various teams. Although the games are designed to model an entire organization, they can often be categorized on the basis of their functional purpose (Wexley & Latham, 2002). Thus there are many types of management games, such as marketing, finance, production-management, and quality-management games. These games are often well received by trainees because they are interesting to participate in and are perceived as relevant and realistic. They are also effective in helping employees understand the complexities and interdependence of the different departments within organizations. Although there has been little empirical evaluation of management games, some critics argue that trainees often become so interested in the competition that they lose sight of the general principles that the game was designed to teach (Goldstein & Ford, 2002). Of course, as with simulators, the effectiveness of management games is clearly linked to their fidelity—that is, how realistic they are and how well they reflect the KSAOs necessary to do the job.

Corporate Universities. Many companies have begun making long-term investments in their workforce through, in part, the development of institutes or "universities" focused on continuous training and development. These corporate classrooms have modern facilities with up-to-date technology that allow for effective learning and transfer on site. Motorola has been at the forefront of this movement and has a campus setting at each major company site worldwide (El-Tannir, 2002). Further, they have made some progress in taking this corporate

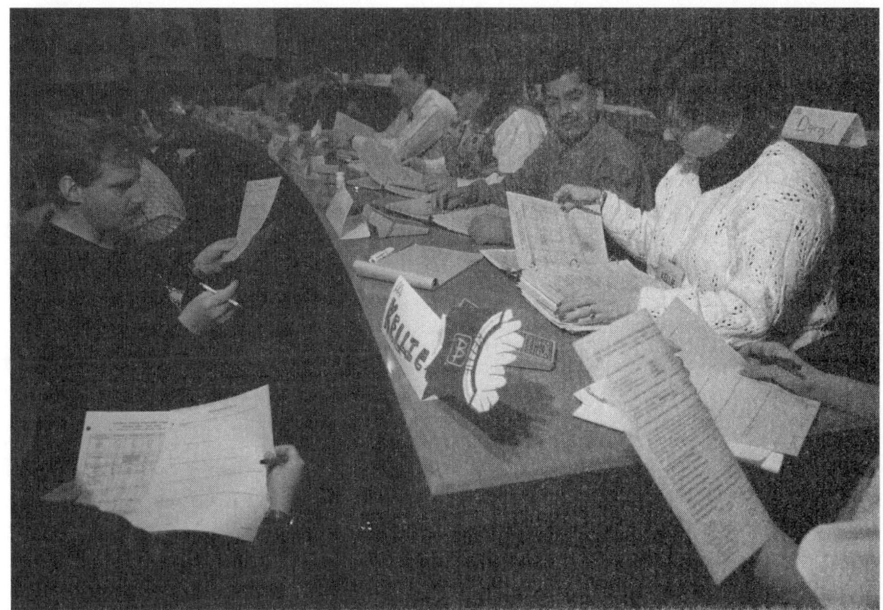

Corporate universities such as McDonald's Hamburger University have become popular ways to train employees in the 21st century.

university idea to the World Wide Web and extending it to other DL approaches; again, Motorola continues to be at the cutting edge in this regard. Other famous corporate universities include McDonald's Hamburger University in Virginia, Xerox's Document University in Illinois, and the Caterpillar Training Institute in Illinois, but the number of corporate universities in the United States has grown to 1,800 (Anderson, 2000). As organizations continue to become more focused on continuous learning and the management of knowledge within the company, corporate universities should grow in importance. In fact, a framework suggested by Prince and Stewart (2002) places the corporate university at the center of organizational learning, having implications for knowledge systems, networks and partnerships, learning processes, and people processes. The corporate university appears to be here to stay!

NEW CONTENT FOR THE NEW MILLENNIUM

Diversity issues related to race, ethnicity, age, and gender have become increasingly important to organizations and employees alike. In this section, two newer areas of training are discussed: sexual harassment and workplace diversity.

Sexual Harassment Training

As we discussed in Chapter 7, sexual harassment is prohibited by the Civil Rights Act and includes behaviors of a sexual nature, submission to or rejection of which affects one's job or creates an offensive work environment (EEOC, 1997). Sexual harassment has received a great deal of attention in recent years because of the Clarence Thomas confirmation hearings, the Tailhook scandal that plagued the military, and harassment allegations made against President Clinton and former Senator Robert Packwood. In an interesting review (Gutek & Koss, 1993), the consequences of sexual harassment are categorized in terms of three dimensions. First, harassment has widespread implications on *work outcomes* such as interpersonal relationships at work, an alteration in the direction of one's career, satisfaction with the job, and commitment to the organization. Second, *psychological and somatic outcomes* result from sexual harassment. For instance, it appears that women who are sexually harassed experience reductions in self-esteem, life satisfaction, home satisfaction, and self-confidence, sometimes also becoming angry, hostile, irritable, and depressed. Physical symptoms that emerge as a result of sexual harassment include gastrointestinal problems, teeth grinding, nausea, weight loss, and an inability to sleep. Finally, sexual harassment has negative effects on the *organization* (Gutek & Koss, 1993). Turnover and absenteeism attributable to harassment incur direct costs; indirect costs also accrue in the form of low motivation, inability to focus on work, and time spent on reacting to the harassment. Finally, organizations can be torn apart by sexual harassment investigations, resulting in a divided workforce and increased conflict among employees.

Because prevention is the best tool against sexual harassment, one option encouraged by the EEOC and other agencies is sexual harassment training. In fact, many organizations offer sexual harassment training programs; most of these employ behavior modeling through the use of videotapes (Meyer, 1992). In one recent study, for example, researchers predicted that participants who saw a sexual harassment training film would perceive sexually oriented work behaviors as incidents of sexual harassment to a greater extent than would individuals who did not see the film (Blakely, Blakely, & Moorman, 1998). Indeed, their findings supported this prediction. Thus the authors concluded that the film sensitized the participants to sexual harassment and what constitutes it. In addition, they found that males who had not viewed the film tended to rate items such as "making sexually suggestive remarks or behaviors around a female subordinate" as less sexually harassing than did males who had seen the film and females in both the film training group and the control group. A more recent review of the literature supports these findings, and an empirical study accompanying this review demonstrates the same effect in a large sample of government employees (Antecol & Cobb-Clark, 2003). Overall, these intriguing results suggest that (1) behavior modeling may help some individuals become more sensitive to sexual harassment behaviors and (2) males and females may view behaviors differently with respect to their potential for sexual harassment. Obviously, a great deal more work is necessary in the area of sexual harassment training, but this is one area in which such work promises to pay huge dividends for organizations and their employees.

The Clarence Thomas confirmation hearings brought sexual harassment to the public's attention.

WORKPLACE DIVERSITY MANAGEMENT AND TRAINING

That demographic changes are affecting the nature of the workforce is not news to anyone. These changes are expected to continue through the early part of the 21st century. Data and projections from the Bureau of Labor Statistics present an especially interesting picture in this regard. Women are entering the workforce at a faster rate than men; by 2006, the Hispanic labor force is expected to be larger than the African-American labor force; and from 1996 to 2006, the Asian and Hispanic workforces will increase at rates of 41% and 36%, respectively, whereas the white and black workforces will increase at rates of 9% and 14%, respectively (Fullerton, 1997).

The changing nature of the workforce necessitates new HR approaches to managing that workforce. Diversity must become a bottom-line issue if companies are going to be able to compete for—and keep—the best and the brightest. Diversity training has burst on the scene; estimates are that it is now a more than $10 billion a year industry (Von Bergen, Soper, & Foster, 2002). Most government agencies and 60% of Fortune 500 companies provide some type of diversity training (Roberson, Kulik, & Pepper, 2003). Here are a few examples of what some of the most competitive companies are doing with respect to diversity (Hemisphere, 1999).

1. *Xerox* maintains that its reputation as a leader in the area of diversity is an important competitive advantage in terms of recruiting talent in a very competitive market. Among the strategies used by Xerox are (1) outreach programs targeted at minority colleges, (2) in-house diversity groups involving senior management leaders, (3) active support of minority professional associations,

and (4) partnerships with newly formed diversity groups such as the Institute for Women and Technology.

2. *Ford Motor Company* has developed a strategic communication plan in which senior managers teach employees why diversity is so important to Ford's success. The program provides five half-hour modules dealing with such themes as leadership, diverse work environments, diverse work teams, and the role of work/life balance in diversity. Each module includes video presentations and group discussions led by supervisors. Also offered are a diversity council, a website, and a speaker series called "Dialogues on Diversity."
3. Selected from among 200,000 federal contractors, *DaimlerChrysler* was one of five winners of a prestigious award given by the EEOC. The goal at DaimlerChrysler is to develop "a workforce that reflects the communities we serve," according to Monica Emerson, director of the diversity and work/family division. Incredibly, 20% of the company's workforce are women and 27% are people of color. More than 50% of the employees hired since 1990 have been women or minorities. Recognizing that the best and the brightest have many avenues of choice, DaimlerChrysler wants to create an environment so desirable that these individuals seek out its company in particular. As Emerson puts it, "Our culture is dynamic and values people with different backgrounds and different lifestyles. When people feel valued and respected, they become a more inspired workforce—they feel passionate about our products and services."
4. With respect to diversity, *Hyatt Hotels and Resorts* is an industry leader. Overall, 62% of Hyatt's 40,000-employee workforce are ethnic minorities and 49% are female; in fact, women make up nearly half of its senior management! Soon after being hired, employees attend mandatory diversity awareness and sensitivity training programs that help them to work better together and to recognize the diversity of their clientele.
5. *IBM* focuses a great deal of time and money on diversity, as evidenced by its theme: "None of us is as strong as all of us." IBM uses task forces to spread its corporate message regarding diversity and enables everyone to be a part of the dialogue. Its Global Diversity Council has targeted six global workforce challenges: (1) work/life balance, (2) a global marketplace, (3) cultural awareness/acceptance, (4) diversity of the management team, (5) advancement of women, and (6) integration of people with disabilities.

As you can see from these examples, the most successful companies in the world are focusing on diversity issues by emphasizing recruitment, selection, retention, and training. The last of these categories, diversity training, has three primary objectives: (1) increasing awareness about diversity issues, (2) reducing biases and stereotypes that interfere with effective management, and (3) changing behaviors so that a diverse workforce can be more effectively managed (Hanover & Cellar, 1998). Among the few studies conducted to evaluate the effectiveness of diversity training, Jeanne Hanover and Doug Cellar (1998) took a nice first step by developing a diversity training program that included presentations, videotapes, case studies, simulations, role plays, and group discussions. About 50 middle managers experienced this diversity training (experimental group); another 50 did not (control group). The results of this study indicated that the training program affected attitudes toward diversity-related management practices. Specifically, the managers exposed to the training viewed a series of diversity-related practices as more important than they had prior to the training and were more likely to report a positive change in their tendency to engage in diversity-related practices. By contrast, managers in the control group demonstrated no changes in either attitude or behavior.

In another interesting study, over 700 HR professionals were asked a series of questions about diversity practices (Rynes & Rosen, 1995). The researchers found significant relationships between perceived success of the diversity training and the following variables: (1) diverse top management teams, (2) high priority given to diversity relative to other business issues, (3) top management support, (4) managerial rewards for supporting diversity, (5) presence of a diversity manager, and (6) mandatory managerial attendance. Interestingly, when we look back at the diversity "top guns" we discussed earlier, such as IBM and Ford, we find that many of these variables are included in their work. This explains why such companies have been so successful in the diversity area. Perhaps somewhat surprisingly, Sara Rynes and Benson Rosen (1995) have discovered that only a minority of organizations are conducting diversity training and only about a third of these seem to be experiencing positive long-term success. (Indeed, the fact that most are experiencing positive short-term success suggests that these companies need to concentrate on ensuring positive long-term benefits.) Finally, the variable that turns up over and over again as most important to the adoption and success of diversity training programs is the support of top management. In short, when a company is initiating a diversity training program, its first order of business should be to gain the support of top management.

TRAINING EVALUATION

Any intervention employed in an organization needs to be evaluated. A careful evaluation is really the only way that the organization and employees can be certain that the intervention has been effective. Accordingly, I have two objectives in this section: (1) to discuss the criteria used to evaluate training programs and (2) to present a few evaluation designs that are used in these evaluations.

TRAINING CRITERIA

By this time, you certainly recognize the importance of criteria (see Chapter 4). The criteria for training programs are just as important as the criteria used to evaluate employees or validate selection systems. The "criteria for the criteria" apply here as well. Indeed, the criteria used in the evaluation of training programs, as with all other criteria, have to be relevant, reliable, sensitive, practical, and fair.

Kirkpatrick's Taxonomy. By far the most frequently used categorizational scheme of training criteria is based on the work of Donald Kirkpatrick in the late 1950s and early 1960s. (For a nice summary, see Kirkpatrick, 1976.) Recognizing that training is a multifaceted endeavor, Kirkpatrick identified four types of criteria to use in the evaluation of training programs. The first type, **reaction criteria,** have traditionally involved trainees' attitudinal reactions to the training program. These are measured with survey or questionnaire items that tap trainees' feelings about the training. Overall, organizations hope that their training program is liked by the trainees and that the trainees value the experience. However, evaluating a training program at the reaction level is probably not enough to provide solid evidence that the training program has been effective.

reaction criteria
In Kirkpatrick's taxonomy, trainees' attitudinal reactions to the training program.

The second type, **learning criteria,** reflect how much of the material is actually learned in the training program, as measured by a knowledge test at the conclusion of the training program. The idea here is that because the training program was designed to teach certain material, a test is needed to measure the extent to which the trainees learned that material. Sometimes this knowledge test is given prior to the training program (as well as afterward) so that trainees' improvement can serve as an index of how much learning occurred. According to Kurt Kraiger, Kevin Ford, and Eduardo Salas (1993), such learning can be categorized or measured in terms of (1) *cognitive outcomes,* such as amount of knowledge gained; (2) *skill-based outcomes,* such as speed of performance as a result of training; and (3) *affective outcomes,* such as the strength or centrality of trainees' attitudes about the content presented during training.

learning criteria
In Kirkpatrick's taxonomy, criteria that reflect how much of the material is actually learned in the training program.

The third type, **behavioral criteria,** involve changes that take place back on the job. These are the criteria most closely linked to transfer of training. Given our emphasis on the importance of positive transfer throughout this chapter, it should be clear that an evaluation of a training intervention that didn't include measures of behavioral criteria would be seriously flawed, because, from the organization's standpoint, learning without transfer is not very useful. For instance, imagine an electrician who learns all of the proper skills and appears to have mastered the knowledge necessary to wire a house for electricity, but when she goes out on an actual job she is unable to use what she learned and complete the task successfully. As a result, the homeowner is constantly frustrated because certain outlets don't work and some light switches short out other outlets. In this case, even if evaluation at the level of learning criteria indicated that the training worked, evaluation at the level of behavioral criteria would have revealed job performance no better than it was prior to training, leading us to conclude that the training did not work.

behavioral criteria
In Kirkpatrick's taxonomy, criteria that refer to changes that take place back on the job.

The fourth and final type level of criteria, **results criteria,** refer to the ultimate value of the training program to the company. Recall that in Chapter 7 we discussed the *utility* of a selection system. It is the utility of a training program that results criteria focus on, as summed up by the organization's question: "Was the

results criteria
In Kirkpatrick's taxonomy, the ultimate value of the training program to the company.

TABLE 8.2 Training Criteria Frameworks

Kirkpatrick's Taxonomy	Augmented Framework of Alliger et al.
Reactions	Reactions
	Affective Reactions
	Utility Judgments
Learning	Learning
	Immediate Knowledge
	Knowledge Retention
	Behavior/Skill Demonstration
Behavior	Transfer
Results	Results

Source: Alliger et al. (1997).

training worth it?" Even if the evaluation indicates that ratees responded favorably to the training program (reaction criteria), learned the material well (learning criteria), and used what they learned to improve their performance on the job (behavioral criteria), the training program is arguably *unsuccessful* if the costs incurred in developing and conducting the training far outweighed the performance improvements. In other words, although the training may appear to have worked in many ways, it still wasn't "worth it" from the organization's perspective.

Note, however, that as these four sets of criteria are not always related to one another, an evaluation of a training program on the basis of just one or two would probably be insufficient. Indeed, although many training evaluation programs focus exclusively on reaction and learning criteria (sometimes called *internal criteria* because they exist within the training program), doing so is problematic because organizations are often most interested in behavioral and results criteria (*external criteria*), as these are more relevant for the conduct of the organizations' business.

Augmented Framework. G. M. Alliger and his colleagues (Alliger & Janak, 1989; Alliger, Tannenbaum, Bennett, Traver, & Shotland, 1997) have worked extensively with Kirkpatrick's taxonomy of criteria. They presented an augmented framework, which is summarized in Table 8.2 alongside Kirkpatrick's traditional framework. Here I want to highlight just some of the differences. First, the new framework recategorizes reactions in terms of affective reactions and utility reactions. *Affective reactions* are the attitudes or feelings that Kirkpatrick referred to in his original conceptualization of reactions, whereas *utility reactions* are trainees' beliefs about the transferability or utility of the training program. Alliger et al. (1997) suggest that the latter are important elements of training evaluation and different enough from trainees' feelings to be considered separately. A recent study by Ronald Morgan and Wendy Casper (2000) also reports empirical support for multiple dimensions of the reactions level, including one dimension that they call utility reactions (Morgan & Casper, 2000).

Second, Alliger et al. (1997) recategorized learning criteria in terms of three distinct types: (1) *immediate posttraining knowledge* measures, which resemble the traditional Kirkpatrick criterion and usually refer to multiple-choice tests of knowledge; (2) *knowledge retention* measures, which are similar to immediate posttraining knowledge measures except that they are administered at a point later than immediately after training and thus give a better indication of the extent to which the information learned during training is retained for some time after training; and (3) *behavior/skill demonstration* measures, which more precisely evaluate behavior in the training context and differentiate it from behavior exhibited on the job. The final change reflected in the augmented framework involved a change in terminology from *behavioral criteria* to *transfer criteria.* Here, too, the intention was to differentiate behavioral changes that take place in training from behavior transfer that takes place on the job.

The Alliger et al. (1997) meta-analysis reveals, at best, only modest correlations among the various criteria. Affective and utility reactions were correlated more strongly with each other ($r = .34$) than with other criteria, as we would expect. But utility reactions correlated more strongly with on-the-job performance (i.e., transfer) than did affective reactions, immediate learning, or retained learning, suggesting that this new category of utility reactions is more useful for the prediction of job performance than more traditional criteria such as affective reactions and learning criteria. Additional research is likely to continue examining these issues.

A recent meta-analysis of about 160 studies is among the first thorough quantitative review of training effectiveness to be published (Arthur et al., 2003). A couple of interesting results emerged. First, the effect sizes for training effectiveness across Kirkpatrick's four criteria ranged from .60 to .63, indicating a medium to large effect of training. In other words, whether measuring reaction, learning, behavioral, or results criteria, training clearly works. Second, as noted earlier in this chapter, although the lecture method of training delivery has the reputation of being boring, the data indicate that it is a very effective technique. Thus perhaps this "low tech" approach still has much to offer.

Evaluation Designs

Once we have chosen how to specifically measure training effectiveness (at the reactions, learning, behavioral, or results level), we turn to identifying an effective design or experimental methodology to employ. Quasi-experiments—which resemble true experiments, but without random assignment (see Chapter 2)—are the most viable alternatives for the evaluation of training programs. Table 8.3 summarizes three such designs. First, let's say that we have four work groups in our organization (all of which are to undergo training at the same time) and that we are interested in finding out whether the training results in *changes* in various criteria. For instance, do the trainees know more about the material on which they were trained after participating in the training program (a question of learn-

TABLE 8.3 Training Evaluation Designs

Design	Group	Time 1	Training Intervention	Time 2
1. *Pre/Post Design*	Experimental	M_1	Training	M_2
2. *Pre/Post Design with a Control Group*	Experimental	M_1	Training	M_2
	Control	M_3		M_4
3. *Solomon Four-Group Design*	Experimental I	M_1	Training	M_2
	Control I	M_3		M_4
	Experimental II		Training	M_5
	Control II			M_6

ing criteria), and do they perform better on the job after participating in the training program (a question of behavioral or transfer criteria)? In this situation, we would use what is called a *pre/post design,* which allows us to measure these various criteria prior to training (M_1) and again after training (M_2). The change on these measures (an improvement, we hope) would be indicated by a larger M_2 than M_1 and would reflect the effectiveness of the training program. One weakness with this design, however, is the lack of a control group, which prevents us from drawing a direct comparison between our training participants and others who did not experience training.

Second, let's say that we have two work groups that we assign to the training condition and two others that we assign to the no-training condition. This design, often described as a *pre/post design with a control group,* is very similar to the previous design except that it involves a control group. In other words, measures are obtained both prior to and after training, but this time they apply to both the experimental condition and the control condition. In addition, the control group can be provided with some other kind of training, such as an old training program, in an attempt to compare the effectiveness of the old program with the newly designed one. Recall that internal validity is the extent to which we can draw causal inferences—or, for the purposes of this training situation, the extent to which the changes reflected in the criteria are due to the training and not to something else. With the addition of a control group, this design is stronger in terms of internal validity than the previous design because we are able to make not only pre- and postcomparisons ($M_2 - M_1$ versus $M_4 - M_3$ in Table 8.3) but also comparisons between the experimental and control groups ($M_2 - M_4$). If the difference between M_2 and M_1 is larger than the difference between M_4 and M_3, and if M_2 is greater than M_4, we can feel pretty certain that the training program was effective in terms of the criteria that we evaluated.

The third design presented in Table 8.3 is called the *Solomon four-group design.* In terms of internal validity, this is a superb design because it includes two experimental groups as well as two control groups, allowing us to draw *several* useful comparisons. However, it is also very costly in terms of both dollars and resources—precisely because it involves multiple groups, numerous participants, and multiple measures. Thus, although it is a very strong design from a research perspective, organizations find it impractical and are seldom willing to use it for their training evaluation studies.

SUMMARY

This chapter was structured around four major areas. First, we discussed how organizations are diagnosed with respect to training needs. The organizational analysis identifies where training is needed in the organization, the task analysis identifies which behaviors or duties have to be improved through training, and the person analysis identifies those employees who need to be trained (Harvey, 1991). In addition, demographic analysis may indicate the training needs of particular employee populations.

Second, the learning context and its role in training effectiveness were considered. Some learning principles were defined and then applied to specific training issues. As discussed, these principles can play a critical role in the success of a training program. For instance, we noted that trainees may fail to learn effectively if the material to be learned is too large and cumbersome, if the material is not meaningful, if practice is rarely used or done poorly, if the desired behaviors are not overlearned, and if immediate, specific feedback is not provided. We also discovered that the transfer of learned behaviors and skills back to the workplace is contingent on many factors that make up the learning context.

Third, we discussed training delivery methods, categorizing them as traditional, technology-based, or employee development-focused. Many of the most frequently used specific techniques within each category were discussed, along with examples and empirical evidence. Sexual harassment training and diversity management were discussed in light of their growing importance in 21st-century organizations.

The last section of the chapter centered on the evaluation of training programs. In this connection we discussed Kirkpatrick's four levels of criteria (reactions, learning, behavioral, results), as well as the augmented framework presented by Alliger and his colleagues (1997). Finally, we discussed a few commonly used training evaluation designs.

REVIEW QUESTIONS

1. Distinguish among organizational, task, and person analysis.
2. What legal and organizational issues have led to the use of demographic analysis in training?

3. What principles of learning are important in successful training programs?
4. What is instructional design and how does it help define the learning context?
5. Why would you want your employees to overlearn important behaviors?
6. How do positive transfer and negative transfer differ from each other? Provide examples of each.
7. Discuss the role played by trainer characteristics and trainee individual differences in training effectiveness.
8. Discuss the role you believe will be played by sexual harassment training and diversity training in organizations of the 21st century.
9. Discuss the technology-based approaches to training
10. Why are all four traditional criteria important in the evaluation of training programs?
11. How would you design a training evaluation program if you had unlimited resources? What design would you use if your resources were limited?
12. What is a "corporate university" and how is it important for training in the 21st century?

SUGGESTED READINGS

Arthur, W., Bennett, W., Edens, P. S., & Bell, S. T. (2003). Effectiveness of training in organizations: A meta-analysis of design and evaluation features. *Journal of Applied Psychology, 88*(2), 234–245. This quantitative review of training effectiveness will become the most relied-upon resource for drawing inferences about training success.

Goldstein, I. L., & Ford, J. K. (2002). *Training in organizations: Needs assessment, development, and evaluation* (4th ed.). Belmont, CA: Wadsworth. This classic text, in its new and updated version, is as readable as ever and still provides the most thorough treatment of the training area.

Wexley, K. N., & Latham, G. P. (2002). *Developing and training human resources in organizations* (3rd ed.). Upper Saddle River, NJ: Prentice Hall. This thorough treatment of training provides a nice mix of research findings, but it is especially strong in presenting real-world training examples.

Motivation

9

CHAPTER OUTLINE

Whereas the second section of this text focused on industrial psychology, the third section provides an overview of organizational psychology. As I discussed in Chapter 1, it was the Hawthorne Studies in the 1920s and 1930s that provided a stable foundation for organizational psychology. Prior to this work, I/O psychology was largely about industrial psychology. The Hawthorne Studies opened the way for researchers to realize that systems of rewards and punishments created by organizations, relationships among workers, organizational norms, and individuals' perceptions of where they fit into the organization were all key elements of the workplace. As Edgar Schein (1980) noted in his classic book, organizational psychology "is intimately tied to the recognition that organizations are complex social systems, and that almost all questions one may raise about the determinants of individual human behavior within organizations have to be viewed from the perspective of the entire social system" (p. 6). In other words, as organizational psychologists, we cannot study an individual's work behaviors without considering the entire context in which that individual works and lives. **Organizational psychology,** then, can be formally defined as the systematic study of dispositional and situational variables that influence the behaviors and experiences of individuals and groups at work (Lawson & Shen, 1998). Accordingly, this section of the book covers the following topics: motivation, job attitudes, stress and worker well-being, group processes and work teams, leadership, and organizational theory and development. As in the industrial psychology section of the book, much of our discussion will focus on individual performance and organizational effectiveness.

organizational psychology
The systematic study of dispositional and situational variables that influence the behaviors and experiences of individuals and groups at work.

Of all the topics typically considered within the realm of organizational psychology, motivation draws the most interest and attention from both scientists and practitioners alike. Indeed, it is likely that more journal space over the years has been devoted to work motivation than to any other area of organizational psychology (Pinder, 1984; Steers, Mowday, & Shapiro, 2004). The fact that this topic is especially important to management is evidenced by the following quotes by managers from various companies:

> "The workers today aren't willing to put out the extra effort that is required to do a nice job."
>
> "Everybody wants something for nothing—they all want the big pay, nice benefits, and to work in a nice air-conditioned office, but they don't want to work hard for any of those things."
>
> "It's really not that they can't do the work, most of my workers are pretty competent, they just seem to want to take shortcuts around doing the work—they just aren't motivated."
>
> "The only thing that at least half of my workers are motivated to do is to make as much money as possible by doing as little as possible."
>
> "As a manager, the most difficult part of my job is keeping my employees motivated—if I don't stay on top of this, their motivation drops off drastically and it is reflected in performance and attitude problems."

CHAPTER NINE

As an I/O psychologist, I am often asked by organizational managers and executives about what can be done to improve the motivation of their workforce. One theme that I have emphasized throughout this book is the complexity of human behavior at work. This complexity explains why we need to use multiple tests (i.e., a selection battery) for employee selection and why we are fortunate if our battery accounts for 30% of the variance in performance. It also explains why even the most skilled and competent professionals are not always the best performers. Certainly, ability is an important predictor of individual performance, but so is motivation. The brightest and most skilled workers in the world will not be successful if they are not motivated to be successful. It is quite common to hear psychologists discuss performance as being largely a function of ability and motivation, with other elements such as situational constraints playing important but somewhat smaller roles. In this chapter, we thus take a very detailed look at work motivation. Along the way, several theories of motivation will be presented, followed by various applications of these theories to motivational issues in organizations.

work motivation
A force that drives people to behave in a way that energizes, directs, and sustains their work behavior.

Among the many definitions of **work motivation,** one that strikes me as particularly useful is to view it as a force that drives people to behave in a way that energizes, directs, and sustains their work behavior (Steers et al., 2004). Work motivation is *energizing* in that it results in the expenditure of effort. It *directs* effort or behavior in a particular way or channels it toward a particular object or place. In other words, having energy is not sufficient to characterize a worker as being motivated; there must also be some direction or purpose to that energy. Finally, work motivation is not fleeting; rather, it *sustains* effort over a period of time.

Motivation is an abstract concept in that it cannot be seen or touched. It is also an internal concept in that it cannot be measured directly. We infer motivation from employees' behaviors, and we operationalize it by measuring behavior choice, intensity, and persistence. It is important to note that motivation and performance are different constructs, although many individuals seem to confuse the two (Pinder, 1998). It's not unusual for managers to immediately attribute performance problems to the motivation of the employees involved. As I mentioned earlier, performance is much more complicated than that. Motivation is an important antecedent of performance, but so is ability, the right equipment, organizational support, and freedom from organizational constraints. One quote that I did not include before but that I have heard from managers many times goes something like this: "My workers are not performing up to my expectations; *they just aren't as motivated as they need to be.*" This may very well be the case, but managers need to be careful not to fall into the trap of unquestioningly viewing performance problems as being motivational in nature. Throughout the rest of the book, we will discuss many different areas of organizational psychology and gain a better understanding of the complexity of work performance and the multidimensional nature of the antecedents and causes of work performance. Let's start with a detailed look at work motivation.

LEARNING OBJECTIVES

This chapter should help you understand:

- the importance of work motivation to organizational psychology.
- how the three major categories of motivation theories differ from each other.
- the similarities and differences among the various need-motive-value theories of motivation.
- how cognitive choice theories emphasize the rationality of human behavior.
- the similarities and differences between equity theory and expectancy theory.
- how important self-regulatory processes are to work behavior.
- the major principles and findings with respect to goal-setting theory.
- why discrepancies are so important to goal-directed behavior.
- the widespread use and success of organizational behavior management programs for improving motivation and performance.
- how successful goal setting (including management-by-objectives) is as an applied technique for improving motivation and performance.
- what job enrichment approaches have to offer organizations and the various ways in which enrichment can be employed.

THEORETICAL PERSPECTIVES

The following three subsections are based on a framework presented by Ruth Kanfer (1990) that involves three major categories of motivation theories. Each theory is illustrated with examples.

Need-Motive-Value Theories

Approaches to motivation from the need-motive-value perspective emphasize the role of personality traits, stable dispositions, needs, and values as the basis for behavioral differences. In other words, individuals are motivated to perform a particular behavior as a result of these four factors. The most frequently cited theories of work motivation in this category focus on needs, so let's look at needs from a psychological perspective. Henry Murray, a famous personality theorist, defined a **need** as a force that organizes perceptions, beliefs, cognitions, and actions, giving rise to behaviors that reduce the force and bring about a steady state (Pinder, 1984). A need is a hypothetical construct in that we can never measure it directly or describe what it looks like; thus we are left to infer it from a person's behavior. It is something internal to individuals that leads or pushes them to exhibit certain behaviors, which in turn reduce the need and satisfy the individual. Let's look now at four need-motive-value theories of work motivation.

need
A force that organizes perceptions, beliefs, cognitions, and actions, giving rise to behaviors that reduce the force and bring about a steady state.

Maslow's Hierarchy of Needs. This theory of human motivation was popular in organizational psychology during the 1950s and 1960s, but it has since fallen into disfavor. Yet despite criticisms from the scientific community, it is still a favorite of the business world (Kiel, 1999; Payne, 2000). Maslow's theory assumes, in part, that we are all aroused by needs that are biological and instinctive in nature. People behave as they do in order to satisfy those needs. For example, an individual who is hungry is experiencing a hunger need, and the behavioral pattern that follows that experience of hunger (which may include walking to the refrigerator and grabbing a snack) is exhibited to reduce or satisfy that hunger need. Hunger is one of the physiological needs at the bottom of Maslow's hierarchy of needs (see Figure 9.1). *Physiological* needs are the needs for food, shelter, and water—the basic needs for existence. *Safety* needs, one level up, are the needs to be free from threat and danger. Then come *love* needs (sometimes called social needs), which have to do with our needs for affiliation, belongingness, and friendship. The *esteem* needs, at the next level, are the needs for respect from others, self-confidence, and belief in oneself. Finally, at the top of the hierarchy are the needs for *self-actualization,* the definition of which Maslow was not clear about. However, it appears that he was referring to fulfillment of one's potential. Quite a few years ago the Army ran an advertising campaign that included the jingle "Be all that you can be"—this is what I think Maslow meant by self-actualization.

Maslow argued that humans are motivated first by lower-order needs and that when these needs are met, higher-order needs become more important as

FIGURE 9.1 Maslow's Hierarchy of Needs

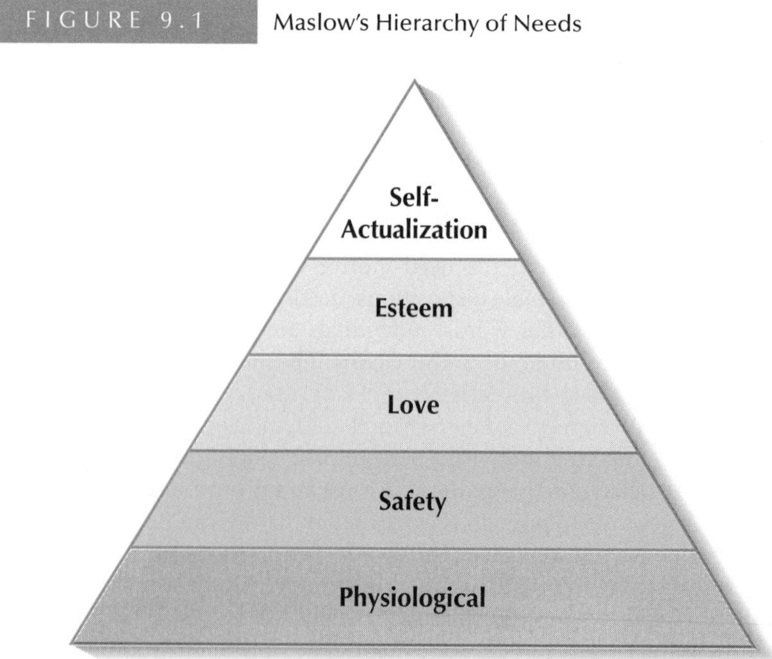

motivators of behavior. Thus, if someone is dying of hunger, the need for food will take precedence over all the other needs above it; but once this need is satisfied, the safety needs become more important, and then the love needs, and so forth up the hierarchy. One organizational implication of this theory is that different employees are likely to be at different places in the hierarchy, such that no one thing can be assumed to motivate *all* employees. For instance, one employee may be motivated to earn money that he needs right now to pay for his wife's cancer surgery, whereas a second employee may be focused on gaining the respect of her peers because she is at a different stage in her life. This employee, then, would be motivated to behave in ways that result in her being respected and appreciated by her colleagues—she would be motivated by esteem needs, whereas the first employee would be focused on physiological and safety needs. There isn't much empirical support for Maslow's theory. In fact, few empirical tests of this theory have ever been conducted. The reason has to do with the difficulty of testing needs theories—and, indeed, with the hypothetical nature of needs themselves: We can't see or touch them, or manipulate them, or measure them—and this makes it very hard to empirically test whether needs are important causes of human behavior at work. Yet, as suggested earlier, Maslow's theory is popular among managers and students of organizational behavior (Pinder, 1998). Let's examine a reformulation of Maslow's theory.

Alderfer's ERG Theory. Whereas Maslow's theory was chiefly rooted in his own clinical observations, Alderfer set out to empirically generate a theory of motivation—a theory focused on the subjective states of need satisfaction and desire. He proposed that satisfaction is an internal state that results from obtaining what one was seeking. Desire is similar to such concepts as want or intensity of need strength. Alderfer developed three categories of needs that somewhat parallel Maslow's five levels. First there are *existence* needs, the same kinds of needs that Maslow referred to as physiological and safety needs. Examples include pay and fringe benefits. Second are *relatedness* needs, which correspond to Maslow's love needs and are focused on social relationships. Finally, *growth* needs parallel Maslow's esteem and self-actualization needs. The focus here is on interacting successfully with one's environment through exploration and mastery of it.

One difference between the two theories is that ERG theory suggests that all three categories of needs can be operating simultaneously rather than in the sequence suggested by Maslow. Thus, for instance, an employee can be motivated at the same time by existence, relatedness, and growth needs. A second difference is that Alderfer posited a *frustration-regression hypothesis,* which allows for situations in which an individual who is frustrated at a higher level of need then refocuses energy on satisfying a lower-level need. For example, someone who is frustrated over not being able to satisfy her growth needs at work may take a step back and focus instead on continuing to satisfy her relatedness needs. This hypothesis has a lot of intuitive appeal because it makes sense to think that when we are frustrated over trying to do too much or to be too successful, we can focus instead on maintaining excellence in another way until we are reenergized to resume our attack on the higher-order needs. More research has been directed at Alderfer's theory than at Maslow's theory, but with few exceptions it was conducted by Alderfer himself, with very mixed results. Some of his predictions were supported; others weren't. For that matter, the problems inherent in testing need theories emerge here as well. We will revisit these shortly.

Herzberg's Two-Factor Theory. In the 1950s Frederick Herzberg and his colleagues (1959) proposed that the determinants of job satisfaction were different from those of job dissatisfaction. In other words, providing employees with some things will result in job satisfaction and motivation, whereas *not* providing the same things will *not* lead to job dissatisfaction but will instead lead to some degree of neutrality. This was a rather controversial statement at the time because it suggested that job satisfaction and job dissatisfaction were not at opposite ends of a continuum but, rather, were different constructs entirely. Two-factor theory suggests that *motivators* are the things that lead employees to be satisfied with and motivated by their jobs—things like recognition, interesting work, responsibility, reinforcement for work well done, and potential advancement. Motivators have to do with job content: Their presence results in job satisfaction and motivation, but their absence results only in neutrality. *Hygienes,* on the other hand, are related to job context. Examples include supervisory problems, poor interpersonal relations at work, low salary, and poor working conditions. The presence of hygienes results in job dissatisfaction, but their absence leads not to job satisfaction or motivation—only to neutrality.

Figure 9.2 shows how these two categories of needs map onto the other need theories that we've discussed. The implication from two-factor theory should be obvious: To ensure that your workforce will be satisfied and motivated to perform, it is not enough to provide for a reasonable context by altering working conditions and pay. Indeed, the content of the job, such as interpersonal relationships and recognition for one's contributions to the workplace, must be taken into account as well.

There has been considerably more empirical investigation of this theory than of the other need theories we've discussed, but the results have done no better than to demonstrate mixed support. Nevertheless, although this is purely anecdotal, I have heard many practitioners argue (sometimes convincingly) that they see two-factor theory play out before them every day in their organizations. Some, for instance, have dealt with employees for whom a decent office and wage prevent them from being dissatisfied but for whom these are not sufficient to make them truly satisfied with their jobs or to motivate them to do their jobs well.

Job Characteristics Theory. In this more contemporary example of need-motive-value theories, the emphasis is on matching individuals to jobs or changing jobs to better fit individuals. In proposing their *job characteristics theory,* building on Herzberg's earlier work, Richard Hackman and Greg Oldham (1980)

FIGURE 9.2 Overview of Need Theories

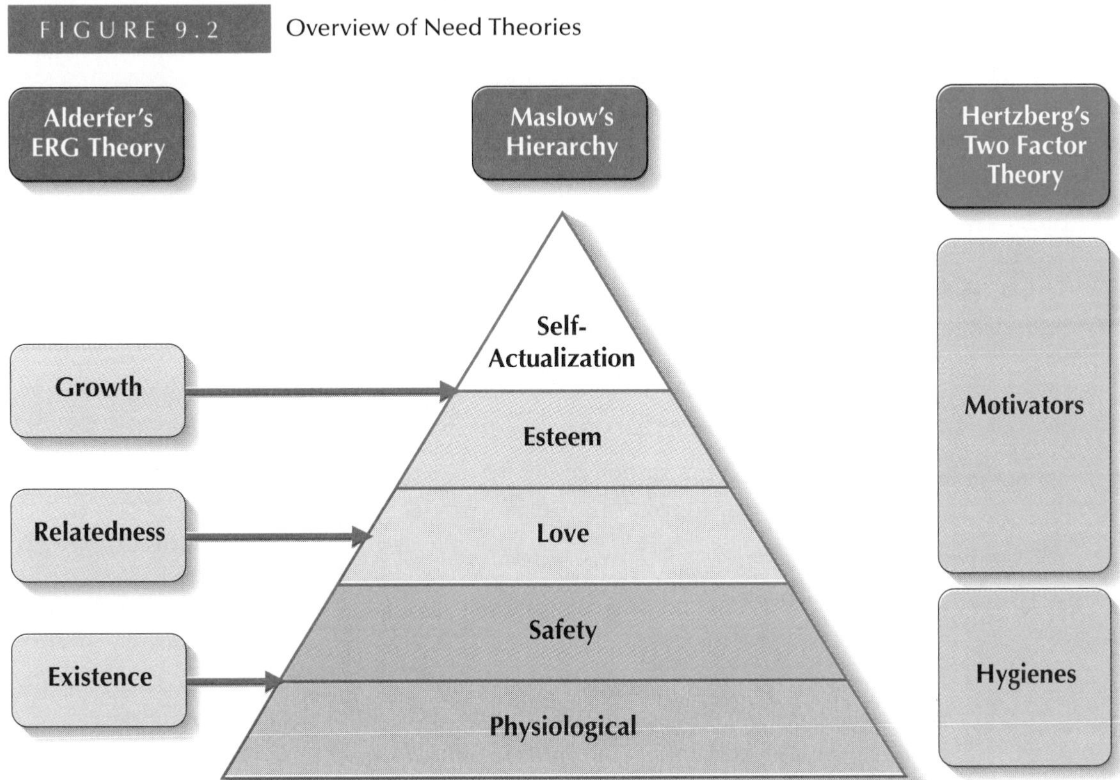

argued that motivation is determined by the joint effects of individual differences in personality and characteristics of the job; they also developed a model (see Figure 9.3) that explains how jobs influence attitudes and behaviors. Any job, they said, can be described by five *core job dimensions:* skill variety, task identity, task significance, autonomy, and feedback. Jobs vary along these dimensions: Some have more of one, others have less of another. These dimensions influence the three *critical psychological states* that are necessary for motivation. In particular, jobs that appear *meaningful* to employees, generate *personal responsibility* on the part of employees for the outcomes they produce, and provide employees with *knowledge of the results* of their efforts are more likely to motivate the employees to put forth some effort. Such jobs would be described as having high motivating potential. Figure 9.3 shows how the five core job dimensions map onto these psychological states. For instance, employees are more likely to experience meaningfulness at work if their job requires skill variety (and thus doesn't involve the same old thing every day), provides task identity (such that employees can point to some aspect of their work as being the result of their own efforts), and provides task significance (such that employees' tasks appear to matter to co-workers or others in society at large). The final element of the model concerns the *personal*

FIGURE 9.3 The Job Characteristics Model

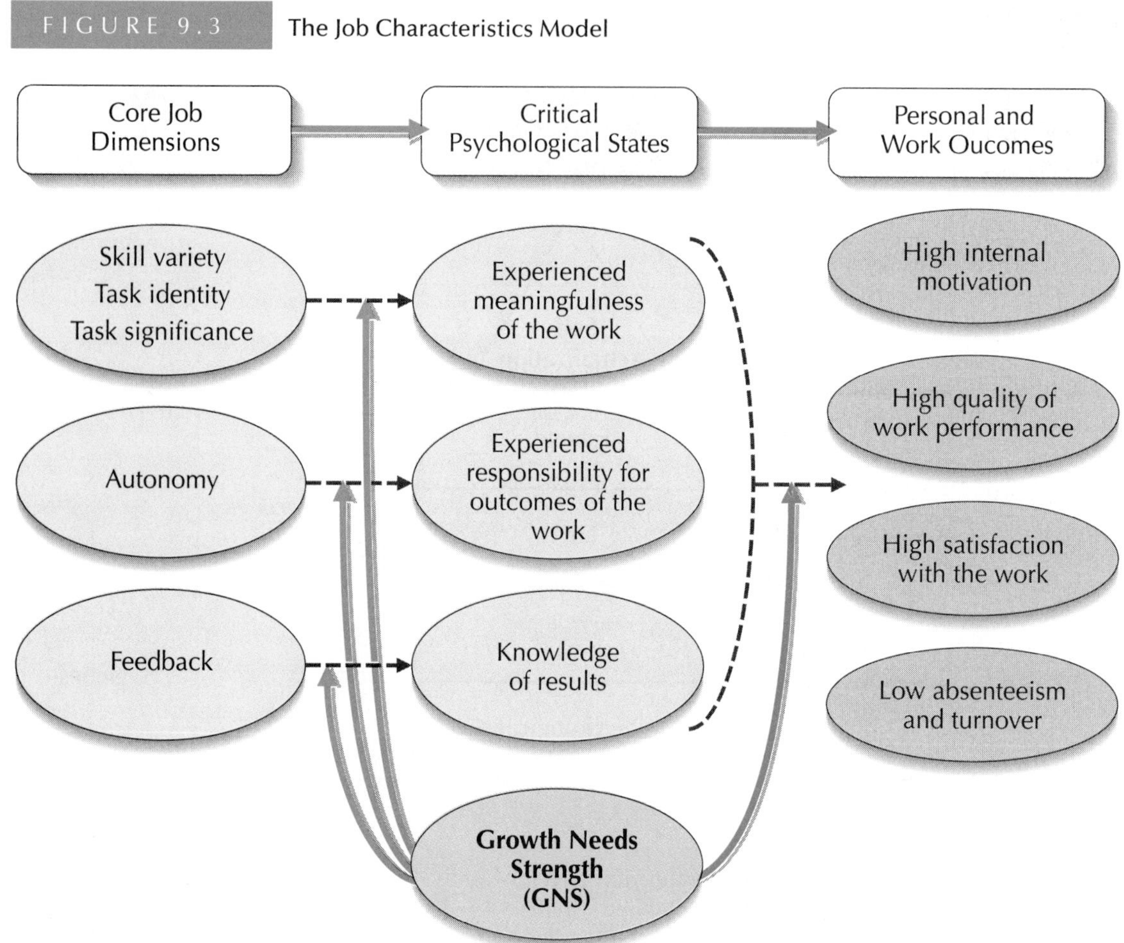

Source: *Hackman & Oldham (1976).*

and work outcomes that follow from the psychological states. These include high internal motivation to work hard and excel, high quality of work performance, high satisfaction with the work, and low absenteeism and turnover.

This model has at least two major implications. The first is that jobs should be designed with the core dimensions in mind. Because positive outcomes are believed to follow from these core dimensions, then it seems reasonable to design and redesign jobs to be high on skill variety, task identity, task significance, autonomy, and feedback. (We will talk more about this issue in the applications section of the chapter.) Second, some thought should be given to the placement of employees in jobs. Although the core dimensions are arguably positive for most employees, there are likely to be individual differences among them. For instance,

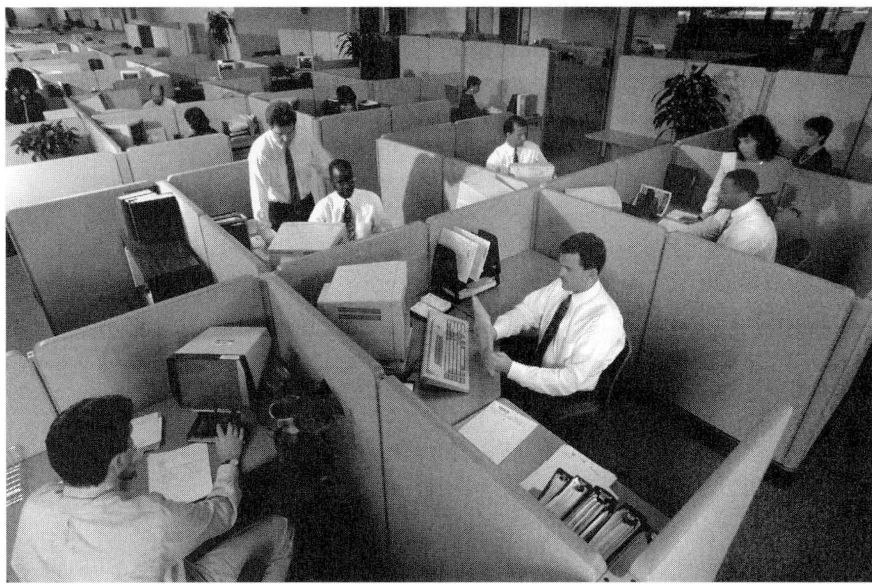

Characteristics of jobs, such as the office layout, can affect one's motivation.

autonomy may be much more important to one employee than to another, suggesting that the first employee should be placed in a job involving a great deal of autonomy, while the second employee should be given a job in which he simply follows someone else's direction. Furthermore, if task significance, say, is the key dimension for this second employee, a job as a key member of the disaster relief team (even though he may not have much autonomy) might fit his needs quite well. According to Hackman and Oldham, **growth need strength,** or the extent to which individuals value or desire fulfilling higher-order needs, moderates the relationships among the variables in the model. For instance, if fulfilling higher-order needs is not an important goal for a particular employee, then meaningfulness of work probably doesn't matter much for that employee. Many studies have provided support for parts of this model (e.g., Pollock, Whitbred, & Contractor, 2000), but research has not found consistent support for the full model. However, most experts would agree that job characteristics play some role in the motivation of employees.

growth need strength
The extent to which individuals value or desire fulfilling higher-order needs.

Job characteristics theory is considered a theory of intrinsic motivation because of its emphasis on personal mastery and control. Another popular theory of intrinsic motivation is Deci's (1975) cognitive evaluation theory, which assumes that individuals adopt either an intrinsic or extrinsic motivational orientation. Ryan and Deci (2000) describe this theory as being focused on specifying factors that explain variability in intrinsic motivation. The theory postulates that social-contextual events (e.g., reception of feedback or rewards) that enhance perceptions of competence improve intrinsic motivation. However, perceptions of competence must be believed to be self-determined or attributed to one's own

TABLE 9.1 Overjustification Effect

More Noise, please. . . .

Mr. Warren was an elderly man who lived alone on a dead-end street. All the children in the neighborhood gathered to play at the end of the street every day after school, making a lot of noise outside Mr. Warren's house. One day Mr. Warren came out of his house and explained to the boys that he loved hearing them having fun outside, and so he would pay them all 50 cents to come back and do it again the next day. The kids were excited, and the first thing they did after school the next day was to gather outside Mr. Warren's house and made even more noise. Mr. Warren followed through on his promise and encouraged the boys to come back again the next day for additional money. However, when they came back the next day, Mr. Warren explained that he didn't have much money and he was only able to give them each 40 cents this time, but he would pay them again tomorrow. When the boys came the next day and made as much noise as ever, he explained that he could only give them each a quarter. The boys weren't very happy, but they decided to come back the next day and see how much money Mr.Warren had for them. Mr. Warren met them on the street after the boys played noisily for about an hour and told them that he only had a dime for each child. The boys were very disappointed and their leader, a young boy named Jerry, protested, saying that it wasn't worth their time and they wouldn't be back to make the noise for Mr. Warren any more. The boys left and never played in front of Mr. Warren's house again. Mr. Warren looks more rested these days since he has returned to getting in his late-afternoon nap every day without interruption!

abilities or effort in order for intrinsic motivation to follow. Research in this area continues to examine when and how individuals become intrinsically motivated, as well as when providing external reinforcement reduces intrinsic motivation. This latter phenomenon is called the overjustification effect and is illustrated with the story in Table 9.1.

Cognitive Choice Theories

Cognitive processes involved in decision making and choice are the focus of this next approach to motivation. The assumption here is that people are neither passively driven by inner needs nor controlled by their environment. Rather, people are active decision makers who strive to be rational in choosing what to do, how much effort to exert, and so on. Two cognitive choice theories—equity theory and expectancy theory—are discussed in the following sections.

Equity Theory. In the early 1960s, J. Stacy Adams proposed a model of motivation, called equity theory, that focused on social justice. According to this model, behavior is initiated, directed, and maintained by the attempts of individuals to preserve some internal psychological balance (Adams, 1965). Equity theory stemmed in part from the earlier work of Leon Festinger, who developed the theory of cognitive dissonance—a theory that explains how and why we change our behaviors or beliefs to be consistent with other behaviors or beliefs. The idea behind equity theory is that people's perceptions and beliefs about the fairness of their treatment at work affects their motivation, attitudes, and behaviors. We have all experienced situations at work or at school in which we have felt mistreated. Have you ever thought that you worked too hard on a class project to get a C, whereas someone else in the class didn't work very hard at all and yet received a B? Have you ever noticed that your co-worker in the cubicle next to you always comes in late, whereas you are there 15 minutes before work officially begins—and you are both paid the same wage? In such cases you may have perceived inequity. How did you respond? At school, did you talk to the teacher about how unfair the grading was? Did you stop taking classes from that instructor? And at your job, did you stop working so hard? Did you ask for a raise? There are many ways to respond to situations in which we feel that we are not being treated fairly. Let's look at the mechanics of equity theory a bit more closely.

Equity theory is based on the notion that we compare the ratios of what we bring to a situation (i.e., inputs) and what we get out of it (i.e., outcomes) with what others bring to and get out of the situation. Underlying these comparisons are four main postulates:

1. People strive to maintain a state of equity.
2. When inequity is perceived, a state of tension results.
3. When faced with this tension, people are motivated to reduce the tension.
4. The greater the magnitude of the perceived inequity, the greater the motivation to act to reduce the tension.

In an organizational setting, inputs can include abilities, effort, resources such as money or education level, and anything employees possess that help prepare them to do their jobs. Outcomes include wages, benefits, feelings of satisfaction, and anything the employees receive as a result of their inputs. Table 9.2 presents lists of potential inputs and outcomes. Suppose Bill is an accountant for the city of Akron, Ohio, and works with three other accountants who are at approximately the same level in the organization. Bill has a master's degree and five years of experience with the city; he puts in overtime and believes that he works very hard and is quite competent. He makes $46,000 per year but feels that he doesn't get many benefits, accolades for his hard work, or sufficient appreciation. He notices that no one else in his group has a master's degree and that no one else has more than three years of experience. However, all four accountants make the same salary, and Bill thinks that Carmen is the favorite of the bosses, receives more awards, and is more appreciated. In this situation Bill perceives inequity because when he compares his input/outcome ratio to that of his coworker's, the ratios aren't equal. He brings more to the job but gets no more than the others and, compared with at least one other person, actually gets less. In fact, this is a classic case of inequity, but not because Bill gets less than he deserves; rather,

TABLE 9.2 Potential Inputs and Outcomes

Inputs	Outcomes
Education	Compensation
Effort	Benefits
Ability	Recognition
Skills	Self-Concept
Knowledge	Experience
Experience	Learning
Diversity	Opportunities
Vision	Satisfaction

inequity has resulted because, compared with what others have to offer, what Bill has to offer gets him *relatively* less than they get.

Employees can reduce perceived inequity in several different ways. Let's apply a few of these to Bill's situation. The first thing he can do is *change his inputs.* Bill can stop working so hard and avoid working overtime. Of course, with respect to changing inputs, he is limited to altering his effort. He can't suddenly not have a master's degree anymore—this input is relatively fixed. On the other hand, if Bill felt that he was getting *more* than he deserved, he could reduce the inequity by going back to school and obtaining more training, thereby increasing his inputs. A second way to reduce perceived inequity is to *change outcomes.* Bill can present his concerns to his boss and ask for a raise, a promotion, additional benefits, more recognition, and so on. Obviously, Bill is dependent on his boss for increasing the outcomes, but he can certainly get the ball rolling by asking for them. A third way, though perhaps not always a wise one, is to *alter his perceptions.* Bill can attempt to convince himself that his ratio is about the same as his co-workers'. In other words, he can decide that he doesn't really work any harder than they do and, although he has a master's degree, they have more practical experience from previous jobs than he does. Although this may seem like he's "tricking" himself, this option can be reasonably successful in the short term by reducing the tension that arises from perceived inequity. Whether there are long-term costs associated with this strategy is another matter.

Empirical support for equity theory is generally mixed (Pinder, 1998). According to some studies, when people who are paid on the basis of how much they produce (i.e., on a piece-rate system) feel that their rate of pay is not enough, they tend to produce more but at a lower quality (Mowday, 1991). There is some evidence, though not a great deal, that when individuals believe that their hourly pay rate is too low, they tend to reduce their inputs—for example, by reducing their effort (Mowday, 1991). Another study has demonstrated that inequity can have important motivational effects and may lead to resentment, absenteeism, and turnover (Cropanzano & Greenberg, 1997). One problem with equity theory, however, is that it predicts that if individuals believe they are *paid too much,* they will change their inputs to make the situation more equitable. In other words, if you believe that you are getting more and better outcomes from your job than those received by your co-workers, all of whom have the same inputs as you, you will be motivated to make this situation more fair either by working harder to *earn your extra outcomes* or by telling your boss that you are being paid too much for what you do. As you can imagine, there isn't much research to substantiate this prediction. Have you ever worked with people who thought they were overpaid and offered to take a cut in pay? Such situations are rare, but recent studies have shown that inequity in either direction (i.e., getting too little or too much) led to burnout in a sample of professionals (van Dierendonck, Schaufeli, & Buunk, 2001) and negative organizational outcomes (Scheer, Kumar, & Steenkamp, 2003).

A newer construct called **equity sensitivity** has been developed to account for the notion that people differ in terms of their sensitivity to over-reward or under-reward situations (O'Neill & Mone, 1998). This construct has been quite useful in predicting attitudes and behaviors as a function of various inequitable situations. Depending on how employees score on equity sensitivity measures, they are classified as *benevolents,* who tend to be more tolerant of under-reward inequity; as *entitleds,* who always want over-reward; or as *equity-sensitives,* who truly desire the state of equity or balance. Recent research has shown a relationship between these categories and such factors as job satisfaction, effort, organizational commitment, and turnover (Allen & White, 2002; King & Miles, 1994). This relationship is an element of equity theory that will continue to be the focus of research for years to come.

equity sensitivity
An individual difference indicating the extent to which people are affected by over-reward or under-reward situations.

Equity theory has served as the foundation for one of the "hottest" topic areas in 21st-century organizations—**organizational justice,** which is the term used to refer to the role of fairness in the workplace. The term was coined by Jerry Greenberg in the 1980s to describe individuals' interest in and concern with fairness-related activities that take place at work. Organizational justice is viewed as a class of motivated behavior or attitudes that are engaged by different individual and contextual characteristics (Levy & Norris-Watts, in press). Justice perceptions result in both affective and cognitive responses that determine ensuing behaviors. Adams's (1965) work on equity theory focused on fairness with respect to outcomes, which has become known as *distributive justice.* More recently, researchers and practitioners alike have become interested in *procedural justice,* or the extent to which the procedures and processes used at work are perceived to be fair by employees. Finally, a third dimension of organizational justice has received considerable interest in recent years—*interactional justice,* or the way in which decisions and procedures are communicated to employees. This last dimension is focused more on the extent to which individuals are provided information about the rationale and purpose of organizational decisions. In fact, this dimension has been further divided by some scholars and researchers into interpersonal and informational subdimensions. Organizational justice is one of the most heavily researched topics in organizational psychology today, with hundreds of articles published per year on this topic and many, many books published annually, as well. For those interested in more depth and breadth regarding this topic, I would

organizational justice
The study of people's perceptions of fairness in organizational contexts.

refer the reader to the works of Russell Cropanzano, Jerry Greenberg, Rob Folger, and Allan Lind.

expectancy An individual's belief about the likelihood of achieving a desired performance level when exerting a certain amount of effort.

Expectancy Theory. One of the most popular theories of work motivation is based on the modern work of Victor Vroom (1964) and stems from the much earlier work of Edward Tolman (see Tolman, 1932). Vroom's expectancy theory includes a model termed Valence-Instrumentality-Expectancy (VIE). The major premise of this model is that people's behaviors result from conscious choices among alternatives and that these alternatives are evaluated with respect to valence, instrumentality, and expectancy. Its basic assumption, to which its critics have objected, is that individuals are rational and make rational decisions. We know that this isn't always the case, but it certainly is some of the time. **Expectancy**

FIGURE 9.4 Expectancy Theory: Concepts and Examples

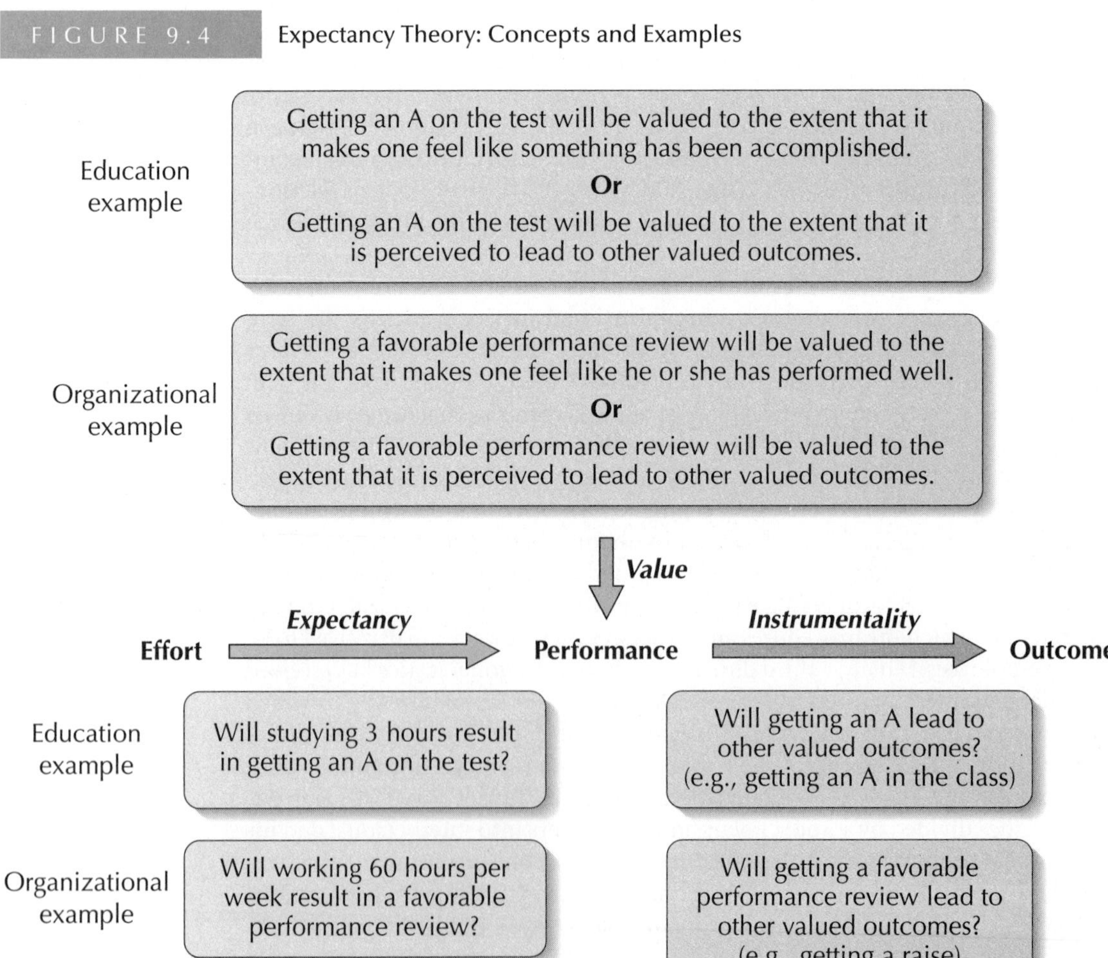

is defined as an individual's belief about the likelihood of achieving a desired performance level when exerting a certain amount of effort. Figure 9.4 presents the VIE model, along with two examples. A student might ask how likely it is that studying 3 hours for a test will result in getting an A on the test, whereas a computer programmer might ask how likely it is that working 60 hours a week for the next 3 months will result in performance that is good enough to receive a favorable performance review. Expectancy is sometimes referred to as the effort→performance link—a link that should be clear from these two examples.

Instrumentality is the perceived relationship between the performance of a particular behavior and the likelihood that a certain outcome will result from that behavior. This is sometimes viewed as the performance→outcome link. In our school example, instrumentality is the extent to which getting an A on the test is likely to lead to other favorable outcomes, such as an A for the course or graduating with honors. In the workplace example, it is the extent to which getting a favorable performance review is likely to result in a pay raise or a promotion. In both of these examples, instrumentality is reflective of one outcome leading to another outcome.

instrumentality
The perceived relationship between the performance of a particular behavior and the likelihood that a certain outcome will result from that behavior.

Valence, which literally means "value," is the expected level of satisfaction to be derived from some outcome. An outcome is positively valued if an individual expects to be satisfied by obtaining it. As Vroom (1964) noted, an outcome is more likely to be valued if other positive outcomes are likely to stem from it. In other words, if one outcome is instrumental for other outcomes, that first outcome is likely to be positively valued. In our school example, getting an A on the test may be valued in and of itself because it makes a student feel as though she has accomplished something important. In addition, if getting an A on the test is

valence (or value)
The expected level of satisfaction to be derived from some outcome.

The motivation to study is affected by valence, expectancy, and instrumentality.

likely to lead to getting an A in the course (instrumentality) and getting an A in the course is important to her (value), then getting an A on the test is positively valued as well. Similarly, our computer programmer may value a positive performance review because it makes him feel that he is doing a good job. In addition, he is likely to value a positive performance review if he believes that the review will result in a large pay raise (instrumentality) and if the pay raise is important to him (value).

Putting all of this together, Vroom (1964) suggests that individuals' beliefs about values, instrumentalities, and expectancies interact psychologically to create the motivational force to act in such a way as to bring pleasure and avoid pain. In other words, we tend to do things that make us happy, pleased, and proud and to not do things that displease us, disappoint us, or make us unhappy. Motivation is a multiplicative function of these three concepts, which means that if any of the three is 0, there is no motivation. For instance, if getting an A on the test is *valued* and believed to be *instrumental* for obtaining other valued outcomes such as an A in the course but the student believes that it is completely unrealistic to *expect* that pulling an all-nighter is going to result in getting an A on the test, then she won't pull an all-nighter. Although she perceives high levels of value and instrumentality, her 0 expectancy results in the choice not to exhibit the behavior (i.e., pulling an all-nighter). Alternatively, if the computer programmer knows that hard work will be reflected in a favorable performance review but he is certain that the performance review will not lead to any other important outcomes, then he may choose not to work so hard. Which factor is 0 in this example? Instrumentality. The computer programmer believes that the performance review will not lead to anything valued, so there is no performance→outcome link.

A major implication of the VIE model is that if the organization can identify the weak link in the chain, it can work to rectify it. I chose the performance review example because this is an area in which motivation often breaks down. Although some employees may value a favorable performance review in and of itself, most value it only if it leads to something else. (See Chapter 5 for more details about performance appraisal.) The organization needs to recognize that employees are not likely to exert great effort at work if they don't see the performance review leading to something else of value, such as a pay raise, a promotion, additional benefits, a better job situation, or increased responsibility and autonomy. Indeed, the organization can fix this instrumentality problem by clarifying the links between performance and other outcomes. For instance, the performance review can be used as a basis for important organizational rewards, and employees can be made explicitly aware of this link. The motivational force to work hard will be stronger if employees believe that they can work hard enough to attain a desirable level of performance and if that level of performance is linked to favorable work-related outcomes.

A meta-analysis exploring the results of almost 80 studies that tested all or part of the VIE model (Van Eerde & Thierry, 1996) uncovered a few important findings. First, the relationship between the individual VIE components (valence, instrumentality, expectancy) and the work-related outcomes is stronger than that between a score that combines the VIE components and the work-related outcomes. Second, many of the studies reviewed were flawed because they examined the model in terms of comparisons between people rather than in terms of predicting how an individual person is likely to behave. The model was developed by Vroom to account for how motivated an individual is to exhibit a certain behavior versus a different behavior—it was not developed to compare one person's motivation to perform a particular behavior with another person's motivation to perform that same behavior. Finally, the correlations between the VIE components and attitudes/intentions were stronger than those between the VIE components and behaviors (e.g., performance, effort, and choice). Based on these findings, the authors concluded that the VIE components are clearly related to work criteria. VIE theory has since been applied to a diverse set of work-related criteria, such as occupational choices, managers' intentions to use a particular system, job choices, decisions to participate in an employee involvement program, votes in a union election, strategic decision making (Ambrose & Kulik, 1999), and test-taking motivation (Sanchez, Truxillo, & Bauer, 2000).

Self-Regulation Theories

Self-regulation theories revolve around goal-directed behaviors. The idea here is that motivation is directly linked to **self-regulation,** or the manner in which individuals monitor their own behaviors and make adjustments to those behaviors in the pursuit of goals. Motivation is translated into behavior as a result of self-governing cognitive mechanisms. Unlike the needs-motives-values theories and the cognitive choice theories, self-regulation theories come into play after a goal has been chosen. They explain how time and effort are allocated across various activities, all of which are directed toward attaining that goal. And whereas the former theories deal with intentions or choices, self-regulation theories deal with *volition* or will (Kanfer, 1990). That is, given the choice to pursue a particular goal or exhibit a particular behavior, how do we go about pursuing that goal or exhibiting that behavior?

self-regulation
The manner in which individuals monitor their own behaviors and make adjustments to those behaviors in the pursuit of goals.

Goal-Setting Theory.

Kurt Lewin's early work on "level of aspiration" (Lewin, Dembo, Festinger, & Sears, 1944) provided the foundation for the most researched and well-established theory of work motivation—goal-setting theory. Largely developed by Edwin Locke over the past 35 years, this model suggests that goals affect behavior in four ways. First, goals direct our attention to a particular task or element of a task. Second, goals mobilize on-task effort. In other words, they allow us to focus our effort appropriately to move toward their attainment. Third, goals enable us to be persistent as we strive toward their attainment. Without goals we would often give up and move on to something else. Finally, goals help us to facilitate strategies that can be used at a higher cognitive level to move toward their attainment.

Locke and others have conducted empirical research in this area for over 35 years (for a review, see Locke and Latham, 2002). This wealth of data has provided us with a great deal of useful information, but I will summarize only a few of the major findings. First, people tend to perform better when they are assigned or choose difficult, specific goals than when they are assigned or choose easy goals or no goals. Second, the goal-setting effect—namely, improved performance as a result of difficult, specific goals—occurs only when individuals accept and are committed to those goals. (For this reason, providing your employees with a difficult, specific goal that they don't accept and don't care about achieving will not result in increased motivation or performance.) Third, feedback about a person's performance in relation to the goal positively affects that performance.

These three well-supported propositions combine to produce goal-setting theory's key statement: *Motivation is enhanced when employees accept and are committed to specific, difficult goals and when feedback about progress toward those goals is provided.* This effect has been found in literally hundreds of studies in both the laboratory and the field, in both the United States and elsewhere; and it holds true for over 100 different tasks, as well as for diverse samples along dimensions of race, gender, age, mental ability, and work experience (for a review, see Locke, 1990). More recently, the effect has been extended into such areas as group goal setting (Durham, Locke, Poon, & McLeod, 2000) and goal strategies of athletes (Hodge & Petlichkoff, 2000). Goal-setting theory is not only one of the most successful motivation theories in terms of demonstrating consistent support for its propositions, but it is also among the simplest. It is this simplicity (along with its strong results) that has made it a favorite technique for practitioners who are interested in altering the behavior or effort of their employees. We will discuss some applications of goal-setting theory a bit later in the book.

Social Cognitive Theories. Social cognitive theories, which gained prominence in the 1960s, stressed the interplay of both behavioral and cognitive elements in motivation. Emerging as a result of dissatisfaction with the way in which behaviorism ignored the role of cognitive processes in motivation, this approach emphasizes the cognitive, behavioral, individual, and environmental factors that work together in determining motivation (Kanfer, 1990).

The most important of these social cognitive theories was developed by Albert Bandura (1986), who views self-regulation as composed of three major components. The first is *self-observation,* which refers to the extent to which we pay attention to specific aspects of our behavior. Because we are limited processors of information, we cannot attend to all dimensions of our behavior and thus have to choose which ones will occupy our attention. It is through this process that we are able to monitor our behavior, performance, feedback, and goals to allow for motivational strategies to develop. The second component is *self-evaluation,* which accounts for the attention that individuals devote to feedback processes. Specifically, it is how we evaluate our own performance and effort. Third, *self-reactions* are the internal responses to self-evaluation. Some of these are affective reactions, such as being disgruntled with our performance toward a goal or being overjoyed with the progress that is being made. Others are behavioral reactions, which may involve an increase in effort, a goal shift, or abandonment of the goal altogether.

Another crucial element of Bandura's theory is what he called **self-efficacy expectations**—that is, individuals' perceptions of their ability to successfully complete a task or attain a goal. Bandura (1986) has argued that strengthening one's self-efficacy enhances motivation to attain a particular goal, and other researchers view self-efficacy as being intimately related to the *expectancy* component of VIE theory. Indeed, people do tend to be more motivated to take on a particular task when they feel competent to do that task and expect that they can do it well. Bandura's social cognitive theory specifically views motivation as resulting from the joint influence of self-efficacy expectations and self-reactions to discrepancies between current performance and some standard or goal (Kanfer, 1990). Bandura and Locke (2003) argue that a strong belief in one's performance efficacy or ability is essential to mobilize and sustain effort necessary to succeed (remember our definition of motivation presented earlier in the chapter?). We form intentions, along with plans and strategies for carrying out our intentions. As self-regulators, we adopt personal standards (i.e., goals) and monitor our actions by self-reactive influence.

self-efficacy expectations
Individuals' perceptions of their ability to successfully complete a task or attain a goal.

In keeping with Bandura's emphasis on self-efficacy, some social cognitive researchers have begun linking motivational principles to other individual-difference variables. For instance, *learning goal orientation* (i.e., the extent to which individuals approach problems with an emphasis on learning and developing) has been linked to both motivation and affect in the performance of complex tasks, and *performance goal orientation* (i.e., the extent to which individuals approach problems with a focus solely on performance) has been linked to motivation and affect in the performance of simple tasks (Steele-Johnson, Beauregard, Hoover, & Schmidt, 2000). Bell and Kozlowski (2002) have argued that goal orientation, self-efficacy, and ability interact in affecting performance. Specifically, they found that a learning goal orientation was adaptive for high-ability individuals but not so for low-ability individuals. Further, high-ability individuals experienced a decrement in performance that was determined by high levels of performance orientation. Finally, Van Yperen and Janssen (2002) found that high job demands felt by those employees who were high on performance orientation and low on learning orientation resulted in low job satisfaction but that the same was not true for those low on performance orientation and high on learning orientation.

Several researchers have proposed and developed *control theory*, which is essentially a social-cognitive motivational theory with a negative feedback loop at its core (see Carver & Scheier, 1981; Klein, 1989; Lord & Hanges, 1987; Powers, 1973). The basic premise of control theory is that this negative feedback loop results from the comparison of performance feedback with some goal or standard. If people perceive a discrepancy between the feedback and the standard, they are motivated to reduce that discrepancy in some way. The objective in such cases is to control the situation so that the feedback and the standard match—or, in control theory lingo, to keep the sensed values (feedback) in conformity with the reference value (standard). Control theory is certainly not limited to the social sciences; in fact, it did not even originate there. Rather, control theory in the social sciences has developed from work done in technical areas such as engineering, which employs the term *control system* to illustrate the process in question. The best example of a control system is a thermostat that operates by sensing the temperature in the room and comparing it with the standard or preset temperature. If the preset temperature is higher than the sensed temperature, the thermostat turns on the furnace to reduce this discrepancy, bringing the sensed temperature (feedback) in line with the preset temperature (standard). Now, what does a thermostat have to do with motivation? (See Bandura and Locke, 2003, for criticisms of this approach as too mechanical.) A quick look at one of the best articulated and empirically supported control theories of motivation—developed by Charles Carver and Michael Scheier—will provide an answer.

According to Carver and Scheier (1998), most behaviors entail feedback control. Consider the following scenario:

> If your standard for a day's work is to "be productive," how do you decide at day's end whether you've met your goal? You look at the hard evidence of what you've done, and you look at some concrete comparison point (guidelines provided by a work assignment, or perhaps performance of other people engaged in similar activity). In sum, to compare your behavior against an abstract standard, you often seek out concrete information that facilitates the abstract comparison. (Carver & Scheier, 1998, p. 32)

This very simple principle has given rise to a complicated but useful theory of motivation. The basics of Carver and Scheier's theory stem largely from earlier work on control theory, but these authors have developed many important related issues that have helped researchers gain a better understanding of motivation. For instance, they have conducted many studies demonstrating that the more self-focused individuals are, the more often they engage the feedback loop and concentrate on comparisons that reveal information about existing discrepancies (Carver & Scheier, 1998). By *self-focused* the authors mean simply the degree to which individuals focus attention on themselves. Being self-focused, they argue, is more likely than not being self-focused to lead to reactions (both affective and behavioral) that stem from perceiving a discrepancy (when a discrepancy exists) between one's standard and feedback.

The scenario I just borrowed from Carver and Scheier seems quite simple, but their theory points out that the process of gathering, receiving, and interpreting feedback from various sources is quite complex. Think back to Chapter 5, in which we discussed the use of 360-degree feedback in organizations for the purposes of individual development, as well as more formal performance-appraisal processes. Obviously, individuals are presented with a wealth of feedback from a 360-degree system, and sorting out and choosing which feedback to use in the feedback loop is a complicated issue. I mention this here only to reiterate that although examples can be simplified to better illustrate control theory and its processes, the theory's operation is, in actuality, much more complex. Diefendorff and Lord (2003), for example, have used control theory to focus on the volitional and intellectual elements of motivation. They demonstrated that individuals who formed implemental intentions (i.e., specific goals and a plan for acting on those goals) performed better than those who did not, regardless of their particular strategy. However, strategy quality interacted with implemental intentions to result in the best performance. Thus both volitional and intellectual domains are important parts of the motivational system.

Carver and Scheier (1998) have argued that people are goal-directed and that we use not only goals but also intentions, values, and wishes in our daily lives to move forward. Furthermore, Diefendorff and Gosserand (2003) present an interesting application of control theory to emotions, in which they present a control theory model that explains the process through which individuals regulate their emotional displays over time. However, the use of intentions, values, wishes, and emotions for motivated processes doesn't always work. We don't always reach our goals—and when it appears as though we aren't going to make it, we have an important decision to make: Persevere or throw in the towel? This decision has implications for everything that follows. If we choose to give up, our behavior and attitudes will be considerably different from those associated with the choice to continue putting forth the effort to attain our goal. But Carver and Scheier suggest that giving up—what they call *disengagement*—is not always a bad thing. Indeed, they argue that it is a natural and necessary part of self-regulation. There are times when a goal is unattainable, and continuing to shoot for it can have serious detrimental effects on one's psychological well-being and ultimate success. Sometimes we have to let go and start over again with some other goal or direction (Carver & Scheier, 1998). Of course, giving up too soon can have detrimental effects as well. But the essential point here is that both continued effort and giving up are necessary parts of adaptive self-regulation. Each has its place and can serve us well in the appropriate situation.

Think about the time you were shooting for an A in a particular class but kept getting Cs on the exams. At some point, revisiting your goal and making an adjustment to it probably helped you to move forward (perhaps you passed the course with a B and learned something about yourself in the meantime); but if you had continued shooting for that A and had continued making no progress toward it, your progress (as well as your attitude, self-confidence, and mood!) would have been thwarted. A similar process would be at work in a situation in which you are focused on achieving $10,000 in sales for the quarter, but as weeks go by it becomes clear that this goal is unattainable (because of downturns in the economy, new products produced by your competitor, and an increase in the prices of your products). Are you better served by continuing to bang your head against the wall or by reevaluating your goal and attempting to move forward toward another reasonable goal? Hopefully, you see that the answer to this question is to go easy on your head and come up with an alternative goal that is still motivating, resulting in individual and organizational productivity. As Carver and Scheier (1998) note, although the feedback loop is the very foundation of motivation as viewed from a control theory perspective, an "override" of some sort has to take over from the feedback loop and cause disengagement—an outcome that actually furthers progress rather than frustrating it.

APPLICATIONS OF MOTIVATIONAL THEORIES TO ORGANIZATIONAL PROBLEMS

I have spent the first part of this chapter presenting and explaining many of the most common theories of work motivation. Given that I/O psychology is an applied field with applied goals and issues, I'd like to devote the rest of the chapter to applications of a few of these theories to real-world organizational problems. Case studies and empirical research will be discussed where appropriate.

ORGANIZATIONAL BEHAVIOR MANAGEMENT

organizational behavior management (OBM) The application of the principles of behavioral psychology to the study and control of individual and group behavior within organizational settings.

The **organizational behavior management (OBM)** approach to improving motivation and performance in organizations is based in large part on reinforcement theory—particularly operant conditioning, in which desired behaviors are rewarded. OBM can be defined as the application of the principles of behavioral psychology to the study and control of individual and group behavior within organizational settings. One approach to OBM that has been applied to organizations across the globe is called *applied behavior analysis,* in which the focus is on the ABC model: "A" stands for the antecedents of the behavior, "B" stands for the behavior itself, and "C" stands for the consequences of the behavior. It is important that the antecedents for desired behaviors be in place within the organization. For instance, employees must have the equipment and training to be able to do the job well. The consequences are perhaps the most important part of this approach, as they are the rewards that follow the desired behaviors. These can range from seemingly small rewards such as verbal recognition to large rewards such as a salary bonus or additional vacation days. (See "Practitioner Forum" for some interesting examples.)

This behavioral approach to the management of human resources can be summarized in five steps (Stajkovic & Luthans, 1997). First, the behaviors that need to be changed must be targeted. This step is much like a needs analysis that is done in the area of training (see Chapter 8). Second, the targeted behaviors are measured so that the organization has a baseline against which to compare behaviors that occur after the intervention. Third, the links between both current rewards and punishments and behaviors are examined. Fourth, the organization intervenes with a program that sets goals on the targeted behaviors and links various rewards to the attainment of those goals. Finally, there is an evaluation phase in which the success of the intervention is determined by comparing resultant behaviors with baseline behaviors in terms of the program's goals.

Two priorities are instrumental in this context. First, the targeted behaviors need to be specific. Goals like "more sales" or "safety is our top priority" are too general to be useful in an OBM program. Second, managers and supervisors need to be trained to acknowledge the importance of recognition. At BankBoston, for instance, managers are given Employee Recognition Toolkits that contain information about simple and creative ways to recognize and praise employees, a set of thank-you cards, three acknowledgment ribbons, and a list of suggested gifts and rewards (Gross, 1999). By and large, it is important to employees that they be recognized for the contributions they make to their company.

OBM has been used extensively in organizations (Bucklin, Alvero, Dickinson, Austin, & Jackson, 2000). Let's look at one example in the area of safety improvement, in which OBM has been very popular (Grindle, Dickinson, & Boettcher, 2000). An injury prevention model was applied in a large industrial plant to reduce lost time due to injuries and to increase safety behaviors (Sulzer-Azaroff, Loafman, Merante, & Hlavacek, 1990). Three departments with the highest injury rates were identified; the number of employees totaled about 250. Safety charts (24" × 36" weekly feedback posters) and low-cost tangible rewards such as luncheons, coffee, pens, and ice scrapers were used in this approach. The researchers identified behavioral targets for each department and observed behaviors such as safe lifting of heavy materials, use of safety glasses and appropriate safety shoes, immediate cleaning of wet floors, and storage of chemicals in designated areas. In addition, they recorded accident data, including medical visits and lost time due to injuries or accidents. After implementing the intervention program, which included meetings about safety, weekly safety posters, small rewards and reinforcements, and setting of goals, the researchers noted some drastic improvements. First, safe behavior goals were attained at a rate of over 90% across departments. Second, this period was the best in the history of the company in terms of injury rate and person-hours worked. And, third, workers' comments about the program and the improvements were overwhelmingly positive. Results like these are typical of OBM programs, demonstrating the usefulness of

Rewards and awards can be powerful motivators.

PRACTITIONER FORUM

PATRICK SHANNON

Ph.D., 1988, I/O Psychology, University of Minnesota
Principal with Mercer HR Consulting's Performance, Measurement and Rewards Practice

What motivates people? Some would say money, money, and more money! Yes, that's a narrow perspective, but to some extent, it's true. I know strong leadership, meaningful work assignments, and the opportunity to make a difference are valued motivators as well, but for most of us, money is an especially powerful one.

I work for Mercer Human Resources Consulting, as a consultant in our Performance, Measurement and Rewards practice. One area in which we assist companies is in developing incentive compensation programs. The effectiveness of these programs is well documented, and these days more and more companies are offering cash incentives to their employees.

In compensation terms, an incentive refers to a situation in which you have an opportunity to earn a reward for achieving a *preestablished* goal. For example, if you mow the lawn, I will pay you $15. Or, if our team achieves a customer satisfaction rating of 90% or better for the next quarter, we will each receive a cash award of $500. Both the goal and the potential payout are clearly communicated beforehand. An incentive is different from a bonus or recognition award, in which an individual is rewarded, without prior expectations, for delivering superior performance. Incentive programs have direct motivational value.

At Mercer, we often work with organizations that want to connect and align their employees with key business strategies. We do this by designing performance systems that link individual employee goals with annual business plans. To strengthen this connection and motivate employees to achieve their goals, many organizations also choose to offer incentive pay.

I recently worked with a consumer products company that wanted to motivate its workforce to increase production, cut waste, and improve safety. Certainly there was value in clearly communicating to employees the company's specific goals and what each employee could do to influence these goals. But employees got really excited and involved when they learned they would have an opportunity—through a new annual incentive plan—to share in the company's success. At the end of year, the targeted results were achieved, and employees received cash bonuses: a win-win situation for the company and its workforce.

Several of the theoretical perspectives discussed in this chapter are useful in explaining why incentive systems work. To me, goal-setting and expectancy theories seem particularly relevant. If I accept my goals, have the necessary tools and resources, receive feedback on my progress, and value the rewards that I can receive for achieving my goals, I'll be one highly motivated employee!

APPLYING YOUR KNOWLEDGE

1. Why do incentive systems work?
2. What is it about linking goals to incentives that results in increased motivation?
3. How do incentive systems tie into VIE theory?

this approach in improving motivation and performance behaviors. In fact, a meta-analysis (Stajkovic & Luthans, 1997) reported an average effect of one-half a standard deviation on performance (d effect size = .51). What this tells us is that the use of OBM resulted in a sizable performance improvement in the various companies studied.

Goal Setting and Management-by-Objectives

Goal-setting theory has received considerable attention from practitioners and has been applied across the world in every type of organization imaginable with very consistent success. (For a review, see Locke, 1990.) Let's look at one recent example. Since pizza delivery has become such a huge industry (perhaps nowhere more so than on college campuses!), delivery drivers' safety has become a subject of concern. Pizza deliverers have accident rates that are three times higher than the national average, resulting in fatalities and personal injuries that cost companies millions of dollars (Ludwig & Geller, 1997, 2000). In a 1997 study, pizza deliverers ($N = 324$) from three different pizza stores were observed going out on and returning from deliveries. Observers were stationed in the windows of nearby businesses with a clear view of the streets on which the pizza stores were situated. Three specific behaviors were observed: (1) whether the drivers used their seat

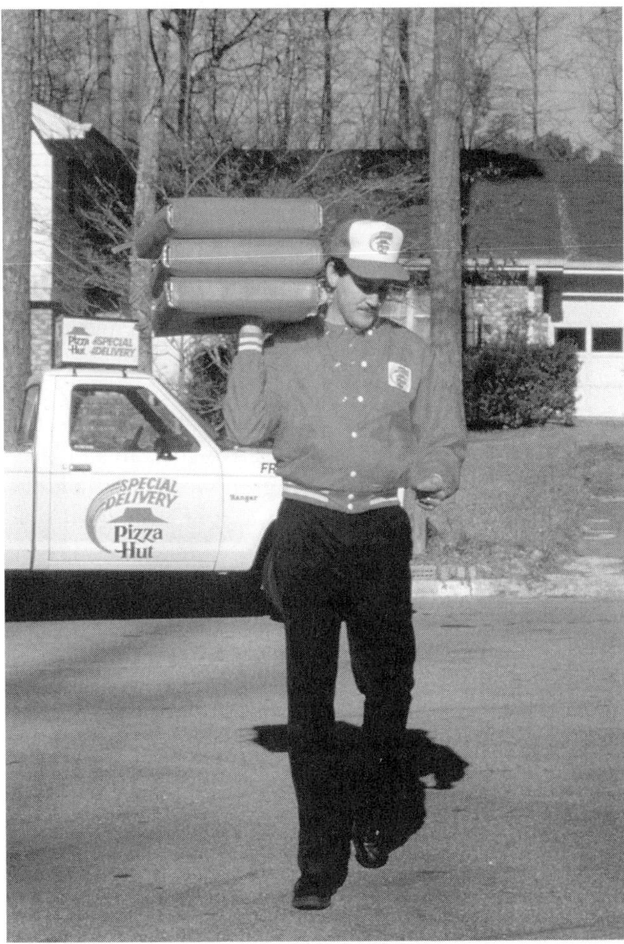

Because pizza deliverers have such high accident rates, psychologists have targeted them for behavioral change.

FIGURE 9.5 Pizza Delivery Results—Intersection Stops

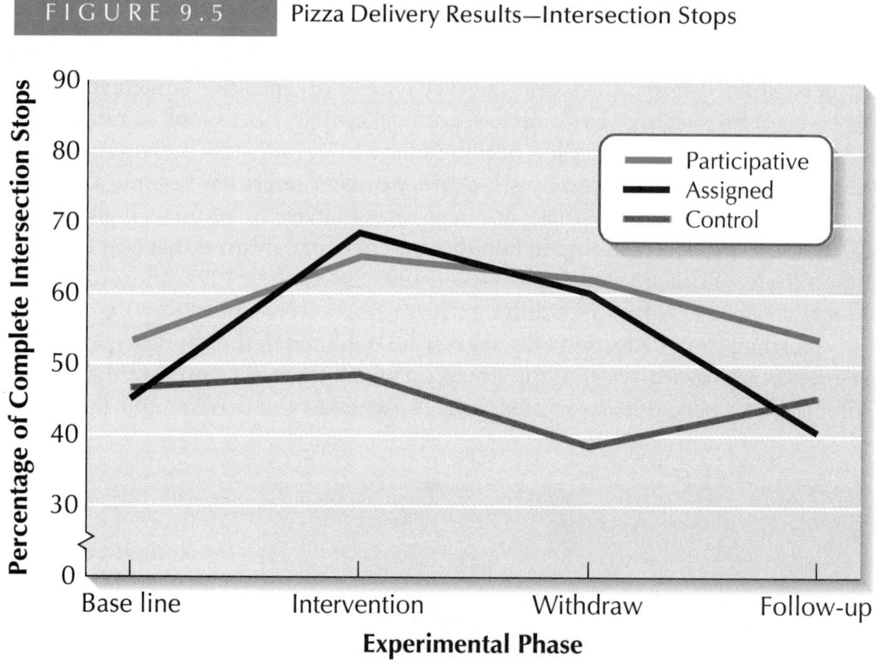

Source: Ludwig & Geller (1997).

belts, (2) whether the drivers used their turn signals when leaving or entering the pizza store's parking lot, and (3) whether the drivers made a complete, slow-rolling, or fast-rolling stop when entering the street from the store's parking lot.

These three behaviors were observed for 6 weeks to establish a baseline. At this point, deliverers were randomly assigned into a participative-goal, an assigned-goal, or a control condition. Those in the participative group took part in a discussion-based meeting, participative goal setting, and 4 weeks of group feedback. Those in the assigned-goal group took part in a lecture-based meeting, were assigned a goal (the same goal that was arrived at participatively in the participative group), and underwent 4 weeks of group feedback. The control group received no intervention at all. The targeted behavior in all three conditions was the percentage of complete stops, and the goal in both goal-setting conditions was 75%. Figure 9.5 presents a summary of the observation data for four periods: the 6-week baseline phase, the 4-week intervention phase, the 4-week withdrawal phase (after the feedback posters were removed), and the 10- to 11-week follow-up phase. The data clearly indicate that both the participative-goal and assigned-goal groups made a larger number of complete intersection stops and that this improvement in safety behavior continued for some time (though for longer in the participative condition than in the assigned-goal condition). Interestingly, the observers also coded other behaviors that were not part of the intervention, in-

FIGURE 9.6 Pizza Delivery Results—Seat Belt Use

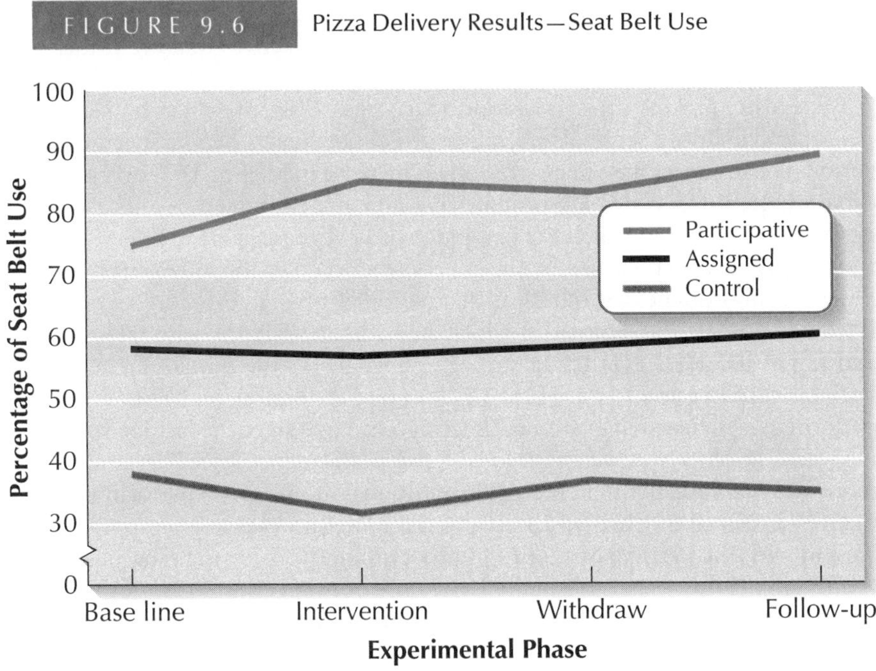

Source: Ludwig & Geller (1997).

cluding seat-belt use. (Although seat-belt use was observed, it was never mentioned in the meetings, nor was group feedback ever presented on this behavior.) Figure 9.6 presents the relevant data for seat-belt use. Here, only participative goal setting seemed to improve safety behaviors and to maintain that improvement—an especially interesting outcome given that seat-belt use was not part of the intervention. Apparently, participative goal setting that focused on one particular safety behavior improved other safety behaviors as well. (Similar results were found for turn-signal use.) The power of goal-setting programs like this one is very clear: People respond very effectively to feedback that is coupled with difficult, specific goals.

Another practical application of goal setting involves what is called *management by objectives (MBO),* a managerial technique widely used in the Western world since the late 1950s (Pinder, 1998). MBO dates back to the work of Peter Drucker at both General Motors and General Electric (cited in Greenwood, 1981). Drucker's approach to management centers on the importance of performance objectives and involves two essential factors: (1) a system for establishing work-related goals and (2) a procedure for assessing a person's performance as compared with those goals. Additional though somewhat less pervasive factors include (1) a periodic review of the objectives, (2) a specific time period for goal accomplishment, (3) quantifiable and verifiable indicators of results, (4) objectives that are flexible across situations, (5) objectives that include an "action plan" or statement for how they will be accomplished, and (6) objectives that are prioritized (Pinder, 1998).

The MBO process consists of four basic stages. First, managers and subordinates participatively set goals/objectives for subordinates over a specified time period. For instance, they may agree on an increase in sales of 15% over the next 6-month period. Second, subordinates develop an action plan or "how to" map describing the ways in which they intend to achieve these goals. This action plan, which is frequently reviewed by the supervisor, becomes the blueprint to be followed by subordinates for the stipulated period of time. In our current example, it would stipulate the manner in which subordinates will increase sales by 15% and might include a marketing strategy, subgoals for the development of new business contacts, and so on. Third, at the end of the period, managers conduct a performance review that examines the progress made since the last formal meeting when the objectives were set. (Ideally, this performance review is handled in a more participative manner than the traditional "top-down" performance appraisals discussed in Chapter 5.) Finally, the process comes to a temporary conclusion with the participative setting of goals/objectives for the next period. By "temporary" I mean that this phase is the only one that ends; MBO continues in a cyclical manner with the development of new objectives, action plans, and evaluations over time.

Let's look at a couple of good examples of applications of MBO. One of these concerns Southern California Edison (SCE), which was unhappy with its performance management and motivational system and thus began implementing an MBO program (Moravec, Juliff, & Hesler, 1995). First, it conducted in-depth interviews with employees to gather important data on their attitudes, beliefs, and future outlooks with regard to SCE. This step introduced participation into SCE. Second, consultants were hired to conduct a task force (consisting of 40 employee volunteers) to help generate some solutions to the performance management problems. The members of this task force encouraged everyone in the organization to provide input and to add their own perspective to the important issues under discussion. They concluded that the organization needed a system in which (1) employees (in addition to supervisors) assume responsibility; (2) the focus is on values and future growth, not past problems; and (3) the discussion is not a control tool but, rather, supports a partnership between employees and supervisors. The new MBO system (the task force called it the "Performance Enhancement Process") emphasized that supervisors and employees should work together to improve performance together. In other words, they should collaboratively define objectives, develop strategies to attain the objectives, determine ways to measure performance relative to the objectives, and then periodically reevaluate the objectives and adjust them where appropriate. Both supervisors and employees have reported on the success of this program, noting that they feel energized by becoming active participants and that they appreciate the enhanced openness that has become the culture in the company.

A survey of over 500 cities and municipalities found that almost half are currently using an MBO program; 54% reported that the MBO program focuses attention on top management priorities, 42% indicated that the MBO program had a strong impact on coordinating goals and objectives across departments, and over 90% viewed the MBO program as effective (Poister & Streib, 1995). One of these cities, Milwaukee, Wisconsin, has implemented an MBO program as part of a restructuring of its performance management and motivational system (Weber, 1995). This program emphasizes the following elements: (1) the use of positive behaviors as ratable factors, (2) customer satisfaction ratings, (3) recognition for ongoing process improvements, (4) peer and subordinate feedback, (5) empowerment of subordinates for personal development, and (6) continuous evaluation of progress toward objectives. Here, as before, we see a few of the key elements of MBO programs, such as emphasis on participation, emphasis on objectives, and the continuous evaluation of performance with respect to those objectives.

According to a meta-analysis of the MBO literature, 97% of the evaluation studies reviewed found increases in productivity; the mean rise in productivity across those studies with quantitative measures of performance was over 40% (Rodgers & Hunter, 1991). This finding suggests that an organization that is producing 100 units of its product per month prior to an MBO intervention is likely to produce 140 units per month after the intervention. The meta-analysis also revealed that MBO programs tend to result in greater performance improvement when they were supported by upper-level management. This observation is consistent with what we know about most organizational interventions: Support from the top is often necessary for their success. We will see other examples of this in the remainder of the book.

Job Enrichment

We have already discussed Hackman and Oldham's (1980) model of job design called job characteristics theory, which stemmed from Herzberg's earlier work on two-factor theory. One way in which organizations apply this approach to job design is through job enrichment. **Job enrichment** is the process of increasing the motivating potential of jobs—specifically, by strengthening the key motivating characteristics identified by job characteristics theory. Let's briefly look at a few organizational interventions along these lines.

job enrichment
The process of increasing the motivating potential of jobs, often by strengthening the key motivating characteristics identified by job characteristics theory.

We'll start with an example of job enrichment that, although not a direct application of job characteristics theory, emphasizes many of the same general principles. Fleet Financial Group was interested in improving quality-of-life issues and reducing stress while maintaining productivity (Anonymous, 1998). Fleet's site in Framingham, Massachusetts, included a 20-person loan underwriting team. The workers complained of long commutes, administrative overloads, and difficulty in scheduling their work. These distractions seemed to negatively affect their primary jobs. Input was provided by all of the employees, and changes were made to the design of their jobs such that administrative tasks were reassigned, the loan monitoring process was revised, and telecommuting was made available to employees. At Fleet's site in Providence, Rhode Island, 35 employees were stressed about the demand for faster reporting of bank information. Flex-time schedules, telecommuting, revised paperwork procedures, and more timely information about client needs were among the design changes made for these financial managers. Their jobs were enriched by the following desired outcomes: (1) reduction of stress, (2) maintenance of productivity, (3) more time to spend with family members, and (4) higher morale (Anonymous, 1998). As Fleet executive vice president Anne Szostak notes, this kind of job enrichment has provided Fleet with a competitive advantage in attracting and maintaining a highly competent workforce.

Our second example concerns an article about improving the teaching of psychology that argues for the use of job characteristics theory for "course enrichment"—a process similar to job enrichment. Its author, Diane Catanzaro (1997), specifically proposes the job characteristics model as a theoretical framework for increasing the motivational potential of college courses. She suggests that instructors can increase skill variety among students by requiring a wider range of skills through varied written and oral assignments. For instance, in an I/O course, the instructor could (1) ask students to write about how theories of motivation are used by employers and employees at their place of employment; (2) structure a debate that considers the pros and cons of affirmative action; (3) illustrate task significance through applications of what is learned in class and discussions of their implications for organizations and employees; or (4) give an assignment that requires students to conduct a job analysis of some real job (e.g., interviewing incumbents) or to develop a proposal that outlines a potential selection battery for their current position. Each of the five core job dimensions we discussed earlier (skill variety, task identity, task significance, autonomy, feedback) could be emphasized in the design of such a course in order to enrich its content and increase its motivating potential. A recent study found that four of these five core dimensions were related to outcome measures such as course motivation, satisfaction, and performance in a sample of over 200 psychology students (Bloom, Yorges, & Ruhl, 2000).

Our final example involves the Hamot Medical Center in Erie, Pennsylvania, which recently undertook an extensive job redesign effort to reduce costs within two intensive care units (ICUs) of the hospital (Pedersen & Antoon, 1997). Employees recorded their activities in five-minute blocks of time and summarized this information weekly, thus providing a snapshot of the time they spent on various activities at different levels in the ICU. This information was then evaluated by both employees and management. As a result of this information, employee responsibilities, procedures, and behaviors were made more consistent with the hospital's job descriptions. In 1993, prior to this job design process, registered nurses (RNs) had been spending only about 40% of their time doing RN-valued tasks, whereas in 1995, after the job design process, the same RNs were spending almost 60% of their time doing these tasks. The redesigned jobs are now more

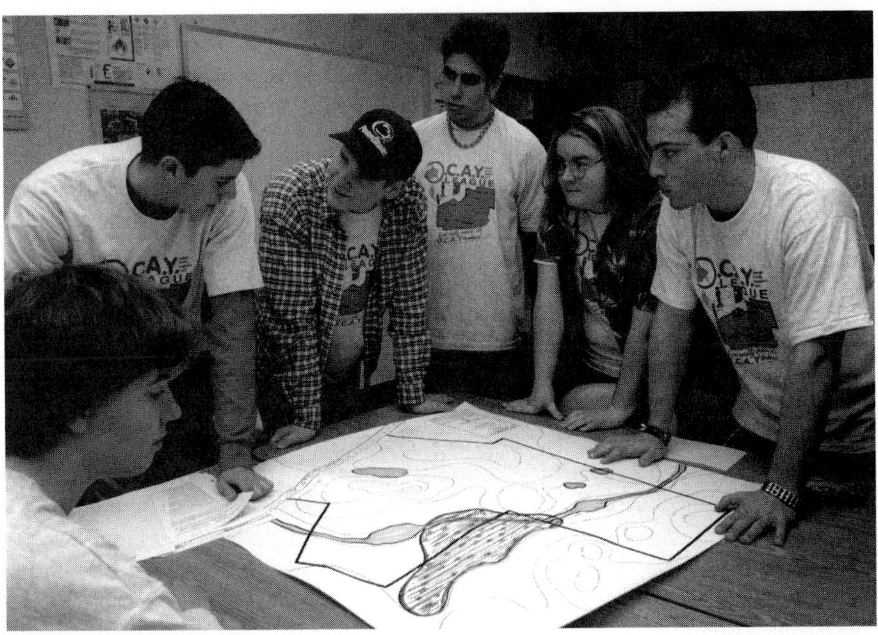

In addition to traditional writing and testing assignments, making use of a diverse variety of class assignments, such as designing a golf course, may improve students' motivation.

cost-effective and continue to make the best use of employees' skills, training, and abilities. Clearly, job enrichment is a viable way of improving employee motivation and morale, as well as organizational productivity and effectiveness.

SUMMARY

Few topics in I/O psychology have been as thoroughly explored as work motivation. In the first part of this chapter I presented the most commonly cited theories of work motivation, and in the second part I focused on applications of these theories to organizational problems. Three sets of theories were considered: need-motive-value theories, cognitive choice theories, and self-regulation theories. Although need-motive-value theories are no longer as well accepted by researchers and academics as they were 40 years ago, they are still popular in business settings. First we discussed Maslow's hierarchy of needs; then we examined two approaches that are related to Maslow's work, ERG theory and two-factor theory. Job characteristics theory and cognitive evaluation theory were also considered in this category, as they clarify the different motivational potentials that are inherent in jobs and people.

Cognitive choice theories, which view motivation and behavior as rational processes rather than as a function of inherent needs or values, were discussed in terms of two important theories: equity theory and expectancy theory. The latter—presented in the context of VIE theory—was described as the most rational theory of them all. Each of its three components was explained, illustrated with examples, and discussed in terms of recent meta-analytic research on expectancy theory. The conclusion drawn was that these three components seem related to motivation, though not always in the multiplicative manner predicted by the theory.

Self-regulation theories were discussed last. In this context, goal-setting theory was presented as one of the simplest and most empirically supported models of work motivation. Social cognitive theories were described as extensions of goal-setting theory that provide potential explanations for why goals are so important to individual motivation and performance. All three sets of theories have received a great deal of attention in the literature, some of which was reviewed in the text.

In the second part of the chapter I presented applications of motivation theories to organizations. OBM was discussed as a very successful technique (particularly in the area of improving organizational safety) that stems from reinforcement theory. An overview of this technique was described, along with some recent applications. A similar approach was followed with respect to goal setting and management-by-objectives. There appears to be a great deal of support for these goal-based interventions as well. Finally, I discussed job enrichment and its potential for organizational improvement. Although the empirical results are not as impressive as those associated with other methods, the applications we considered suggest that enriching jobs may improve employees' motivation levels. An interesting extension of this approach involves enrichment of university courses so as to improve their motivating potential for students.

REVIEW QUESTIONS

1. Why is work motivation viewed as so important to organizational functioning? Is it ever overemphasized by managers?
2. How would you describe motivation theories that are categorized as need-value-motive theories?
3. Discuss the differences among Maslow's hierarchy of needs, ERG theory, and two-factor theory.
4. Identify the chief emphasis of cognitive choice theories of work motivation.
5. What major predictions are made by equity theory?
6. What do V, I, and E stand for, and how are they reflected in work motivation?
7. What do the self-regulation theories have in common?
8. Discuss the potential difficulties involved in applying motivational theories to organizational problems.

9. How would you explain the success of goal-setting and MBO programs?

10. What is the most important element of job enrichment programs, and why?

SUGGESTED READINGS

Kanfer, R. (1990). Motivation theory and industrial and organizational psychology. In M. Dunnette & L. Hough (Eds.), *Handbook of industrial and organizational psychology* (2nd ed., Vol. 1, pp. 75–170). Palo Alto, CA: Consulting Psychologists Press. This chapter provides a very detailed review of motivational theories as they have been developed and investigated within I/O psychology. It is a sophisticated account of the content area.

Pinder, C. C. (1998). *Work motivation in organizational behavior.* Saddle River, NJ: Prentice-Hall. My personal favorite! I've used Pinder's earlier book in my classes for almost 15 years and highly recommend this newer version as well. It is a very complete treatment of motivation, written at a level that makes it accessible for undergraduates and graduate students.

Steers, R. M, Mowday, R. T., & Shapiro, D. L. (2004). Introduction to Special Topic Forum: The future of work motivation theory. *Academy of Management Review, 29*(3), 379–387. This is the introduction to a special issue on work motivation in one of the field's most respected journals. This paper gives a nice overview of the historical development of work motivation, and the other papers spend considerable time looking to the future and setting a research agenda for the field.

Job Attitudes: Antecedents and Consequences

10

CHAPTER OUTLINE

Have you ever had a job that you didn't like? Did the fact that you didn't like the job affect your performance? Why didn't you like the job? Was it your supervisor, co-workers, the work itself, or the pay that led to your dissatisfaction? Do you say good things to people about your current company, or do you give the impression that you'd rather work anywhere but there? Do you identify with your job, profession, or occupation? In other words, is what you do an important part of who you are, or is it just something you do? All of these questions have to do with job attitudes, which are the focus of this chapter.

Like most of us, you have probably experienced the anger and frustration that come with working in a job that you don't like. There's the feeling that you're wasting your time, and each minute of the day seems like an hour. Even routine tasks, which by themselves should not be so unpleasant, become unbearable when you are "stuck" in a job you don't like. These negative experiences can become so pervasive that their effects trickle into other elements of your life. Before you know it, you are arguing with your spouse more frequently and running out of patience with your children more quickly. You are becoming that unhappy, grouchy neighbor who lived up the street while you were growing up—you know, the neighbor all the kids talked about as being "mad at the world." The person you always thought seemed so unhappy with his work, his family, and his position in life. On the other hand, when you really love your job, it's easy to get up in the morning; the minutes, hours, and days seem to fly by, and your thoughts are occupied not with the tasks or jobs you have to do at work but, rather, with the opportunities and programs that you get to experience. You go home wanting to talk about work, and you want your spouse and children to understand what it is that you do for a living and why it's the best job in the world.

The difference between a job that we hate and one that we love is a very real difference. In this chapter we will discuss job satisfaction, because this is the attitude that organizations seem most interested in and researchers know the most about. We will also discuss organizational commitment, a job-related attitude that captures the attention of practitioners and researchers alike. Organizational justice, work centrality, job involvement, perceived organizational support, and emotional labor are covered as well.

LEARNING OBJECTIVES

This chapter should help you understand:

- the role played by attitudes in predicting behavior.
- why attitudes are sometimes unrelated to behavior.
- what job satisfaction is and how it is measured.
- what determines a person's level of job satisfaction.
- how job satisfaction affects important organizational outcome variables such as performance and withdrawal behaviors.
- what the three major components of organizational commitment are.
- what determines a person's commitment to his or her organization.
- how organizational commitment affects important organizational outcome variables such as performance and withdrawal behaviors.

- what types of withdrawal behaviors are important to organizations.
- what types of counterproductive behaviors are important to organizations.
- the role played by emotional labor in organizations.
- the effect that perceived organizational support has on employee attitudes and behaviors.

ATTITUDES, INTENTIONS, AND BEHAVIORS

attitude
The degree of positive or negative feeling a person has toward a particular person, place, or thing.

In I/O psychology, when we talk of attitudes we are usually interested in the relationship between attitudes and intentions or behaviors. An **attitude** can be defined as the degree of positive or negative feeling a person has toward a particular person, place, or thing (Fishbein & Ajzen, 1975). As you might imagine, humans have many work-related attitudes. These have to do with supervisors, coworkers, the job environment, the work that is done on the job, and even the amount of respect received on the job. However, before delving into a discussion of specific job-related attitudes, we need to back up a bit and examine a popular model of the attitude-behavior relationship.

A Useful Model

Known as the *theory of planned behavior,* this model was developed from an earlier model called the theory of reasoned action by Icek Ajzen and his colleagues (Ajzen & Fishbein, 1980; Ajzen & Madden, 1986; Fishbein & Ajzen, 1975). It is a rational choice model much like expectancy theory and equity theory, which we talked about in Chapter 9 in the context of cognitive choice theories of motivation. These researchers subscribe to the view that people consider the implications of their actions before deciding to engage or not engage in a particular behavior (Ajzen & Fishbein, 1980). From this perspective, the determinants of an action are one's intentions to perform the action (Ajzen & Fishbein, 1980). Thus, in a sense, predicting behaviors is not that difficult; if we want to predict whether an employee will work hard on a particular project, the most efficient approach is to ask her whether she intends to work hard. All else being equal, there should be a pretty strong relationship between her intention and her behavior.

Because our goal is to understand human behavior, just knowing that someone does what she intends to do is not that illuminating. We need to be able to predict the intention as well. This is where attitudes come into play. The theory of planned behavior is useful here because it depicts the relationships among attitudes, intentions, and behaviors (Ajzen & Madden, 1986; Fishbein & Ajzen, 1975). Figure 10.1 presents a simplified version of the model, which clearly shows

FIGURE 10.1 Theory of Planned Behavior

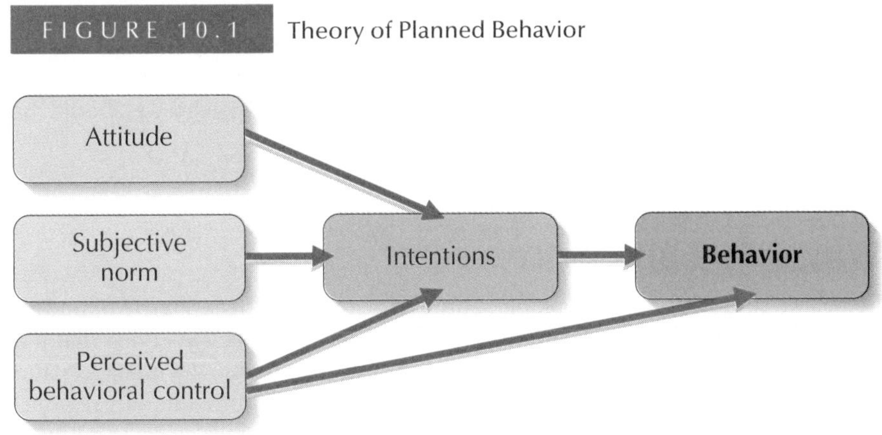

that attitudes and subjective norms affect intentions, which in turn affect behaviors. A **subjective norm** is an individual's perception of the social pressures to perform or not perform a particular behavior. The theory of planned behavior maintains that a person's intention to act is a function of both the subjective norm for that act and his attitude toward that act. For example, he will intend to meet his deadline if meeting deadlines is the norm at his office and if he has a positive attitude about meeting deadlines. The theory also maintains that his intention to meet the deadline is the best predictor of whether his actions will result in his meeting the deadline—because intention predicts behavior.

subjective norm
An individual's perception of the social pressures to perform or not perform a particular behavior.

As shown in Figure 10.1, **perceived behavioral control** is an important element to the theory as well. Perceived behavioral control is the individual's belief as to how easy or difficult performance of the behavior is likely to be (Ajzen & Madden, 1986). Although an individual may be favorably disposed to a particular act and perceive the social norms as being in favor of the act, he may not perceive that he has any control over performance of the act. For instance, a factory worker may recognize that the norm is to produce 200 units of product per 8-hour shift; he may also want to achieve this level of performance. But if he believes that this action is out of his control because of equipment breakdowns, this perceived behavioral control should be considered when predicting his behavior. In effect, he won't produce 200 units because of a lack of control. This calls to mind the role played by expectancy in the motivational model known as VIE theory (see Chapter 9). You may recall that no matter how valued or instrumental a certain performance level is, if the individual does not believe that a particular amount of effort can lead to that performance level, there will be no motivation to exhibit that level of effort. The theory of planned behavior goes one step further in suggesting that even if an employee has an intention to exhibit the behavior, if she perceives that she can't do so because of a lack of control, she won't.

perceived behavioral control
An individual's belief as to how easy or difficult performance of a behavior is likely to be.

The work of Ajzen and his colleagues is important as we proceed with our discussion of crucial job attitudes. The theory of planned behavior will become even more useful as we try to make sense of the relationships between job attitudes and job behaviors. We will revisit this theory from time to time as a way of explaining some of the empirical findings in the I/O literature on attitudes and behaviors. Meanwhile, however, you might be wondering why we should be studying job attitudes in the first place.

Why Study Job Attitudes?

Before we spend more time talking about job attitudes, it makes sense to understand why such attitudes are important. First, it has long been assumed that job attitudes influence work behavior. This assumption explains why managers and executives are so interested in job attitudes. Second, for humanitarian reasons, improvement of employees' job attitudes is a desirable goal alone. As Edwin Locke (1976) notes, happiness is the goal of life—and making people happy at work should be a goal of organizations. Third, studying job attitudes can help us to understand not only the complexities of our work lives but also the complexities of our nonwork lives. For these reasons and others, researchers and practitioners alike have been, and continue to be, very interested in job attitudes. Let's turn to the most important of these attitudes: job satisfaction.

Job Satisfaction

Job satisfaction is one of the most researched areas of I/O psychology in part because it has long been viewed as relevant for organizational effectiveness—it is an aspect of the attitude-behavior link that we talked about earlier, but in an applied setting. Job satisfaction is something that everyone seems both interested in and an expert on. Managers, employees, neighbors, cousins: They all seem to have something to say about job satisfaction. Some insist that the key to job satisfaction is money; others claim that it's working conditions; still others believe that it's employee participation. The list goes on and on. The point here, however, is that job satisfaction interests all of us, and we all have an opinion on the subject—which makes for lively discussions at work and in the grocery store but does not always help us to understand the construct. So let's get a bit more scientific. According to Locke (1976), **job satisfaction** can be defined as a pleasurable, positive emotional state resulting from the cognitive appraisal of one's job or job experiences. The same author notes that job satisfaction stems from our perceptions that our jobs are fulfilling. In other words, we tend to be satisfied in our jobs if we believe that we are getting what we want out of them.

job satisfaction
A pleasurable, positive emotional state resulting from the cognitive appraisal of one's job or job experiences.

ANTECEDENTS

Figure 10.2 presents a framework for studying and thinking about job satisfaction. On the left side of the figure are the antecedents of job satisfaction—these are the characteristics or factors that lead to job satisfaction. On the right side are the consequences—the outcomes or results of job satisfaction. Below I discuss the research in support of these antecedents and consequences, but due to space constraints I consider only a sampling of the specific antecedents and consequences themselves. Let's start with some of the antecedents to job satisfaction.

Job Characteristics. The first category of antecedents consists of *job characteristics*, which include not only the five core job dimensions postulated by Richard Hackman and Greg Oldham's (1980) job characteristics theory but also stress and workload. The premise here is that one's satisfaction with a job is affected by the structure of the job and what it provides. Look back at Figure 9.3 and you will

FIGURE 10.2 Framework for Job Satisfaction

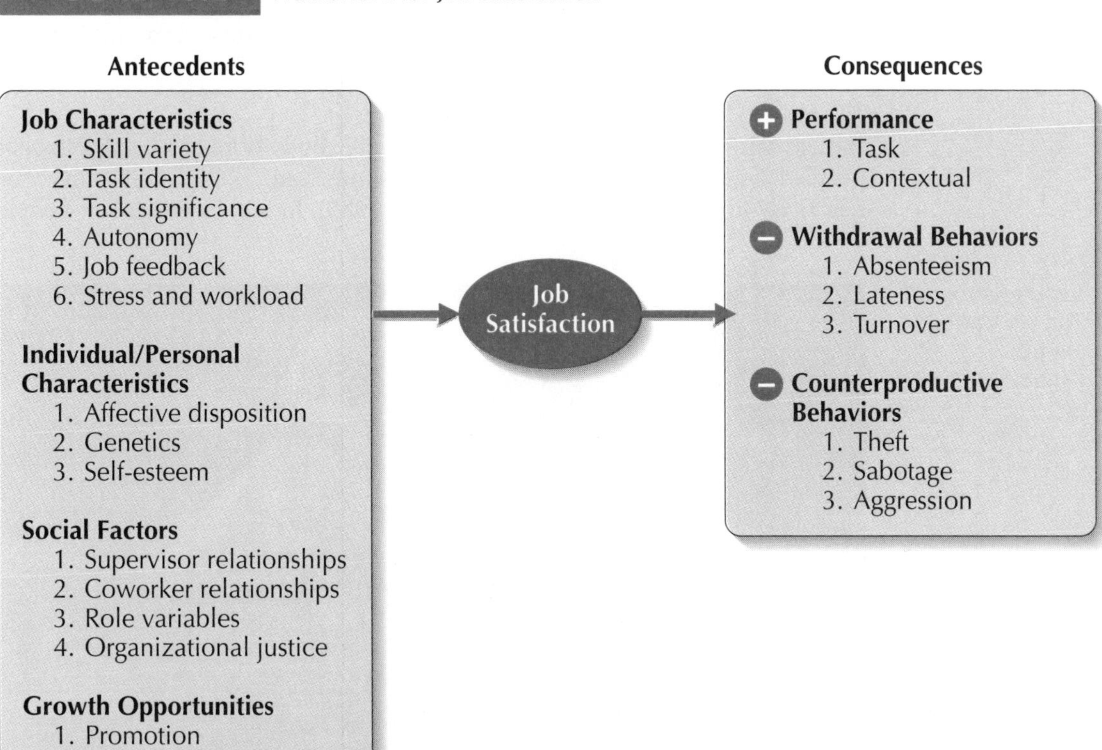

notice that satisfaction is one of the hypothesized outcomes in job characteristics theory. Research has demonstrated a consistent relationship between employees' perceptions of the characteristics of their jobs and their level of job satisfaction (Spector & Jex, 1991). The more employees perceive that their jobs provide autonomy, task identity, task variety, task significance, and job feedback, the more satisfied they report being with their jobs. A meta-analysis that reviewed 28 studies found that correlations between the core job dimensions and job satisfaction ranged from .32 (task identity) to .46 (autonomy; Loher, Noe, Moeler, & Fitzgerald, 1985). A recent study reported that the match between worker preferences regarding work schedule, shift, number of hours, and so forth and organizational staffing policies regarding those same variables was positively related to employee attitudes such as job satisfaction (Holtom, Lee, Tidd, 2002). Thus it is clear that job satisfaction is related, at least in part, to employees' perceptions of the characteristics of their jobs. Other studies indicate that employees who feel overloaded and stressed at work tend to be dissatisfied with their jobs. For instance, Peter Hart (1999) found that low levels of job satisfaction were consistently reported by employees who experienced high levels of "daily hassles" (negative events that are harmful to well-being). Recent work has further indicated that personality traits such as self-esteem affect job satisfaction through their effects on job characteristics (Judge, Bono, & Locke, 2000). Stress is also important in this context, but we will hold off on discussing that until Chapter 11.

Individual/Personal Characteristics. A sizable body of research suggests that people have stable characteristics that predispose them to respond positively or negatively to job contexts (e.g., Staw & Ross, 1985). In other words, some people

Characteristics of jobs can affect one's job satisfaction.

tend to be satisfied with their jobs over the course of their careers, and others tend to be dissatisfied. Barry Staw and Jerry Ross (1985) found moderate correlations between satisfaction measures over time and even saw evidence of this stability in job satisfaction scores when individuals changed jobs. Yet other research has shown that job enrichment and other organizational interventions designed to "improve" jobs still have the potential to raise individuals' levels of satisfaction (Gerhart, 1987; Newton & Keenan, 1991). One longitudinal study (Steel & Rentsch, 1997) that examined the stability of job satisfaction scores over 10 years found that the scores were quite stable over the entire period. Interestingly, however, the data also showed that job characteristics accounted for variance in job satisfaction at Time 2 even after controlling for job satisfaction at Time 1. Finally, whereas satisfaction appeared to be stable for some individuals such that job enrichment was not likely to have much effect on their satisfaction score, for others whose satisfaction scores were not so stable, job enrichment seemed very promising for improving satisfaction levels. In short, there appears to be some stability in job satisfaction scores over time, but this stability varies across people, and it does not rule out the importance of job characteristics in affecting or changing one's level of job satisfaction.

Some researchers in this area have argued that the stability we see in job satisfaction scores over time stems from **affective disposition** or the tendency to respond to classes of environmental stimuli in predetermined affect-based ways (Judge & Hulin, 1993). Quite a few studies conducted by Tim Judge and his colleagues have demonstrated that one's affective disposition is related to one's level of job satisfaction (Judge, 1993; Judge & Hulin, 1993; Judge, Locke, Durham, & Kluger, 1998). In other words, some individuals respond to the world in a favorable way, while others respond in an unfavorable way. Affective disposition thus seems to explain at least some individuals' stable levels of job satisfaction. Recall that we discussed the Big Five theory of personality in Chapter 6. Judge and his colleagues (Judge, Heller, & Mount, 2002) have demonstrated relationships between some Big Five factors and job satisfaction. For instance, those employees who are high on extraversion, agreeableness, and conscientiousness tend to be more satisfied at work, whereas those high on neuroticism tend to be less satisfied. This is considered as more evidence for the dispositional view of job satisfaction.

affective disposition
The tendency to respond to classes of environmental stimuli in predetermined affect-based ways.

Another group of researchers has taken a slightly different perspective, focusing on genetic differences as an explanation for the stability in job satisfaction. In particular, they argue that genetic factors might influence the way in which individuals respond to their work contexts (Arvey, Bouchard, Segal, & Abraham, 1989). We know that genes affect intelligence, personality, interests, and attitudes—so why not job satisfaction? These researchers used an often-studied group of twins from the Minnesota Study of Twins Reared Apart to examine the extent to which twins who were separated at (or soon after) birth had similar levels of job satisfaction much later in life. They found that the proportion of variance in satisfaction resulting from genetic factors was about 30%, a statistically significant number. Thus there appears to be some genetic contribution to an individual's level of job satisfaction (Ilies & Judge, 2003).

The remaining dispositional variables I'd like to discuss have to do with self-esteem. First, some attention has been paid to the idea that individuals with high self-esteem tend to be satisfied with their jobs (Brockner, 1988; Lopez & Greenhaus, 1978). In a recent study, researchers examined the role played by core self-evaluations in both job satisfaction and life satisfaction (Judge et al., 1998). By *core self-evaluations* the authors mean the fundamental evaluations that we make about ourselves—a concept that includes self-esteem and generalized self-efficacy (Bono & Judge, 2003; Judge, Erez, Bono, & Thoresen, 2003). Their results strongly support the link between self-esteem (and other core self-evaluations) and both job and life satisfaction. The authors concluded that core evaluations of the self have consistent effects on job satisfaction regardless of the job. In other words, how people view (or evaluate) themselves directly affects how they experience their jobs and their lives.

organization-based self-esteem (OBSE) A measure of how valuable employees view themselves as organization members.

A second, related variable is **organization-based self-esteem (OBSE),** which concerns employees' perceptions of their value as organization members (Pierce, Gardner, Cummings, & Dunham, 1989). In other words, OBSE reflects one's degree of work-related self-esteem. It seems reasonable to expect that individuals who view themselves as valuable to the organization would also report higher levels of job satisfaction than would individuals who don't perceive themselves as valuable. This is exactly what researchers found in a recent study of health care workers (Chen, Goddard, & Casper, 2004). OBSE was strongly correlated with job satisfaction ($r = .58$) and even predicted job satisfaction, organizational commitment, and job involvement after first controlling for work locus of control and job self-efficacy. Other work has found OBSE to be related not only to job satisfaction but also to performance in a sample of utility employees (Gardner & Pierce, 1998) and to organizational justice in a sample of employees in diverse occupations and industries (McAllister & Bigley, 2002).

Social Factors. Other antecedents of job satisfaction can be considered social factors; these include interactional and relational variables at work. For instance, the relationships that employees have with their supervisors and co-workers seem to be important indicators of whether these employees are satisfied with their jobs. Think back to a job that you really liked—one in which you were really motivated to work hard, looked forward to going to work, and never "watched the clock." I've asked many students over the years to do the same, and when I then requested that they describe what made the job so great, most started by saying something like "I had this great boss" or "My manager was a great woman who really knew how to work with people and didn't play head games with us." The role played by such relationships in affecting job satisfaction is supported by more than just anecdotes of this kind. For instance, research indicates that job satisfaction is affected by the demographic similarity between supervisors and subordinates (Wesolowski & Mossholder, 1997), by the way in which supervisors assign tasks (Balu, 1999), and by the extent to which subordinates and supervisors like and respect each other (Murphy & Ensher, 1999). Clearly, the relationship we have with our bosses has an important effect on how we react to our jobs.

The next thing people with great jobs often tell me is that they like their co-workers. It's nice, they say, working with a great group of people who pitch in for each other and make work fun. You can look at this from another perspective, too. Think of a job that you really disliked and ask yourself what was so bad about it. If you're like most people, you'll say that the people you worked with in this job were a big reason for your dissatisfaction because they were not supportive, helpful, trustworthy, or enjoyable to be around. Again, the evidence goes beyond anecdotes. Research definitely supports the importance of co-worker relations as an antecedent to job satisfaction. According to one study, for instance, the extent to which individuals are satisfied with their pay levels is partly determined by their comparisons with, as well as beliefs and attitudes about, their co-workers (Taylor & Vest, 1992). Another study proposed that organizational restructuring that influences the nature of interactions at work affects co-worker relationships, which, in turn, affect job satisfaction (Howard & Frink, 1996). Indeed, this study found that after the departments in a few city governments were restructured, attitudes about co-workers predicted job, as well as life, satisfaction.

Role variables also affect job satisfaction. If you have ever had a job in which you were not completely sure what your role or function in the organization was, you can understand the negative effect that such ambiguity has on job satisfaction. Ambiguity is something that most people feel very uncomfortable with, especially with respect to the expectations associated with one's job.

Another important variable is organizational justice or fairness, now one of the most investigated concepts in I/O psychology (see Chapter 9). Studies have examined the role of this variable in determining employees' levels of job satisfaction and other work-related attitudes (e.g., Schappe, 1998). By **organizational justice** I mean simply the role of fairness in the workplace. The question here is whether employees' perceptions of the fairness of policies, procedures, and treatments affect their attitudes, behaviors, and performance. Recently, a scale has been developed to measure these perceptions (Donovan, Drasgow, & Munson, 1998). In validating this scale, the authors found that it was strongly correlated with various job satisfaction measures. Even after affective disposition had been controlled for, the justice scale was still correlated with various job satisfaction measures, indicating that justice is an important predictor of job satisfaction regardless of one's affective disposition. Further research has demonstrated that organizational fairness affects job satisfaction through its effect on perceived organizational support and leader-member relationships (Masterson, Lewis, Goldman, & Taylor, 2000; Rhoades & Eisenberger, 2002).

organizational justice
The role of fairness in the workplace.

In sum, employees' levels of job satisfaction are likely to be affected by the quality of the interpersonal relationships that they experience at work. These relationships are affected by how well the employees get along with their supervisors and co-workers, as well as by their perceptions of role clarity, organizational fairness, and organizational support.

Bad bosses, such as J. Jonah Jameson, played by J. K. Simmons in the *Spiderman* movies, and good bosses, such as Capt. John Miller, played by Tom Hanks in *Saving Private Ryan*, can have strong effects on employees' work experiences.

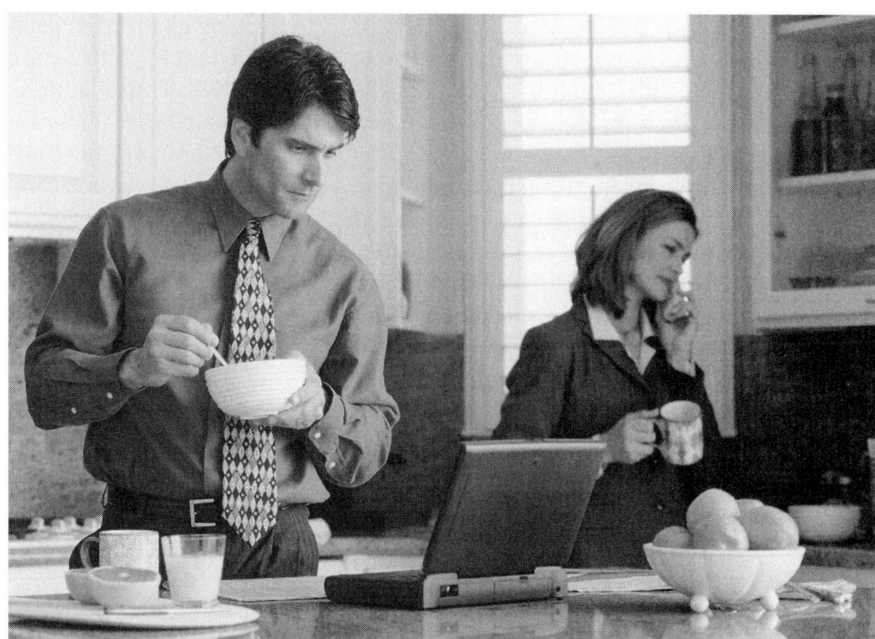

Many 21st-century families are characterized by dual-career couples, which can complicate things at work and at home.

Growth Opportunities. The last group of factors that can affect job satisfaction are what I call growth opportunities, such as the employee's perception that there is potential to grow, advance, or be promoted within the organization. The obvious antecedents here include whether someone is paid well, is provided excellent benefits, and has the opportunity for advancement or promotion. Each of these factors is related to job satisfaction. For instance, one study has demonstrated that employees' satisfaction with their pay and benefits are significant predictors of job satisfaction (Huber, Seybolt, & Venemon, 1992). Another study shows that attitudes about pay are better predictors of job satisfaction than attitudes about benefits, although both make significant contributions to predicting satisfaction (Howard, 1999). Finally, a study of MBAs that examined the impact of career mobility on job satisfaction reported data over a 7-year period demonstrating that the more promotions these managers received, the more satisfied they were (Murrell, Frieze, & Olson, 1996). However, this study also found that lateral transfers (i.e., changes in jobs within the company that aren't promotions) and moves to other organizations had small negative effects on job satisfaction. Perhaps the instability of moving around too much can alter employee attitudes for the worse.

In the next chapter, on work-related stress, we will discuss many issues related to work-family conflict. For now, however, note that the conflict or stress one experiences as a function of valuing both one's family and one's job affects both job and life satisfaction (Bruck, Allen, & Spector, 2002). According to a recent meta-analysis, work-family conflict was negatively correlated with both job satisfaction ($r = -.31$) and life satisfaction ($r = -.36$; Kossek & Ozeki, 1998). Thus it appears that employees with high levels of conflict tend to be less satisfied with their jobs (and their lives in general) than employees with low levels of conflict. Other findings suggest that this relationship is slightly stronger for men than for women and considerably stronger for dual-career couples than for single-career couples. In addition, the conflict appears to be more strongly related to satisfaction if it is the work domain that is "interfering" with the family domain rather than the other way around. We'll revisit these interesting findings in Chapter 11.

MEASUREMENT AND DIMENSIONS

We have been discussing job satisfaction without considering the manner in which it can be measured. More important, we have been conceptualizing job satisfaction in a general sense so that the antecedents could be considered separately from the complexities inherent in the measurement process. At this point, however, we need to consider the measurement of job satisfaction from a multidimensional standpoint. Traditionally, job satisfaction has been assessed at the global level with questionnaire items like "In general, I like my job" or at the facet level with items determining how satisfied employees are with their pay, supervisor, and so on. Both approaches seem reasonable, so the choice may depend on what the organization's purpose is. But I would also argue that including measures at the facet level provides more fine-grained or specific data that can be useful in diagnosing organizational problems and developing organizational interventions.

One of the most frequently used and best validated measures of job satisfaction is the Job Descriptive Index, or JDI (Kinicki, McKee-Ryan, Schriesheim, & Carson, 2002; Stanton, Sinar, Balzer, Julian, Thoresen, Aziz, et al., 2002). It was developed in the 1960s (Smith, Kendall, & Hulin, 1969) and measures satisfaction along five dimensions: satisfaction with the type of work itself, satisfaction with pay, satisfaction with promotion opportunities, satisfaction with supervision, and satisfaction with co-workers. Figure 10.3 presents sample items from each facet. A more recent version of the JDI includes a general measure of job satisfaction called the "Job in General" scale (Ironson, Smith, Brannick, & Gibson, 1989). A scale along similar lines was developed by Hackman and Oldham (1980) in connection with their Job Diagnostic Survey (JDS), which measures job characteristics (see Chapter 9). This latter scale measures satisfaction as a function of pay, security, social factors, supervision, and growth (see Figure 10.4). There are many other measures of facet satisfaction, but the JDI and the JDS are well known and psychometrically sound.

Overall measures of job satisfaction are plentiful as well. For instance, the JDS includes a measure of overall job satisfaction that taps the extent to which employees are satisfied and happy with their jobs. This measure is presented in Fig-

FIGURE 10.3 Sample Items from the JDI

Think of the work you do at present. How well does each of the following words or phrases describe your job? In the blank beside each word or phrase below, write

__Y__ for "Yes" if it describes your work
__N__ for "No" if it does not describe your work
__?__ for "?" if you cannot decide

Work on Present Job

_____ Fascinating
_____ Pleasant
_____ Can see results

Supervision

_____ Doesn't supervise enough
_____ Around when needed
_____ Knows job well

Present Pay

_____ Barely living on income
_____ Bad
_____ Well paid

Co-workers

_____ Stimulating
_____ Unpleasant
_____ Smart

Opportunities for Promotion

_____ Opportunities somewhat limited
_____ Promotion on ability
_____ Regular promotions

Job in General

_____ Pleasant
_____ Worse than most
_____ Worthwhile

Source: Bowling Green State University (1975, 1985, 1997).

ure 10.5. Another large-scale approach to measuring job attitudes is related to L. H. Lofquist and R. V. Dawis's (1969) theory of work adjustment, which proposes that employees seek to maintain correspondence with their environment. The idea here is that employees want their jobs to fulfill their needs and desires. The Minnesota Satisfaction Questionnaire, which was developed on the basis of this theory, totals 100 items that measure 20 different facets of satisfaction. However, a short form of the scale (with just 20 items) has also been used very successfully for measuring overall satisfaction. Three versions of the Faces Scale (Dunham & Herman, 1975; Kunin, 1955; Kunin, 1998) are depicted in Figure 10.6 and have also been frequently used to measure overall satisfaction. This scale

FIGURE 10.4 Sample Items from the JDS

How satisfied are you with this aspect of your job?						
Extremely dissatisfied	Dissatisfied	Slightly dissatisfied	Neutral	Slightly satisfied	Satisfied	Extremely satisfied
1	2	3	4	5	6	7

Pay

❑ The amount of pay and fringe benefits I receive.

Security

❑ The amount of job security I have.

Social

❑ The chance to get to know other people while on the job.

Supervisory

❑ The amount of support and guidance I receive from my supervisor.

Growth

❑ The amount of personal growth and development I get in doing my job.

measures the affective component of job satisfaction rather than the cognitive component, which is tapped by the other scales (Fisher, 2000). The Faces Scale can be used in many different situations because it is largely nonverbal and thus easier for verbally unskilled employees to complete. It is easily adapted for measuring various facets of satisfaction as well.

Consequences

Now that we've talked about what job satisfaction is, what factors determine it, and how to measure it, we need to consider the consequences of job satisfaction for organizations and employees. In our discussion of the theory of planned behavior, I noted that we would come back to this theory when we began to consider the role of work-related attitudes in organizations. If you look back at Figure 10.1, you'll see that attitude is only one of four variables that are instrumental in the prediction of an individual's behavior. Although we hope that an employee's attitude will strongly predict her behavior, we have to realize that behavior is very complicated and that other important variables will also play a part

FIGURE 10.5 JDS Measure of Overall Job Satisfaction

Disagree strongly	Disagree	Disagree slightly	Neutral	Agree slightly	Agree	Agree strongly
1	2	3	4	5	6	7

- ☐ 1. Generally speaking, I am very satisfied with this job.
- ☐ 2. I frequently think of quitting this job. (R)
- ☐ 3. I am generally satisfied with the kind of work I do in this job.
- ☐ 4. Most people on this job are very satisfied with the job.
- ☐ 5. People on this job often think of quitting. (R)

FIGURE 10.6 Three Versions of the Faces Scale

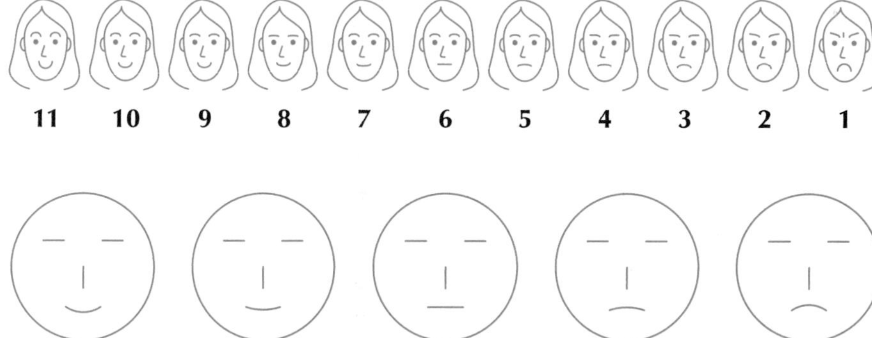

Put a check under the face that expresses how you feel about your **job in general,** including the work, the pay, the supervision, the opportunities for promotion and the people you work with.

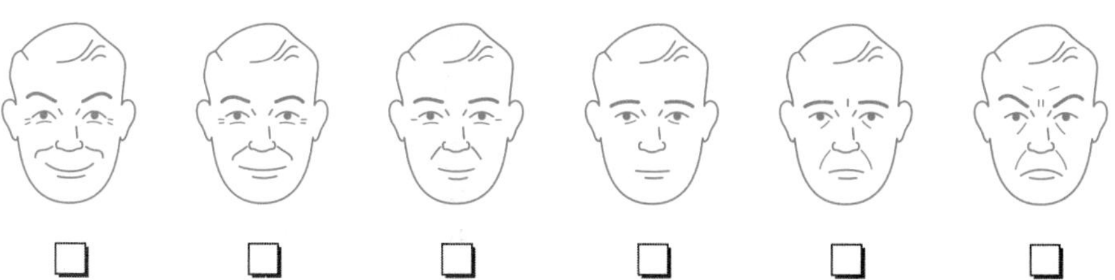

Source: Kunin (1955); American Psychological Association (1975).

in the prediction. Thus, for instance, "a satisfied worker is a productive worker," as the old axiom goes; but what if that satisfied worker is incapable of doing what is required on her job? What if, despite her satisfaction, the norm at work is to do just enough to get by? What if she is really pleased with her job, but this satisfaction does not lead to an intention to work hard because her supervisor doesn't require much effort to get a favorable performance review? In all of these situations, despite a high level of satisfaction, this employee is not likely to perform well, and the attitude-behavior relationship is thus small or nonexistent. Full coverage of this relationship is beyond the scope of the book, but I do want you to consider the complexities of behavior, the fact that there are many antecedents to behavior other than attitudes, and that expecting a strong relationship between attitudes and behaviors might be unrealistic in many situations. With this observation in mind, let's now talk about some of the potential consequences of job satisfaction.

Performance. I have just suggested that the satisfied worker may or may not be a productive worker—an outcome that depends on many other variables. Think about this. Have you ever had a job in which you were not very satisfied but still did decent work? For that matter, did you sometimes perform better than others who were much more satisfied than you? Sometimes, our performance is not a function of our job satisfaction at all but, instead, is determined by the constraints we perceive at work; the skills we possess to do a particular task; the health problems of our children, which prevented us from getting any sleep the night before; our misunderstanding of what is expected with respect to particular tasks; our lack of motivation, resulting from the company's new policy to limit salary increases to 1%; and so on. In other words, satisfaction is a good predictor of performance some of the time, but not all of the time, and, in any case, there are always other important predictors involved (see Schleicher, Watt, & Greguras, 2004, for an example).

To talk in a general sense about the satisfaction-performance relationship is to ignore all of these other potential variables. It's reasonable to do this as long as we keep in mind that these variables exist and that we shouldn't expect an extremely strong relationship between satisfaction and performance. A good general estimate of the relationship (i.e., the correlation) between satisfaction and performance is hard to nail down, but we can be reasonably certain that it lies somewhere between .14 and .30 (Iaffaldano & Muchinsky, 1985; Petty, McGee, & Cavender, 1984). In the most recent and comprehensive meta-analysis of the job satisfaction–performance link, Judge, Thoresen, Bono, and Patton (2001) report an overall correlation of .30. Further, the correlation tended to be stronger for employees in highly complex jobs ($r = .52$). A recent study of hotel managers discovered complex relationships among job satisfaction, affective disposition, and value attainment on performance (Hochwarter, Perrewe, Ferris, & Brymer, 1999). In particular, it found that the strongest relationship was between job satisfaction and performance when both value attainment and positive affect were high. In other words, job satisfaction predicted performance best for those who had positive affect and who reported that their jobs helped them to attain valued outcomes. In sum, there appears to be a direct relationship between job satisfaction and performance, but that relationship is moderated (or affected) by other variables (Schleicher et al., 2004).

Another variable to consider is *contextual performance,* also known as *organizational citizenship behavior* or *OCB* (see Chapter 4). Contextual performance refers to behaviors that are not formally part of one's job description—in other words, to behaviors that have more to do with social elements at work than with task elements. Research has examined the relationship between job satisfaction and contextual performance as well; in fact, the most studied antecedent of contextual behaviors is job satisfaction. For instance, in a recent study of machine operators, satisfaction with co-workers, supervision, and pay were significantly correlated with various dimensions of OCB (Lowery, Beadles, & Krilowicz, 2002). Further, in a study of U.S. government employees and various kinds of employees in Saudi Arabia and Egypt, moderate to strong correlations were found between job satisfaction and OCBs (Tang & Ibrahim, 1998). These correlations ranged from .22 to .57, depending on the type of satisfaction and the type of OCBs measured. Indeed, the relationship between job satisfaction and contextual performance appears to be stronger than the relationship between job satisfaction and task performance.

Withdrawal Behaviors. Performance is one outcome variable of interest to organizations, but withdrawal behaviors are important as well. The three most common withdrawal behaviors are absenteeism, tardiness, and turnover. Let's look at absenteeism first.

We have all missed a few days of work here and there because of illnesses or other uncontrollable events such as a funeral, jury duty, a doctor's appointment, or our child's play or pageant. No one would suggest that employees should come to work every day regardless of illness, personal problems, or other important considerations. The Bureau of Labor and Statistics reports that, on average, employees are absent about 4 days per year due to illness or personal concerns. This doesn't sound like much, but absenteeism does cost companies a great deal of money. It's hard to determine the total costs incurred, but one source estimates that costs resulting from absent employees caring for aging loved ones alone amount to over $12 billion per year (Bisio, 1999), while another source estimates that injuries due to disorders like carpal tunnel syndrome cost companies over $60 billion annually in workers' compensation claims (Tyler, 1998).

A survey by the Commerce Clearing House found that only 28% of unscheduled time off was due to personal illness, which means that there are other explanations for 72% of this time off (Reisenwitz, 1997). A popular model of absenteeism developed by Richard Steers and Susan Rhodes (1978) provides some of these alternative explanations. A simplified version of this model is depicted in Figure 10.7. First, notice that *job satisfaction* is an integral variable in the model, but also notice that it is rather far removed from *employee attendance* and that there are many variables in between. Some studies have found low to moderate correlations ($r = -.15$ to $-.25$) between job satisfaction and absenteeism (Hackett & Guion, 1985; Scott & Taylor, 1985), whereas others have demonstrated a stronger relationship. For instance, in a study based on the personnel records of over 300 city employees in Israel, a moderate negative correlation ($r = -.47$) was found between job satisfaction and voluntary absence (this includes everything but excused absence due to sickness or family obligations; Sagie, 1998). Still other studies have reported relationships close to zero (e.g., Goldberg & Waldman, 2000).

Second, notice that in Figure 10.7 the closest predictor to attendance is *attendance motivation.* This should remind you of the work of Ajzen and his colleagues (Ajzen & Fishbein, 1980; Ajzen & Madden, 1986; Fishbein & Ajzen, 1975), who argued that the best predictor of a behavior is the intention to exhibit that behavior. In Ajzen's models, attitude leads to intention, which affects behavior, much like satisfaction leads to attendance motivation, which then influences attendance. Third, notice that attendance motivation is affected by *pressure to attend.* For example, if an individual has very little money and depends on his job to buy food and shelter, then he is unlikely to behave in ways that might cost him his job, such as being consistently absent from work. This individual would experience pressures to attend that might not be experienced by someone who is independently wealthy. Fourth, notice that *ability to attend* takes into account whether employees actually have control over their attendance behavior. (Think back once more to Ajzen's work and you'll find that this variable is similar to the notion of

FIGURE 10.7 Steers & Rhodes's (1978) Attendance Model

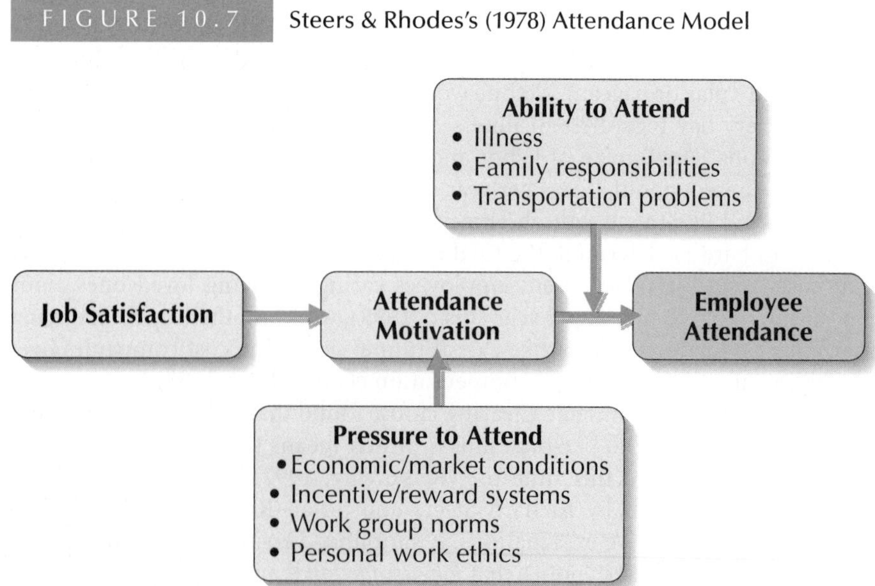

perceived behavioral control.) In short, attendance motivation is likely to affect attendance behavior only if the employees involved have control over their ability to attend. Consider the case of an employee who is very motivated to attend but who has a son with chicken pox who needs her to stay home and take care of him. This lack of ability to attend would affect the relationship between the employee's attendance motivation and her attendance behavior. The employee doesn't go to work, but it's not because she's unmotivated to attend work; rather, it's because she's unable to attend work due to family responsibilities. In fact, research on more than 200 employed, married parents has found positive relationships between the number of children under 6 years of age and absence and between child-care difficulties and absence (Erickson, Nichols, & Ritter, 2000).

The Steers and Rhodes model of absenteeism makes it very clear that although job satisfaction can be an important predictor of absenteeism, the absenteeism process is much more complicated than that. As discussed in the section on satisfaction and performance, expecting a strong direct relationship between satisfaction and any outcome variable is unreasonable given the complexities of human behavior.

Much less research has been conducted on tardiness or lateness, but some work by Gary Blau (1994) has proved especially interesting. Blau suggests that there are different types of lateness and that one common type, which he calls "chronic lateness," is significantly predicted by job satisfaction. In his study of hospital employees, he found a –.39 correlation between job satisfaction and one's tendency to be late. In addition, a meta-analysis found a relationship of about –.21 between various facet satisfactions and lateness (Koslowsky, Sagie, Krausz, & Singer, 1997). The Steers and Rhodes model of absence has also been applied to lateness; here, the results indicate that job satisfaction has a small direct effect on attendance but that both motivation to be on time and ability to be on time are important determinants of lateness (Bardsley & Rhodes, 1996). Again, although the correlation between satisfaction and lateness is not large, we need to consider the vast array of other potential variables when predicting lateness behavior. The Steers and Rhodes model might help in this endeavor.

One last withdrawal behavior is a very important one: turnover. Turnover can have huge cost implications for organizations. Think of some of the major areas we have talked about so far in this book. Organizations invest a great deal of time and effort in things like recruitment, testing and selection, training, and performance evaluation. When an employee is hired, trained, and evaluated, a great deal of money has been invested in that employee. If the employee chooses to leave the company, not only is that money no longer working for the company, but the process must begin again in terms of recruitment, selection, and training—such that, in effect, the company is spending considerable additional money. Further, because it usually takes a while for the recruitment-selection-training process to identify someone to fill the position, for a period of a few months the company has to train someone internally to fill that position. You should be getting the picture by now—turnover is a real concern for organizations. Of course, the flip side of all this is that turnover can be good for companies if those employees who

Turnover costs organizations millions of dollars, but sometimes ineffective performers or unpopular employees leave, which could have positive effects on the organization and its employees.

turned over are ineffective and can be replaced by more effective employees. This is often the case when employees are fired or when ineffective employees select themselves out of the organization. For our present purposes, however, let's think about situations in which organizations lose employees whom they would have preferred to keep.

Traditionally, researchers have looked at two main antecedents of turnover: (1) perceived ease of movement, or the extent to which employees can find alternative jobs; and (2) perceived desirability of movement, which has largely been operationalized with respect to job satisfaction. In general, a modest relationship has been found between job satisfaction and turnover (Griffeth, Hom, & Gaertner, 2000; Lee, Mitchell, Holtom, McDaniel, & Hill, 1999), with correlations between –.20 and –.30. One approach to turnover, developed by Peter Hom and Ricky Griffeth (1991), includes job satisfaction as an important element, among others. Figure 10.8 presents a simplified version of their model; as you can see, "job satisfaction" is at the beginning of the model, and "quitting or staying" is at the end. Along one path to turnover, job satisfaction affects the extent to which an individual begins thinking about quitting; a second path leads from job satisfaction to a job search and comparisons of alternatives. Both paths eventually result in a decision to stay or go.

Job satisfaction is indeed often integral to the turnover process, but we must also realize that some individuals leave companies because they can't pass up an incredible opportunity or want to relocate back home to take care of an ailing parent. In other words, turnover may be less related to the current job than to alternative job opportunities or personal circumstances. For an example, consider recent cutting-edge work on turnover, involving what Tom Lee and his colleagues call the *unfolding model* (Mitchell, Holtom, Lee, Sablynski, & Erez, 2001; Sablynski, Lee, Mitchell, Burton, & Holtom, 2002), in which four different paths to turnover are hypothesized. Along the first path, turnover results from a *shock to the system* (e.g., an unsolicited job offer, a change in one's marital state, a job transfer, a firm merger), and job satisfaction is completely irrelevant. This model provides other turnover paths and some interesting alternatives to traditional beliefs about the turnover process and, along with the work of Hom and Griffeth (1991), demonstrates the complexity of the turnover process.

FIGURE 10.8 Hom & Griffeth's (1991) Modified Model of Turnover

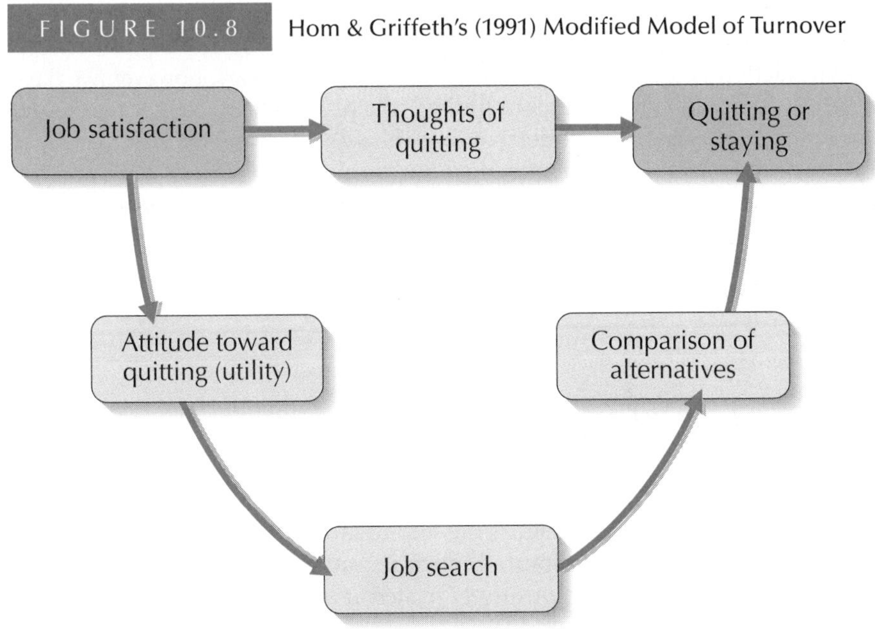

Counterproductive Behaviors. There are various terms for the kinds of behaviors that employees engage in that are detrimental to the organization, including antisocial behaviors and dysfunctional behaviors. Here I use the phrase **counterproductive behaviors,** defined as any behaviors that bring, or are intended to bring, harm to an organization, its employees, or stakeholders. Counterproductive behaviors include arson, blackmail, bribery, sabotage, theft, fraud, psychological withdrawal, and interpersonal violence (Giacalone & Greenberg, 1997). Paul Spector (1997) has presented a model of antisocial behaviors in which frustration is the centerpiece. He argues that when an employee is frustrated and thus dissatisfied (i.e., when something interferes with his goals or objectives), his potential for antisocial behaviors is increased. In their review of the literature, Lau, Au, and Ho (2003) found that young, dissatisfied employees are most likely to engage in counterproductive work behaviors, and Salgado (2002) demonstrated that individuals low on conscientiousness tended to be most likely to exhibit counterproductive behaviors. More generally, the correlations between job satisfaction and counterproductive behaviors range from –.10 to –.25 (Boye & Jones, 1997). Although relatively little empirical research has been conducted in this area (because measuring counterproductive behaviors requires "catching" people actually committing the behaviors), the notion that employees' work-related attitudes play a role seems reasonable and is becoming the focus of more recent research.

counterproductive behaviors
Any behaviors that bring, or are intended to bring, harm to an organization, its employees, or stakeholders.

In sum, job satisfaction is an important organizational variable. However, although we know a great deal about the antecedents and consequences of job satisfaction, we have probably been guilty in the past of expecting too much from it (Fisher, 2003). That is, we have anticipated very strong relationships between job satisfaction and organizational behaviors. In recent years, however, we have begun to realize the important, but limited role played by job satisfaction in organizational processes. Our understanding of how satisfaction fits into the bigger picture of organizational and individual functioning continues to grow, and the interest of researchers and practitioners in job satisfaction is not likely to decline. The questions that we have asked in the past about the small direct effects of job satisfaction on various outcomes have led the way for research that is now helping to build more accurate models of organizational functioning.

ORGANIZATIONAL COMMITMENT

Organizational commitment (OC) is the second most frequently studied attitude in the workplace, but it has captured much less attention than job satisfaction. These two attitudes tend to be positively related at a moderate level with correlations around .30 to .40. However, there has been some controversy over the causal order of these two variables (Kinicki et al., 2002) without a resolution as to which variable causes the other or whether there is a particular causal order. Organizational commitment is broader in scope than job satisfaction given that the target is the "organization" rather than the "job." Further, it is often reported that OC is more stable over time than is job satisfaction, which can fluctuate with daily or even hourly changes at work; OC doesn't fluctuate quite so much. In this section, I will define the various dimensions of organizational commitment and present a brief discussion of some of its antecedents and consequences. **Organizational commitment** can be defined as the relative strength of an individual's identification with and involvement in a particular organization. However, to really understand this attitude we need to consider three components of commitment that have been defined in the literature.

organizational commitment
The relative strength of an individual's identification with and involvement in a particular organization.

affective commitment
Emotional attachment to an organization, characterized by a strong belief in and acceptance of the organization's goals and values; a willingness to exert effort on behalf of the organization; and a strong desire to remain a part of the organization.

COMPONENTS

In recent years, John Meyer and Natalie Allen have studied organizational commitment more thoroughly than anyone else in the field, so this section borrows extensively from their work (Allen & Meyer, 1996; Meyer & Allen, 1997; Meyer, Stanley, Herscovitch, & Topolnytsky, 2002). Meyer and Allen conceptualize commitment as having three components, and they have developed a measure of each one. Figure 10.9 presents these measures, which are the most frequently used and accepted in the literature (Meyer & Allen, 1997). The first and most studied component of organizational commitment, **affective commitment,** is characterized by (1) a strong belief in and acceptance of the organization's goals and val-

PRACTITIONER FORUM

SCOTT GOODMAN

Ph.D., 1995, I/O Psychology, University of Akron
Principal, Shaker Consulting Group

As you've learned in this chapter, a person's intention to act is a function of both the subjective norm for that act and of his attitude toward that act. In our consulting engagements we've applied this theory of planned behavior to assist clients in delivering on the promise of their brand.

Companies today see their brand as a strategic asset, as is the case with Disney, Coca-Cola, Microsoft, McDonald's, Apple, and Nike, to name a few. Each interaction between an employee and customer or prospect can enhance or erode the brand, improve or weaken customer loyalty, and affect business results for better or worse.

Companies that fail to deliver the promise of their brand often do so because they are unable to operationalize it in a meaningful way. Our first step in helping clients deliver on their brand promise is to convert the brand promise into concrete brand behaviors. This is really about establishing subjective norms, which subsequently affect intentions and job behaviors.

After operationalizing the brand promise, our next step is to create a measure that will accurately assess employee brand behaviors as they relate to the customer experience. Employees' interactions with customers are observed, and employees are given specific feedback on how well they exhibited the brand behaviors (e.g., did they encourage customers to ask questions, etc.). This is an excellent way of helping employees to understand how a customer experience can be better and where specific improvements can be made. The process helps change the way employees think (i.e., their attitude) and behave as they go about their daily activity. This results in creating a brand culture in which all activities center on delivering the brand promise to customers. The most successful brand cultures are those in which every employee thinks and acts as if he or she is the brand. Southwest Airlines is a good example of this.

After creating the brand promise and operationalizing the required behaviors, the real value is in demonstrating the business impact of living the brand. In our work we have been able to link brand behaviors to customer satisfaction and ultimately customer outcomes such as sales and retention. In short, we have been able to help companies quantify both the emotional and business importance of their brand.

Once these linkages between brand behaviors and business outcomes are established, the next step is to make sure training and development programs, performance management systems, and compensation programs are designed to reinforce and promote brand behavior.

APPLYING YOUR KNOWLEDGE

1. What is a company's "brand"?
2. In what ways do Shaker consultants attempt to get clients to make good on their brand promise?
3. What role do you think the brand might have on employees' job attitudes?

ues, (2) a willingness to exert effort on behalf of the organization, and (3) a strong desire to remain a part of the organization (Mowday, Steers, & Porter, 1979). This component can be thought of as the employee's emotional attachment to the organization. Second is **continuance commitment,** which has to do with the costs that are associated with leaving the organization. This component is sometimes referred to as "sunk-costs" commitment, because it concerns attachment to an

continuance commitment
Attachment to an organization as a function of what the employee has sunk into it.

organization as a function of what the employee has sunk into it (Shore, Tetrick, Shore, & Barksdale, 2000). An employee might have high continuance commitment because to leave the organization would cost her a great deal in retirement earnings and other benefits that come with seniority. Third is **normative commitment,** which reflects one's obligation to continue employment with the organization. This component is sometimes called "moral commitment." Individuals who are high on normative commitment tend to believe that they ought to stay with the company regardless of what it offers them.

normative commitment
Attachment to an organization that reflects one's obligation to continue employment with the organization.

ANTECEDENTS

Figure 10.10 presents a heuristic framework for thinking about and studying organizational commitment. On the left side of the figure, antecedents are grouped into three categories to enhance the understanding of the commitment construct. We will discuss each of these categories in turn.

Organizational Mechanisms. Have you ever noticed all the little things that organizations seem to be doing these days to get employees committed to the company? Some organizations have "company stores" that sell merchandise with the company logo emblazoned all over them. (Do you have a coffee cup with your company's logo on it? How about a sweatshirt or T-shirt? Maybe a bumper sticker or a hat?) The use of logos and insignias on merchandise for employees and their children (What "organizational team player" wouldn't want his or her child to have a hat that says Xerox or AT&T?) may serve various purposes, but one is clearly to increase the commitment of employees. No empirical studies have examined the success of this approach thus far; but, speaking for myself, I proudly wear a sweatshirt from Virginia Tech (where I went to school), and when people stop me to say that it's a great school or that their daughter got a great education there or that it has a great football program, I probably become even a little more committed. The same process occurs with respect to organizations. Newsletters can also increase the strength of employees' identification with or involvement in the organization. Hearing about the charity work that the company has done, the new employees who have been hired, the employees who are retiring after 30 years of distinguished service to the company, the company's goals and objectives over the next 5 years, and how the CEO is a great champion for the company in the local community can all help to increase employees' commitment to the organization.

Of course, there are more formal mechanisms as well, in the form of reward systems that give employees trips for positive performance, provide gift certificates for employees of the month, pay for furthering employees' education, and so on. Meyer and Allen (1997) view such mechanisms as leading to affective commitment—specifically, by communicating to employees that the organization is supportive of them, by treating them fairly, and by enhancing their sense of personal

FIGURE 10.9 Affective, Continuance, and Normative Commitment Scales

Disagree strongly	Disagree	Disagree slightly	Neutral	Agree slightly	Agree	Agree strongly
1	2	3	4	5	6	7

Affective Commitment

- ☐ 1. I would be very happy to spend the rest of my career in this organization.
- ☐ 2. I really feel as if this organization's problems are my own.
- ☐ 3. I do not feel like "part of the family" at my organization. (R)
- ☐ 4. I do not feel "emotionally attached" to this organization. (R)
- ☐ 5. This organization has a great deal of personal meaning for me.
- ☐ 6. I do not feel a strong sense of belonging to my organization. (R)

Continuance Commitment

- ☐ 1. It would be very hard for me to leave my organization right now, even if I wanted to.
- ☐ 2. Too much of my life would be disrupted if I decided I wanted to leave my organization right now.
- ☐ 3. Right now, staying with my organization is a matter of necessity as much as desire.
- ☐ 4. I believe that I have too few options to consider leaving this organization.
- ☐ 5. One of the few negative consequences of leaving this organization would be the scarcity of available alternatives.
- ☐ 6. If I had not already put so much of myself into this organization, I might consider working elsewhere.

Normative Commitment

- ☐ 1. I do not feel any obligation to remain with my current employer. (R)
- ☐ 2. Even if it were to my advantage, I do not feel it would be right to leave my organization now.
- ☐ 3. I would feel guilty if I left my organization now.
- ☐ 4. This organization deserves my loyalty.
- ☐ 5. I would not leave my organization right now because I have a sense of obligation to the people in it.
- ☐ 6. I owe a great deal to my organization.

FIGURE 10.10 Framework for Organizational Commitment

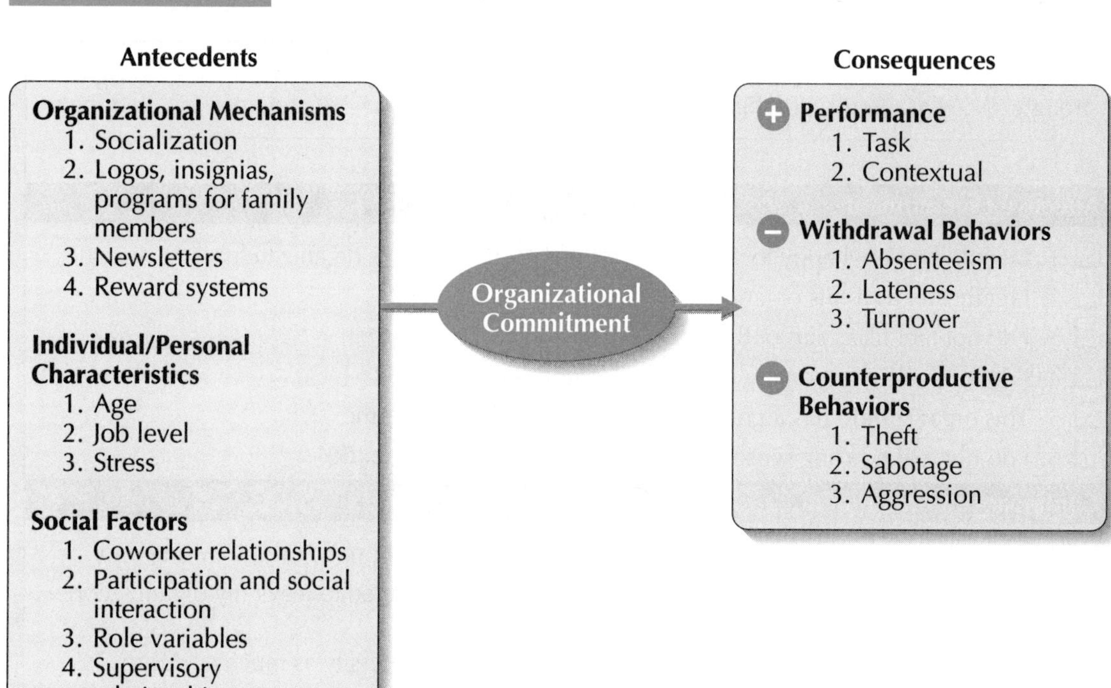

importance and competence. Other research, too, has demonstrated that affective commitment is influenced by employees' perception that organizational policies, procedures, and programs are fair (Konovsky & Cropanzano, 1991; Sweeney & McFarlin, 1993).

Individual/Personal Characteristics. Examining situational characteristics such as the organizational mechanisms discussed previously would be incomplete without considering individual characteristics as well. Individual employees bring to their jobs many qualities, attitudes, beliefs, and skills—what we often refer to as *individual differences*—and these differences are often related to job attitudes such as organizational commitment. In perhaps the largest meta-analysis done in the area of commitment, John Mathieu and Dennis Zajac (1990) identified certain individual-difference variables that appear to be important predictors of organizational commitment. Across 26 different samples they found a .22 correlation between age and affective commitment, indicating that the older employees are, the more affectively committed they are. This could be the result of more experience or tenure on the job, or it could be that as we age we are increasingly likely

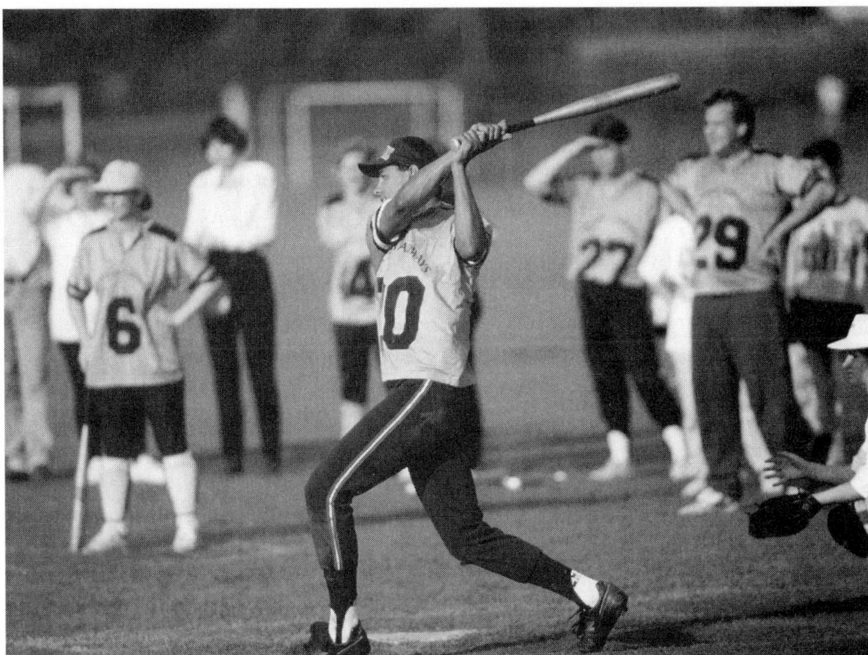

Employee's commitment is developed in many ways, including the use of company logos and competitive events against other companies.

to end up in a job that we like and thus we become emotionally attached to it. One exception was uncovered in a recent study that reported that the affective commitment of police officers decreases with additional tenure in the law enforcement organization (Beck & Wilson, 2000). Thus there are still questions left to be answered.

In their meta-analysis Mathieu and Zajac also found a .21 correlation between job level and affective commitment, suggesting that individuals in higher-level jobs are more committed to the organization than are individuals in lower-level jobs. Specifically, they discovered a stronger relationship between organizational tenure and continuance commitment than between organizational tenure and affective commitment, thus supporting what we know about these two components of commitment: As employees' tenure with an organization increases, their sunk costs—and hence their continuance commitment—also increase. Finally, they calculated that stress was negatively related to both affective commitment ($r = -.32$) and continuance commitment ($r = -.35$), suggesting that individuals who are stressed at work tend to develop neither an emotional attachment to the organization nor one based on sunk costs. In other words, there is no bond between the employee and the company if the employee is quite stressed on the job.

Although less is known about normative commitment than about the other two components, some antecedents have emerged in the literature. For instance, whereas there is no direct evidence that parental values or early socialization affect normative commitment, there is some indirect evidence demonstrating that employees who report an ingrained belief in the need to fulfill their obligations to others are more likely to be normatively committed to their organization than employees who do not report such a belief (Meyer & Allen, 1997). The implication is that this individual difference may have been developed by employees' parents during child rearing and early socialization experiences.

Social Factors. The last category of antecedents revolves around social interactions and relationships. One consistent antecedent of organizational commitment is the nature and quality of the employee-supervisor relationship. For instance, the extent to which a boss is considerate in his treatment of his employees ($r = .34$) and communicates often and openly with them ($r = .45$) is related to the employees' level of organizational commitment (Mathieu & Zajac, 1990). Role variables are similarly important antecedents, given consistent negative correlations between concepts—like role ambiguity (when employees are not sure what is expected of them) and role conflict (when role expectations are inconsistent)—and organizational commitment. Another example in this category has to do with relationships among co-workers. An interesting study found that employees' normative commitment levels were correlated with the normative commitment levels of their co-workers, suggesting that co-workers' attitudes and beliefs were somehow affecting each other (Dunham, Grube, & Castaneda, 1994).

Consequences

In Figure 10.10 the potential consequences of organizational commitment are divided into three categories. Let's discuss each of these in turn.

Performance. Comprehensive reviews of the literature on the consequences of organizational commitment include Mathieu and Zajac's (1990) meta-analysis of the commitment literature, Allen and Meyer's (1996) summary of their three-component model of organizational commitment, and an important book by the last two authors (Meyer & Allen, 1997). I rely on these and several other sources in the following discussion.

It is reasonable to assume that any work-related attitude will be more favorably viewed by organizational practitioners if that attitude is directly related to job performance. However, as we noted in an earlier section, expecting strong direct relationships between job satisfaction and performance outcome variables is not reasonable given the complexity of performance. The same advice holds for organizational commitment: Don't expect a strong direct relationship between commitment and performance. Still, we can try to understand what the empirical data indicate about the relationship that does exist. First, recent studies report correlations between affective commitment and task performance of between .15

and .25 (for reviews, see Allen & Meyer, 1996; Riketta, 2002). Similarly, contextual performance appears to be consistently related to affective commitment in a positive way, less consistently related to normative commitment, and unrelated or somewhat negatively related to continuance commitment (Allen & Meyer, 1996). A meta-analysis reported that affective commitment was related to both altruistic OCBs ($r = .23$) and compliance (similar to what we have called conscientiousness earlier) OCBs ($r = .30$; Organ & Ryan, 1995). The same meta-analysis found a weaker positive relationship between normative commitment and OCBs and no support for a relationship between continuance commitment and OCBs. Riketta's (2002) review found a stronger relationship between OC and performance when performance was extra-role (i.e., OCBs) rather than in-role (i.e., task performance) and when employees were in white-collar rather than blue-collar jobs. Finally, another study found that even after controlling for procedural justice and job satisfaction, affective commitment accounted for a significant amount of variance in altruistic OCBs, suggesting that it might be more important than satisfaction or justice in predicting OCBs (Schappe, 1998). The author of this study concluded that employees' feelings about their organization may manifest themselves in terms of contextual behaviors that are important to organizational functioning.

Withdrawal Behaviors. Affective commitment and absence appear to be correlated to a small but significant degree. For instance, one study found a –.18 correlation between affective commitment and the frequency of absence incidents over a 12-month period (Gellatly, 1995), while a second found a –.22 correlation between the affective commitment of bus drivers and the frequency of absence incidents that were under the drivers' control (Hackett, Bycio, & Hausdorf, 1994). Again, if you think back to the attendance model in Figure 10.7 and recall the many variables other than attitudes that play a part in determining absence behavior, a direct correlation of about –.20 should not be surprising. Another study suggests an even stronger direct relationship than the research just reviewed. Abraham Sagie (1998) collected absence data from the personnel files of city government employees in Israel and found that affective commitment was strongly related to these objective measures of voluntary absence ($r = -.54$). His results suggest that the relationship of both affective commitment and job satisfaction with voluntary or controllable absence may be stronger than previously believed. Research indicates that continuance commitment does not appear to be related to absenteeism. Further, so little research has looked at the role of normative commitment that no conclusion can be drawn about its relationship with absenteeism.

Organizational commitment has a long-standing association with turnover (see Mowday et al., 1979). This association is clear in my earlier presentation of the three characteristics that define a highly committed employee, the last of which is *a strong desire to remain a part of the organization.* By definition, organizational commitment should be negatively related to the turnover process. The aforementioned meta-analysis by Mathieu and Zajac (1990) uncovered strong support for the role of organizational commitment in the turnover process, finding organizational commitment to be strongly related to intent to search for a new job (–.60), intent to leave one's current job (–.46), and turnover (–.28). And according to Allen and Meyer's (1996) more recent review, the relationship between affective commitment and turnover intentions ranges from –.29 to –.61 and is statistically significant in each of the 12 studies uncovered since 1991. A more recent study has found similar and consistently strong effects in a Chinese sample (Cheng & Stockdale, 2003). For normative commitment Meyer and his colleagues have found a similar pattern but weaker relationships, with correlations ranging from –.20 to –.38. They also found 9 recent studies that looked at the relationship between continuance commitment and turnover, finding correlations ranging from .00 to –.42.

Ellen Whitener and Pat Waltz (1993) measured actual turnover 1 year after measuring both continuance and affective commitment in a sample of bank tellers. They found a –.19 relationship between continuance commitment and actual turnover and a –.26 relationship between affective commitment and actual turnover. These results suggest reasonably direct effects, even in light of the fact that the turnover process is quite complex and includes many other important variables. In sum, individuals who are committed to the organization through an emotional attachment or a moral obligation tend not to search for jobs, intend to stay in their current jobs, and actually do remain with the organization, whereas those who are committed due to sunk costs may have similar inclinations, but the relationships are clearly not as consistent.

Counterproductive Behaviors. Although little research has investigated the role of organizational commitment in counterproductive behavior, there are various reasons to expect a relationship. One model of counterproductive behavior that emphasizes the role of frustration in the process suggests a likely relationship between frustration and a lack of commitment to the organization (Spector, 1997). Other recent work indicates that the values and goals communicated by an organization have a significant effect on the frequency of counterproductive behaviors. Because one important characteristic of an organizationally committed employee is a strong belief in and acceptance of the organizational's goals, it follows that commitment ought to be related to the frequency of counterproductive behavior. Indeed, companies that espouse such organizational values as treating employees with fairness, empowering employees, and demonstrating interpersonal cooperation report higher levels of trust than do companies that do not emphasize these values (Boye & Jones, 1997). In the near future, we can expect to see the development of a research base focusing on this important relationship between organizational commitment and counterproductive behaviors.

ADDITIONAL JOB ATTITUDES

Job Involvement and Work Centrality

Although job satisfaction and organizational commitment have received by far the most attention from employee attitude researchers, a few other attitudes deserve mention. Two constructs in particular—job involvement and work centrality—are closely related to each other and to organizational commitment and have a long history in I/O psychology. **Job involvement** is the extent to which employees are cognitively engaged in their jobs (Paullay, Alliger, & Stone-Romero, 1994). In extreme cases, the employees become *workaholics,* whose work completely dominates their lives. **Work centrality,** on the other hand, is defined as the degree of importance that work holds in one's life (Paullay et al., 1994). This attitude usually develops as a result of socialization, reflecting the nature of our individual role models as we grow and mature. One distinction between job involvement and work centrality is that the former focuses on one's particular job, whereas the latter concerns work in general. Although we know less about these two constructs than about the others we've talked about in this chapter, research is continuing to illuminate the role they play in organizations. According to two studies, for instance, job involvement, work centrality, and organizational commitment are moderately intercorrelated, with relationships between .25 and .45 (Hirschfeld & Feild, 2000; Paullay et al., 1994). In the more recent study, which examined over 300 employees, Robert Hirschfeld and Hubert Feild (2000) concluded on the basis of the relationships among these three constructs that affectively committed employees tend to identify with their work roles (work centrality) and are engaged in their jobs (job involvement).

job involvement
The extent to which employees are cognitively engaged in their jobs.

work centrality
The degree of importance that work holds in one's life.

Second, a recent investigation of over 280 public-sector employees found that job involvement moderated the effect of job insecurity on outcomes such as negative job attitudes, health problems, and psychological distress (Probst, 2000). In particular, job insecurity had stronger effects on these outcomes for individuals who were highly involved in their jobs. This makes a great deal of sense: If you are invested in your job and engaged by it, job insecurity is more likely to lead to negative attitudes and both physical and psychological distress. On the other hand, if you aren't all that invested in your job to begin with, job insecurity is not likely to be very relevant for you and, therefore, won't lead to negative outcomes. Another recent study found that job involvement was significantly related to OCBs and task performance. The job involvement–OCB relationship was also stronger for women than it was for men (Diefendorff, Brown, Kamin, & Lord, 2002).

For a conceptual framework of job involvement and a meta-analysis, I encourage you to read Brown (1996). Some work has also begun to focus on the extreme job involvement known as workaholism. For instance, Janet Spence and Ann Robbins (1992) have argued that there are different kinds of workaholics and even suggest that certain types of workaholism may not be so bad. The key distinction among these various types of workaholics is enjoyment. Employees who are driven by their work, involved in their work, and enjoy their work are termed *enthusiastic workaholics,* whereas the more traditional workaholics are driven and involved but report that they do not enjoy their work. In a sample of over 500 MBA graduates in Canada, enthusiastic workaholics reported higher levels of emotional and psychological well-being than did traditional workaholics (Burke, 2000). This finding suggests that being driven by and heavily involved in your job can have favorable outcomes, provided that you also enjoy your job. Employees whose workaholism results in psychological, emotional, and even physical problems tend to be those who do not like what it is they are driven by and involved in.

Perceived Organizational Support

perceived organizational support (POS)
Employees' global beliefs concerning the extent to which the organization values and cares about them.

Perceived organizational support (POS) has been defined as employees' global beliefs concerning the extent to which the organization values their contributions and cares about their well-being (Rhoades & Eisenberger, 2002). These authors' recent review identified over 70 empirical studies measuring POS. They conclude from their review that the major antecedents of POS include fair organizational procedures, supervisor support, and favorable rewards/job conditions, whereas the most strongly related consequences include organizational commitment, increased performance, and reduced withdrawal behaviors (e.g., turnover, intentions, tardiness). For instance, Allen, Shore, and Griffeth (2003) found that POS was strongly related to other attitudes, such as job satisfaction and organizational commitment, but that it also predicted turnover intentions and actual turnover behavior 1 year later. Finally, in an interesting study of perceptions of politics and POS, Hochwarter, Kacmar, Perrewe, and Johnson (2003) found that perceptions of politics in the organization affected job satisfaction, organizational commitment, stress, and performance through its effect on POS. In other words, employees who worked in a "political" environment felt very little organizational support and tended to be stressed at work, low on job satisfaction, low on organizational commitment, and low performers.

Emotions at Work

emotion regulation
The ways in which individuals monitor their emotions and the expression of those emotions.

emotional labor
The effort, planning, and control required by employees to express organizationally desired emotions during interpersonal interactions.

In recent years, the role of emotions in the workplace has attracted a great deal of research attention; accordingly, I end this chapter with a brief discussion of this subject. One topic of interest is generally referred to as **emotion regulation,** or the ways in which individuals monitor their emotions and the expression of those emotions (Gross, 1998). As you know, emotions play an important role in our day-to-day functioning—and this is certainly the case in the workplace. **Emotional labor** is a slightly more specific term and is defined as the effort, planning, and control required by employees to express organizationally desired emotions during interpersonal interactions (Morris & Feldman, 1996). It is believed that there are two forms of emotion regulation: *amplification,* or faking/exaggerating pleasant emotions, and *suppression,* or hiding displays of felt emotions such as anger or jealousy (Cote & Morgan, 2002). Much of the work on the regulation of emotions or emotional labor has focused on service jobs that emphasize interactions with customers, because it is believed that employees in these jobs must constantly regulate their emotions and the expression of them.

Some research suggests that emotional labor is linked to substance abuse, absenteeism, work-related stress, and psychological well-being, whereas other research has not found these relationships to be strong and consistent (Zapf, 2002). One consistent finding, however, is that employees who experience "emotional dissonance"—whose true feelings are different from the emotions they project on the job—experience higher rates of stress (Grandey & Brauburger, 2002). For example, people who tend to see the world in rather rigid and negative ways may experience emotional dissonance as customer service representatives who are required by their job to be pleasant, helpful, and encouraging. This disconnect between their feelings and what's required of them at work is likely to lead to stress, burnout, and, ultimately, poor customer service. (See Chapter 11 for a more detailed discussion of stress.) In an interesting recent study of employees in the service industry, it was demonstrated that the suppression of unpleasant emotions led to job dissatisfaction, which resulted in strong intentions to quit. On the other hand, the amplification of pleasant emotions led to increases in job satisfaction (Cote & Morgan, 2002).

Psychologists in general know a good deal about emotions, but as I/O psychologists in particular, we don't yet know much about emotional labor. The authors of a recent review make the argument that we need considerably more empirical research on this topic, with a focus on how emotional labor affects individual and organizational functioning (Grandey & Brauburger, 2002). This growing area of study promises to be at the forefront of job-related attitude research in the 21st century.

The existing work on emotional labor has relevant applications as well. For instance, emotional dissonance, given its links to stress and burnout, has implications for selection systems that determine how well employees fit into the hiring organization—a factor known as *person-organization fit.* Not surprisingly, customer service representatives are likely to be more successful at their jobs if their emotional makeup is somewhat consistent with the emotional regulation required in those jobs. These requirements, of course, should be identified by a job analysis, which in turn could be used in developing predictors on which applicants are measured. Ideally, applicants who believe that people should help themselves and not expect others to help them at all, who don't enjoy interacting with people, and who believe that customers are never right should be screened out by such predictors. In this way, emotional dissonance can be avoided, along with the potentially negative consequences that follow from it. Think about it: How many times in the past few weeks have you walked into a store and been "served" by a customer service employee who was clearly unable to do the emotional labor required of that job and really didn't care much about you as a customer? This kind of problem is certainly a relevant subject for study in I/O psychology, and the area of emotional labor, more generally, promises to enhance our understanding of organizations and increase organizational effectiveness.

SUMMARY

This chapter is divided into four sections. First, I presented some background information on attitudes, behaviors, and the relationship between them. At the outset I discussed a popular model of this relationship and then referred to it throughout while trying to make sense of the links between work-related attitudes and organizational outcomes. The work of Ajzen and Fishbein provided a nice foundation for the more work-specific issues that were discussed later in the chapter.

Second, after considering various reasons why I/O researchers and practitioners are interested in job attitudes, I presented a detailed overview of job satisfaction, using Figure 10.2 as a basis for discussion. I cited research dealing with the four main classes of antecedents to job satisfaction: job characteristics, individual/personal characteristics, social factors, and growth opportunities. All of these antecedents appear to make important contributions to employees' levels of job satisfaction. I also discussed a few scales that measure job satisfaction, included examples of those scales, and considered the multidimensional nature of job satisfaction. To conclude this section on job satisfaction, I discussed at length three classes of organizational outcome variables (consequences) that appear to be substantively linked to job satisfaction: performance, withdrawal behaviors, and counterproductive behaviors.

In the third section, I presented Figure 10.10 as a working heuristic for our discussion of organizational commitment. Throughout this discussion, I reviewed Meyer and Allen's three-component model: affective commitment, continuance commitment, and normative commitment. I also classified the antecedents of organizational commitment as organizational, individual, or social in nature. Each of these sets of variables seems to have potential effects on organizational commitment. Indeed, recent research in this area demonstrates that performance, withdrawal behaviors, and counterproductive behaviors are all influenced by organizational commitment. Finally, in the context of other work attitudes, I discussed the role played by job involvement, perceived organizational support, and emotions in the workplace.

REVIEW QUESTIONS

1. Discuss the relationship between attitudes and behaviors.
2. Why should I/O psychologists study work attitudes in the first place?

3. How would you define job satisfaction?
4. What role do individual characteristics play in determining one's level of job satisfaction?
5. What role do social factors and organizational factors play in affecting one's job satisfaction?
6. Identify the best estimate of the relationship between job satisfaction and each of the following: performance, turnover, and absence.
7. Describe the three-component model of organizational commitment.
8. How do organizations attempt to increase employees' commitment levels?
9. What consequences follow from low levels of organizational commitment?
10. What role does POS play in organizations?
11. What is emotional labor? Discuss its implications for organizational life.

SUGGESTED READINGS

Lee, T. W., Mitchell, T. R., Holtom, B. C., McDaniel, L. S., & Hill, J. W. (1999). The unfolding model of voluntary turnover: A replication and extension. *Academy of Management Journal, 42*(4), 450–462. This cutting-edge look at turnover modeling appears to be the new wave of the study of turnover.

Locke, E. A. (1976). The nature and causes of job satisfaction. In M. D. Dunnette (Ed.), *Handbook of industrial and organizational psychology* (1st ed., pp. 1297–1349). Chicago: Rand McNally. This classic chapter on job satisfaction provides a very thorough review. The information presented here is still important and relevant today.

Meyer, J. P., & Allen, N. J. (1997). *Commitment in the workplace: Theory, research, and application.* Thousand Oaks, CA: Sage. Now that the three-component model has emerged as the leader in the field, I recommend this well-written and comprehensive book for its review of the commitment literature and suggestions for future research.

Lord, R. G., Klimoski, R. J., & Kanfer, R. (Eds.). (2002). *Emotions in the workplace: Understanding the structure and role of emotions in organizational behavior.* San Francisco: Jossey-Bass. A hallmark piece of scholarship written by top-notch researchers and theoreticians that summarizes what we know and don't know about emotions in the workplace.

Stress and Worker Well-Being

11

CHAPTER OUTLINE

Has something like this ever happened to you? You wake up in the morning and just don't feel right. You get out of bed and notice that you have a little headache. After your shower, you sit down to eat breakfast with the morning newspaper and notice that you can't seem to finish an article—your mind keeps wandering. Before leaving for the office you pull out your daily calendar and realize (actually, you knew this all along!) that your day includes: a meeting with a supervisor who usually asks to see you only when she has a problem with your work; a meeting with a disgruntled subordinate who thinks he should have been promoted and who you think should be fired; about four hours of administrative paperwork; a sexual harassment training session because your department has been guilty of some serious violations in this area; and an appointment with a few executives from the home office you need to show around the office and socialize with.

Or how about something like this? After waking with a headache, probably the result of staying up until 3 A.M. studying for two final exams that happen to fall on the same day, you go downstairs for some breakfast but find that there's no cereal and no milk. You gobble down your Pop-Tart while looking over your notes for your psych exam—and suddenly realize that you never got the notes for the day you missed for your grandmother's funeral. After unsuccessfully trying to call a couple of friends in the hopes of catching a quick glimpse of their notes, you go back to studying and get frustrated because you just can't seem to remember all the definitions that are likely to be on the exam. Finally, you grab your backpack and head out for the bus. As you close the door behind you and step onto the porch, your foot sinks about 8 inches into snow that you hadn't even realized had fallen overnight. It's almost 9 A.M., and you realize that if the bus doesn't come on time, you will be late for the 10 A.M. exam and your psych prof makes no exceptions for makeups or tardiness.

Both of these situations involve stress—a word that we throw around a great deal. In fact, we all know what stress is when we feel it. In this chapter I will define stress in a more formal way and discuss stress as it relates to work. In addition, I consider some modifications that organizations are making to reduce the stress that is so prevalent in today's workplaces. The chapter concludes by focusing on one of the most terrifying outcomes of excessive stress—workplace violence.

LEARNING OBJECTIVES

This chapter should help you understand:

- the difference between stress and strains.
- why so many Americans are "working scared" and how best to deal with this situation.
- how coping skills help individuals to handle stress.
- what Warr's environmental determinants of well-being are.
- many of the important issues that are involved in work-family conflict.

- the importance of family-friendly employee benefits.
- the ways in which companies are helping employees balance their work and family lives with as little stress as possible.
- the particular complexities faced by dual-earner couples.
- why job loss is one of the most severe sources of stress that individuals ever experience.
- the factors that trigger workplace violence in the United States today.

STRESS AND STRAINS

stress
Any force that pushes a psychological or physical function beyond its range of stability, producing a strain within the individual.

strains
Undesirable personal outcomes resulting from the combined stressful experiences of various life domains.

Stress refers to any force that pushes a psychological or physical function beyond its range of stability, producing a strain within the individual (Cartwright & Cooper, 1997). In other words, we experience stress when we feel "stretched too thin." The two scenarios that began this chapter presented many examples of stressful events and elements, such as multiple meetings in one day, missing class notes, and so on. **Strains,** on the other hand, are undesirable personal outcomes resulting from the combined stressful experiences of various life domains (Bhagat, Allie, & Ford, 1995). In other words, stress leads to strains. Employees who are particularly stressed at work may experience sickness, low-quality performance, increased absence, poor communication, and many other strains.

STRESS

There are many models of workplace stress. Each has unique elements, but most share several elements as well. Figure 11.1 was developed on the basis of two such models (see Bhagat et al., 1995; Cartwright & Cooper, 1997). Though not perfect, this figure presents a reasonable picture of the sources and outcomes of stress, along with two of the most important coping strategies. In particular, note that the sources of stress are categorized in ways that we have seen elsewhere in the book (e.g., in Chapter 10's discussion of job satisfaction). Intrinsic factors such as poor working conditions (e.g., low lighting, excessive noise and dirt, and poorly designed office space) tend to lead to perceived stress, as do long hours, excessive travel, work overload, lack of input into the decision processes at work, and lack of control over one's job. This last factor—lack of control—has been found to play an especially important role in employees' stress levels. According to Robert Karasek's (1990) demand-control model of stress, for example, stress is a function of the psychological demands of work and the amount of decision latitude (i.e., control) that employees are provided (see also Theorell & Karasek, 1996). Since the inception of this model, many studies have demonstrated links between

FIGURE 11.1 General Stress Model

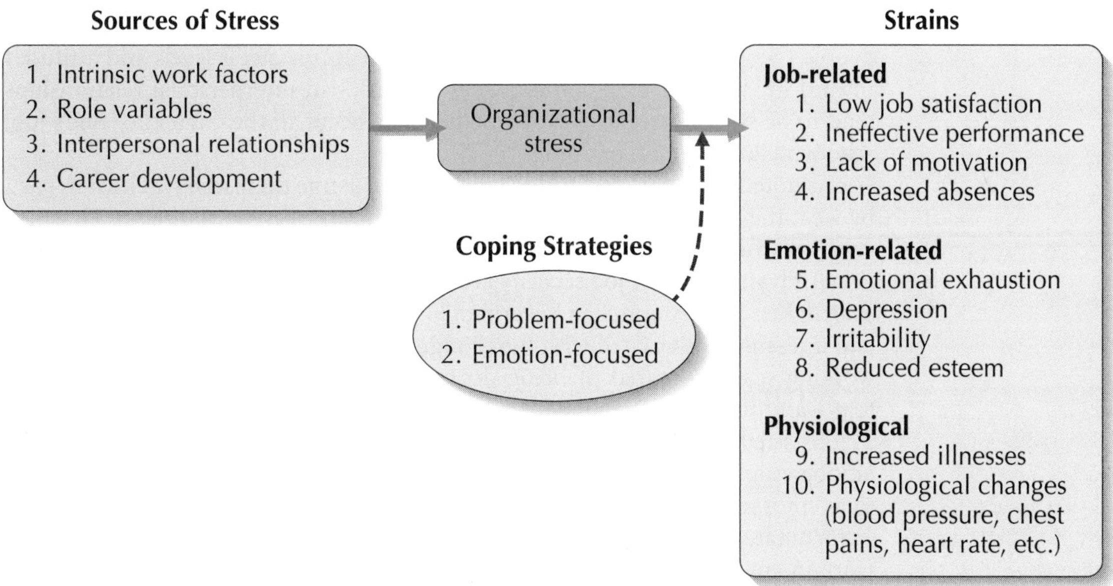

low levels of workplace control and psychological and physical problems such as coronary heart disease, depression, exhaustion, job dissatisfaction, stomach ailments, and absenteeism (reviewed in Karasek, 1990). For instance, a recent survey conducted by the Families and Work Institute (Galinsky, Kim, & Bond, 2001) discovered that employees who perceive a lack of control at work are much more likely to report feeling overworked, a situation that is linked to such various work and personal outcomes as making mistakes at work, feeling anger toward coworkers, increased work-life conflict, and disrupted sleep patterns.

Role variables are important as well. A **role** is a set of behaviors expected of a person who occupies a particular position in a group. **Role ambiguity** results when role expectations are unclear and employees are thus not sure what is expected of them. **Role conflict,** on the other hand, occurs when role expectations are inconsistent, as when a supervisor sends employees mixed messages about their roles. For instance, your boss might tell you to be creative and to take initiative—but when you do so, he says that you aren't following company policy. Alternatively, you may get conflicting messages about your role from two different people, such that your subordinate sees your role one way and your boss sees it another way. Needless to say, both role ambiguity and role conflict can lead to workplace stress.

Another source of stress has to do with interpersonal relationships at work. Employees who have bad relationships with their supervisors and their co-workers

role
A set of behaviors expected of a person who occupies a particular position in a group.

role ambiguity
A situation that results when role expectations are unclear and employees are thus not sure what is expected of them.

role conflict
A situation that results when role expectations are inconsistent, as when a supervisor sends employees mixed messages about their roles.

tend to be more stressed than individuals whose interpersonal relationships are more favorable. If you can recall a stressful job situation that you have experienced, it is likely that you can also recall relationships with your colleagues at that job that were contentious or lacking in trust. It has always been my belief that the people I work with actually have more to do with my stress levels and attitudes toward my job than the job itself does. Indeed, bad interpersonal relationships tend to be stressful regardless of whether they occur in the context of one's job, school, neighborhood, or family.

As noted in an earlier chapter, many people define themselves, at least in part, by what they do. Our jobs and careers are important parts of our lives. Thus it is very stressful to reach a point in one's career at which opportunities for additional advancement or job security are lacking. In their aptly titled book *Working Scared,* Ken Wexley and Stan Silverman (1993) argue that the stress, nervousness, and uneasiness associated with the changing nature of work have left many of us working scared—scared of being downsized, fired, or considered less competent—and thus more expendable—than younger and cheaper employees. Table 11.1 lists eight major areas of change in organizations that have given rise to stress among employees. Because they are sources of stress, these changes are referred to as *stressors* (Wexley & Silverman, 1993). It isn't fun to be working scared, but unfortunately many of us are. We have less supervision than we used to have, we work in environments in which doing more with less is expected of us, and we witness many of our co-workers being "let go" to save the bottom line. Table 11.1 also provides some suggestions for dealing with these stressors.

Strains

Strains are everywhere in the workplace. A partial list is presented in Figure 11.1, which groups them into three categories. First, there are the job-related strains. For instance, when you are employed in a job that creates a great deal of stress for you, you probably aren't either terribly satisfied with that job or motivated by it. Indeed, a lack of satisfaction and motivation often leads to low effort, high absenteeism, high turnover, and low productivity or ineffective performance (Cartwright & Cooper, 1997). Stress-related absence alone costs the U.S. economy many tens of billions of dollars each year (Warr, 1999).

burnout
A condition that occurs when employees become so stressed that they experience emotional exhaustion, depersonalization, and a sense of reduced personal accomplishment.

The second category of strains is emotional strains. Stress certainly takes a toll on us emotionally. One clear indicator that I'm stressed at work is that I have much less patience with my children and become irritable. After a particularly stressful day at work, when my kids act up (as five-, eight-, and eleven-year-olds tend to do), I am very quick to lose my temper and seem unable to understand that they are doing exactly what little children always do. Sometimes employees become so stressed that they experience **burnout,** a condition that is characterized by (1) *emotional exhaustion,* or being overextended by one's work; (2) *depersonalization,* or a cynical view of others and the work role that often results in

TABLE 11.1 21st-Century Organizational Changes (Stressors) That Lead to Stress

Organizational Change	Techniques for Dealing with These Stressors
1. Less Supervision: As organizations downsize and cut back, managers have more subordinates and have less time for each.	1a. Develop your own responsibilities and objectives. 1b. Seek high-quality feedback from co-workers, supervisors, and subordinates.
2. Team Culture: It's typical for employees today to work in a team environment, and being a team player can be difficult.	2a. Be prepared for and accept empowerment. 2b. Improve your communication skills.
3. Focus on Quality: Many employees are learning new methods and approaches to ensure that the organization is doing "quality" work.	3a. Don't wait for training—start learning on your own. 3b. Look for ways to improve your work—slowly, but steadily.
4. Downsizing: Organizations feel the need to get "lean and mean," leaving many employees without jobs and others as layoff survivors.	4a. Be aware of rumors, but don't let them overcome you. 4b. Work hard and creatively to prove your worth to the organization.
5. Mergers and Acquisitions: Companies are buying each other out, resulting in very different companies—a situation that affects employees.	5a. Learn as much as possible about the other company. 5b. Be prepared and receptive to organizational changes.
6. Diversity: As the workforce becomes more diverse, employees are working more with co-workers who have backgrounds different from theirs.	6a. Become more aware of your own values and prejudices. 6b. Consider the many benefits that come from diversity, including increasing productivity.
7. International Environment: Companies are becoming more international, and employees often find themselves working in a different culture.	7a. Be honest in considering whether an overseas assignment might work for you and your family. 7b. Expect six difficult months at first, with serious adjustments necessary on your part.
8. Innovative Pay Strategies: Employees are faced with different payment plans, such as gainsharing and bonuses.	8a. Understand the organization's new pay strategy. 8b. Ask for periodic performance reviews.

detachment; and (3) *reduced personal accomplishment*, or the belief that one is no longer very useful or successful at one's job. Burnout was originally believed to be limited to the helping professions, such as medicine and psychology (Cordes & Dougherty, 1993). More recently, however, it has been recognized as a more widespread phenomenon (Demerouti, Bakker, Nachreiner, & Schaufeli, 2001) and linked to characteristics of jobs (e.g., workload, control, rewards, social relationships, fairness, and values) rather than dispositions of people (Maslach, 2003). Work-related stress can be so overwhelming that some individuals lose a sense of themselves or begin to lack self-esteem. In cases of chronic high stress they may

Sometimes our own jobs can become overwhelming and even result in burnout.

even become depressed. These are all common elements of burnout. In addition to psychological problems such as lowered self-esteem and depression, burnout has been linked to physical health problems such as fatigue, insomnia, headaches, and gastrointestinal disorders (Cordes & Dougherty, 1993).

The third category of strains is physiological in nature. There is considerable evidence for the role of stress in physical conditions. One study, for instance, found both life stress and work stress to be significant predictors of the frequency of serious illnesses (Bhagat et al., 1995). In the United Kingdom alone, over 500 people die each day from heart disease (Cartwright & Cooper, 1997). Stress plays an integral role in heart disease, and workplace stress is a major culprit. Indeed, employees whose work is demanding but who have little control over the work are more likely than their counterparts to suffer from high blood pressure and other precipitating factors for coronary heart disease (Hasselhorn, Hammar, Alfredsson, Westerholm, & Theorell, 1998; Sleek, 1999).

In addition, there is substantial evidence that managers experience a great deal of stress and that this level of stress has been increasing in recent years (Cohen, 1997). A recent study of more than 800 upper-level managers reported some interesting results along these lines (Cavanaugh, Boswell, Roehling, & Boudreau, 2000). According to the researchers, stress is either *challenge related* or *hindrance related.* What they found is that challenge-related stress—which results from time pressures at work, high levels of responsibility, and job overload—is positively related to job satisfaction and negatively related to searching for a new job. In other words, stress related to being challenged at work has positive outcomes for the manager and for the organization. The researchers also found that hindrance-related stress—which results from constraints that interfere with one's work—are negatively related to job satisfaction and positively related to job searching and voluntary turnover. Hindrance-related stress is often due to red tape, organizational politics, and job insecurity. In fact, employees who reported high levels of hindrance-related stress tended to be much less satisfied than those who reported low levels of hindrance-related stress; they were also much more likely to search for new jobs and to leave their existing jobs (Cavanaugh et al., 2000). Clearly, these two types of stress have potentially important differential effects on outcome variables.

Coping with Stress

Stress is clearly a problem for many employees, but fortunately there are coping mechanisms to which they can turn. **Coping** is defined as efforts that help people manage or reduce stress. Some of these techniques are listed in Table 11.1. For instance, to deal with the stress that comes with being provided less supervision because of cutbacks in managerial positions, employees can develop their own responsibilities and objectives and seek high-quality feedback from co-workers, supervisors, and subordinates.

coping
Efforts that help people manage or reduce stress.

Coping mechanisms take two general forms: problem-focused coping and emotion-focused coping. **Problem-focused coping** is a coping style that involves behaviors or actions targeted toward solving or handling the stress-inducing problem itself. One example might be compromising with a co-worker with whom one is experiencing conflict. **Emotion-focused coping** on the other hand, involves cognitive or thought-related strategies that minimize the emotional effects of stress-inducing events. Examples of emotion-focused coping include rationalizing or intellectualizing, looking for the "silver lining," and making the best of a bad situation.

problem-focused coping
A coping style that involves behaviors or actions targeted toward solving or handling the stress-inducing problem itself.

emotion-focused coping
A coping style that involves cognitive or thought-related strategies that minimize the emotional effects of stress-inducing events.

One study indicates that work stress linked to serious illness can be moderated by problem-focused coping (Bhagat et al., 1995). In other words, among individuals who use problem-focused coping, stress is less likely to lead to serious illness. The same study found that although emotion-focused coping can be useful as well, it is not as successful in reducing stress levels or preventing stress from leading to strains. Another recent study suggests that the effectiveness of coping depends on the coping method, the particular stressor, and one's view of oneself (i.e., self-efficacy; Jex, Bliese, Buzzell, & Primeau, 2001). Finally, Fugate, Kinicki, and Scheck (2002) show the coping process to be very complex in situations in which employees have to adjust to an organizational merger over time.

In addition to coping styles, social support can play a huge role in helping us deal with stress. I'm sure that you have experienced this firsthand. It's always easier to handle stress-inducing events or situations if you have others around to provide the kind of support you need. In the workplace, for instance, credible senior-level employees or peers who make an effort to convince you that you can be successful at work may help you push through stressful situations and rise to the occasion. Quite a few studies have demonstrated the importance of social support in dealing with stress (e.g., Bliese & Britt, 2001; Zellars & Perrewe, 2001). Even family support can be instrumental to a low-stress experience at work. As I mentioned earlier, when I'm stressed I also become more irritable than usual, and this mood sometimes spills over into my personal life. But the other side of the coin is that I am often better able to deal with stress at work because of support from my family. For instance, it's hard for me to be stressed and to let that affect me very much when I go home and find three little boys ready to play and talk about their incredibly exciting days at school. Our personal lives can act as a buffer that helps us to reduce our stress and also to prevent the stress from leading to serious strains. Indeed, a recent meta-analysis (Viswesvaran, Sanchez, & Fisher, 1999) found that social support has a direct effect on strains by mitigating or preventing them and that it also affects the stress process by reducing stress levels and moderating the stress-strain relationship.

ENVIRONMENTAL DETERMINANTS OF WELL-BEING

As I pointed out in the first chapter of this book, employment is a central element of our lives. Certainly, there is some variability in the sense that some individuals are more apt than others to define and view themselves with respect to their jobs or occupations; but all in all, our work is important to most of us. In his research and writing, Peter Warr takes a very useful approach toward helping I/O psychologists gain an understanding about work processes. He has spent years developing his model of the environmental determinants of well-being (Warr, 1987; 1990) and has applied this model to job-related well-being, which is a function of people's feelings about themselves in relation to their jobs (Warr, 1999). Indeed, Warr argues that the workplace is central to mental health. His framework provides a way of further investigating how individuals interact with the workplace.

Warr's 10 environmental determinants of well-being are listed in Table 11.2. The more employees experience these determinants on the job, the less likely they are to experience negative well-being, which, according to Warr, is reflected in anxiety, displeasure, and depression rather than enthusiasm, pleasure, and comfort. Let's consider each of the determinants in turn. *Opportunity for personal control* refers to one's ability to control situations and events at work. We have talked in various chapters of this book (and earlier in this chapter) about the importance of participation, freedom to choose, and job autonomy. These are all consistent with Warr's notion of the importance of control. *Opportunity for skill use* is the extent to which employees are encouraged to use and develop skills. Not having

TABLE 11.2 Warr's Environmental Determinants of Well-Being

Environmental Determinants	Links to I/O Theory
1. Opportunity for personal control	Job characteristics theory
2. Opportunity for skill use	Job characteristics theory
3. Variety	Job characteristics theory
4. Environmental clarity	Job characteristics theory
5. Valued social position	Job characteristics theory
6. Externally generated goals	Intrinsic motivation and reinforcement theories
7. Availability of money	Intrinsic motivation and reinforcement theories
8. Physical security	Maslow's Hierarchy of Needs, ERG
9. Supportive supervision	
10. Opportunity for interpersonal contact	

the opportunity to develop their skills can be stifling for employees, resulting in a negative sense of well-being. Employees who enjoy *variety* at work don't do the same old thing each day but, rather, have an assortment of tasks and responsibilities. *Environmental clarity* has to do with whether employees have a clear understanding of current and future expectations, as reflected in the amount and quality of feedback that they receive at work. *Valued social position* is the extent to which employees gain prestige or sense of accomplishment from their work.

Do these first five determinants remind you of anything? They should send you back to Chapter 9, where we discussed job characteristics theory and talked about the effect of factors like feedback, autonomy, skill variety, task significance, and task identity on certain psychological states, which lead to outcomes such as job satisfaction, high motivation, and high work quality. In this sense, the work of Warr is consistent with job characteristics theory, which has received considerable attention in I/O psychology. Table 11.2 lists this theory and others in relation to each of Warr's environmental determinants.

Externally generated goals and the *availability of money* may be familiar from previous discussions about motivation. In this context, goals have to do with task demands; a job that requires very little from employees is not likely to be challenging or stimulating. And although having money doesn't guarantee positive well-being, not having what one considers to be enough money can result in a devastatingly negative sense of well-being. Much the same can be said about *physical security,* which has to do with working conditions and safety.

The last two determinants, *supportive supervision* and *opportunity for interpersonal contact,* deal with the social atmosphere at work. As discussed in previous chapters in the context of interpersonal relationships, having a boss who is understanding, supportive, and effective is quite important to employees' well-being, as are their opportunities for social interactions with peers, supervisors, subordinates, and customers.

Warr (1999) has reviewed dozens of empirical studies demonstrating the relevance of these factors to well-being in the workplace. For the most part, the more one's job provides these factors, the more positive one's well-being is likely to be. However, where some of these determinants are concerned, there may be a point at which more *isn't* better. For instance, employees tend to be favorably disposed toward jobs that demand a lot from them and provide a good deal of responsibility. However, too many demands and too much responsibility can easily result in overload, stress, and a negative sense of well-being. In fact, jobs that combine very high demands with very low opportunity for control tend to be extremely stressful. You can see how various combinations of these 10 determinants might have significant effects on an individual's well-being. Although Warr places considerable emphasis on the environmental (i.e., job-related) determinants of well-being, he also makes it clear that one's job environment and experiences are not wholly independent of other life experiences. We turn now to a discussion of the two most salient elements of individuals' lives, work and family, which appear to be quite closely linked.

WORK-FAMILY CONFLICT

Never before has the interplay between work and family been the focus of so much talk at work, at home, in the neighborhood, at churches, and, especially, in research labs across the United States (Allen, Herst, Bruck, & Sutton, 2000). In the last 20 to 30 years, the American family has undergone some significant changes that have had widespread impact on organizational life as well. In this section, I consider some of these changes and what they typically mean for today's employees who try so hard to successfully juggle their work and family responsibilities. According to one survey, the number-one priority for 78% of all employees is to successfully balance their work and personal lives (Gregg, 1998). Other surveys report that 42% of employees think that their work interferes with their personal lives, and 22% say that they can't have a good family life and still get ahead in their company (Gregg, 1998).

work-family conflict
A model of work-family relations in which work and family demands are incompatible

work-family enrichment
A model of work-family relations in which positive attitudes and behaviors are believed to carry over from one domain to the other.

Recent models of work-family conflict have begun to examine its bidirectional nature. In other words, family life affects work life, and work life affects family life. The model presented in Figure 11.2 clearly shows that both organizational and personal variables have an impact on work-family conflict and work-family enrichment, which have both organizational and personal outcomes. **Work-family conflict** exists when the two domains don't fit well together and results in one role having a negative effect on the other (Hammer, Cullen, Neal, Sinclair, & Ahafiro, in press). **Work-family enrichment** occurs when attitudes and

FIGURE 11.2 Conceptual Model of Work-Family Interface

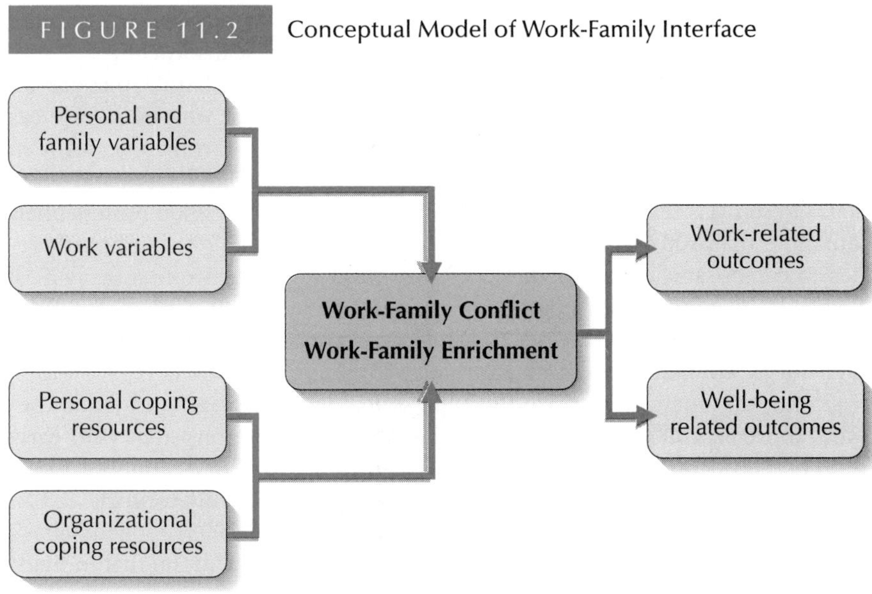

behaviors are believed to have a positive carryover from one domain to the other (Greenhaus & Powell, in press). Traditionally, this kind of approach was termed a *spillover model*. A different approach is taken by two other models: the *compensation model*, which suggests that the domains of work and family operate in a counterbalancing manner such that what is lacking in one domain can be emphasized or made up for by the other; and the *segmentation model*, which proposes that work and family issues are kept separate such that there isn't much overlap at all.

Considerable research support exists for the effects of work-family conflict on both personal and organizational outcomes. For instance, according to a large meta-analysis of research in this area, employees with high levels of work-family conflict tend to be less satisfied with their jobs ($r = -.31$) and their lives ($r = -.36$) than their low-conflict counterparts (Kossek & Ozeki, 1998). Further, the spillover was stronger for work-to-family conflict than for family-to-work conflict. A recent study of over 300 government employees found that values are also very important. For instance, when family is highly valued, work antecedents like time demands and role ambiguity have a more salient effect on work-to-family conflict and job satisfaction. The opposite pattern appears to hold for employees who value work as a central interest (Carlson & Kacmar, 2000). Recent research has found negative relationships between work-family conflict and variables such as family-related satisfaction and job performance (Wayne, Musisca, & Fleeson, 2004). As Mike Frone (2000) has reported on the basis of a national sample of over 2,700 employees, both work-to-family conflict and family-to-work conflict are positively related to mood, anxiety, and substance abuse disorders.

The common belief has always been that women give their family roles greater priority than do men, even when individuals are compared who both have careers outside the home. It follows that career satisfaction of women versus men should be more affected by work-family conflict. Martins, Eddleston, and Veiga (2002) found this to be the case in their survey of more than 1,000 professionals from more than 100 organizations: Work-family conflict was not significantly related to career satisfaction for men ($r = -.07$), but it was for women ($r = -.23$). Further, they found that this pattern held up for women at all ages, but for older men work-family conflict became more important. That is, for men over 40, work-family conflict was significantly related to career satisfaction ($r = -.26$), suggesting that men reprioritize their life domains as they age, and family becomes more central. The authors note that this finding is consistent with early theoretical work suggesting that men are less willing to sacrifice family relationships later in their lives and thus are less tolerant of work-family conflict.

In another interesting study, Baltes and Heydens-Gahir (2003) applied Baltes's *life management theory* to work-family conflict. Basically, they found that individuals who identify and set goals, who develop and refine strategies for achieving those goals, and who are flexible enough to employ alternative approaches when the initial targeted approach isn't working both perceive less job and work stress and report low levels of work-family conflict.

Earlier, I discussed the importance of social support in relieving stress; this seems particularly important with respect to work-family conflict. A recent study that surveyed over 400 government employees who were married and/or had children at home (Carlson & Perrewe, 1999) found that social support lowered the stress levels of these employees by reducing the likelihood that they would even notice the role stress and time demands in their environment. In other words, individuals who develop strong social support networks at work and at home perceive less stress in both their organizational and family lives (Carlson & Perrewe, 1999).

It seems that work-family research has traditionally focused on work-family conflict, but experts in this area have become increasingly aware that to understand work-family dynamics requires more research on work-family enrichment (Hammer et al., in press). Although not much research has examined work-family enrichment yet (Greenhaus & Powell, in press), we do know that it is positively related to physical and mental health, as well as to job and family satisfaction, and negatively related to problem drinking and depression (see Hanson, Hammer & Colton, 2004, for similar results and the validation of a new measure of work-family enrichment).

According to a 1997 Families and Work Institute report based on a study of more than 3,000 workers, addressing work-family issues keeps employees happy (Gregg, 1998). Ellen Galinsky, the institute's president and coauthor of the report, says it best: "Demanding and hectic jobs lead to negative spillover into workers' personal lives, jeopardizing their personal and family well-being. And when workers feel burned-out by their jobs, when they don't have the time and energy for their families, these feelings spill back into the workplace, reducing job performance" (quoted in Gregg, 1998). In a recent special issue of the *International Journal of Stress and Management*, O'Driscoll et al. (2003) found that organizational and supervisory support for family life were related to key stress and strain variables, suggesting an important role for family-friendly policies in organizations.

Many companies offer family-friendly programs, or what are often called *work-life supports* (Sahibzada, Hammer, Neal, & Kuang, in press) to alleviate some of the stress experienced by workers. Table 11.3 provides a list of some of these programs. Although great progress has been made in this area over the past 20 years, some of the results from the Families and Work Institute's 1998 Business Work-Life Study may be surprising with respect to the frequency with which

TABLE 11.3 Work-Life Supports Offered by Organizations

Traditional Benefits	Nontraditional Benefits
1. Child-Care Benefits • on-site child-care centers • informational assistance • financial assistance • sick-child care	1. Convenience Benefits • on-site physicians, dry cleaning, postal services, etc. • take-home meals • preferred banking
2. Elder-Care Benefits • counseling • informational assistance • geriatric care management • financial assistance	2. Health Promotion Benefits • on-site fitness centers • health screening • flu shots • counseling services
3. Flexible Work Arrangements • flextime • part-time options • job-sharing • telecommuting	3. Education Assistance Benefits • tutoring • tuition reimbursement • scholarships • student loan assistance
4. Leave/Time-Off Policies • maternity leaves • family and medical leaves • parental leaves • educational leaves	4. Housing Assistance Programs • relocation programs • seminars • home-purchase savings accounts • preferred mortgage arrangements
	5. Group Purchase Programs • discounts at local merchants • auto-purchase arrangements • group auto and home insurance

PRACTITIONER FORUM

E. JEFFREY HILL

Ph.D., Family and Human Development, 1995, Utah State University
Consultant, Work and Family Issues
IBM Global Workforce Diversity
Associate Professor, School of Family Life, Brigham Young University

I have worked at IBM for 26 years. When I started, "IBM" stood for "I've Been Moved." In one five-year stretch I had five different IBM jobs, and we lived in Washington, Utah, New York, Georgia, and Arizona. I traveled extensively and worked long hours.

I found myself becoming a casual occupant in our home. Sometimes the kids would still be asleep when I left for work in the morning and already be in bed by the time I returned. I missed birthdays, ball games, plays, concerts, recitals, and parent-teacher conferences. I began to worry that I was living to work instead of working to live.

In 1990 I was offered a promotion to do employee surveys for IBM. But the job was in New York, the commute horrendous, and the cost of living out of sight. Still, I hated to turn it down. In a moment of clear "outside-the-box" insight, I decided to accept the job with conditions. I reasoned with my future boss that I could better design surveys and analyze results through a modem from my home in the West than from an expensive office in the East. I told her that telecommuting was the wave of the future. To my surprise, she agreed to let me try it.

The difference in my life was immediate. Instantly I gained an hour and a half a day because I didn't have to drive to and from work. Instead of dragging into the office after a "fast-lane" commute, I could roll out of bed early with an exciting idea and immediately type it into the laptop. So what if I was still in my pajamas?! A little later I would get the kids up and together we ate breakfast.

I became more focused, energized, and productive at work. Without the constant interruptions of co-workers, I was able to deliver higher-quality surveys and analyses in less time. My manager made the comment, "He does the work of two people." The arrangement worked so well that soon four of my colleagues were working from home as well.

In the mid-1990s, IBM began to implement what was called the "virtual office" in a big way. Soon 25,000 IBMers no longer had dedicated IBM offices but were given laptops, cell phones, and pagers. They could work wherever and whenever it made sense: from home, a customer location, a hotel, or at IBM. To my delight, I was given the assignment to research telecommuting.

Controlled research findings were similar to my personal experience. On the work side, telecommuting at IBM was associated with increased productivity, higher morale, greater organizational commitment, and better customer relationships. The only negative was that telecommuters had more difficulty establishing close-knit relationships with their co-workers.

On the family side, telecommuting was found to have a positive influence on family relationships and well-being. Many telecommuters reported that they were thriving because the flexibility of the virtual office enabled them to be more involved in family life and helped them to take care of family needs.

Sure, it's true that telecommuting works better in some jobs than others. But for me and thousands of telecommuters I have studied at IBM and in other companies, the flexibility alluded to in this chapter has been a positive step toward resolving work-family conflict.

Let me close with my real-life telecommuting story, an abbreviated version of which appeared in *Reader's Digest* in January 1998:

Working from home is not without its difficult moments. I was recording my daily voice-mail greeting from my home office in the basement. Across the hallway my wife, Juanita, was folding clothes in the laundry room. My six-year-old daughter Emily had just taken a bath, couldn't find the clothes she wanted in her bedroom, and so came downstairs to the laundry room wrapped in just a towel. When my wife saw Emily, she exclaimed something about Emily's lack of clothing. After several colleagues and co-workers left funny messages suggesting that I listen to my voice-mail greeting, I did so, and this is what I heard:

Male voice: This is Jeff Hill with IBM Global Employee Research.

Giggly female voice in background: Look at you! You have no clothes on!

Male voice: I'm not available right now. . . .

APPLYING YOUR KNOWLEDGE

1. Discuss Dr. Hill's experience of telecommuting in the context of the benefits described in this chapter.
2. Why is schedule flexibility so important to workers in the 21st century?
3. What are the potential long-term benefits of telecommuting for IBM (or any other company)?

these programs are provided by employers. For instance, (1) 36% of the employees surveyed reported having access to dependent-care benefits such as referrals and other information regarding child care, (2) 23% reported elder-care services, (3) only 9% reported having access to child-care services on or near the worksite, and (4) 56% reported having access to an Employee Assistance Program to help employees deal with problems affecting their work or personal lives. The most popular work-family benefit appears to revolve around flexible scheduling. For instance, 88% of the employees report being given time off from work to attend school functions, 68% report that traditional flextime work schedules are allowed, and over 50% report being allowed to work from home occasionally. Another recent survey from a Washington, D.C.–based think tank (Employment Policy Foundation) reported that 15% of the workforce works from home at least one day per week. Forty percent of the teleworkers reported that they were more productive working from home than they were working from the office, and 30% estimated productivity to be about the same (Robinson, 2004). See the "Practitioner Forum" for an interesting example of the importance of flexible scheduling at IBM.

Additional examples of work-family programs are provided in a recent article about what some companies are doing to help employees deal with some of the stressors that arise from work-family issues (Lobel & Faught, 1996) and how valuable the companies believe these programs are. First, work-family programs benefit the organizations that provide them. Corning, the glassware manufacturer, reported a reduction in the turnover of female employees from 16.2% to 7.6% after three years of intensive work-family and diversity programming. PCA International, a color-photography company, reported that parents using their on-site child-care center had a 25% lower turnover rate than those who did not use the site. And Lotus, the software manufacturer, reported a 4–5% turnover rate for users of their on-site child-care center—a rate that is considerably lower than the industry turnover rate of 18%. Second, high-performing employees tend to respond favorably to family-friendly benefits. At IBM, high-performing employees ranked work-family programs second in importance, after compensation, as a factor contributing to their desire to stay with the company; IBM employees in general ranked it fifth. . Highest-performing Johnson & Johnson employees also used and reported liking family programs more than other employees did. Finally, Corning found that usage of work-family programs was correlated with high job performance.

Let's look at a few particularly innovative programs that, at a minimum, should prevent the circumstances depicted in the Dilbert cartoon on page 336. The first of these, at PepsiCo, is a concierge service to help employees run errands (lining up a babysitter, getting an oil change, etc.). PepsiCo believes it has a more focused workforce because employees can concentrate on their work instead of worrying about many of the little things that can lead to distractions at work (Sladek, 1995). Second, Goodyear offers an on-site physician, an on-site fitness center, a go-cart track, an 18-hole golf course, a stocked fishing lake, a jogging trail, and archery and shooting ranges. And third, Rhone-Poulenc Rorer provides

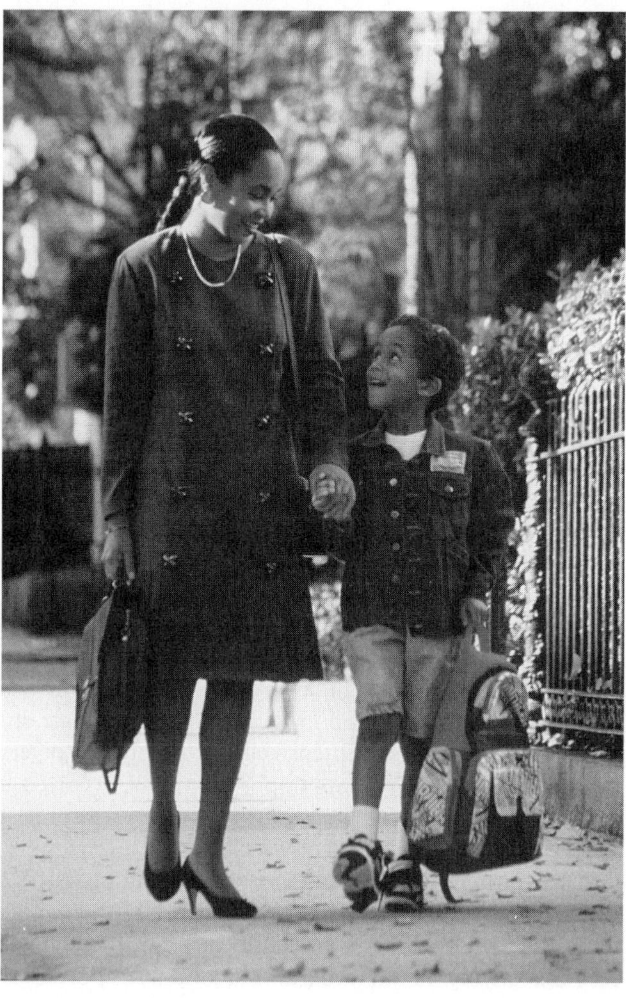

A growing number of 21st-century workers juggle work and family responsibilities.

Certainly, most managers have a better handle on the importance of work-family issues than Dilbert's boss does.

on-site services like shoe repair, dry cleaning, car servicing, jewelry repair, take-home meals, and a 400-square-foot company store on the assumption that employees will stay at work longer if they don't need to rush out to run errands (Sladek, 1995).

We now turn to a more detailed discussion of three work-family supports that are being more frequently offered by organizations.

Family-Leave Policies

As we discussed in Chapter 7, the first piece of legislation passed by President Clinton was the Family and Medical Leave Act (FMLA), which allows eligible employees to take job-protected, unpaid leave for up to 12 weeks because of family-related issues such as the birth of a child, serious health conditions of a family member, or one's own serious health condition. The United States is actually a late arrival in this respect; many other countries have had formal family-leave programs and laws in place for over 30 years. Nevertheless, many U.S. companies provided some form of family leave to their employees before it was mandated by law; indeed, many states have had family-leave policies for state employees since 1978. New York State, for instance, had a family sick leave policy in place before the FMLA was enacted in 1993. A recent evaluation of the frequency and pattern of leaves taken by New York State employees provides some interesting information (Kim, 1998). First, over 4,000 state employees took leave under the FMLA between 1994 and 1996. Second, the largest age group taking advantage of this program comprised those between 18 and 34, and 87% of these were women. Obviously, childbirth and child rearing were partially driving these figures. Third, when asked their reason for taking leave, 74% of employees (both male and female) specified personal health. Finally, women took leave for childbirth and care of family members 22% of the time, compared with only 4% of the time among men.

Hungary and Sweden first introduced parental leave in 1967 and 1974, respectively. **Parental leave** was developed to enable employees to combine work and family responsibilities related to child rearing; many countries provide for this type of leave for children up to the age of 3 and, in some cases, until school age (Anonymous, 1997). Belgium has a rather distinctive program: Employees can take a *career break,* with an allowance payable by unemployment insurance, provided that the employer hires an unemployed person to replace the worker on leave.

parental leave
A program offered by organizations that enables employees to combine work and family responsibilities related to child rearing.

Although family-leave programs can provide great relief for many employees for whom juggling family and work responsibilities is a major priority and an increasingly complex task, such programs are not without their problems. About 40% of employees taking advantage of the FMLA are forced to cut their leave short because they can't afford to go without pay during the entire leave—and 25% actually borrow money to make ends meet. Some experts in this area are advocating making family leave affordable for the majority of workers who cannot utilize it in its current form. Somewhat like the Belgian system just discussed is the Family Income to Respond to Significant Transitions Insurance Act (FIRST, 2001), drafted by Senator Chris Dodd (D-CT). FIRST would provide six months of paid leave (as opposed to 12 unpaid weeks), and funding would rely on disability insurance or unemployment insurance (Schroeder, 1999). The latest rendition of this bill, called the Family and Medical Leave Expansion Act, was introduced on February 5, 2003, but has yet to be written into law ("Murray Marks a Decade," 2004). Of course, many foresee this kind of law as resulting in huge unemployment costs to employers. More generally, however, we should all keep our eyes open for potential developments in this area, as changes to existing family-leave laws are certainly possible.

Child-Care Benefits

If you have children and work outside the home, then you know how frustrating it can be to balance your work responsibilities with the care that you want to provide for your kids. Many studies have linked child-care difficulties not only to employee absenteeism, tardiness, productivity, and leaving work early but also to indirect effects on co-workers' productivity (e.g., Erickson, Nichols, & Ritter, 2000; Tetrick, Miles, Marcil, & Van Dose, 1994). In fact, a general conclusion is that an employee who fills the dual role of full-time employee and parent (i.e., who has a child under 18 living at home) tends to experience lower psychological well-being, decreased life and marital satisfaction, and increased work-family conflict (Sahibzada et al., in press). Given the effect of child-care problems on employee morale, productivity, and well-being, many companies have begun to give serious attention to child-care benefits and other child-care programming.

Four of these child-care benefits are listed in Table 11.3. Some organizations provide resources that help employees become aware of other child-care facilities in the area. They may also provide some financial assistance to employees to help cover the high costs of child care. But perhaps the most interesting benefit is the on-site child-care center, which has begun to receive some empirical examination. In a survey of employees who worked at hospitals with on-site child-care centers, Ellen Kossek and Victor Nichol (1992) found that employees who were active users of the on-site center were more likely to believe that the center was a good recruitment and retention tool for the company than were those who were not actively using the center. Also, those using the center held more positive attitudes toward managing their work and family responsibilities than did those who weren't using the center. Finally, the study suggested that the on-site center was especially valuable for employees who did not have adequate family resources to care for their children (e.g., those who didn't have assistance from family members). Other studies, too, have found increased organizational commitment and job satisfaction among employees who have access to an on-site child-care center (for a review, see Grover & Crooker, 1995). For example, according to a recent

Child care has become a very important issue as the increase in dual-earner couples continues. Some companies have even developed on-site child-care centers for their employees.

survey of individuals employed by two companies with on-site child-care centers (Rothausen, Gonzalez, Clarke, & O'Dell, 1998), current, future, and past users of the centers had more positive reactions to the center than did nonusers. In particular, they were more likely than nonusers to report that the centers were associated with recruitment and retention benefits and that they were pleased with the company's support of the centers.

Although the studies just discussed provide some convincing evidence of the positive role played by on-site child-care centers, they also suggest a potential "backlash" on the part of those who aren't using the centers. Kossek and Nichol (1992) present data suggesting the existence of this backlash. An organization called "The Childfree Network," an advocacy group of approximately 5,000 members, was founded in 1992 and is a manifestation of the resentment felt by some employees who don't have children and feel that organizations are spending too much money and attention on those who do (Parker & Allen, 2001; Rothausen et al., 1998). Indeed, childless workers are increasingly expressing the feeling of being second-class citizens and complaining that, compared to employees with children, they are asked to work and travel more, are transferred more, and are less likely to be granted flexible schedules (Picard, 1997). Some of these employees have urged companies to change their focus from work-family issues to work-life issues and to include policies and benefits that go beyond family life per se, such as convenience benefits, health promotion benefits, and education assistance. Many companies are now carefully considering how best to make all of this work so that no group of employees feels alienated or discriminated against. Among these companies are Marriott, Corning, Quaker Oats, and Eastman Kodak, which have made the transition to nontraditional work-life benefits in place of traditional work-family ones (Picard, 1997). Examples of these nontraditional benefits are listed on the right side of Table 11.3.

Elder-Care Assistance

Some might say that child care was the family-friendly emphasis of the 1980s and 1990s (Perry-Jenkins, Repetti, & Crouter, 2000), but for the first few decades of the 21st century, the emphasis will most certainly be on elder care. According to a major study by the National Alliance for Caregiving and the American Association of Retired Persons (AARP), there are 22.4 million U.S. households providing caregiving to elderly relatives or friends. Here is the typical profile of a caregiver: a 46-year-old employed woman who spends about 18 hours per week caring for her mother who lives nearby. Her mother is 77 years old, lives alone, and has a chronic illness (Timmermann, 1999). Seventy-two percent of caregivers are women, and over 60% of the caregivers work full time. Even more problematic is the fact that 41% of these caregivers are caring for children under 18 at the same time they are caring for their elderly parent! The members of this generation of baby boomers (born between 1946 and 1964) have been labeled the *sandwiched generation* because they are providing care to both their children and their parents—and often feel stuck in the middle. Obviously, financing child care and elder care at the same time can be extremely costly, and the enormous stress these caregivers experience often results in health problems.

The statistics are amazing. The U.S. Census Bureau projects that there will be 39.4 million Americans over 65 by 2010 and over 70 million by 2030—doubling in the 30 years between 2000 and 2030 (Seaward, 1999). Further, the fastest-growing subpopulation of elderly comprises people over 75, who are the most likely to need caregiving services. Given these demographics, employers have begun to respond to elder-care needs; according to one estimate, over 50% of employers now offer some form of elder-care services, up from 40% in 1998 (Gonzalez, 2004). As more and more employers begin to recognize the importance of elder-care benefits to employees and to the organizations themselves, this percentage should increase considerably (much as the percentage of child-care programs has done). Some recent data are likely to motivate employers to move quickly in this direction: The MetLife Study of Employer Costs for Working Caregivers has found that caregiving responsibilities result in lost productivity to U.S. businesses on the order of at least $11.4 billion per year. Other estimates range as high as $29 billion per year, depending on what costs are included (Timmermann, 1999); according to one study, companies lose $3,142 per year for each worker who has elder-care responsibilities (Pearson, 1999), and caring for elderly parents from afar costs companies 15 million work days per year, according to the National Council on

Aging (Gonzalez, 2004). The major costs include replacement costs for employees who quit as a result of caregiving responsibilities, absenteeism costs, costs due to workday interruptions, costs due to elder-care crises and emergencies, and costs associated with supervising employed caregivers (Boles, 1997).

The most prevalent elder-care services offered by organizations are resource and informational assistance, dependent-care accounts, seminars, counseling, and long-term insurance. Some employers have begun reimbursing their employees for elder-care expenses, with a limit on the funds provided, and certain large companies have even established on-site intergenerational day-care centers. Perhaps the fastest growing benefit is geriatric care management, in which the employer provides certified professionals to go to an elderly person's home and assess his or her well-being and specific needs. Further, the professional may also provide an on-site review of an elder-care facility for the employee (Gonzalez, 2004). Experts who work in the areas of family-friendly benefits and elder care argue that caregiving for the elderly directly affects employees' performance, causing them to report late for work, to work fewer hours, and, sometimes, to resign or retire early (Seaward, 1999). Of the 22.4 million individuals who indicated on the AARP survey that they were providing care to an older parent or friend, about half reported that they took time off, came in late, and worked fewer hours because of their caregiving responsibilities. Conversely, employees who don't have to worry about caring for an elderly individual are more satisfied with their jobs, as well as more productive (Seaward, 1999). According to Ceridian Corporation, the largest dependent-care resource provider, 16% of employee caregivers leave the workforce to provide full-time care (Gonzalez, 2004).

Empirical work has indeed begun to examine the impact of elder-care responsibilities on workplace functioning. For example, a comprehensive survey was administered to over 400 employees from various organizations across the United States in an attempt to examine organizational responses to employees' growing elder-care concerns (Goodstein, 1995). Among its interesting findings were the following. First, the more female employees there were in the organization, the more likely the company was to be involved in elder-care issues. Second, the more work-family benefits the organization provided, the more likely the organization was to provide elder-care benefits as well. Third, the more the company perceived that elder-care benefits improve productivity, the higher the level of company involvement in elder care was. Fourth, and perhaps most interesting, the more the company worked with other companies that emphasized work-family issues, the more likely the company was to become involved in elder care. This last finding suggests that an organization is somewhat affected by the values, attitudes, and benefits associated with its clients and business partners.

A second study surveyed more than 60 employees from three different companies in the Midwest, all of whom were currently caring for an elderly dependent (Kossek, DeMarr, Backman, & Kollar, 1993). Some interesting results emerged here as well. First, the more problems that employees had arranging for the care of their elderly dependent, the more days they were absent from work.

Second, the more frustrating they found their elder-care responsibilities to be, the higher their absenteeism rate was. Finally, those employees most likely to be negatively affected by elder-care responsibilities were women, single parents or dual-career parents, employees who used paid care in the home, and employees whose parents lived with them. These survey results led the authors to conclude that the most important thing a company can do to help employees is to be flexible when elder-care problems arise. This includes flexibility in terms of work schedules, absence policies, and deadlines.

Dual-Earner Couples

dual-earner couples
Couples in which both members are employed and maintain a family life.

We turn now to a discussion of dual-earner couples, a recent trend in the world of work that is clearly and logically linked to work-family conflict. **Dual-earner couples** refers to couples in which both members are employed and maintain a family life. In this section, we have been talking about the changing nature of work and the demographic characteristics of the current labor force. Let's add a few more statistics to the mix. In 1994, 75% of all women between the ages of 25 and 54 were in the U.S. labor force, and 70% of those in this age category had children under the age of 18 (U.S. Bureau of Labor Statistics, 1995). In 1996, the percentage of married couples who both worked was more than 60%; today it is 78% (Bond, Thompson, Galinsky, & Prottas, 2002). In 1997, according to the Census Bureau, only 17% of U.S. households conformed to the traditional model of a dad who brought home the wages and a mom who stayed home and took care of the kids. Currently, dual-earner couples constitute over 45% of the labor force (Kate, 1998). A survey by Catalyst, a research group that focuses on working women, found that 85% of the respondents listed increased income as the biggest advantage of a dual-earner situation and that 56% noted that a lack of time was the biggest challenge (Kate, 1998). As one IBM executive put it: "Dual-career couples are telling us that they're not cash-poor. They're telling us, 'We make enough money, but we don't have time to spend it, because we're focused on our jobs and the demands of those jobs'" (Vogl & Budman, 1997).

In a recent interview in *Forbes* magazine, Ralph Gomory, president of the Sloan Foundation and former director of the research labs at IBM, provided an interesting take on the notion that everyone is working harder and putting in more hours: "It's not that one individual is working longer so much as that two people are now doing three jobs. In the past, one person did the working job and the other one brought up the family, took care of the home, built a social network or anything else you want to describe in that category. It was never recognized as a job. But it was" (Machan, 1999). In other words, the dual-earner couple has added a third job to what used to be only two—two jobs outside the home and one inside. Needless to say, this situation takes more effort and is more difficult. As for the job of taking care of the home and the kids, men still do less than their fair share—even when their wives are working full time. In 1977 American men spent a little over 1 hour per day doing household tasks; today they spend a little more than 2 hours per day. Women, on the other hand, average about 3 hours per day on chores (Ebenkamp, 1999). The disparity is much worse in Japan, where a government survey found that husbands in dual-earner families devote less than 8 minutes per day to housework, while their income-earning wives spend over 3 hours on domestic duties (Beck, 1998).

Although little academic research has focused on dual-earner couples in the past, interest has increased of late. One recent study, for instance, looked at the effects of work and nonwork influences on the career satisfaction of dual-earner couples in Hong Kong and found some interesting results (Aryee & Luk, 1996). First, work-related variables are better predictors of career satisfaction than nonwork-related variables. Among the predictors for both husbands and wives are supervisor support, the extent to which employees' skills are made the most of on the job, and the extent to which employees feel they are an important part of the organization. Second, the only nonwork-related variable that was important to both husbands and wives was satisfaction with child-care arrangements. Given the previous discussion about child-care benefits, this finding makes a great deal of sense. Third, and this surprised the authors, results for both husbands and wives were parallel. In other words, the same variables seemed to be important predictors of career satisfaction for both husbands and wives, indicating considerable agreement about what these partners see as integral to making their dual-earner situation successful.

A second recent study also surveyed dual-earner couples, but its focus was on predictors of marital satisfaction rather than career satisfaction (Mauno & Kinnunen, 1999). Recall that in a previous section we talked about spillover effects and how work-related stress can affect one's family life and vice versa. This study looked at the spillover of work to family with respect to dual-earner couples and found that job insecurity, time pressures at work, poor supervisor-subordinate relations, and work-family conflict affected marital satisfaction. These difficulties were experienced indirectly, however, through their effects on job exhaustion and psychosomatic symptoms like headaches and heart palpitations. In other words, husbands and wives who perceived a lack of job security, who worked under time pressure, who didn't get along with their supervisors, and who experienced work-family conflict in general tended to be tired at work and to report a greater tendency toward headaches and the like. When the stress associated with these various work elements was so severe as to result in exhaustion and psychosomatic symptoms, these individuals were also more likely to report lower levels of marital satisfaction. Moreover, the situation was exactly the same for men as for women—a finding that parallels the career satisfaction results just discussed. The authors of this study concluded that gender differences in work experiences, though still present, are diminishing.

Third, in a national sample of 234 sandwiched-generation dual-earner couples, Hammer et al. (in press) uncovered longitudinal crossover effects regarding both work-family conflict and work-family enrichment. Crossover effects refer to the transmission of stress, strain, and depression from one member of a couple to the other. For instance, they found that husbands' work-family enrichment (i.e., positive spillover) was negatively related to wives' depression 1 year later; a parallel effect was found from wives' family-work enrichment to husbands' depression. This is the first study highlighting the important role of a dyad members' positive spillover from work to family or family to work to the well-being of the other member of the dyad. The authors encourage future research on the marital dyad when examining work-family issues.

A fourth recent study has taken a different approach by surveying over 170 career-oriented college women in the United States about their expectations and desires regarding future careers and family life (Hallett & Gilbert, 1997). Participants were limited to those who reported that they envisioned themselves in a dual-career marriage. Based on their responses, the authors classified each student as expecting either a *conventional dual-career marriage,* in which the female maintains primary responsibility for the home and the children while simply adding a career to her responsibilities, or a *role-sharing dual-career marriage,* in which both spouses actively pursue careers and actively involve themselves in the household and parenting.

One interesting finding was that women who expected a role-sharing marriage were significantly more likely than their conventional counterparts to be committed to a lifelong, time-consuming career. They were also higher in self-esteem, suggesting that this attribute in these women allowed them to consider a less conventional option (Hallett & Gilbert, 1997). In addition, having a spouse who would involve himself in managing the household and parenting the children was more important to those women looking for a role-sharing marriage than to those looking for a more conventional dual-career relationship. The authors concluded that many college-educated women today are thinking about their futures in ways quite different from those of earlier generations. No longer must women choose between a career and a family; today's college-educated women believe that both are possible. Fortunately, many are leading the way in demonstrating how to make this work so that everyone involved can benefit.

I will wrap up this section on work-family conflict with a quote from Robert Haas, chairman of Levi Strauss:

> We used to think you could separate the soft stuff from the hard stuff—the soft stuff was our commitment to the workforce—and the hard stuff—what really mattered—was getting pants out the door. No more. Now we know you can't get stuff out the door unless your employees are 100% committed and free of home life distractions. And the way you get them there is simple. You do everything you can to help them handle those home life issues. So work and family can co-exist, successfully. (quoted in MacGregor, 1999)

I don't think it's much of a stretch to predict that the companies emerging as national and world leaders in the 21st century are likely to be the ones that subscribe to the simple but accurate reflections of Mr. Haas. In fact, a close look at the really top-drawer companies of today suggests that this is already happening. In *Fortune* magazine's "100 Best Companies to Work For," a list it publishes every year, its most important criterion is the extent to which these companies are helping employees to balance work and life issues (Levering & Moskowitz, 2000). Its list for the year 2000 includes some companies you will recognize: Starbucks, Qualcomm, J. M. Smucker, Microsoft, S. C. Johnson & Son, Federal Express, Amercian Express, Timberland, and Nordstrom (Levering & Moskowitz, 2005.)

PSYCHOLOGICAL EFFECTS OF JOB LOSS

You might recall that way back in Chapter 1, when I was highlighting the reasons for which I/O psychology is important and relevant to most of us, I focused on the fact that a large part of who we are is, in some way or another, tied to what we do. Remember when I described myself in the following way?

> My name is Paul Levy. I have been fortunate enough to be married to Sylvia Chinn-Levy for 16 years and have three terrific young boys named Christopher, Sean, and Jared. I am a psychology professor at The University of Akron, where I specialize in industrial/organizational psychology. I teach both undergraduate and graduate students and do research in the area of performance appraisal and feedback. I'm a big sports fan, coach youth sports, play basketball, and am a fanatic about the Baltimore Orioles.

In particular, I talked about how being a psychology professor is an integral part of who I am. It affects not only the way I live my life but also my perceptions, beliefs, and attitudes. Is the same true for you? Certainly, some of us identify with our occupation or job more than others; but I really believe that, for the overwhelming majority of us, our occupation is central to who we are. That said, it shouldn't be a surprise to learn that losing one's job is a profoundly stressful event. In fact, research has consistently found job loss to be among the 10 most stressful events in a person's life (Maysent & Spera, 1995). For some, it can be almost as stressful as the loss of a loved one.

Jobs are important to us for a variety of reasons. First, of course, they provide the financial means for living our lives in the manner that we desire. Second, they provide time structure to our day. They determine what time we get up, when we eat lunch, what we do in the afternoon, and when we are available to be home for dinner. If we were to suddenly lose our jobs, this structure would fall apart and leave us demotivated and without direction to our day (Cartwright & Cooper, 1997). Third, jobs provide us with an opportunity to use our existing skills and to develop new ones. Without this opportunity, people can become stagnant and bored. Fourth, for most of us, an important feature of our jobs is social interaction with people outside our family. Human beings are social animals, and we all need some degree of social interaction. Our jobs provide an opportunity to interact not only with people who have interests and skills in common but also with those who differ from us in these respects. In other words, at work we have the opportunity to interact with various kinds of people. Fifth, our jobs help provide a purpose to our lives—in the form of both short-term day-to-day goals and long-term goals regarding career development and advancement. A sense of purpose is crucial; without it, individuals can get stuck "spinning their wheels." Finally, we tend to get a sense of identity and even prestige from our jobs. Being a professor is important to me in part because it is a job that I value and a job that many others in society value—I am pleased with the prestige that goes with being a professor. I didn't choose this profession for that reason alone, of course; but the sense of identity that I receive from my job is very important for my sense of well-being.

The Hard Facts

Whether we call it "rightsizing," "downsizing," "layoffs," or "reductions in force," there's no denying that U.S. corporations have been reducing the size of their workforces at alarming rates since the late 1980s. From July 1989 to June 1990 alone, nearly 81,000 positions were eliminated in 1,219 U.S. corporations (Schwartz, 1990). Some of the most stable and reliable companies in the world—including United Airlines, DuPont, and General Electric—have laid off workers in record numbers. In the final months of 1998, Kodak, Woolworth, Citicorp, Fruit of the Loom, Montgomery Ward, and Levi Strauss also announced major reductions in force (Fisher & White, 2000), and Montgomery Ward finally went out of business, with all employees there losing their jobs. According to one estimate, over 43 million jobs were lost in the United States from 1979 to 1999 (McKinley, Zhao, & Rust, 2000). About 80,000 people lost their jobs because of layoffs in each month of 2004 (Weber, 2004). For instance, Maytag, the giant appliance maker, laid off over 1,100 employees due to slow sales in the first half of 2004 alone. Worse still, a recent study using a very large employment database has reported that U.S. workers are even more concerned about losing their jobs than the data suggest they should be—anxiety about job loss continues to rise (Rudisill & Edwards, 2002; Schmidt, 1999). Carol Wilson, a vice president of a firm specializing in employee assistance, says that when a layoff is announced in a company, 20% of the remaining employees leave the organization either physically or emotionally, and another 60% take a "wait and see approach" (Wilson, 2004).

The data presented here indicate that many employees are being laid off across all of the major industries of the United States and that employees are stressed about this fairly recent turn of events. In addition to those people who have become accustomed to having a job and are experiencing layoffs, there are individuals who tend to be more chronically unemployed. The bottom line is that many more Americans have to deal with the threat of being unemployed today than have had to in the recent past. Let's consider some empirical work that looks at the effect of unemployment on stress levels, as well as on attitudes and behaviors.

There are no "good ways" to lay off employees, but relying on an approach made famous by a series of recent TV shows is certainly a "bad way."

First, Sally Grant and Julian Barling (1994) tested a model in which they proposed that the subjective experience of unemployment leads to depression, which leads to negative interactions with one's spouse, which in turn leads to marital dissatisfaction. They found that unemployed individuals' perceptions of time use and negative life events were strong predictors of depressive symptoms. In other words, unemployed individuals who reported that their days were without much time structure and who reported frequent negative life events were also likely to report symptoms of depression such as a lack of desire to do anything at all and a belief that they were incapable of doing anything valuable. These depressive symptoms in turn predicted negative behaviors such as yelling at, becoming angry with, and being disrespectful toward one's spouse. And, finally, these negative behaviors directed toward one's spouse were strongly linked to marital dissatisfaction. This study demonstrates the indirect effects that unemployment can have on both behaviors toward one's spouse and marital satisfaction.

Second, in a recent study of employees who had lost their jobs as a result of a company closing, coping resources were examined as predictors of distress and reemployment (Gowan, Riordan, & Gatewood, 1999). The researchers operationalized problem-focused coping as job search activity and emotion-focused coping as distancing oneself from the job loss. Their results indicated that the more social support employees had, the better able they were to distance themselves from the job loss. Social support (along with lack of financial resources) also led to job search activities. But employees' ability to distance themselves from the job loss (measured by items like "I remind myself that other people have been in this situation and that I can probably do as well as they did") appeared to be the key variable, as it was negatively related to distress about the job loss and positively related to reemployment. This study suggests that although stress is likely to follow job loss (and, again, note that the participants were employees who had all recently lost their jobs because their company closed), coping strategies like getting distance from the event can help to alleviate the stress and make a new job more likely through more effective interview behavior and more reasonable decisions about job search activities (Gowan et al., 1999).

Third, a recent line of research has focused on the stress and pressure involved in being layoff survivors—that is, employees who have survived a layoff but who are left at the workplace to deal with its aftereffects. In a review of the literature in this area, it was reported that layoff survivors tend to be less productive, less trusting of the organization and supervisors, more angry and anxious about their futures, and more likely to suffer from low morale and low job satisfaction (Grunberg, Anderson-Connolly, & Greenberg, 2000). In addition, Joel Brockner and his colleagues, who have been leaders in the scientific study of layoff survivors, have reported that employees' perceptions of the fairness of the process, employees' organizational commitment levels prior to the layoff, and employees' levels of self-esteem affect how survivors respond to the layoffs (see Brockner, Wiesenfeld, & Martin, 1995; Wiesenfeld, Brockner, & Martin, 1999). In one of their more recent papers, Brockner and his colleagues examined *managers* as layoff survivors, giving careful consideration to procedural justice, organizational commitment, and ensuing managerial behavior (Wiesenfeld, Brockner, & Thibault, 2000). The results from the two studies reported in this paper indicated that managers (as opposed to nonmanagers) who perceive injustice in how layoffs are handled tend to report low self-esteem, which seems to be partly a function of their high levels of organizational commitment. They also exhibit less effective managerial behaviors than are necessary in times of organizational change and direct these less effective behaviors toward subordinates, who report a less supportive work environment. A series of recent studies has shown perceptions of justice to be very important in determining how employees respond to various organizational changes such as the violation of one's psychological contract and layoffs (Edwards, Rust, McKinley, & Moon, 2003; Kickul, Lester, & Finkl, 2002).

Environmental Determinants—Revisited

Let's close this section by returning briefly to Warr's environmental determinants of well-being (see Table 11.2). As you may recall, Warr argues that the more employees experience these determinants on the job, the more likely they are to experience positive well-being. Another way to look at the importance of work in our lives is to consider the potential effect that losing one's job has on each of these determinants, along with the more general effect of job loss on overall well-being.

First, work tends to provide people with *opportunity for control;* but when they lose their jobs they experience a considerable loss of control, which certainly affects their well-being. Second, job loss largely eliminates *opportunity for skill use,* causing some individuals to feel that their skills are being wasted. Third, we noted that *variety* was important and that doing the same old thing has a negative effect on job-related well-being. But when one's job is lost, doing the same old thing becomes more the norm than the exception and often involves unappealing activities like standing in unemployment lines and searching the newspaper for potential jobs. Fourth, *environmental clarity* helps employees define their roles, but without jobs, they lose all sense of their roles and lack environmental clarity altogether. Fifth, the sense of *valued social position* that employees derive from their jobs is damaged when they lose their jobs, thereby affecting their general sense of esteem and self-worth. Sixth, people without jobs tend to lose focus on their *externally generated goals;* because there are no demands placed on them by their jobs, supervisors, or organizations, they engage in little activity or achievement. Certainly, job security provides both the *availability of money* and *physical security,* the seventh and eighth factors in Warr's list; but when people lose their jobs, both are gone, creating anxiety-arousing circumstances that affect every facet of their lives. Ninth, *supportive supervision*—a form of social support—is obviously relinquished when a job is lost. The tenth and last determinant of job-related well-being is *opportunity for interpersonal contact*—one of the main benefits provided by a job. When employees lose their jobs, they are cut off from the outside world, or at least from a circle of people who were an important part of their lives. For some, a large void is left. For others, interpersonal contact is experienced through job-search behaviors, but the quality and depth of that contact pales by comparison to what used to occur at work.

I have reviewed these environmental determinants to demonstrate how significant job loss can be. When we look at Warr's model, what becomes quite clear is how much we actually receive or gain from our jobs. When we lose our jobs, we lose a great deal—more than any of us (including myself) can understand until it happens to us. The last area that needs to be covered in this chapter on stress stems in part from our discussion of how damaging job loss can be. In very extreme situations, it can even result in workplace violence.

WORKPLACE VIOLENCE

Violence in the workplace has become a very important topic to organizations, employees, and researchers. The trends are indeed staggering. Every year, nearly

1,000 workers are murdered and over a million are assaulted (Biles, 1999; see also Laurent, 1996). According to the U.S. Bureau of Labor Statistics, homicide is one of the leading causes of death among American employees. In 2003, 631 people were murdered at their places of employment (National Census of Fatal Occupational Injuries, 2003). About 20 employees are murdered each week while working or on duty (LeBlanc & Kelloway, 2002). Of the 6,218 fatal work injuries in the United States in 1997, 856 (14%) were homicides. Retail sales workers are the most frequently assaulted or threatened; indeed, job-related homicides in retail account for almost half of all workplace homicides (many of which occur during robberies).

In July 1993, Northwestern National Life Insurance Company conducted the first comprehensive assessment of fear and violence in the workplace. It surveyed 600 full-time American workers and, in generalizing these data to the U.S. workforce as a whole, uncovered some startling facts. First, during the preceding 12-month period, more than 2 million American workers were victims of physical attacks, 6 million were threatened, and 16 million were harassed (Northwestern National Life, 1993). This amounts to one out of every four full-time U.S. workers between July 1992 and July 1993. Of those individuals who reported being attacked, almost 80% were affected psychologically, 40% found their work lives disrupted by the experience, and 28% were physically injured or sick as a result of the attack. A strong relationship between job stress and workplace violence was also found. Employees whose companies had effective grievance, harassment, and security programs reported lower levels of job dissatisfaction, lower burnout rates, and lower levels of stress-related illnesses than those whose companies did not have such programs (Northwestern National Life, 1993). The National Institute for Occupational Safety and Health (NIOSH) lists the following risk factors for the likelihood of being assaulted at work (Biles, 1999):

- Contact with the public
- Exchange of money
- Delivery of passengers, goods, and services
- Having a mobile workplace (e.g., taxicab or police cruiser)
- Working with unstable persons (e.g., health care, social services, criminal justice settings)
- Working alone or in small numbers

A recent study developed and validated a measure for identifying the risk for workplace violence by focusing on 28 different job characteristics that have been reported in the literature as being related to workplace violence (LeBlanc & Kelloway, 2002). Along with those characteristics listed by NIOSH, this new measure asks about whether the job involves: serving alcohol, the emotional/physical care of others, disciplining others, handling weapons, and making decisions that influence other people's lives. The study reported significant correlations between 22 of the job characteristics and reports of violence. Further, they found that the new scale was more strongly related to violence from individuals outside the or-

In the movie *Falling Down,* Michael Douglas plays a worker so frustrated with his job that he becomes quite violent.

ganization (e.g., customers) than from those inside the organization (e.g., employees). Other research has shown that most violence at work is initiated by what are called "organizational outsiders" rather than "organizational insiders" (LeBlanc & Barling, 2004). Finally, LeBlanc and Barling (2004) make it clear that even though insider-initiated violence is not as frequent (nor, usually, as deadly) as outsider-initiated violence, it still frequently occurs and has devastating effects for its victims.

Interest in workplace violence has taken off only in the past 20 years. In fact, prior to the events in Edmund, Oklahoma, in 1986, most Americans weren't even aware of the potential impact of workplace violence. It was at the Edmund Post Office that Patrick Sherrill went on a rampage that resulted in the death of 14 of his co-workers before he took his own life. What set Sherrill off isn't completely clear, but we do know that his performance record at work was spotty and that he wanted to get revenge on his shift supervisor, who was his first victim in the onslaught. This atrocious crime is the first well-known incident of workplace violence in the United States, and it marks the beginning of the escalating trend toward workplace violence that we just discussed. In recent years, I/O psychologists, social psychologists, organizational development experts, and others have begun a systematic examination of this phenomenon. The remainder of this section briefly highlights the results of their research.

Figure 11.3 presents a profile of the dangerous employee. This profile is consistent with a 1995 study published by the U.S. Department of Justice and the FBI that discovered some interesting trends after reviewing 89 incidents of serious violence in the workplace (Duncan, 1995). First, 97% of the murderers were male, and over 70% were white. Second, the average age of the perpetrators (nearly 40) was a bit higher than that of non-workplace murderers (under 30). Third, in each of the 89 incidents, a firearm was used to commit the crime. Fourth, almost 90% of the perpetrators were current or former employees. Fifth, many of the perpetrators had a history of psychological or personality disorders and an affinity for weapons. Sixth, they often exhibited warning signs, such as extremely erratic behavior, threats of violence, irrational thought processes, and agitated mood, just prior to the incident.

organization-motivated aggression
Attempts by someone inside or outside the organization to cause injury or to be destructive as a result of some organizational factor.

organization-motivated violence
The negative effects on people or property that result from organization-motivated aggression.

A useful model along these lines has been developed by Anne O'Leary-Kelly, Ricky Griffin, and D. J. Glew (1996), who use the term **organization-motivated aggression** to refer to attempts by someone inside or outside the organization to cause injury or to be destructive as a result of some organizational factor and the term **organization-motivated violence** to refer to the negative effects on people or property that result from the aggression. Figure 11.4 presents their model of organization-motivated aggression, which demonstrates the importance of both the organizational environment and individual characteristics. Some individuals are clearly more disposed toward violent or aggressive behavior than others (again, see Figure 11.3), but organizations that are rigid, punitive, and aggressive themselves may also encourage aggressive behavior on the part of employees (Tobin, 2001). The model further indicates that the way in which the organization responds to the aggressive behavior moderates the extent to which the aggression results in violence and other negative outcomes. On the basis of this model and various psychological theories relevant to aggressive behavior, O'Leary-Kelly, Griffin, and Glew (1996) have generated a series of propositions that, in my opinion, ought to be the focus of future research. One of these is that aversive treatment and aggressive models act as triggers to organization-motivated aggression; another is that when aggression is instigated by aversive treatment, it is more likely to be directed at a very specific source. The accuracy of this latter proposition has been borne out by many major incidents of organization-based aggression in which employees who felt maligned (because they had been passed over for promotion, fired, or written up) attacked the person whom they held responsible for the mistreatment (usually their supervisors).

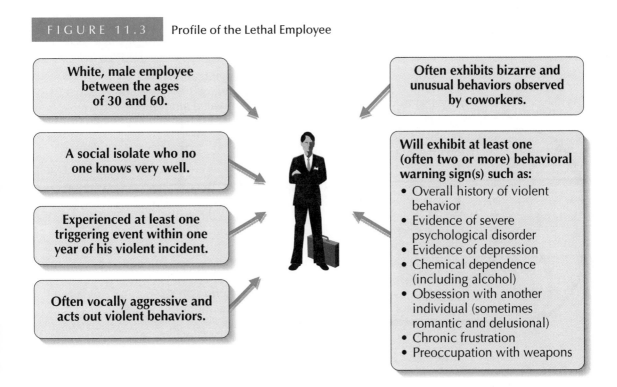

FIGURE 11.3 Profile of the Lethal Employee

White, male employee between the ages of 30 and 60.

A social isolate who no one knows very well.

Experienced at least one triggering event within one year of his violent incident.

Often vocally aggressive and acts out violent behaviors.

Often exhibits bizarre and unusual behaviors observed by coworkers.

Will exhibit at least one (often two or more) behavioral warning sign(s) such as:

- Overall history of violent behavior
- Evidence of severe psychological disorder
- Evidence of depression
- Chemical dependence (including alcohol)
- Obsession with another individual (sometimes romantic and delusional)
- Chronic frustration
- Preoccupation with weapons

A second model of organizational aggression has been developed by Mark Martinko and Kelly Zellars (1998). Though extremely complex, this model builds on the work of O'Leary-Kelly and her colleagues (1996) by focusing on the individual characteristics specified in the earlier model (again, see Figure 11.4). Martinko and Zellars grouped their findings into three categories: *reliable findings,* which are findings for which sufficient research evidence has verified their accuracy; *tentative findings,* which are findings supported by the literature but for which the evidence is insufficient to verify their accuracy; and *propositions,* which are potential findings that need to be tested with future research. Their literature review led to four reliable findings: (1) High levels of frustrating events in the workplace lead to a greater incidence of aggression and violence; (2) employees who tend to exhibit violent and aggressive behavior also tend to have been rewarded in the past for this pattern of behavior and to have had role models who were violent and aggressive; (3) employees who believe that what happens to them is beyond their control (i.e., those who are high on external locus of control) are more likely than others to respond to negative events in an aggressive or violent way; and (4) males are considerably more likely than females to be aggressive and violent in the workplace.

FIGURE 11.4 A Model of Organization-Motivated Aggression

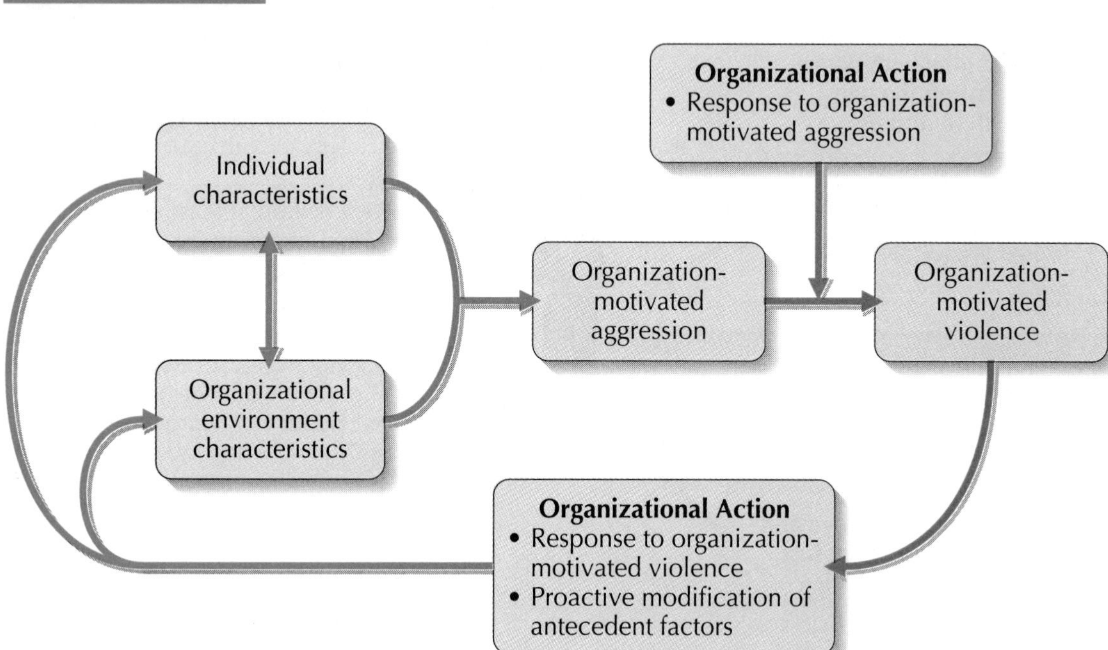

Source: Adapted from O'Leary-Kelly, Griffin, & Glew (1996).

Martinko and Zellars' literature review has also given rise to a few tentative findings. For instance, a series of seemingly minor frustrations at work may serve as a trigger for aggression (Tobin, 2001). Individuals who exhibit a high degree of negative affectivity—that is, who see their lives and the world around them in an unfavorable light—are more likely to respond to aversive outcomes (e.g., being laid off) with aggressive behavior than are those who exhibit a low degree of negative affectivity. Similarly, individuals who tend to be impulsive are more likely to react to aversive outcomes in violent ways than are those who tend not to be impulsive.

Martinko and Zellars have developed a series of propositions as well. First, they argue that some aggressive behaviors happen without conscious thought on the part of the perpetrator; in effect, these behaviors are purely emotional reactions to a trigger event. Second, they propose that individuals who are emotionally susceptible (i.e., easily affected by events happening around them) are more likely to perceive workplace incidents as trigger events than are those who are not emotionally susceptible. Third, they suggest that in ambiguous situations, perpetrators may attribute negative outcomes to a general cause such as "management," such that personnel who are most like management are likely to be blamed for the trigger events.

Both of these models provide useful summaries of what we know about workplace aggression and violence. But even more important, they provide directions for future work in this area. One final point: We must not assume that all (or even most) aggressive behaviors in the workplace involve fatal physical assaults. In actuality, such incidents often entail subtle, covert, or verbal types of aggression, the majority of which are directed at co-workers rather than at supervisors (Neuman & Baron, 1998). But of course it is the heinousness of the murders and rampages, in combination with the media spotlight, that makes them more salient than more typical incidents such as verbal threats, arguments, paybacks, and assaults among co-workers.

SUMMARY

The purpose of this chapter was to discuss stress as it manifests itself in the workplace. I began the chapter with a look at stress, strains, and coping. After defining these important terms and briefly considering stress in general, I presented a model that indicates various sources and outcomes of job-related stress. Then, in the second section, I highlighted Warr's model of environmental determinants of well-being as a way of thinking about how employees' jobs can affect their well-being. (Later in the chapter the same model is used to show how job loss can result in anguish.)

In the third section I focused on work-family conflict. Given the importance of this area to both employees and organizations, I devoted a substantial amount of space to discussing it. In particular, I defined work-family conflict and enrichment, presented a conceptual model to demonstrate how work and family interact with each other and related variables, and emphasized the various struggles faced by people who are working and nurturing a family at the same time. I then discussed the benefits that some organizations are currently providing to employees to help them deal with this conflict—benefits such as family-leave policies, child care, and elder care. Because more and more married people are dual-earner couples, I also considered some of the issues that make this situation stressful and explained how companies can help reduce the stress associated with juggling multiple careers and family responsibilities. Throughout this section, specific companies were highlighted to provide a sense of the many family-friendly benefits and services being offered to help reduce employees' stress.

Whereas in the second and third sections it was somewhat exciting to see what companies are doing to help employees deal with work-family issues, the last two sections of the chapter were quite somber. First I discussed the psychological effects of job loss in light of the increased number of layoffs at major U.S.

corporations and the perceived threat of being laid off experienced by so many employees in the 21st century. Then I presented some incredible statistics indicating the rise of workplace violence. In this context, employees at risk of becoming perpetrators were profiled, some recent research was reviewed, and a discussion was presented of two recent theoretical works that attempt to model the process through which workplace aggression and violence occur.

REVIEW QUESTIONS

1. Discuss the differences between stress and strains.
2. What does it mean to be "working scared"?
3. Differentiate between problem-focused and emotion-focused coping.
4. What are Warr's environmental determinants of well-being?
5. Why is work-family conflict such an important issue in I/O psychology?
6. What is work-family enrichment?
7. What are some of the family-friendly benefits being provided by organizations?
8. What does it mean to be a dual-earner couple? Discuss the problems often faced by such individuals.
9. What are some of the psychological effects of job loss, and how do they relate to Warr's environmental determinants of well-being?
10. How prevalent is workplace violence today, and what is the most typical type of violence enacted against employees?
11. Describe the profile of an employee who is likely to engage in severe workplace aggression.

SUGGESTED READINGS

Cartwright, S., & Cooper, C. L. (1997). *Managing workplace stress.* Thousand Oaks, CA: Sage. This book provides a readable treatment of stress at work and offers approaches and techniques for dealing with stress.

***Public policy, work, and families: The report of the APA presidential initiative on work and families.* APA 2004.** This new report presents cutting-edge knowledge and a thorough summary of the social science research on the challenges faced by working families and their employers. It's a very readable account of what we know and don't know about some very complicated and important issues.

Warr, P. (1999). Well-being and the workplace. In D. Kahneman, E. Diener, & N. Schwartz (Eds.), *Well-being: The foundations of hedonic psychology.* New York: Russell Sage Foundation. Peter Warr is one of the most interesting writers on this topic. The chapter cited here focuses on well-being at work and ties in nicely with Warr's more general models of well-being and health. Accordingly, it serves as a good place to begin reading and learning about how work affects our lives.

Wexley, K. N., & Silverman, S. B. (1993). *Working scared: Achieving success in trying times.* San Francisco: Jossey-Bass. This timely book, written by respected I/O psychologists, portrays the state of many 21st-century organizations. A very easy read, it can be used as a "how to" book for dealing with workplace stress caused by recent changes in organizations.

Group Processes and Work Teams

12

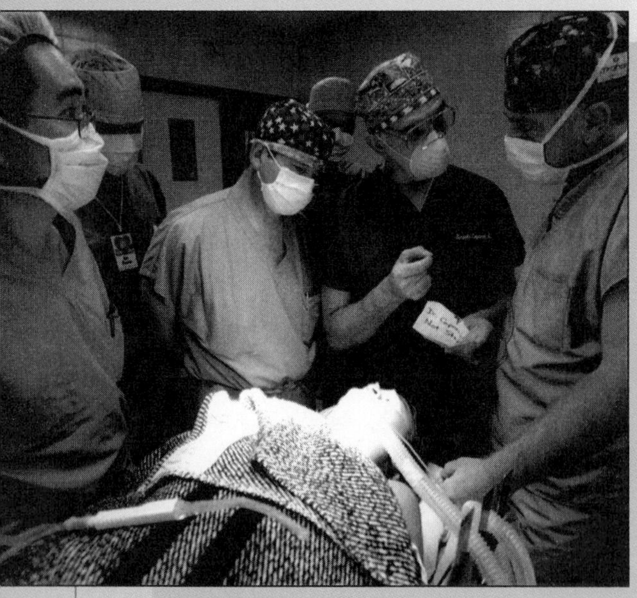

CHAPTER OUTLINE

At some point during your education you have probably worked with other students on a group project. It may have been a book report in the 5th grade, a science project in the 10th grade, or a term paper in your freshman year of college. Group projects have been a common way for students to learn about relevant material, develop interpersonal skills, and achieve goals that may have been more difficult and less likely on an individual basis. Groups are quite prevalent in our day-to-day lives as well. I was a member of a softball team for over 10 years, participate in various groups at church, and have done some volunteer work as part of a group. You may have been a member of the Boy Scouts or Girl Scouts. Perhaps your parents belonged to the Rotary Club or a Masonic group.

Groups, it seems, have always played a role in people's lives, from play groups in early childhood to social or service groups in late adulthood. In the years between, they join the workforce and experience groups at work. Though more typically considered a specialty area within social psychology, group processes have been extensively examined by industrial/organizational psychologists interested in organizations that utilize work groups. In this chapter I deal with the role of such groups in organizations. Specifically, I review some of the basics of group processes, apply them to groups at work, consider what I/O psychologists know about work teams, and discuss the great potential that teams have for transforming organizations.

LEARNING OBJECTIVES

This chapter should help you understand:

- how social influence affects group behavior.
- what group cohesion is and how important it is to group processes.
- the stages of group development.
- the implications for work groups of social loafing and free riding.
- the stages of effective decision making.
- why groups don't always make good decisions.
- what groupthink is and how it can affect organizations.
- why one current trend in organizational processes is the use of work teams.
- how to differentiate among the various types of work teams.
- what self-managed work teams are, along with some of the processes involved in their success.
- how to measure work-team effectiveness and what factors affect it.
- the implications that work teams have for employee selection and placement.

GROUPS VERSUS TEAMS

work group
An interdependent collection of individuals who share responsibility for specific outcomes for their organizations.

A **work group** is "an interdependent collection of individuals who share responsibility for specific outcomes for their organizations" (Sundstrom, DeMeuse, & Futrell, 1990). Other definitions, too, emphasize that members of work groups have interrelated goals; in short, a collection of people is not a group unless the individuals share common goals that affect one another. For instance, five people sitting in close proximity on a subway do not constitute a group, but they become a group when the subway doors get stuck and they work together to achieve such interrelated goals as getting the door open, contacting emergency personnel and family members who may be worried, and so on. *Formal groups* are subunits of the organization that the organization has actually established (e.g., committees, small departments, work crews), whereas *informal groups* develop apart from the official structure of the organization and exist relatively independently of it. Informal groups often emerge among employees who work in close proximity to one another and interact frequently. They may consist of employees who get together for a working lunch, go through training together, or study together for a certification exam.

All organizations have both formal and informal groups. Formal groups are discussed at greater length in this chapter, but first we need to recognize how powerful and important informal groups can be. Informal groups serve a variety of functions, including the following:

1. They satisfy social needs such as friendship and companionship.
2. They satisfy security needs in that they make employees feel safe and connected.
3. They facilitate cooperation among employees.
4. They regulate social and task behaviors such that organizational norms and procedures are disseminated.

In the past, researchers drew a distinction between work groups and work teams, arguing that the former consist of individuals who work together but can do their respective jobs without the other members of the group, whereas the latter consist of individuals who are truly interdependent such that they are required to "work together" in order to get their jobs done. Many contemporary researchers, however, use these terms interchangeably, arguing that the distinction is unnecessary, sloppy, and not widely recognized (Sundstrom, McIntyre, Halfhill, & Richards, 2000). I myself use both terms to refer to the same idea: *Work groups* were defined at the beginning of the chapter, and *work teams* are discussed later on in the context of organizations, but I do not mean to imply any qualitative difference between the two terms.

Although there are many people on this New York subway, it doesn't meet the definition of a *group* because these individuals are not involved in a common task.

SOCIAL INFLUENCE IN GROUPS

Social psychologists spend a great deal of time studying the ways in which groups affect individual behaviors. In this section we will review some major concepts related to group processes that have traditionally been studied by social psychologists and are now applied by I/O psychologists to organizations.

Norms

Norms are shared expectations about appropriate ways of responding in a group. As such, they are guidelines that serve an important organizational function, sometimes by stipulating certain behaviors as off-limits or not appropriate. *Descriptive norms* define what most people tend to do, feel, or think in a particular situation, while *prescriptive norms* suggest what people *should* do, feel, or think in a particular situation (Forsyth, 1999). As you might imagine, employees who violate descriptive norms are viewed as unusual or different, but those who violate prescriptive norms are viewed as dysfunctional—as bad employees.

norms
Shared expectations about appropriate ways of responding in a group.

Sometimes groups sit down and list their norms; but more often, norms develop gradually as group members become more comfortable with their place in the organization—and more comfortable with each other. Norms may also be passed down by employees who were members of the group at an earlier time. New employees, rather than changing existing norms, tend to adapt or adjust to them. I have had experience with an organization in which the norm was for employees not to use their sick days at all. It was very clear to new employees that unless they had to be hospitalized, they were expected to be present at work, and their sick days would accumulate for years and years. Many of the employees in this organization intended to work there until they retired, anticipating that they would "turn in" their sick days and, in effect, retire earlier than they otherwise could. However, new employees who did not see the value in carrying over their sick days and who preferred to stay home when ill (so as to get better sooner and to avoid infecting co-workers) essentially violated a prescriptive norm at this organization, leading at times to interpersonal conflict. Indeed, as this example illustrates, work-group norms can powerfully affect employees' behaviors and other social elements of the workplace.

Roles

We have discussed roles elsewhere in this text (see especially Chapter 11), but let's take a more formal look at them here. First, consider the context of behavior. An individual's behavior is jointly determined by internal forces (e.g., values, attitudes, and needs) and external forces (e.g., social pressure and job requirements). In other words, behavior is a function of both the person and the situation. Kurt Lewin (1951), widely recognized as the leader of the scientific study of groups, put it a bit differently: Behavior is a function of the person and the environment, or

$$B = f(P,E).$$

Second, role concept is used to describe how people perceive the various situational forces acting upon them. For example, my role as a father is composed of what I think a father is supposed to do and, in particular, what I think *I* am supposed to do as a father. Similarly, my role as a psychology professor consists of how I interpret the expectations and demands of the environment to arrive at what I think I am supposed to do, how I should behave, and what my chief purpose is as a psychology professor.

role differentiation
The process by which a group or organization establishes distinct roles for various members of the group or organization.

Third, as defined in Chapter 11, a *role* is a set of behaviors expected of a person who occupies a particular position in a group or organization. The process by which a group or organization establishes distinct roles for various members of the group or organization is called **role differentiation.** This is accomplished through formal job descriptions, rules, and task requirements, as well as by supervisors, subordinates, and co-workers who communicate expectations and beliefs to individual employees. Thus, for example, a computer programmer knows what her role is at Microsoft not only because it is spelled out in the job description and other formal organizational documents but also because it is defined through discussions and interactions that she's had with her supervisor and other computer programmers.

Especially when combined with the work stress caused by role conflict and role ambiguity (again, see Chapter 11), role differentiation within work groups can become quite complicated. With this in mind, let's now examine one of the more important dimensions of groups—cohesion.

Cohesion

At some point in your life, you have probably been part of a group in which the members were very close-knit, expressed a unified commitment to the group, and shared similar beliefs about issues relevant to the group. You may also recall that morale was generally high in that group. All of these elements are related to **cohesion,** defined as the strength of members' motivation to maintain membership in a group and of the links or bonds that have developed among the members. As Donelson Forsyth (1999) points out, based on his review of the literature, cohesion is seen (1) as both a binding force that pushes members together and as a combative force that tries to pull them apart; (2) as group unity or "we-ness" in which group members feel such a strong sense of belongingness that they put the goals of the group above their own; (3) as a special type of interpersonal attraction; and (4) as an aspect of "teamwork." Kenneth Dion agrees that cohesion is multidimensional, arguing that some groups are cohesive because they consist of close personal friends, others are cohesive because the members feel a strong sense of belongingness, and still others are cohesive as a result of great teamwork (Cota, Evans, Dion, Kilik, & Longman, 1995).

cohesion
The strength of members' motivation to maintain membership in a group and of the links or bonds that have developed among the members.

Cohesion has been demonstrated to have both positive and negative consequences for groups and organizations. The negative consequences, which are largely related to group decision making, are discussed in a later section. For now, however, I focus on the positive consequences. Most managers, if asked to choose between supervising a cohesive work group and supervising a noncohesive work group, would quickly opt for the former. Faced with a similar choice, you would probably do the same. What, then, are the positive consequences of cohesion?

First, a great deal of research across athletic, industrial, and educational settings demonstrates that members of cohesive groups report being more satisfied than do members of noncohesive groups (Forsyth, 1999). Think about your own experiences in this regard. I would predict that you have more positive things to say about the cohesive groups you've belonged to than about the noncohesive groups. There tends to be less tension and anxiety in cohesive groups because their members get along, like each other, have similar goals and objectives, and work well together.

Second, group cohesion is positively linked to performance (Kerr & Tindale, 2004). One of the truly great groups of our time was the Disney group that worked together in the early days of Walt Disney's success (Bennis & Biederman, 1997). Creative, hard-working, and cohesive, this group made incredible contributions to the world of animation and film. As Warren Bennis and Patricia Ward Biederman (1997) point out, other accomplished groups of our time have also tended to be very cohesive. Indeed, two meta-analyses support a positive relationship between cohesiveness and performance (Evans & Dion, 1991; Mullen & Copper, 1994). Both meta-analyses have identified a series of moderators that affect the strength of this relationship. In addition, the relationship is reciprocal such that cohesion affects performance and performance affects cohesion (Mullen & Copper, 1994). Meanwhile, other research has demonstrated that cohesiveness affects organizational citizenship behaviors (OCBs) and that the relationship between job satisfaction and OCBs is stronger among members of cohesive work groups than among members of noncohesive work groups (Kidwell, Mossholder, & Bennett, 1997).

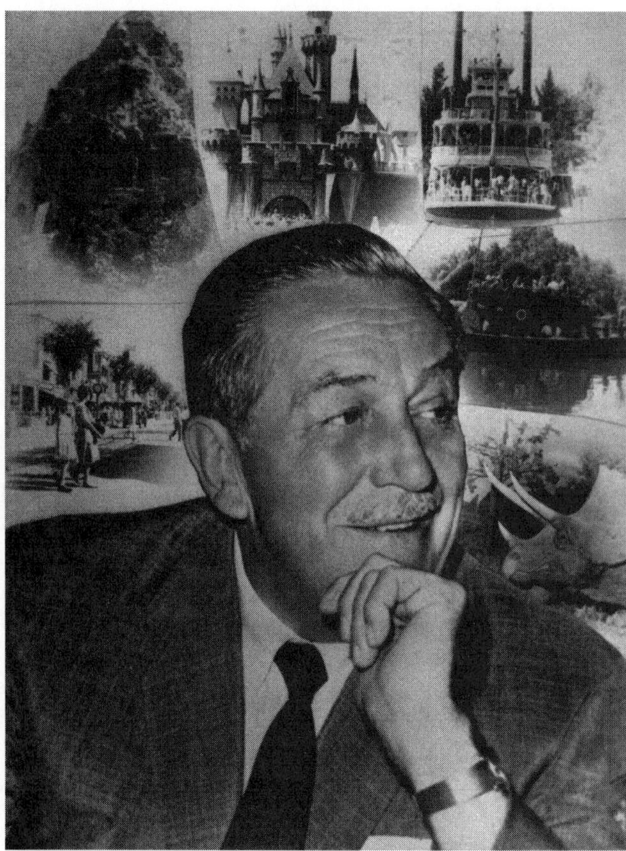

Walt Disney developed and nurtured creative work groups that changed the world of animation.

Examples of cohesive work groups are widespread; think of the many work groups depicted on television. *E.R.*, for instance, routinely presents the emergency-room employees as belonging to a very cohesive group whose members get along well; are committed to one another, the patients, and the hospital; share similar beliefs about medicine and patient treatment; and are clearly motivated to maintain affiliation with the group. Interestingly, some of the storylines of this popular TV show are about the conflict that results when someone disrupts the cohesiveness of the group by disagreeing with other group members or violating a group norm. In reality, of course, many work groups are not very cohesive. They consist of employees who don't get along all that well, see things very differently, and remain affiliated with other group members only because doing so is part of their jobs. In other words, they aren't committed to the group but, rather, are simply focused on keeping their jobs. Have you experienced both cohesive and noncohesive groups at work, at school, or in social circles? If so, you know that the differences between the two types of groups are striking. How do cohesive groups develop? The answer will become clear in the following discussion of how groups in general are formed and develop.

Group Development

Traditionally, theories and models of group development agree that groups pass through various stages as they develop. One model that many group researchers have endorsed is the five-stage version proposed by Bruce Tuckman in the 1960s (Tuckman, 1965; see also Tuckman & Jensen, 1977). We'll examine this model in detail because it provides a solid general view of group development.

Tuckman believed that groups develop while passing through five stages over time (see Table 12.1). In the first stage, groups go through an orientation period that Tuckman referred to as *forming;* group members spend time getting to know each other. At this point their interactions are rather polite, tentative, and exploratory as members tactfully try to gain some understanding of one another. This is followed by a period of conflict called the *storming* stage, in which group members have moved beyond polite conversation and actually begin disagreeing with each other, questioning each other's ideas and beliefs, and openly revealing who they are. This second stage results in tension and stress within the group and can also lead to the formation of coalitions—small cohesive groups—within the larger group.

In the third stage, a structure-building stage that Tuckman referred to as *norming,* group members become more cohesive and establish unity among themselves. Trust increases, roles are defined, norms develop, and the group members become more "tightly knit" as they begin to understand what their roles, goals, and procedures are. During the fourth stage, members are focused on productivity, or *performing.* It typically takes a while before a group is productive; after the members have a better feel for each other, have formed some bonds, and have developed a sense of organizational structure, performance can follow. Of course,

TABLE 12.1 Tuckman's Five Stages of Group Development

Stage	Group Processes
1. Forming	• Members get acquainted. • Interactions are polite, tentative, exploratory, and sometimes guarded.
2. Storming	• Interactions are characterized by disagreement. • Members question each other more pointedly. • Some conflict emerges.
3. Norming	• Unity is established. • Members become more cohesive. • Roles, standards, and relationships develop. • Trust increases.
4. Performing	• Members become focused on productivity and goal achievement.
5. Adjourning	• Task orientation is high. • Roles are terminated. • Relationships weaken, and members become much less dependent on each other or the group. • Some degree of stress or tension is likely.

some groups never make it to this stage; having stagnated at the norming stage, they fail to reach their potential in terms of productivity. Examples of unproductive groups can be found in numerous studies of combat groups, civic groups, and personal-growth groups (reviewed in Forsyth, 1999). On the other hand, we have all experienced groups that were truly productive and reached the performing stage. It is exhilarating, indeed, to be part of a group that grows and matures into a productive arm of society, whether at work, church, home, or school.

The final stage involves the dissolution of the group, or what Tuckman called *adjourning*. This stage can be planned for, as when a work group charged with a particular project dissolves because the project is finished or when a student group breaks up because the class is over and there is no other reason for the group to exist. Sometimes, however, groups dissolve due to lack of performance, lack of funding, or group members' dissatisfaction. The organization itself may decide that a particular group is no longer successful or useful and reassign its members to other projects and perhaps other groups. (We will revisit this topic later in the context of different functions and types of work teams in organizations.) At other times, work groups are dissolved for financial reasons, as when group members are laid off or asked to take on more work that necessitates their being pulled out of the group.

Change is stressful regardless of the context, especially when one has spent considerable time as a member of a group, only to see it disband. The stress that accompanies the dissolution of a team was made very clear to me by my son when he was 8 years old. He loved playing baseball and soccer in the local recreation leagues, and every time the season would end, he would become very sad and tell me how much he was going to miss his teammates and the fun that comes from working together to score more than the other teams. I always pointed out that he would see the same guys in school, at church, and around the neighborhood, but he would say that it wasn't the same because they wouldn't be a team anymore. Indeed, when we affiliate with others in close situations and work interdependently to achieve a goal, it's hard to end that relationship.

Earlier, I presented Tuckman's model of the process through which groups develop—but we need to be careful about generalizing this process to all groups all the time. Some groups may go through the five stages in a different order and spend more time at one stage than at another. Other groups may stop short of making it through all of the stages; still others may skip a stage or two. Regardless of which stage theory of development we're dealing with (e.g., Piaget's theory of cognitive development, Maslow's theory of motivation, Kohlberg's theory of moral development), we need to recognize that there are exceptions to the process. In general, however, the five stages presented by Tuckman describe the process that many groups experience.

Models of *punctuated equilibrium* present an alternative in which groups fluctuate more quickly among these and other stages of development (Gersick, 1989). For instance, a particular group may oscillate between the norming and performing stages as interpersonal and task-oriented issues compete for dominance within the group. This model has become extremely popular as a useful description of how groups form and is certainly in contrast to the more traditional linear stage process views such as Tuckman's, which soon fell out of favor. However, a recent paper has suggested that groups may actually develop in a way that combines these two approaches. Chang, Bordia, and Duck (2003) contrasted Gersick's punctuated equilibrium model with a stage approach and found that the two models together explain group formation pretty well. They argued and demonstrated that each model is useful when looking at a particular unit of analysis. For instance, the punctuated equilibrium model describes the discontinuous changes in a group's pacing and task activities over time, but a stage model describes the continuous manner in which a group's structure changes over time. So the pendulum swung away from linear stage models like Tuckman's and toward Gersick's punctuated equilibrium model in the 1990s, but today some researchers and theoreticians have argued that it may have swung too far and that the models complement each other in gaining a better understanding of group functioning. Future research will continue to explore the various ways in which groups evolve and develop.

Social Loafing

The idea of social loafing was first analyzed and presented in the early 1900s by Max Ringelmann, who noticed that individual effort in a wide variety of tasks often decreased with increases in the size of the group. The term he coined, **social loafing,** refers to the reduction in individual effort that occurs when people work in groups compared with working alone. The point here is not that groups, as a whole, work less hard than individuals but, rather, that individuals, in many situations, work less hard in groups than they do when working alone. Ringelmann and others noticed this effect across a variety of tasks such as rope pulling and clapping.

social loafing
The reduction in individual effort that occurs when people work in groups compared with working alone.

Since Ringelmann's early work, social loafing has been empirically demonstrated by additional researchers on such tasks as making noise, working on mazes, writing, swimming, and problem solving (for a review, see Karau & Williams, 1993). Although there are various explanations for this effect (Pinder, 1998), most researchers agree that people are less likely to "loaf" (1) when they believe that their individual efforts can be identified and (2) when others are going to be personally affected by their effort. Indeed, S. J. Karau and K. D. Williams (1993) argue that social loafing is especially pervasive in groups and usually occurs because people don't expect their efforts in group tasks to be as directly tied to valued outcomes as their efforts on individual tasks. You may recognize this explanation as being based on the expectancy theory of motivation (see Chapter 9).

When Steve Zaccaro (1984) conducted a study in which students were given the opportunity to "loaf" in groups, he found that social loafing occurred only among group members who were working on a task low in attractiveness. The opposite effect, *social enhancement,* occurred among group members who were working on a task that was high in attractiveness. In the latter case, individuals in larger groups performed better than those in smaller groups. Recent research has also demonstrated that social loafing is less likely to occur in cohesive groups than in noncohesive groups (Karau & Hart, 1998; Karau & Williams, 1997); thus variables other than task attractiveness may affect the likelihood of social loafing in any given situation (Goren, Kurzban, & Rapoport, 2003). Finally, according to Miriam Erez and Anit Somech (1996), social loafing occurs less frequently than previously believed and tends not to occur when communication, incentives, and specific goals are present.

free-riding
A situation that occurs when employees do less than their share of the work but still share equally in the rewards.

sucker effect
An outcome that occurs when group members become concerned that their co-workers are holding back, at which point they reduce their own efforts to the level they believe is being exhibited by their co-workers.

Group dynamics can get even more complicated than that. Sometimes, for instance, employees do less than their share of the work but still share equally in the rewards. Known as **free-riding,** this situation appears to happen when employees perceive that their efforts are not necessary to group success and rewards. In such cases, other group members become concerned that their co-workers are holding back, at which point they reduce their own efforts to the level they believe is being exhibited by their co-workers. This outcome, called the **sucker effect,** occurs when group members decide that they will no longer be played for a sucker and reduce their effort, even if it results in failure on the task. Kerr and Tindale (2004) discuss other complex group effects such as *social compensation,* which occurs when individuals increase their efforts on collective tasks because they don't anticipate much help from their group members. You can see, then, how complicated social processes can become, with potentially far-reaching effects on organizational functioning.

GROUP DECISION MAKING

Think about the roles that groups play throughout the world. We often give our greatest responsibility to groups. Groups run our major national and international companies, affecting our economy and lives (e.g., board of directors); groups run our universities and colleges, influencing our education and the education of our children (e.g., board of regents); groups decide the fate of our accused criminals and provide the only means of protection for those of us who are unjustly accused (e.g., juries); groups make life-changing decisions about such fundamental things as our basic rights and responsibilities (e.g., the Supreme Court); groups make the laws that we live by (e.g., Congress); and we even trust our physical health and well-being to groups when faced with serious illness (e.g., surgical teams). Although most of us would agree that as citizens of the United

We entrust some of our most important decisions to groups such as this jury.

States we live in an individualistic society, we must not lose sight of the importance of groups—especially considering the power and responsibility that we give to them to make crucial decisions. In this section we will consider both effective and ineffective group decision making.

Effective Decision Making

Although no two groups make decisions in exactly the same way, certain elements can be said to characterize most successful decision making. There are various ways to break these elements down; I do so by relying on the five steps outlined in Table 12.2.

First, before any intensive work can be done to solve a problem by making a particular decision, groups must begin *diagnosing the problem.* Group members must come to some agreement about the nature of the problem, about the goals of the group with respect to this problem, and about the obstacles the group needs to be sensitive to and prepared to overcome. Although at first glance this step in the process appears rather straightforward, research indicates that many groups don't spend enough (or any!) time on it (Forsyth, 1999). Some common mistakes at this stage include confusing facts with opinions and looking for scapegoats. For instance, the members of a salary-equity task force charged with identifying and resolving apparent differences in pay between men and women may mistake as a fact what is merely the members' opinion that the pay differences are based purely on skills and experience, thus distorting their perception of the problem.

The second step of effective decision making is *generating solutions.* This discussion-oriented stage involves communication among group members in which they process the problem and group goals while trying to identify potential solutions. A useful technique here is **brainstorming,** in which all members of a group generate potential solutions without the fear of having their suggestions criticized by other members. The purpose is to create an atmosphere in which each group member feels comfortable generating solutions—and, indeed, the group is arguably best served by having a long list of such solutions. One mistake sometimes made at this stage, however, is to raise irrelevant solutions, thereby throwing the group off task. Another mistake is to rely on "old" solutions that have been used in the past rather than remaining open and willing to think creatively about the problem. In general, research suggests that the effectiveness of brainstorming is reduced when (1) members have to wait their turn or are otherwise delayed in their opportunity to share, thus blocking the free flow of ideas (this is called *production blocking*); (2) members are apprehensive about voicing their ideas to the group; and (3) members are more motivated by concern for how "good" they look in comparison with others than by concern for generating viable solutions (Forsyth, 1999).

brainstorming
A technique in which all members of a group generate potential solutions without the fear of having their suggestions criticized by other members.

Several decades of research have shown many instances in which brainstorming results in worse performance than that of nominal groups (i.e., individuals

TABLE 12.2 Five Steps to Effective Group Decision Making

Step	Description	Common Mistakes
1. Diagnosing the Problem	Group members come to an agreement on the nature of the problem.	• Confusing facts with opinions • Confusing symptoms with causes
2. Generating Solutions	Group interaction is focused on understanding the problem well enough to identify potential solutions.	• Suggesting irrelevant solutions • Looking at what should have been done rather than looking forward
3. Evaluating Solutions	Group members consider each solution in terms of its potential for success and failure.	• Failure to consider potential downside to each solution • Attacking the person who proposed a particular solution rather than focusing on the solution itself
4. Choosing a Solution	Group members come to some agreement on the best solution.	• Allowing powerful members of the group to dictate the solution chosen; biasing a particular solution because it's politically correct
5. Developing an Action Plan and Implementation	Group members determine steps to follow in carrying out the decision and monitoring progress.	• Preventing some members from being involved even though they were part of the decision process

not working together). This performance decrement has been the major criticism of brainstorming. More recent work, however, has begun to challenge these negative findings and provide some solutions to improving the effectiveness of this technique, such as employing a trained facilitator to minimize production blocking (Kerr & Tindale, 2004). Perhaps the most intriguing solution is the recent development of "electronic brainstorming," in which software allows individuals to type in their ideas without production blocking, with anonymity, and with group members' ideas available to them at any time on the screen. Recent research has demonstrated the superiority of this electronic brainstorming approach to the use of nominal groups (for a review, see Nijstad, Stroebe, and Lodewijkx, 2003), which may result in greater interest in this approach in the future.

The third step, *evaluating solutions,* follows directly from the previous one. Specifically, the group critically evaluates each of the solutions proposed during the brainstorming procedure, accepting the ones that seem workable and rejecting the ones that do not. At this point it's important for the group to consider the worst-case scenario regarding each alternative when deciding whether to eliminate it from further consideration. For instance, if our salary-equity task force decides to explain pay differences in terms of the importance of jobs held by the respective genders, the result could be a worst-case scenario involving angry female employees whose commitment to the organization is compromised, leading to dissatisfaction with their jobs, a decrement in performance, high turnover rates, potential suits brought against the company, and depleted morale. *Choosing a solution* from those on the list is the fourth step of the process. After considering the potential benefits and weaknesses of each alternative and eliminating those that are not workable or that would have negative consequences, the group must compare the remaining solutions and pick the best one for implementation. Groups choose solutions in various ways. Forsyth (1999) discusses some common approaches:

- *Delegating:* The group provides information to the chairperson of the group, who makes the decision. (Alternatively, a subcommittee speaks for the whole group.)
- *Averaging individual inputs:* Group members make individual private decisions, which are then averaged to arrive at a group-level decision.
- *Majority rules:* The group votes, and the majority viewpoint becomes the group's choice.
- *Group consensus:* The group members discuss the issue until they arrive at a unanimous agreement.

Potential mistakes at this stage include allowing those with power to dictate the chosen solution and biasing the benefits and weaknesses to support a "favorite" solution.

Finally, after the decision has been made to enact a particular solution, the group begins *developing an action plan and implementation* of that solution. Detailed action steps and methods for monitoring and evaluating progress toward the solution are developed. Let's say our salary-equity task force decides to conduct a reevaluation of job classifications and wage scales; toward this end it must develop a plan that includes timelines, steps in the process, and objectives for each step. After the action plan is ready, implementation begins, with each step monitored and evaluated along the way.

Although success is not guaranteed, consideration of the issues raised in each of the preceding five steps is certainly more likely to result in effective decisions than ignoring such issues. Of course, groups can also undergo these steps with varying degrees of commitment, which explains why some decisions are good ones and others are not so good.

Ineffective Decision Making

The fact that groups are asked to make many of our important decisions doesn't mean that they always do it well. Indeed, in American culture we often poke fun at groups, especially committees, through comics, such as the *Cathy* strip in this chapter, and jokes; Forsyth (1999), for instance, quotes the all-too-common view that "committees consist of the unfit appointed by the unwilling to do the unnecessary." Now perhaps that is a bit extreme, but we have all had bad experiences being part of a group decision-making effort or been affected adversely by an inadequate group decision-making process.

Process Loss. In 1972, Ivan Steiner suggested the following *law of group performance:*

Actual Productivity = Potential Productivity – Losses Due to Faulty Processes

Here, "potential productivity" refers to all of the positive things that can come from group work, such as shared responsibilities and the variety of skills brought to bear on a particular problem. At the end of the equation, however, is the category of "losses due to faulty processes," or **process loss,** which refers to any nonmotivational element of a group situation that detracts from the group's performance. For example, coordination problems among group members result in process loss, as when one employee works on her part of a group task without coordinating her efforts with other members who are doing related parts of the task. Actual productivity is adversely affected by process loss, a key element that groups need to be aware of so that they can take advantage of the benefits of group processes rather than being limited by potential disadvantages. A recent program of research by James Larson and his colleagues (1998a, 1998b) has focused on the factor of shared versus unshared information in terms of its effect on decision making. *Unshared information* is information held by only one group member, while *shared information* is information held by all group members.

process loss
Any nonmotivational element of a group situation that detracts from the group's performance.

cathy® by Cathy Guisewite

Group decision making, for both unimportant decisions such as choosing one's lunch order to more serious ones such as how to solve an organizational problem, can be quite complex.

According to these researchers, one reason we entrust important decisions to groups is that we assume that a larger pool of relevant information is being brought to bear on the problem. As their studies have shown, however, groups are not particularly effective at pooling unshared information; indeed, group decisions tend to be determined more by shared information. This finding is ironic given that the notion of pooling unshared information is one of the assumed strengths of group decision making. Larson and his colleagues argue that to improve the quality of group decision making, the pooling of valuable unshared information should be encouraged (see also Brodbeck, Kerschreiter, Mojzisch, Frey, & Schulz-Hardt, 2002). One technique they suggest is for leaders to employ a "participative" style of leadership. This method has received some qualified support in their most recent research (Larson et al., 1998b), but more work still needs to be done regarding how to encourage groups to take advantage of one of their potential benefits—the pooling of unshared information.

groupthink
A mode of thinking that individuals engage in when the desire to agree becomes so dominant in a cohesive group that it tends to override the realistic appraisal of alternative courses of action.

Groupthink. Without a doubt the most talked about group decision-making error is **groupthink,** which was defined by Irving Janis (1972) as a mode of thinking that individuals engage in when the desire to agree becomes so dominant in a cohesive group that it tends to override the realistic appraisal of alternative courses of action. In such instances, group members become so focused on sticking together and following through as a cohesive group that their decision making is clouded or biased. Indeed, groupthink has been presented (by Janis and others) as an explanation for various poor decisions made throughout the history of the United States. An especially compelling example has to do with Japan's attack on Pearl Harbor on December 7, 1941. U.S. military commanders in Hawaii had been provided with a great deal of information about Japan's buildup for this attack; as a group, however, they never really took the situation seriously. They didn't strategically place aircraft carriers in the Pacific where they could have provided some warning of the attack, and they didn't deem the threat real enough to warrant any buildup on the part of the United States. Thus there was absolutely no warning at all until the Japanese bombers were directly overhead attacking our defenseless ships and airfields (Janis & Mann, 1977). Other historical examples of groupthink include President Johnson's handling of the Vietnam conflict, the 1980 attempt to rescue hostages in Iran, and the Watergate fiasco.

Although the most publicized examples of groupthink tend to be large-scale historical/political blunders, groupthink is quite relevant to your job and mine. Let's return to our example of the task force charged with evaluating pay-equity issues. Groupthink would be a likely outcome if (1) this group is very cohesive, with a few members strongly convinced that there is no gender discrimination at the company; (2) the group does not solicit information from employees outside the group; (3) the group doesn't allow individual group members to present opinions that differ from the majority opinion; or (4) the group has a strong leader who is able to sway everyone in his or her direction. Although some researchers argue that the empirical data about groupthink are mixed at best and

The USS *Missouri,* where Japan and the United States signed the agreement to end World War II, approaches the USS *Arizona* Memorial, which pays tribute to the ship sunk by the Japanese attack on Pearl Harbor.

perhaps better characterized as weak (e.g., Paulus, 1998), others suggest that additional research is needed, both to examine the theoretical variables involved and to expand these variables to include other potentially important constructs (Raven, 1998). Many experts agree, however, that the groupthink construct presents a useful framework for analyzing group decisions and structuring decision-making processes.

Have you ever tried to get an established rule changed at work and run into a brick wall? For example, it might make perfect sense to you and many others that employees be allowed to pick and choose their benefits from a cafeteria-style list of benefits (e.g., vision care, dental care, work-family benefits, different types of insurance, etc.)—within limits, of course. However, you find that the personnel committee doesn't want to hear anything about this new approach and seems to work very hard to present a united front that prevents new and different information from being presented, new employees from being heard, and alternative ideas from being considered. This is probably an example of groupthink. Regarding the *antecedents* of groupthink, what do you think are some of the factors likely to lead to this phenomenon? Not surprisingly, Janis has presented a list of these factors in his model of groupthink (see Figure 12.1). The primary necessary antecedent for groupthink to occur is *cohesion* (Janis, 1982). Members of cohesive groups often feel such a strong sense of belongingness that they put group goals above their own. The implication here is that group members may even choose to avoid expressing a dissenting opinion because they believe group unity to be more important; in this case, group cohesion is problematic. Groupthink is also more likely in groups that are *isolated* from others. This makes sense, given that

FIGURE 12.1 Janis's Model of Groupthink

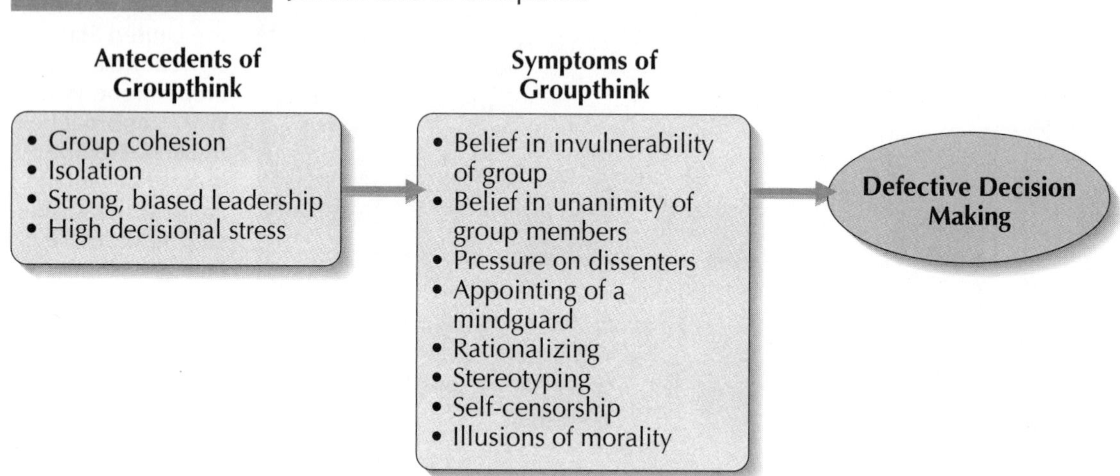

Source: Adapted from Janis & Mann (1977), p. 132.

isolation from others limits the dissenting opinions that could be shared with the group. *Strong, biased leadership* is another important antecedent of groupthink. Strong leaders have a tendency to "dictate" the direction of the group and even some of its opinions. In your own experience, have you ever tried to get a group to listen to your opinion about something, only to be silenced by the group leader, who had a seemingly solid explanation of why your opinion wasn't relevant? The last antecedent of groupthink is *high decisional stress,* which refers to situations in which a decision needs to be made quickly and the context in which it exists is very important and emotionally charged.

As for the *symptoms* of groupthink, take another look at Figure 12.1, in which eight such symptoms are listed. Limited space prevents me from discussing all of these, but I will mention briefly a few of the more interesting ones. First, in situations involving groupthink, members tend to believe that they are *invulnerable* to harm and *unanimous* in their beliefs. I always think of Watergate as a great example of this; the accounts and interviews of those involved with the Nixon White House—the principal players on the Committee to Reelect the President (CREEP)—make it very clear that these people never considered the possibility that they could be caught, brought down, and damaged, much less that they were doing anything "wrong."

Two other symptoms that seem to go hand-in-hand with the ones just discussed are *pressure on dissenters* and *appointing of a mindguard.* When groupthink occurs, there is usually a great deal of pressure put on members whose opinions seem at odds with those of the rest of the group. In other words, when a group is experiencing groupthink, it is not unusual for dissenters in the group to be coerced through guilt or some other means to "join the rest of the group" and contribute to the unanimity. Related to this is the group's formal or informal appointment of a **mindguard,** a member of a cohesive group whose job it is to protect the group from outside information that is inconsistent with the group's views. Obviously, this approach maintains the cohesiveness of the group and keeps it isolated from outside influences that might otherwise negatively affect the perceived unanimity of the group.

mindguard
A member of a cohesive group whose job it is to protect the group from outside information that is inconsistent with the group's views.

Finally, the steps to effective decision making presented earlier (see Table 12.2) should be followed in the hopes of eliminating or preventing groupthink altogether. The more carefully the problem is diagnosed, the more tightly focused the group is on identifying potential solutions, the more critically the potential solutions are evaluated, the more carefully a final solution is chosen, and the more precisely the action plan and implementation are carried out, the less likely groupthink is to emerge.

WORK TEAMS OF THE 21ST CENTURY

Although I made it clear at the outset that I would use the terms *work group* and *work team* interchangeably, I predominantly use the latter in this last section in order to be consistent with the growing I/O literature. In this literature, work teams are essentially defined as work groups in which the actions of individuals are interdependent and coordinated, each member has a specified role, and the team has common goals and objectives. But regardless of the specifics of the definition, a growing organizational trend that cannot be denied is the steady increase in work teams across every segment of the industrial sector. In the 1980s only about 5% of American organizations used work teams; by 1992 this figure had grown to about 20% (Mohsen & Nguyen, 1999). Ed Lawler (2001) reports that 72% of Fortune 1000 companies had at least one self-managed work team (SMWT) in 1999, up from 28% in 1987 (SMWTs are discussed in more detail later). And the Center for Collaborative Organizations (formerly the Center for the Study of Work Teams) at the University of North Texas estimates that about 80% of Fortune 500 organizations have at least half of their employees in work teams (Johnson, 1999). Corning, Xerox, Chrysler, Monsanto, Apple Computer, Motorola, Texas Instruments, and Frito-Lay are among the leaders at the forefront of the teams movement (see "Practitioner Forum"). This emphasis on teams reflects the growing realization that the complexity of work in the 21st century requires collaboration (Wheelan, Murphy, Tsumura, & Kline, 1998). Work is complicated today—so many different skills and so much knowledge are required that individuals can no longer accomplish certain tasks on their own. As Manfred De Vries (1999) puts it, "One way of managing for continuity, one way of creating companies that last, is through teamwork. Companies that gain the tools of effective teamwork have a distinct competitive advantage, a leg up toward organizational success."

Types of Work Teams

As I/O psychologists began studying work teams more intensively, it became clear that such teams could be grouped into five different categories (Sundstrom et al., 2000). These are summarized in Table 12.3. First, *production teams* are groups of employees who produce the output. They tend to be front-line employees in that they are responsible for production at the front end; in other words, they get their hands dirty making the ball bearings, computer chips, or automobile parts. Second, *management teams* coordinate workers who report to them as the product is being made, developed, or refined. They aren't on the front line but, instead, are responsible for the planning, staffing, budgeting, and logistics of work projects. Third, *service teams* consist of employees who work together to attend to the needs of customers. One example of a service team is the group of flight attendants who

TABLE 12.3 Types of Teams

Production Teams	• Front-line employees producing tangible output • Often self-managed, self-led, self-directed • Examples: electronics assembly units, coal mining crews, candy production crews
Management Teams	• Corporate executive teams; regional steering committees • Coordinate other work units under their direction • Responsibilities include planning, budgeting, staffing • Examples: top management teams, military command teams, health-care teams
Service Teams	• Attend to the needs of customers • Serve many customers at one time • Examples: flight attendants, hospital emergency units, retail sales groups
Project Teams	• Created for the duration of a project • Cross-functional • Disband at completion of project • Examples: new product teams, research units, research and design project groups
Advisory Teams	• Solve problems and recommend solutions • Very popular in organizations • Temporary • Examples: quality circles, employee involvement teams, university advisory group to the president

PRACTITIONER FORUM

TOM RUDDY

Ph.D., Industrial/Organizational Psychology, 1989, Bowling Green State University
Senior Director of Executive Development and Learning at Siemens Corporation

Much of what you've learned in this chapter about work teams rings true in the "real world" of corporate America. At Xerox and Siemens, I became familiar with these concepts while implementing empowered teams for over 14 years in over 36 countries worldwide. In Xerox, the empowered team implementation process we used in our global Customer Service organization (an organization with over 24,000 employees) consisted of several steps: (1) Form teams (controlling size and composition); (2) understand and communicate the company vision; (3) develop a team mission; (4) define team goals; (5) establish team norms of behavior; (6) clarify team member roles; and (7) document and follow key work processes (e.g., communication, meeting, and work processes). We used these team start-up steps during team training as a way to get teams up and functioning. We sometimes found that there was a lack of clarity in one of these key areas, which affected the team's success. For example, a group may not have agreed upon a set of norms regarding how to act in particular situations, resulting in conflicts. The completion and monitoring of these process steps would often ensure effective team functioning.

This chapter's review of the research on team cohesiveness is consistent with my experience. As my own study and observation of over 3,000 teams has demonstrated, team members' ability to follow agreed-upon processes and norms is more predictive of good team functioning than the extent to which team members "like" each other on a personal level. While positive personal relationships do not hurt team functioning, such relationships are not necessary or sufficient to create high-performance work teams. My work at Siemens with virtual teams that operate across multiple countries and time zones has highlighted that well-defined processes and behavioral expectations, especially in the areas of communciation and action item follow-up, are the critical factor in making teams successful.

While the chapter notes that Tuckman's five-stage model of team development has been popular, it also suggests that the model is limited because teams may undergo these stages in different orders. I fully agree with this statement and would go even further by proposing that most teams are simultaneously in all stages, with their level of functioning dependent upon the task at hand. I have often seen "high-performing" teams receive a new team task (e.g., realigning territories, giving peer performance feedback , facing tight product development timelines) and revert to so-called "storming" behavior in a very short time.

Also discussed in this chapter is the research of Sundstrom and his colleagues, who cite the importance of organizational context, team composition, processes, and support structures. This model of team performance is consistent with our data, which is based on over 16 separate research studies on Xerox and Siemens teams. This research has identified the following critical organizational context factors in team performance: (1) team-based support structures (e.g., team-based incentives, performance feedback systems), (2) management leadership and coaching, and (3) technical resources (e.g., pagers, laptops, real time communication devices). The presence or absence of these factors has an impact on the ability of teams to develop effective team processes (i.e., the seven start-up steps discussed previously) and drives performance (e.g., customer satisfaction, employee satisfaction, and expense management).

APPLYING YOUR KNOWLEDGE

1. Why is team cohesiveness related to tasks more important than general liking among team members?
2. In what ways are Dr. Ruddy's experiences regarding team development consistent with the punctuated equilibrium model?
3. What kinds of support structures are most relevant to the effective functioning of teams?
4. How do virtual teams differ from traditional face-to-face teams with regard to the importance of team processes and organizational context factors?

assist you and other passengers on an airplane; another is the technical support team that addresses a software problem you have e-mailed them about. Service teams have become very popular in organizations because they provide fast and efficient service to a large number of customers with minimal costs.

cross-functional teams Work teams that are composed of members from diverse departments of the organization, each with their own function.

Fourth, *project teams* are put together to carry out specific projects only and are dissolved upon their completion. These may also be referred to as **cross-functional teams,** especially when they involve team members from diverse departments of the organization, each with their own function. For instance, a book publisher might assign to a particular book a cross-functional team that will handle all of the procedures necessary to get the finished product in the stores. Members of this team might include someone from production who is responsible for making sure the book is edited and ready to go by the deadline, someone from marketing who is responsible for the design of the marketing campaign, someone from finance who knows all about the costs and budget of this particular project, and someone from circulation who is in charge of making sure that the book is in targeted stores when it should be. These various team members are responsible for working with each other while at the same time focusing on their individual responsibilities to best serve the company's interest with respect to this one particular book or project. Harley-Davidson, for example, uses cross-functional teams extensively in the production of its motorcycles. Typically, each line of motorcycle is designed, manufactured, and marketed by a specific team consisting of a program manager from the design department, a representative from the manufacturing department, a representative from the purchasing de-

Harley-Davidson makes extensive use of cross-functional teams in the production of motorcycles.

partment, and a marketing representative to handle the advertising end of the product (Brunelli, 1999).

Finally we come to the category of *advisory teams,* sometimes called parallel teams because they are developed to work separate from and in parallel to production processes (Sundstrom et al., 2000). A company may have an employee involvement team, for example; or a college may have an advisory group whose chief focus is to keep the president informed about morale on campus and other faculty/student issues. This group would also likely provide guidance and counsel to the president on how to handle these issues. Typically, members of advisory teams serve for a limited term, after which they are replaced by new members. The popularity of advisory teams is indicated by a 1990 survey of Fortune 1000 companies in which over 90% of the participating companies reported using some form of advisory teams (Lawler, Mohrman, & Ledford, 1992). A recent book called *The Third Opinion* by Saj-Nicole Joni describes advisory team members as external thinking partners who may help the executive deal with a particular problem or with big-picture issues (Joni, 2004).

In their review of work-team literature published between 1980 and 1999, E. Sundstrom and his colleagues (2000) reported that 33% of the research focused on service teams, 17% on production teams, 14% on management teams, and 14% on project (or cross-functional) teams. Interestingly, despite the obvious popularity of advisory teams, very few studies have formally examined this newer approach to management and productivity. Future research is certainly called for, given the prevalence of these teams in organizations today. It would be helpful to know how successful these teams are, how they are received by employees, and how they are viewed by upper-level management.

We have just discussed one popular scheme for categorizing work teams (again, see Table 12.3). But another important dimension along which teams differ has also received both popular and scientific attention—namely, the extent to which work teams are self-managing, self-directing, self-leading, and self-regulating. These terms, which are often used interchangeably, refer to work teams that assume complete responsibility for a final product or an ongoing process (Mohsen & Nguyen, 1999). In short, the **self-managed work team (SMWT)** is responsible for monitoring and controlling the overall process or product, as well as for doling out specific tasks to team members. These teams often schedule their own work, do routine housekeeping, and maintain their own equipment; some may even participate in discussions of budgets, performance appraisals, or training (Sundstrom et al., 2000).

self-managed work team (SMWT)
A work team that is responsible for monitoring and controlling the overall process or product, as well as for doling out specific tasks to team members.

Traditionally, organizations have taken a "command and control" approach to operations. Generally, organizations have been viewed as machine-like systems that were all about order, predictability, and control (Ashmos & Nathan, 2002). Some recent theorizing suggests that in the current global environment of rapid and discontinuous change, organizations and their constituencies will be better served via "sense making," in which people try to make sense out of organizational life (Weick, 1995). The emphasis is on being flexible enough to change as the organization encounters more complex and varied situations. Ashmos and

Nathan have suggested that an alternative way to characterize effective teams is as sense makers. In this way, teams can help the organization get to know itself, its history, and its future. To serve this purpose teams need to be flexible, independent, and self-empowered rather than a command-and-control arm of the organization.

SMWTs seem to fit this sense-making framework quite well. They are often referred to as autonomous work teams or empowered work teams because autonomy and empowerment are two essential features of these teams. In fact, some research has demonstrated that autonomy and empowerment are positively related to team effectiveness. Bradley Kirkman and Benson Rosen (1999) found that empowered teams were not only more productive than less empowered teams but also had higher levels of customer service and more favorable attitudes. Similarly, Claus Langfred (2000) found that, in cases in which team members' tasks were interdependent, autonomy had a positive effect on work-team effectiveness. In other words, when team members were dependent on each other for the completion of their tasks, their autonomy as a team was an important predictor of team success.

An example is provided by Chevron Oil Company, which has recently made a transition to the SMWT approach. The original 80-member team, called the Kern River Asset Team, consisted of 80 members and was charged with the task of producing oil from Chevron properties in Bakersfield, California (Mohsen & Nguyen, 1999). However, this 80-member team was not as efficient as the company had hoped it would be, so in 1995 a restructuring was initiated with a focus on self-managed work process teams (or what would be product teams in the preceding categorization) through empowerment. Each SMWT was supplied with an outside coach who met regularly with the team and provided some leadership. Training programs were available to help team members with their communication, conflict-management, and time-management skills. Some frustrations and problems were experienced throughout the transition; but as an overall result of the creation of SMWTs, the progress was clear and steady, with tangible improvements in terms of better maintenance of oil pumps, better usage of the pumps, and better quality control. The Kern River Asset Team is now a model of reengineering at Chevron, and company executives are quite pleased with the effect of this new approach on employee morale, efficiency, product quality, and economic savings (Mohsen & Nguyen, 1999).

Work-Team Effectiveness

An important question is how to evaluate the effectiveness of work teams. Among the various ways to do so, one of the best is a framework developed by Susan Cohen (Cohen, 1994; Cohen & Bailey, 1997). According to this framework, there are three major dimensions of work-team effectiveness: (1) *team performance,* which concerns how well the team is performing and includes such variables as productivity, quality of output, and the degree to which costs are controlled in this process; (2) *attitudes* of team members, which reflect such variables as quality of work life, trust in management, organizational commitment, and job satisfaction; and (3) *withdrawal* behaviors, such as turnover, absence, and tardiness.

Another useful way to think about the effectiveness of teams is to consider two types of behaviors described by Robert McIntyre and Eduardo Salas (1995): **taskwork,** which involves the task-oriented aspects of work, and **teamwork,** which involves the process-oriented aspects of work. Whereas taskwork entails specific individual behaviors or duties that are required for success, teamwork includes the wide range of activities aimed at maintaining and enhancing team performance. Teamwork revolves around communication and coordination among team members, feedback, team cohesion, and norms (Levy & Steelman, 1997). Most team experts argue that both taskwork and teamwork are integral to successful team performance. In other words, if teams are to be successful, it isn't enough for members to fulfill their individual duties; they must also work together toward common goals. Whether we use the term *teamwork* to describe a great NBA team, the board of directors of General Electric, or the cross-functional groups at Harley-Davidson, the importance of teamwork is clear. Further insights in this area are likely to emerge from research that has begun to examine the level at which team data should be analyzed—for example, at the level of individual perceptions, perceptions aggregated across team members, and perceptions combined across teams at the organizational level.

taskwork
Activities, behaviors, or actions that involve the task-oriented aspects of work.

teamwork
Activities, behaviors, or actions that involve the process-oriented aspects of work.

A second important question concerns the factors involved in increasing work teams' effectiveness. There are many different models and theories dealing with this issue as well, but fortunately the work of making sense out of all of them has been done for us already. In their extensive review of the literature on work teams, Sundstrom and his colleagues (2000) identified five categories of factors that appear to be important predictors of work-team effectiveness: organizational context, group composition and size, group work design, intragroup processes, and external group processes. Table 12.4 presents some examples of each of these categories.

One category in particular has received considerable attention as of late: group composition. A series of recent studies have built on this notion, paying particular attention to personality traits of team members. For instance, Mohammed, Mathieu, and Bartlett (2002) found that team personality variables predicted team effectiveness. In particular, extraversion and neuroticism were significantly related to leadership performance, and agreeableness predicted contextual performance. In another interesting study, Porter et al. (2003) demonstrated that when an individual perceived that his or her team member really needed help with a task—what the literature calls "backup behavior"—the personalities of the helper and the recipient of help play an important role. For instance, teams higher on conscientiousness delivered more backup to each other, whether it was really needed or not, and those who were high on extraversion secured more backup from others, regardless of their true need for help, than did those low on

TABLE 12.4 Predictors of Work-Team Effectiveness

Organizational Context	• Rewards • Goals and feedback • Training
Group Composition and Size	• Cognitive ability of group members • Personality traits of group members • Demographic characteristics of group members
Group Work Design	• Member task interdependence • Member goal interdependence
Intragroup Processes	• Group cohesion • Group efficacy or communication processes
External Group Processes	• Communication outside the group • External interaction patterns

Source: Adapted from Sundstrom et al. (2000).

extraversion. There are many other interesting (and complex!) findings from these studies, but both studies presented here serve as good examples of the recent work exploring Sundstrom's notion of the importance of group composition (see also Bunderson & Sutcliffe, 2002; Ellis et al., 2003).

Finally, another interesting empirical investigation also revealed potential factors influencing work-team effectiveness. In what they called a Group Development Profile, David Hyatt and Tom Ruddy (1997) used roundtable sessions and employee interviews to identify six important factors, developed survey items to tap employees' opinions about the degree to which these factors were present in their work teams, and, finally, measured team performance in a variety of ways. Table 12.5 presents the six factors that emerged from this study, along with two examples of survey items used to measure each factor. Notice that several of these factors are related to the predictors identified in the literature by Sundstrom and his colleagues (2000). Indeed, there seems to be a good deal of agreement about the variables influencing work-team effectiveness. Hyatt and Ruddy (1997) found a positive correlation between the presence of their Group Development Profile factors and managers' ratings of team effectiveness. These six factors also predicted objective measures of performance such as the time it took a service technician to respond to the service call. Thus, although we can argue about what constitutes the *most* important predictors of work-team effectiveness, the literature clearly indicates that the variables listed in Tables 12.4 and 12.5 are important to varying degrees.

TABLE 12.5 Factors in the Group Development Profile

Process Orientation	• We can be counted on to follow agreed-upon work processes. • We consistently follow the agreed-upon practices.
Work-Group Support	• We are treated with respect by our manager. • We receive honest feedback from our manager.
Goal Orientation	• We have a documented plan for achieving goals. • We have established plans to obtain the skills needed to be effective.
Work-Group Confidence	• We have structured our work group to maximize performance. • We are confident that we can succeed as a work group.
Customer Orientation	• We are committed to meeting customer requirements. • We accept that they are responsible for ensuring 100% customer satisfaction.
Interpersonal Work-Group Processes	• We engage in open and honest communications. • We share and accept constructive criticisms without making it personal.

Source: Adapted from Hyatt & Ruddy (1997).

Future Trends

Regarding important future trends in this field, Sundstrom and his colleagues (2000) suggest, first, that the use of work groups or teams will continue to expand in the areas of service, production, and project completion. Second, work teams will continue to become more fluid; in other words, the teams will be assembled in such a way as to make use of various people, including employees from other units and other companies. (Even today, some organizations are using teams as a way to link or partner with other organizations. Perhaps the definition, development, and use of teams will change as organizations find new and interesting ways to make use of them.) Third, with the increase in telecommuting and electronic work, the use of virtual teams (already a reality) promises to expand (Zaccaro & Bader, 2003). Virtual teams are composed of members who work in different cities or countries and communicate via e-mail, fax, Web pages, and video conferencing. Indeed, it's not unusual for team members to be working on the same sales account or for the same client but to be doing all their communicating in ways other than face-to-face.

One other trend worth discussing has to do with selecting employees to work in the team environment. Think back to Chapters 6 and 7, in which we talked about the various predictors and procedures used for selecting employees into organizations. As you might recall, the selection process always begins with a job analysis to identify what tasks are done on the job (job description) and what Knowledge, Skills, Abilities, and Other characteristics (KSAOs) employees need to have in order to do the job successfully (job specification). We also talked about the use of ability tests, personality tests, work sample tests, and so on as techniques for predicting how effective or successful particular individuals are likely to be in a particular job. Given this background and review, what additional kinds of information might we want to know about applicants prior to hiring them into a job that exists within a team-based environment? I certainly wouldn't want to hire onto a production team someone who is focused solely on himself and cannot or will not get along with others. In short, it makes sense from a selection standpoint to consider applicants in light of their interest, desire, and ability to work in a team environment.

Some recent work has begun to examine this issue, which I view as an important and growing trend in the team area. For instance, a laboratory experiment in which students worked together on group decision-making tasks found that work-team performance was predicted by students' preferences for and attitudes about working in teams, as well as by their perceptions of group confidence and ability (Jung & Sosik, 1999). The authors of this study argued that group preference appears to be a stable individual disposition and thus can be used to select individuals for group membership, increasing the likelihood that those selected will be suitable for and perform well in team-based work environments. Another study examined the mental abilities and Big Five personality traits (see Chapter 6) of more than 600 employees to determine the relationship between these variables and group performance (Barrick, Stewart, Neubert, & Mount, 1998). The authors concluded on the basis of their data that selecting team members with higher levels of general mental ability, conscientiousness, agreeableness, and emotional stability appears to improve team performance—and that just one team member who was low on agreeableness, conscientiousness, or extroversion can result in increased stress and decreased performance among team members.

George Neuman and Julie Wright (1999) elaborated on the study just mentioned (Barrick et al., 1998) by demonstrating that even when cognitive ability and job-related skill were controlled for, personality variables predicted the performance of department-store employees at the team level. Based on this finding, they concluded that personality measures should be used in team selection systems for certain jobs and tasks and that agreeableness and conscientiousness are the personality traits most important to performance in a team-based work environment. Here, however, we need to keep in mind the legal and ethical guidelines discussed in earlier chapters regarding employee selection and placement: Only by using job analysis and linking these particular traits to job performance in a team environment can a company reasonably use such predictors. As with any selection situation, it is imperative that predictors be linked to criteria; indeed, the organization must assume responsibility for demonstrating this link when it chooses its predictors.

Others have begun developing an instrument specifically geared toward identifying individuals likely to be successful in a team environment. Thus, rather than relying on, say, agreeableness in general, a personnel manager could use a measure that provides information about how an employee feels about working on teams *in particular* and then use this information to predict team performance. In fact, Michael Stevens and Mike Campion (1999) have developed such a measure. Known as the Teamwork Test, it identifies KSAOs that more effectively predict teamwork than taskwork. The following KSAOs are tapped by this measure: conflict resolution, collaborative problem solving, communication, goal setting and performance management, and planning and task coordination.

The Teamwork Test itself is a situational judgment test in which respondents are provided with hypothetical teamwork situations and asked to select, from multiple solutions, which one they would be likely to use. Correct answers were determined on the basis of the research literature. The authors found that scores on the Teamwork Test were correlated with ratings of teamwork performance and that these ratings were predicted even after aptitudes and abilities measured by nine different tests had been controlled for. The implication is that the Teamwork Test can be used for selection purposes in identifying individuals who are most likely to thrive in a team environment (Miller, 2001). Perhaps further research would provide an even better understanding of the entire process of team management and both the legal and ethical guidelines involved in selection processes.

SUMMARY

The purpose of this chapter was to introduce the concepts of work groups and work teams and to discuss the processes involved in the use of such groups in organizations. I began the chapter by defining work groups and reviewing group processes. Then I discussed social influence in groups in the context of norms, roles, cohesion, and social loafing, and applied those elements to organizational functioning. I also presented Tuckman's model of group development and the popular punctuated equilibrium model.

Group decision making was another area emphasized in this chapter. Because groups are entrusted with important organizational decisions, I spent considerable time discussing a process that, when followed, is likely to result in effective decision making. This five-step process emphasizes the quality of the social interaction among group members—an issue I discussed in connection with some of the common mistakes made at certain points in the process. This topic led logically into the next one: ineffective decision making, with a particular emphasis on groupthink. Here I presented historical examples of groupthink and discussed its antecedents and symptoms in light of organizational situations.

In the last section of the chapter I focused on work teams, which have become incredibly popular in modern-day organizations. I discussed a variety of types of work teams and gave examples of each, placing particular emphasis on self-managed work teams both because of their prevalence in organizations and because of their inherent complexities. I also provided a few examples of organizations currently using work teams and identified the determinants of work-team effectiveness. I concluded the chapter with a discussion of future trends, as well as future research needs, in the work-team arena.

REVIEW QUESTIONS

1. What is a work group? Discuss what needs are fulfilled by work groups in organizations.
2. Can you differentiate between norms and roles?
3. What is group cohesion, and why is it so important to group functioning?
4. How are groups formed? Describe the process in detail.
5. Distinguish among social loafing, free-riding, and the sucker effect.
6. What are the five major steps to effective group decision making?
7. Discuss the potential impact of groupthink on organizations.
8. What are self-managed work teams, and why are they so popular in organizations?
9. What factors complicate the operationalization and measurement of team effectiveness?
10. Discuss the implications of work teams for the employee selection process, and describe the recent research in this area.

SUGGESTED READINGS

De Vries, M. F. R. K. (1999). High performance teams: Lessons from the Pygmies. *Organizational Dynamics*, Winter, 66–75. An interesting, albeit unusual, application of work teams by an expert in the area.

Forsyth, D. (1999). *Group dynamics* (3rd ed.). Belmont, CA: Brooks/Cole. Far and away the best book on the psychology of groups. It's very readable and has good examples.

Hyatt, D. E., & Ruddy, T. M. (1997). An examination of the relationship between work group characteristics and performance: Once more into the breech. *Per-*

***sonnel Psychology, 50,* 553–585.** A nicely done empirical study on work groups using real-world data; this article is more readable than much of the academic literature. Both authors are practitioners who have had experience with groups and teams.

Sundstrom, E., McIntyre, M., Halfhill, T., & Richards, H. (2000). Work groups: From the Hawthorne Studies to work teams of the 1990s and beyond. *Group Dynamics: Theory, Research, and Practice, 4*(1), 44–67. An excellent review and discussion of work teams that serves as a good place to start for those interested in this area.

Leadership

13

CHAPTER OUTLINE

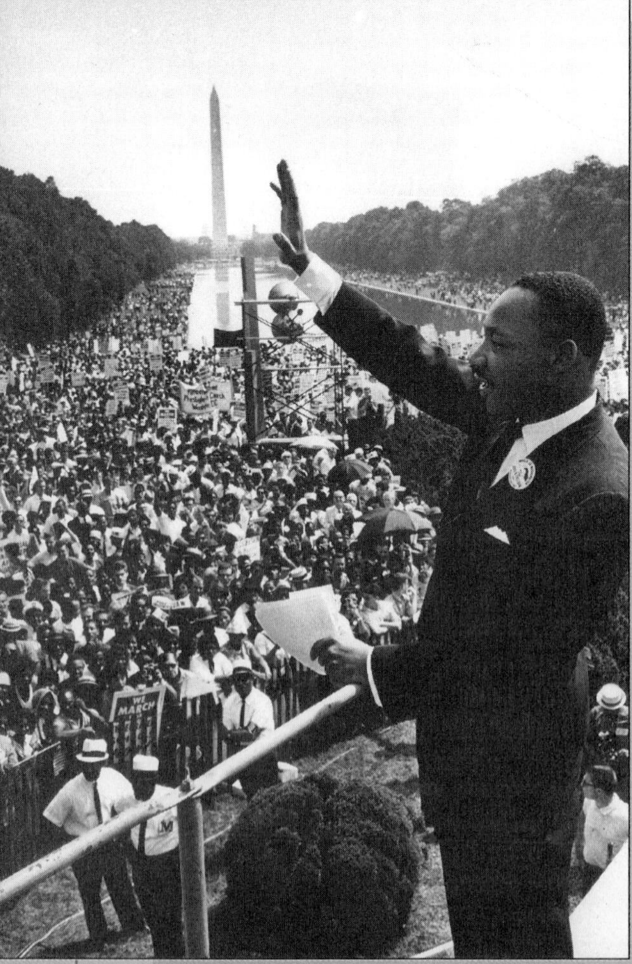

Certainly the use of the term *leadership* is not limited to academic circles. Walk into your favorite neighborhood bookstore, go to the "business management" section, and one thing you will notice immediately is the number of books that deal with leadership. Leadership is an especially hot topic during political elections. We heard a great deal about the leadership style and qualities of John Kerry versus George W. Bush during the U.S. presidential election of 2004. The leadership of these two men was a central focus of campaign advertising and was constantly debated on the CNN and MSNBC news shows. We are fascinated by leadership—leadership in government, leadership in the community, leadership in the boardroom, leadership on the baseball diamond, and leadership on the shop floor. Leadership is an important dimension along which people are evaluated in all walks of life.

Have you had the good fortune to spend time with a really terrific leader? What was this person like? If a boss of yours, was this person able to motivate you to work hard and remain committed to the company? As this last question implies, leadership is intricately linked to other topics in organizational psychology such as work motivation and job attitudes.

Many of us have also known people who appeared to be terrible leaders. These individuals most likely had poor relationships with others, were not respected or trusted, and seemed unable to identify the best way to get work done. Although at times it might seem easy to classify people as good or bad leaders,

Leadership was a major focus of the 2004 U.S. presidential election.

we'll see in this chapter that the issue is more complex than that. For an example, let's return to the political arena: One of the debates that will define the next decade or so is whether William Jefferson Clinton was a good leader. The fact that people disagree strongly over this question suggests that identifying good leaders is not always easy. Defining leadership is no simple matter, either: Most historians would agree that Martin Luther King, Jr., Abraham Lincoln, and Mother Teresa were outstanding leaders, yet their styles, personalities, and backgrounds were extremely different.

Accordingly, we will spend considerable time in this chapter talking about leadership theories and the research that has been conducted about leadership; much of this research provides a foundation for the application of leadership theories to organizations. Then, in Chapter 14, we will discuss organizational development techniques and discover how the leadership theories presented in this chapter are applied to organizations.

LEARNING OBJECTIVES

This chapter should help you understand:

- what leadership is and how the effectiveness of leaders is evaluated.
- the various types of power and how they are employed by leaders.
- the major elements of the various leadership theories.
- the historical development of leadership research and conceptualization.
- how to distinguish between leader traits and behaviors.
- what kinds of contingencies affect leadership processes.
- the most recent theories about leadership such as leader-member exchange theory, implicit leadership theory, and transformational leadership theory.
- why implicit leadership theory is fundamentally different from the leadership theories that came before it.
- the differences between transformational and transactional leaders.
- how both gender and culture affect leadership processes.
- the extent to which gender and culture are likely to determine the agenda for future leadership research.

WHAT IS LEADERSHIP?

leadership
A social process through which an individual intentionally exerts influence over others to structure their behaviors and relationships.

Among the many different definitions of leadership, the one I prefer is this: **Leadership** is a social process through which an individual intentionally exerts influence over others to structure their behaviors and relationships. As I pointed out at the beginning of this chapter, there are good leaders and bad leaders; merely being given the responsibility and status of a leader doesn't make a person a good leader. Rather, **effective leadership** is a function of the outcomes produced by those who are being led, usually operationalized as the successful long-term performance of the leader's work group or subordinates. The core of leadership, then, is influence over others. To understand this influence we need to examine the issue of power in organizations.

effective leadership
Usually operationalized as the successful long-term performance of the leader's work group or subordinates.

THEORIES

Power is defined as an individual's potential influence over the attitudes and behavior of one or more other individuals (Yukl, 2002). It is a resource that leaders can use to exert influence over their followers or subordinates. Although power is often viewed as something inherently negative (see the *Dilbert* cartoon on page 394), organizations could not survive without power as the basis of influence (Steers, Porter, & Bigley, 1996). John French and Bertram Raven (1958) have put forth the most often cited and discussed typology of power in the literature. This typology identifies five major bases of power (see Table 13.1), each of which has the potential to play an important role in the leadership and dynamics of an organization.

power
An individual's potential influence over the attitudes and behavior of one or more other individuals.

The first base, *legitimate power,* is the power bestowed on an individual by the organization. This is what we think of when we talk about authority. When we question whether a particular employee has the authority to make an important decision, we are asking whether the organization has provided this person with the legitimate power to make that decision. We can certainly think of individuals who, based on the nature of their job titles and responsibilities, have legitimate power. However, they do not necessarily use that power—or use it in effective ways. Some individuals think that all they need to be successful and respected leaders is the legitimate power provided by the company; but as we will soon see, a good deal more than this is required for successful leadership. The second base, *reward power,* is simply the power that results from controlling the rewards or outcomes that others receive. Parents have almost unlimited reward power over their kids because they can provide the candy, hours of TV watching, and Yu-Gi-Oh or

TABLE 13.1 Bases of Power

Legitimate Power	Conferred on a person by the organization
Reward Power	Exists when an individual controls the reward of others
Coercive Power	Exists when an individual controls the punishment of others
Expert Power	Held by those who have specific expertise or proficiencies
Referent Power	Gained when one is shown respect and admiration by others

Source: French & Raven (1958).

Leadership and coaching have less to do with the abuse of power and more to do with trust and communication.

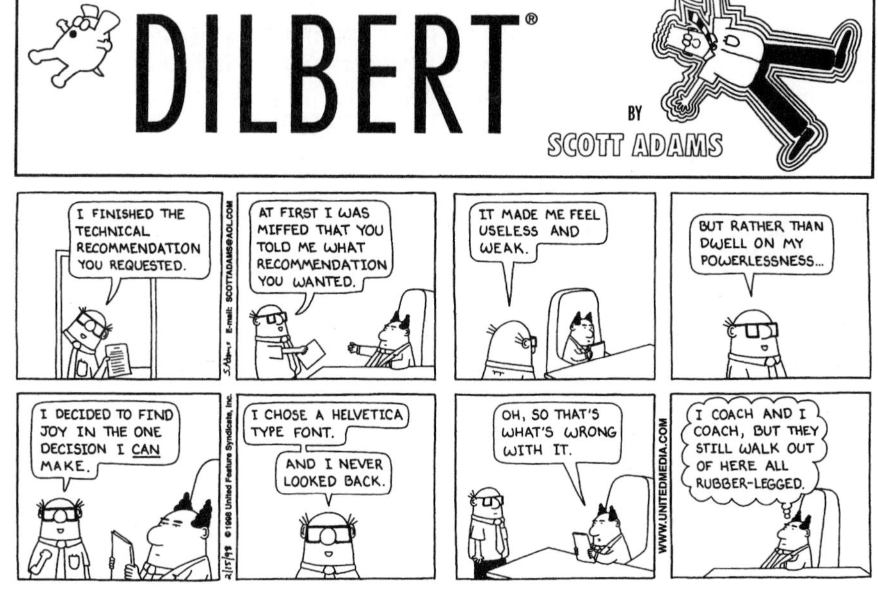

Sesame Street paraphernalia that children covet. In organizations, the person who makes decisions about employees' raises, promotions, and assignments is said to have reward power. The other side of this coin, however, is the third base: *coercive power.* People with coercive power have control over punishments, which they often use to get others to do what they want them to. The manager who consistently intimidates employees by arousing fear in them and insinuating that if they don't produce at a particular level they will be written up, forced to work additional hours, or transferred to a less desirable position is someone who manages through coercion.

Expert power, the fourth base of power, is affiliated with special knowledge or proficiency. Expert power is not limited to those at the top of an organizational hierarchy. Consider computer technicians, for instance. They're not at the top of the organizational structure, but they have a great deal of expert power that is essential for the functioning of the organization. Without their knowledge, the organization could be crippled. Expert power at lower levels of the organization sometimes balances the legitimate power at upper levels (Steers et al., 1996). The fifth base, *referent power,* is power gained through respect or admiration. Though strongly related to reputation and status, referent power can be obtained by anyone in the organization, regardless of hierarchical position. For example, an employee who is not high up in the organization and thus has low legitimate, reward, and coercive power may nevertheless have a high level of referent power because she is a well-respected team player who always seems to say and do the right things and is considerate of others' needs and perspectives. One final point about power: To be effective, leaders need to have some power at their disposal, and they are likely to use different types of power in managing their subordinates across different situations. However, it does not necessarily follow that more power is always better. I can think of situations in which a leader had so much power that subordinates became skeptical of his goals and behaviors, and the leader took both his power and his subordinates for granted. In all such cases, the result was highly ineffective leadership.

In the remaining sections of this chapter I will trace the historical development of various leadership theories and summarize the empirical evidence for and against these theories. (For a complete overview, see Chemers, 2000.) Before we get started, however, think about the successful leaders to whom you've been exposed and consider their similarities and differences. Although you may be able to identify some similarities, such as being conscientious and having good people skills (although I can think of successful leaders that I didn't like very much and who did not have good people skills), I'm quite certain that you can also identify many differences in style, approach, beliefs, values, vision, and behaviors among those effective leaders. In short, there isn't one "best" way to lead. As we proceed with our review of the leadership research, this fact will become clear to you. Indeed, the complexity of effective leadership is what makes studying, predicting, and understanding it both interesting and challenging.

Trait Theories

The first systematic study of leadership began in the 1930s with the development of **trait theories,** which focus on identifying the individual characteristics that made people good leaders. The central question posed by such research concerned what effective leaders had in common. Was it intelligence? Was it a domineering personality? Was it aggressiveness? This trait approach to leadership, sometimes called the "good man/good woman" theory, dominated leadership research into the 1950s. During this beginning phase, the research was largely atheoretical (House & Aditya, 1997), based mostly on common-sense notions of leadership and social interactions. Numerous individual characteristics were studied, including gender, dominance, intelligence, appearance, physical energy, need for power, and need for achievement. In 1948 a seminal review was published by R. M. Stogdill, who uncovered studies in which traits such as intelligence and dominance were significantly related to leader effectiveness. However, the overall results were not very supportive of these relationships, and there didn't appear to be much consistency in the findings. Scholars concluded that there were few, if any, universal traits that predicted leadership (Stogdill, 1948).

trait theories
Leadership theories that focus on identifying the individual characteristics that make people good leaders.

Interest in traits waned as a result of reviews like Stogdill's, but their potential role in leadership has become a renewed focus of attention in recent years. One contemporary review concluded that factors such as intelligence, dominance, and masculine orientation were consistent predictors not of effective leadership but of the type of person who tends to emerge as a leader in small groups

(Lord, DeVader, & Alliger, 1986). That is, in groups without an assigned leader, men viewed as more intelligent and dominant than the others tend to take on the leadership role. In other studies, Dave Kenny and his colleagues demonstrated that behavioral flexibility—the extent to which an individual is willing and able to consider what behaviors and approaches might work best in a particular situation—is a very useful predictor of who emerges as a leader in small groups (Kenny & Zaccaro, 1983; Zaccaro, Foti, & Kenny, 1991). Jeff Smith and Roseanne Foti (1998) found that individuals high on dominance, intelligence, and self-efficacy were more likely to emerge as leaders than those with other personality trait patterns. And Stogdill himself concluded in 1974 that his earlier paper may have painted too negative a conclusion regarding the role of traits in leadership. Thus it appears that traits play a larger role in leadership processes than was believed in the 1950s after the publication of reviews like Stogdill's (see "Practitioner Forum").

The most recent chapter in this story suggests that traits—in particular, the Big Five—actually play an important role in leadership. Judge, Bono, Ilies, and Gerhardt (2002) conducted a meta-analysis of more than 70 studies and found that the Big Five traits accounted for 53% of the variance in leader emergence and 39% in leader effectiveness. In particular, extraversion and conscientiousness appeared to be the most important and consistent predictors. The pendulum appears to have swung back toward traits as a relevant focus in the study of leadership.

Behavior Theories

behavior theories
Leadership theories that focus on identifying what leaders actually do, in the hope that this approach will provide a better understanding of leadership processes.

In the 1950s, after researchers had come to the conclusion that there weren't any traits that consistently predicted effective leadership, a new direction was taken. Now the emphasis was on leader *behaviors.* Indeed, the rationale for **behavior theories** was that if traits aren't all that useful in helping us understand the leadership process and what makes a good leader, perhaps we should begin to look at what leaders actually do, with the hope that this approach will provide a better understanding. Much of the research in this area was conducted at The Ohio State University, the University of Michigan, and the University of Iowa. The Iowa studies, led by Kurt Lewin, examined three types of leadership styles: authoritarian, democratic, and laissez-faire. They revealed that most subordinates prefer democratic leaders but that there isn't much of a relationship between leader style and subordinate behaviors. The conclusions of the Ohio State and Michigan studies were very similar, and I focus here on the former because Ohio State was the location of the most extensive program ever conducted on leader behaviors. Stogdill was a part of the research group at this institution, having shifted gears somewhat after becoming convinced that traits were not that important in determining leadership effectiveness (Stogdill & Coons, 1957).

The Ohio State studies gathered self-reports of leader behaviors using a survey called the Leader Opinion Questionnaire (LOQ), as well as observations and ratings of leader behaviors using a questionnaire called the Leader Behavior Descriptive Questionnaire (LBDQ). The LBDQ items were rated on a 5-point scale

PRACTITIONER FORUM

RHONDA GUTENBERG

Ph.D., Industrial/Organizational Psychology, 1982, University of Houston
Western Region Director—Talent Advantage Solutions
Personnel Decisions International

This chapter provides a nice textbook description of the important leadership theories and issues, but let me assure you that leadership is a hot topic in the corporate world as well. I have spent most of my career consulting to organizations of all types (big, small, public-sector, private-sector, domestic, international) and in many industries. In the past few years, one of the most common requests I have received is to develop leadership "competencies" that describe what it takes to be an effective leader within the organization.

Competencies are primarily behavioral in description but may have a traits flavor as well, depending upon how they are labeled and defined. I would like to share two examples of projects designed to develop leadership competencies.

The first project involved a global pharmaceutical company that was interested in defining the leadership competencies required of the top-level leaders in the organization (worldwide). First, we formed a group of subject-matter experts consisting of executives representing various countries as well as various functions (e.g., finance, research). Then, over the course of several half-day sessions, we developed and defined organizational capabilities—things required of the whole organization to achieve competitive advantage in the 21st century (e.g., Create Leverage, Innovation). These organizational capabilities were used as a context for developing leadership competencies including Vision and Strategic Thinking, Drive for Results, and Inspiring People.

At this point we gave each competency a behavioral definition, followed by key behaviors that would span across all senior leaders. After that, we conducted focus groups with other leaders to more fully define what "high-," "medium-," and "low"-level performance would look like for each of the competencies—also referred to as behavioral anchors. This model of leadership and the behaviorally defined levels of performance were then integrated into the performance management and career development systems for current and aspiring executives in the organization.

The second project involved a regional airline. In this case, leadership competencies were not limited to top-tier leaders but, rather, were applied to all levels of leaders. Using subject-matter-expert focus groups (incumbents and managers of incumbents), we defined competencies that spanned all types of leaders in the organization. We then created behavioral anchors (high-, medium-, and low-performance levels) for each competency for each level of leader (i.e., for supervisors, managers, and directors). This additional work allowed each competency definition to come to life for a specific level of leader. As you might imagine, these competencies (e.g., Communication, Coaching) were a bit more generic in nature than those in the first example; however, the behavioral anchors allowed us to tailor them for each leadership level. These competencies were also used for performance management.

In short, while situation and culture can certainly play a role in the definition of effective leadership, it is also possible to span those boundaries within a specific organizational context.

APPLYING YOUR KNOWLEDGE

1. What do competencies have to do with leadership?
2. In Dr. Gutenberg's examples, why were the competencies given behavioral definitions?
3. How are leadership competencies linked to performance management?

ranging from "Never" to "Always." After hundreds of different leader behaviors had been accumulated and many dimensions examined, they were categorized in terms of two major dimensions (Fleishman & Harris, 1962). The first dimension, **initiating structure,** refers to behaviors through which leaders define the roles played by themselves and their subordinates in achieving the group's formal goals. Examples of initiating-structure behaviors include assigning specific tasks to subordinates, planning ahead for the next job to be done, pushing for higher production by setting difficult goals, defining procedures, and so on. The second dimension, **consideration,** concerns the extent to which leaders act in a supportive way and show concern and respect for their subordinates. Examples of consideration behaviors include emphasizing participative decision making, establishing two-way communication, and working to establish a favorable rapport with subordinates. Interestingly, the University of Michigan studies identified two very similar dimensions: *task-oriented behaviors* and *relationship-oriented behaviors.* The terms from the two sets of studies (initiating structure/task oriented and consideration/relationship oriented) are often used interchangeably.

initiating structure
Behaviors through which leaders define their roles and their subordinates' roles in achieving the group's formal goals.

consideration
The extent to which leaders act in a supportive way and show concern and respect for their subordinates.

The consideration and initiating-structure dimensions of the LBDQ are shown in Table 13.2, along with 10 behavior statements related to each. Consideration is clearly reflected in such statements as "Is friendly and approachable," "Does little things to make it pleasant to be a member of the group," "Puts suggestions made by the group into operation," and "Gives advance notice of changes." Indicative of initiating structure are statements like "Lets group members know what is expected of them," "Makes his or her attitudes clear to the group," "Decides what shall be done and how it will be done," and "Assigns group members to particular tasks." One thing to keep in mind is that leaders are not necessarily one or the other: For instance, a leader can be either high or low on both initiating structure and consideration. In fact, there tends to be a small positive correlation between the two dimensions. Can you think of a boss you've worked with who was very directive in terms of deadlines and goals but also supportive in his or her interactions with employees? If so, then you have an example of a supervisor who is high on both facets of leadership behaviors. Of course, there are other leaders who have been known to lean pretty far in one direction or the other. For instance, Generals George Patton and Omar Bradley were both extremely successful and respected military generals during World War II, but Patton was low on consideration and high on initiating structure, whereas Bradley was high on consideration and relatively low on initiating structure. In short, these were leaders in the same field at the same time who attained impressive goals in very different ways.

The most important contribution of the behavioral approach to leadership has been the classification of leader behaviors in terms of the two broad dimensions just discussed. Unfortunately, specific findings have been inconsistent. For instance, some studies have found a negative correlation between consideration behaviors and leader effectiveness, whereas others have found a positive correlation (see Bass, 1985, for a review). Most of this research was conducted in the 1960s and 1970s, but recent studies have continued to examine leader behaviors (e.g., Van Vugt & De Cremer, 1999). In a survey of workers in an employment agency, for example, the most favorable attitudes were expressed by those who

TABLE 13.2 Items from the Leadership Behavior Description Questionnaire (LBDQ)

My Leader/Boss:	Never 1	2	3	4	Always 5
Consideration					
1. Is friendly and approachable.					
2. Does little things to make it pleasant to be a member of the group.					
3. Puts suggestions made by the group into operation.					
4. Treats all group members as his or her equals.					
5. Gives advance notice of changes.					
6. Keeps to him- or herself. (R)					
7. Looks out for the personal welfare of group members.					
8. Is willing to make changes.					
9. Refuses to explain his or her actions. (R)					
10. Acts without consulting the group. (R)					
Initiating Structure					
1. Lets group members know what is expected of them.					
2. Encourages the use of uniform procedures.					
3. Tries out his or her ideas in the group.					
4. Makes his or her attitudes clear to the group.					
5. Decides what shall be done and how it will be done.					
6. Assigns group members to particular tasks.					
7. Makes sure that his or her part in the group is understood by group members.					
8. Schedules the work to be done.					
9. Maintains definite standards of performance.					
10. Asks that group members follow standard rules and regulations.					

Source: Stogdill (1963).

worked for leaders high in both interpersonal orientation and task orientation. This relationship varied as a function of the leader's gender, however: Employees working for female leaders who were high on both interpersonal orientation and task orientation did not report more organizational commitment than did employees working for female leaders who were low in both leadership dimensions (Hutchison, Valentino, & Kirkner, 1998). In other words, interpersonal orientation and task orientation didn't matter as much among female leaders as among male leaders.

In the most recent work in this area, Judge, Piccolo, & Ilies (2004) examined the relationships between both consideration and initiating structure and a set of leadership effectiveness indicators via a meta-analysis. In arguing that these leadership behaviors are important and should not be viewed as relevant only to the history of leadership, they reported correlations from .22 to .78 between these behaviors and constructs such as follower job satisfaction, follower motivation, leader performance, and leader effectiveness. They concluded that research that reexamines consideration and initiating-structure behaviors could benefit the leadership field.

However, as with trait theory, no one set of behaviors has emerged as being consistently predictive of effective leadership across a series of studies. This inconsistency may be due to the use of several different measures of leader behaviors (Schreisheim, House, & Kerr, 1976), the use of questionnaires that relied on participants' recall of behaviors, and a chief focus on lower-level managers (House & Aditya, 1997). It may also be due to the impact of situational variables on the leadership process, and this is where the journey takes us next—to contingency theories.

Contingency Theories

Because researchers were unable to discover a specific set of traits or behaviors that predicted effective leadership, they began to consider the role of the situation. In the 1960s, contingency theories grew out of this new approach to the study of leadership. **Contingency theories** differ from both trait and behavioral theories by formally taking into account situational or contextual variables. The central question, in other words, is whether leadership is contingent on the context or situation in which it takes place. We now turn to a discussion of two of the best-known contingency theories: Fiedler's contingency theory and path-goal theory.

contingency theories
Leadership theories that differ from both trait and behavioral theories by formally taking into account situational or contextual variables.

Fiedler's Contingency Theory. In 1967 Fred Fiedler published his contingency theory of leader effectiveness, which maintains that effective leadership is a joint function of the characteristics of the leader and the features of the situation. Specifically, he argued that task-oriented leaders are best suited for some situations and that relationship-oriented leaders are best suited for other situations. This was the first theory to consider how leader characteristics (i.e., traits and behaviors) might interact with situational variables to determine leader effectiveness. Given that leadership research to this point was dominated by trait and behavioral theories, it was a groundbreaking approach.

Fiedler's theory is graphically summarized in Figure 13.1. Here, situational variables are described in terms of *situational favorability*, which is a function of the leader's perception of *situational control*. A favorable situation is defined in

FIGURE 13.1 Fiedler's Contingency Theory

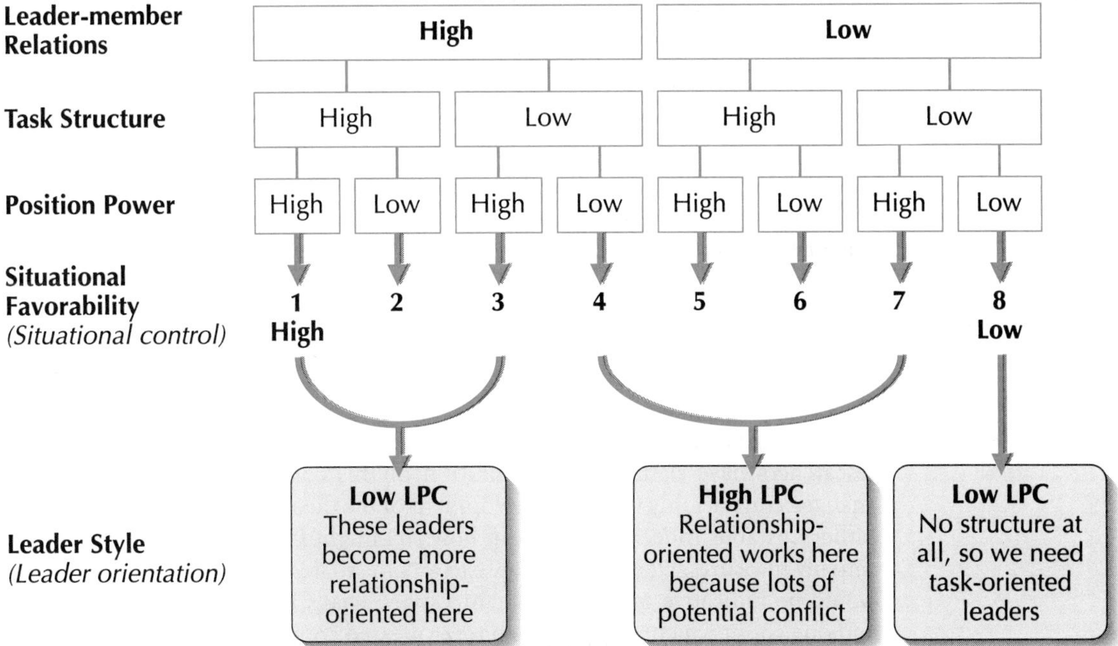

terms of three dimensions. The first and most important of these concerns *leader-member relations,* or the extent to which the leader has a positive relationship with subordinates such that the subordinates trust the leader. This dimension is related to group cohesion in the sense that the work group is either unified or not unified in its support of the leader. The second dimension concerns the amount of *task structure* that is present in subordinates' jobs—a variable that includes clarity of goals and procedures. And the last dimension concerns the *position power* possessed by the leader. (In terms of the five bases of power that we reviewed earlier, position power is probably related to both legitimate power and reward power.) Thus the situation is favorable (i.e., controllable by the leader) if the leader has a positive relationship with subordinates, if the subordinates' tasks are well defined, and if the leader has the power to make important decisions. As shown in Figure 13.1, each of these three dimensions can be described as either high or low, resulting in eight different degrees of situational favorability.

These degrees of situational favorability match up with leader style or orientation, which can be measured by the *least preferred co-worker (LPC)* scale. On this scale, which contains a list of bipolar adjectives, the leader is asked to describe the single worst co-worker that he or she has ever encountered. However, as the construct measured by this scale has never been very well defined, Fiedler's theory has come under criticism (e.g., Hosking & Schriesheim, 1978). Suppose you were asked to evaluate your least preferred co-worker on the basis of 15 or 20 bipolar adjectives such as the following:

Pleasant	1 2 3 4 5 6 7 8	Unpleasant
Friendly	1 2 3 4 5 6 7 8	Unfriendly
Cooperative	1 2 3 4 5 6 7 8	Uncooperative

If I were to sum up your scores across these adjectives, what would the result tell me about you? According to Fiedler, rather than measuring a leader's attitudes directly, the LPC scale requires that we infer the leader's investment in task accomplishment through his or her reactions to a co-worker who gets in the way of accomplishments. For example, if a leader gave the LPC a very negative rating, we would infer that the rating reflected the leader's frustration or anger (Ayman, Chemers, & Fiedler, 1995). We would also conclude that the leader is task-oriented, meaning that the leader prefers to work toward goals by structuring and controlling tasks. Alternatively, if the leader rated the LPC in favorable terms, the leader would be considered person-oriented, meaning that the leader prefers to reach group goals by working closely with people on an interpersonal basis. Many researchers have criticized the definition of this construct, noting that it has changed considerably with the development of the theory and at times has seemed rather unstable. Indeed, think about how *you* might fill out the LPC and what it actually measures. Does it make sense to assume that your responses on this scale would be indicative of your leadership style? That's really the central question and one about which many critics have expressed concern.

Note that Figure 13.1 also shows how the match between situational control and leader style influences work-group effectiveness. There has been some support for this aspect of the model, but it is largely mixed (for some of the eight quadrants there has been no support at all). Fiedler maintains that task-oriented leaders perform best in situations of high and low control, whereas relationship-oriented leaders perform best in situations of moderate control. These more global predictions have been consistently supported with respect to measures of work-group performance (House & Aditya, 1997). So, in the final analysis, despite the many criticisms of Fiedler's theory, it was the first approach to leadership to consider *both* situational and individual factors, and it should thus be considered an important historical contribution to the development of the field.

In an interesting twist, a recent meta-analysis has found support for Fiedler's cognitive resource theory, which focuses on intelligence as an important element of leadership. Fiedler (1995) argued, consistent with his contingency theory, that the effect of leader intelligence on leader success was contingent on other variables. In their meta-analysis, Judge, Colbert, and Ilies (2004) found support for this contingency approach by showing that intelligence had a moderately positive effect on leadership success when leaders were under low stress but no effect on leadership success when leaders were under high stress. This supports Fiedler's theory that in stressful situations an individual uses intelligence to deal with the stress, which makes that resource unavailable for leadership, while the stress distracts the individual from the tasks at hand. Judge et al. also found support for Fiedler's notion that intelligence of the leader results in success only if the leader is directive and is unrelated to success when the leader is nondirective.

Path-Goal Theory. Given that leadership is the process of motivating subordinates, an effective leader is one who adopts whatever approach is most likely to accomplish this goal. With this in mind, Bob House (1971) presented his path-goal theory of leader effectiveness. This theory emerged from a historical context in which results regarding leader behaviors on work-group performance and subordinate satisfaction were very inconsistent and in which a cognitive emphasis was inherent in the popular motivational theories of the day. In particular, the path-goal theory arose out of the motivational concepts related to the expectancy theory of Victor Vroom (1964; see also Chapter 9). As you may recall, expectancy theory maintains that individuals are motivated to exhibit particular behaviors if they expect positive outcomes to come from exhibiting those behaviors and if they value those outcomes. As House (1996) explains:

> [T]he essential notion underlying the path-goal theory is that individuals in positions of authority, supervisors, will be effective to the extent that they complement the environment in which their subordinates work by providing the necessary cognitive clarifications to ensure that subordinates expect that they can attain work goals and that they will experience intrinsic satisfaction and receive valent rewards as a result of work goal attainment. (p. 326)

The path-goal theory specifies a number of situational moderators that influence the relationship between leadership behaviors and their effectiveness. It also identifies four kinds of leader behaviors: *directive leader behaviors, achievement-oriented leader behaviors, supportive leader behaviors,* and *participative leader behaviors* (House, 1996). These categories are presented and defined in Table 13.3. It is interesting to note that directive leader behavior is analogous to initiating-structure behavior (task orientation), while supportive leader behavior is akin to consideration behavior (relationship orientation). Figure 13.2 depicts the interactions between situational moderators and leader behaviors. Note that the leader behaviors are predicted to have direct effects on subordinates' expectancies and values (as moderated by both subordinate and environmental characteristics) and that subordinates' perceptions regarding these expectancies and values affect their satisfaction, effort, and performance (as would be predicted by expectancy theory).

The results of the 40 to 50 studies that have tested various propositions of the path-goal theory are mixed. A meta-analysis of these studies found support for the basic propositions related to directive behaviors, task characteristics, and employee satisfaction; however, the results for predicting performance, as well as those involving supportive behaviors as predictors, were much less consistent (Schriesheim & Neider, 1996). Recent reviews and critical evaluations of the

TABLE 13.3 Path-Goal Theory: Leader Behaviors

Directive Leader Behaviors	Provide structure by clarifying subordinates' performance goals and clarifying standards used to evaluate subordinates
Achievement-Oriented Leader Behaviors	Stress personal accomplishments and encourage performance excellence
Supportive Leader Behaviors	Focus on interpersonal relations and provide psychological and emotional support for subordinates
Participative Leader Behaviors	Encourage subordinates to take an active role through mentoring, guidance, and coaching

theory and its accompanying research indicate that the theory has not been well tested owing to methodological problems such as poor measures of the constructs, lack of attention to intermediate variables (i.e., subordinate expectancies and perceptions of values), and lack of control regarding other relevant variables (House, 1996; Schriesheim & Neider, 1996). These criticisms and the absence of valid tests of the path-goal theory led House (1996) to reformulate the theory and call for more careful testing. The jury is still out with respect to the validity of this revised theory, but current and future empirical research will help provide a more useful evaluation of its contribution to our ability to understand and predict effective leadership.

FIGURE 13.2 Path-Goal Theory

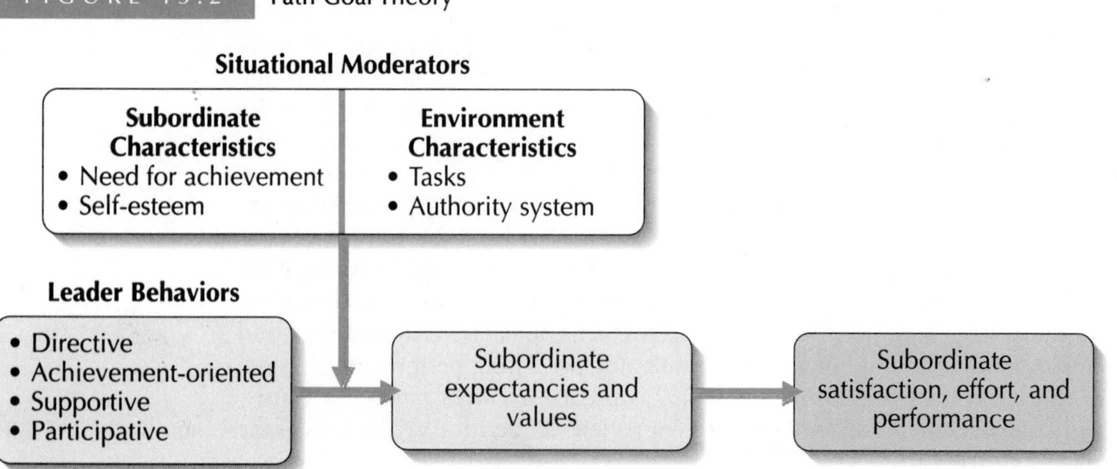

Contemporary Theories

Newer leadership theories developed in the past 25 years have captured the attention of leadership researchers and practitioners alike. In this section I will talk about three of these theories in particular: leader-member exchange theory, implicit leadership theory, and transformational leadership theory.

Leader-Member Exchange Theory.

We have talked about leadership as being based on behaviors, traits, and interactions between the individual and the situation. Leadership researchers have also begun to view leadership as a reciprocal interaction between two parties (Lord, 2000). **Leader-member exchange (LMX) theory,** for instance, is a theory about work dyads that focuses on the relationships among subordinates and leaders rather than on leader behaviors or traits. A precursor to LMX, developed in the 1970s, was called vertical dyad linkage (VDL) theory (Dansereau, Graen, & Haga, 1975). A major premise of VDL theory that has carried over to LMX is the notion that leaders have different relationships with different subordinates. Whereas both trait and behavior-based theories assume that leaders use the same style or orientation (called "average leadership style") with all of their subordinates, VDL suggests that their styles vary across subordinates. This results in subordinates being placed or classified in the in-group or the out-group. Subordinates in the in-group tend to have good relationships with their leaders based on mutual trust, shared responsibility, and support, whereas those in the out-group do not experience particularly strong relationships with their supervisors and tend to be treated in a more task-oriented fashion (Yukl, 2002).

leader-member exchange (LMX) theory
A theory about work dyads that focuses on the relationships among subordinates and leaders rather than on leader behaviors or traits.

According to LMX theory, the quality of the leader-follower relationship is predictive of individual-, group-, and organizational-level outcomes (Gerstner & Day, 1997). According to a recent meta-analysis of about 80 LMX studies, the quality of LMX relationships was significantly related to such outcomes as subordinate performance ratings, job satisfaction, organizational commitment, role clarity, role conflict, and turnover intentions. (In the case of the latter two outcomes, the relationship was negative.) The authors concluded that having a high-quality relationship with one's boss can affect the entire work experience in a very positive way (Gerstner & Day, 1997). Recent work has begun teasing out the effects of LMX on performance-related factors (Hofmann, Morgeson, & Gerras, 2003). For example, Kacmar, Witt, Zivnuska, and Gully (2003) replicated previous work, finding that positive LMX relationships were related to favorable performance ratings (see Chapter 5). However, they also found that this relationship was enhanced by the frequency of communication between the leader and the follower. In other words, LMX was more strongly related to performance ratings if the members of the dyad communicated frequently. This suggests the potential importance and breadth of LMX effects.

To this point we have talked only about the effects of LMX on outcomes. However, from both a theoretical and a practical standpoint, it is important to investigate how LMX develops over time and what the antecedents of high-quality LMX relationships are. Not much research has been done in this area; the aforementioned meta-analysis found very few studies that examined antecedents (Gerstner & Day, 1997), and a more recent review of the literature suggests that although LMX appears to be positively related to various organizational outcome variables, additional work is necessary on the theoretical side to formulate more testable models of the development of LMX relationships (Schriesheim, Castro, & Cogliser, 1999). Nevertheless, a couple of recent studies have tried to tackle this issue. In one, both demographic and organizational factors were theorized as important for the development of LMX relationships. When the authors examined some of these factors in a survey of 208 public library employees (Green, Anderson, & Shivers, 1996), they found support for one demographic variable as a predictor of LMX quality: Specifically, gender dissimilarity between leader and member resulted in lower-quality relationships than did gender similarity. (In this study, gender dissimilarity was operationalized primarily in terms of male leaders and female subordinates.) The authors also uncovered three important organizational factors: First, the quality of LMX relationships was negatively affected both by the number of subordinates who reported to each supervisor and by the workload of employees. Finally, the amount of available resources was positively related to the quality of the LMX relationship, indicating that, like anything else worth pursuing, development of positive LMX relationships requires effort and resources. The authors of this study argued that such organizational factors provide boundaries or constraints on the development of LMX relationships—a topic that promises to become important in the 21st century as organizations move toward structures in which leaders supervise the work of many more subordinates than has been typical in the past. If the leader's discretion is limited by these factors, the potential quality of the LMX relationship will be limited as well.

Another study that has examined antecedents to LMX relationships (Murphy & Ensher, 1999) involved a survey of 56 leader-member pairs in a media company. A few interesting results emerged. First, LMX quality was strongly related to the perceived similarity between leader and member from the perspective of either. In other words, subordinates who believed that their attitudes, outlooks, perspectives, and problem-solving methods were similar to those of their supervisors (and vice versa) reported better quality LMX relationships than those who did not perceive this similarity. Second, subordinates who were high on self-efficacy tended to be rated by supervisors as being involved in high-quality LMX relationships. And, third, subordinates low on self-efficacy at Time 1 tended to be significantly higher on self-efficacy at Time 2 if they were fortunate enough to experience a high-quality LMX relationship in the interim. These findings clearly suggest that the relationship between leaders and followers is an important element of the leadership process—especially given its impact on employee attitudes and organizational outcomes.

Implicit Leadership Theory (ILT). A very different approach to leadership has been developed by Bob Lord and his colleagues (Lord, Foti, & DeVader, 1984;

Lord & Maher, 1991) at the University of Akron. This approach—known as **implicit leadership theory (ILT)**—emphasizes subordinates' perceptions of leader behaviors, in contrast to the theories we've previously discussed, which maintain that leaders affect the performance of subordinates through leader behaviors, traits, charismatic qualities, and the ability to structure situations and define roles (Lord, 2000). Specifically, ILT views leadership as the outcome of a perceptual process involving both leaders and subordinates. Lord and Maher (1991) actually define leadership in terms of whether one is perceived by others as a leader. In his most recent work, Lord defines leadership as a process through which the leader changes the way followers envision themselves (Lord & Brown, 2004).

implicit leadership theory (ILT)
A leadership theory that views leadership as the outcome of a perceptual process involving both leaders and subordinates.

The central idea here is that we all hold implicit beliefs about the personal qualities and behaviors of leaders. These beliefs develop over time and are influenced by experience and socialization. The word **prototype** is sometimes used to refer to one's mental representation of a leader. (My own prototype of a leader, for instance, is someone who is intelligent, has excellent communication skills, is committed to the work that needs to be done and to the people who do the work, and knows how to motivate employees.) Lord and his colleagues (1984) have demonstrated in experimental studies that when people observe someone behaving in a way that is consistent with their prototype for an effective leader, they conclude that this person is an effective leader. The implication is that leadership effectiveness may be more about followers' perceptions than about leaders' actions. Further, more recently, they have begun to focus on how the follower's self-concept works along with leadership perceptions in affecting attitudes and behaviors (Lord & Brown, 2004).

prototype
One's mental representation of something or someone, such as a leader.

Other research (Phillips & Lord, 1981) has demonstrated that people develop global impressions of leader effectiveness based on the extent to which a particular leader matches their prototype. Even more important, however, is the finding that people use that global impression to describe the leader and to recall leader behaviors and traits—and that in doing so, they often make errors. An example is presented in Figure 13.3, which concerns my perceptions of my boss, Jared. My experience with Jared's behaviors are evaluated in light of my effective leader prototype (Box A), and I have decided that Jared is an effective leader (Box C) because he matches up with salient parts (Box B) of that prototype (i.e., intelligent, excellent communication skills, committed). Now, suppose that I'm asked to rate Jared on whether he is a *self-starter,* or to rate any other dimension of his behavior that I have not observed. I decide that because Jared is an effective leader, and because being a self-starter is part of my effective-leader prototype, Jared himself must also be a self-starter (Box D).

The process that I've just described is akin to the cart pulling the horse: Jared's behaviors are not driving my ratings of him, but, rather, my global impression of him as an effective leader colors my ratings of him on other, unseen dimensions. The implications of this process are pretty serious: When subordinates are asked to rate their leaders on scales such as the LBDQ, we can't be sure whether they are providing valid ratings of their leaders' behaviors. Perhaps they are relying instead on their general impression of their leader as effective or ineffective based on their leadership prototype and how well the leader seems to match that prototype—or,

FIGURE 13.3 Implicit Leadership Theory and Leadership Ratings

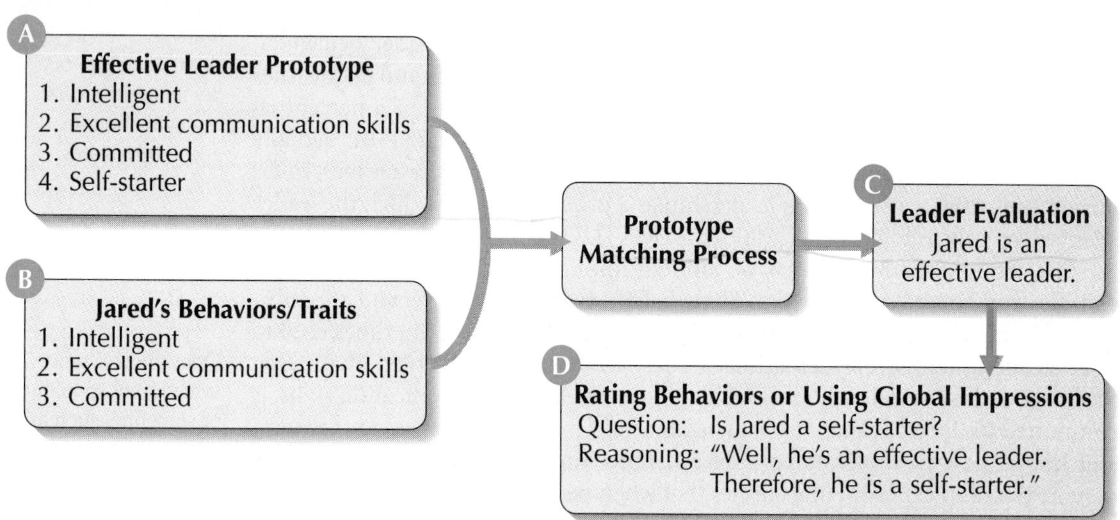

worse, only a few dimensions of that prototype. Lord's work on ILT has been at the center of leadership research over the past two decades and clearly raises many important issues for future research to consider. Recently the role of affect and emotions has begun to attract research attention within this ILT framework, as well as other leadership theories (Dasborough & Ashkanasy, 2002).

ILT has been applied to the issue of gender as well. Let's look at one such example. In a laboratory investigation that examined the role of gender in leader perceptions (Hall, Workman, & Marchioro, 1998), several groups consisting of two men and two women were assigned to work on either a masculine-typed or feminine-typed task. Leader ratings were provided by each group member of every other group member. Overall, men were rated higher on leadership scales than women; they were also more likely to emerge as leaders. Specifically, men emerged as leaders in about 70% of the groups. The relationship of gender to leadership ratings was also moderated by task type, such that the differences between males and females on leadership dimensions were greatest when the groups were working on a masculine-typed task. In a more recent study, Powell, Butterfield, and Parent (2002) noted that the proportion of women managers has more than doubled from 1976 to 1999 (21% to 46%). However, although participants seemed less likely to build managerial stereotypes around masculinity than they were a few decades ago, effective managers were still perceived as predominatly masculine. Gender and type of task thus appear to be related in a way that affects leadership perceptions and emergence. Because the issue of gender is so important to the workplace of the 21st century, we will discuss it in more detail later.

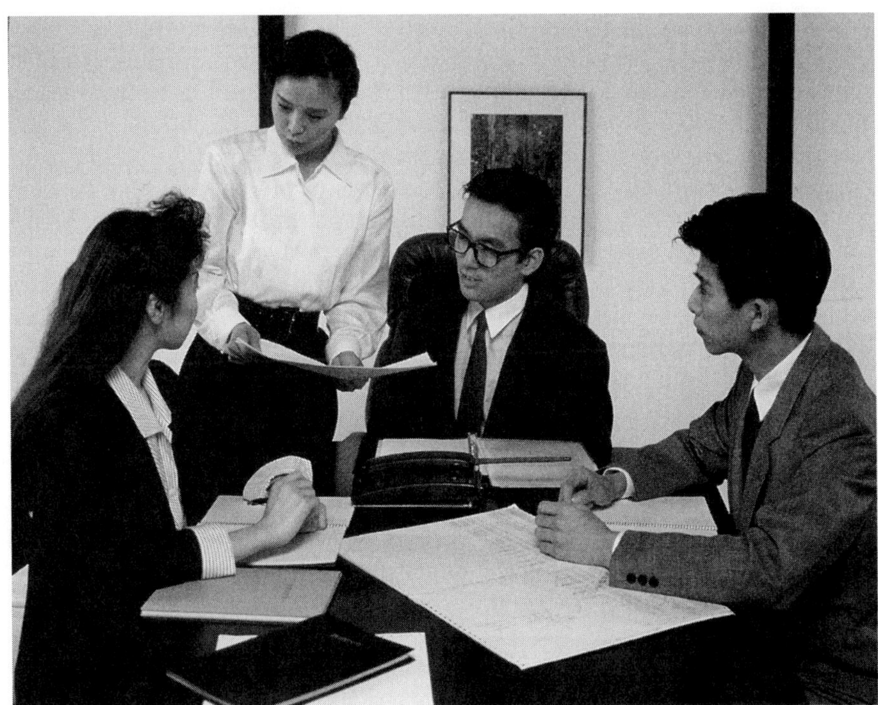

Gender sometimes plays a role in individuals' perceptions of leadership.

Transformational Leadership Theory. According to House, a major paradigm shift occurred in the leadership work of the mid-1970s, resulting in a class of theories referred to as the "New Leadership theories" (House & Aditya, 1997). These theories have the following four characteristics in common: (1) They explain how leaders can take organizations to new heights; (2) they explain how certain leaders are able to achieve extraordinary levels of motivation, commitment, dedication, and so on; (3) they stress emotionally appealing behaviors such as empowering, developing a vision, and role modeling for their subordinates; and (4) they encourage increased follower self-esteem and satisfaction, as well as identification with the leader's values and vision (House & Aditya, 1997).

Transformational leadership theory is one of the best known of this group of leadership theories. One of its strongest proponents and developers, Bernie Bass (1985), defines **transformational leadership** as a form of leadership in which the interaction of leader and follower raises both to higher levels of motivation and morality than they would achieve individually. In effect, transformational leaders attempt to motivate subordinates to transcend their self-interests and achieve more than they think is possible. Both the leader and follower are thus *transformed* or changed in some noticeable and important way. President John F. Kennedy is a good historical example of this type of leader. Individuals who worked for or with Kennedy, as well as citizens who lived during his time, talk about how he

transformational leadership
A form of leadership in which the interaction of leader and follower raises both to higher levels of motivation and morality than they would achieve individually.

raised their self-esteem and got them involved—he truly seemed able to change people for the good. Bass and his colleagues distinguish transformational leadership from **transactional leadership,** in which the relationship between leader and follower is based on exchanges and not much more (Bass, 1985; Bass & Steidlmeier, 1999). For instance, leaders who are more transactional than transformational tend to tell their subordinates what is expected of them and what they will get if they meet these expectations rather than emphasizing how the subordinates can grow and develop within the organization. In short, transactional leaders operate on the basis of *contingent reinforcement,* rewarding subordinates for specific behaviors. In real life, all leaders are partly transformational and partly transactional; thus, for example, when I speak of a "transformational leader" I am referring to a leader who tends to be more transformational than transactional.

transactional leadership
A form of leadership in which the relationship between leader and follower is based chiefly on exchanges, with an emphasis on contingent reinforcement.

Transformational leadership can be described in terms of four main components (Bass & Steidlmeier, 1999). The first of these, *idealized influence,* refers to the charisma brought to a relationship by a leader who arouses in the follower a strong desire to identify with or emulate the leader. Leaders who provide the second component, *inspirational motivation,* give followers challenges and a reason to engage in shared goals. Their inspirational appeal focuses on the best in people, such as harmony, charity, and good works (Bass & Steidlmeier, 1999). The third component, *intellectual stimulation,* refers to the process through which transformational leaders increase follower awareness of problems from a new perspective. This approach helps followers to think critically and to approach problems with an open and flexible mind, thus encouraging creative problem solving. Finally, *individualized consideration* is what leaders share with followers when they treat each as an individual, providing support, encouragement, and growth experiences to all. Overall, transformational leaders concentrate their efforts on long-term goals, develop and articulate a vision to share, inspire followers to enthusiastically pursue that vision, and coach followers to take greater responsibility for their own and others' development. They go the extra yard and do more than just *motivate* their followers; they *inspire* them.

Research has connected transformational leadership to important organizational outcomes like job satisfaction, organizational commitment, and workgroup performance (House & Aditya, 1997). A meta-analysis has demonstrated that the four main transformational behaviors—idealized influence, inspirational motivation, intellectual stimulation, and individualized consideration—are significantly correlated with leadership effectiveness (Lowe, Kroeck, & Sivasubramaniam, 1996). And House concludes that transformational leadership results in a high level of subordinate motivation and commitment, in addition to well-above-average performance (House & Aditya, 1997). Of course, elements of transactional leadership are important, too, such as reinforcing subordinates based on their performance. Thus transformational leaders are more successful if they exhibit some transactional behavior as well, but transactional leadership alone is typically not so successful (Bass, 1985). Bass, Avolio, Jung, and Berson (2003) recently showed that in military platoons under stressful situations, the best performance resulted from platoon leaders and sergeants who exhibited transactional contingent reward and transformational behaviors.

Research on transformational leadership continues at a blistering clip (Antonakis, Avolio, & Sivasubramaniam, 2003). Let's look at a few recent examples. First, because transformational leadership is believed to bring followers to a higher level regarding commitment to and identification with the leader and organization, it seems reasonable to expect that it will influence organizational citizenship behaviors (OCBs). Recall that OCBs are behaviors that seem to go above and beyond the call of duty—though not necessarily included in one's job description, they tend to be in the best interests of both the organization and one's co-workers. A recent study using two samples—one consisting of employees from an employment agency and the other consisting of employed students—found support for a model in which transformational leadership led to higher perceptions of procedural justice, higher levels of trust, and, finally, increased frequency of OCBs (Pillai, Schriesheim, & Williams, 1999). In other words, transformational leadership behaviors are viewed as procedurally fair by employees who grow to trust their leader as a result of these behaviors and are then motivated to go beyond the call of duty and exhibit various OCBs.

A second study applies transformational leadership theory to the political arena. In this case, the researchers were interested in determining whether voters' perceptions of the extent to which a particular leader was transformational or charismatic affected their intentions to vote for the candidate as well as their actual voting behavior. Rajnandini Pillai and Ethlyn Williams (1998) surveyed over 260 business students about their perceptions of Bill Clinton and Bob Dole 1 week prior to the 1996 U.S. presidential election. Then, 1 week after the election, they collected data on actual voting behavior. The preelection survey asked questions about the extent to which each candidate (1) is able to get others committed to his dream, (2) provides a good model for his followers to follow, (3) shows respect for his followers' personal feelings, and (4) has stimulated followers to rethink the way they do things. The theory of transformational leadership predicts that voters who view the candidate in these transformational terms are more likely not only to intend to vote for him but also to actually vote for him. This is exactly what the researchers found: Transformational leadership ratings were significantly related to both the intent to vote and the actual vote for a particular candidate. As you might imagine, party affiliation was important, too. Republicans were more likely to intend to vote and to actually vote for Bob Dole, and Democrats were more likely to intend to vote and to actually vote for Bill Clinton. But the most interesting finding was that transformational ratings predicted both intent to vote and actual voting behavior even after party affiliation was controlled for. In other words, regardless of political affiliation, voters tended to vote for the candidate whom they viewed as the more transformational of the two.

Third, Kark, Shamir, and Chen (2003) suggest that transformational leadership can actually result in two conflicting outcomes: dependence on the leader and empowered self-direction. These scholars suggest that transformational leadership can lead to such a strong personal identification with the leader that the followers become dependent on her. On the other hand, transformational leadership can also lead to social identification with co-workers and the organization, resulting in an increase in self-efficacy and self-esteem. In their study of Israeli midlevel managers, they found empirical support for these theoretical relationships. Future research seems necessary to uncover the contextual variables that are likely to result in transformational leadership leading to more empowerment than dependence and vice versa. Of course, too, links from dependence and empowerment to follower behaviors would be an interesting avenue for additional research, as well.

NEW DIRECTIONS IN LEADERSHIP RESEARCH

Now that we have discussed the various leadership theories at length, I will take a closer look at the impact of gender issues on leadership—a topic with significant implications for the effectiveness of 21st-century organizations. After that, we will consider a related subject: the influence of culture on leadership.

GENDER AND LEADERSHIP

Certainly, we are all aware of the changing nature of our workforce. Women and minorities are currently being employed at rates far greater than this country has ever seen before. Six out of every 10 women age 16 and over were labor-force participants in 2002; they also made up 47% of the labor force, and that number is projected to increase (U.S. Department of Labor, 2004).

The Department of Labor has established a category of work known as executive, administrative, and managerial (EXAM) occupations that includes fast-food restaurant managers, CEOs of large corporations, accountants, financial managers, and health managers. This is the category in which managers are typically placed; it is also especially relevant to our discussion of gender and leadership, given that women made up 46% of the total number of EXAM workers in 2002—up from 39% in 1988 (U.S. Department of Labor, 2004). Specific occupations are listed in Table 13.4, along with the percentages of women holding those jobs in 2002.

The Glass Ceiling Commission was established in 1991 to study the barriers preventing women from rising to the top of the corporate ladder. Its report indicated that although women made up 43% of EXAM workers at that time, they held only 3–5% of the top executive positions. Further, surveys of Fortune 1500 companies over the past decade have indicated that 95–97% of senior managers—vice presidents and higher—were men (U.S. Department of Labor, 1997). Other relevant data include the fact that only 14% of the members of the U.S. House of Representatives and 14% of the members the U.S. Senate are women (U.S. Government, 2004); women make up over 40% of college faculty but only 19% of college presidents (ACE News, 2000); and although about 42% of the associates in our nation's law firms are women, only 16% are partners (American Bar Asso-

TABLE 13.4 Employment by Gender

Occupations	Total Persons Employed	Women as Percent of Total
Officials and administrators in public administration	720,000	52.6
Financial managers	803,000	50.5
Managers in marketing, advertising, and public relations	735,000	38.4
Managers in medicine and health	828,000	78.4
Accountants and auditors	1,720,000	59.4
Management analysts	545,000	42.2
Personnel, training, and labor relations specialists	624,000	74.9

Source: U.S. Department of Labor (2004).

ciation, 2004). Thus, despite great progress for women in the workforce and in management positions, there is still a long way to go. Indeed, the increased number of women in leadership positions demands additional leadership research in which gender is considered an important and relevant variable of interest.

Alice Eagly has been a leader herself in bringing issues of gender to the front and center of leadership studies. In a series of meta-analyses she and her colleagues identified the important variables and summarized the big picture involved in linking gender to leadership. Let's review some of this work. First, Eagly and Blair Johnson (1990) looked at the role of gender in leadership style and found consistent (albeit small) differences between men and women, including the fact that women are more participative and interpersonally oriented than men. The largest differences tended to be seen in laboratory studies rather than organizational studies, indicating that when individuals are selected or trained to be leaders within an organization, they are not provided the opportunity to lead or manage in a gender-stereotypic manner; but when they are left to their own devices in laboratory studies, stereotypic differences between the genders do emerge. Their results also demonstrated that in situations that were congenial to a particular gender—such that the characteristics of the situation matched well with the gender roles (e.g., women in the role of head nurse and men in the role of construction manager)—both men and women leaders tended to be task oriented. This last finding is consistent with Eagly's work on gender role theory. The authors concluded from their extensive review that women tend to lose authority or legitimate power if they employ feminine (participative and interpersonally oriented) styles of leadership in male-dominated roles (Eagly & Johnson, 1990). Of course, the position of a leader has traditionally been viewed by the general

Women are underrepresented in many executive-level and senior-leadership positions, such as the U.S. Congress.

public as being masculine, and a recent study of male cadets in the United States Air Force Academy supports this notion (Boyce & Herd, 2003); so the fact that women have been hindered from obtaining and being successful in leadership roles has more to do with stereotypes about leadership than about women's actual ability to lead. This is consistent with Lord's work on ILT discussed earlier in the chapter.

Second, using gender role theory as a background, Eagly and Steven Karau (1991) predicted that men would emerge as leaders in contexts or situations that were consistent with male gender roles and that women would emerge as leaders in contexts or situations that were consistent with female gender roles. An extensive meta-analysis of the existing literature supported their predictions: Men emerged more often as leaders in task-oriented situations, whereas women emerged more often as leaders in socially oriented situations. Like the earlier meta-analysis (Eagly & Johnson, 1990), this one suggests that perceptions of leadership tasks and gender characteristics play an important role in leadership processes and provides some support for the basic tenets of implicit leadership theory.

An even more recent meta-analysis has looked at the role of gender in leadership effectiveness (Eagly, Karau, & Makhijani, 1995). In this work, Eagly and her associates asked two very important questions: (1) Are leaders of one gender more effective than leaders of the other gender? And (2) do situations or contexts affect the likelihood that leaders of one gender or the other will be more effective leaders? Based again on gender role theory, these researchers predicted that men would be more effective—or at least *perceived* to be more effective—than women in leadership roles that have been defined in masculine terms. In other words, they anticipated that gender congeniality would moderate the relationship between gender and leader effectiveness.

Some interesting results emerged. First, women and men did not differ overall in terms of their perceived effectiveness as leaders. Second, whether the study took place in the laboratory or in an organization didn't seem to matter. Third, gender congeniality did moderate the gender/leader effectiveness relationship: Male leaders were perceived as more effective in contexts that were congenial to men and female leaders were perceived as more effective in contexts that were congenial to women (Eagly et al., 1995). This last finding is especially interesting; it suggests that both men and women are unlikely to be perceived as effective leaders in situations that are not traditionally viewed as gender-congruent. Of course, considering that leadership tends to be defined in masculine terms, women are already at a disadvantage in many leadership situations: In order to behave in a way that is consistent with prototypical leadership (e.g., being aggressive and directive), they must behave in contrast to their gender roles (e.g., being nurturing, supportive, and participative). Thus women are criticized for not being "leader-like" due to their feminine characteristics—but when they adjust and take on more masculine traits in order to be viewed as "leader-like," they are criticized for not being true to their femininity. This conflict is at the root of the stress and struggles faced by many women in leadership positions today.

Some have argued over the years for the "feminine advantage" perspective to leadership effectiveness (Yukl, 2002). The notion is that because women are more adept at being inclusive, interpersonally sensitive, and nurturing than men, they should be better leaders. Vecchio (2002) argues convincingly against this perspective by citing a good deal of research that does not find these differences between the genders. However, Eagly, Johannesen-Schmidt, and van Engen's (2003) meta-analysis of leadership behaviors across genders finds that female leaders tend to exhibit higher levels of transformational leadership behaviors and transactional contingent reward behaviors than do male leaders, who tend to exhibit higher levels of the typically less effective transactional behaviors (i.e., management by exception) than do female leaders. Although these differences were generally small, they were statistically significant, and there were also small statistical differences between genders on leadership outcomes such as effectiveness, with females performing better than males. Obviously, Vecchio's analysis and Eagly et al.'s review lead to different conclusions, suggesting the need for additional research and better conceptual development.

Genuineness plays an important role in the perceived effectiveness of female leaders. In one study, for example, Christine Kawakami and her colleagues manipulated the way in which women delivered leadership speeches (Kawakami, White, & Langer, 2000). They attempted to deal with the so-called double bind that women leaders are in: To be perceived as effective leaders, they have to take on male characteristics, because leadership has traditionally been viewed as male in nature; but to "act male" they must behave in ways that are inconsistent with their gender roles, resulting in negative evaluations. Kawakami argued that women may be able to overcome this double bind by taking on male traits while also behaving in a genuine or mindful manner. She and her associates manipulated genuineness by giving some women the freedom to deliver a leadership speech in their own way and restricting others to a very close reading of a prepared script. Their argument was that women leaders with masculine traits would be perceived as more effective if they also showed genuineness. The results strongly supported this prediction. Additional research is necessary before any firm conclusions can be drawn, but this approach certainly seems to hold promise for helping women leaders overcome the barriers preventing them from being perceived as effective leaders.

Culture and Leadership

Although cultural issues were ignored by leadership researchers for many years, they have recently become the focus of research (Dickson, Hanges, & Lord, 2000) due to the global economy and the increased diversification of organizations in the new millennium. Dickson, Den Hartog, and Mitchelson (2003) refer to the recent interest in cross-cultural leadership as an "explosion" in the field. Substantial evidence now indicates that cultures vary in terms of the extent to which they value different traits, leadership behaviors, and incentives (House, Wright, & Aditya, 1997). Indeed, Bob House and his colleagues have put forth a theory of cross-cultural leadership, which maintains that expected, accepted, and effective leader behavior varies by culture (House & Aditya, 1997). According to these authors, what a particular culture values in its leaders is based on the implicit leadership theory endorsed by that culture. This idea is, of course, an extension of Lord's work on ILT (Lord, 2000; Lord, Foti, & DeVader, 1984; Lord & Maher, 1991). An interesting study by Ensari and Murphy (2003) demonstrated that leadership prototypes develop through different processes in individualistic versus collectivistic cultures. Ideas along these lines constitute one focus of the ongoing Global Leadership and Organizational Behavior Effectiveness (GLOBE) research project, which involves 60 countries and more than 180 researchers led by House. These researchers argue that although some leader behaviors or traits are universally accepted and effective, there are many others for which acceptance and effectiveness are more culture specific (House & Aditya, 1997). Dickson et al. (2003) argue that future research from the GLOBE project should show with increasing frequency the many leadership effects or processes that are moderated by culture.

Interestingly, Bass (1997) has found that behaviors or traits that appear to be important across all cultures are precisely those behaviors or traits that are integral to transformational leadership as we have discussed it here. Some of the early data coming out of the GLOBE research project provide support for this argument (House et al., 1999): A total of 22 leadership attributes consistent with transformational leadership were universally endorsed by middle-level managers across 60 countries.

Nevertheless, it is likely that many other traits and behaviors vary across cultures. A study by Charlotte Gerstner and Dave Day (1994) demonstrates some of these expected differences. When these researchers administered a survey measuring 59 leadership traits to a sample of international and American graduate students (the international sample consisted of students from China, France, Germany, Honduras, India, Japan, and Taiwan), they found that the traits seen as most characteristic of business leaders varied across cultures. This result suggests that leadership prototypes also vary across cultures. For instance, the five most prototypical traits identified by Japanese participants were *disciplined, intelligent, trustworthy, educated,* and *responsible,* while those identified by U.S. participants were *persistent, industrious, good verbal skills, goal-oriented,* and *determined.* In short, there are clear differences between these two cultures in terms of what they view as prototypical leadership. Two other findings are interesting. First, no single trait emerged in the top-five category across all eight countries, indicating the considerable variability of leadership prototypes, but *goal-oriented* was the trait seen as prototypical in the largest number of countries. Second, categorizing cultures as either Western or Eastern resulted in some consistency within these two subgroups. In cultures categorized as Western (i.e., France, Germany, Honduras,

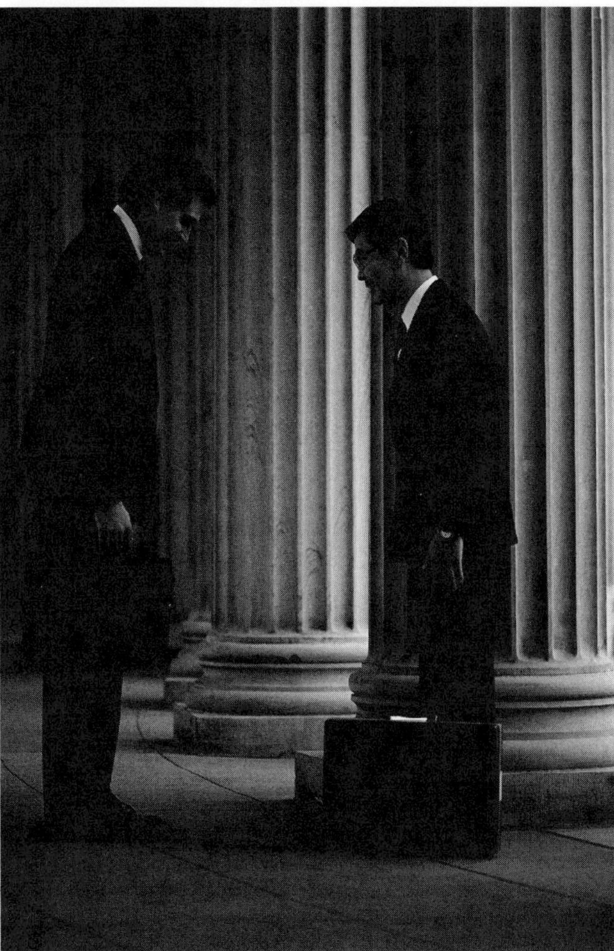

Some recent work suggests that leadership perceptions and processes differ across cultures.

India, and the United States), *determined* was highly prototypical, while in those categorized as Eastern (i.e., Taiwan, China, and Japan), *intelligence* was highly prototypical. The authors of this study concluded that there are reliable differences in leadership perceptions across cultures. The implication is that we need to understand these and other differences much more thoroughly if we are to comprehend the true nature of leadership processes. Indeed, a heightened awareness of such differences may help employees to better understand their co-workers and organizations to better understand their employees as the 21st-century workplace continues to become more diverse and global in nature.

SUMMARY

This chapter provides an overview of leadership with an emphasis on the theoretical and empirical work done in the field. I began by defining leadership and demonstrating how the concept of power and its different types relate to leadership processes. I then emphasized that leaders use different types of power in different situations and that some leaders rely on some types of power more than other types.

Next, I presented the major theories of leadership with an eye toward tracing their historical development; my rationale here was that history provides clues about how our thinking on leadership has evolved and become more sophisticated. I then described trait theories as the first real systematic approach to leadership, explaining that because no traits consistently emerged as necessary to be a good leader, this approach was largely abandoned (albeit revived later) in favor of research on leadership behaviors. The latter has revealed that some effective leaders exhibit mostly consideration behaviors, whereas others exhibit mostly initiating-structure behaviors. Taking a different direction, I then considered research on situational and individual moderators, as well as contingencies. In particular, I presented Fiedler's theory as an important new approach that eventually came under criticism—with the result that leadership advocates began looking elsewhere for a theoretical orientation.

In a later section I spent considerable time discussing three contemporary theories—LMX theory, ILT, and transformational leadership theory—that have great potential for helping us to understand leadership processes. I also noted that the perspective on leadership taken by both LMX and ILT is very different from that of more traditional theories. At the conclusion of the chapter, I described two cutting-edge issues in leadership that promise to be relevant in the 21st century—gender and culture. Both of these issues merit further study, as an understanding of their impact on leadership processes promises to enhance organizational practice.

REVIEW QUESTIONS

1. How would you evaluate a leader's effectiveness?
2. What are the five bases of power?
3. Differentiate between the trait and behavior approaches to leadership.
4. What are contingency theories of leadership? Give two examples.
5. What is the basic principle of LMX theory?
6. How is ILT different from earlier leadership theories?
7. What matters more in terms of effective leadership: leader behaviors or leader prototypes?
8. Distinguish between transformational and transactional leaders.
9. Why is gender an important issue in leadership research?
10. In what ways do cross-cultural issues complicate the study and understanding of leadership?

SUGGESTED READINGS

House, R. J., & Aditya, R. N. (1997). The social scientific study of leadership: Quo vadis? *Journal of Management, 23*(3), 409–473. A great review of leadership theories—and one that presents current research relevant to each theory.

Lord, R. G., & Maher, K. J. (1991). *Leadership and information processing: Linking perception and performance.* Boston: Unwin Hyman. Though complex, this is the most complete description of Lord's work on ILT and other information-processing issues.

Steers, R. M., Porter, L. M., & Bigley, G. A. (1996). *Motivation and leadership at work* (6th ed.). New York: McGraw-Hill. An easy read that covers all the major theories in the areas of both motivation and leadership.

Lord, R. G., & Brown, D. J. (2004). *Leadership process and follower identity.* Mahwah, NJ: Erlbaum. Lord's latest scholarly take on the leadership field is both fascinating and very readable.

Organizational Theory and Development

14

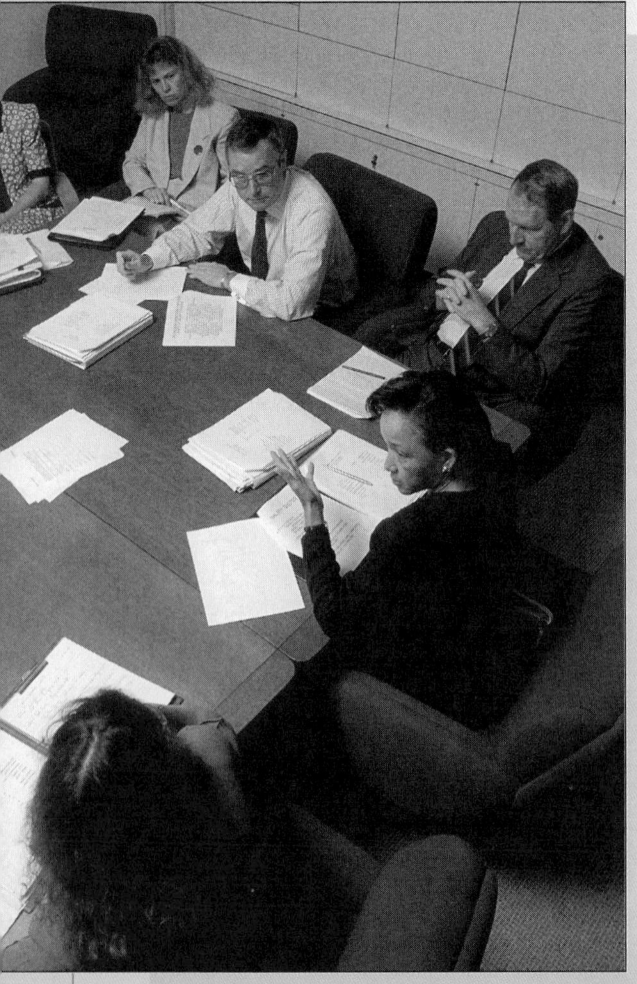

CHAPTER OUTLINE

What do you think about the company you work for? Is it a good company? Is it a company for which you expect to work for a long time, or is it just serving your needs right now? If your company is a good one to work for, what is it that makes it good? Is it financially successful? Does it treat its employees with respect and dignity? Do employees have input into the company's direction? I think these are all good questions, and the answers say a great deal about the organization that employs you. Over the course of the past decade, Southwest Airlines has been at or near the top of *Fortune* magazine's list of 100 Best Companies to Work For, has been listed as the second most admired company in the world (again, by *Fortune*), and has been cited as having one of the best national reputations of any company by the *Wall Street Journal* (Southwest Airlines, 2000). Cisco Systems, a worldwide leader in computer networking, has also been consistently rated as one of the best 100 companies to work for ("America's most admired companies," 2004) and the 2004 Most Admired Company; for the past five years it has been named one of the 100 Best Corporate Citizens by *Business Ethics* Magazine ("100 best corporate citizens," 2004). What do these companies have in common that allows them to be so successful—not only economically and competitively but also from the perspective of employees and applicants? In addition to providing employee-centered benefits such as medical benefits, fitness centers, on-site stores, profit sharing, and elder-care assistance (as we have discussed in earlier chapters), these companies emphasize the culture or environment in which their employees work. Indeed, to remain competitive in an economic sense and both desirable and valued by employees and applicants, organizations today must be willing and able to change their environment—a move that sometimes necessitates a complete alteration of their direction. As a reflection of the need to change, this chapter discusses organizational theories that are used to categorize, analyze, and improve organizations, with a focus on how and why organizations change or develop.

We have examined most issues in this text from either an individual perspective or a group perspective. In this chapter on organizational development, I take more of an organizational perspective. Rather than discussing how to appraise employees' performance, how to test employees to determine if we should hire them, how to motivate employees to work hard for the organization, or how to develop a work team, increase the productivity of a work team, or train individuals to work well in a team environment, I talk about how organizations operate, how they change and develop, and what techniques they can use to operate more effectively and efficiently. One theme throughout this text has been that given the changes confronting the world of work (e.g., downsizing, empowerment, global competition, diversity), organizations need to be forward looking. Accordingly, I devote this last chapter to a discussion of what organizations are doing, need to be doing, and should be doing in order to compete in this changing and increasingly competitive environment.

LEARNING OBJECTIVES

This chapter should help you understand:

- the various organizational theories and how they have developed.
- the differences between bureaucratic theory and scientific management.
- how Theory X differs from Theory Y.
- how open-system theory provides a useful framework for thinking about organizations.
- what organizational development is and why it is so important for the long-term success of organizations.
- the basic premises on which organizational change is based.
- the major principles of many organizational development interventions, as well as some benefits of each.
- some of the specifics concerning organizational development interventions, such as total quality management and gainsharing.
- technostructural interventions such as reengineering.
- how culture-change interventions and knowledge-management interventions can act to transform organizations profoundly.

ORGANIZATIONAL THEORY

organizational theory
A set of propositions that explains or predicts how groups and individuals behave in varying organizational structures and circumstances.

Organizational theory is defined as a set of propositions that explains or predicts how groups and individuals behave in varying organizational structures and circumstances (Shafritz & Ott, 1996b). It is not a stretch to say that much of how the world behaves is relevant to the study of organizational theory. From the community association to which we belong to our local church (or its parent organization), our government agencies, our local and national charities, and the workplace, organizational theory can help explain and predict behaviors that take place in many aspects of our lives. I discuss organizational theory specifically in the context of the last category, the workplace, in order to understand the structure and functioning of organizations. *Classical organizational theory*—one of three major organizational approaches—is important in this context.

Classical Organizational Theory

Some scholars have argued that organizational theory has its roots in ancient or medieval times, but the formal study of organizational theory appears to have begun when factories became popular in Great Britain in the 1700s (Shafritz & Ott,

1996a). Classical organizational theory, the first type of organizational theory to develop, has four basic tenets (Shafritz & Ott, 1996a):

- Organizations exist for economic reasons and to accomplish productivity goals.
- Scientific analysis will identify the one best way to organize for production.
- Specialization and the division of labor maximize production.
- Both people and organizations act in accordance with rational economic principles.

With the beginning of large, complex factories came a multitude of new and sophisticated problems with which managers had to deal. To be successful in this new economy, industrial and mechanical engineers needed to organize production systems to keep the machines busy and work flowing. Toward this end, workers were viewed as merely part of the mix—as interchangeable cogs in an organization-wide machine. In fact, a common argument was that organizations should work like machines, with people and technology as their components. The four preceding tenets helped maintain this focus. Two particular developments occurred within classical organizational theory: scientific management and bureaucracy. We will consider each in turn.

Scientific Management. In the late 1800s and early 1900s, Frederick Taylor provided a framework that he believed would be useful in structuring organizations. From the perspective of this framework, which he called *scientific management,* the organization is a machine—a pragmatic machine whose focus is simply to run more effectively. The scientific-management school conducted time and motion studies and analyzed temperature, illumination, and other conditions of work, all the while looking at the effects of these conditions on productivity and efficiency. "Taylorism," as this approach was sometimes called, had as its premise the notion that there is one best way to get the job done. And its tactics, given this premise, were quite simple: Conduct studies that gather data indicating what the fastest and most efficient method is, and then implement that method. In short, Taylorism maintained that factory workers would be much more productive if their work was designed scientifically. In the early 1900s this notion became a movement; sweeping through our nation's factories, it had a profound—almost revolutionary—effect on the business field (Shafritz & Ott, 1996a).

Scientific management can be summarized in terms of four principles (Taylor, 1916/1996). First, management gathers data from the workers, who are in the best position to understand the job duties and tasks. These data are analyzed and reduced to laws and rules, which are applied to workers' jobs in the form of detailed procedures and how-to explanations. Second, workers are selected carefully—or, as Taylor put it, "scientifically"—and then trained so that they become more efficient than ever before. Third, scientific selection, data collection, and training are combined to enhance efficiency. Taylor argued that these processes must be brought together because science and workers are not a "natural combination."

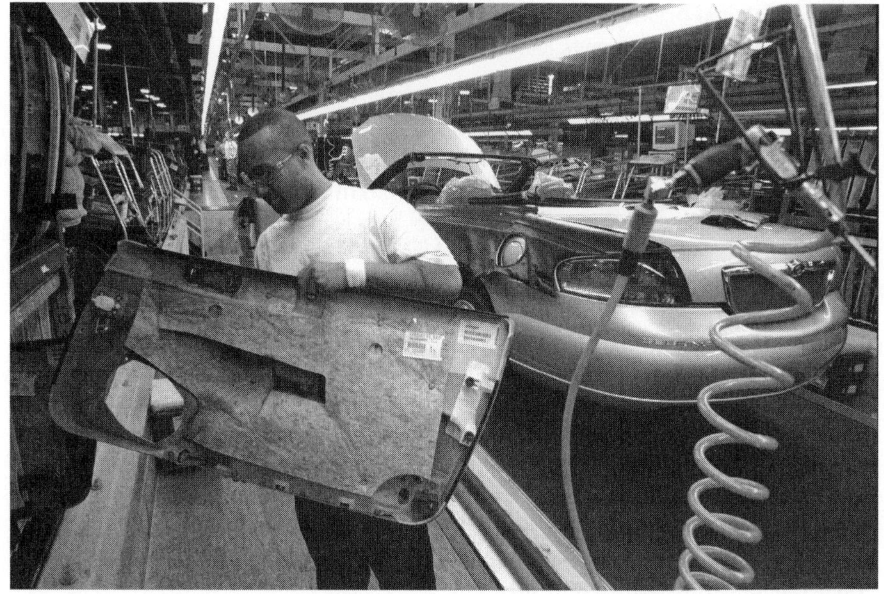

Frederick Taylor's principles of scientific management were instrumental in improving the efficiency of assembly lines in the U.S. factories of the early 1900s.

Finally, the work itself is redistributed, with management taking over tasks previously left to subordinates (e.g., factory workers). Taylor emphasized that cooperation and genuine sharing of the labor was important if the overall process was to work.

In one of his last addresses before he died in 1915, Taylor gave an example of how scientific management, when applied to the "science of shoveling," had worked at Bethlehem Steel (Taylor, 1916/1996). Taylor noticed that there was great variability in the loads that men placed on their shovels, and he proceeded to scientifically study this process by paying a couple of employees to shovel for a specified period of time with varying loads. What he found was that efficiency—that is, amount shoveled in a specified amount of time—varied as a function of the size of shovel load (see Figure 14.1). The employees started with a 38.5-pound load, using increasingly smaller loads as testing continued. As the loads got smaller, efficiency improved, due largely to the greater strength and energy that was available to the employees. However, at about 20 pounds, efficiency began to decrease. The optimum shovel load turned out to be about 20.5 pounds—the weight at which the most ore or coal could be moved in a fixed amount of time. Taylor then developed shovels with a maximum capacity of 21 pounds and taught employees how to use them. The use of these new shovels resulted in an almost immediate increase in efficiency: Each shoveler's daily yield of coal went from 16 tons to 59 tons! The science of shoveling provides a nice example of how Taylorists went about improving the efficiency of organizations. As for the long-term success of scientific management, we will consider that question a bit later on in the chapter.

FIGURE 14.1 An Example of Taylorism

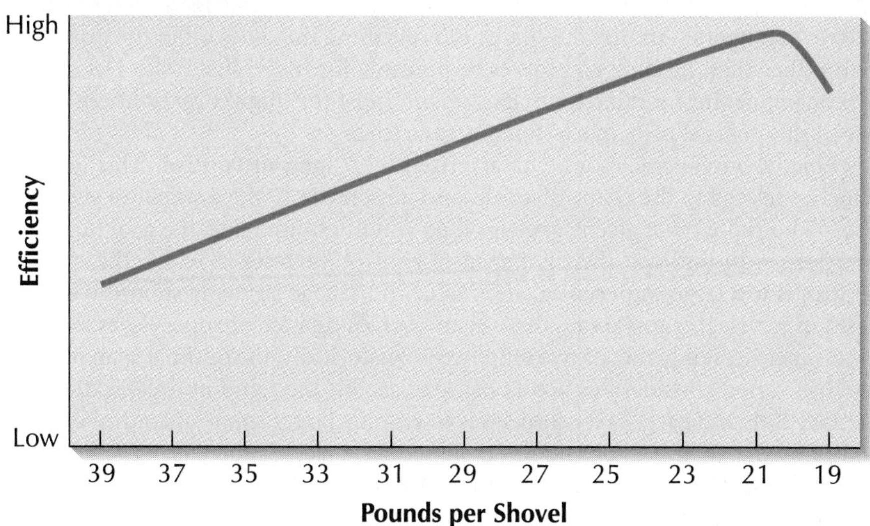

Bureaucracy. Max Weber was a German sociologist who studied organizations in the late 1800s and early 1900s. Specifically, he analyzed historically large and efficient organizations such as the Egyptian empire, the Prussian army, and the Roman Catholic Church (Wagner & Hollenbeck, 1998). Weber used these careful analyses to develop the notion of *bureaucracy,* which, in his view, described the structure, organization, and operation of many efficient organizations. Let's consider four major features of a bureaucratic organization.

First, each job in a bureaucratic organization is a specialized position with its own set of responsibilities and duties. Weber called this idea **division of labor**—a rather simple approach in which employees are narrowly trained to do the particular tasks and duties assigned to their jobs only. Dividing up tasks in this manner allows the organization to take advantage of individuals' particular strengths and to avoid the problems that result from asking people to do tasks that require skills they don't have. Of course, one potential difficulty in bureaucracies involves the coordination of various tasks handled by various employees. In other words, it is good that each employee has his or her particular task to do, but it can be difficult to coordinate the many tasks done by all employees while at the same time ensuring a particular outcome or end product for the organization.

division of labor
An approach whereby each job in a bureaucratic organization is a specialized position with its own set of responsibilities and duties.

Second, bureaucracies tend to be top-down pyramidal organizations like the one depicted in the top panel of Figure 14.2. At every level (except for the very top) of the organization, employees report to a person one level up in the chain of command. According to Weber, this hierarchical system of supervision is necessary if the division of labor is to be beneficial. Third, bureaucracies rely on the principle of **delegation of authority,** an approach whereby supervisors provide

delegation of authority
An approach whereby supervisors provide particular tasks to separate employees and hold them responsible for completing these tasks.

particular tasks to separate employees and hold them responsible for completing these tasks rather than trying to do everything themselves. We have all experienced managers who are incapable of delegating; these managers—often called **micro-managers**—try to take charge of everything that goes on in the organization rather than holding employees responsible for individual tasks. Delegation is very important for effective management; most top-flight organizations make use of this general principle of bureaucratic theory.

micro-managers
Managers who, instead of delegating tasks to individual employees, try to take charge of all tasks.

Finally, bureaucracies are characterized by a **span of control.** This feature, which is related to the chain-of-command idea, refers to the number of subordinates who report to a given supervisor. As you might imagine, the goal for organizations is to find just the right span of control. In cases in which the span of control is too large, supervisors are unable to manage so many subordinates; in cases in which it is too small, there is an overabundance of supervisors because each supervises only one or two employees. Historically, the optimal span of control has varied considerably across companies, but the trend in organizations of the late 20th and early 21st centuries is to employ larger spans of control as a result of smaller numbers of middle-level managers (see Chapter 1). A comparison of the top and bottom panels in Figure 14.2 shows what happens to the span of control when layoffs or organizational restructuring result in the reduction of middle-level management, as happened dramatically in the United States during the 1990s. Obviously the trick is to establish a span of control that works for your particular organization such that (1) supervisors are able to effectively manage all

span of control
The number of subordinates who report to a given supervisor.

FIGURE 14.2 Contrasting Organizational Structures

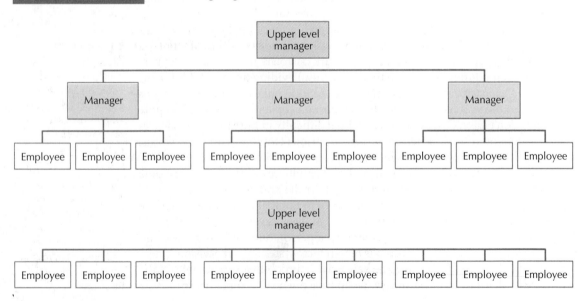

of their subordinates (with respect to oversight, delegation of tasks, etc.) and (2) the organization does not become "top heavy" with supervision.

In a classic text on the psychology of organizations, Daniel Katz and Robert Kahn (1978) emphasize two additional issues that are important to Weberian bureaucracy: *standardization of tasks* and *centralized decision making.* Task standardization is analogous to Taylor's notion of the "one best way" to get a job done, in that it pertains to the training of employees toward that end. And related to the notion of a chain of command is the idea that decision making should be centralized. I noted earlier that it can be hard to coordinate the many tasks done by individual employees while at the same time moving the work of the organization along. This becomes easier in a bureaucratic system, in which major decisions are made by one or more individuals who are centralized under one command. In other words, rather than allowing different people in different parts of the organization to make final decisions, bureaucracies give this responsibility to one person or one group of people, such as a board of trustees. A good analogy is the military, in which all major decisions are made by the central command.

It is no secret that bureaucracies today are viewed with skepticism and perhaps even disdain. The U.S. government and even the universities we participate in are often described as excessively bureaucratic. Here, too, however, we need to consider the historical period in question—specifically, the context in which Weber developed his model of bureaucracy and in which Taylor developed the concept of scientific management. At this point in the late 19th and early 20th centuries, there were no theories of organizations and no reliable format or framework to follow in developing an organization or improving organizational functioning. The industrial revolution had begun in the 1700s, and large factories were coming into their own at this time and throughout the 1800s. During these early

The military uses a central decision-making body reflective of a bureaucratic system.

years there was little or no sense as to how industrial organizations should be run, and disorder and chaos were prevalent. Indeed, scientific management and bureaucracies were developed to provide these directionless organizations with formal, orderly, and efficient functioning.

In more modern times, however, theorists have begun to argue that bureaucracies are ineffective for organizations operating in rapidly changing environments, such as the high-tech industry (Schellenberg & Miller, 1998). In fact, Weber himself warned that work in a bureaucracy can be so simplified and unchallenging that workers might become dissatisfied and demotivated, resulting in lower productivity overall (Wagner & Hollenbeck, 1998). Arguably, it was these basic criticisms of both bureaucracy and scientific management that led to the development of alternative theories of organizations.

Humanistic Theory

The human relations movement resulted, in part, from a reaction to the rigidity of classical organizational theory. Factors that were not even remotely associated with the classical approach to organizations, such as employees' motives, goals, and aspirations, were emphasized by those in the human relations movement (Katz & Kahn, 1978). The relationship between supervisor and subordinate has been especially instrumental in the humanistic theory of organizations, which explains organizational success in terms of employee motivation and the interpersonal relationships that emerge within the organization.

Perhaps the best example of humanistic theory is D. M. McGregor's (1960) work on Theory X and Theory Y. McGregor argued that the beliefs and assumptions that managers hold about employees determine how they behave toward those employees. Managers' behaviors, of course, affect employees' attitudes and behaviors, which in turn affect managers' attitudes, beliefs, and behaviors. This cycle is illustrated in Figure 14.3, which clearly shows the importance of the interaction between employees and management. This interaction often involves a *self-fulfilling prophecy* in which employees, over time, learn to act and believe in ways consistent with how managers think they act and believe—even if this wasn't the case initially. According to McGregor, employees were traditionally viewed as lazy, interested only in what's best for themselves, inherently uninterested in work, lacking in ambition, and not very intelligent. Management's job, therefore, was to control and direct employees in order to make economic profits. Without a firm hand, it was thought, employees would be passive and unresponsive to the organization's needs. This perspective is what McGregor refers to as *Theory X*, and he argues that it was the most prevalent set of beliefs about employees from the birth of industry until the middle 1900s.

In order for organizations to get ahead and to have an opportunity to develop and become truly effective, a different approach was needed—and, according to McGregor, management's view of employees was where this had to start. In the 1950s and 1960s, when McGregor was writing about his ideas, he did not dispute

FIGURE 14.3 Self-fulfilling Theory X Cycle

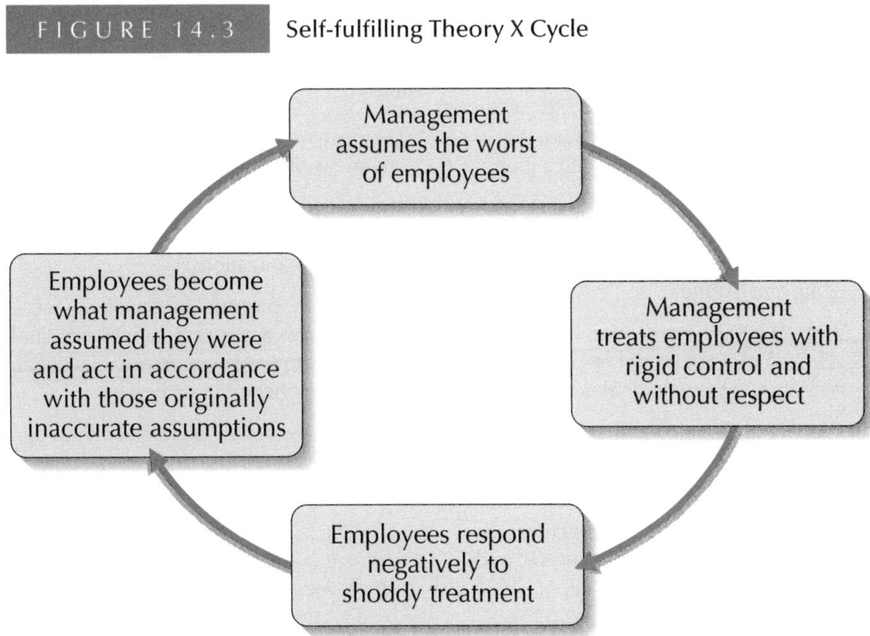

the notion that employees lacked ambition and were somewhat lazy; but he argued that they had developed these behaviors because of the way they were treated by managers, whose behaviors in turn stemmed from their preconceived notions about employees. So, again, we see the vicious cycle depicted in Figure 14.3. McGregor proposed *Theory Y* as a new perspective that was needed to improve both employees and organizations. Table 14.1 presents the assumptions and responsibilities of management under both Theory X and Theory Y. The differences are clear: Compared to Theory X, Theory Y takes a much more humanistic and developmental orientation, emphasizing not only the inherent goodness, capacity, and potential of employees but also their readiness to be developed. Theory Y also emphasizes management's responsibility for nurturing those qualities and providing opportunities for employees to develop their inherently positive characteristics in the workplace (McGregor, 1957). Throughout this text we have talked about many "new" approaches to management, including empowerment, participation, self-managed work teams, transformational leadership, self-assessment, and organizational citizenship behavior. If you think back to our discussion of these and other developments in I/O psychology, you can see that they are all consistent with the human relations movement, or what McGregor has called the Theory Y approach to organizational management. Most of McGregor's work was done in the late 1950s and early 1960s (in fact, he died in 1964 at only 58 years of age), but it has taken on great importance since it first came on the scene, shaping to a considerable degree the approach taken by many successful organizations worldwide.

TABLE 14.1 Theory X and Theory Y

Theory X	Theory Y
1. Management is responsible for the economic well-being of the organization.	1. Management is responsible for the economic well-being of the organization.
2. Management of employees requires directing, controlling, motivating, and modifying their behavior to fit the needs of the organization.	2. Employees have become passive and resistant only as a result of their experience in organizations.
3. Without active intervention by management, employees would be passive and resistant to organizational needs.	3. Motivation, potential for development, capacity for assuming responsibility, and readiness to work toward organizational goals are inherent in employees.
4. The average employee is lazy, works as little as possible, lacks ambition, and dislikes responsibility.	4. It is management's job to allow employees to recognize and develop the characteristics listed above.
5. The average employee is self-centered, indifferent to organizational needs, and, by nature, resistant to change.	5. The chief job of management is to arrange organizational conditions so that employees can achieve their own goals by directing their own efforts.
6. The average employee is gullible and not very bright.	

The humanistic movement has been applied by organizations and consultants to many different situations. An especially interesting example is the work of Monty Roberts, the horse trainer on whom Robert Redford's character in the movie *The Horse Whisperer* was loosely based. Roberts wrote a bestseller, *The Man Who Listens to Horses,* in which he described his amazing ability to train horses without breaking their spirit. Breaking in horses so that they can be saddled and ridden is a very difficult thing to do; it has traditionally involved breaking their spirit and often takes many months or years. Roberts, however, has a truly novel approach in which he never raises his voice, treats the horses with respect, emphasizes that they can trust him above all else, and trains them in 30 to 45 minutes! You're probably wondering what all of this has to do with I/O psychology; at first, so was I. As it turns out, Roberts has packaged his horse-training method as a metaphor for the humanistic style of management. He argues that what he does with horses has a parallel in people: In short, you get more out of people by winning them over than by ordering them around (Marsh, 1998). This sounds much like the distinction between Theory Y and Theory X. Hundreds of Fortune 500 companies, including Disney, Merrill Lynch, AT&T, and General Motors, have gone to Roberts's ranch to view and experience his demonstrations.

Volkswagen is an example of a company that has traditionally used a Theory X approach to management and has been successful with that approach. Recently, however, Volkswagen of America was faced with declining sales and organizational problems, prompting the company to take a different approach. At that point Clive Warrilow was brought in to save the floundering U.S. operation. When Warrilow observed Roberts's horse demonstration, he declared that it was an "aha" experience (Marsh, 1998). This experience helped bring into focus the kinds of improvements Warrilow had tried to introduce into organizations throughout his career. He made it clear to the VW employees that he would emphasize trust, understanding, and autonomy to get things turned around. He also made some structural and procedural changes, such as giving supervisors more control over budgets, and altered the overall culture of the organization dramatically. Since then, Volkswagen of America has come back! In 1997 the company sold $5 billion worth of cars, compared to $2 billion worth in 1993. And in 1999, its strongest year in more than a quarter-century, it sold over 315,000 cars, up 43% from 1998, which was considered a very successful year (Volkswagen Press, 2000). Sales of Volkswagen cars in North America since 2000 have averaged more than 600,000 cars per year! Although these results are not directly attributable to Monty Roberts, his work did demonstrate in a dramatic way what can happen in organizations that are willing to take the risk of changing their general approach and trying to win people over rather than ordering them around.

Open-System Theory

It is important to recognize that organizations are not always well defined by the purposes for which they were developed. On the contrary, organizations develop and change over time as a result of both internal and external forces. This is the basic premise of Katz and Kahn's (1978) open-system theory of organizations (see Figure 14.4). The three key elements of open-system theory are inputs, throughputs, and outputs. *Inputs* are transformed during the *throughputs* stage into *outputs,* which in turn are brought back into the process as additional inputs—and thus the process continues. For example, a car manufacturer who uses production processes to transform raw materials into automobiles is, in effect, using throughputs to transform inputs into outputs. The outputs (automobiles) are then sold for money, which is reinvested as inputs into the system—and transformation or production continues. Katz and Kahn (1978) point out that organizations thrive only as long as there is a continuous flow of energy from the external environment into the system and a continuous export of products out of the system. In our car manufacturer scenario, for example, the organization would be headed toward eventual death if the automobiles stopped bringing in money and production was negatively affected. This simple principle is at the heart of several disciplines, including economics, psychology, and biology. Indeed, open-system theory was adapted by Katz and Kahn on the basis of biology, which defines all living things as open systems. Plants and animals, for instance, both give to and take from the environment in which they exist—and well-run organizations operate in a very similar way.

FIGURE 14.4 The Cycle of Open-System Theory

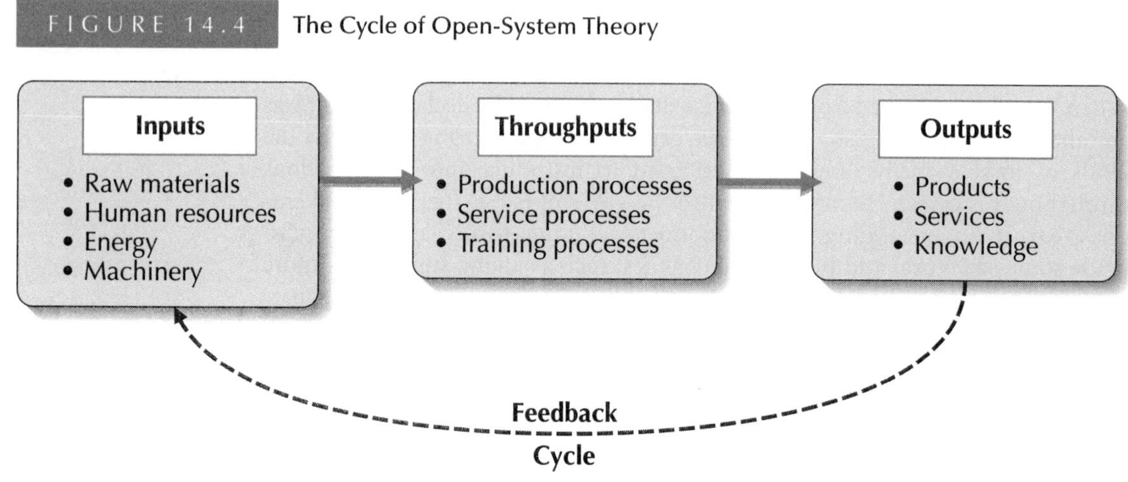

Table 14.2 presents the 10 characteristics of open systems as presented by Katz and Kahn (1978). We've already discussed inputs, throughputs, outputs, and the cyclic nature of the process, but there are other important characteristics of open systems, too—such as *negative entropy.* Entropy is a universal law of nature that posits that all forms of organization move toward disorganization or death (Katz & Kahn, 1978), whereas the principle of negative entropy suggests that organizations must avoid this movement toward death by continuing to import energy from outside the system. Thus, for example, our car manufacturer must continue to transform raw materials (inputs) into cars (outputs)—for if this cycle is broken, entropy will follow and the company will crumble. What companies often do to avoid entropy is to store up resources during good times so that they can be used to maintain the cycle during bad times.

Information input and *negative feedback* are also important parts of the open-system cycle. Recall our discussion of control theory in Chapter 9, in which we talked about how the negative feedback loop is instrumental in determining individuals' motivation to exhibit particular behaviors. In an organizational context, the negative feedback loop provides information about where and how the organization is getting off-course. For instance, if outputs are not bringing in sufficient resources to enable continual production of those outputs, changes need to be made at the input or throughput stage. The last characteristic that I'll mention here is *equifinality,* the notion that a system can reach the same end state in different ways. In other words, there isn't just one way to achieve a particular outcome. Note that this is inconsistent with the basic premise of scientific management, which is that there is "one best way" to do everything. The idea of equifinality reflects the human element in organizations, providing more flexibility and allowing for more creativity in their development and operations. Given this human element, the only stable aspect of organizations and the environment they

TABLE 14.2 Characteristics of Open Systems

Importation of Energy	Bring energy from the external environment for use by the system.
The Throughput	Transform that energy.
The Output	Export a product or service.
Systems as Cycles	The pattern of importation of energy and exportation of products and services continues.
Negative Entropy	Reverse the tendency of all systems to move eventually toward death.
Information Input and Negative Feedback	Information input and negative feedback allow the system to correct or adjust its course.
The Steady State	Surviving open systems are characterized by a balance in energy exchange.
Differentiation	Open systems move toward more specialized functions.
Integration and Coordination	Bringing the system together as a unified process is necessary for the system to continue.
Equifinality	The notion that there are many ways within the system to get to the same conclusion or end point.

interact with is that they change—they change a lot and often! Thus being limited to "one best way" tends not to result in effective organizations.

ORGANIZATIONAL DEVELOPMENT

Defining organizational development is not an easy thing to do, but let's use this definition: **Organizational development (OD)** is a planned, organization-wide effort to increase organizational effectiveness through behavioral science knowledge and technology (Beckhard, 1969). Many argue that OD is really about promoting positive humanistic changes in organizations; that is, it's as much about helping the people in an organization as it is about helping make the organization more productive (Church, Waclawski, & Seigel, 1999). OD programs share some important characteristics. In particular, they tend to:

- involve the total organization.
- be supported (and initiated) by top management.
- entail a diagnosis of the organization, as well as an implementation plan.

organizational development (OD) A planned, organization-wide effort to increase organizational effectiveness through behavioral science knowledge and technology.

- be long-term processes.
- focus on changing attitudes, behaviors, and performance of groups/teams.
- emphasize the importance of goals, objectives, and planning.

These characteristics explain what OD is. What it *isn't* is a short-term patch to hide an organizational problem. In fact, when OD fails, it is often because the characteristics just listed have been ignored in favor of superficial changes that have very little impact on the organization's effectiveness and result in greater stress and lower morale at the company. If anything, bad OD programs take organizations back a few steps rather than moving them forward. New CEOs are frequently expected by their boards to initiate successful organizational change efforts, but these efforts are rarely successful because changing organizations is such a complex thing (Greiner, Cummings, & Bhambri, 2002), especially for new leaders.

Why Organizations Need Organizational Development

Organizations embark upon OD interventions for many reasons, but much of the time it is because of changes in the environment in which organizations operate. Like everything else we've covered in this book, organizational practices and programs operate not in a vacuum but, rather, in a context or environment that affects those practices and programs. Whether social, technical, economic, or political in nature, this environment sometimes undergoes changes requiring development of the organization so that it will become more effective. Can you think of any creatures—or technologies, for that matter—durable enough to survive without adapting to new environments? Certainly humans and computers have evolved. In order for organizations to survive, they too must be adaptable enough to change over time.

In a thought-provoking and very readable analysis of management in the new millennium, Michael Hitt (2000) discusses changes that have taken place in the last 15 to 20 years, changes that will take place in the next 20 to 30 years, and challenges that organizations are facing. In fact, this section of the chapter is partly based on this fascinating article. We often hear about how much things have changed in recent years. Here is an incredible example: In 1990, use of the Internet was limited to scientific exchanges and some government correspondence—and that's all! A decade later, we entered the 21st century with almost 1 billion people communicating and conducting business on the Internet. When I started my job in 1989 at the University of Akron, I had some access to an archaic e-mail system from a computer lab in our department but no access at all from my office, and I had very little idea what the Internet was. Now, my 5-year-old uses the mouse like he was born with it in his hand, my 8-year-old knows enough to be dangerous, and my 11-year-old makes frequent use of it for school projects. In the mid-1980s, IBM and Apple Computer were the undeniable leaders in the high-tech market, and they competed fiercely in the PC and software markets.

About 20 years later, these two giants are still players in these markets, but not really among the industry leaders, having been replaced by the likes of Dell, Gateway, Microsoft, and Sun.

Hitt (2000) argues that the competitive landscape of the new millennium will be characterized by substantial and sporadic changes. He focuses on two major changes in this landscape that successful companies will need to navigate through organizational development. The first change concerns the technological revolution and the knowledge explosion that accompanies it; according to one estimate, due to incredible advances in medicine, communications, and technology, we double our knowledge every 50 years! The second change concerns globalization, which will become (if it hasn't already) the norm for successful organizations as additional countries become a more active part of the world economy, different economies and markets develop, and new economic rules and alliances emerge. We have talked historically about the "Fortune 500"; we are begining now to focus more on the "Global 500"—companies that are active across the globe and not just in the United States. Companies that aren't ready to make the changes necessitated by the technological revolution and globalization can quickly lose their competitive advantage. For instance, Levi Strauss's stock increased from $2.53 per share in 1985 to $265.00 per share in 1996, but in 1997 it closed 29 manufacturing plants and laid off over 16,000 employees (Hitt, 2000). Increased competition from Tommy Hilfiger and Gap—both of which took a different approach, emphasizing a greater diversity of product—took its toll as Levi Strauss maintained its traditional approach based on a very narrow product line. Gap's sales increased from $7 billion in 1995 to over $40 billion in 1998.

One result of the technological revolution is the incredible speed with which products become obsolete. The technology changes so quickly that last year's cutting-edge product, which seemed to secure the future of one company, is completely replaced by this year's cutting-edge product, which may be developed and manufactured by a different company. If the first company is not prepared for this advance in technology, it can be left behind (as happened to Levi Strauss, IBM, and Xerox) and lose its competitive advantage to other companies that are more prepared and willing to change with the environment. The rise and fall of the dot-coms (i.e., Internet companies such as E-Toys.com, Pets.com, and CDWorld.com) exemplify this rapid change. When they were launched, these companies seemed to be market leaders with a long future; less than 1 year later most of them no longer existed. One obvious example of rapid product obsolescence has to do with computers. I am currently writing this chapter on a computer that will probably be obsolete (or, at best, quite limited and slow) by the time this book is actually on the shelves in bookstores! Indeed, just as today's microchip is tomorrow's old news, the only companies that will survive as competitive forces are the ones that continue to invest in research and development, work to establish favorable work environments for employees, and think flexibly about their future direction.

Of course, one other rapid change that we've talked about in this book has to do with the increasing diversity of the workforce—in terms of age, gender, race,

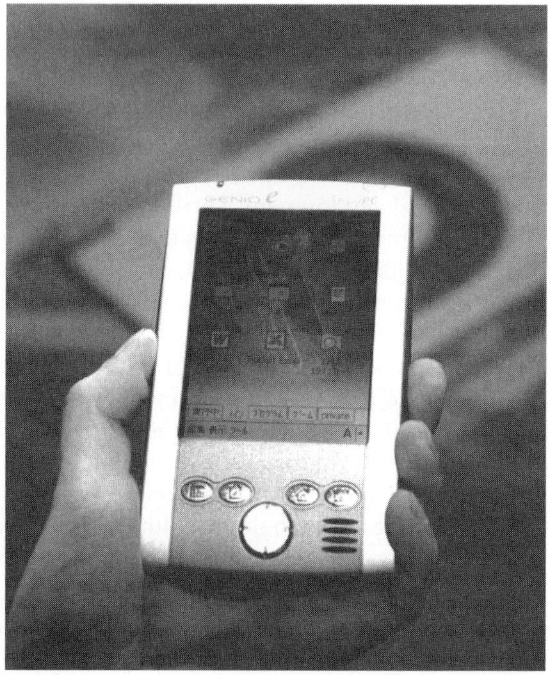

Perhaps no industry has changed as much in the past 50 years as the computer industry.

ethnicity, and mental and physical disability. Because today's workforce is so different from the workforce of previous generations, organizations need to make adjustments in the way they operate. In fact, the most competitive leaders are likely to be those that use this incredible diversity to increase knowledge, creativity, and overall effectiveness. Organizations have to find ways to turn this diversity into a 21st-century advantage. (Recall that we discussed some of these changes in Chapter 11 when we examined family-friendly policies in the context of diversity.)

As for how to deal with these many fast-paced changes in the workplace, Hitt (2000) makes a few interesting suggestions. First, managers need to adopt new forms of managerial thinking that are global in orientation and allow for strategic flexibility, as well as new organizational structures. Similarly, managers have to be able to operate and thrive in environments characterized by ambiguity and uncertainty because the changes occurring in these environments are neither predictable nor amenable to deliberate step-by-step procedures. Second, organizations must have highly developed human capital. Indeed, well-trained and highly skilled employees are important if companies are to maintain a competitive edge. Achieving this goal, of course, requires careful and thorough recruitment, selection, placement, training, and development of employees. Some companies on the cutting edge actually try to stockpile employees with a vast array of knowledge and skills because they recognize that, as things change, individuals with a variety of skills and knowledge bases will become especially valuable. The ability to "think outside the box" is also important; in other words, employees and managers must be capable of coming up with creative and novel ideas. Sometimes, the old ways and old approaches don't work anymore; to stay ahead, companies need to be flexible. Finally, an emphasis on continuous learning and knowledge delivery throughout the organization is what will set successful companies apart from those that don't survive. It's not enough that only a few employees continue learning; rather, this new knowledge needs to be shared throughout the organization. (We'll revisit this point later in the chapter.) In addition, Greiner et al. (2002) emphasize the match between CEO's orientation, organizational flexibility, characteristics of the team members, and the organization's change history as important to successful organizational development.

Hitt (2000) concludes by saying that "[m]anagement in the new millennium must build an organization that is constantly being transformed. It must develop and respond continuously to new technologies, new markets, new businesses, and new people in the form of employees and customers" (p. 15). Organizational development and change are the means by which we can accomplish this. Before we discuss some of the more common organizational development interventions, let's review how organizations actually change.

Models of Organizational Change

Organizational development interventions are focused on making changes in organizations. To understand how organizations change, we must understand three basic elements of the process. First, the **change agent** (sometimes called the *interventionist*) is the individual who initiates the change process. Usually this person is external to the organization, as in the case of organizational consultants; less often it is someone internal to the organization. On the whole, however, this person is significantly involved in diagnosing and classifying the organization's problems so as to define what changes need to be made. As the recipient of the *change effort,* the **client** is also central to the process. This effort is most likely to have an effect if the client is receptive to it; thus the client needs to be kept abreast of whatever ideas are being considered by the change agent. The client may be a particular individual, a work team, or perhaps the entire organization. Finally, the **intervention** is the program or initiative suggested or implemented by the change agent; it is what the change agent does for the client. An intervention consists of sequenced activities intended to help an organization increase its effectiveness (Cummings & Worley, 2001). As such, it intentionally disrupts the status quo in its attempt to change the organization.

There are two very well-established models of organizational change, both of which stem from the early work of Kurt Lewin. Let's consider each in turn.

change agent
The individual who initiates the change process in an organization.

client
The recipient of an organizational change effort in an organization.

intervention
The program or initiative that is suggested or implemented by the change agent in an organizational change intervention.

Lewin's Change Model. Lewin is considered a pioneer of I/O psychology owing to his interests in organizational change, as well as his work on group processes and leadership. He characterized change as a matter of modifying those forces that are acting to keep things stable (Lewin, 1951). Any behavioral situation, according to Lewin, is characterized both by forces operating to maintain stability or equilibrium and forces pushing for change. Stability results when the former win out over the latter. Lewin suggested that for planned change to occur in organizations with the least amount of tension and resistance, it is best to try to modify the forces that are maintaining the status quo rather than dramatically increasing the forces for change. The three steps in his change process are depicted in the top panel of Figure 14.5. In the first of these steps, known as *unfreezing,* the forces maintaining the status quo are broken down, and the system is opened up for change. This step is often accomplished by demonstrating that the behaviors and outcomes that are prevalent in the organization are not consistent with the organization's goals and objectives. Once the organization has been opened up for change, the second step of the process, *moving,* begins. At this point, real organizational change begins to happen as reflected in the new attitudes, values, and

FIGURE 14.5 Change Models

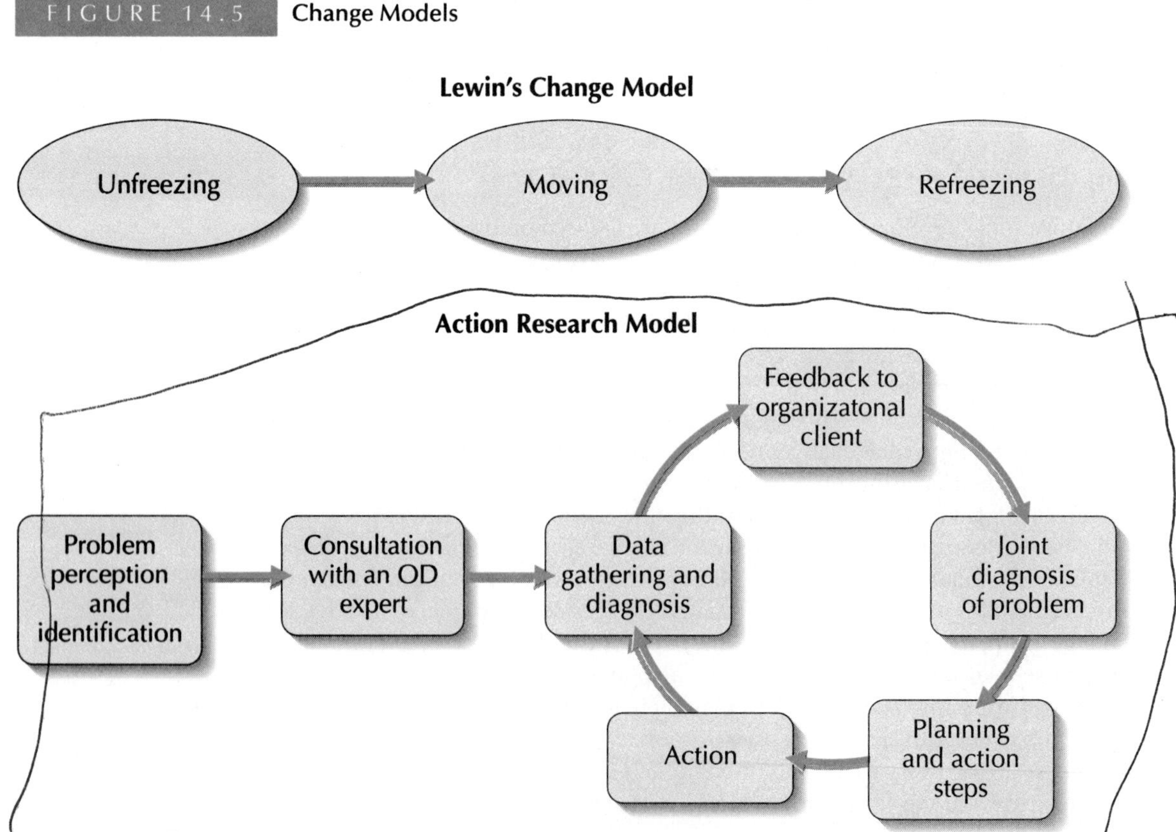

behaviors that have resulted from the intervention. During the final step, called *refreezing,* the changes that were implemented become stabilized, and the organization reaches a new level of equilibrium. Organizational policies, norms, and structures are used to support these changes, resulting in a new sense of stability. This basic three-step model, though still a major factor in organizational change processes, has been developed and enhanced by other theorists, resulting in more steps but holding to the basic premises of Lewin's early work.

Action Research Model. In the 1940s Lewin developed a second model of organizational change—the action research model. In this case he was motivated by what he viewed as social problems that needed to be addressed from both a methodological and social perspective. Toward this end he called for social scientists to take a more active role by combining theory building with research on real-world practical problems. Lewin died before he was able to fully develop and expand his ideas for action research, but others have followed his lead. The major characteristic of the action research model is its cyclical nature. Initial research about the organization is the foundation on which subsequent action is built. The

Kurt Lewin was one of the leaders in the early development of organizational psychology.

results of this action, in turn, provide information that can be used to guide further action—and the cyclical process continues. The various steps in the action research model are presented in the bottom panel of Figure 14.5. Here we can clearly see a research orientation with multiple data-gathering and problem-diagnosis stages. Lewin's idea was that research informs practice—a central theme of his model. He conceived of a process whereby I/O psychologists could attain a deeper understanding of an organizational phenomenon through cycles of fact finding and taking action (Dickens & Watkins, 1999).

Some contemporary adaptations of the action research model are worthy of note. One such adaptation has resulted in a dramatic increase in the participation of employees. In the past, consultants worked chiefly with management; in this more contemporary approach, other employees are involved. In short, the consultant and employees are co-learners such that neither party takes complete charge of the change process (Cummings & Worley, 2001). Another contemporary adaptation is called *appreciative inquiry.* It differs from traditional action research, which focused exclusively on what needed to be changed, by emphasizing what the company is doing well and using this information to paint a picture of the organization at its successful best. In effect, this is a picture of what the organization can become through a change process that reinforces and supports its strengths (Cummings & Worley, 2001).

Organizational Development Interventions

Effective interventions can be described as those that (1) fit the needs of the organization, (2) are based on causal knowledge of intended outcomes, and (3) transfer change-management competence to organization members (Cummings & Worley, 2001). The first criterion suggests that not all interventions are right for all organizations. Indeed, an intervention is more likely to succeed if it fits with what organization members believe and perceive is appropriate—and if they are committed to being a part of it and its eventual success. The second criterion implies that because interventions usually have goal- or objective-based outcomes, the interventions themselves must be based on the knowledge that these outcomes will reasonably result from them. Of course, we don't always know with certainty that a particular intervention will work—especially given the complexity of human behavior in both our personal lives and our work lives. As for the last criterion, which implies that organizational members should be better able to carry out planned change activities on their own following an intervention (Cummings & Worley, 2001), OD interventions are developed and implemented in such a way that they eventually become part of the organization's routine and thus less driven by the OD consultant. In fact, one sign that an OD intervention has succeeded is that the OD consultant becomes more and more expendable with the passage of time. (This point needs qualifying, of course, because in situations in which new opportunities for change have developed, the further expertise of OD consultants is necessary.)

There are many different OD interventions available, and numerous experts have proposed categorical schemes for how to organize them. However, I will focus on only six classes of interventions that are among the most prevalent and most researched.

Survey Feedback. One widely used intervention strategy involves the systematic collection of data via organizational surveys. These data are then summarized, analyzed, fed back to people employed by the organization, and used as a basis for planning purposes, with the outcome being a framework for organizational changes. The steps involved in survey feedback are rather simple:

- Top management supports and actively participates in the survey process.
- An anonymous survey is administered to organization members, tapping their attitudes, perceptions, and beliefs.
- Survey results are compiled by department, plant, or demographic segment.
- The consultant provides feedback to organizational members in the form of compilation and summary of data.
- Managers, task forces, and other employees meet with the consultant to identify potential changes for implementation.

I myself have been involved in many survey feedback programs while doing work for various organizations. For instance, I recently did some survey work for a provider of clinical and behavioral services—a mental health clinic. I met with the chair of the task force that was charged with gathering information from employees as an evaluation of the company's strengths and weaknesses. After a couple of meetings with this individual and other task force members, I developed a 140-item survey that measured employees' levels of job satisfaction, trust in management, stress and tension, attitudes toward the team emphasis, beliefs about organizational citizenship behaviors (OCBs), and so on. Demographic data such as gender, age, experience, and education were also gathered. After surveying about 200 employees, I compiled the data and presented the task force with a detailed written report of my findings; in addition, I made an oral presentation on-site to the task force members. All employees had access to the complete report, as well as to a memo that I had written directly to the employees summarizing the data. Finally, I made a series of recommendations based on the data that I thought would enhance the effectiveness, morale, and productivity of this particular organization. Some of my recommendations were implemented, and I was hired 2 years later to develop and conduct a follow-up survey. This survey revealed that, although some employees still had concerns, the organization overall experienced sizable improvements as a result of this OD intervention.

Team Building. As you may recall, we discussed the organizational role played by teams in Chapter 12. Here, we're concerned specifically with **team building,** a technique used by organizations to develop teams or to enhance the effectiveness of existing teams. Most of the experts in this area assume that in order for work

team building
A technique used by organizations to develop teams or to enhance the effectiveness of existing teams.

groups or teams to be successful, the members must collaborate and be interdependent. One of the best parallel examples of team building is the process through which sports teams develop. Whether they're involved in Little League, high school, college, or professional sports, team members must learn how to pool their individual abilities, coordinate their individual efforts, strive for agreed-upon goals, and establish a uniform set of work patterns and structures to maximize team performance (Forsyth, 1999). Specifically, team-building interventions focus on the following objectives:

- clarifying role expectations and responsibility among team members
- improving supervisor-subordinate relations
- improving problem solving, decision making, and planning by team members
- reducing conflict among team members
- developing a vision, mission, or set of goals
- building cohesion and unity within the team.

Team building is an extremely popular OD intervention and has been used in a variety of industries such as hotel management, manufacturing, urban transit, health, and sports (Salas, Rozell, Mullen, & Driskell, 1999). Despite widespread enthusiasm on the part of practitioners for the effectiveness of team building, there has been little in the way of well-controlled research. Nevertheless, a recent meta-analysis that reviewed the studies that do exist found strong support for the impact of team building on team performance (Svyantek, Goodman, Benz, & Gard, 1999). This review also took an applied perspective and examined the role played by different organizational characteristics in affecting the relationship between team building and team performance. The results indicated that team building had a stronger impact on team performance when (1) it was initiated to correct existing problems; (2) it was combined with other OD interventions; (3) the intervention was strongly supported by members of the organization, including the immediate team supervisor; (4) it was implemented in a participative management climate; and (5) performance was measured at the group level (Svyantek et al., 1999). *Outdoor experiential training (OET)* is a newly developed approach to team building that makes use of the outdoors and involves a variety of physical and mental exercises, as well as group activities. A recent review uncovered some support for its effectiveness and even suggested that this approach has a positive effect on the organization's return on investment (ROI; Williams, Graham, & Baker, 2003).

total quality management (TQM)
An initiative that focuses on employee involvement in the control of quality in organizations.

Total Quality Management. **Total quality management (TQM)**—also called *continuous improvement* or *quality management*—focuses on employee involvement in the control of quality in organizations. Many organizations have implemented a quality initiative in which all of the organization's activities concentrate on the quality of products made or services provided. This emphasis on quality was spearheaded by the work of W. Edwards Deming and Joseph M. Juran, who presented their ideas to U.S. companies during World War II. However, their ideas were much better received by the Japanese than by Americans (Cummings & Worley, 2001). As Japanese companies became increasingly formidable in their competition with American companies (especially in the automobile industry), American executives began to take notice. Eventually, Deming's ideas were also well received in the United States. In fact, they are now so popular that the U.S. government gives an award to companies that best meet the ideals of the TQM movement—namely, the Malcolm Baldrige National Quality Award. The criteria used for the Baldrige Award are (1) the extent to which quality values are communicated throughout the organization, (2) the organization's ability to meet customer needs, (3) the extent and caliber of the approaches used to monitor the quality of goods and services produced, (4) the use of data supporting the TQM system, and (5) the extent to which the full potential of employees has been utilized (Tata, Prasad, & Thorn, 1999). TQM has become a vast enterprise as we enter the 21st century, including consulting firms that specialize in quality work, nationwide training programs on the basic principles of TQM, and numerous national associations, including the American Society for Quality and the Association for Quality and Participation.

TQM interventions are typically conducted in a series of stages. They begin, like many of the other programs discussed throughout this book, with the support of top management. This means that senior management must receive training on what TQM is, how it operates, and what their responsibilities are. During the second stage, employees are trained on quality methods such as *statistical process control*—a technique proposed by Deming that focuses on identifying problems reflective of a low-quality product or service. A recent empirical investigation found that individual differences among those involved in the TQM effort predicted its success. In particular, employees' trust in colleagues, commitment to the organization, and higher-order-need strength were more strongly related to the effectiveness of TQM than were situational variables. Given that individual differences in the TQM process have received very little research attention, these findings suggest that we need a stronger conceptual understanding of how these and other variables operate in this context (Coyle-Shapiro & Morrow, 2003).

The third, or active, stage involves the actual implementation of TQM processes and procedures. At this time, employees identify not only areas in which their department or division excels but also deviations from quality standards (i.e., error). The potential causes of these deviations, or *output variations*, are examined, corrected, and brought within the range of acceptable quality. The fourth stage in the process is a self-comparison analysis whereby the organization compares its effectiveness to that of competitors that set the goals or benchmarks for the industry. For instance, an organization attempting to work on its customer-service performance is likely to compare its performance to Disney's benchmarks, because Disney is widely recognized as a world leader in customer service (Cummings & Worley, 2001). Then, during the final stage of the process, rewards are linked to the achievement of the TQM intervention's process goals. This, of course, is the main point of the whole process. Because the focus is on developing or employing a work process that produces high-quality goods and services that are as good as or better than those produced by the competition, the rewards are linked to processes that achieve those results. In the airline industry, for example, these processes would include being on time most often, having the lowest rate of lost luggage, having the fewest customer complaints, and having the smallest percentage of canceled flights. One criticism of TQM is that it is so rational and technical in its approach that it ignores the importance of social-political conditions and the consequences of change (Knights & McCabe, 2002).

gainsharing
An OD intervention that involves paying employees a bonus based on improvements in productivity.

Gainsharing. **Gainsharing** is an OD intervention that involves paying employees a bonus based on improvements in productivity. This approach to increasing employee participation and benefits while also improving organizational productivity was first documented in 1935 by the Nunn-Bush Shoe Company of Milwaukee. And one of the most frequently used varieties of gainsharing—the Scanlon Plan—was developed a few years later by Joseph Scanlon of Empire Steel and Tin Plate Company of Cleveland (Gowen, 1991). The use of gainsharing continued to grow quickly after that; in fact, many contemporary organizations, such as General Electric, Georgia-Pacific, TRW, Huffy Bicycle Company, DuPont, Motorola, and General Motors, have instituted some form of gainsharing. In 1990 about 47% of American companies used some form of variable pay program, but that has increased to almost 80% today (Kuhn & Yockey, 2003).

Gainsharing plans have as their basic premise a link between pay and performance—the assumption being that this link will lead to increased employee involvement and job satisfaction, as well as improved productivity and self-management. Although there are a few different types of gainsharing plans, and even these are sometimes altered to be organization-specific, most such plans have the following components in common. The first is a *suggestion system* that encourages employees to think about and share any ideas they might have about improving productivity. The second is an election of *department teams* composed of nonmanagement employees who are charged with overseeing the formal procedures used in considering, evaluating, and implementing the employees' suggestions. The third is a *review board* composed of both management and nonmanagement employees as a way to improve communication between the two groups and to allow management to answer questions posed by nonmanagement. By means of this review board, the two groups can educate each other about how the "other half" lives and what issues are important to them. Finally, all gainsharing plans are based on a formula that generates a bonus pool of dollars that are then distributed among employees. This *group bonus* is really the central element of all gainsharing plans. Although different formulae are used, experts suggest that the calculation should be based on matters that employees have some direct impact on or control of and that employees should be active participants in determining the formula (Collins, 1995).

In essence, gainsharing revolves around two factors that we've talked about at length throughout this text: participation and justice. According to a recent sur-

Because Disney is so highly regarded for its customer service, it is often used as a benchmark by other companies looking to improve their customer service.

vey, the gainsharing plan at one public organization was unsuccessful in part because employees perceived that they had very little participation in and control over the group bonus formula (Patton & Daley, 1998). This finding is consistent with a meta-analysis indicating that gainsharing programs tend to be more successful when companies provide formal avenues for employee participation in the development and implementation of the program (Bullock & Tubbs, 1990). Gainsharing programs also create a sense of justice or fairness by distributing "gains" equally between the employer and employees. Indeed, a recent study found some support for the role of justice in employees' satisfaction with a gainsharing program. In particular, both distributive justice and procedural justice were correlated with gainsharing satisfaction across two different gainsharing organizations. Interestingly, in the organization in which the bonus payout was quite small, procedural justice seemed to matter more than distributive justice (Welbourne, 1998)—a result that parallels the justice literature in which bad outcomes (e.g., low bonus payout) can sometimes be "made up for" by fair procedures. (For a review, see Brockner & Wiesenfeld, 1996.) From their research, Coyle-Shapiro, Morrow, Richardson, and Dunn (2002) conclude that gainsharing and profit sharing are successful when employees have favorable reactions to them, because these reactions lead to organizational commitment and trust in management, which results in greater effort and performance. The role of trust in organizational change has been highlighted in a recent paper that places it at the center of organizational changes processes (Morgan & Zeffane, 2003). Finally,

Kuhn and Yockey (2003) demonstrated that individuals opted for pay alternatives that, although more risky, had a greater potential payoff, with the payoff tied to individual rather than group performance.

Technostructural Interventions. OD interventions that focus on the technology and structure of organizations have increased in popularity as organizations have become more and more focused on effectiveness, efficiency, and productivity. One basic technostructural intervention has to do with the structural design of organizations. Structural design is what determines how the work of organizations progresses throughout the various layers of the organization. Some OD practitioners alter this structural design to meet particular needs or goals of an organization and its employees. The most basic version—the *functional* organizational design—is structured according to the various functions of the employees. Figure 14.6 provides an example of this design. Notice that the president/CEO has a number of employees (all vice presidents) below him or her and that each of these, in turn, is responsible for a particular function within the organization. For instance, someone is in charge of the manufacturing process, and someone else is in charge of marketing. The responsibilities for these different functions are independently held by various employees. Although this structure prevents duplication of labor by keeping in the same department employees who are doing the same or similar jobs, it can also result in departments that become very limited or narrow in their views and approaches because they don't interact as much with employees in other departments.

FIGURE 14.6 Functional Organizational Design

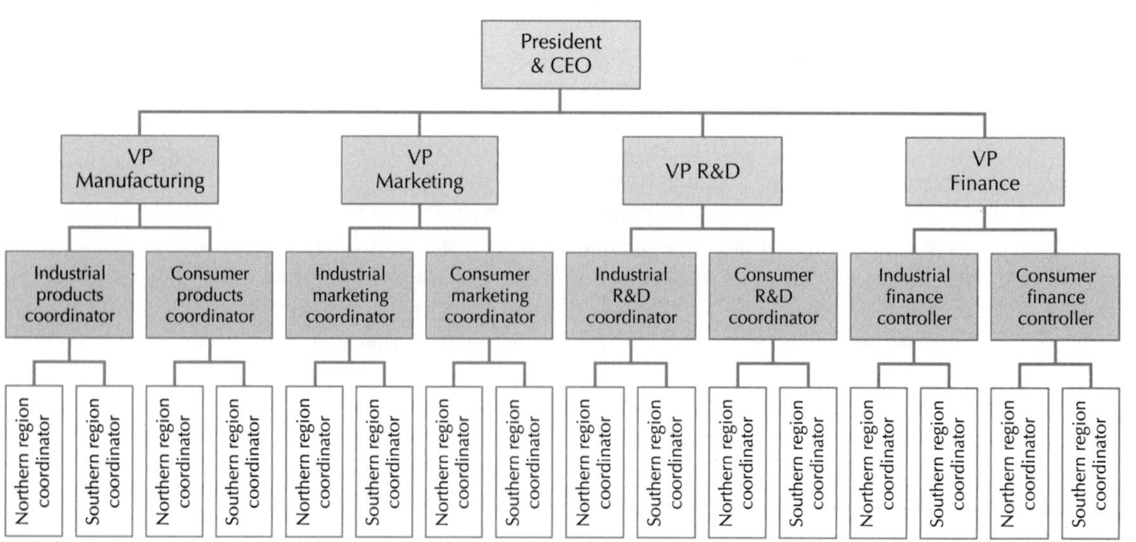

Other organizations are structured by *product* rather than by function, as shown in Figure 14.7, which depicts an organization that produces three different products. For each product there is a separate director of manufacturing, a separate director of marketing, and so on. It's as if there are separate divisions or subcompanies for each product, enabling all of the jobs associated with a particular product to be housed within one division. This design allows the managers of a particular division to focus exclusively on that division; it also creates the potential for greater commitment and cohesion within the division. However, there is also a greater potential for duplication of effort and costs. For example, similar research and development (R&D) equipment for each division is probably necessary, along with perhaps more R&D personnel than would be required by a functional design. Another drawback is that potential communication across product lines can be problematic, resulting in coordination difficulties and conflict across these lines.

A more recent organizational design sometimes employed by OD practitioners is called the *matrix structure.* This design combines the function and product structures we've just talked about. Figure 14.8 presents an example of a matrix organizational design; as you can see, the manufacturing employees for Product A work for both the VP of manufacturing and the Product A coordinator. In effect, the employees have two bosses; but this also means that the bosses—in this case, the VP of manufacturing and the Product A coordinator—have to work together as supervisors because neither has ultimate authority. Reading across Figure 14.8 demonstrates product-based authority; reading down demonstrates

FIGURE 14.7 Product-Based Organizational Design

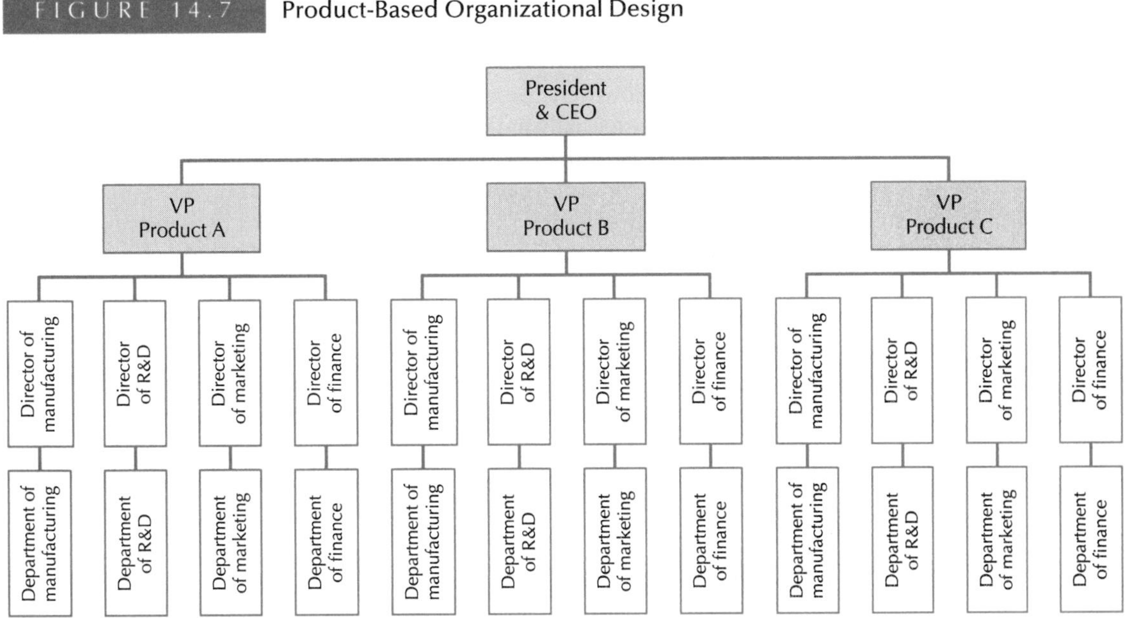

FIGURE 14.8 Matrix Organizational Design

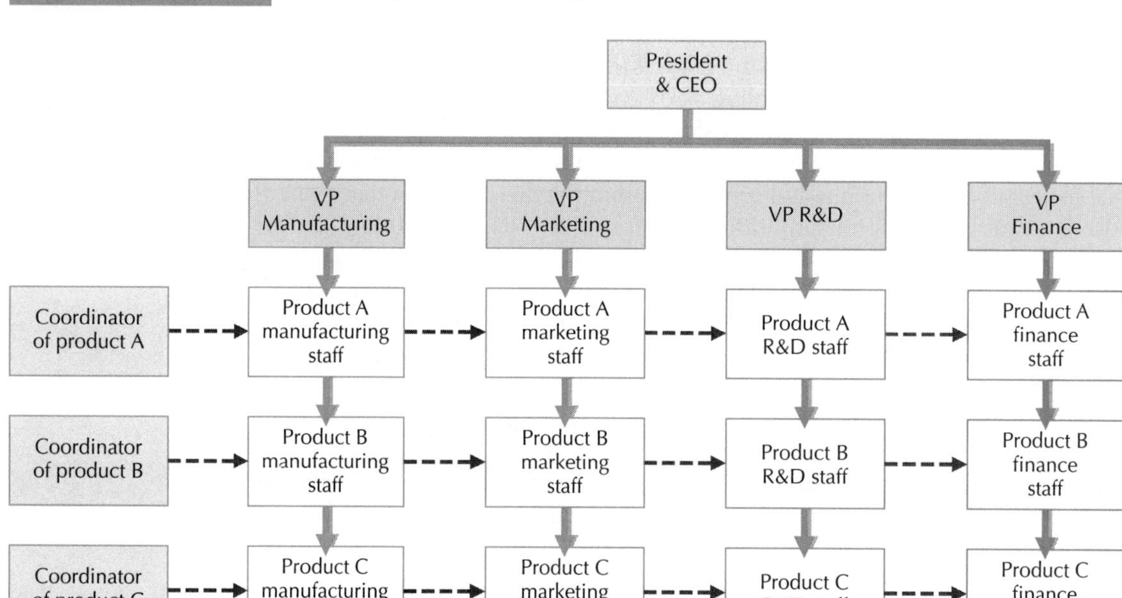

functional-based authority. Certainly, this structure is more complex than either of the other two structures that combine to form this matrix. One advantage of this approach is that it encourages communication and cooperation between managers, thereby maintaining consistency across product lines and across functional departments. However, given its complexity, a matrix structure can be very difficult to introduce, especially in the absence of a preexisting supportive culture.

reengineering
The fundamental rethinking and redesign of business processes to improve critical performance as measured by cost, quality, service, and speed.

The last technostructural intervention we will consider is **reengineering,** also known as *business process redesign,* which involves the fundamental rethinking and redesign of business processes to improve critical performance as measured by cost, quality, service, and speed (Hammer & Champy, 1993). C. D. Beugre (1998) summarizes the four elements of reengineering. First is the *fundamental* element, an examination of what the company does and why. Second is the *radical* element, a willingness to make crucial and far-reaching organizational changes rather than merely superficial changes. Third is the *dramatic* element, which focuses on making striking performance improvements rather than slight performance improvements. And the last element is the idea that the reengineering intervention is centered on the *processes* of the organization, not just the tasks, jobs, or structures.

Reengineering generally implies a revolutionary change in the operation of the organization. The organization alters its overall structure, as well as the way in which its work is structured (see the "Practitioner Forum" for an example). Most of the reengineering currently taking place in organizations revolves around

information technology (IT), which is typically defined as "the new science of collecting, storing, processing, and transmitting information" (McDonagh & Coghlan, 1999, p. 41). Any drastic change in the way an organization functions that is related to information gathering, storing, processing, or transmitting would qualify as an IT intervention. This type of reengineering occurs, for example, when a company computerizes all of its files and records or switches from a manual inventory and bookkeeping procedure to a computer-based one. These kinds of changes certainly alter the company's entire structure and way of doing business. However, despite great hope in the promise of IT as a way of dramatically improving business, many experts believe that to this point it has fallen far short of that promise (e.g., Beugre, 1998; Moosbruker & Loftin, 1998). Explanations for IT's lack of success include the following: (1) insufficient emphasis on organizational justice in the implementation of reengineering (Beugre, 1998); (2) the fact that IT specialists and OD practitioners speak different "languages," have different views of the organization, use different tools, and have different values (Moosbruker & Loftin, 1998); and (3) IT specialists' failure to recognize the importance of human, social, and organizational factors in the reengineering process (McDonagh & Coghlan, 1999).

information technology (IT)
The new science of collecting, storing, processing, and transmitting information.

Organizational Transformation. To this point we have discussed organizational development in a somewhat traditional way. Now, however, we turn to the recent work of Jerry Porras, a leader in the OD field, who draws a distinction between OD and what he says is at the cutting edge of OD—namely, **organizational transformation** (Porras & Silvers, 1991). Organizational transformation refers to any intervention primarily directed toward creating a new vision for an organization and changing its beliefs, purpose, and mission. OD, by contrast, focuses more on work-setting variables that are mismatched with the organization's desires (although some would say that organizational transformation is OD at a deeper level). Porras himself suggests that organizational transformation is an approach that will continue to grow in popularity as more upper-level executives recognize the need for and potential benefit of profound shifts in the vision and direction of their organizations (Porras & Silvers, 1991). Such shifts are indeed becoming commonplace in organizations of the 21st century.

organizational transformation
A term that refers to any intervention primarily directed toward creating a new vision for an organization and changing its beliefs, purpose, and mission.

Organizational transformation usually results from a serious jolt to a company that prompts the CEO and other senior executives to change their business strategy and, with that, their mission and vision for the company. At the forefront of many attempts at organizational transformation is **culture change,** the alteration of a pattern of beliefs, values, norms, and expectations shared by organizational members. The culture of an organization evolves historically, stemming directly from the leaders, and often founders, of a company. Several companies are famous for their organizational cultures; examples include Disney, Nordstrom, IBM, and Hewlett-Packard. In some cases, the culture is so much a part of the company that it can't be changed. In fact, there are experts who believe that culture change, in general, is too difficult to be reasonable. Others, however, recognize its

culture change
The alteration of a pattern of beliefs, values, norms, and expectations shared by organizational members.

difficulty but embrace its potential and believe in its usefulness. Although an organization's culture can be instrumental to a company's success (as is true of the companies just mentioned), it can also be detrimental, leading companies to attempt to change the ineffective culture. Finally, because of the complexities involved, culture change itself can lead to many unintended consequences, such as behavioral compliance and cultural erosion (Harris & Ogbonna, 2002).

T. G. Cummings and C. G. Worley (2001) present an excellent list of the determinants of successful culture change. First, the organization and change agent must develop a clear vision of the new strategy, as well as of the shared values, attitudes, and action steps needed to make it a reality. Second, as with any organizational intervention, culture change is likely to succeed only with top-management support; in fact, this is especially the case with culture change. Third, senior executives not only have to support the culture-change efforts but also must live by them. Instead of just paying lip service to the changes in attitudes and behaviors, these executives need to implement them, believe in them, and demonstrate their complete alignment with them in their day-to-day activities. Fourth, the supportive systems of the organization must also be intricately involved in the financial and control systems, and management systems must provide the support and resources necessary to give the culture change an opportunity for success. The fifth determinant of culture change has to do with issues of selection. Because it is important that new hires be socialized into the new culture rather than into the culture that is being left behind, consideration should be given to hiring employees (especially at higher levels) based on their match or consistency with the new shared values, beliefs, and behaviors. Further, employees who don't fit with the new culture should be let go. Senior employees who prefer the old culture and don't see the need or opportunity for change are often leaders in the resistance against change—a situation that is very detrimental to the change process. Finally, as with all interventions, it is incumbent upon the organization to ensure that employees' rights and responsibilities are maintained. The organization should be sure to avoid making promises it can't keep and encouraging expectations that are unlikely to be met.

knowledge management
A method in which organizations enhance their operations through attempts to develop, disseminate, and use knowledge.

A second approach to organizational transformation that has taken companies by storm is **knowledge management**—a method in which organizations enhance their operations through attempts to develop, disseminate, and use knowledge. It is a conscious effort to get the right knowledge to the right people at the right time so that information can be put into action to improve the organization's performance (Seng, Zannes, & Pace, 2002). Although there is widespread belief in the effectiveness of knowledge management and its close cousin, the development of *learning organizations,* these concepts are still so new as to be lacking empirical support. Nevertheless, experts agree that learning organizations tend to be characterized by (1) an organizational structure that facilitates learning, (2) a sophisticated information system that allows companies to manage knowledge for a competitive advantage, (3) a human resources system that promotes and rewards employees for continuous learning and knowledge manage-

PRACTITIONER FORUM

JOSELITO C. LUALHATI
Ph.D., Industrial/Organizational Psychology, 2000, University of Illinois
Global Skills X-change

When I was in grad school, I believed that a "good" solution was one that solves the problem. I now know that a "good" solution is one that solves the problem *and* doesn't lead to other problems. This shift reflects my greater appreciation of organizations as open systems. Organizational problems have multiple causes—some known, some unknown; some under control, some not; some with potential solutions that have intended consequences, others having unintended consequences. Let me provide you with a real-life example.

Due to external and internal pressures, a group in my former organization decided to redesign how it structured its work. Once the redesign was completed, I was brought in to figure out what competencies were required to perform the restructured jobs and identify from the current set of employees those with the required competencies to perform the restructured jobs. Simply put, my role was to develop a process that would result in the *intended consequence* of matching the "right people" to the "right job."

I would have treated this project differently years ago. I would have done a job analysis and then developed a solution that would have fit the needs of the client. In this more recent case, however, I knew better than to stop there. I knew that the process I developed would not be implemented in a vacuum. It would be implemented in a complex environment—a work organization. I was worried about the *unintended consequences* of the process I developed and about the possibility that factors not under my control, such as employees' perceptions of the redesign, would affect my piece of the project.

With that in mind, I implemented a series of surveys to gather employees' impressions of the different components of the redesign. The first survey provided important negative feedback. Although my clients were openly communicating with their employees and the employees were participating in the redesign, almost 68% of the employees did not understand why it was occurring and 75% of the employees did not understand the need for the matching process I was about to implement. Based on this information, my clients and I postponed the implementation of the matching process. Moving ahead with the implementation would have been a disaster. It would have erased the intended positive effect of the matching process by potentially creating new problems. Instead, we spent time meeting with employees to talk about the need for change, focusing on why the status quo would lead to the demise of the organization. The second survey showed that this "mini-intervention" partially worked. Eighty percent of the employees now understood the reasons for the redesign. And although many were still apprehensive about the matching process, 78% understood the reasons for its implementation. This signaled that we could move on to implementation. The matching process resulted in a very small number of displaced employees—most were placed in other groups within the organization. Today, this group appears to be successfully fulfilling its mission.

I recently saw one of the employees displaced by the process I developed. After some pleasantries, she told me that the process had been nerve-racking but was "roughly right." I asked her what she meant. She said that she wished it had turned out differently, but that she wasn't sure it could have—some things were simply not under anyone's control. When doing organizational change, OD practitioners need to remember how important it is to control the things they can and to recognize and monitor the things they can't control.

APPLYING YOUR KNOWLEDGE

1. Why are the effects of an open system important for organizational development?
2. Describe how Dr. Lualhati used the technique of survey feedback.
3. What important elements of an OD intervention might be difficult to control by the OD practitioner?

ment, (4) a strong organizational culture that fosters openness and creativity, and (5) supportive leaders who are active participants in learning and knowledge management (Cummings & Worley, 2001).

As Lew Platt, former CEO of Hewlett-Packard (HP), put it: "Successful companies of the 21st century will be those who do the best jobs of capturing, storing, and leveraging what their employees know" (quoted in Martiny, 1998, p. 71). In 1996 Hewlett-Packard embarked on a knowledge-management initiative that was designed to deliver more value to customers, bring more intellectual capital to solutions, and create an enthusiastic environment about knowledge sharing. The HP credo for this initiative was to make the "knowledge of the few, the knowledge of the many" (Martiny, 1998, p. 72). Knowledge management has been successfully integrated into the business strategy of HP and many other organizations as well. Its importance at General Electric, for example, is attested to by the fact that knowledge management was one of three business processes that former CEO Jack Welsh took personal responsibility for (employee development and allocating resources were the others; Stewart, 2000).

In 1998, by emphasizing knowledge management and using tools already in place at BP Amoco, Kent Greenes and his team of knowledge workers saved nearly $700 million in the bottom line (Stewart, 1999). Greenes employed rather simple techniques such as asking individuals who had successfully turned around another part of the business to brief others on their approach—in other words, to share their knowledge with their co-workers, who in turn could use this knowledge when they encountered a situation that called for it. He also created linked lists of individuals who had knowledge to share so that they could be contacted easily by co-workers in need of such knowledge. Knowledge management has become such an integral part of organizations that many companies have created a new position—that of "chief knowledge officer" (not to be confused with the "knowledge assets" in the *Dilbert* cartoon below), who is responsible for spearheading an emphasis on knowledge and learning. This position seemed to spring up first in professional service firms such as accounting firms and stock brokerages.

At Caterpillar, Inc., the Fortune 100 company that makes heavy construction equipment, the management of knowledge has become so important that the company has introduced the Knowledge Network, an intranet-based system designed to provide the structure for knowledge management throughout the cor-

The management of knowledge, not the labeling of employees as "knowledge assets," has become very important to many of the world's dynamic organizations.

poration. The Network is supported by knowledge experts at their corporate university (Ardichvili, Page, & Wentling, 2003). Employees at Caterpillar are motivated to contribute to the electronic sharing of information out of a moral obligation, community interest, a belief in giving back to the organizational community, and a desire to develop one's expertise at work (Ardichvili et al., 2003). A recent model of the knowledge management process has suggested that the psychological contract between the employee and the organization plays an important role through the employees' level of organizational commitment, which affects their willingness to share knowledge (Hislop, 2003). Perhaps this model will help set a research agenda resulting in more empirical work in this area.

According to John Peetz, the chief knowledge officer at Ernst & Young, knowledge management is one of four core work processes at that company: sell work, do work, manage people, and manage knowledge. Among his job duties are evangelizing about the importance of sharing knowledge, as well as managing and backing projects that find, publish, and distribute knowledge throughout the firm (Stewart, 1998). Although it appears clear to organizations that managing and sharing knowledge are important to maintaining a competitive edge, one successful and respected management guru, Jeffrey Pfeffer, suggests that organizations need to go one step beyond knowledge management. Pfeffer argues that knowing what to do is not enough; organizations must also put that knowledge to good use. In short, truly successful and cutting-edge organizations must work to bridge the knowing-doing gap (Pfeffer & Sutton, 1999). Perhaps putting knowledge to work will be the next trend in this exciting and dynamic field.

SUMMARY

This chapter presents information about two related organizational topics: organizational theory and organizational development. These I defined and discussed in terms of their importance to the effectiveness of organizations. I then presented three organizational theories: classical organizational theory, with its emphasis on scientific management and bureaucracy, and the more recent approaches known as humanistic theory and open-system theory.

Before discussing various techniques of organizational development, I spent considerable time highlighting reasons why companies, if they are to be successful, must pursue OD. I also presented examples of companies that have succeeded in part because of OD, as well as examples of companies that did not succeed owing to a lack of flexibility and willingness to change. In this context I provided a detailed discussion of Lewin's general change model and the more well-developed action research model.

Next, I considered some of the most frequently used OD interventions, such as survey feedback, team building, total quality management, and gainsharing; empirical support was cited along with a description of their potential benefits and disadvantages. I also introduced more recently conceived OD interventions such as reengineering and information technology. Finally, I discussed organizational transformation in the context of interventions that profoundly change the nature of the organization. Here I presented culture change and knowledge management as two examples of organizational transformation.

REVIEW QUESTIONS

1. Discuss the differences between scientific management and bureaucracy.
2. How does Theory X differ from Theory Y?
3. Describe some of the characteristics of an open system.
4. Define OD, and discuss some of the major reasons that organizations need it.
5. Who is involved in organizational change, and what theories help explain how change happens in organizations?
6. How can survey feedback be used to benefit an organization?
7. What is team building, and why has it become so important in recent years?
8. What are the major principles of TQM?
9. How does gainsharing work, and what role should employees play in it?
10. Provide an example of organizational transformation, and discuss how this approach differs from OD interventions.

SUGGESTED READINGS

Cummings, T. G., & Worley, C. G. (2001). *Organization development and change* (7th ed.). Cincinnati, OH: South-Western College Publishing. An extremely readable overview of organizational change and OD.

Hitt, M. A. (2000). The new frontier: Transformation of management for the new millennium. *Organizational Dynamics,* Winter, 7–17. This stimulating review of issues confronting organizations includes suggestions from an expert about how to approach such issues in the 21st century.

Katz, D., & Kahn, R. L. (1978). *The social psychology of organizations* (2nd ed.). New York: Wiley. Though not an easy read, this classic text is still recognized as the authority on organizational topics such as change, development, power, structure, and groups.

Pfeffer, J., & Sutton, R. I. (1999). Knowing "what" to do is not enough: Turning knowledge into action. *California Management Review, 42*(1), 83–108. A very interesting discussion of the importance of knowledge to organizations and what needs to be done if companies are to move ahead successfully.`

actual criterion Our best real-world representative of the ultimate criterion, which we develop to reflect or overlap with the ultimate criterion as much as possible.

adverse impact The most accepted operationalization of discrimination, defined in the Guidelines as the "80% rule of thumb." A selection battery exhibits adverse impact (i.e., discriminates) against a group if the selection rate for that group is less than 80% of the selection rate for the group with the highest selection rate.

affective commitment Emotional attachment to an organization, characterized by a strong belief in and acceptance of the organization's goals and values; a willingness to exert effort on behalf of the organization; and a strong desire to remain a part of the organization.

affective disposition The tendency to respond to classes of environmental stimuli in predetermined affect-based ways.

affirmative action A practice employed in many organizations to increase the number of minorities or protected class members in targeted jobs.

archival research Research relying on secondary data sets that were collected either for general or specific purposes identified by an individual or organization.

Army Alpha and Army Beta Mental ability tests developed by I/O psychologists during World War I that were used to select and classify army personnel.

assessment center (AC) An approach or method in which multiple raters (*assessors*) evaluate applicants or incumbents (*assessees*) on a standardized set of predictors (*exercises*).

attitude The degree of positive or negative feeling a person has toward a particular person, place, or thing.

attribute A dimension along which individuals can be measured and along which individuals vary.

base rate The percentage of current employees who are successful on the job.

behavioral criteria In Kirkpatrick's taxonomy, criteria that refer to changes that take place back on the job.

behavior theories Leadership theories that focus on identifying what leaders actually do, in the hope that this approach will provide a better understanding of leadership processes.

BioData Personal history information obtained through a biographical information blank (BIB) that asks respondents about their attitudes, hobbies, experiences, and so on.

biographical information In the context of selection, any information that is descriptive of an individual's personal history.

brainstorming A technique in which all members of a group generate potential solutions without the fear of having their suggestions criticized by other members.

burnout A condition that occurs when employees become so stressed that they experience emotional exhaustion, depersonalization, and a sense of reduced personal accomplishment.

case studies Examinations of a single individual, group, company, or society.

causal inference A conclusion, drawn from research data, about the likelihood of a causal relationship between two variables.

central tendency The tendency to use only the midpoint of the scale in rating one's employees.

change agent The individual who initiates the change process in an organization.

clerical ability A specific cognitive ability relevant for jobs such as secretary, administrative assistant, and bookkeeper involving a focus on both perceptual speed and accuracy in processing verbal and numerical data.

client The recipient of an organizational change effort in an organization.

coaching The process by which supervisors provide subordinates with advice and information about current performance and discuss ideas and goals for improving that performance.

coefficient of determination The percentage of variance in a criterion that is accounted for by a predictor.

cohesion The strength of members' motivation to maintain membership in a group and of the links or bonds that have developed among the members.

Common-Metric-Questionnaire A newly developed worker-oriented job-analysis instrument that attempts to improve the generalizability of worker-oriented approaches through the use of items focused on slightly less general work behaviors.

comparable worth A doctrine maintaining that jobs of equal (or comparable) worth to the organization should be compensated equally.

compensable factors Dimensions or factors that are used to rate jobs, indicating that employees are compensated based on these factors. Examples include effort, skill, responsibility, and working conditions.

competencies The skills, behaviors, and capabilities that allow employees to perform specific functions.

composite criterion A weighted combination of multiple criteria that results in a single index of performance.

concurrent validity The extent to which a test predicts a criterion that is measured at the same time that the test is conducted.

consideration The extent to which leaders act in a supportive way and show concern and respect for their subordinates.

construct An abstract quality, such as intelligence or motivation, that is not observable and is difficult to measure.

construct validity The extent to which a test measures the underlying construct that it was intended to measure.

content validity The degree to which a test or predictor covers a representative sample of the quality being assessed.

context The social-psychological climate in which performance appraisal takes place.

contextual performance Activities performed by employees that help to maintain the broader organizational, social, and psychological environment in which the technical core operates.

contingency theories Leadership theories that differ from both trait and behavioral theories by formally taking into account situational or contextual variables.

continuance commitment Attachment to an organization as a function of what the employee has sunk into it.

convergent validity The degree to which a measure of the construct in which we are interested is related to measures of other, similar constructs.

coping Efforts that help people manage or reduce stress.

correlation coefficient A statistic that measures the strength and direction of the relationship between two variables.

counterproductive behaviors Any behaviors that bring, or are intended to bring, harm to an organization, its employees, or stakeholders.

criteria Evaluative standards that can be used as yardsticks for measuring an employee's success or failure.

criterion contamination A condition in which things measured by the actual criterion are not part of the ultimate criterion.

criterion deficiency A condition in which dimensions in the ultimate measure are not part of or are not captured by the actual measure.

critical incidents Examples of job performance used in behaviorally anchored rating scales or job-analytic approaches.

cross-functional teams Work teams that are composed of members from diverse departments of the organization, each with their own function.

culture change The alteration of a pattern of beliefs, values, norms, and expectations shared by organizational members.

deduction An approach to science in which we start with theory and propositions and then collect data to test those propositions—working from theory to data.

delegation of authority An approach whereby supervisors provide particular tasks to separate employees and hold them responsible for completing these tasks.

dependent variable The variable of interest, or what we design our experiments to assess.

***Dictionary of Occupational Titles* (DOT)** A tool developed by the Department of Labor in the 1930s that has been used to classify occupations and jobs, consisting of narrative descriptions of tasks, duties, and working conditions of about 12,000 jobs.

disparate impact cases Cases involving a minority group discriminated against or unfairly affected by employment procedures that appear to be unintentional.

disparate treatment cases Cases involving discrimination that results from intentional differential treatment or behavior.

dissertation A unique piece of scholarly research that is usually the last hurdle before obtaining a Ph.D.

distance learning (DL) The delivery of material to all participants at the same time even though participants are separated by geographical distance.

distributed practice Training in which the practice is divided into segments, usually with rest periods in between.

distributional errors Rating errors, such as severity, central tendency, and leniency, that result from a mismatch between actual rating distributions and expected rating distributions.

divergent validity The degree to which a measure of the construct in which we are interested is *not* related to measures of other, dissimilar constructs.

division of labor An approach whereby each job in a bureaucratic organization is a specialized position with its own set of responsibilities and duties.

dual-earner couples Couples in which both members are employed and maintain a family life.

dynamic criteria Measures reflecting performance levels that change over time.

effective leadership Usually operationalized as the successful long-term performance of the leader's work group or subordinates.

element In job analysis, the smallest unit of work activity.

emotional labor The effort, planning, and control required by employees to express organizationally desired emotions during interpersonal interactions.

emotion-focused coping A coping style that involves cognitive or thought-related strategies that minimize the emotional effects of stress-inducing events.

emotion regulation The ways in which individuals monitor their emotions and the expression of those emotions.

employment at-will A common law doctrine stating that employers and employees have the right to initiate and terminate the employment relationship at any time, for any reason or for no reason at all.

equity sensitivity An individual difference indicating the extent to which people are affected by over-reward or under-reward situations.

essential functions Tasks that are significant and meaningful aspects of the job.

expectancy An individual's belief about the likelihood of achieving a desired performance level when exerting a certain amount of effort.

experimental methods Research procedures that are distinguished by random assignment of participants to conditions and the manipulation of independent variables.

external validity The extent to which the results obtained in an experiment generalize to other people, settings, and times.

extraneous variable Anything other than the independent variable that can contaminate our results or be thought of as an alternative to our causal explanation.

Frame of Reference (FOR) Training A type of training designed to enhance raters' observational and categorizational skills so that all raters share a common frame of reference and improve rater accuracy.

free-riding A situation that occurs when employees do less than their share of the work but still share equally in the rewards.

Functional Job Analysis A highly structured job-oriented approach developed by Sidney Fine in which data are obtained about *what* tasks a worker does and *how* those tasks are performed.

gainsharing An OD intervention that involves paying employees a bonus based on improvements in productivity.

group tests Tests on which many applicants can be tested at one time.

groupthink A mode of thinking that individuals engage in when the desire to agree becomes so dominant in a cohesive group that it tends to override the realistic appraisal of alternative courses of action.

growth need strength The extent to which individuals value or desire fulfilling higher-order needs.

halo The rating error that results from either (1) a rater's tendency to use his or her global evaluation of a ratee in making dimension-specific ratings for that ratee or (2) a rater's unwillingness to discriminate between independent dimensions of a ratee's performance.

hypothesis A tentative statement about the relationship between two or more variables.

implicit leadership theory (ILT) A leadership theory that views leadership as the outcome of a perceptual process involving both leaders and subordinates.

in-basket An individual exercise in which an assessee is asked to act as if he or she is a manager in a particular company with certain issues or ideas that need to be considered and responded to.

incumbents In job analysis, employees who are currently occupying the job of interest.

independent variable A variable that is systematically manipulated by the experimenter or, at the least, measured by the experimenter as a precursor to other variables.

individual tests Tests that are administered to one person at a time.

induction An approach to science that consists of working from data to theory.

industrial/organizational (I/O) psychology The application of psychological principles and theories to the workplace.

information technology (IT) The new science of collecting, storing, processing, and transmitting information.

initiating structure Behaviors through which leaders define their roles and their subordinates' roles in achieving the group's formal goals.

instructional design A set of events that facilitate training through their impact on trainees.

instrumentality The perceived relationship between the performance of a particular behavior and the likelihood that a certain outcome will result from that behavior.

integrity tests Tests used in an attempt to predict whether an employee will engage in counterproductive or dishonest work-related behaviors like cheating, stealing, or sabotage.

internal consistency An indication of the extent to which individual test items seem to be measuring the same thing.

internal validity The extent to which we can draw causal inferences about our variables.

interrater reliability The extent to which multiple raters or judges agree on ratings made about a particular person, thing, or behavior.

intervention The program or initiative that is suggested or implemented by the change agent in an organizational change intervention.

interviews A procedure designed to predict future performance based on an applicant's oral responses to a series of oral questions.

job A collection of positions similar enough to one another to share a common job title.

job analysis The process of defining a job in terms of its component tasks or duties and the knowledge or skills required to perform them.

job description As an outcome of job analysis, a written statement of what jobholders actually do, how they do it, and why they do it.

Job Element Method (JEM) A worker-oriented approach to job analysis that was designed to identify the characteristics of superior workers in a particular job.

job enrichment The process of increasing the motivating potential of jobs, often by strengthening the key motivating characteristics identified by job characteristics theory.

job evaluation As an outcome of job analysis, a technique that attempts to determine the value or worth of particular jobs to organizations so that salaries can be set accordingly.

job involvement The extent to which employees are cognitively engaged in their jobs.

job-oriented Referring to approaches to job analysis that focus on describing the various tasks that are performed on the job.

job satisfaction A pleasurable, positive emotional state resulting from the cognitive appraisal of one's job or job experiences.

job specifications An outcome of job analysis delineating the KSAOs deemed necessary to perform a job.

knowledge management A method in which organizations enhance their operations through attempts to develop, disseminate, and use knowledge.

leaderless group discussion (LGD) A group exercise designed to tap managerial attributes that requires the interaction of a small group of individuals.

leader-member exchange (LMX) theory A theory about work dyads that focuses on the relationships among subordinates and leaders rather than on leader behaviors or traits.

leadership A social process through which an individual intentionally exerts influence over others to structure their behaviors and relationships.

learning The relatively permanent change in behavior that occurs as a result of experience or practice.

learning criteria In Kirkpatrick's taxonomy, criteria that reflect how much of the material is actually learned in the training program.

leniency The rating error that results when (1) the mean of one's ratings across ratees is higher than the mean of all ratees across all raters or (2) the mean of one's ratings is higher than the midpoint of the scale.

manipulation The systematic control, variation, or application of independent variables to different groups of participants.

massed practice Training in which all the practice takes place at the same time, without breaks.

mean The arithmetic average of a group of scores, typically the most useful measure of central tendency.

measurement The assignment of numbers to objects or events using rules in such a way as to represent specified attributes of the objects.

mechanical ability A specific cognitive ability involving a focus on mechanical relations, recognition of tools used for various purposes, and sometimes actual mechanical skills.

median The score in the middle of the distribution.

meta-analysis A methodology that is used to conduct quantitative literature reviews.

micro-managers Managers who, instead of delegating tasks to individual employees, try to take charge of all tasks.

mindguard A member of a cohesive group whose job it is to protect the group from outside information that is inconsistent with the group's views.

mode The most frequent single score in a distribution.

multiple cutoff approach A noncompensatory model of employee selection in which "passing scores," or cutoffs, are set on each predictor.

multiple hurdle approach A rendition of the multiple cutoff approach in which the predictors are administered in a predetermined order and applicants are measured on the next predictor only if they scored above the cutoff on the previous predictor.

multiple regression A statistical technique that, when used in the selection context, allows us to estimate how well a series of predictors forecasts a performance criterion.

need A force that organizes perceptions, beliefs, cognitions, and actions, giving rise to behaviors that reduce the force and bring about a steady state.

normal distribution A mathematically based distribution depicted as a bell-shaped curve, in which most of the observations cluster around the mean and there are few extreme observations.

normative commitment Attachment to an organization that reflects one's obligation to continue employment with the organization.

norms Shared expectations about appropriate ways of responding in a group.

objective criteria Performance measures that are based on counting rather than on subjective judgments or evaluations.

organizational behavior management (OBM) The application of the principles of behavioral psychology to the study and control of individual and group behavior within organizational settings.

organizational commitment The relative strength of an individual's identification with and involvement in a particular organization.

organizational development (OD) A planned, organization-wide effort to increase organizational effectiveness through behavioral science knowledge and technology.

organizational justice The study of people's perceptions of fairness in organizational contexts.

organizational psychology The systematic study of dispositional and situational variables that influence the behaviors and experiences of individuals and groups at work.

organizational socialization The process by which an individual acquires the attitudes, behavior, and knowledge needed to participate as an organizational member.

organizational theory A set of propositions that explains or predicts how groups and individuals behave in varying organizational structures and circumstances.

organizational transformation A term that refers to any intervention primarily directed toward creating a new vision for an organization and changing its beliefs, purpose, and mission.

organization-based self-esteem (OBSE) A measure of how valuable employees view themselves as organization members.

organization-motivated aggression Attempts by someone inside or outside the organization to cause injury or to be destructive as a result of some organizational factor.

organization-motivated violence The negative effects on people or property that result from organization-motivated aggression.

overlearning The process of giving trainees continued practice even after they have appeared to master the behavior, resulting in high levels of learning.

paper-and-pencil tests Frequently used tests in which individuals respond to questions in a test booklet or mark answers on computer sheets to be scanned.

parallel forms reliability The extent to which two independent forms of a test are equivalent measures of the same construct.

parental leave A program offered by organizations that enables employees to combine work and family responsibilities related to child rearing.

perceived behavioral control An individual's belief as to how easy or difficult performance of a behavior is likely to be.

perceived organizational support (POS) Employees' global beliefs concerning the extent to which the organization values and cares about them.

performance Actual on-the-job behaviors that are relevant to the organization's goals.

performance appraisal The systematic review and evaluation of employees' job performance, as well as the provision of feedback to the employees.

performance management A system of individual performance improvement that typically includes (1) objective goal setting, (2) continuous coaching and feedback, (3) performance appraisal, and (4) development planning.

performance tests Tests that require the manipulation of an object or a piece of equipment.

personality tests Tests in which numbers are systematically assigned to individuals' characteristics.

physical fidelity The extent to which the operation of equipment in training mimics that in the real world.

point system The most common approach to job evaluation, which involves estimating the value of jobs based on points assigned to various predetermined dimensions.

position An individual's place in the organization defined by the tasks performed.

Position Analysis Questionnaire (PAQ) A widely used job analysis instrument that focuses on general work behaviors.

power An individual's potential influence over the attitudes and behavior of one or more other individuals.

power test A test with no fixed time limits and relatively difficult items.

predictive validity The extent to which test scores obtained at one point in time predict criteria obtained in the future.

problem-focused coping A coping style that involves behaviors or actions targeted toward solving or handling the stress-inducing problem itself.

process loss Any nonmotivational element of a group situation that detracts from the group's performance.

prototype One's mental representation of something or someone, such as a leader.

psychological fidelity The extent to which the essential behavioral processes needed to be successful on the job are also necessary for success on the training simulation.

psychomotor tests Tests that measure both the speed and the accuracy of motor and other sensory coordination.

quasi-experiment A research design that resembles an experimental design but does not include random assignment.

random assignment The procedure by which research participants, once selected, are assigned to conditions such that each one has an equally likely chance of being assigned to each condition.

range The simplest measure of dispersion, reflecting the spread of scores from the lowest to the highest.

Rater Error Training (RET) A type of training originally developed to reduce rater errors by focusing on describing errors like halo to raters and showing them how to avoid making such errors.

reaction criteria In Kirkpatrick's taxonomy, trainees' attitudinal reactions to the training program.

readiness Possessing the background characteristics and necessary level of interest that makes learning possible.

realistic job preview (RJP) During an employment interview, the presentation of an accurate glimpse of what the job would be like.

reasonable accommodations Changes or exceptions made by an employer that allow qualified disabled individuals to successfully do a job.

recruitment The process of encouraging potentially qualified applicants to seek employment with a particular company.

reengineering The fundamental rethinking and redesign of business processes to improve critical performance as measured by cost, quality, service, and speed.

reliability The consistency or stability of a measure.

results criteria In Kirkpatrick's taxonomy, the ultimate value of the training program to the company.

role A set of behaviors expected of a person who occupies a particular position in a group.

role ambiguity A situation that results when role expectations are unclear and employees are thus not sure what is expected of them.

role conflict A situation that results when role expectations are inconsistent, as when a supervisor sends employees mixed messages about their roles.

role differentiation The process by which a group or organization establishes distinct roles for various members of the group or organization.

science A process or method for generating a body of knowledge.

scientist/practitioner model An approach used to train I/O psychologists that maintains that because I/O psychologists are both generators and consumers of knowledge, training must be focused on both theory and application.

selection battery A set of predictors, or tests, that are used to make employee hiring decisions.

selection ration The number of job openings divided by the number of applicants.

self-efficacy expectations Individuals' perceptions of their ability to successfully complete a task or attain a goal.

self-managed work team (SMWT) A work team that is responsible for monitoring and controlling the overall process or product, as well as for doling out specific tasks to team members.

self-regulation The manner in which individuals monitor their own behaviors and make adjustments to those behaviors in the pursuit of goals.

severity The tendency to use only the low end of the scale or to give consistently lower ratings to one's employees than other raters do.

sexual harassment Behaviors such as unwelcome sexual advances, requests for sexual favors, and other conduct of a sexual nature, submission to or rejection of which affects one's job or creates an offensive work environment.

situational specificity The belief that test validities are specific to particular situations.

social loafing The reduction in individual effort that occurs when people work in groups compared with working alone.

span of control The number of subordinates who report to a given supervisor.

spatial ability A specific cognitive ability involving a focus on geometric relations such as visualizing objects and rotating them spatially to form a particular pattern.

speed test A test containing relatively easy items in which individuals are told to complete as many as they can in a given time period.

standard deviation A measure of dispersion that is calculated as the square root of the variance.

statistic An efficient device for summarizing in a single number the values, characteristics, or scores describing a series of cases.

strains Undesirable personal outcomes resulting from the combined stressful experiences of various life domains.

stress Any force that pushes a psychological or physical function beyond its range of stability, producing a strain within the individual.

subjective criteria Performance measures that are based on the judgments or evaluations of others rather than on objective measures such as counting.

subjective norm An individual's perception of the social pressures to perform or not perform a particular behavior.

subject matter experts Individuals who participate in job analyses as a result of their job-related expertise.

sucker effect An outcome that occurs when group members become concerned that their co-workers are holding back, at which point they reduce their own efforts to the level they believe is being exhibited by their co-workers.

surveys A data collection technique that involves the selection of a sample of respondents and the administration of some type of questionnaire.

task A work activity that is performed to achieve a specific objective.

Task Inventory Approach A job-oriented approach to job analysis in which task statements are generated by experts who are familiar with the job in question.

task performance The work-related activities performed by employees that contribute to the technical core of the organization.

taskwork Activities, behaviors, or actions that involve the task-oriented aspects of work.

team building A technique used by organizations to develop teams or to enhance the effectiveness of existing teams.

teamwork Activities, behaviors, or actions that involve the process-oriented aspects of work.

test A systematic procedure for observing behavior and

describing it with the aid of numerical scales or fixed categories.

test-retest reliability The stability of a test over time; often referred to as a *coefficient of stability.*

theory A set of interrelated constructs (concepts), definitions, and propositions that present a systematic view of a phenomenon by specifying relations among variables, with the purpose of explaining and predicting the phenomenon.

360-degree feedback A method of performance appraisal in which multiple raters at various levels of the organization evaluate a target employee and the employee is provided with feedback from these multiple sources.

total quality management (TQM) An initiative that focuses on employee involvement in the control of quality in organizations.

training The formal procedures that a company utilizes to facilitate learning so that the resultant behavior contributes to the attainment of the company's goals and objectives.

trait theories Leadership theories that focus on identifying the individual characteristics that make people good leaders.

transactional leadership A form of leadership in which the relationship between leader and follower is based chiefly on exchanges, with an emphasis on contingent reinforcement.

transfer of training The extent to which the material, skills, or procedures learned in training are taken back to the job and used by the employee in some regular fashion.

transformational leadership A form of leadership in which the interaction of leader and follower raises both to higher levels of motivation and morality than they would achieve individually.

true halo Halo that results from accurate intercorrelations among performance dimensions rather than from rating error.

ultimate criterion A theoretical construct encompassing all performance aspects that define success on the job.

undue hardship An accommodation for the disabled that would result in significant difficulty or expense given the employer's size and financial resources.

unobtrusive naturalistic observation An observational technique whereby the researcher unobtrusively and objectively observes individuals but does not try to blend in with them.

upward appraisal ratings Ratings provided by individuals whose status, in an organizational-hierarchy sense, is below that of the ratees.

utility The degree to which a selection battery is useful and cost efficient.

valence (or value) The expected level of satisfaction to be derived from some outcome.

validity coefficient A correlation that serves as an index of the relationship between a predictor and a criterion, used by selection researchers and practitioners as evidence that a particular test is a valid predictor of a performance criterion.

validity generalization A statistical approach used to demonstrate that test validities do not vary across situations.

validity shrinkage A statistical phenomenon reflecting the likelihood that a given selection battery will demonstrate lower validity when employed with a different sample.

variance A useful measure of dispersion reflecting the sum of the squared differences between each score and the mean of the group divided by the number of total scores.

work centrality The degree of importance that work holds in one's life.

worker-oriented Referring to approaches to job analysis that examine broad human behaviors involved in work activities.

work-family conflict A model of work-family relations in which work and family demands are incompatible

work-family enrichment A model of work-family relations in which positive attitudes and behaviors are believed to carry over from one domain to the other.

work group An interdependent collection of individuals who share responsibility for specific outcomes for their organizations.

work motivation A force that drives people to behave in a way that energizes, directs, and sustains their work behavior.

work sample tests Tests that attempt to duplicate performance criteria measures and use them as predictors, thus forming miniature replicas of the job.

REFERENCES

Aberson, C. L. (2003). Support for race-based affirmative action: Self-interest and procedural justice. *Journal of Applied Social Psychology, 33*(6), 1212–1225.

*ACE News. (2000). *ACE study shows gains in number of women college presidents, smaller gains for minority CEOs.* Retrieved September 17, 2004, from *http://www.acenet.edu/news/press_release/2000/09september/college-president.html.*

Adams, J. S. (1965). Inequity in social exchange. In L. Berkowitz (Ed.), *Advances in experimental psychology.* New York: Academic Press.

Ajzen, I., & Fishbein, M. (1980). *Understanding attitudes and predicting social behavior.* Englewood Cliffs, NJ: Prentice-Hall.

Ajzen, I., & Madden, T. J. (1986). Prediction of goal-directed behavior: The role of intention, perceived control, and prior behavior. *Journal of Experimental Social Psychology, 22,* 453–474.

Allen, D. G., Shore, L. M., & Griffeth, R. W. (2003). The role of perceived organizational support and supportive human resource practices in the turnover process. *Journal of Management, 29*(1), 99–118.

Allen, N. J., & Meyer, J. P. (1996). Affective, continuance, and normative commitment to the organization: An examination of construct validity. *Journal of Vocational Behavior, 49,* 252–276.

Allen, R. S., & White, C. S. (2002). Equity sensitivity theory: A test of responses to two types of under-reward situations. *Journal of Managerial Issues, 14*(4), 435–451.

Allen, T. D., Herst, D. E. L., Bruck, C. S., & Sutton, M. (2000). Consequences associated with work-to-family conflict: A review and agenda for future research. *Journal of Occupational Health Psychology, 5*(2), 278–308.

Alliger, G. M., & Dwight, S. A. (2000). A meta-analytic investigation of the susceptibility of integrity tests to faking and coaching. *Educational and Psychological Measurement, 60*(1), 59–72.

Alliger, G. M., & Janak, E. A. (1989). Kirkpatrick's levels of training criteria: Thirty years later. *Personnel Psychology, 42,* 331–342.

Alliger, G. M., Tannenbaum, S. I., Bennett, W., Jr., Traver, H., & Shotland, A. (1997). A meta-analysis of the relations among training criteria. *Personnel Psychology, 50,* 341–358.

Allworth, E., & Hesketh, B. (2000). Job requirements biodata as a predictor of performance in customer service roles. *International Journal of Selection and Assessment, 83*(3), 137–147.

Ambrose, M. L., & Kulik, C. T. (1999). Old friends, new faces: Motivation research in the 1990s. *Journal of Management, 2*(3), 231–292.

American Bar Association. (2004). *Commission on women in the profession.* Retrieved 9/14/04. *http://www.abanet.org/women/glance2003.pdf.*

American Institutes for Research. (1996, September 13). *Occupational Classification Systems Review List.* Available online at *http://www.air-dc.org/ssa/air_ocs2.html* [2001, January 11].

American Psychological Association. (2001). *Publication manual of the American Psychological Association* (5th ed.). Washington, DC: American Psychological Association.

America's most admired companies. (2004). Retrieved September 21, 2004, from *http://www.fortune.com/fortune/mostadmired. 100 best corporate citizens.* (2004). Retrieved September 21, 2004, from *http://www.business-ethics.com/100best.htm.*

Anderson, L. (2000, October 23). Business education survey: Corporate universities. *Financial Times.*

Anonymous. (1997). Perspectives: Parental leave. *International Labour Review, 136*(1), 109–128.

Anonymous. (1998). Working better by design. *USBanker, 108*(5), 14–15.

Antecol, H., & Cobb-Clark, D. (2003). Does sexual harassment training change attitudes? A view from the Federal level. *Social Science Quarterly* (Vol. 84, pp. 826–842): Blackwell.

Antonakis, J., Avolio, B. J., & Sivasubramaniam, N. (2003). Context and leadership: An examination of the nine-factor full-range leadership theory using the Multifactor Leadership Questionnaire. *Leadership Quarterly, 14*(3), 261–295.

Ardichvili, A., Page, V., & Wentling, T. (2003). Motivation and barriers to participation in virtual knowledge-sharing communities of practice. *Journal of Knowledge Management, 7*(1), 64–77.

Aronson, E., Wilson, T. D., & Akers, R. M. (1997). *Social Psychology* (2nd ed.). New York: Longman.

Arthur, W., Bennett, W., Edens, P. S., & Bell, S. T. (2003). Effectiveness of training in organizations: A meta-analysis of design and evaluation features. *Journal of Applied Psychology, 88*(2), 234–245.

Arthur, W., Day, E. A., McNelly, T. L., & Edens, P. S. (2003). A meta-analysis of the criterion-related validity of assessment center dimensions. *Personnel Psychology, 56*(1), 125–154.

Arthur, W., Jr., Woehr, D. J., & Maldegen, R. (2000). Convergent and discriminate validity of assessment center dimensions: A conceptual and empirical reexamination of the assessment center construct-related validity paradox. *Journal of Management, 26*(4), 813–835.

Arvey, R. D., & Begalla, M. E. (1975). Analyzing the homemaker job using the Position Analysis Questionnaire (PAQ). *Journal of Applied Psychology, 60,* 513–517.

Arvey, R. D., Bouchard, T. J. J., Segal, N. L., & Abraham, L. M. (1989). Job satisfaction: Environmental and genetic components. *Journal of Applied Psychology, 74*(2), 187–192.

Aryee, S., & Luk, V. (1996). Work and nonwork influences on the career satisfaction of dual-earner couples. *Journal of Vocational Behavior, 49,* 38–52.

Ash, R. A., & Edgell, S. L. (1975). A note on the readability of the Position Analysis Questionnaire (PAQ). *Journal of Applied Psychology, 60,* 765–766.

Ashmos, D. P., & Nathan, M. L. (2002). Team sense-making: A mental model for navigating uncharted territories. *Journal of Managerial Issues, 14*(2), 198–217.

Athey, T. R., & McIntyre, R. M. (1987). Effect of rater training on rater accuracy: Levels of processing theory and social facilitation theory perspectives. *Journal of Applied Psychology, 72,* 567–572.

Atkins, P. W. B., & Wood, R. E. (2002). Self- versus others' ratings as predictors of assessment center ratings: Validation evidence for 360-degree feedback programs. *Personnel Psychology, 55*(4), 871–904.

Atwater, L. E., Daldman, D. A., Atwater, D., & Cartier, P. (2000). An upward feedback field experiment: Supervisors' cynicism, reactions, and commitment to subordinates. *Personnel Psychology, 53,* 275–297.

Austin, J. T., & Davies, S. A. (2000). History of Industrial-organizational psychology. In A. E. Kazdin (Ed.), *Encyclopedia of Psychology* (Vol. 4, pp. 252-255). Oxford: Oxford University Press.

Austin, J. T., & Villanova, P. D. (1992). The criterion problem: 1917–1992. *Journal of Applied Psychology, 77,* 836–874.

Austin, J. T., Villanova, P. D., & Hindman, H. G. (1995). Legal requirements and technical guidelines involved in implementing performance appraisal systems. In G. R. Ferris & M. R. Buckley (Eds.), *Human resource management: Perspectives, context, functions, and outcomes.* Boston: Allyn & Bacon.

Avolio, B. J., Waldman, D. A., & McDaniel, M. A. (1990). Age and work performance in nonmanagerial jobs: The effects of experience and occupational type. *Academy of Management Journal, 33*(2), 407–422.

Awoniyi, E. A., Griego, O. V., & Morgan, G. A. (2002). Person-environment fit and transfer of training. *International Journal of Training and Development* (Vol. 6, p. 25): Blackwell.

Ayman, R., Chemers, M. M., & Fiedler, F. (1995). The contingency model of leadership effectiveness: Its level of analysis. *Leadership Quarterly, 6*(2), 147–167.

Babbie, E. (1998). *The practice of social research.* Belmont, CA: Wadsworth Publishing Company.

Bailey, C., & Fletcher, C. (2002). The impact of multiple source feedback on management development: Findings from a longitudinal study. *Journal of Organizational Behavior, 23*(7), 853–867.

Baldwin, T. P., & Ford, J. K. (1988). Transfer of training: A review and directions for future research. *Personnel Psychology, 41,* 63–105.

Baltes, B. B., & Heydens-Gahir, H. A. (2003). Reduction of work-family conflict through the use of selection, optimization, and compensation behaviors. *Journal of Applied Psychology, 88*(6), 1005–1018.

Bandura, A. (1986). *Social foundations of thought and action.* Englewood Cliffs, NJ: Prentice-Hall.

Bandura, A., & Locke, E. A. (2003). Negative self-efficacy and goal effects revisited. *Journal of Applied Psychology, 88*(1), 87–99.

Bardsley, J. J., & Rhodes, S. R. (1996). Using the Steers-Rhodes (1984) framework to identify correlates of employee lateness. *Journal of Business and Psychology, 10*(3), 351–365.

Barrett, G. V., Caldwell, M. S., & Alexander, R. A. (1985). The concept of dynamic criteria: A critical reanalysis. *Personnel Psychology, 15,* 93–97.

Barrett, G. V., & Kernan, M. C. (1988). Performance appraisal and terminations: A review of court decisions since *Brito v. Zia* with implications for personnel practices. *Personnel Psychology, 40*(3), 489–503.

Barrick, M. R., & Mount, M. K. (1991). The Big Five personality dimensions and job performance: A meta-analysis. *Personnel Psychology, 44,* 1–26.

Barrick, M. R., Stewart, G. L., Neubert, M. J., & Mount, M. K. (1998). Relating member ability and personality to work-team processes and team effectiveness. *Journal of Applied Psychology, 83*(3), 377–391.

Bass, B. M. (1985). *Leadership and performance beyond expectations.* New York: Free Press.

Bass, B. M. (1997). Does the transactional-transformational leadership paradigm transcend organizational and national boundaries? *American Psychologist, 52*(2), 130–139.

Bass, B. M., Avolio, B. J., Jung, D. I., & Berson, Y. (2003). Predicting unit performance by assessing transformational and transactional leadership. *Journal of Applied Psychology, 88*(2), 207–218.

Bass, B. M., & Steidlmeier, P. (1999). Ethics, character, and authentic transformational leadership behavior. *Leadership Quarterly, 10*(2), 181–217.

Bassi, L. J., & Van Buren, M. E. (1998). *Sharpening the leading edge.* American Society for Training and Development (ASTD). Available online at *http://www.astd.org/CMS/templates/template_1.html?articleid=20940* [1999, May 19].

Bates, R. (2002). Liking and similarity as predictors of multi-source ratings. *Personnel Review, 31*(5), 540–552.

Bates, S. (2003). Forced rankling. *HR Magazine, 48*(6), 62–68.

Bauer, T. N., Morrison, E. W., & Callister, R. R. (1998). Organizational socialization: A review and directions for future research. In G. R. Ferris (Ed.), *Research in personnel and human resources management* (Vol. 16, pp. 149–214). Stamford, CT: JAI Press.

Baumohl, B. (1993). When downsizing becomes "dumbsizing." *Time,* 55.

Beck, B. (1998). Women and work: At the double. *The Economist, 348*(8077), S12–S15.

Beck, K., & Wilson, C. (2000). Development of affective organizational commitment: A cross-sequential examination of change with tenure. *Journal of Vocational Behavior, 56*(1), 114–136.

Beckhard, R. (1969). *Organization development: Strategies and models.* Reading, MA: Addison-Wesley.

Bell, B. S., & Kozlowski, S. W. J. (2002). Adaptive guidance: Enhancing self-regulation, knowledge, and performance in technology-based training. *Personnel Psychology, 55*(2), 267–306.

Bell, B. S., & Kozlowski, W. J. (2002). Goal orientation and ability: Interactive effects on self-efficacy, performance, and knowledge. *Journal of Applied Psychology, 87*(3), 497–505.

Benitez, E. (2004). Personal Communication. Bowling Green, OH: SIOP.

Bennis, W., & Biederman, P. W. (1997). *Organizing genius: The secrets of creative collaboration.* Reading, MA: Addison-Wesley.

Bernardin, H. J. (1978). Effects of rater training on leniency and halo errors in student ratings of instructors. *Journal of Applied Psychology, 63*(3), 301–308.

Bernardin, H. J., & Beatty, R. W. (1984). *Performance appraisal: Assessing human behavior at work.* Boston: Kent.

Bernardin, H. J., & Buckley, M. R. (1981). Strategies in rater training. *Academy of Management Review, 6,* 205–212.

Bernardin, H. J., Cooke, D. K., & Villanova, P. D. (2000). Conscientiousness and agreeableness as predictors of rating leniency. *Journal of Applied Psychology, 85*(2), 232–236.

Bernardin, H. J., Orban, J., & Carlyle, J. (1981). Performance ratings as a function of trust in appraisal and rater individual differences. Paper presented at the 41st annual meeting of the Academy of Management.

Bernardin, H. J., & Pence, E. C. (1980). Effects of rater training: Creating new response sets and decreasing accuracy. *Journal of Applied Psychology, 65,* 60–66.

Bettenhausen, K. L., & Fedor, D. B. (1997). Peer and upward appraisals: A comparison of their benefits and problems. *Group and Organization Management, 22*(2), 236–263.

Beugre, C. D. (1998). Implementing business process reengineering: The role of organizational justice. *Journal of Applied Behavioral Science, 34*(3), 347–360.

Bhagat, R. S., Allie, S. M., & Ford, D. L., Jr. (1995). Coping with stressful life events: An empirical analysis. In R. Crandall & P. L. Perrewe (Eds.), *Organizational Stress: A handbook.* Washington, DC: Taylor & Francis.

Biles, M. A. (1999). *OSHA workplace violence prevention guidelines.* American Psychological Association, Public Interest Directorate. Available online at *http://www.apa.org/pi/wpo/niosh/abstract12.html* [2000, January 20].

Bisio, J. (1999). The age boom. *Risk Management, 46*(2), 22–27.

Blakely, G. L., Blakely, E. H., & Moorman, R. H. (1998). The effects of training on perceptions of sexual harassment allegations. *Journal of Applied Social Psychology, 28*(1), 71–83.

Blau, G. (1994). Developing and testing a taxonomy of lateness behavior. *Journal of Applied Psychology, 79*(6), 959–970.

Blau, G. (1999). Testing the longitudinal impact of work variables and performance appraisal satisfaction on subsequent overall job satisfaction. *Human Relations, 52*(8), 1099–1113.

Bliese, P. D., & Britt, T. W. (2001). Social support, group consensus, and stressor-strain relationships: Social context matters. *Journal of Organizational Behavior, 22,* 425–436.

Bloom, A. J., Yorges, S. L., & Ruhl, A. J. (2000). Enhancing student motivation: Extensions from job enrichment theory and practice. *Teaching of Psychology, 27*(2), 135–137.

Bloom, D. E. (1998). Technology, experimentation, and the quality of survey data. *Science, 280*(5365), 847–848.

Blum, M. L., & Naylor, J. C. (1968). *Industrial psychology.* New York: Harper & Row.

Boles, M. (1997). Elder care is everyone's responsibility. *Workforce, 76*(10), 23.

Bolino, M. C., Turnley, W. H., & Bloodgood, J. M. (2002). Citizenship behavior and the creation of social capital in organizations. *Academy of Management Review, 27*(4), 505–522.

Bond, J. T., Thompson, C., Galinsky, E., & Prottas, D. (2002). *Highlights of the National Study of the Changing Workforce Executive Summary.* Retrieved August 15, 2004, from Families and Work Institute website: *http://www.familiesandwork.org.*

Bono, J. E., & Judge, T. A. (2003). Core self-evaluations: A review of the trait and its role in job satisfaction and job performance. *Personality and Industrial, Work and Organizational Applications, 17*(Suppl. 1), S5–S18.

Borman, W. C., Buck, D. E., Hanson, M. A., Motowidlo, S. J., Stark, S., & Drasgow, F. (2001). An examination of the comparative reliability, validity, and accuracy of performance ratings made using computerized adaptive rating scales. *Journal of Applied Psychology, 86*(5), 965–973.

Borman, W. C., Hanson, M. A., & Hedge, J. W. (1997). Personnel selection. In J. T. Spence, J. M. Darley, & D. J. Foss (Eds.), *Annual Review of Psychology* (Vol. 48, pp. 299–337). Palo Alto, CA: Annual Reviews, Inc.

Borman, W. C., & Motowidlo, S. J. (1997). Task performance and contextual performance: The meaning for personnel selection research. *Human Performance, 10*(2), 99–109.

Boudreau, J. W., & Ramstad, P. M. (2003). Strategic industrial and organizational psychology and the role of utility analysis models. In W. C. Borman, D. R. Ilgen, & R. Klimoski (Eds.), *Handbook of psychology: Vol. 12. Industrial and organizational psychology* (pp. 193–221). New York: Wiley.

Boyce, L. A., & Herd, A. M. (2003). The relationship between gender role stereotypes and requisite military leadership characteristics. *Sex Roles, 49*(7-8), 365–378.

Boye, M. W., & Jones, J. W. (1997). Organizational culture and employee counterproductivity. In R. A. Giacalone & J. Greenberg (Eds.), *Antisocial behavior in organizations.* Thousand Oaks, CA: Sage Publications.

Brannick, M. T., & Levine, E. L. (2002). *Job analysis: Methods, research, and applications for human resource management in the new millennium.* Thousand Oaks, CA: Sage.

Bray, D. W., Campbell, R. J., & Grant, D. L. (1974). *Formative years in business: A long-term AT&T study of managerial lives.* New York: Wiley.

Breaugh, J. A., Greising, L. A., Taggart, J. W., & Chen, H. (2003). The relationship of recruiting sources and pre-hire outcomes: Examination of field ratios and applicant quality. *Journal of Applied Social Psychology, 33*(11), 2267–2287.

Brennan v. Prince William Hospital Corp., 503 F. 2d 282 (4th Cir. 1974).

Briel, J. B., O'Neill, K., & Scheuneman, J. D. (Eds.). (1993). *GRE technical manual.* Princeton, NJ: Educational Testing Service.

Britannica Online. (1998a). *Nicolaus Copernicus. http://www.eb.com:180/cgi-bin/g?DocF=macro/5001/53.html* [1998, November 9].

Britannica Online. (1998b). *Ptolemy. http://www.eb.com:180/cgi-bin/g?DocF=micro/485/40.html* [1998, November 9].

Brockner, J. (1988). *Self-esteem at work.* Lexington, MA: Lexington Books.

Brockner, J., & Wiesenfeld, B. M. (1996). An integrative framework for explaining reactions to decisions: Interactive effects of outcomes and procedures. *Psychological Bulletin, 120*(2), 189–208.

Brockner, J., Wiesenfeld, B. M., & Martin, C. L. (1995). Decision frame, procedural justice, and survivors' reactions to job layoffs.

Organizational Behavior and Human Decision Processes, 63, 59–68.

Brodbeck, F. C., Kerschreiter, R., Mojzisch, A., Frey, D., & Schulz-Hardt, S. (2002). The dissemination of critical, unshared information in decision-making groups: The effects of prediscussion dissent. *European Journal of Social Psychology, 32,* 35–56.

Brown, J. (2002). Training needs assessment: A must for developing an effective training program. *Public Personnel Management, 31*(4), 569–578.

Brown, M., & Benson, J. (2003). Rated to exhaustion? Reactions to performance appraisal processes. *Industrial Relations Journal, 34,* 67.

Brown, S. P. (1996). A meta-analysis and review of organizational research on job involvement. *Psychological Bulletin, 120*(2), 235–255.

Bruck, C. S., Allen, T. D., & Spector, P. E. (2002). The relation between work-family conflict and job satisfaction: A finer-grained analysis. *Journal of Vocational Behavior, 60*(3), 336–353.

Brunelli, M. (1999). How Harley-Davidson uses cross-functional teams. *Purchasing,* November 4, 144.

Bucklin, B. R., Alvero, A. M., Dickinson, A. M., Austin, J., & Jackson, A. K. (2000). Industrial-organizational psychology and organizational behavior management: An objective comparison. *Journal of Organizational Behavior Management, 20*(2), 27–75.

Bullock, R. J., & Tubbs, M. E. (1990). A case meta-analysis of gainshairing plans as organizational development interventions. *Journal of Applied Behavioral Science, 26*(3), 383–404.

Bunderson, J. S., & Sutcliffe, K. M. (2002). Comparing alternative conceptualizations of functional diversity in management teams: Process and performance effects. *Academy of Management Journal, 45*(5), 875–893.

Burgess, J. R. D., & Russell, J. E. A. (2003). The effectiveness of distance learning initiatives in organizations. *Journal of Vocational Behavior, 63*(2), 289–303.

Burke, R. J. (2000). Workaholism in organizations: Psychological and physical well-being consequences. *Stress Medicine, 16,* 11–16.

Burnett, J. R., & Motowidlo, S. J. (1998). Relations between different sources of information in the structured selection interview. *Personnel Psychology, 51,* 964–983.

Cable, D. M., & Turban, D. B. (2003). The value of organizational reputation in the recruitment context: A brand-equity perspective. *Journal of Applied Social Psychology, 33*(11), 2244–2266.

Campbell, J. P. (1990). Modeling the performance prediction problem in industrial and organizational psychology. In M. Dunnette & L. M. Hough (Eds.), *Handbook of industrial and organizational psychology* (2nd ed., Vol. 1, pp. 687–732). Palo Alto, CA: Consulting Psychologists Press.

Campbell, J. P., Gasser, M. B., & Oswald, F. L. (1996). The substantive nature of job performance variability. In K. R. Murphy (Ed.), *Individual differences and behavior in organizations* (pp. 258–299). San Francisco: Jossey-Bass.

Campbell, J. P., McCloy, R. A., Oppler, S. H., & Sager, C. E. (1993). A theory of performance. In N. Schmitt & W. C. Borman (Eds.), *Personnel selection in organizations.* San Francisco: Jossey-Bass.

Campbell, J. P., McHenry, J. J., & Wise, L. L. (1990). Modeling performance in a population of jobs. *Personnel Psychology, 43,* 313–333.

Cardy, R. L., & Dobbins, G. H. (1994). *Performance appraisal: Alternative perspectives.* Cincinnati: South-Western Publishing.

Carlson, D. S., & Kacmar, K. M. (2000). Work-family conflict in the organization: Do life role values make a difference? *Journal of Management, 26*(5), 1031–1054.

Carlson, D. S., & Perrewe, P. L. (1999). The role of social support in the stressor-strain relationship: An examination of work-family conflict. *Journal of Management, 25*(4), 513–540.

Carroll, S. J., & Schneier, C. E. (1982). *Performance appraisal and review systems: The identification, measurement, and development of performance in organizations.* Glenview, IL: Scott, Foresman.

Cartwright, S., & Cooper, C. L. (1997). *Managing workplace stress.* Thousand Oaks, CA: Sage Publications.

Carver, C. S., & Scheier, M. F. (1981). *Attention and self-regulation: A control-theory approach to human behavior.* New York: Springer-Verlag.

Carver, C. S., & Scheier, M. F. (1998). *On the self-regulation of behavior.* Cambridge, England: Cambridge University Press.

Cascio, W. F. (1995). Whither industrial and organizational psychology in a changing world of work. *American Psychologist, 50*(11), 928–939.

Cascio, W. F. (1998). *Applied psychology in human resource management* (5th ed.). Upper Saddle River, NJ: Prentice-Hall.

Catanzaro, D. (1997). Course enrichment and the job characteristics model. *Teaching of Psychology, 24*(2), 85–87.

Cattell, R. B., Eber, H. W., & Tatsuoka, M. M. (1970). *Handbook for the Sixteen Personality Factor Questionnaire.* Champaign, IL: Institute for Personality and Ability Testing.

Cavanaugh, M. A., Boswell, W. R., Roehling, M. V., & Boudreau, J. W. (2000). An empirical examination of self-reported work stress among U.S. managers. *Journal of Applied Psychology, 85*(1), 65–74.

Cawley, B. D., Keeping, L. M., & Levy, P. E. (1998). Participation in the performance appraisal process and employee reactions: A meta-analytic review of field investigations. *Journal of Applied Psychology, 83*(4), 615–633.

Chambers, B. A., & Schmitt, N. (2002). Inequity in the performance evaluation process: How you rate me affects how I rate you. *Journal of Personnel Evaluation in Education, 16*(2), 103–112.

Chan, D., & Schmitt, N. (2002). Situational judgment and job performance. *Human Performance, 15*(3), 233–254.

Chang, A., Bordia, P., & Duck, J. (2003). Punctuated equilibrium and linear progression: Toward a new understanding of group development. *Academy of Management Journal, 46*(1), 106–117.

Chemers, M. M. (2000). Leadership research and theory: A functional integration. *Group Dynamics, 4*(1), 27–43.

Chen, G., Goddard, T. G., & Casper, W. J. (2004). Examination of the relationships among general and work-specific self-evaluations, work-related control beliefs, and job attitudes. *Applied Psychology: An International Review, 53*(3), 349–370.

Cheng, Y., & Stockdale, M. S. (2003). The validity of the three-component model of organizational commitment in a Chinese context. *Journal of Vocational Behavior, 62*(3), 465–489.

Christensen, L. B. (1994). *Experimental Methodology.* Boston: Allyn and Bacon.

Chronicle of Higher Education. (1998). Almanac. *Chronicle of Higher Education, 45*(1).

Church, A. H., & Bracken, D. W. (1997). Advancing the state of the art of 360-degree feedback: Guest editors' comments on the research and practice of multirater assessment methods. *Group and Organization Management, 22*(2), 149–161.

Church, A. H., Waclawski, J., & Seigel, W. (1999). Will the real O.D. practitioner please stand up? *Organization Development Journal, 17*(2), 49–59.

Clarke, N. (2002). Job/work environment factors influencing training transfer within a human service agency: Some indicative support for Baldwin and Ford's transfer climate construct. *International Journal of Training and Development, 6*(3), 146–162.

Cleverly v. Western Electric, 594 F. 2d 638 (8th Cir. 1979).

Cober, R. T., Brown, D. J., Blumental, A. J., Doverspike, D., & Levy, P. E. (2000). The quest for the qualified job surfer: It's time the public sector catches the wave. *Public Personnel Management, 29*(4), 479–496.

Cober, R. T., Brown, D. J., Keeping, L. M., & Levy, P. E. (2004) Recruitment on the net: How do organizational web site characteristics influence applicant attraction. *Journal of Management. 30(5),* 623-646.

Cober, R. T., Brown, D. J., Levy, P. E., Cober, A. B., & Keeping, L. M. (2003). Organizational web sites: Web site content and style as determinants of organizational attraction. *International Journal of Selection and Assessment, 11*(2/3), 158–169.

Cohen, A. (1997). Facing pressure. *Sales and Marketing Management, 149,* 30–38.

Cohen, S. G. (1994). Designing effective self-managing work teams. In M. M. Beyerlein & D. A. Johnson (Eds.), *Advances in interdisciplinary studies of work teams* (Vol. 1, pp. 67–102). Greenwich, CT: JAI Press.

Cohen, S. G., & Bailey, D. (1997). What makes teams work: Group effectiveness research from the shop floor to the executive suite. *Journal of Management, 23,* 239–290.

College Board. (2003). *SAT Verbal and Math scores up significantly as a record-breaking number of students take the test.* Retrieved April 28, 2004, from *www.collegeboard.com/press/article/0,3183,26858,00.html.*

Collins, C. J., & Stevens, C. K. (2002). The relationship between early recruitment-related activities and the application decisions of new labor-market entrants: A brand equity approach to recruitment. *Journal of Applied Psychology, 87*(6), 1121–1133.

Collins, D. (1995). Death of a gainsharing plan: Power politics and participatory management. *Organizational Dynamics, 24*(1), 23–38.

Collins, J. M., & Schmidt, F. L. (1993). Personality, integrity, and white collar crime: A construct validity study. *Personnel Psychology, 46,* 295–311.

Cook, T. D., & Campbell, D. T. (1979). *Quasi-Experimentation: Design and analysis issues for field settings.* Boston: Houghton Mifflin.

Cordes, C. L., & Dougherty, T. W. (1993). A review and an integration of research on job burnout. *Academy of Management Review, 18*(4), 621-656.

Cortina, J. M., Goldstein, N. B., Payne, S. C., Davison, H. K., & Gilliland, S. W. (2000). The incremental validity of interview scores over and above cognitive ability and conscientiousness scores. *Personnel Psychology, 53*(2), 325–351.

Cota, A. A., Evans, C. R., Dion, K. L., Kilik, L., & Longman, R. S. (1995). The structure of group cohesion. *Personality and Social Psychology Bulletin, 21*(6), 572–580.

Cote, S., & Morgan, L. M. (2002). A longitudinal analysis of the association between emotion regulation, job satisfaction, and intentions to quit. *Journal of Organizational Behavior, 23*(8), 947–962.

Cox, Matthews, & Associates. (2003). *Black issues in higher education.* Retrieved April 28, 2004, from *www.findarticles.com/cf_dls/m0DXK/15_20/109165562/p1/article.jhtml.*

Coyle-Shapiro, J. A.-M., Morrow, P. C., Richardson, R., & Dunn, S. R. (2002). Using profit sharing to enhance employee attitudes: A longitudinal examination of the effects on trust and commitment. *Human Resource Management, 41*(4), 423–439.

Coyle-Shapiro, J. A.-M., & Morrow, P. C. (2003). The role of individual differences in employee adoption of TQM orientation. *Journal of Vocational Behavior, 62*(2), 320–340.

Cronbach, L. J. (1990). *Essentials of psychological testing* (5th ed.). New York: Harper & Row.

Cropanzano, R. (Ed.). (2001). *Justice in the workplace: From theory to practice* (Vol. 2). Mahwah, NJ: Erlbaum.

Cropanzano, R., & Greenberg, J. (1997). Progress in organizational justice: Tunneling through the maze. In C. L. Cooper & I. T. Robertson (Eds.), *International review of industrial and organizational psychology.* Chichester, England: Wiley.

Cummings, T. G., & Worley, C. G. (2001). *Organization development and change* (7th ed.). Cincinnati: South-Western College Publishing.

Cunningham, J. W. (1989). Applied measurement issues in job analysis. Paper presented at the annual meeting of the American Psychological Association, New Orleans.

Dansereau, F., Graen, G. B., & Haga, W. (1975). A vertical dyad linkage approach to leadership in formal organizations. *Organizational Behavior and Human Performance, 13,* 46–78.

Dasborough, M. T., & Ashkanasy, N. M. (2002). Emotion and attribution of intentionality in leader-member relationships. *Emotions and leadership, 13*(5), 615–634.

De Vries, M. F. R. K. (1999). High performance teams: Lessons from the Pygmies. *Organizational Dynamics,* Winter, 66–75.

Deadrick, D. L., Bennett, N., & Russell, C. J. (1997). Using hierarchical linear modeling to examine dynamic performance criteria over time. *Journal of Management, 23*(6), 745–757.

Deadrick, D. L., & Madigan, R. M. (1990). Dynamic criteria revisited: A longitudinal study of performance stability and predictive validity. *Personnel Psychology, 43,* 717–744.

Deci, E. L. (1975). *Intrinsic motivation.* New York: Plenum Press.

Demerouti, E., Bakker, A. B., Nachreiner, F., & Schaufeli, W. B. (2001). The job demands–resources model of burnout. *Journal of Applied Psychology, 86*(3), 499–512.

DeNisi, A. S., Cafferty, T., & Meglino, B. (1984). A cognitive view of the performance appraisal process: A model and research propositions. *Organizational Behavior and Human Decision Processes, 33,* 360–396.

DeNisi, A. S., & Kluger, A. N. (2000). Feedback effectiveness: Can 360-degree appraisal be improved? *Academy of Management Executive, 14*(1), 129–139.

Department of Labor. (2000). *Balancing the needs of families and employers.* Available online at *http://www.dol.gov/dol/public/fmla/main.htm* [2001, January 15].

Diaz v. Pan American World Airways, Inc., 442. F. 2d 385 (5th Cir. 1971).

Dickens, L., & Watkins, K. (1999). Action research: Rethinking Lewin. *Management Learning, 30*(2), 127–140.

Dickson, M. W., Den Hartog, D. N., & Mitchelson, J. K. (2003). Research on leadership in a cross-cultural context: Making progress, and raising new questions. *Leadership Quarterly, 14,* 729–768.

Dickson, M. W., Hanges, P. J., & Lord, R. G. (2000). Trends, developments and gaps in cross-cultural research on leadership. In W. Mobley (Ed.), *Advances in global leadership* (Vol. 2, pp. 2–22). Stamford, CT: JAI Press.

Diefendorff, J. M., Brown, D. J., Kamin, A. M., & Lord, R. G. (2002). Examining the roles of job involvement and work centrality in predicting organizational citizenship behaviors and job performance. *Journal of Organizational Behavior, 23*(1), 93–108.

Diefendorff, J. M., & Gosserand, R. H. (2003). Understanding the emotional labor process: A control theory perspective. *Journal of Organizational Behavior, 24*(8), 945–959.

Diefendorff, J. M., & Lord, R. G. (2003). The volitional and strategic effects of planning on task performance and goal commitment. *Human Performance, 16*(4), 365–387.

Dipboye, R. L., & dePontbriand, R. (1981). Correlates of employee reactions to performance appraisals and appraisal systems. *Journal of Applied Psychology, 66,* 248–251.

Dobbins, G. H., Cardy, R. L., & Platz-Vieno, S. J. (1990). A contingency approach to appraisal satisfaction: An initial investigation of the joint effects of organizational variables and appraisal characteristics. *Journal of Management, 16,* 619–632.

Dobbins, G. H., Lane, I. M., & Steiner, D. D. (1988). A note on the role of laboratory methodologies in applied behavioural research: Don't throw out the baby with the bath water. *Journal of Organizational Behavior, 9,* 281–286.

Donovan, J. J., & Radosevich, D. J. (1999). A meta-analytic review of the distribution of practice effect: Now you see it, now you don't. *Journal of Applied Psychology, 84*(5), 795–805.

Donovan, M. A., Drasgow, F., & Munson, L. J. (1998). The Perceptions of Fair Interpersonal Treatment scale: Development and validation of a measure of interpersonal treatment in the workplace. *Journal of Applied Psychology, 83*(5), 683–692.

Duarte, N. T., Goodson, J. R., & Klich, N. R. (1993). How do I like thee? Let me appraise the ways. *Journal of Organizational Behavior, 14*(3), 239–249.

Duncan, T. S. (1995). Death in the office—Workplace homicides. *Law Enforcement Bulletin, 64*(4), 20–25.

Dunford, B. B., & Devine, D. J. (1998). Employment at-will and employee discharge: A justice perspective on legal action following termination. *Personnel Psychology, 51,* 903–934.

Dunham, R. B., Grube, J. A., & Castaneda, M. B. (1994). Organizational commitment: The utility of an integrative definition. *Journal of Applied Psychology, 79,* 370–380.

Dunham, R. B., & Herman, J. B. (1975). Development of a female Faces Scale for measuring job satisfaction. *Journal of Applied Psychology, 60*(5), 629–631.

Dunnette, M. D. (1962). Personnel management. *Annual Review of Psychology, 13,* 285–314.

Durham, C. C., Locke, E. A., Poon, J. M. L., & McLeod, P. L. (2000). Effects of group goals and time pressure on group efficacy, information-seeking strategy, and performance. *Human Performance, 13*(2), 115–138.

Eagly, A. H., Johannesen-Schmidt, M. C., & van Engen, M. L. (2003). Transformational, transactional, and laissez-faire leadership styles: A meta-analysis comparing women and men. *Psychological Bulletin, 129*(4), 569–591.

Eagly, A. H., & Johnson, B. T. (1990). Gender and leadership style: A meta-analysis. *Psychological Bulletin, 108*(2), 233–256.

Eagly, A. H., & Karau, S. J. (1991). Gender and the emergence of leaders. *Journal of Personality and Social Psychology, 60*(5), 685–710.

Eagly, A. H., Karau, S. J., & Makhijani, M. G. (1995). Gender and the effectiveness of leaders: A meta-analysis. *Psychological Bulletin, 117*(1), 125–145.

Ebenkamp, B. (1999). And now, a word from Dad. *Brandweek, 40*(3), 19.

Eder, R. W., & Fedor, D. B. (1990). Priming performance self-evaluations: Moderating effects of rating purpose and judgment confidence. *Organizational Behavior and Human Decision Processes, 44*(3), 474–493.

Edwards, J. C., Rust, K. G., McKinley, W., & Moon, G. (2003). Business ideologies and perceived breach of contract during downsizing: The role of the ideology of employee self-reliance. *Journal of Organizational Behavior, 24*(1), 1–23.

EEOC Updates. (2002, December 12). *EEOC updates guidance on National Origin discrimination.* Retrieved May 20, 2004, from *http://www.epexperts.com/print.php?sid=1124.*

E.E.O.C. v. Atlas Paper Box, Co., 868 F. 2d 1487 (6th Cir. 1989)

E.E.O.C. v. Univ. of Texas Health Science Center at San Antonio, 710 F. 2d 1091 (5th Cir.1983).

Ehrenreich, B. (2001). What are they probing for? *Time South Pacific, 22,* 112–113.

Ellis, A. P. J., Hollenbeck, J. R., Ilgen, D. R., Porter, C. O. L. H., West, B. J., & Moon, H. (2003). Team learning: Collectively connecting the dots. *Journal of Applied Psychology, 88*(5), 821–835.

El-Tannir, A. A. (2002). The corporate university model for continuous learning, training and development. *Education and Training, 44*(2), 76–81.

Engle, E. M., & Lord, R. G. (1997). Implicit theories, self-schemas, and leader-member exchange. *Academy of Management Journal, 40*(4), 988–1010.

Ensari, N., & Murphy, S. E. (2003). Cross-cultural variations in leadership perceptions and attribution of charisma to the leader. *Organizational Behavior and Human Decision Processes, 92*(1-2), 52–66.

Equal Employment Opportunity Commission. (1978). Uniform guidelines on employee selection procedures. *Federal Register, 43,* 38290-38315.

Equal Employment Opportunity Commission. (2004, January 6). *Age discrimination.* Retrieved May 22, 2004, from *http://www.eeoc.gov/types/age.html.*

Equal Employment Opportunity Commission. (2004, January 6). *Disability discrimination.* Retrieved May 22, 2004, from *http://www.eeoc.gov/types/ada.html.*

Equal Employment Opportunity Commission. (2004, January 14). *National origin discrimination.* Retrieved May 22, 2004, from *http://www.eeoc.gov/types/origin.html.*

Equal Employment Opportunity Commission. (2004, January 15). *Pregnancy discrimination.* Retrieved May 22, 2004, from *http://www.eeoc.gov/types/pregnancy.html.*

Equal Employment Opportunity Commission. (2004, January 16). *Religious discrimination.* Retrieved May 22, 2004, from *http://www.eeoc.gov/types/religion.html.*

Equal Employment Opportunity Commission. (2004, January 6). *Sexual harassment.* Retrieved May 22, 2004, from *http://www.eeoc.gov/types/harassment.html.*

Equal Employment Opportunity Commission. (2004). *U.S. Equal Employment Opportunity Commission: An overview.* Retrieved May 22, 2004, from *http://www.eeoc.gov/overview.html.*

Erez, M., & Somech, A. (1996). Is group productivity loss the rule or the exception? Effects of culture and group-based motivation. *Academy of Management Journal, 39*(6), 1513–1537.

Erickson, R. J., Nichols, L., & Ritter, C. (2000). Family influences on absenteeism: Testing an expanded process model. *Journal of Vocational Behavior, 57,* 246–272.

Ethridge v. Alabama, 860 F. Supp. 808 (M.D. Ala 1998).

Evans, C., & Dion, K. (1991). Group cohesion and performance: A meta-analysis. *Small Group Research, 22*(175–186).

Evans, D. C. (2003). A comparison of the other-directed stigmatization produced by legal and illegal forms of affirmative action. *Journal of Applied Psychology, 88*(1), 121–130.

Families and Work Institute. (1998). *Business work-life study.* Available online at: *http://www.familiesandwork.org/summary/worklife.pdf;* 1998 Business work-like study, accessed on 11/9/04.

Farr, J. L., & Levy, P. E. (in press). Performance appraisal. In L. L. Koppes (Ed.), *The science and practice of industrial-organizational psychology: The first hundred years.* Mahwah, NJ: Erlbaum.

Fiedler, F. E. (1967). *A theory of leadership effectiveness.* New York: McGraw-Hill.

Fiedler, F. E. (1995). Cognitive resources and leadership performance. *Applied Psychology: An International Review, 44*(1), 5-28.

Findley, H. M., Giles, W. F., & Mossholder, K. W. (2000). Performance appraisal process and system facets: Relationships with contextual performance. *Journal of Applied Psychology, 85*(4), 634–640.

Fine, S. A. (1988). Functional job analysis. In S. Gael (Ed.), *The job analysis handbook for business, industry, and government* (Vol. 2). New York: John Wiley.

Fishbein, M., & Ajzen, I. (1975). *Belief, attitude, intention and behavior: An introduction to theory and research.* Reading, MA: Addison-Wesley.

Fisher, C. D. (2000). Mood and emotions while working: Missing pieces of job satisfaction. *Journal of Organizational Behavior, 21,* 185–202.

Fisher, C. D. (2003). Why do lay people believe that satisfaction and performance are correlated? Possible sources of a commonsense theory. *Journal of Organizational Behavior, 24*(6), 753–777.

Fisher, S. R., & White, M. A. (2000). Downsizing in a learning organization: Are there hidden costs? *Academy of Management Journal, 25*(1), 244–251.

Flanagan, J. C. (1956). The evaluation of methods in applied psychology and the problem of criteria. *Occupational Psychology, 30,* 1–9.

Fleishman, E. A., & Harris, E. F. (1962). Patterns of leadership behavior related to employee grievances and turnover. *Personnel Psychology, 15,* 43–56.

Fletcher, C., & Anderson, N. (1998, May 14). A superficial assessment. *People Management, 4* (10), 44–46.

Fletcher, C., & Baldry, C. (1999). Multi-source feedback systems: A research perspective. *International Review of Industrial and Organizational Psychology, 14,* 149–193.

Folger, R., Konovsky, M., & Cropanzano, R. (1992). A due process metaphor for performance appraisal. In B. Staw & L. Cummings (Eds.), *Research in organizational behavior* (Vol. 14, pp. 129–177). Greenwich, CT: JAI Press.

Forsyth, D. (1999). *Group Dynamics* (3rd ed.). Belmont, CA: Brooks/Cole.

Fortune. (2000). *100 Best Companies to Work For.* Time, Inc. Available online at *http://www.fortune.com/fortune/bestcompanies/index.html* [2000, October 27].

Franklin, & Gringer. (1999). *Key provisions of the Family and Medical Leave Act of 1993.* Available online at *http://www.frankgrin.com/famact.html* [1999, February 11].

French, J., & Raven, B. H. (1958). The bases of social power. In D. Cartwright (Ed.), *Studies of social power.* Ann Arbor, MI: Institute for Social Research.

Frone, M. R. (2000). Work-family conflict and employee psychiatric disorders: The National Comorbidity Survey. *Journal of Applied Psychology, 85*(6), 888–895.

Frone, M. R., Yardley, J. K., & Markel, K. S. (1997). Developing and testing an integrative model of the work-family interface. *Journal of Vocational Behavior, 50,* 145–167.

Fugate, M., Kinicki, A. J., & Scheck, C. L. (2002). Coping with an organizational merger over four stages. *Personnel Psychology, 55*(4), 905–928.

Fullerton, H. N., Jr. (1997). Labor Force 2006: Slowing down and changing composition. *Monthly Labor Review* (November), 23–38.

Funderburg, S. A., & Levy, P. E. (1997). The influence of individual and contextual variables on 360-degree feedback system attitudes. *Group and Organization Management, 22*(2), 210–235.

Gagne, R. M., Briggs, L. J., & Wager, W. W. (1992). *Principles of instructional design* (4th ed.). Fort Worth, TX: Harcourt Brace Jovanovich.

Galinsky, E., Kim, S. S., & Bond, J. T. (2001). *Feeling overworked: When work becomes too much.* Retrieved August 19, 2004, from Families and Work Institute website: *http://www.familiesandwork.org.*

Ganzach, Y., Kluger, A. N., & Klayman, N. (2000). Making decisions from an interview: Expert measurement and mechanical combination. *Personnel Psychology, 53,* 1–20.

Gardner, D. G., & Pierce, J. L. (1998). Self-esteem and self-efficacy within the organizational context. *Group and Organization Management, 23*(1), 48–70.

Gardner, S. E., & Daniel, C. (1998). Implementing comparable worth/pay equity: Experiences of cutting-edge states. *Public Personnel Management, 27*(4), 475–489.

Gatewood, R. D., & Feild, H. S. (2001). *Human resource selection* (5th ed.). Fort Worth, TX: Harcourt College Publishers.

Gaugler, B. B., Rosenthal, D. B., Thornton III, G. C., & Bentson, C. (1987). Meta-analysis of assessment center validity. *Journal of Applied Psychology, 72*(3), 493–511.

Gellatly, I. R. (1995). Individual and group determinants of employee absenteeism: Test of a causal model. *Journal of Organizational Behavior, 16,* 469–485.

Gerhart, B. (1987). How important are dispositional factors as determinants of job satisfaction? Implications for job design and other personnel programs. *Journal of Applied Psychology, 72*(3), 366–373.

Gersick, C. J. G. (1989). Making time: Predictable transitions in task groups. *Academy of Management Journal, 32,* 274–309.

Gerstner, C. R., & Day, D. V. (1994). Cross-cultural comparison of leadership prototypes. *Leadership Quarterly, 5*(2), 121–134.

Gerstner, C. R., & Day, D. V. (1997). Meta-analytic review of leader-member exchange theory: Correlates and construct issues. *Journal of Applied Psychology, 82*(6), 827–844.

Ghorpade, J. (2000). Managing five paradoxes of 360-degree feedback. *Academy of Management Executive, 14*(1), 140-150.

Giacalone, R. A., & Greenberg, G. (1997). *Antisocial behavior in organizations.* Thousand Oaks, CA: Sage Publications.

Giles, W. F., & Mossholder, K. W. (1990). Employee reactions to contextual and session components of performance appraisal. *Journal of Applied Psychology, 75,* 371–377.

Gilmer, B. V. H. (1981). The early development of industrial-organizational psychology. In J. A. Sgro (Ed.), *Virginia Tech Symposium on Applied Behavioral Science* (Vol. I, pp. 3–16). Lexington, MA: Lexington Books.

Goffin, R. D., Jelley, R. B., & Wagner, S. H. (2003). Is halo helpful? Effects of inducing halo on performance rating accuracy. *Social Behavior and Personality, 31*(6), 625–636.

Goldberg, C. B., & Waldman, D. A. (2000). Modeling employee absenteeism: Testing alternative measures and mediated effects based on job satisfaction. *Journal of Organizational Behavior, 21,* 665–676.

Goldstein, H. W., Zedeck, S., & Goldstein, I. L. (2002). Is this your final answer? *Human Performance, 15*(1-2), 123–142.

Goldstein, I. L., & Ford, J. K. (2002). *Training in organizations: Needs assessment, development, and evaluation* (4th ed.). Belmont, CA: Wadsworth.

Gonzalez, G. (2004). Elder care resources offer comfort to workers. *Business Insurance, 38*(13), 11–12.

Goodstein, J. (1995). Employer involvement in eldercare: An organizational adaptation perspective. *Academy of Management Journal, 38*(6), 1657–1671.

Goren, H., Kurzban, R., & Rapoport, A. (2003). Social loafing vs. social enhancement: Public goods provisioning in real-time with irrevocable commitments. *Organizational Behavior and Human Decision Processes, 90*(2), 277–290.

Gowan, M. A., Riordan, C. M., & Gatewood, R. D. (1999). Test of a model of coping with involuntary job loss following a company closing. *Journal of Applied Psychology, 84*(1), 75–86.

Gowen, C. R., III. (1991). Gainsharing programs: An overview of history and research. *Journal of Organizational Behavior Management, 11*(2), 77–99.

Grandey, A. A., & Brauburger, A. L. (in press). The emotion regulation behind the customer service smile. In R. G. Lord, R. J. Klimoski, & R. Kanfer (Eds.), *Emotions in the workplace: Understanding the structure and role of emotions in organizational behavior.* San Francisco: Jossey-Bass.

Grant, S., & Barling, J. (1994). Linking unemployment experiences, depressive symptoms, and marital functioning: A mediational model. In G. P. Keita & J. J. Hurrell, Jr. (Eds.), *Job stress in a changing workforce: Investigating gender, diversity, and family issues.* Washington, DC: American Psychological Association.

Gratz v. Bollinger, 539 U.S. 244 (2003).

Green, S. G., Anderson, S. E., & Shivers, S. L. (1996). Demographic and organizational influences on leader-member exchange and related work attitudes. *Organizational Behavior and Human Decision Processes, 66*(2), 203–214.

Greenhaus, J. H., & Powell, G. N. (in press). When work and family are allies: A theory of work-family enrichment. *Academy of Management Review.*

Greenwald, J. (2001). Rank and fire. *Time,* June 18, 38–40.

Greenwood, R. G. (1981). Management by objectives: As developed by Peter Drucker, assisted by Harold Smiddy. *Academy of Management Review, 6,* 225–230.

Gregg, L. (1998). *Humanity in the workplace: When work/family becomes an HR issue.* Credit Union Executive. Available online at *http://proquest.umi.com/pqdlink?Ver...3Fliqez3U2%2fTTGT91Y6%2fEdu97o0ag* [1999, December 29].

Greguras, G. J., Robie, C., Schleicher, D. J., & Goff, M. (2003). A field study of the effects of rating purpose on the quality of multisource ratings. *Personnel Psychology, 56*(1), 1–21.

Greiner, L., Cummings, T., & Bhambri, A. (2003). When new CEOs succeed and fail: 4-D theory of strategic transformation. *Organizational Dynamics, 32*(1), 1–16.

Griffeth, R. W., Hom, P. W., & Gaertner, S. (2000). A meta-analysis of antecedents and correlates of employee turnover: Update, moderator tests, and research implications for the next millennium. *Journal of Management, 26*(3), 463–488.

Griggs v. Duke Power, 401 U.S. 424 (1971).

Grindle, A. C., Dickinson, A. M., & Boettcher, W. (2000). Behavioral safety research in manufacturing settings: A review of the literature. *Journal of Organizational Behavior Management, 20*(1), 29–68.

Gross, J. (1998). Antecedent- and response-focused emotion regulation: Divergent consequences for experience, expression, and physiology. *Journal of Personality and Social Psychology, 74*(1), 224–237.

Gross, K. M. (1999). Positive reinforcement. *Executive Excellence, 16*(2), 12–13.

Grover, S. L., & Crooker, K. J. (1995). Who appreciates family-responsive human resource policies? The impact of family-friendly policies on the organizational attachment of parents and non-parents. *Personnel Psychology, 48,* 271–288.

Grunberg, L., Anderson-Connolly, R., & Greenberg, E. S. (2000). Surviving layoffs: The effects of organizational commitment and job performance. *Work and Occupations, 27*(1), 7–31.

Grutter v. Bollinger, 539 U.S. 306 (2003).

Gully, S. M., Payne, S. C., Koles, K. L. K., & Whiteman, J.-A. K. (2002). The impact of error training and individual differences on training outcomes: An attribute-treatment interaction perspective. *Journal of Applied Psychology, 87*(1), 143–155.

Gutek, B. A., & Koss, M. P. (1993). Changed women and changed organizations: Consequences of and coping with sexual harassment. *Journal of Vocational Behavior, 42,* 28–48.

Gutman, A. (2000). EEO law and personnel practices (2nd ed.). Thousand Oaks, CA: Sage.

Gutman, A. (2003). The Grutter, Gratz, & Costa rulings. *Industrial-Organizational Psychologist, 41*(2), 117–127.

Hackett, R. D., Bycio, P., & Hausdorf, P. A. (1994). Further assessments of Meyer and Allen's (1991) three-component model of organizational commitment. *Journal of Applied Psychology, 79,* 15–23.

Hackett, R. D., & Guion, R. M. (1985). A reevaluation of the absenteeism-job satisfaction relationship. *Organizational Behavior and Human Decision Processes, 35,* 340–381.

Hackman, J. R., & Oldham, G. R. (1980). *Work redesign.* Reading, MA: Addison-Wesley.

Hall, R. J., Workman, J. W., & Marchioro, C. A. (1998). Sex, task, and behavioral flexibility effects on leadership perceptions. *Organizational Behavior and Human Decision Processes, 74*(1), 1–32.

Hallett, M. B., & Gilbert, L. A. (1997). Variables differentiating university women considering role-sharing and conventional dual-career marriages. *Journal of Vocational Behavior, 50,* 308–322.

Hammer, L. B., Cullen, J. C., Neal, M. B., Sinclair, R. R., & Shafiro, M. V. (in press). The longitudinal effects of work-family conflict and positive spillover on depressive symptoms among dual-earner couples. *Journal of Occupational Health Psychology.*

Hammer, M., & Champy, J. (1993). *Reengineering the corporation: A manifesto for business revolution.* New York: HarperCollins.

Hanover, J. M. B., & Cellar, D. F. (1998). Environmental factors and the effectiveness of workforce diversity training. *Human Resource Development Quarterly, 9*(2), 105–124.

Hansen, J. C., & Campbell, D. P. (1985). *Manual for the SVIB-SCII* (4th ed.). Palo Alto, CA: Consulting Psychologists Press.

Hanson, G. C., Hammer, L. B., & Colton, C. L. (2004). *Development and validation of a multidimensional scale of work-family enrichment.* Unpublished manuscript, Portland State University.

Harris, L. C., & Ogbonna, E. (2002). The unintended consequences of culture interventions: A study of unexpected outcomes. *British Journal of Management, 13*(1), 31–49.

Hart, P. M. (1999). Predicting employee life satisfaction: A coherent model of personality, work and nonwork experiences, and domain satisfactions. *Journal of Applied Psychology, 84*(4), 564–584.

Harvey, R. J. (1991). Job analysis. In M. D. Dunnette & L. M. Hough (Eds.), *Handbook of industrial and organizational psychology* (2nd ed., Vol. 2, pp. 71–163). Palo Alto, CA: Consulting Psychologists Press.

Harvey, R. J. (1998). *Research Monograph: The development of the Common-Metric Questionnaire (CMQ).* Personnel Systems & Technologies Corporation and Virginia Tech. Available online at *http://www.pstc.com/CMQmonograph.html* [1998, December 8].

Hasselhorn, H., Hammar, N., Alfredsson, L., Westerholm, P., & Theorell, T. (1998). *Differences in the impact of self-rated and externally-rated job strain on risk factors for coronary heart disease.* American Psychological Association. Available online at *http://www.apa.org/pi/wpo/niosh/abstracts1.html* [2000, January 20].

Hattrup, K., O'Connell, M. S., & Wingate, P. H. (1998). Prediction of multidimensional criteria: Distinguishing task and contextual performance. *Human Performance, 11*(4), 305–319.

Hauenstein, N. M. A. (1992). An information-processing approach to leniency in performance judgments. *Journal of Applied Psychology, 77*(4), 485–493.

Hauenstein, N. M. A. (1998). Training raters to increase the accuracy of appraisals and the usefulness of feedback. In J. W. Smither (Ed.), *Performance appraisal: State of the art in practice.* San Francisco: Jossey-Bass Publishers.

Hauenstein, N. M. A., & Foti, R. J. (1989). From laboratory to practice: Neglected issues in implementing Frame-of-Reference rater training. *Personnel Psychology, 42,* 359–378.

Hedge, J. W., & Borman, W. C. (1995). Changing conceptions and practices in performance appraisal. In A. Howard (Ed.), *The changing nature of work.* San Francisco: Jossey-Bass.

Hedge, J. W., & Teachout, M. S. (2000). Exploring the concept of acceptability as a criterion for evaluating performance measures. *Group and Organizational Management, 25*(1), 22–44.

Hemisphere (1999). *Building a competitive workforce.* Hemisphere Inc. Available online at *http://www.DiversityInc.com/forbes.htm* [1999, June 2].

Herold, D. M., Davis, W., Fedor, D. B., & Parsons, C. K. (2002). Dispositional influences on transfer of learning in multistage training programs. *Personnel Psychology, 55*(4), 851–869.

Herzberg, F., Mausner, B., & Snyderman, B. (1959). *The motivation to work.* New York: Wiley.

Highhouse, S. (1999). The brief history of personnel counseling in industrial-organizational psychology. *Journal of Vocational Behavior, 55*(3), 318–336.

Highhouse, S., Hoffman, J. R., Greve, E. M., & Collins, A. E. (2002). Persuasive impact of organizational value statements in a recruitment context. *Journal of Applied Social Psychology, 32*(8), 1737–1755.

Hinkin, T. R. (1998). A brief tutorial on the development of measures for use in survey questionnaires. *Organizational Research Methods, 1*(1), 104–121.

Hirschfeld, R. R., & Feild, H. S. (2000). Work centrality and work alienation: Distinct aspects of a general commitment to work. *Journal of Organizational Behavior, 21,* 789–800.

Hislop, D. (2003). Linking human resource management and knowledge management via commitment: A review and research agenda. *Employee Relations, 25*(2), 182–202.

Hitt, M. A. (2000). The new frontier: Transformation of management for the new millennium. *Organizational Dynamics,* Winter, 7–17.

Hochwarter, W. A., Perrewe, P. L., Ferris, G. R., & Brymer, R. A. (1999). Job satisfaction and performance: The moderating effects of value attainment and affective disposition. *Journal of Vocational Behavior, 54,* 296–313.

Hochwarter, W. A., Witt, L. A., & Kacmar, K. M. (2000). Perceptions of organizational politics as a moderator of the relationship between conscientiousness and job performance. *Journal of Applied Psychology, 85*(3), 472–478.

Hodge, K., & Petlichkoff, L. (2000). Goal profiles in sport motivation: A cluster analysis. *Journal of Sport and Exercise Psychology, 22*(3), 256–272.

Hoffman, D. A., Jacobs, R., & Gerras, S. J. (1992). Mapping individual performance over time. *Journal of Applied Psychology, 77*(2), 185–195.

Hoffman, D. H., Jacobs, R., & Baratta, J. E. (1993). Dynamic criteria and the measurement of change. *Journal of Applied Psychology, 78,* 194–204.

Hofmann, D. A., Morgeson, F. P., & Gerras, S. J. (2003). Climate as a moderator of the relationship between leader-member exchange and content specific citizenship: Safety climate as an exemplar. *Journal of Applied Psychology, 88*(1), 170–178.

Hogan, R., & Hogan, J. (1995). *Hogan Personality Inventory manual.* (2nd ed.). Tulsa: Hogan Assessment Systems.

Hogan, R., Hogan, J., & Roberts, B. W. (1996). Personality measurement and employment decisions: Questions and answers. *American Psychologist, 51*(5), 469–477.

Holtom, B. C., Lee, T. W., & Tidd, S. T. (2002). The relationship between work status congruence and work-related attitudes and behaviors. *Journal of Applied Psychology, 87*(5), 903–915.

Hom, P. W., & Griffeth, R. W. (1991). Structural equations modeling test of a turnover theory: Cross-sectional and longitudinal analyses. *Journal of Applied Psychology, 76*(3), 350–366.

Hosking, D. M., & Schriesheim, C. A. (1978). Improving leadership effectiveness: The leader match concept—A book review. *Administrative Science Quarterly, 23,* 496–505.

Hough, L. (1998). Personality at work: Issues and evidence. In M. Hakel (Ed.), *Beyond multiple choice: Evaluating alternatives to traditional testing for selection.* Hillsdale, NJ: Erlbaum.

House, R. J. (1971). A path-goal theory of leader effectiveness. *Administrative Science Quarterly, 16,* 321–338.

House, R. J. (1996). Path-goal theory of leadership: Lessons, legacy, and a reformulated theory. *Leadership Quarterly, 7*(3), 323–352.

House, R. J., & Aditya, R. N. (1997). The social scientific study of leadership: Quo vadis? *Journal of Management, 23*(3), 409–473.

House, R. J., Hanges, P. J., Ruiz-Quintanilla, S. A., Dorfman, P. W., Javidan, M., Dickson, M. W., & GLOBE. (1999). Cultural influences on leadership: Project GLOBE. In W. Mobley (Ed.), *Advances in global leadership* (Vol. 1, pp. 171–233). Stamford, CT: JAI Press.

House, R. J., Wright, N., & Aditya, R. N. (1997). Cross-cultural research on organizational leadership: A critical analysis and a proposed theory. In P. C. Earley & M. Erez (Eds.), *New perspectives on international industrial and organizational psychology.* San Francisco: Jossey-Bass.

Howard, J. L., & Frink, D. D. (1996). The effects of organizational restructure on employee satisfaction. *Group and Organization Management, 21*(3), 278–303.

Howard, L. (1999). Validity evidence for measures of procedural/distributive justice and pay/benefit satisfaction. *Journal of Business and Psychology, 14*(1), 135–147.

Hoyt, W. T. (2000). Rater bias in psychological research: When is it a problem and what can we do about it? *Psychological Methods, 5*(1), 64–86.

Huber, V. L., Seybolt, P. M., & Venemon, K. (1992). The relationship between individual inputs, perceptions, and multidimensional pay satisfaction. *Journal of Applied Social Psychology, 22,* 1356–1373.

Hunter, J. E., & Hunter, R. F. (1984). Validity and utility of alternative predictors of job performance. *Psychological Bulletin, 96*(1), 72–98.

Hunter, J. E., & Schmidt, F. L. (1990). *Methods of meta-analysis: Correcting error and bias in research findings.* Newbury Park, CA: Sage.

Hurtz, G. M., & Donovan, J. J. (2000). Personality and job performance: The Big Five revisited. *Journal of Applied Psychology, 85*(6), 869–879.

Hutchison, S., Valentino, K. E., & Kirkner, S. L. (1998). What works for the gander does not work as well for the goose: The effects of leader behavior. *Journal of Applied Social Psychology, 28*(2), 171–182.

Hyatt, D. E., & Ruddy, T. M. (1997). An examination of the relationship between work group characteristics and performance: Once more into the breech. *Personnel Psychology, 50,* 553–585.

Iaffaldano, M. T., & Muchinsky, P. M. (1985). Job satisfaction and job performance: A meta-analysis. *Psychological Bulletin, 97*(2), 251–273.

Ilgen, D. R., Barnes-Farrell, J. L., & McKellin, D. B. (1993). Performance appraisal process research in the 1980s: What has it contributed to appraisals in use? *Organizational Behavior and Human Decision Processes, 54,* 321–368.

Ilgen, D. R., Fisher, C. D., & Taylor, M. S. (1979). Consequences of individual feedback on behavior in organizations. *Journal of Applied Psychology, 64,* 349–371.

Ilies, R., & Judge, T. A. (2003). On the heritability of job satisfaction: The mediating role of personality. *Journal of Applied Psychology, 88*(4), 750–759.

Institute for Women's Policy Research. (2003). The gender wage gap: Progress of the 1980s fails to carry through. *IWPR Publication #C353.*

Ironson, G. H., Smith, P. C., Brannick, M. T., & Gibson, W. M. (1989). Construction of a Job in General scale: A comparison of global, composite, and specific measures. *Journal of Applied Psychology, 74*(2), 193–200.

Judge, T. A., & Hulin, C. L. (1993). Job satisfaction as a reflection of disposition: A multiple-source causal analysis. *Organizational Behavior and Human Decision Processes, 56,* 388–421.

Judge, T. A., Locke, E. A., Durham, C. C., & Kluger, A. N. (1998). Dispositional effects on job and life satisfaction: The role of core evaluations. *Journal of Applied Psychology, 83*(1), 17–34.

Judge, T. A., Piccolo, R. F., & Ilies, R. (2004). The forgotten ones? The validity of consideration and initiating structure in leadership research. *Journal of Applied Psychology, 89*(1), 36–51.

Judge, T. A., Thoreson, C. J., Bono, J. E., & Patton, G. K. (2001). The job satisfaction–job performance relationship: A qualitative and quantitative review. *Journal of Applied Psychology, 127,* 376–407.

Jung, D. I., & Sosik, J. J. (1999). Effects of group characteristics on work group performance: A longitudinal investigation. *Group Dynamics: Theory, Research, and Practice, 3*(4), 279–290.

Jackson, S. E., & Schuler, R. S. (2000). *Managing human resources: A partnership perspective* (7th ed.). Cincinnati: South-Western College Publishing.

Janis, I. L. (1972). *Victims of groupthink.* Boston: Houghton Mifflin.

Janis, I. L. (1982). *Groupthink.* Boston: Houghton Mifflin.

Janis, I. L., & Mann, L. (1977). *Decision making: A psychological analysis of conflict, choice, and commitment.* New York: Free Press.

Jeanneret, P. R., & Strong, M. H. (2003). Linking O*NET job analysis information to job requirement predictors: An O*NET application. *Personnel Psychology, 56,* 465–492.

Jex, S. M., Bliese, P. D., Buzzell, S., & Primeau, J. (2001). The impact of self-efficacy on stressor-strain relations: Coping style as an explanatory mechanism. *Journal of Applied Psychology, 86*(3), 401–409.

Johnson, C. (1999). Teams at work. *HRMagazine, 44*(5), 30–36.

Joni, S.-N. (2004). *The third opinion: How successful leaders use outside insight to create superior results.* Penguin.

Judge, T. A. (1993). Does affective disposition moderate the relationship between job satisfaction and voluntary turnover? *Journal of Applied Psychology, 78*(3), 395–401.

Judge, T. A., Bono, J. E., Ilies, R., & Gerhardt, M. W. (2002). Personality and leadership: A qualitative and quantitative review. *Journal of Applied Psychology, 87*(4), 765–780.

Judge, T. A., Bono, J. E., & Locke, E. A. (2000). Personality and job satisfaction: The mediating role of job characteristics. *Journal of Applied Psychology, 85*(2), 237–249.

Judge, T. A., Colbert, A. E., & Ilies, R. (2004). Intelligence and leadership: A quantitative review and test of theoretical propositions. *Journal of Applied Psychology, 89*(3),542–552.

Judge, T. A., Erez, A., Bono, J. E., & Thoresen, C. J. (2003). The Core Self-Evaluations Scale: Development of a measure. *Personnel Psychology, 56*(2), 303–331.

Judge, T. A., & Ferris, G. R. (1993). Social context of performance evaluation decisions. *Academy of Management Journal, 36,* 80–105.

Judge, T. A., Heller, D., & Mount, M. K. (2002). Five-factor model of personality and job satisfaction: A meta-analysis. *Journal of Applied Psychology, 87*(3), 530–541.

Kacmar, K. M., Witt, L. A., Zivnuska, S., & Gully, S. M. (2003). The interactive effect of leader-member exchange and communication frequency on performance ratings. *Journal of Applied Psychology, 88*(4), 764–772.

Kanfer, R. (1990). Motivation theory and industrial and organizational psychology. In M. Dunnette & L. Hough (Eds.), *Handbook of industrial and organizational psychology* (2nd ed., Vol. 1, pp. 75–170). Palo Alto, CA: Consulting Psychologists Press.

Kanter, R. M. (1999). Change is everyone's job: Managing the extended enterprise in a globally connected world. *Organizational Dynamics, 28*(1), 7–23.

Karasek, R. (1990). Lower health risk with increased job control among white-collar workers. *Journal of Organizational Behaviour, 11,* 171–185.

Karau, S. J., & Hart, J. W. (1998). Group cohesiveness and social loafing: Effects of a social interaction manipulation on individual motivation within groups. *Group Dynamics: Theory, Research, and Practice, 2*(3), 185–191.

Karau, S. J., & Williams, K. D. (1993). Social loafing: A meta-analytic review and theoretical integration. *Journal of Personality and Social Psychology, 26,* 377–384.

Karau, S. J., & Williams, K. D. (1997). The effects of group cohesiveness on social loafing and social compensation. *Group Dynamics: Theory, Research, and Practice, 1*(2), 156–168.

Kark, R., Shamir, B., & Chen, G. (2003). The two faces of transformational leadership: Empowerment and dependency. *Journal of Applied Psychology, 88*(2), 246–255.

Kate, N. T. (1998). Two careers, one marriage. *American Demographics, 20*(4), 28.

Katz, D., & Kahn, R. L. (1978). *The social psychology of organizations* (2nd ed.). New York: Wiley and Sons.

Katzell, R. A., & Austin, J. T. (1992). From then to now: The development of industrial-organizational psychology in the United States. *Journal of Applied Psychology, 77*(6), 803–835.

Kaufman, A. S. (1994). *Intelligent testing with the WISC-III.* New York: John Wiley & Sons.

Kaufman, A. S., & Lichtenberger, E. (1999). *Essentials of WAIS-III Assessment.*

Kawakami, C., White, J. B., & Langer, E. J. (2000). Mindful and masculine: Freeing women leaders from the constraints of gender roles. *Journal of Social Issues, 56*(1), 49–63.

Keeping, L. M., & Levy, P. E. (2000). Performance appraisal reactions: Measurement, modeling, and method bias. *Journal of Applied Psychology, 85*(5), 708–723.

Kenny, D. A., & Zaccaro, S. J. (1983). An estimate of the variance due to traits in leadership. *Journal of Applied Psychology, 68*(4), 678–685.

Kerlinger, F. N. (1986). *Foundations of behavioral research* (3rd ed.). Fort Worth, TX: Holt, Rinehart and Winston.

Kerr, N. L. & Tindale, R. S. (2004). Group performance and decision making. In S. T. Fiske , D. L. Schachter, & C. Zahn-Waxler (Eds.), *Annual Review of Psychology, 55*, 623–655.

Kickul, J., Lester, S. W., & Finkl, J. (2002). Promise breaking during radical organizational change: Do justice interventions make a difference? *Journal of Organizational Behavior, 23*, 469–488.

Kidwell, R. E., Jr., Mossholder, K. W., & Bennett, N. (1997). Cohesiveness and organizational citizenship behavior: A multilevel analysis using work groups and individuals. *Journal of Management, 23*(6), 775–793.

Kiel, J. M. (1999). Reshaping Maslow's hierarchy of needs to reflect today's educational and managerial philosophies. *Journal of Instructional Psychology, 26*(3), 167–168.

Kim, S. (1998). Toward understanding family leave policy in public organizations: Family leave use and conceptual framework for the family leave implementation process. *Public Productivity and Management Review, 22*(1), 71–87.

King, W. C., Jr., & Miles, E. W. (1994). The measurement of equity sensitivity. *Journal of Occupational and Organizational Psychology, 67*, 133–142.

Kinicki, A. J., McKee-Ryan, F. M., Schriesheim, C. A., & Carson, K. P. (2002). Assessing the construct validity of the Job Descriptive Index: A review and meta-analysis. *Journal of Applied Psychology, 87*(1), 14–32.

Kirkman, B. L., & Rosen, B. (1999). Beyond self-management: Antecedents and consequences of team empowerment. *Academy of Management Journal, 42*(1), 58–74.

Kirkpatrick, D. L. (1976). Evaluation of training. In R. L. Craig (Ed.), *Training and development handbook* (pp. 18–27). New York: McGraw-Hill.

Klein, H. (1989). An integrated control theory model of work motivation. *Academy of Management, 14*, 150–172.

Klein, H. J., & Weaver, N. A. (2000). The effectiveness of an organizational-level orientation training program in the socialization of new hires. *Personnel Psychology, 53*, 47–66.

Knights, D., & McCabe, D. (2002). A road less travelled: Beyond managerialist, critical and processural approaches to total quality management. *Journal of Organizational Change Management, 15*(3), 235–254.

Konovsky, M. A., & Cropanzano, R. (1991). Perceived fairness of employee drug testing as a predictor of employee attitudes and job performance. *Journal of Applied Psychology, 76*, 698–707.

Koppes, L. L. (Ed.). (in press). *The science and practice of industrial and organizational psychology: Historical aspects of the first 100 years*. Mahwah, NJ: Erlbaum.

Korsgaard, M. A., & Roberson, L. (1995). Procedural justice in performance evaluation: The role of instrumental and non-instrumental voice in performance appraisal discussions. *Journal of Management, 21*, 657–669.

Koslowsky, M., Sagie, A., Krausz, M., & Singer, A. D. (1997). Correlates of employee lateness: Some theoretical considerations. *Journal of Applied Psychology, 82*(1), 79–88.

Kossek, E. E., DeMarr, B. J., Backman, K., & Kollar, M. (1993). Assessing employees' emerging elder care needs and reactions to dependent care benefits. *Public Personnel Management, 22*(4), 617–638.

Kossek, E. E., & Nichol, V. (1992). The effects of on-site child care on employee attitudes and performance. *Personnel Psychology, 45*, 485–509.

Kossek, E. E., & Ozeki, C. (1998). Work-family conflict, policies, and the job-life satisfaction relationship: A review and directions for organizational behavior–human resources research. *Journal of Applied Psychology, 83*(2), 139–149.

Kraiger, K., Ford, K., & Salas, E. (1993). Application of cognitive, skill-based, and affective theories of learning outcomes to new methods of training evaluation. *Journal of Applied Psychology, 78*(2), 311–328.

Kuhn, K. M., & Yockey, M. D. (2003). Variable pay as a risky choice: Determinants of the relative attractiveness of incentive plans. *Organizational Behavior and Human Decision Processes, 90*(2), 323–341.

Kuncel, N. R., Campbell, J. P., & Ones, D. S. (1998). Validity of the Graduate Record Examination: Estimated or tacitly known? *American Psychologist, 53*(5), 567–568.

Kunin, T. (1955). The construction of a new type of attitude measure. *Personnel Psychology, 8*, 65–77.

Kunin, T. (1998). The construction of a new type of attitude measure. *Personnel Psychology, 51*, 823–824.

Landy, F. J. (2003). Validity generalization: Then and now. In K. R. Murphy, (Ed.), *Validity generalization: A critical review* Mahwah, NJ: Lawrence Erlbaum Associates, 155–195.

Landy, F. J., & Farr, J. L. (1980). Performance rating. *Psychological Bulletin, 87*, 72–107.

Langfred, C. W. (2000). Work-group design and autonomy: A field study of the interaction between task interdependence and group autonomy. *Small Group Research, 31*(1), 54-70.

Larson, J. R., Jr., Christensen, C., Franz, T. M., & Abbott, A. S. (1998a). Diagnosing groups: The pooling, management, and impact of shared and unshared case information in team-based medical decision making. *Journal of Personality and Social Psychology, 75*, 93–108.

Larson, J. R., Jr., Foster-Fishman, P. G., & Franz, T. M. (1998b). Leadership style and the discussion of shared and unshared information in decision-making groups. *Personality and Social Psychology Bulletin, 24*(5), 482–495.

Latham, G. P. (1988). Human resource training and development. *Annual Review of Psychology, 39*, 545–582.

Latham, G. P., & Saari, L. M. (1979). The application of social learning theory to training supervisors through behavior modeling. *Journal of Applied Psychology, 64*, 239–246.

Lau, V. C. S., Au, W. T., & Ho, J. M. C. (2003). A qualitative and quantitative review of antecedents of counterproductive behavior in organizations. *Journal of Business and Psychology, 18*(1), 73–99.

Laurent, A. (1996). Short fuse. *Government Executive, 28*(12), 12–20.

Lawler, E. E. (2001). *Organizing for high performance.* San Francisco: Jossey-Bass.

Lawler, E. E., Mohrman, S. A., & Ledford, G. E. (1992). *Employee involvement and total quality management: Practices and results in Fortune 1000 companies.* San Francisco: Jossey-Bass.

Lawler, E. E., & Porter, L. W. (1967). The effects of performance on job satisfaction. *Industrial Relations, 7,* 20–28.

Lawson, R. B., & Shen, Z. (1998). *Organizational psychology: Foundations and applications.* New York: Oxford University Press.

LeBlanc, M. M., & Barling, J. (2004). Workplace aggression. *Current Directions in Psychological Science, 13*(1), 9–12.

LeBlanc, M. M., & Kelloway, E. K. (2002). Predictors and outcomes of workplace violence and aggression. *Journal of Applied Psychology, 87*(3), 444–453.

Lee, B. A. (2003). A decade of the Americans with Disabilities Act: Judicial outcomes and unresolved problems. *Industrial Relations: A Journal of Economy & Society, 42*(1), 11–30.

Lee, T. W., Mitchell, T. R., Holtom, B. C., McDaniel, L. S., & Hill, J. W. (1999). The unfolding model of voluntary turnover: A replication and extension. *Academy of Management Journal, 42*(4), 450–462.

Levering, R., & Moskowitz , M. (2000, January 10). 100 best companies to work for. *Fortune, 141.*

Levering, R., & Moskowitz, M. (2001). America's top employers. *Fortune, 143*(1), 148–149.

Levy, P. E., & Norris-Watts, C. (in press). Workplace justice. In C.D. Spielberger (Ed.), *Encyclopedia of applied psychology.* San Diego, CA: Academic Press.

Levy, P. E., & Steelman, L. A. (1994). Determinants of feedback seeking: Costs, environment, and the performance appraisal process. Paper presented at the 9th annual meeting of the Society for Industrial and Organizational Psychology, Nashville, TN.

Levy, P. E., & Steelman, L. A. (1997). Performance appraisal for team-based organizations: A prototypical multiple rater system. In M. Beyerlein, D. Johnson, & S. Beyerlein (Eds.), *Advances in interdisciplinary studies of work teams: Team Implementation Issues* (Vol. 4, pp. 141–165). Greenwich, CT: JAI Press.

Levy, P. E., & Williams, J. R. (1998). The role of perceived system knowledge in predicting appraisal reactions, job satisfaction, and organizational commitment. *Journal of Organizational Behavior, 19,* 53–65.

Levy, P. E., & Williams, J. R. (2004). The social context of performance appraisal: A review and framework for the future. *Journal of Management. 30*(6) 881–905.

Lewin, K. (1951). *Field theory in social science.* New York: Harper.

Lewin, K., Dembo, T., Festinger, L., & Sears, P. (1944). Level of aspiration. In J. M. Hunt (Ed.), *Personality and the behavior disorders* (Vol. 1). New York: Ronald.

Lievens, F., & Highhouse, S. (2003). The relation of instrumental and symbolic attributes to a company's attractiveness as an employer. *Personnel Psychology, 56*(1), 75–102.

Littlefield, D. (1995, January 26). Menu change at Novotel. *People Management, 1* (2), 34—36.

Lobel, S., & Faught, L. (1996). Four methods for proving the value of work/life interventions. *Compensation and Benefits Review, 28*(6), 50–57.

Locke, E. A. (1976). The nature and causes of job satisfaction. In M. D. Dunnette (Ed.), *Handbook of industrial and organizational psychology* (1st ed., pp. 1297–1349). Chicago, IL: Rand McNally.

Locke, E. A. (1990). *A theory of goal setting and task performance.* Englewood Cliffs, NJ: Prentice-Hall.

Locke, E. A. (1991). The motivation sequence, the motivation hub, and the motivation core. *Organizational Behavior and Human Decision Processes, 50,* 288–299.

Locke, E. A., & Latham, G. P. (2002). Building a practically useful theory of goal setting and task motivation: A 35-year odyssey. *American Psychologist, 57*(9), 705–717.

Lofquist, L. H., & Dawis, R. V. (1969). *Adjustment to work: A psychological view of man's problems in a work-oriented society.* New York: Appleton-Century-Crofts.

Loher, B. T., Noe, R. A., Moeler, N. L., & Fitzgerald, M. P. (1985). A meta-analysis of the relation of job characteristics to job satisfaction. *Journal of Applied Psychology, 70*(2), 280–289.

London, M., & Smither, J. W. (2002). Feedback orientation, feedback culture, and the longitudinal performance management process. *Human Resource Management Review, 12*(1), 81.

Longenecker, C. O., Sims, H. P., & Gioia, D. A. (1987). Behind the mask: The politics of employee appraisal. *Academy of Management Executive, 1,* 183–193.

Lopez, E. M., & Greenhaus, J. H. (1978). Self-esteem, race, and job satisfaction. *Journal of Vocational Behavior, 13,* 75–83.

Lord, R. G. (2000). Leadership. In A. E. Kazdin (Ed.), *Encyclopedia of Psychology* (Vol. 3, pp. 775–786). Washington, DC: American Psychological Association.

Lord, R. G., & Brown, D. J. (2004). *Leadership processes and follower self-identity.* Mahwah, NJ: Lawrence Erlbaum Associates.

Lord, R. G., DeVader, C. L., & Alliger, G. M. (1986). A meta-analysis of the relation between personality traits and leadership perceptions: An application of validity generalization procedures. *Journal of Applied Psychology, 71*(3), 402–410.

Lord, R. G., Foti, R. J., & DeVader, C. L. (1984). A test of leadership categorization theory: Internal structure, information processing, and leadership perceptions. *Organizational Behavior and Human Performance, 34,* 343–378.

Lord, R. G., & Hanges, P. J. (1987). A control systems model of organizational motivation: Theoretical development and applied implications. *Behavioral Science, 32,* 161–178.

Lord, R. G., & Maher, K. J. (1991). *Leadership and information processing: Linking perception and performance.* Boston: Unwin Hyman.

Lowe, G. S. (1987). *Women in the administrative revolution: The feminization of clerical work.* Oxford: Polity Press.

Lowe, K. B., Kroeck, K. G., & Sivasubramaniam, N. (1996). Effectiveness correlates of transformational and transactional leadership: A meta-analytic review of the MLQ. *Leadership Quarterly, 7,* 385–425.

Lowery, C. M., Beadles, N. A. I., & Krilowicz, T. J. (2002). Note on the relationships among job satisfaction, organizational commitment, and organizational citizenship behavior. *Psychological Reports,* 91(2), 607–617.

Lowman, R. L., Kantor, J., & Perloff, R. (in press). History of I-O psychology educational programs. In L. L. Koppes (Ed.), *The science and practice of industrial and organizational psychology: Historical aspects from the first 100 years.* Mahwah, NJ: Erlbaum.

Ludwig, T. D., & Geller, E. S. (1997). Assigned versus participative goal setting and response generalization: Managing injury control among professional pizza deliverers. *Journal of Applied Psychology, 82*(2), 253–261.

Ludwig, T. D., & Geller, E. S. (2000). Intervening to improve the safety of delivery drivers: A systematic behavioral approach. *Journal of Organizational Behavior Management, 19*(4), 1–124.

MacGregor, R. (1999). *Work and family policies: A "win-win" formula for business and society.* Minnesota Center for Corporate Responsibility. Available online at http://www.cyfc.umn.edu/work/ [2000, January 28].

Machan, D. (1999). A dyed-in-the-wool skeptic. *Forbes, 163*(1), 96–98.

Mael, F. A. (1991). A conceptual rationale for the domain and attributes of biodata items. *Personnel Psychology, 44,* 763–792.

Makiney, J. D., & Levy, P. E. (1998). The influence of self ratings versus peer ratings on supervisors' performance judgments. *Organizational Behavior and Human Decision Processes, 74,* 212–228.

Malos, S. B. (1998). Current legal issues in performance appraisal. In J. W. Smither (Ed.), *Performance appraisal: State of the art in practice.* San Francisco: Jossey-Bass Publishers.

Marsh, A. (1998). The man who listens to horses. *Forbes, 161*(9), 122–126.

Martin v. PGA Tour, Inc., 994 F. Supp. 1242 (D. Or 1998).

Martinko, M. J., & Zellars, K. L. (1998). Toward a theory of workplace violence and aggression: A cognitive appraisal perspective. In R. W. Griffin, A. O'Leary-Kelly, & J. M. Collins (Eds.), *Dysfunctional behavior in organizations: Violent and deviant behavior.* Stamford, CT: JAI Press.

Martiny, M. (1998). Knowledge management at HP consulting. *Organizational Dynamics,* Autumn, 71–77.

Masterson, S. S., Lewis, K., Goldman, B. M., & Taylor, M. S. (2000). Integrating justice and social exchange: The differing effects of fair procedures and treatment on work relationships. *Academy of Management Journal, 43*(4), 738–748.

Mathieu, J. E., & Zajac, D. M. (1990). A review and meta-analysis of the antecedents, correlates, and consequences of organizational commitment. *Journal of Applied Psychology, 108*(2), 171–194.

Mathiowetz, V., Rogers, S. L., Dowe-Keval, M., Donahoe, L., & Rennels, C. (1986). The Purdue Pegboard: Norms for 14- to 19-year-olds. *American Journal of Occupational Therapy, 3,* 174–179.

Mauno, S., & Kinnunen, U. (1999). The effects of job stressors on marital satisfaction in Finnish dual-earner couples. *Journal of Organizational Behavior, 20,* 879–895.

Maurer, T. J., Barbeite, F. G., & Mitchell, D. R. D. (2002). Predictors of attitudes toward a 360-degree feedback system and involvement in post-feedback management development activity. *Journal of Occupational and Organizational Psychology,* 75, 87.

Martins, L. L., Eddleston, K. A., & Veiga, J. F. J. (2002). Moderators of the relationship between work-family conflict and career satisfaction. *Academy of Management Journal, 45*(2), 399–409.

Maslach, C. (2003). Job burnout: New directions in research and intervention. *Current Directions in Psychological Science, 12*(5), 189–192.

Mayer, R. C., & Davis, J. H. (1999). The effect of the performance appraisal system on trust for management: A field quasi-experiment. *Journal of Applied Psychology, 84*(1), 123–136.

Maysent, M., & Spera, S. (1995). Coping with job loss and career stress: Effectiveness of stress management training with outplaced employees. In L. R. Murphy, J. J. Hurrell, Jr., S. L. Sauter, & G. P. Keita (Eds.), *Job stress interventions.* Washington, DC: American Psychological Association.

McAllister, D. J., & Bigley, G. A. (2002). Work context and the definition of self: How organizational care influences organization-based self-esteem. *Academy of Management Journal, 45*(5), 894–904.

McCormick, E. J. (1976). Job and task analysis. In M. D. Dunnette (Ed.), *Handbook of industrial and organizational psychology* (1st ed., pp. 651–696). Chicago: Rand McNally.

McCormick, E. J., Jeanneret, P. R., & Mecham, R. C. (1972). A study of characteristics and job dimensions as based on the Position Analysis Questionnaire (PAQ). *Journal of Applied Psychology, 56,* 347–368.

McDaniel, M. A., Morgeson, F. P., Finnegan, E. B., Campion, M. A., & Braverman, E. P. (2001). Use of situational judgment tests to predict job performance: A clarification of the literature. *Journal of Applied Psychology, 86*(4), 730–740.

McGregor, D. M. (1960). *The human side of enterprise.* New York: McGraw-Hill.

McHenry, J. J., Hough, L. M., Toquam, J. L., Hanson, M. A., & Ashworth, S. (1990). Project A validity results: The relationship between predictor and criterion domains. *Personnel Psychology, 43,* 335–354.

McIntyre, R. M., & Salas, E. (1995). Measuring and managing for team performance: Emerging principles from complex team environments. In R. A. Guzzo & E. Salas (Eds.), *Team effectiveness and decision making in organizations* (pp. 9–45). San Francisco: Jossey-Bass.

McKinley, W., Zhao, J., & Rust, K. G. (2000). A sociocognitive interpretation of organizational downsizing. *Academy of Management Review, 25*(1), 227–243.

Meisler, A. (2003). Dead man's curve. *Workforce Management, 82*(7), 44–49.

Meritor Savings Bank v. Vinson, 477 U.S. 57 (1986).

Meyer, A. (1992). Getting to the heart of sexual harassment. *HR Magazine, 37,* 82–84.

Meyer, H. H. (1991). A solution for the performance appraisal feedback enigma. *Academy of Management Executive, 5,* 68–76.

Meyer, J. P., & Allen, N. J. (1997). *Commitment in the workplace: Theory, research, and application.* Thousand Oaks, CA: Sage Publications.

Meyer, J. P., Stanley, D. J., Herscovitch, L., & Topolnytsky, L. (2002). Affective, continuance, and normative commitment to the organization: A meta-analysis of antecedents, correlates, and consequences. *Journal of Vocational Behavior, 61*(1), 20–52.

Milkovich, G. T., & Newman, J. M. (1984). *Compensation.* Plano, TX: Business Publications.

Miller, D. L.(2001). Reexamining teamwork KSAs and team performance. *Small Group Researach, 32*(6), 745–766.

Mitchell, J. V. (Ed.). (1998). *Mental measurement yearbook* (13th ed.). Lincoln, NE: Buros Institute of Mental Measurements.

Mitchell, T. R., Holtom, B. C., Lee, T. W., Sablynski, C. J., & Erez, M. (2001). Why people stay: Using job embeddedness to predict voluntary turnover. *Academy of Management Journal, 44*(6), 1102–1121.

Mohammed, S., Mathieu, J. E., & Bartlett, A. L. B. (2002). Technical-administrative task performance, leadership task performance, and contextual performance: Considering the influence of team- and task-related composition variables. *Journal of Organizational Behavior, 23*(7), 795–814.

Mohsen, A., & Nguyen, T. T. (1999). Succeeding with self-managed work teams. *Industrial Management, 41*(4), 24–28.

Moosbruker, J. B., & Loftin, R. D. (1998). Business process redesign and organization development: Enhancing success by removing the barriers. *Journal of Applied Behavioral Science, 34*(3), 286–304.

Moravec, M., Juliff, R., & Hesler, K. (1995). Partnerships help a company manage performance. *Personnel Journal, 74*(1), 104–107.

Moreland, R. L., & Myaskovsky, L. (2000). Exploring the performance benefits of group training: Transactive memory or improved communication. *Organizational Behavior and Human Decision Processes, 82*(1), 117–133.

Morgan, D. E., & Zeffane, R. (2003). Employee involvement, organizational change and trust in management. Trust in the Workplace. *International Journal of Human Resource Management, 14*(1), 55–75.

Morgan, R. B., & Casper, W. J. (2000). Examining the factor structure of participant reactions to training: A multidimensional approach. *Human Resource Development Quarterly, 11*(3), 301–317.

Morris, J. A., & Feldman, D. C. (1996). The dimensions, antecedents, and consequences of emotional labor. *Academy of Management Review, 21*(4), 986–1010.

Motowidlo, S. J. (2003). Job perfromance. In W. C. Borman, D. R. Ilgen, & R. J. Klimoski (Eds.), *Handbook of psychology: Industrial and organizational psychology* (Vol. 12, pp. 39–53). New York: Wiley.

Motowidlo, S. J., Borman, W. C., & Schmit, M. J. (1997). A theory of individual differences in task and contextual performance. *Human Performance, 10*(2), 71–83.

Mount, M. K., Witt, L. A., & Barrick, M. R. (2000). Incremental validity of empirically keyed biodata scales over GMA and the Five Factor personality constructs. *Personnel Psychology, 53*(2), 299–323.

Mowday, R. T. (1991). Equity theory predictions of behavior in organizations. In R. M. Steers and L. W. Porter (Eds.), *Motivation and work behavior* (5th edition, pp. 111–130). New York: McGraw-Hill.

Mowday, R. T., Steers, R. M., & Porter, L. W. (1979). The measurement of organizational commitment. *Journal of Vocational Behavior, 14*, 224–247.

Mueller-Hanson, R., Heggestad, E. D., & Thornton, G. C. I. (2003). Faking and selection: Considering the use of personality from select-in and select-out perspectives. *Journal of Applied Psychology, 88*(2), 348–355.

Mullen, B., & Copper, C. (1994). The relation between group cohesiveness and performance: An integration. *Psychological Bulletin, 115*, 210–227.

Munsterberg, H. (1913). *Psychology and industrial efficiency.* Boston: Houghton Mifflin.

Murphy, K. R. (2002). Can conflicting perspectives on the role of g in personnel selection be resolved? *Human Performance, 15*(1-2), 173–186.

Murphy, K. R., & Cleveland, J. N. (1995). *Understanding performance appraisal: Social, organizational, and goal-based perspectives.* Thousand Oaks, CA: Sage Publications.

Murphy, K. R., & Jako, B. (1989). Under what conditions are observed intercorrelations greater than or smaller than true intercorrelations? *Journal of Applied Psychology, 74*, 827–830.

Murphy, K. R., & Reynolds, D. H. (1988). Does true halo affect observed halo? *Journal of Applied Psychology, 73*, 235–238.

Murphy, S. E., & Ensher, E. A. (1999). The effects of leader and subordinate characteristics in the development of leader-member exchange quality. *Journal of Applied Social Psychology, 29*(7), 1371–1394.

Murray marks a decade of FMLA, urges expansion of act. (2003). Retrieved August 10, 2004, from the Web site of U. S. Senator Patty Murray: *http://murray.senate.gov/news.cfm?id=191243.*

Murrell, A. J., Frieze, I. H., & Olson, J. E. (1996). Mobility strategies and career outcomes: A longitudinal study of MBAs. *Journal of Vocational Behavior, 49*, 324–335.

National Census of Fatal Occupational Injuries in 2003. *http://www.bls.gov/news.release/pdf/cvoi.pdf.* Accessed February 11, 2005. Released September 22, 2004.

Neuman, G. A., & Wright, J. (1999). Team effectiveness: Beyond skills and cognitive ability. *Journal of Applied Psychology, 84*(3), 376–389.

Neuman, J. H., & Baron, R. A. (1998). Workplace violence and workplace aggression: Evidence concerning specific forms, potential causes, and preferred targets. *Journal of Management, 24*(3), 391-419.

Newton, T., & Keenan, T. (1991). Further analyses of the dispositional argument in organizational behavior. *Journal of Applied Psychology, 76*(6), 781–787.

Nijstad, B. A., Stroebe, W., & Lodewijkx, H. F. M. (2003). Production blocking and idea generation: Does blocking interfere with cognitive processes? *Journal of Experimental Social Psychology, 39*(6), 531–548.

Noonan, L. E., & Sulsky, L. M. (2001). Impact of frame-of-reference and behavioral observation training on alternative training effectiveness criteria in a Canadian military sample. *Human Performance, 14*(1), 3–26.

Northwestern National Life. (1993). *Fear and violence in the workplace: A survey documenting the experience of American workers.* Minneapolis: Northwestern National Life, Employee Benefits Division.

O'Driscoll, M. P., Poelmans, S., Spector, P. E., Kalliath, T., Allen, T. D., Cooper, C. L., et al. (2003). Family-responsive interventions, perceived organizational and supervisor support, work-family conflict, and psychological strain. *Stress and Its Management in Occupational Settings, 10*(4), 326-344.

O*NET Online. (2000). *Welcome to the O*NET online!* Department of Labor. Available online at *http://online.onetcenter.org/main.html* [2004, March 30].

O'Leary-Kelly, A. M., Griffin, R. W., & Glew, D. J. (1996). Organization-motivated aggression: A research framework. *Academy of Management Review, 21*(1), 225–253.

O'Neill, B. S., & Mone, M. A. (1998). Investigating equity sensitivity as a moderator of relations between self-efficacy and workplace attitudes. *Journal of Applied Psychology, 83*(5), 805–816.

Occupational Information Network. (1998, November 25). *The nation's new resource of occupational information.* Available online at *http://www.doleta.gov/programs/onet/* [1998, December 8].

Ones, D. S., Viswesvaran, C., & Schmidt, F. L. (1993). Comprehensive meta-analysis of integrity test validities: Findings and implications for personnel selection and theories of job performance. *Journal of Applied Psychology, 78*(4), 679–703.

Organ, D. W., & Ryan, K. (1995). A meta-analytic review of attitudinal and dispositional predictors of organizational citizenship behavior. *Personnel Psychology, 48,* 775–802.

Ostroff, C., & Atwater, L. E. (2003). Does whom you work with matter? Effects of referent group gender and age composition on managers' compensation. *Journal of Applied Psychology, 88*(4), 725–740.

Parker, L., & Allen, T. D. (2001). Work/family benefits: Variables related to employees' fairness perceptions. *Journal of Vocational Behavior 58,* 453–468.

Patton, K. R., & Daley, D. M. (1998). Gainsharing in Zebulon: What do workers want? *Public Personnel Management, 27*(1), 117–131.

Paullay, I. M., Alliger, G. M., & Stone-Romero, E. F. (1994). Construct validation of two instruments designed to measure job involvement and work centrality. *Journal of Applied Psychology, 79*(2), 224–228.

Paulus, P. B. (1998). Developing consensus about groupthink after all these years. *Organizational Behavior and Human Decision Processes, 73*(2/3), 362–374.

Payne, R. L. (2000). Eupsychian management and the millennium. *Journal of Managerial Psychology, 15*(3), 219–226.

Pearson, R. L. (1999). Long-term care: Addressing the real issues. *Compensation and Benefits Review, 31*(5), 69–73.

Pedersen, A., & Antoon, M. J. L. (1997). A 4-year history of work redesign in two ICUs. *Nursing Management, 28*(10), 32–34.

Penttila, C. (2000). Testy, testy (weighing the value of employee drug testing). *Entrepreneur, 28*(6), 130.

Perry-Jenkins, M., Repetti, R. L., & Crouter, A. C. (2000). Work and family in the 1990s. *Journal of Marriage and the Family, 62,* 981–998.

Petit v. City of Chicago, 352 F. 3d 1111 (7th Cir. 2003).

Petty, M. M., McGee, G. W., & Cavender, J. W. (1984). A meta-analysis of the relationships between individual job satisfaction and individual performance. *Academy of Management Review, 9*(4), 712–721.

Pfeffer, J. (1998). Seven practices of successful organizations. *California Management Review, 40*(2), 96–124.

Pfeffer, J., & Sutton, R. I. (1999). Knowing "what" to do is not enough: Turning knowledge into action. *California Management Review, 42*(1), 83–108.

Phillips, J. S., & Lord, R. G. (1981). Causal attributions and perceptions of leadership. *Organizational Behavior and Human Performance, 28,* 143–163.

Picard, M. (1997). No kids? Get back to work! *Training, 3*(9), 33–40.

Piedmont, R. L. (1998). *The revised NEO Personality Inventory: Clinical and research applications.* New York: Plenum Press.

Pierce, J. L., Gardner, D. G., Cummings, L. L., & Dunham, R. B. (1989). Organization-based self-esteem: Construct definition, measurement, and validation. *Academy of Management Journal, 32*(3), 622–648.

Pillai, R., Schriesheim, C. A., & Williams, E. S. (1999). Fairness perceptions and trust as mediators for transformational and transactional leadership: A two-sample study. *Journal of Management, 25*(6), 897-933.

Pillai, R., & Williams, E. A. (1998). Does leadership matter in the political arena? Voter perceptions of candidates, transformational and charismatic leadership, and the 1996 U.S. presidential vote. *Leadership Quarterly, 9*(3), 397–416.

Pinder, C. (1984). *Work Motivation: Theories, issues and applications.* Dallas: Scott, Foresman and Company.

Pinder, C. C. (1998). *Work motivation in organizational behavior.* Saddle River, NJ: Prentice-Hall.

Podsakoff, P. M., MacKenzie, S. B., Paine, J. B., & Bachrach, D. G. (2000). Organizational citizenship behaviors: A critical review of the theoretical and empirical literature and suggestions for future research. *Journal of Management, 26*(3), 513–563.

Poister, T. H., & Streib, G. (1995). MBO in municipal government: Variations on a traditional management tool. *Public Administrative Review, 55*(1), 48–53.

Pollock, T. G., Whitbred, R. C., & Contractor, N. (2000). Social information processing and job characteristics: A simultaneous test of two theories with implications for job satisfaction. *Human Communication Research, 26*(2), 292–330.

Popovich, P. M., Scherbaum, C. A., Scherbaum, K. L., & Polinko, N. (2003). The assessment of attitudes toward individuals with disabilities in the workplace. *Journal of Psychology, 137*(2), 163–177.

Popper, K. (1959). *The logic of scientific discovery.* New York: Basic Books.

Porras, J. I., & Silvers, R. C. (1991). Organization development and transformation. In M. R. Rosenzweig & L. W. Porter (Eds.), *Annual Review of Psychology* (Vol. 42, pp. 51–78). Palo Alto, CA: Annual Reviews, Inc.

Porter, C. O. L. H., Hollenbeck, J. R., Ilgen, D. R., Ellis, A. P. J., West, B. J., & Moon, H. (2003). Backing up behaviors in teams: The role of personality and legitimacy of need. *Journal of Applied Psychology, 88*(3), 391–403.

Posthuma, R. A. (2002). Employee selection procedures and the business necessity defense. *Applied H.R.M. Research, 7*(1-2), 53–63.

Powell, G. N., Butterfield, D. A., & Parent, J. D. (2002). Gender and managerial stereotypes: Have the times changed? *Journal of Management, 28*(2), 177–193.

Powers, W. T. (1973). *Behavior: The control of perception.* Chicago: Aldine.

Primoff, E. S., & Eyde, L. D. (1988). Job element analysis. In S. Gael (Ed.), *The job analysis handbook for business, industry, and government* (Vol. 2, pp. 807–824). New York: John Wiley.

Prince, C., & Stewart, J. (2002). Corporate universities: An analytical framework. *Journal of Management Development, 21*(10), 794–811.

Probst, T. M. (2000). Wedded to the job: Moderating effects of job involvement on the consequences of job insecurity. *Journal of Occupational Health Psychology, 5*(1), 63–73.

Psychological Corporation. (1979). *Revised manual for the Minnesota Clerical Test.* San Antonio, TX: The Psychological Corporation.

Psychological Corporation. (1980). *The Bennett Mechanical Comprehension Test manual.* San Antonio, TX: The Psychological Corporation.

Pulakos, E. D. (1984). A comparison of rater training programs: Error training and accuracy training. *Journal of Applied Psychology, 69,* 581–588.

Pulakos, E. D. (1986). The development of training programs to increase accuracy. *Organizational Behavior and Human Decision Processes, 38,* 76–91.

Raven, B. H. (1998). Groupthink, Bay of Pigs, and Watergate reconsidered. *Organizational Behavior and Human Decision Processes, 73*(2/3), 352–361.

Ree, J. M., Earles, J. A., & Teachout, M. S. (1994). Predicting job performance: Not much more than *g. Journal of Applied Psychology, 79*(4), 518–524.

Rees, C. J., & Metcalfe, B. (2003). The faking of personality questionnaire results: Who's kidding whom? *Journal of Managerial Psychology, 18*(2), 156–165.

Reilly, R. R., & McGourty, J. (1998). Performance appraisal in team settings. In J. W. Smither (Ed.), *Performance appraisal: State of the art in practice.* San Francisco: Jossey-Bass.

Reisenwitz, E. M. (1997). Absence/lost time management: Strategies to keep the workforce productive. *Benefits Quarterly, 13*(4), 19–25.

Rhoades, L., & Eisenberger, R. (2002). Perceived organizational support: A review of the literature. *Journal of Applied Psychology, 87*(4), 698–714.

Riketta, M. (2002). Attitudinal organizational commitment and job performance: A meta-analysis. *Journal of Organizational Behavior, 23*(3), 257–266.

Roberson, L., Kulik, C. T., & Pepper, M. B. (2003). Using needs assessment to resolve controversies in diversity training design. *Group and Organization Management, 28*(1), 148–174.

Robinson, K. (2004, May). Where did everybody go? *HR Magazine,* 38.

Roch, S. G., & O'Sullivan, B. J. (2003). Frame of reference rater training issues: Recall, time and behavior observation training. *International Journal of Training and Development, 7*(2), 93–107.

Rodgers, R., & Hunter, J. E. (1991). Impact of management by objectives on organizational productivity. *Journal of Applied Psychology, 76*(2), 322–336.

Roethlisberger, F. J., & Dickson, W. J. (1939). *Management and the worker.* Cambridge, MA: Harvard University Press.

Rosenthal, R. (1991). *Meta-analytic procedures for social research* (rev. ed.). Newbury Park, CA: Sage.

Roth, P. L., Bobko, P., & Mabon, H. (2002). Utility analysis: A review and analysis at the turn of the century. In N. Anderson, D. S. Ones, C. Viswesvaran, & H. K. Sinangil (Eds.), *Handbook of industrial, work and organizational psychology: Volume 1. Personnel psychology* (pp. 383–384). Thousand Oaks, CA: Sage.

Rothausen, T. J., Gonzalez, J. A., Clarke, N. E., & O'Dell, L. L. (1998). Family-friendly backlash—Fact or fiction? The case of organizations' on-site child-care centers. *Personnel Psychology, 51,* 685–706.

Rotundo, M., & Sackett, P. R. (2002). The relative importance of task, citizenship, and counterproductive performance to global ratings of job performance: A policy-capturing approach. *Journal of Applied Psychology, 87*(1), 66–80.

Rudisill, J. R., & Edwards, J. M. (2002). Coping with job transitions. *Consulting Psychology Journal: Practice and Research, 54*(1), 55–64.

Ryan, R. M., & Deci, E. L. (2000). Self-determination theory and the facilitation of intrinsic motivation, social development, and well-being. *American Psychologist, 55*(1), 68–78.

Rynes, S. L., & Cable, D. M. (2003). Recruitment research in the twenty-first century. In W. C. Borman, D. R. Ilgen, & R. Klimoski (Eds.), *Handbook of psychology: Vol. 12. Industrial and organizational psychology* (pp. 55–76). New York: Wiley.

Rynes, S., & Rosen, B. (1995). A field survey of factors affecting the adoption and perceived success of diversity training. *Personnel Psychology, 48,* 247–270.

Saal, F. E., Downey, R. G., & Lahey, M. A. (1980). Rating the ratings: Assessing the quality of rating data. *Psychological Bulletin, 88,* 413–428.

Sablynski, C. J., Lee, T. W., Mitchell, T. R., Burton, J. P., & Holtom, B. C. (2002). Turnover: An integration of Lee and Mitchell's unfolding model and job embeddedness construct with Hulin's withdrawal construct. In J. M. Brett & F. Drasgow (Eds.), *The psychology of work: Theoretically based empirical research* (pp. 189–203). Mahwah, NJ: Erlbaum.

Sackett, P. R. (1994). *The content and process of the research enterprise within industrial and organizational psychology (Presidential Address).* Paper presented at the 9th Annual Conference of the Society for Industrial and Organizational Psychology, Nashville, TN.

Sackett, P. R., & DeVore, C. J. (2002). Counterproductive behaviors at work. In N. Anderson, D. S. Ones, H. K. Sinangil, & C. Viswesvaran (Eds.), *Handbook of industrial, work, and organizational psychology: Vol. 1. Personnel Psychology* (pp. 145–164). Thousand Oaks, CA: Sage.

Sackett, P. R., & Laczo, R. M. (2003). Job and work analysis. In W. C. Borman, D. R. Ilgen, & R. J. Klimoski (Eds.), *Handbook of psychology: Industrial and organizational psychology* (Vol. 12, pp. 21–37). New York: Wiley.

Sagie, A. (1998). Employee absenteeism, organizational commitment, and job satisfaction: Another look. *Journal of Vocational Behavior, 52,* 156–171.

Sahibzada, K., Hammer, L. B., Neal, M. B., & Kuang, D. C. (in press). The moderating effects of work-family role combinations and work-family organizational culture on the relationship between family-friendly workplace supports and job satisfaction. *Journal of Family Issues.*

Salam, S., Cox, J. F., & Sims Jr., H. P. (1997). In the eye of the beholder: How leadership relates to 360-degree feedback system attitudes. *Group and Organization Management, 22*(2), 185–209.

Salas, E., Rozell, D., Mullen, B., & Driskell, J. E. (1999). The effect of team building on performance: An integration. *Small Group Research, 30*(3), 309–329.

Salgado, J. (2002). The Big Five personality dimensions and counterproductive behaviors. *International Journal of Selection and Assessment. 10*(1–2), 117–125.

Salgado, J. F., & Anderson, N. (2003). Validity generalization of GMA tests across countries in the European Community. *European Journal of Work and Organizational Psychology, 12*(1), 1–17.

Sanchez, R. J., Truxillo, D. M., & Bauer, T. N. (2000). Development and examination of an expectancy-based measure of test-taking motivation. *Journal of Applied Psychology, 85*(5), 739–750.

Schappe, S. P. (1998). Understanding employee job satisfaction: The importance of procedural and distributive justice. *Journal of Business and Psychology, 12*(4), 493–503.

Scheer, L. K., Kumar, N., & Steenkamp, J.-B. E. M. (2003). Reactions to perceived inequity in U.S. and Dutch interorganizational relationships. *Academy of Management Journal, 46*(3), 303–316.

Schein, E. H. (1980). *Organizational psychology* (3rd ed.). Englewood Cliffs, NJ: Prentice-Hall.

Schellenberg, K., & Miller, G. A. (1998). Turbulence and bureaucracy. *Journal of Applied Behavioral Science, 34*(2), 202–221.

Schippmann, J. S., Ash, R. A., Battista, M., Carr, L., Eyde, L. D., Hesketh, B., Kehoe, J., Pearlman, K., Prien, E. P., & Sanchez, J. I. (2000). The practice of competency modeling. *Personnel Psychology, 53*, 703–740.

Schleicher, D. J., Day, D. V., Mayes, B. T., & Riggio, R. E. (2002). A new frame for frame-of-reference training: Enhancing the construct validity of assessment centers. *Journal of Applied Psychology, 87*(4), 735–746.

Schleicher, D. J., Watt, J. D., & Greguras, G. J. (2004). Reexamining the job satisfaction–performance relationship: The complexity of attitudes. *Journal of Applied Psychology, 89*(1), 165–177.

Schmidt, F. L., & Hunter, J. E. (1998). The validity and utility of selection methods in personnel psychology: Practical and theoretical implications of 85 years of research findings. *Psychological Bulletin, 124*(2), 262–274.

Schmidt, F. L., & Kaplan, L. B. (1971). Composite vs. multiple criteria: A review and resolution of the controversy. *Personnel Psychology, 24*, 419–434.

Schmidt, F. L., Law, K., Hunter, J. E., Rothstein, H. R., Pearlman, K., & McDaniel, M. A. (1993). Refinements in validity generalization methods: Implications for the situational specificity hypothesis. *Journal of Applied Psychology, 78*, 3–12.

Schmidt, S. R. (1999). Long-run trends in workers' beliefs about their own job security: Evidence from the General Social Survey. *Journal of Labor Economics, 17*(4), S127–S141.

Schmitt, N., Gooding, R. Z., Noe, R. A., & Kirsch, M. (1984). Meta-analyses of validity studies published between 1964 and 1982 and the investigation of study characteristics. *Personnel Psychology, 37*, 407–422.

Schneider, B., Hanges, P. J., Goldstein, H. W., & Braverman, E. P. (1994). Do customer service perceptions generalize? The case of student and chair ratings of faculty effectiveness. *Journal of Applied Psychology, 79*(5), 685–690.

Schneider, R. J., Goff, M., Anderson, S., & Borman, W. C. (2003). Computerized adaptive rating scales for measuring managerial performance. *International Journal of Selection and Assessment, 11*(2/3), 237–246.

Schreisheim, C., House, R. J., & Kerr, C. (1976). Leader initiating structure: A reconciliation of discrepant research results and some empirical tests. *Organizational Behavior and Human Performance, 15*(2), 297–321.

Schriesheim, C. A., Castro, S. L., & Cogliser, C. C. (1999). Leader-member exchange (LMX) research: A comprehensive review of theory, measurement, and data-analytic practices. *Leadership Quarterly, 10*(1), 63–113.

Schriesheim, C. A., & Neider, L. L. (1996). Path-goal leadership theory: The long and winding road. *Leadership Quarterly, 7*(3), 317–321.

Schroeder, S. (1999). Improving family leave. *Risk Management, 46*(10), 46.

Schuerger, J. M. (1995). Career assessment and the Sixteen Personality Factor Questionnaire. *Journal of Career Assessment, 3*(2), 157–175.

Scullen, S. E., Mount, M. K., & Judge, T. A. (2003). Evidence of the construct validity of developmental ratings of managerial performance. *Journal of Applied Psychology, 88*, 50.

Schwartz, J. (1990, November). How safe is your job? *Newsweek, 5*, 44–47.

Scott, K. D., & Taylor, G. S. (1985). An examination of conflicting findings on the relationship between job satisfaction and absenteeism: A meta-analysis. *Academy of Management Journal, 28*(3), 599–612.

Scott, W. D. (1903). *The Theory of Advertising.* Boston: Small, Maynard.

Scullen, S. E., Mount, M. K., & Goff, M. (2000). Understanding the latent structure of job performance ratings. *Journal of Applied Psychology, 85*(6), 956–970.

Seaward, M. R. (1999). The sandwich generation copes with elder care. *Benefits Quarterly, 15*(2), 41–48.

Selection test increase. (2003). *Personnel Today*, p. 51, 3/11/2003.

Seng, C. V., Zannes, E., & Pace, R. W. (2002). The contributions of knowledge management to workplace learning. *Journal of Workplace Learning, 14*(4), 138–147.

Shafritz, J. M., & Ott, J. S. (1996a). Classical organization theory. In J. M. Shafritz & J. S. Ott (Eds.), *Classics of organization theory* (4th ed., pp. 29–37). Belmont, CA: Wadsworth Publishing.

Shafritz, J. M., & Ott, J. S. (1996b). Introduction. In J. M. Shafritz & J. S. Ott (Eds.), *Classics of organization theory* (4th ed., pp. 1–28). Belmont, CA: Wadsworth Publishing.

Shore, L. M., Tetrick, L. E., Shore, T. H., & Barksdale, K. (2000). Construct validity of measures of Becker's Side Bet Theory. *Journal of Vocational Behavior, 57*, 428–444.

Silverman, S. B. (1991). Individual development through performance appraisal. In K. N. Wexley (Ed.), *Developing human resources* (Vol. 5, pp. 120–151). Washington, DC: The Bureau of National Affairs, Inc.

Simons, T., & Roberson, Q. (2003). Why managers should care about fairness: The effects of aggregate justice perceptions on organizational outcomes. *Journal of Applied Psychology, 88*(3), 432–443.

Sladek, C. (1995). A guide to offering work/life benefits. *Compensation and Benefits Review, 27*(1), 41–45.

Slaughter, J. E., Sinar, E. F., & Bachiochi, P. D. (2002). Black applicants' reactions to affirmative action plans: Effects of plan content and previous experience with discrimination. *Journal of Applied Psychology, 87*(2), 333–344.

Sleek, S. (1999, February). *Concern for job stresses goes global.* American Psychological Association. Available online at *http://www.apa.org/monitor/feb99/global.html* [2000, January 20].

Smith, J. A., & Foti, R. J. (1998). A pattern approach to the study of leader emergence. *Leadership Quarterly, 9*(2), 147–160.

Smith, P. C., & Kendall, L. M. (1963). Retranslation of expectations: An approach to the construction of unambiguous anchors for rating scales. *Journal of Applied Psychology, 47,* 149–155.

Smith, P. C., Kendall, L. M., & Hulin, C. L. (1969). *Measurement of satisfaction in work and retirement.* Chicago, IL: Rand McNally.

Smither, J. W., London, M., Flautt, R., Vargas, Y., & Kucine, I. (2003). Can working with an executive coach improve multisource feedback ratings over time? A quasi-experimental field study. *Personnel Psychology, 56*(1), 23–44.

Snell, A. F., Sydell, E. J., & Lueke, S. B. (1999). Towards a theory of applicant faking: Integrating studies of deception. *Human Resource Management Review,* 219–242.

Society for Industrial and Organizational Psychology. (1987). *Principles for the validation and use of personnel selection procedures.* College Park, MD: SIOP.

Society for Industrial and Organizational Psychology. (1999). *Guidelines for Education and Training at the Doctoral Level in Industrial-Organizational Psychology.* SIOP. Available online at *http://www.siop.org/PhDGuidelines98.html.*

Society for Industrial and Organizational Psychology. (2000). *Graduate Training Programs in Industrial-Organizational Psychology and Related Fields.* SIOP. Available online at *http://www.siop.org/gtp/Default.htm* [2001, April 3].

Society for Industrial and Organizational Psychology. (2003). *Building better organizations.* Retrieved March 17, 2004, from *http://www.siop.org/visibilitybrochure/memberbrochure.htm.* Sokora v. Dayton Hudson, Cal. H143579-3 (1989).

Southwest Airlines. (2000, July 25). *Southwest Airlines fact sheet.* Southwest Airlines. Available online at *http://www.southest.com/about_swa/press/factsheet.html* [2000, October 27].

Spector, P. E. (1997). The role of frustration in antisocial behavior at work. In R. A. Giacalone & J. Greenberg (Eds.), *Antisocial behavior in organizations.* Thousand Oaks, CA: Sage Publications.

Spector, P. E., & Jex, S. M. (1991). Relations of job characteristics from multiple data sources with employee affect, absence, turnover intentions, and health. *Journal of Applied Psychology, 76,* 46–53.

Spector, P. R., & Wanek, J. E. (1996). New developments in the use of measures of honesty, integrity, conscientiousness, dependability, trustworthiness, and reliability for personnel selection. *Personnel Psychology, 49,* 787–829.

Spence, J. T., & Robbins, A. S. (1992). Workaholism: Definition, measurement, and preliminary results. *Journal of Personality Assessment, 58* (160–178).

Spool, M. D. (1978). Training programs for observers of behavior: A review. *Personnel Psychology, 31*(4), 853–888.

Stajkovic, A. D., & Luthans, F. (1997). A meta-analysis of the effects of organizational behavior modification on task performance. *Academy of Management Journal, 40*(5), 1122–1149.

Stanton, J. & Coovert, M. D. (2004). Introduction to special issue: Information Technology and Human Resources. *Human Resource Management Journal,* 43(2&3), 121–125.

Stanton, J. M., Sinar, E. F., Balzer, W. K., Julian, A. L., Thoresen, P., Aziz, S., et al. (2002). Development of a compact measure of job satisfaction: The abridged Job Descriptive Index. *Educational and Psychological Measurement, 62*(1), 173–191.

Staw, B. M., & Ross, J. (1985). Stability in the midst of change: A dispositional approach to job attitudes. *Journal of Applied Psychology, 70*(3), 469–480.

Steel, R. P., & Rentsch, J. R. (1997). The dispositional model of job attitudes revisited: Findings of a 10-year study. *Journal of Applied Psychology, 82*(6), 873–879.

Steele-Johnson, D., Beauregard, R. S., Hoover, P. B., & Schmidt, A. M. (2000). Goal orientation and task demand effects on motivation, affect, and performance. *Journal of Applied Psychology, 85*(5), 724–738.

Steele-Johnson, D., Osburn, H. D., & Pieper, K. F. (2000). A review and extension of current models of dynamic criteria. *International Journal of Selection and Assessment, 8*(3), 110–136.

Steelman, L. A., Levy, P. E., & Snell, A. F. (2004). The feedback environment scale (FES): Construct definition, measurement, and validation.. *Educational and Psychological Measurement, 64(1),* 165–184.

Steers, R. M., Mowday, R. T., & Shapiro, D. L. (2004). Introduction to Special Topic Forum: The future of work motivation theory. *Academy of Management Review, 29*(3), 379–387.

Steers, R. M., & Rhodes, S. R. (1978). Major influences on employee attendance: A process model. *Journal of Applied Psychology, 63*(4), 391–407.

Steiner, I. D. (1972). *Group process and productivity.* New York: Academic Press.

Sternberg, R. J., & Williams, W. M. (1997). Does the Graduate Record Examination predict meaningful success in the graduate training of psychologists? *American Psychologist, 52*(6), 630–641.

Sterns, H. L., Doverspike, D., & Lax, G. (in press). The Age Discrimination in Employment Act. In F. J. Landy (Ed.), *Employment discrimination litigation: Behavioral, quantitative, and legal implications.* San Francisco: Jossey-Bass.

Stevens, M. J., & Campion, M. A. (1999). Staffing work teams: Development and validation of a selection test for teamwork settings. *Journal of Management, 25*(2), 207–228.

Stevens, S. (1968). Measurement, statistics, and the schemapiric view. *Science, 161,* 849–856.

Stewart, T. A. (1998). The leading edge: Is this job really necessary? *Fortune, 137*(1), 154–157.

Stewart, T. A. (1999). The leading edge: Telling tales at BP Amoco. *Fortune, 139*(11), 220–222.

Stewart, T. A. (2000). The house that knowledge built. *Fortune, 142*(7), 278–279.

Stogdill, R. M. (1948). Personal factors associated with leadership: A survey of the literature. *Journal of Psychology, 25,* 35–71.

Stogdill, R. M. (1974). *Handbook of leadership: A survey of theory and research.* New York: Free Press.

Stogdill, R. M., & Coons, A. E. (1957). *Leader behavior: Its descrip-*

tion and measurement. Columbus: Ohio State University Press for Bureau of Business Research.

Stokes, G. S., & Cooper, L. A. (1994). Selection using biodata: Old notions revisited. In G. S. Stokes, M. M. Mumford, & W. A. Owens (Eds.), *Biodata handbook: Theory, research, and use of biographical information in selection and performance prediction.* Palo Alto, CA: Consulting Psychologists Press.

Strong, E. K. (1927). Vocational interest test. *Educational Record, 8,* 107–121.

Sulsky, L. M., & Day, D. V. (1994). Effects of frame-of-reference training and cognitive categorization: An empirical investigation of rater memory issues. *Journal of Applied Psychology, 79,* 535–543.

Sulzer-Azaroff, B., Loafman, B., Merante, R. J., & Hlavacek, A. C. (1990). Improving occupational safety in a large industrial plant: A systematic replication. *Journal of Organizational Behavior Management, 11*(1), 99–120.

Sundstrom, E., DeMeuse, K. P., & Futrell, D. (1990). Work teams: Applications and effectiveness. *American Psychologist, 45,* 120–133.

Sundstrom, E., McIntyre, M., Halfhill, T., & Richards, H. (2000). Work groups: From the Hawthorne Studies to work teams of the 1990s and beyond. *Group Dynamics: Theory, Research, and Practice, 4*(1), 44–67.

Sutton, J. (2004, April). BellSouth business technical training transformation. *In Practice, www.astd.org/astd/publications/ASTD_Links/April2004/InPractice_April04.*

Sutton v. United Air Lines, 525 U.S. 805 (1999).

Svyantek, D. J., Goodman, S. A., Benz, L. L., & Gard, J. A. (1999). The relationship between organizational characteristics and team building success. *Journal of Business and Psychology, 14*(2), 265–283.

Sweeney, P. D., & McFarlin, D. B. (1993). Workers' evaluations of the "ends" and the "means": An examination of four models of distributive and procedural justice. *Organizational Behavior and Human Decision Processes, 55,* 23–40.

Tang, T. L., & Ibrahim, A. H. S. (1998). Antecedents of organizational citizenship behavior revisited: Public personnel in the United States and in the Middle East. *Public Personnel Management, 27*(4), 529–550.

Tata, J. (2002). The influence of managerial accounts on employees' reactions to negative feedback. *Group and Organization Management, 27*(4), 480–503.

Tata, J., Prasad, S., & Thorn, R. (1999). The influence of organizational structure on the effectiveness of TQM programs. *Journal of Managerial Issues, 11*(4), 440–453.

Taylor, F. W. (1916/1996). The principles of scientific management. In J. M. Shafritz & J. S. Ott (Eds.), *Classics of organization theory* (4th ed., pp. 66–79). Belmont, CA: Wadsworth Publishing. (Reprinted from the Bulletin of the Taylor Society, 1916.)

Taylor, G. S., & Vest, M. J. (1992). Pay comparisons and pay satisfaction among public sector employees. *Public Personnel Management, 21*(4), 445–454.

Taylor, H. C., & Russell, T. (1939). The relationship of validity coefficients to the practical effectiveness of tests in selection: Discussion and tables. *Journal of Applied Psychology, 23,* 565–578.

Tepper, B. J., Lockhart, D., & Hoobler, J. (2001). Justice, citizenship, and role definition effects. *Journal of Applied Psychology, 86* (4), 789–796.

Tetrick, L. E., Miles, R. L., Marcil, L., & Van Dose, C. M. (1994). Child-care difficulties and the impact on concentration, stress, and productivity among single and nonsingle mothers and fathers. In G. P. Keita & J. J. Hurrell, Jr. (Eds.), *Job stress in a changing workforce: Investigating gender, diversity, and family issues.* Washington, DC: American Psychological Association.

Tett, R. P., Jackson, D. N., & Rothstein, M. (1991). Personality measures as predictors of job performance: A meta-analytic review. *Personnel Psychology, 44,* 703–742.

Theorell, T., & Karasek, R. A. (1996). Current issues relating to psychosocial job strain and cardiovascular disease research. *Journal of Occupational Health Psychology, 1*(1), 9–26.

Thorndike, R. L. (1949). *Personnel selection.* New York: Wiley.

Timmermann, S. (1999). From childcare to eldercare: Our turn to care for mom and dad. *Journal of Financial Service Professionals, 53*(5), 28–31.

Tobin, T. J. (2001). Organizational determinants of violence in the workplace. *Aggression and Violent Behavior, 6,* 91–102.

Tolman, E. C. (1932). *Purposive behavior in animals and men.* New York: Century.

Tuckman, B. W. (1965). Developmental sequences in small groups. *Psychological Bulletin, 63,* 384–399.

Tuckman, B. W., & Jensen, M. A. C. (1977). Stages of small group development revisited. *Group and Organizational Studies, 2,* 419–427.

Tyler, K. (1998). Sit up straight. *HRMagazine, 43*(10), 122–128.

U.S. Bureau of Labor Statistics. (1995). *Women in the workforce: An overview.* Washington, DC: Government Printing Office.

U.S. Department of Labor. (1997, April). *Women in Management.* U.S. Department of Labor, Women's Bureau. Available online at *http://www.dol.gov/wb/public/wb_pubs/wmgt97.htm* [2000, August 28].

U.S. Department of Labor. (2000, March). *20 facts on women workers.* U.S. Department of Labor, Women's Bureau. Available online at *http://www.dol.gov/wb/public/wb_pubs/20fact00.htm* [2000, August 28].

U.S. Department of Labor. (2004). *Women in the labor force: A databook.* Retrieved 9/13/04. *http://www.bls.gov/cps/wlf-databook.htm.*

U.S. Government (2001, January 3). *Current Congressional Profile.* U.S. Government. Available online at http://clerkweb.house.gove/mbrcmtee/statsanswers.htm [2001, March 19].

U.S. Government. (2004). *Congressional profile.* Retrieved September 12, 2004, from *http://clerk.house.gov/members/congProfile.html.*

Van Aken v. Young, 750 F. 2d 430 (6th Cir. 1982).

van Dierendonck, D., Schaufeli, W., B., & Buunk, B. P. (2001). Burnout and inequity among human service professionals: A longitudinal study. *Journal of Occupational Health Psychology, 6*(1), 43–52.

Van Eerde, W., & Thierry, H. (1996). Vroom's expectancy models and work-related criteria. *Journal of Applied Psychology, 81*(5), 575–586.

Van Vugt, M., & De Cremer, D. (1999). Leadership in social dilemmas: The effects of group identification on collective actions to provide public goods. *Journal of Personality and Social Psychology, 76*(4), 587–599.

Van Yperen, N. W., & Janssen, O. (2002). Fatigued and dissatisfied or fatigued but satisfied? Goal orientations and responses to high job demands. *Academy of Management Journal, 45*(6), 1161–1171.

Vecchio, R. P. (2002). Leadership and gender advantage. *Leadership Quarterly, 13*(6), 643–671.

Villanova, P., & Bernardin, H. J. (1989). Impression management in the context of performance appraisal. In R. A. Giacalone & P. Rosenfeld (Eds.), *Impression management in the organization* (pp. 299–314). Hillsdale, NJ: Erlbaum.

Villanova, P. D., Bernardin, H. J., Dahmus, S. A., & Sims, R. L. (1993). Rater leniency and performance appraisal discomfort. *Educational and Psychological Measurement, 53*(3), 789–799.

Vinchur, A. J., Schippmann, J. S., Switzer III, F. S., & Roth, P. L. (1998). A meta-analytic review of predictors of job performance for salespeople. *Journal of Applied Psychology, 83*(4), 586–597.

Viswesvaran, C. (2002). Assessment of individual job performance: A review of the past century and a look ahead. In N. Anderson, D. S. Ones, H. K. Sinangil, & C. Viswesvaran (Eds.), *Handbook of industrial, work, and organizational psychology: Vol. 1. Personnel Psychology* (pp. 110–126). Thousand Oaks, CA: Sage.

Viswesvaran, C. (2003). Introduction to special issue: Role of technology in shaping the future of staffing and assessment. *International Journal of Selection and Assessment, 11*(2-3), 107–112.

Viswesvaran, C., Sanchez, J. I., & Fisher, J. (1999). The role of social support in the process of work stress: A meta-analysis. *Journal of Vocational Behavior, 54*, 314–334.

Vogl, A. J., & Budman, M. (1997). Can we have it all? *Across the Board, 34*(8), 16–23.

Volkswagen Press. (2000). Press release. Volkswagen Press. Available online at *http://dealer.vw.com/vwpress/fullstoryA.html?release_id=3682* [2000, November 1].

Von Bergen, C. W., Soper, B., & Foster, T. (2002). Unintended negative effects of diversity management. *Public Personnel Management, 31*(2), 239–251.

Vroom, V. (1964). *Work and motivation.* New York: Wiley.

Wagner, J. A., & Hollenbeck, J. R. (1998). *Organizational behavior: Securing competitive advantage.* Upper Saddle River, NJ: Prentice-Hall.

Warr, P. (1999). Well-being and the workplace. In D. Kahneman, E. Diener, & N. Schwartz (Eds.), *Well-being: The foundations of hedonic psychology.* New York: Russell Sage Foundation.

Warr, P. B. (1987). *Work, unemployment, and mental health.* Oxford: Oxford University Press.

Warr, P. B. (1990). The measurement of well-being and other aspects of mental health. *Journal of Occupational Psychology, 63*, 193–210.

Warr, P., & Hoare, S. (2002). Personality, gender, age and logical overlap in multi-source ratings. *International Journal of Selection and Assessment, 10*(4), 279–291.

Wayne, J. H., Musisca, N., & Fleeson, W. (2004). Considering the role of personality in the work-family experience: Relationships of the big five to work-family conflict and facilitiation. *Journal of Vocational Behavior, 64*(1), 108–130.

Wayne, S. J., & Kacmar, K. M. (1991). The effects of impression management on the performance appraisal process. *Organizational Behavior and Human Decision Processes, 48*, 70–88.

Wayne, S. J., & Liden, R. C. (1995). Effects of impression management on performance ratings: A longitudinal study. *Academy of Management Journal, 38*(1), 232–260.

Weber, A. J. (1995). Making performance appraisals consistent with a quality environment. *Quality Progress, 28*(6), 65–70.

Weber, J. (2004, June). More jobs—and more layoffs. *Business Week Online.*

Weick, K. E. (1995). *Sense-making in organizations.* Thousand Oaks, CA: Sage.

Welbourne, T. M. (1998). Untangling procedural and distributive justice: Their relative effects on gainsharing satisfaction. *Group and Organization Management, 23*(4), 325–346.

Welsh, E. T., Wanberg, C. R., Brown, K. G., & Simmering, M. J. (2003). E-learning: Emerging uses, empirical results and future directions. *International Journal of Training and Development, 7*(4), 245–258.

Werner, J. M., & Bolino, M. C. (1997). Explaining U.S. Courts of Appeals decisions involving performance appraisal: Accuracy, fairness, and validation. *Personnel Psychology, 50*, 1–24.

Wesolowski, M. A., & Mossholder, K. W. (1997). Relational demography in supervisor-subordinate dyads: Impact on subordinate job satisfaction, burnout, and perceived procedural justice. *Journal of Organizational Behavior, 18*, 351–362.

Wexley, K. N., & Klimoski, R. (1984). Performance appraisal: An update. In K. Rowland & G. Ferris (Eds.), *Research in personnel and human resources* (Vol. 2). Greenwich, CT: JAI Press.

Wexley, K. N., & Latham, G. P. (1991). *Developing and training human resources in organizations.* New York: HarperCollins.

Wexley, K. N., & Latham, G. P. (2002). Developing and training human resources in organizations (3rd ed.). Upper Saddle River, NJ: Prentice Hall.

Wexley, K. N., & Silverman, S. B. (1993). *Working scared: Achieving success in trying times.* San Francisco: Jossey-Bass.

Wheelan, S. A., Murphy, D., Tsumura, E., & Kline, S. F. (1998). Member perceptions of internal group dynamics and productivity. *Small Group Research, 29*(3), 371–393.

Whetten, D. A., & Cameron, K. S. (2002). *Developing management skills* (5th ed.). Upper Saddle River, NJ: Pearson Education, Inc.

Whitener, E. M., & Walz, P. M. (1993). Exchange theory determinants of affective and continuance commitment and turnover. *Journal of Vocational Behavior, 42*, 265–281.

Whitney, D. J., Diaz, J., Mineghino, M. E., & Powers, K. (1999). Perceptions of overt and personality-based integrity tests. *International Journal of Selection & Assessment, 7*(1), 35–45.

Wiesenfeld, B. M., Brockner, J., & Martin, C. (1999). A self-affirmation analysis of survivors' reactions to unfair organizational downsizings. *Journal of Experimental Social Psychology, 35*, 441–460.

Wiesenfeld, B. M., Brockner, J., & Thibault, V. (2000). Procedural fairness, managers' self-esteem, and managerial behaviors following a layoff. *Organizational Behavior and Human Decision Processes, 83*(1), 1–32.

Williams, J. R., & Levy, P. E. (1992). The effects of perceived system knowledge on the agreement between self-ratings and supervisor ratings. *Personnel Psychology, 45,* 835–847.

Williams, J. R., & Levy, P. E. (1995). A forgotten dimension: The role of organizational psychology in the performance appraisal process. Paper presented at the 10th annual meeting of the Society for Industrial and Organizational Psychology, Orlando, FL.

Williams, S. D., Graham, T. S., & Baker, B. (2003). Evaluating outdoor experiential training for leadership and team building. *Journal of Management Development, 22*(1), 45–59.

Williamson, I. O., Lepak, D. P., & King, J. (2003). The effect of company recruitment web site orientation on individuals' perceptions of organizational attractiveness. *Journal of Vocational Behavior, 63*(2), 242–263.

Wilson, C. (2004, July). How to heal work force cuts. *Credit Union Executive Newsletter*, 7.

Woehr, D. J., & Arthur, W. (2003). The construct-related validity of assessment center ratings: A review and meta-analysis of the role of methodological factors. *Journal of Management, 29*(2), 231–258.

Wonderlic, E. F. (1984). *Wonderlic Personnel Test manual.* Northfield, IL: Wonderlic & Associates.

Yeager, S. J. (1986). Use of assessment centers by metropolitan fire departments in North America. *Public Personnel Management, 15*(1), 51–64.

Yu, J. H., Albaum, G., & Swenson, M. (2003). Is a central tendency error inherent in the use of semantic differential scales in different cultures? *International Journal of Market Research, 45*(2), 213–228.

Yukl, G. A. (2002). *Leadership in organizations* (5th ed.). Upper Saddle River, NJ: Prentice-Hall.

Zaccaro, S. J. (1984). Social loafing: The role of task attractiveness. *Personality and Social Psychology Bulletin, 10*(1), 99–106.

Zaccaro, S. J., & Bader, P. (2003). E-Leadership and the challenges of leading E-teams: Minimizing the bad and maximizing the good. *Organizational Dynamics, 31*(4), 377–387.

Zaccaro, S. J., Foti, R. J., & Kenny, D. A. (1991). Self-monitoring and trait-based variance in leadership: An investigation of leader flexibility across multiple group situations. *Journal of Applied Psychology, 76*(2), 308–315.

Zaitzow, B. H., & Fields, C. B. (1996). Using archival data sets. In F. T. L. Leong & J. T. Austin (Eds.), *The psychology research handbook.* Thousand Oaks, CA: Sage.

Zapf, D. (2002). Emotion work and psychological well-being: A review of the literature and some conceptual considerations. *Human Resource Management Review, 12*(2), 237–268.

Zellars, K. L., & Perrewe, P. L. (2001). Affective personality and the content of emotional social support: Coping in organizations. *Journal of Applied Psychology, 86*(3), 459–467.

Zickar, M. J. (2001). Using personality inventories to identify thugs and agitators: Applied psychology's contribution to the war against labor. *Journal of Vocational Behavior, 59*(1), 149–164.

Photo and Cartoon Credits

About the Author **p. 1** © Sylvia Chinn-Levy.

Chapter 1 **p. 2** © Bachman/The Image Works. **p. 9** © Mark Richards/PhotoEdit. **p. 18** © Mark Richards/PhotoEdit. **p. 19** © Steve Chenn/CORBIS.

Chapter 2 **p. 22** © Ryan McVay/Getty Images. **p. 27** © Nick Downes from cartoonbank.com. All Rights Reserved. **p. 39** © Billy E. Barnes/PhotoEdit. **p. 43** © Bill Aron/PhotoEdit. **p. 44** © Spencer Grant/PhotoEdit. **p. 57 (top and bottom)** © Sylvia Chinn-Levy.

Chapter 3 **p. 62** © Robertstock.com. **p. 65 (left)** © Tony Freeman/PhotoEdit. **p. 65 (right)** © Rachel Epstein/PhotoEdit. **p. 81 (top)** © Cameramann/The Image Works. **p. 81 (bottom)** © Daemmrich/The Image Works. **p. 82 (top and bottom)** © Steven Rubin/The Image Works.

Chapter 4 **p. 88** © Kevin Horan /Getty Images. **p. 92** © The Far Side by Gary Larson © 1987 FarWorks, Inc. All Rights Reserved. Used with Permission. **p. 93** © 2005 David Madison Sports Images. **p. 97 (left)** © Bill Aron/PhotoEdit. **p. 97 (right)** © Michael Newman/PhotoEdit. **p. 107** © Bill Lai/The Image Works.

Chapter 5 **p. 112** © PhotoEdit. **p. 115 (top)** © Tony Freeman/PhotoEdit. **p. 115 (bottom)** © Betts A. Lohman/PhotoEdit. **p. 132** © Digital Vision/Getty Images. **p. 140** © DILBERT reprinted by permission of United Feature Syndicate, Inc.

Chapter 6 **p. 144** © Daemmrich/The Image Works. **p. 149 (top and bottom)** © Bill Aron/PhotoEdit. **p. 160** © PhotoEdit. **p. 162** © Michael Newman/PhotoEdit. **p. 170** © The Far Side by Gary Larson © 1982 FarWorks, Inc. All Rights Reserved. Used with Permission.

Chapter 7 **p. 176** © Robertstock.com. **p. 181** © PhotoEdit. **p. 198** © The New Yorker Collection 1994 Danny Shanahan from cartoonbank.com. All Rights Reserved. **p. 202** © Jeff Greenberg/PhotoEdit. **p. 203** © Tony Freeman/PhotoEdit. **p. 208** © Jeff Greenberg/PhotoEdit. **p. 210** © Daemmrich/The Image Works.

Chapter 8 **p. 214** © R. W. Jones/Corbis. **p. 217** © DILBERT reprinted by permission of United Feature Syndicate, Inc. **p. 228 (top)** © Tim Barnette/Stock Boston. **p. 228 (bottom)** © David Lassman/The Image Works. **p. 231** © AFP/Corbis. **p. 232** © Courtesy of NASA. **p. 235** © Najlah Feanny/Corbis. **p. 239** © Mark Peterson/CORBIS. **p. 241** © Mark Reinstein/The Image Works.

Chapter 9 **p. 250** © Najlah Feanny/Stock Boston. **p. 259** © Bill Lai/The Image Works. **p. 265** © David H. Wells/Corbis. **p. 273** © Tom McCarthy/PhotoEdit. **p. 275** © Michael Newman/PhotoEdit. **p. 281** © Gary Walts/The Image Works.

Chapter 10 **p. 284 (top)** © Greg Mancuso/Stock Boston. **p. 284 (bottom)** © Dick Blume/The Image Works. **p. 290** © Premium Stock/Corbis. **p. 294 (top and bottom)** © Everett Collection, Inc. **p. 295** © Jeff Zaruba/CORBIS. **p. 304** © DILBERT reprinted by permission of United Feature Syndicate, Inc. **p. 311** © Sean Aidan; Eye Ubiquitous/CORBIS.

Chapter 11 **p. 320** © David Lassman/The Image Works. **p. 326** © Bill Vane/Corbis. **p. 336 (top)** © Ariel Skelley/CORBIS. **p. 336 (bottom)** © DILBERT reprinted by permission of United Feature Syndicate, Inc. **p. 347** © CLOSE TO HOME © 2000 John McPherson. Reprinted with permission of Universal Press Syndicate. All Rights Reserved. **p. 351** © Photofest.

Chapter 12 **p. 358** © Jean Marc/Getty Images. **p. 361** © Will & Deni McIntyre /Getty Images. **p. 364** © Bettman/Corbis. **p. 369** © Comstock Images/ Getty Images. **p. 373** © CATHY © 1990 Cathy Guisewite. Reprinted with permission of Universal Press Syndicate. All Rights Reserved. **p. 375** © Reuters/Kenney Baker/Getty Images. **p. 380** © Tony Arruza/CORBIS.

Chapter 13 **p. 390** © Hulton Archives/Getty Images. **p. 391** © AP/Wide World Photos. **p. 394** © DILBERT reprinted by permission of United Feature Syndicate, Inc. **p. 409** © International Stock. **p. 414** © AP/Wide World Photos. **p. 417** © Corbis.

Chapter 14 **p. 420** © Mike Greenlar/The Image Works. **p. 424** © Tobias Everke. **p. 427** © David Hume Kennerly / Getty Images. **p. 436 (left)** © Hulton Archives/Getty Images. **p. 436 (right)** © Koichi Kamoshida/2001 Getty Images. **p. 439** © Archives of the History of American Psychology, The University of Akron. **p. 445** © Bill Bachman/PhotoEdit. **p. 452** © DILBERT reprinted by permission of United Feature Syndicate, Inc.

Text Credits

Chapter 1 **p. 6** *Guidelines for Education and Training at the Doctoral Level in Industrial/Organizational Psychology,* Society for Industrial and Organizational Psychology, Inc., Bowling Green, OH. Reprinted with permission. **p. 7** O'Connor, Glen T. and Ann Marie Ryan, *Multiple Facets of Industrial-Organizational Psychology.* Copyright © 1996 by Society for Industrial and Organizational Psychology, Inc. Reprinted with permission.

Chapter 3 **p. 73** Reprinted with permission of Dr. Robert J. Harvey.

Chapter 6 **p. 152** This page regarding the Test of Mechanical Concepts has been reproduced with the permission of NCS Pearson, Inc. **p. 153** Copyright © 1975 NCS Pearson, Inc. All rights reserved. Published and distributed exclusively by NCS Pearson, Inc. Reproduced by permission of NCS Pearson, Inc.

Chapter 7 **p. 197** "The Relationship of Validity Coefficients to the Practical Effectiveness of Tests in Selection: Discussion and Tables," by H. C. Taylor and J. T. Russell, 1939, *Journal of Applied Psychology,* 23, pp. 565–578.

Chapter 8 **p. 233** © 1991, *The Washington Post.* Reprinted with permission. **p. 245** © 1991, *The Washington Post.* Reprinted with permission. **p. 247** Alliger, G. M., Tannenbaum, S. I., Bennett, W., Jr., Traver, H., & Shotland, A. (1997), "A meta-analysis of the relations among training criteria," *Personnel Psychology,* 50, p. 343. Copyright © 1997 by *Personnel Psychology.* Reprinted with permission.

Chapter 9 **p. 252** Model from "The Job Characteristics Model," by Hackman and Oldham in *Organizational Behavior and Human Decision Processes,* Volume 16, 256, copyright ©1976 by Academic Press, reproduced by permission of the publisher. **p. 276** Pizza Deliverer Results — Intersection Stops from Ludwig, T. D., and Gellar, E. S. (1997), "Assigned versus Participative Goal Setting and Response Generalization: Managing Injury Control Among Professional Pizza Delivers," *Journal of Applied Psychology,* 82, (2), p. 257, fig. 1. Copyright © 1997 by the American Psychological Association. Reprinted with permission. **p. 277** Pizza Deliverer Results — Seat Belt Use from Ludwig, T. D., and Gellar, E. S. (1997), "Assigned versus Participative Goal Setting Response Generalization: Managing Injury Control Among Professional Pizza Deliverers," *Journal of Applied Psychology,* 82, (2), p. 257, fig. 1. Copyright © 1997 by the American Psychological Association. Reprinted with permission.

Chapter 10 **p. 287** "Theory of Planned Behavior" in *Journal of Experimental Social Psychology,* volume 22, 458, copyright © 1986 by Academic Press, reproduced by permission of the publisher. **p. 298** Copyright © 1997 Bowling Green State University. Reprinted with permission of Bowling Green State University, Department of Psychology, Bowling Green, OH, 43403. **p. 299 (top)** Hackman/Oldham, *Work Redesign,* © 1980. Reprinted by permission of Pearson Education, Inc., Upper Saddle River, New Jersey. **p. 299 (bottom, female faces)** Female Faces Scale from Dunham, R. B., & Herman, J. B. (1975) "Development of a Female Faces Scale for Measuring Job Satisfaction," *Journal of Applied Psychology,* 60 (5), p. 630. Copyright © 1975 by the American Psychological Association. Reprinted with permission. **p. 299 (bottom, female faces)** Copyright © 1975 by the American Psychological Association. Reprinted with permission. **p. 299 (bottom, circular and male faces)** Adapted from "The Construction of a New Type of Attitude Measure," by T. Kunin, 1955, *Personnel Psychology,* 8, pp. 65-77. Reprinted with permission. **p. 302** Attendance Model, adapted from Steers/Rodes (1978), "Major Influences on Employee Attendance: A Process Model," *Journal of Applied Psychology,* 63 (4), p. 391–407. Copyright © 1978 by the American Psychological Association. Reprinted with permission. **p. 309** Meyer, J. P. and Allen, N. J., Commitment in the Workplace: Theory, Research, and Application, p. 118–119, copyright © 1997 by Sage Publications. Reprinted with permission of Sage Publications, Inc.

Chapter 11 **p. 331** Figure from "Developing and testing an integrative model of the work-family interface," by Frone, M. R., Yardley, J. K. & Markel, K. S. in *Journal of Vocational Behavior,* Vol. 50, 145–167, copyright © 1997 with permission form Elsevier. Reprinted by permission of the publisher. **p. 354** Republished with permission of Academy of Management from *Academy of Management Review,* 21 (1), 1996; permission conveyed through Copyright Clearance Center, Inc. **p. 371** Adapted with the permission of The Free Press, a division of Simon & Schuster Adult Publishing Group, from Decision Making: A Psychological analysis of Conflict, Choice, and Commitment by Irving L. Janis and Leon Mann. Copyright © 1977 by The Free Press. All rights reserved.

Chapter 13 **p. 399** Stogdill, R. M. (1963), *Manual for the Leader Behavior Description Questionnaire-Form XII: An Experimental Revision,* Bureau of Business Research, Ohio State University.

NAME INDEX

SUBJECT INDEX

*Note: Page numbers followed by *f* refer to figures and photos; page numbers followed by *t* refer to tables.